ZUNI

CEREMONIALISM

ZUNI

CEREMONIALISM

Ruth L. Bunzel

Introduction by Nancy J. Parezo

University of New Mexico Press
Albuquerque

Library of Congress Cataloging–in–Publication Data

Bunzel, Ruth Leah, 1898–
Zuni ceremonialism / Ruth L. Bunzel ; introduction by Nancy J. Parezo.
p. cm.
This volume contains the complete text of the following 3 studies which were published in 1932 by the Smithsonian Institution, Washington, D.C.: Introduction to Zuñi ceremonialism; Zuñi origin myths; Zuñi ritual poetry.
Includes bibliographical references and index.
ISBN 0–8263–1376–0 (paper)
1. Zuni Indians—Religion and mythology. 2. Zuni Indians—Rites and ceremonies. 3. Zuni Indians—Poetry. 4. Zuni language—Texts. I. Title.
E99.Z9B85 1992 96–10861
978.9′004974—dc20 CIP

Introduction to Zuni Ceremonialism, *Zuni Origin Myths*, and *Zuni Ritual Poetry* were originally published in 1932 in the Forty-seventh Annual Report of the Bureau of American Ethnology, 1929–1930, by the Smithsonian Institution, Washington, D.C. This volume contains the complete text of all three studies.

University of New Mexico Press edition, 1992.

CONTENTS

INTRODUCTION

Ruth L. Bunzel at Zuni: The Search for the Middle Place

by
Nancy J. Parezo
Arizona State Museum
University of Arizona

Zuni culture fascinated me in its externals. There were many beautiful things about it, and I was always intrigued with what it must feel like to live in this culture.
—*Ruth L. Bunzel, 1964*

I

The Zunis have lived in western New Mexico and east-central Arizona for centuries, following the path of the middle place—a life where there is measured harmony. Zuni calls itself "The Middle Place," as both place and community, and considers the pueblo to be the center of the universe. The Zuni have vigorously maintained the core of a Puebloan way of life with a number of economic, material, and technological additions that have resulted from contact with European-based cultures. Living in permanent houses and pursuing an agriculturally based economy, similar to that of the Hopi and Rio Grande Puebloan peoples, the Zuni have successfully retained that which is valued of their indigenous culture, such as their language, while adapting to life in a multicultural society.

In the 1920s when Ruth L. Bunzel visited the Zuni, they numbered approximately 1,900 individuals and lived in a compact village with satellite farming communities that physically reflected an intricate and closely knit social organization (Eggan and Pandey 1979). This social organization has been characterized as an "almost marvelous complexity" (Kroeber 1917:183) of families, clans, fraternities, priesthoods, kiva organizations, and political groups and alliances whose cross-cutting nature has enabled the Zuni to persist despite occasional factional disputes. Like other Puebloan peoples, the Zuni have rich traditions, some shared with their neighbors, some the result of their distinct history and culture. Zunis have a strong sense of community and family; the society has retained its traditional ceremonial and sociopolitical organization.

A dynamic pueblo, Zuni is influenced by employment and school schedules as well as by agricultural cycles. It revolves around communal and familial obligations often expressed in an annual cycle of religious ceremonies. Activities are subordinated to religion; the subsistence economy "receives the full concentration of religious devotion and ritual. In an environment that is fraught with uncertainty regarding the success or failure of the basic means of livelihood, religious activity attempts to force nature to be more bountiful. . . . Activities marginal or unrelated to the basic subsistence economy receive little attention" (Dozier 1950:133). Thus religious obligations and kinship networks form the basis of community life. "The Zuni are a ceremonious people, a people who value sobriety and inoffensiveness above all other virtues. . . . No field of activity competes with ritual for foremost place in their attention" (Benedict 1934:59). As Ruth Bunzel notes in this volume, "All of Zuni life is oriented about religious observance, and ritual has become the formal expression of Zuni civilization" (p.509). "Nowhere in the New World, except in the ancient civilizations of Mexico and Yucatan, has ceremonialism been more highly developed" (p.480).

Given the importance of religion to the Zuni, it is no wonder that many anthropologists who have worked at Zuni since the 1870s have been fascinated by Zuni religion, thought, and ritual. The first ethnographic expedition to the Southwest in 1879 brought James and Matilda Coxe Stevenson and Frank Hamilton Cushing. Cushing is famous for his years spent at Zuni, and Stevenson returned many times over a 25-year period; both studied Zuni ceremonialism and myth. Following in their footsteps came other famous anthropologists—a listing of who's who in the Southwest—Alfred Kroeber, Elsie Clews Parsons, Franz Boas, Edward Sapir, Ruth Benedict, Frederick W. Hodge, Frank H. Roberts, Fred Eggan, Leslie Spier, John Adair, Watson Smith, Loki Pandey, and John Roberts—to name only a few. All studied Zuni religion and values, kinship, social and political organization, economics, culture change and external relations, language and thought—in short, all they could about Zuni life.

One of the finest scholars of Zuni, but unfortunately one of the least known, was Ruth Leah Bunzel. Quiet, shy, dedicated, and extremely private, Ruth Bunzel (1898–1990) is known for her famous work on Zuni pottery, *The Pueblo Potter* (1929a, reissued 1972). This work has had an extensive influence on anthropological theory and methodology (Hardin 1985). Her most substantive works and her most multifaceted contribution to our knowledge of another culture, however, is found in the realm of Zuni religion, particularly in those areas associated with ceremonialism, mythology, and ritual poetry. In a series of important memoirs, *Introduction to Zuni Ceremonialism* (1932a), *Zuni Origin Myths* (1932b), *Zuni Ritual Poetry* (1932c), *Zuni Kachinas* (1932d), and *Zuni Texts* (1933), Bunzel built on the equally extensive contributions of Matilda Coxe Stevenson

(1881, 1887, 1888, 1904), Frank Hamilton Cushing (1883, 1896, 1901, 1902), Elsie Clews Parsons (1916, 1917, 1919, 1922, 1924), and Alfred Kroeber (1916, 1917). She did this by analyzing the formalistic structure of religious activity and grasping the central metaphors, values, and concepts of Zuni religion—the ideas of the middle place, corn, breath and feathers, the journey of the Zuni people on paths, the place of the ancestors, and the role of the kachinas—as exemplified within texts, symbols, and ritual activities (Bunzel 1932c). In all her works there is a search for meanings and values, an attempt to understand the world as a Zuni would, not as an Anglo-American would. Her goal was to understand the search for individual and communal harmony and integration and how this was articulated in ceremonies, prayers, and daily life, in short to "find the middle place" (Bunzel 1985). This was an important search because religion is "of the greatest importance and of absorbing interest to the Zunis" (Smith and Roberts 1954:14).

While anthropologists have used Bunzel's Zuni materials (for example, Benedict 1934, 1935; Li 1937; Parsons 1939; Tedlock 1979), her publications in the massive *Annual Reports of the Bureau of American Ethnology* were published in limited numbers during the Depression. Many people are unaware, therefore, of the richness, detail, and depth of Bunzel's materials, the comprehensiveness of her descriptions, and the beauty of the Zuni texts. Partly because of this and due to the fact that Bunzel has been overshadowed by her colleague Ruth Benedict, Bunzel's contribution to Southwestern ethnography has been undervalued and even ignored (for example, neither Basso [1979] nor Hoebel [1954] mention Bunzel), even though Fred Eggan (1986) has stated that Bunzel is "the greatest ethnographic fieldworker we've had in the Southwest, man or woman." Her willingness to listen, her shyness and reticence, her capacity for comprehending in native terms without imposing inappropriate scientific or Anglo categories on her data, and her ability to contextualize texts with ethnographic detail have rarely been equaled.

This reprint by the University of New Mexico Press of the 1932 publications on Zuni religion—*Introduction to Zuni Ceremonialism*, *Zuni Origin Myths*, and *Zuni Ritual Poetry*—will go a long way toward illuminating Bunzel's contributions. The fourth selection from the Bureau of American Ethnology's 1929 annual report, *The Nature of Kachinas*, is already available in reprint. While *The Nature of Kachinas* stands by itself as a lively publication, it is incomplete because the contextualization to the kachina cult at Zuni is missing. Bunzel wrote these four works in a specific sequence and the reader needs to read and comprehend the first three essays in order to truly appreciate the complexity and beauty of *The Nature of Kachinas*. Thus, in order to make the entire corpus available, to understand the works as a set, and to bring to the fore Bunzel's contributions to Zuni scholarship, we here reprint the first three works on Zuni religion as they were published in 1932. No editing has been done to Bunzel's work.

In order to fully appreciate these contributions to Zuni scholarship we must first understand as much as we can about Ruth Bunzel's life as an anthropologist, her research goals, her experience as an anthropologist at Zuni, and the Zuni's reactions to her and her work. We must also analyze the scope of her works on religion in relation to other scholarly writing on Zuni religion. Scholars build on existing knowledge, reinterpreting what came before in light of contemporary theories and understandings. Bunzel's work should be seen, therefore, as part of the rich literature that was produced by American anthropologists of the "Boasian" school during the 1920s and 1930s. At Columbia University during this time a remarkable group of individuals gathered; these men and women encouraged each other and debated concepts and theories under the leadership of Franz Boas and Ruth Benedict. This was a dynamic period in the history of American anthropology in which anthropologists saw their discipline simultaneously as a scientific and humanistic endeavor, a way to change the world, and a way of life.

> To be young and energetic and bright in the twenties, recalled another Boas protegee, the anthropologist Ruth Bunzel, was to face stirring choices. "Some of us fled to the freer air of Paris," she said, "and eventually retired. Some of us joined radical movements, and sold the *Daily Worker* on street corners, and some of us went into anthropology, hoping that there we might find some answers to the ambiguities and contradictions of our age and the general enigma of human life . . . It was inconceivable that this cultural upheaval would not be reflected in so sensitive a discipline as anthropology." To this third group it appeared that anthropology could be instrumental not only in influencing and manipulating primitive peoples, but in bringing about "self-confrontation." Perhaps, Bunzel said, the important question was less "How can we change others?" than "How can we change ourselves?" In 1983, Bunzel amended that last question to read "How can we understand ourselves?" (Howard 1984:69).

For Bunzel, to understand Zuni religion, values, and morals was a mechanism by which one could understand her own culture. Implicit in her works was a comparison between Zuni culture and middle-class Anglo-American culture and a quest to understand the former as an integrated system of interrelated ideas that could help the latter. Bunzel decided to learn about the wisdom of other peoples in order to teach her own.

II

Ruth Bunzel and Ruth Benedict are linked at Zuni because they traveled together on their first trip (Bunzel came under Benedict's sponsorship) and because they both wanted to understand the aesthetics and poetics of Zuni secular and religious life. In anthropology as well they are often linked because of their associations at Columbia University. Their career paths and Zuni research overlap.

A student of Pueblo art, technology, ceremonialism, economics, individuality, poetry, language, culture, and personality, Bunzel became an anthropologist by accident. Born and raised in New York City, she attended Barnard College with a major in general studies and history. Upon graduating in 1918 she was without definite goals and held a series of temporary clerical jobs.

> I had been in school for a long time and wanted to get out into the world, I thought, and so I had a couple of years in business. I didn't find that very rewarding and I was out of a job, so I went to work for Professor Boas. I hadn't had a course with him, though I had sat in on a course of his rather irregularly when I was an undergraduate (Bunzel quoted in Mead 1964:88–89).

When Esther Goldfrank (another Barnard graduate) left her position as Boas's secretary in 1922, Bunzel was hired, her salary paid by Elsie Clews Parsons.

In the summer of 1924, with Boas traveling to Europe and Benedict to Zuni to collect mythology, Bunzel had little to do. From her years with Boas and her interaction with the dynamic anthropology community in New York City, she began to consider an anthropological career.

> I thought that if I could see an anthropologist at work at the most crucial and mysterious part of his study, and perhaps try a bit on my own, I would know whether or not I wanted to be and could be an anthropologist. So I thought that I would take my vacation time and a few dollars I had saved for a trip to Europe and instead meet Ruth Benedict in Zuni. My plan was not too ambitious—I was a good stenographer and I would take down folk tales and interviews in shorthand, and do all our typing. Ruth Benedict seemed pleased with the suggestion so I took it to Boas (Bunzel quoted in Mead 1959a:33).

Boas, however, felt differently.

> [He] heard me out, snorting in his inimitable fashion and said, "Why do you want to waste your time typing?" He always thought typing a "waste of time" though Heaven knows he wasted enough of his precious time on similar donkey work to know that the gremlins didn't do it after funds were spent on informants (Bunzel quoted in Mead 1959a:33–34).

> He said, "What are you going to do?" And I said, "I don't know." And he said, "Don't waste your time. Do a project of your own." But I said, "Professor Boas, I'm not an anthropologist. I can't do that." He said, "You're interested

> in art. They make pottery there. Go do a project on the relationship of the artist to her work" (Bunzel 1985).

Boas continued,

> "I have always wanted someone to work on the relation of the artist to his work." Boas always had a long list of problems that he hoped someone would work on, things that he had started and hadn't had time to go on with, or things that had just occurred to him (Bunzel quoted in Mead 1959a:34).
>
> So I had a problem to work on, but it was a pretty tall order (Bunzel 1985).

At that time one accepted the problem Professor Boas assigned and then developed it independently. Bunzel decided to study Zuni potters and their works, and to look at the manner in which "individuals operate within the limits of established style" (Bunzel 1929a:1), that is, cultural traditions.

Boas had always been interested in art and at this period was becoming focused on the individual (Mead 1959b). Since his pioneering work (Boas 1908/1940) he had advocated a search for creativity, innovation, and historical change, centering on the individuals who produce art, not only the objects themselves, as he felt had been done in the past (Boas 1927). This did not mean that he neglected tradition and the community, but he felt that one had to find the artists and ask them for their own native explanations to get the "play of the imagination" (Boas 1940:589). Additionally he felt the researcher had to participate in the culture in order to understand the process of creating art within a cultural and social setting. This required firsthand observation, experimentation, in-depth interviewing, rigorous empirical investigation, and insight. His classic work, *Primitive Art* (Boas 1927), reflects these ideas that had been germinating for many years (and, in turn, would be influenced by the success of Bunzel's work at Zuni).

The influence of one scholar on the other is difficult to unravel. Bunzel accepted Boas's basic methodology and his definitions, which delimited her research scope on art and later on religion, economics, and folklore (Hardin 1983:47). Boas's theories, however, were modified and expanded because of Bunzel's creativeness and her Zuni perspective, especially her view of the range of individual creativity within the confines of cultural values, and her analysis of normative and actual behavior. (Bunzel presented her data and findings in graduate seminar sessions after each field season.)

With no formal training in art history, technology, or anthropology, Bunzel "had about four or five weeks to become an anthropologist and plan a project" (Bunzel 1985).

> I was really alone in a big sea and I had to swim. I assumed that the Zuni

> artists were not going to be any more articulate about what they were trying to do than the poets and painters I had met in Greenwich Village, and that direct questioning would get me nowhere (Bunzel quoted in Mead 1959a:34).

Yet with a little help from Boas (i.e., an enjoinder to get going, to read Herman Haeberlin's thesis "The Idea of Fertilization in the Culture of the Pueblo Indians," to examine a book on Northwest Coast basket technology, and to see some pots in the museum) and Benedict about her "ironic dilemma" (Benedict quoted in Mead 1959b:75), Bunzel developed innovative methods, perspectives, and techniques:

> I had to figure out what to do with art. So I spent the next couple weeks down at the American Museum of Natural History photographing all the Zuni pottery—all the Pueblo pottery too. I had all these photographs to take along with me to show to the people to get them started (Bunzel 1985).

"I had to approach the problem indirectly. I decided on three lines of approach—criticism, instruction, and problem solving" (Bunzel quoted in Mead 1959a:33). Her use of photographs to elicit critiques of craftsmanship and aesthetic criteria have become standard. But at the time, Bunzel was apprehensive because as an experiment, her methods were untested and she had little time for refinement for "three weeks later I was on the train to Zuni" (Bunzel quoted in Mead 1959a:34).

Bunzel had another reason for choosing pottery production as her first project, one not influenced by Boas: pottery was made by women. Looking back over the years, she reflected,

> Zuni is a woman's society, and women have a great deal of power and influence. Women don't have access to all the ceremonials and of course the early anthropologists of the Southwest all dealt with ceremonials—the men's part of culture. I felt there was a great lack of knowledge about people's lives—particularly about women. . . . So being a woman, that was the obvious place to start. Of course the ceremonial life in the Pueblos is so spectacular and so elaborate, people just gravitated to that and didn't pay an awful lot of attention to the family life, the private live of the individuals and they knew almost nothing about the women, so that was the obvious place for a woman to start (Bunzel 1985).

Bunzel was also expressing a growing criticism of ethnographers; most scholars dealt with native men and ignored women when they studied other cultures. Bunzel, like other intellectuals reviewing existing knowledge, felt that "society consisted of more than old men with long memories" (Bunzel 1975). Women, too, had long memories and central places in societies, especially in Zuni where women are greatly respected. To ignore them or to marginalize them was to only gain a partial understanding of a culture.

The rationale among male anthropologists of the day was that women were inaccessible. Bunzel accepted but was not limited by this conception. She was cognizant of her access to women, of their knowledge of their culture and social organization. Unlike her friend and colleague Margaret Mead, however, she did not concentrate on "women's issues" such as childbirth and child-rearing. Rather she followed Boas's and Benedict's lead toward understanding the values and the contradictions of societies by using both men and women as sources of information and active cultural actors. For the Zuni she eventually articulated this as the relationship of the individual to others and to culture in a society with a communal rather than an individualistic orientation.

Bunzel decided to focus on an on-going activity rather than search for an "ethnographic present" that no longer, if it had ever, existed. This again was a criticism of ethnographers who devoted their attention solely to searching for the essence of "primitive" culture uncontaminated by European societies. In this she overcame the problem of relying on memory culture and was able to integrate herself into the community by attempting to perform a respected female task. Pottery-making was considered important by the Zuni and an appropriate topic for study. Studying pottery, an activity that was still practiced, if in decline (Hardin 1983), was thus intellectually satisfying and served as a practical means of entry into a community tired of, and disillusioned by, anthropologists. (See next section.) Bunzel could study both actual behavior and idealized behavior.

Bunzel's concern with entry into another culture and research methodology quickly became apparent. Reflecting years later on her first fieldwork endeavor and her subsequent development of methods, she stated:

> Out of all the ways in which one can work in a foreign culture, each anthropologist has one which is preferred (though, of course, not to the exclusion of other methods) and which for him seems most natural and most promising. He will use this method whenever the situation permits, and it is right that he should do so because a person picks up more cues in a field which is familiar and natural to him. I, for instance, am only a moderately good observer. I have had to train myself to look at things, to observe them precisely and attentively. Even so, I miss many subtleties that would be picked up by someone for whom visual experience is the primary method of orienting himself in life. On the other hand, I am naturally very alert to those nuances in verbal communication that can reveal more than the informant intended to say (Bunzel 1952:xiv).

Bunzel learned about Zuni pottery-making and aesthetics in 1924 and 1925 through observation, listening, talking, and participation. She quickly realized, as did Gladys Reichard later with Navajo weavers, that artists like to talk about their work and demonstrate their expertise. Bunzel was recognized at Zuni as a potter—a respected position—and "at one point she could walk about with a pot on her head, and climb a ladder balancing a pot with her hand" (Fawcett and McLuhan 1988:31). She acquired these skills by apprenticing herself.

> I felt that instruction was very important in how they visualized, how they thought about what they were doing. So I said I wanted to learn how to do it and got people to teach me. I was never very good at it (Bunzel 1985).

Bunzel watched pottery being made, noted her own observations, and recorded the comments of Zuni potters in both English and Zuni. In addition she had potters use photographs to classify pots that had been collected by the Stevensons and Cushing in the 1880s for the Bureau of Ethnology and the Smithsonian Institution, as well as paint designs on *papier mâché* models and draw designs.

This perspective and methodology resulted in *The Pueblo Potter* (1929a), which became a landmark in the anthropology of art. By focusing on the artist rather than solely on the object, Bunzel helped free material culture studies from a sterile compendium of type lists and stylistic taxonomies. The act of making pottery became as crucial as the object itself. Her work marked a shift from historic reconstruction to the use of art as a means of understanding human behavior, for this was the first time both art and psychology were combined in a problem-oriented focus (Bunzel 1929b), and the first time the artist was seen as part of a complex social organization.

This same focus on the place of the individual within the system, the amount of "freedom" an individual has with regard to aesthetics and designs, can be seen duplicated in this volume in Bunzel's analysis of *Zuni Ritual Poetry*, and in her analyses of prayer. As with pottery design the ritual poetry analysis combines formalism with individual expression in a search for the boundary between the communal and the individual. This was the first time this analytical framework was applied to folklore and religious rhetoric. It also demonstrated clearly how one scholarly success influences a researcher's later work.

Bunzel proved that Boas's ideas and her expansion of them, combined with an innovative methodology, could produce new insights into culture, especially a culture like Zuni about which a great deal was already known. Modest as always, Bunzel states of her work,

> I was too ignorant at the time to know that I was pioneering; that I was on the frontier of a whole new field of anthropology; that this was the first tentative approach to the study of the individual in culture; the first attempt at a systematic study of behavior. I didn't know that I was employing "participant observation" and "projective techniques" because I had never heard of these things (Bunzel quoted in Mead 1959a:34).

Benedict's tutelage and their discussions on the place of the individual in culture and aesthetic and social patterns also greatly informed Bunzel's analysis and helped guide her to look for the inner feelings of the artist. This perspective constituted the basis of Bunzel's later specialization in culture and personality (Bunzel 1929b, 1938, 1953) and can be seen here in her references to the individual in relation to religious organization and activity. Bunzel attempted throughout her artistic study to focus on the processes by which potters created designs and analyzed design meanings (Hardin 1983:8). This same perspective can be seen in her approach to religion and folklore. More importantly she tried to identify with the women potters, to understand the works as they did: "I guess I was more interested in people than in things, and I wanted to find out what the Zunis were thinking about and why they did the things that they did" (Bunzel 1985).

III

Bunzel did not return to the study of art and material culture per se when she returned to Zuni to begin her next projects. She shifted her attention to values, a topic that she found more interesting and one that would help her discover what the Zunis thought. However her work on religion and texts as the place where values are most clearly expressed must be seen as an outgrowth of her earlier study. Bunzel had learned, although she tried to minimize it (Bunzel 1929a:69), that pottery communicates prayers and stories (Hardin 1986). Religion permeated all of Zuni life, but she was not yet ready to undertake its study.

Bunzel returned to Zuni the next summer as a graduate student in anthropology at Columbia University on another grant from Elsie Clews Parsons (Mead 1959a:33–35). She and Benedict arrived in August 1925:

> We drove in with the rain pouring down in great white separate drops and sunlit clouds, and soft veils of rain sifting and forming against the far off mesas. The red terraced hillock of Zuni never looked better in any setting (Benedict quoted in Mead 1959b:291).

Bunzel had decided to become an anthropologist and like all anthropologists she wanted to be a part of her native community. "I went back to Zuni to learn the language and prepare to find out what it felt like to be a Zuni; I saw this as an extension of the study of the artist" (Bunzel quoted in Mead 1959a:35).

This quest, and her perspective that one should structure "an inquiry within a framework that is meaningful in the culture" (Bunzel 1952:xv), led her, like Stevenson, Cushing, Benedict, Boas, and Parsons, to ceremonialism. "In Zuni, as in all the pueblos, religion spreads wide" (Bunzel

1932a:480). It was the most evident and available road to the inner content and feel of the culture, to finding the middle place, to understanding how one found and followed the completed path.

> I felt that we knew a lot about the external Pueblo life, but there is always more to find out for it is such a rich culture. I guess I just wanted to know what they were thinking about, why they did the things they did, and how they felt about their lives and their work and the things that they did. . . . Especially in ritual because Zuni is such a highly ritualized culture. I felt that to really get people to open up I had to learn the language. So I spent a couple summers on language (Bunzel 1985).

Boas and Benedict encouraged this research agenda. Benedict had been struggling with Zuni for three years and making little progress (Mead 1959b:292). After one summer concentrating on Zuni grammar, Bunzel went to the University of Chicago to study with Edward Sapir. She did this, however, over Boas's objections. Boas argued that she could obtain all the linguistic training she needed from him. Bunzel felt, however, a need to gain new insights and perspectives as well as obtain formal training in linguistics. This was a difficult decision for her—to go against the wishes of the "Great Man" who was simultaneously "the frightening Herr Professor" and "Papa Franz" (Goldfrank 1978:39). But Bunzel began to move toward autonomy and made the right decision; she found her studies with Sapir—the most noted linguist of his time—of great help in writing her Zuni grammar (Bunzel 1935), although a later linguist, Stanley Newman, thought Sapir's influence affected her work negatively.

> The morphology was marred by an overzealous attention to fine shades of meaning and a corresponding inattention to the systematic analysis and classification of forms (Newman 1965:11).

Newman (1954:163) has also stated that he has found Bunzel's "transcribed material highly unreliable" and her system of vowel phonemes "somewhat ambiguous." Today, Bunzel and Sapir's approach is seen as meaningful, the "marring" actually an enhancement to our understanding. In addition other linguists feel Newman missed core elements of Zuni grammar that Bunzel correctly identified (Shaul 1985). Although there may be problems with it, Bunzel's grammar is still a fundamental reference work for Zuni linguistics and the texts that appear later in this book can still be used with confidence. Luckily, Bunzel, like others of her period, provides textual information in Zuni as well as translations so that other scholars can assess the data for themselves.

With the necessary linguistic tools, Bunzel again returned to Zuni in the late 1920s, having completed two years of training at Columbia and one at the University of Chicago.

> I think the year that I went back to Zuni knowing the language and really feeling that I belonged there and could participate in the culture was the most interesting thing that ever happened to me in the field. I felt that I really understood it. I think that was the most rewarding year. The years before, I had plugged away at learning the language and I had done jobs that other people had picked for me. But this was the problem which I had picked for myself (Bunzel quoted in Mead 1964:89–90).

Traveling by herself this time, Bunzel began to gather texts that illustrated the important values in Zuni life and culture. She obtained case studies and life-history materials as a "way of finding out what it was really like to live as a Zuni" (Bunzel quoted in Mead 1964:90). This quickly led to an analysis of religion, emphasizing ceremonialism, mythology, poetry, and the kachina cult (Bunzel 1932a–d, 1933, 1938a).

IV

Ritual was a topic about which the Zuni were more reticent to speak than the production and use of pottery or grammar. Bunzel notes that she, like other anthropologists before her, was watched at night to see who came to work with her. Luckily Bunzel had developed good relations at Zuni during the previous summers, although, as she recalls, this had been anything but easy.

> When Ruth Benedict and I first arrived at Zuni the village was in one of its periodic states of upheaval in which anthropologists figured. The "progressive" faction, favorable to Americans and friendly to anthropologists, had been ousted after unsuccessful attempts by anthropologists to photograph the midwinter ceremonies, and its members were so discredited that any contact with them would have been disastrous. We were consequently faced with the necessity of finding informants among the conservative and traditionally hostile group that was now in power (Bunzel 1952:xv).

The upheaval was deep-seated and bitter. Frederick W. Hodge, an archaeologist who had excavated at Hawikuh from 1917 to 1923 under the auspices of the Museum of the American Indian, Heye Foundation, received permission from the Zuni to film parts of Zuni culture, namely adobe-making, pottery construction, and bread-baking. Then he received permission from the "progressive" faction to film the Shalako ceremony and the pilgrimage to the Great Salt Lake (Fred Eggan 1986). In addition he and his cameraman, Owen Cattel, filmed parts of the summer rain dances and the sacred pilgrimage to Ojo Caliente. The "conservatives" were outraged.

The factionalism between the conservatives and the progressives had a long history (Fergusson 1990). The progressives were anti-Catholics and strongly Protestant; they had opposed the reestablishment of the Roman Catholic mission in 1916 and the Bureau of Indian Affairs' grant of land on which to rebuild Saint Anthony's Church in 1922 (Li 1937; Pandey 1972). Early in his excavations

> when Dr. Hodge was excavating the ruins near Zuni, a Protestant Zuni got the information from him that a sacred object valued by the people was but a small figure of St. Francis, inherited from the early Franciscan padres, and he used this information to discredit his Catholic opponents to his own advantage. Previous to this the priests of Zuni valued the object as indigenous and with this discovery a strife of immense magnitude took place between the Catholic and Protestant elements (Li 1937:64).

This brought the progressives to power and they were in power when Boas visited the community.

The Zunis were sharply divided on these issues that reflected a long pattern of power struggles between Zuni political factions and the community's attempts to determine its own future. This political process had been complicated by the BIA's meddling in the internal affairs of the pueblo. The first attempt to reestablish the mission in 1907 was exacerbated by the BIA superintendent, who was a Catholic (Fergusson 1990).

By 1922 Zuni was ripe for another political confrontation. The Bursum Bill and a tribal land claim were at immediate issue, as was the intrusion of non-Zunis into the society's private affairs. If it had not been Hodge's filming of sacred events that triggered the confrontation, there would have been some other issue. The conservatives confiscated Hodge's and Cattel's cameras and forced Hodge and his associates to leave the reservation. The progressive officials of the secular government were replaced by conservatives when the religious leaders appointed a new governor and Tribal Council. When Benedict and Bunzel arrived, the progressives and their Protestant (i.e., Dutch Reform Church) supporters who had been working with Hodge were no longer in power.

Anthropologists, when they first enter a community, tend to go first to individuals who have most recently helped other anthropologists. But in this case, it was not possible. Luckily, however, Boas had established good relations with the conservative faction, as well as the progressives, when he visited Zuni in 1920.

> When Nick Tumaka paid his official call on us that evening [the first night at Zuni], to find out as governor who we were and what we were doing, we fished around for names that might identify us as acceptable. . . . Finally we mentioned Boas. Boas had spent three days in Zuni when he was working at

> Laguna [1920], but Nick remembered the man with the crooked face who had wanted to hear stories. That turned the trick and we got our visas. We had no further trouble, but, naturally our contacts were somewhat limited by our sponsorship (Bunzel quoted in Pandey 1972:332).

Bunzel and Benedict had intended to stay with Margaret Lewis, a member of the progressive faction, who had worked closely with Elsie Clews Parsons (Pandey 1972:332). Lewis was a Cherokee who had married a Zuni after she came to teach at the Zuni school.

> Well, two days—or is it two years—ago we set up house keeping a la Zuni. Mrs. Lewis is no longer here so we have been thrown on our own resources. It was not a great surprise because Hodge had warned me of the possibility. It seems that Mrs. Lewis has gotten herself badly involved in the religious rumpus, and as a result did not get a school appointment for next year. Nevertheless, our hearts went down into our toes when we got here and actually found her gone, and our letters lying undelivered in the post office (APS: RB to FB, August 6, 1924).

They tried another family at Tumaka's suggestion:

> We soon made contact with a young woman employee of the Government school who spoke English and who was a member of the household of one of the leaders of the ultra-conservative factions (Bunzel 1952:xv).

> We went to Flora [Zuni] as a next resort and were received like princes and rented from her a house on the edge of the village where we are more than comfortable (APS: RB to FB, August 6, 1924).

The sponsoring family defined and limited an anthropologist's social interaction at Zuni, and even the ability to stay. Flora agreed "to serve as our interpreter, but only with members of her own family" (Bunzel 1952:xv).

> We moved in and began work with this family. For the first week it seemed doubtful that we would be able to remain, but through a mixture of caution and luck we survived (Bunzel 1952:xv).

Bunzel, like Benedict, was allowed to stay. Her work progressed because of the personal relationships she cultivated, especially with these two remarkable individuals from two clans, Flora Zuni and Nick Tumaka, and her ability to become quietly part of the community—at least of the conservative faction for the moment. Bunzel decided that she would, as far as possible without actually going "native" as Cushing had, conform to local expectations of gender. Luckily she had an appropriate project—pottery—and a good guide—Flora Zuni (Pandey 1972:322). Her decision made her future research on ceremonialism possible.

Flora Zuni's conservative family and their social network remained methodologically and informationally at the core of Bunzel's and Benedict's Zuni work (Bunzel 1952). Bunzel worked closely with Flora; Clarence [Bunzel does not specify his kinship relationship but he is probably Flora's husband or brother]; Flora's sister, Margaret; their brother, Leo; Flora's mother, Catalina; and Flora's father (Bunzel 1933). She is fondly remembered by them (Margaret Hardin 1986). "Although years later I had many friends at Zuni and was accepted everywhere, our first informant and her family remained the core of our informants and our anchor at Zuni" (Bunzel 1952:xv). The family provided the necessary fictive kinship attachments and roles for single women living in a society where marriage and children were expected.

Bunzel lived for five summer seasons and several winters with the Zuni family (1924–1929) and was formally made a member of Flora's Badger clan in 1926. (Zuni has 13 matrilineal clans.) She was given the name "Maiatitsa," which means "blue bird," in honor of a blue smock that served as her fieldwork uniform (Fawcett and McLuhan 1988:30). Flora and Bunzel developed a lasting friendship.

Flora Zuni, a sewing instructor at the local school, is considered by Triloki Pandey (1978) to be one of the most remarkable women he has ever met. Flora Zuni remembered Bunzel fondly, reporting to Pandey years later (1972:333):

> She was just like a sister to me. We lived together for a while in the old house and then moved to this new house. I washed her hair and my children used to bring her [drinking] water from the day school. She was very hardworking like me. She used to grind cornmeal for our [religious] doings, go to the field with men to work there, and helped my nieces with their homework. Once she got after one of the teachers for giving them too much homework and after that they treated our children nicely.
>
> Bunzel was a good woman. She liked people and was always good to children. She used to go to [the Zuni] night dances in the winter. Once I got after her because she spoiled one of my nicest dresses. She borrowed it for a dance and then sat on the dirt floor wearing my dress. I remember her getting upset only once when she was followed by some boys who said dirty things to her. She talked back to them in Zuni and scolded them. They got scared and ran away. Boys were nice and obedient in those days (Zuni quoted in Pandey 1978:220).

Bunzel, likewise, had fond memories of Flora, but simultaneously retained the objective distance required of a positivist anthropological fieldworker at this time—a relationship with natives was to be "both warm and limited, affectionate but not passionate, friendly but not partisan" (Mead 1986:324).

> Flora is a very shrewd young person. They are rebuilding for Shalako and they have their eyes on a particular field they want to buy—so she is making the most of the gold mine that descended on her. Her chief regret is that each day has only 24 hours that she can work in. . . . Flora is a good story teller and a good interpreter. She is working here now (APS: RB to FB, August 6, 1924).
>
> Flora promptly tried to monopolize me. She is too good a person to alienate, so I continue to work with her. As I expected, I find her an excellent informant for linguistic works, especially analytical work. Her pronunciation, however, according to all the young people, is very bad. It has taken me all this time to realize how bad it is. You may remember that I once said there were no glottalized consonants—Flora and most of the people of her generation simply don't pronounce them, and are equally careless about other things (APS: RB to FB, July 25, 1926).

Bunzel also recognized that Flora was ambivalent about being the source of anthropological information:

> From the first it was apparent that our interpreter and mentor was of two minds about her role. As a conservative Zuni, fully accepting the responsibilities and values of her culture, she was beset by anxieties both social and supernatural. On the other hand, she was attracted to White culture and White people, and saw in her relationship with us an opportunity to advance herself both economically (the custom of paying informants was so well entrenched at Zuni that it took me five years to break it down at certain points), and socially as a leader of what might be called "conservative progressivism" (Bunzel 1952:xv–xvi).

Bunzel (1933:vi) stated in the foreword to *Zuni Texts* that it was Flora Zuni's "patient and intelligent cooperation which alone made progress possible."

It should be acknowledged that Flora Zuni both collected and translated the texts for Bunzel. At the time that Bunzel wrote and published, Native American consultants/informants were not formally acknowledged in introductions or in texts, let alone recognized as coauthors. In fact it is sometimes impossible to figure out which native individuals were involved in the research. In addition to methodological concerns dealing with the number of individuals who were consulted, and the attempts to show cultures as homogeneous wholes without internal variation, one of the reasons for this nonrecognition was that anthropologists were trying to protect the peoples with whom they worked. It was felt that anonymity would screen the individual from government intervention and political pressure within the home community. This practice went so far that some anthropologists even changed the name of the community, although rarely the culture. Because of the animosity toward individuals who worked with anthropologists in the eastern Pueblos, and the oft-repeated rumors of individuals who had been killed or ostracized for revealing information (including at Zuni), keeping the names of informants, translators, and native co-researchers secret was a necessity extended to all Puebloan and even some Apachean communities. At Zuni this concern may have been due to sensitivity on Bunzel's part, to the ambivalence of the Zuni family, to the volatile political situation, or simply the acceptance of standard scientific practice. Nevertheless it is clear that we must consider Flora Zuni and members of her family as Bunzel's peers and coworkers, not only her paid anonymous assistants.

Bunzel later stated that the single-family approach to fieldwork was the one with which she felt most comfortable, even though it had shortcomings (Pandey 1978:221). Because of the necessity of a cultural and linguistic interpreter, she felt that working with a small number of "highly intelligent individuals with whom one is able to form and maintain fairly close personal relationships of mutual trust" (Bunzel 1952:viii) yielded the most valuable data. In order to secure this trust one had to work within and become part of a kinship network, that is, a family or household.

> My preferred method of work is to become attached to a single family, living as intimately as possible within the orbit of their lives, identifying as fully as possible with them and learning to see the culture through their eyes (Bunzel 1952:xiv–xv).

For Bunzel the results were highly productive. She worked closely with Flora's mother, Catalina (or Lina), a 65-year-old woman who spoke no English. Catalina was "an excellent potter and a real artist" (APS: RB to FB, August 6, 1924) "who has been practicing her art for at least forty years. . . . She was an able informant on all matters of religious belief and practice, knew many esoteric ceremonies and imparted freely whatever she knew" (Bunzel 1929a:69). Bunzel published Catalina Zuni's autobiography in *Zuni Texts* (Bunzel 1933:74–96).

Bunzel obtained "from various members of Flora's large family short texts of every day activities—planting-harvesting, housebuilding, baking, cooking—and short simple descriptions of ceremonies" (APS: RB to FB, July 25, 1926). She tried to fit as closely as possible into the orbit of their lives. She participated in the ceremonial activities of Zuni women; she ground corn, prepared and presented food. With the help of Flora Zuni she learned songs and studied the language through the medium of corn because corn is essential to life and is under the direct care of the daylight people—the Zuni themselves. Corn is a metaphor for life, its tassels are the head and the children are the maturing corn ears that the people of the middle place hold in their arms (Pandey 1978; Bunzel 1932c:645,

658). As Cushing documented earlier in his classic *Zuni Breadstuff,* and as Benedict (1935) noted in *Zuni Mythology,* corn is the mother of us all.

> The world then, is as it is, and man's plan in it is what it is. Day follows night and the cycles of the years complete themselves. In the spring the corn is planted, and if all goes well the young stalks grow to maturity and fulfill themselves. They are cut down to serve man for food, but their seeds remain against another planting. So man, too, has his days and his destined place in life. His road may be long or short, but in time it is fulfilled, and he passes on to fill another role in the cosmic scheme (Bunzel 1932a:486).

Factionalism and family rivalries in Zuni had direct consequences for Bunzel's work, however, just as it had for the work of other anthropologists (Smith and Roberts 1954:7). Factionalism meant that anthropologists were ignored by groups who did not get along with the host family. This engendered hostility from rival factions, thus limiting the opportunities of anthropologists to collect information, especially on intercultural variation. The result was often a depiction of a society that appears to be more homogeneous than it actually is. Bunzel tried to overcome this problem by working closely with people outside Flora Zuni's family and in other clans.

Bunzel's most important "outside" consultant was Nick Tumaka, Zuni's governor and one of the few Zuni who knew English in the early 1900s (Pandey 1978:219). Tumaka was one of the most powerful men in the pueblo (Pandey and Eggan 1979:477). He had successfully challenged the authority of the Bow Priests in 1896 and 1897, and had changed the nature of religious politics in the early 1900s (Smith and Roberts 1954). Tumaka had worked with several anthropologists because he was interested in their work. Tumaka was "the outstanding intellectual of Zuni" (Kroeber quoted in Parsons 1939:64), and "a person of great ability, of commanding presence, and with a great personal need for achieving eminence, which he sought primarily in the medicine societies" (Benedict 1935:xxxix). As Benedict noted in a letter to Margaret Mead (quoted in Mead 1959b:292), "There's something impressive in the man's fire. He might have been a really great man. And yet I think any society would have used its own terms to brand him a witch. He's too solitary and too contemptuous." Tumaka worked with Kroeber, Parsons, Boas, and Benedict. He soon became one of Bunzel's primary consultants and closest friends, telling her lengthy tales and prayers. "He is excellent for dictation and translated literally, but gets impatient if I try any work on morphology and begins to gossip about other things" (APS: RB to FB, July 25, 1926). Bunzel was given a second Zuni name, "Tsatitsa," by Tumaka, because he was "jealous of the name bestowed upon her by Flora and her clan" (Fawcett and McLuhan 1988:30). Bunzel and Tumaka became so close that Bunzel told

David Fawcett and Teri McLuhan in 1984 that Nick had wanted to marry her.

Bunzel slowly was accepted (or at least tolerated) among the Zuni and worked with several other individuals during her third field season and thereafter, trying not to align herself exclusively with any single family (APS: RB to FB, July 25, 1926). Of course, as Langness (1970:221) has demonstrated,"there is no way to avoid being identified with a particular group or faction. After only a brief period of residence, one is so strongly identified with his host group that virtually nothing can be done to change the situation." Because of this one of the keys to acceptance was to prove one "was harmless and that the research would be for their [the host culture's] benefit as well as mine" (Bunzel 1985). Trust was built slowly.

> I started off in the first project the first year I was there working on the pottery and that is public. There are no secrets about it. And I learned to make pots and sat with the women and did the whole thing from beginning to end. I think they decided I was harmless. Then I got to make friends. Just by joining in daily activities. I like to do women's things. And of course they spend much of their time grinding corn. It's long hard hours so they were very glad to have someone else do it. So I had to spend hours grinding corn (Bunzel 1985).

Bunzel was realistic about her acceptance. She knew it would never be complete.

> I continue to dance on eggs, carrying water on both shoulders. Of the three families where I work, not one is on speaking terms with either of the others, so navigation is ticklish. I except a grand smashup at any moment. I'm not exactly a popular character in the village. However, a few more people deign to answer my "good morning." I think most of them are coming to regard me as a fairly harmless lunatic. But I am not accepted on a basis of open friendliness anywhere. After all, there is really no adequate answer to the question: "Why do you want to know?" At least none that is comprehensible with people whose world is bounded by the corrals on the edge of the village. I have too much sympathy with this attitude of mind your own business and we will mind ours. Then I felt more than ever before the disabilities of sex. It is hard for a woman to scrape up chance acquaintances in the streets or on the plaza. The first few days I was here I had an endless procession of callers—mostly young men, returned schoolboys, who came snooping. They'd sit around, smoking my cigarettes and trying to worm things out of me. I could never tell whether the visit was friendly or not—but probably not. However for the past week I've been let alone. They have probably decided that I'm harmless because no one even looks in at the windows any more (APS: RB to FB, July 25, 1926).

The year of studying the public domain of pottery and her attempts to speak

Zuni allowed Bunzel to build the trust necessary to study the more private domain of religion.

Bunzel's consultants regarding ritual included both elders and younger men and women, whom she paid by the day. Unlike many other anthropologists, she did not have to and did not want to "take her informants to Albuquerque" to obtain information.

> I ran into a man who will tell me all the prayers I have time to record. . . . None of the Flora family will tell any esoteric texts, but their superstitions apparently do not extend to the point of refusing to translate and interpret what I get from other sources. They all, including the old people, sit around and listen to what I have gotten and I get the benefit of their combined comments and explanations (APS: RB to FB, August 15, 1924).

These commentators included, as far as I can tell because Bunzel's notes on her sources are cryptic, Husteto, a Rain Priest, "who sets the tone for the [Flora Zuni's] family. . . . I am accepted into his house and his son works for me. They are the very core of Zuni religious life but they come in for much criticism from other factions who are hostile to all outsiders" (APS: RB to FB, July 25, 1926). Another young unidentified man drew kachinas for her. These drawings served as the basis for her interviews with other Zuni and as the illustrations for her book *The Nature of Kachinas* (1932d). For her linguistic work she consulted with the Ondulacy family (spelled Andelesis in Bunzel's notes), members of the progressive faction. But persuading them to help proved difficult.

> Warren and his father, but they are hard to get hold of! They are so well off that they don't need the money and will only work in the evenings, and Warren is more likely than not to go right to sleep in the middle of the session. His father is apt to be skittish and is rather scared (APS: RB to FB, July 25, 1926).

Others, whom Bunzel never identified, even in her notes in order to ensure their anonymity, took her to shrines, or led her through the intricacies of Zuni religious life so that she could use "a conceptual scheme native to the culture as the structural framework of research" (Bunzel 1952:xv). For her textual work, she obtained stories primarily from the Zuni family, and from Nick, Clarence, and Walelia (further identification is not given by Bunzel) (Bunzel 1933:ix).

V

Bunzel documented through the three works reprinted in this volume—*Introduction to Zuni Ceremonialism, Zuni Origin Myths, Zuni Ritual*

Poetry—and *The Nature of Kachinas* that the integration and measured harmonious whole which characterized Zuni life must be viewed through both collective and individual activity and knowledge. "At Zuni the same ceremonious collectivism that characterizes social activities is the essence also of all religious participation" (Bunzel 1932a:480); and, in addition to culture displayed as detailed ethnographic facts, Zuni must be understood as "rituals whose richness, variety, and beauty have attracted the attention of poets and artists of all countries" (Bunzel 1932a:480). "It [ceremonialism] pervades all activities, and its very pervasiveness and the rich and harmonious forms in which it is externalized compensate the study of religion for the lack of intensity of that feeling" (Bunzel 1932a:480).

Introduction to Zuni Ceremonialism is one of the best and most readable introductions to Zuni religion—"a description and brilliant analysis of Zuni ceremonial life" according to Edward Dozier (1970:224). Integrating much of the work of her predecessors, Bunzel analyzes the basic organization of Zuni ritual, the cult of the ancestors, and places this within Zuni conceptual categories and simultaneously demonstrates how these relate to social organizations. (At Zuni ceremonial associations are under clan or lineage as well as priesthood control.) This is a crucial analysis, for the clan and the priests are the repositories of ceremonial knowledge and ritual paraphernalia.

In the text Bunzel reveals how the ceremonies bring together the day people (that is, the Zuni) and the world of the ancestors. Ceremonial activity is the people's contribution to maintenance of a harmonious balance, which is believed to be the natural state of affairs. She also documents how other esoteric cults are embedded in the cosmological system and world view. The priesthoods possess complex ritual knowledge that is highlighted in a calendrical cycle of ceremonies (Bunzel 1932a:509), and the welfare of the pueblo rests on the timely observance of this calendar. She categorizes these cults and rituals, noting their functions and purpose, investigates their social organization, and assesses their importance. Special attention is given to the priesthoods and the cult of the kachina, which is described in detail with regard to the Zuni emphasis on weather control, curing, and harmony. The kachina cult receives special attention by Bunzel because it is communitywide and thus a crucial organization for her theory of communal integration. The kachina cult is embedded in her analysis of the cult of the ancestors, for as Bunzel reports, kachinas are supernatural beings vaguely considered to be ancestral spirits. This analysis is expanded in *The Nature of Kachinas*.

Bunzel focuses on the elaborate ceremonies and elucidates the accompanying prayers and ceremonial speeches. These are transcribed and presented word for word as her Zuni respondents said them. "In the end the meaning of the ceremonies as the way of maintaining harmony in the universe, as the Zuni feel them, is made unforgettably clear" (Spicer 1948:85). In *Zuni Origin Myths* Bunzel outlines the religious system as a metaphysical system, and demonstrates that this text provides the basis for Zuni ceremonialism—the rationale for the Zuni concerns of village harmony, weather control, illness, hunting, and the control of fertility in nature and humans. Zuni ritual, Bunzel notes, cannot be understood as a collective and individual activity without an understanding of myth and prayer, the philosophy and ritualistic formulae of Zuni world view. Bunzel's work here is complementary to Benedict's in that it demonstrates that Zuni ceremonialism can best be understood as the general Pueblo concept of the interrelatedness and cooperative nature of the universe. In this book is the justification for the Zuni belief that as long as ceremonies are properly and regularly performed, nature will respond by providing the necessities of life and the world will continue as it should. Universal balance, the middle path will be actively maintained.

Like Benedict, Bunzel is attuned to the nuances of the literary style of Zuni myths, prayers, and stories. Her concern with ethnographic methodology provides a systematic, comparative framework emphasizing problems of translation, interpretation, and internal variation, while increasing our knowledge of Zuni religious texts and poetics. Both authors display a sensitive appreciation of the spoken word and a fascination for form and content as well as the "compulsive force of ritual."

Bunzel's analysis of prayer formulae and ritual poetic structure in *Zuni Ritual Poetry* helped serve as a model for Gladys Reichard's work on Navajo prayer (1944). Likewise Bunzel's work (especially *Introduction to Zuni Ceremonialism*) was influenced by and was intended to be an implicit comparison to Benedict's work on the guardian spirit complex (1923). Bunzel, in turn, influenced Benedict's famous *Patterns of Culture* (1934) and her compendium, *Zuni Mythology* (1935); her research provided a major source of information for Benedict's works (Goldfrank 1978:39).

On another level the prayers scattered throughout these works and highlighted in *Zuni Ritual Poetry* demonstrate how the Zuni system works. By supplication, dramatically and cheerfully rendered without ill feelings toward any one or toward any aspect of the universe, the day people can ask powerful supernaturals to bring rain, cure, and ensure the general well-being of the community. This is thus a very active analysis that documents how formalistic renderings can bring positive results. There is little emphasis on personal feelings, even in individual prayer, as Li (1937:63) notes. Bunzel portrays Zuni prayer as "not a spontaneous outpouring of the heart. It is rather the repetition of a fixed formula" (p.612). Yet this does not mean that there is no room for individual creativity and religious feeling; Bunzel also states that prayers are "individually varied in degree of elaboration," and she quotes a Zuni consultant who remarked that "some men who are smart talk a long time, but some are just like babies." The poetic ability of individuals is further discussed when Bunzel comments that some Zuni are renowned for their ability to handle the poetic medium. The total analysis, however, must be seen as Bunzel's attempt to implicitly compare Zuni to a cultural foil, the Plains vision quest. For both Bunzel and Benedict, Zuni ritual prayer seems "mechanistic," "controlled," "harmonious," "unchanging," and "to lack an intensity of feeling" because it stands in such stark contrast to Plains religious activity. This does not mean that Bunzel found Zuni ritual uninteresting, or lacking an emotional character, only that it differed markedly from the Plains.

Bunzel is especially concerned with detail and precision in her translations because of a Zuni concern, as well as her own desire, for scientific accuracy. As Benedict (1934:63) relates, "This preoccupation with detail is logical enough. Zuni religious practices are believed to be supernaturally powerful in their own right. At every step of the way if the procedure is correct, the costume of the masked god traditional to the last detail, the offerings unimpeachable, the words of the hours-long prayers letter-perfect, the effect will follow according to man's desires . . . Every detail has magical efficacy." Bunzel's pages of description therefore are an attempt to convey to the reader what is important to the Zuni, not only what is important to the anthropologist.

Bunzel's analysis of Zuni kachinas (or *ko'ko*) documents their centrality to Zuni religion and life. A culmination of the preceding studies, it is still the definitive analysis of the most vital, the most spectacular, and the most pervasive of Zuni cults. It was in the kachina cult that Bunzel discovered the inner core of Zuni life; thus the reader should not neglect *The Nature of Kachinas*. This series of studies is the culmination of her work in religion, linguistics, values, and aesthetics, just as *Zuni Texts* (1933) is the culmination of her years of research in folklore with her Zuni families.

In the works reprinted in the volume at hand, Bunzel tried to capture the essence of Zuni religion and world view within the context of Zuni society. Because of previous research on Zuni religion, she could "obtain a deeper understanding, a more dynamic view" (Bunzel 1952:xvi). Her use of metaphor, her descriptions in Zuni terms, her identification of key concepts will be readily apparent. Like her later work these are "attempts to penetrate a culture by looking at it through the eyes of members of it" (Bunzel 1952:viii). Her goals were to understand the patterns and ethos of Zuni, the views of the people, the ideals of life, the institutional framework, and significant relationships, rather than the events of concrete religious behavior (which had fascinated Stevenson). It is through religion, through knowing the origin myth and the prayers that the basic assumptions and expectations of the culture toward the individual are learned. Thus Bunzel came full circle and completed her path. By beginning with the individual as artist she ended with the individual as Zuni.

These essays contain another benefit for the reader who reads critically and closely. In addition to ethnographic descriptions on religion, they are rife with information on kinship, politics, social organization, households, and economics, for Bunzel knew that religion, poetry, and myth could not be understood in isolation from the rest of the culture. Much of this can be found in footnotes, the standard location for this type of information in anthropological publications from the 1920s and 1930s. While the analysis is written and should be seen as a synchronic thesis, the books also contain scattered references of historical interest, especially information on the expansion and contraction of parts of the ceremonial organization due to changes in Zuni society as the people were increasingly integrated into the political and economic system of the Anglo-American world.

Those who have read Ruth Benedict's *Patterns of Culture*, with its emphasis on the strong dominant patterns of a culture, will find much that is familiar in the essays reprinted here. This is because Benedict drew heavily on Bunzel's work for her synthesis of Zuni culture. As Edward Spicer (1948:85) pointed out, "the chapter [on Zuni] in *Patterns of Culture* could not have been written if Ruth Bunzel, one of Benedict's colleagues at Columbia University, had not made her intensive study of Zuni ceremonies, prayers, and the concepts laying back of them." Clearly evident in Bunzel's texts are the noncompetitive character of Zuni life, its rejection of any intense individual emotional experience, the merging of the individual in the family, clan, and ceremonial societies, which, recurrently and in a highly formalistic fashion, brings the Zuni in touch with the supernatural world.

VI

The Zunis have had mixed reactions to Bunzel's work, focusing mainly on the accuracy of the published information, the quality of the interpretations, and the necessity of the fieldwork act itself. According to Pandey (1972:334) there has been, as there has been for all anthropologists who worked with Puebloan peoples, some Zuni criticism of Bunzel's publications on their religion. Wilson (1956:22) contends that upon seeing her publication "the Indians seem to have felt that Miss Bunzel had imposed upon them." Bunzel, however, states that in 1933 a Zuni priest asked her to translate some of the ceremonial texts in *Zuni Ritual Poetry*. After she had, he confirmed that they were correct and left without objection. After Nick

Tumaka's death in the late 1920s, an unnamed Rain Priest, one of her Zuni friends and confidants, came and informed her that Nick had died because he had given away his religion "as if it were of no value" and he subsequently had nothing with which to defend himself. "He was voicing public opinion" (Bunzel 1932a:494fn). "According to Bunzel, her family and many other Zuni blamed her for his [Nick's] death" (Fawcett and McLuhan 1988:32). Bunzel, however, felt she had never violated Zuni trust nor related information that Nick requested she withhold.

> Yesterday started off with an interview that would make better reading than the details of mask decoration but alas! it cannot be published. It ended amicably with the promise of a new shirt—and mutual assurances that we would pray for one another. I kept a straight face through it all but I had some sad moments afterwards in which I decided that all ethnologists should be drawn and quartered for being party to such transactions (APS: RB to FB, August 15, 1925).

Bunzel neither took photographs of esoteric ceremonies nor tried to gain access to kivas as had earlier anthropologists such as Cushing and Stevenson. She was extremely sensitive to the role of intruder and constantly questioned her conflicting loyalties to science and to the people with whom she worked—people who had resisted discussing certain areas of their life. Bunzel also questioned herself as an agent of change.

> In Zuni I encountered informant resistance at all levels. Those whom I interviewed for data on economics and social structure were afraid that their neighbors would think they were telling "secrets"; those who were willing to talk about religious matters feared supernatural punishment; at least two female informants who formed warm personal ties with me found that this relationship intensified their conflicts in regard to cultural loyalties. They became increasingly attracted to White culture at the same time as they became increasingly self-conscious about their own cultural values (Bunzel 1952:xix).

Cultural criticism and ambiguity was conveyed to Bunzel on several levels, as the talk concerning Nick Tumaka's death demonstrates. "There is an ill-defined feeling that in teaching prayers, 'giving them away,' as the Zunis say, the teacher loses some of the power over them, so men are 'stingy' with their religion" (Bunzel 1932a:494). During Tumaka's final illness he related the following dream to Bunzel.

> It happened that I was collecting dreams at that time, and the number of times I appeared, usually under some thin disguise, in the dreams of informants, and their spontaneous comments on these dreams were my first indication of the disturbing character of the informant-anthropologist relationship. One male informant who was seriously ill at the time reported the following dream: "I was lying here in bed and a White girl—not you, but I don't know who it

> was—came into the room and came over and handed me a bundle of prayer-sticks. Then I knew I was going to die because this was the kind of bundle we make for the dead . . . and it is true I will die because I have given away my religion (the esoteric texts he had dictated to me) and I have nothing with which to defend myself." He did die a few days later. He was an old man and his illness was of long standing; he was believed to be a sorcerer and his passing caused no sorrow in the village, although it was believed that he died as a result of betraying secrets. He himself had struggled to break off a relationship that he felt was destructive, but each time he came back of his own accord. Altogether this was a shattering experience for a young anthropologist doing her first intensive field work, and aware for the first time of "informants" as people, and of herself as an object in their emotional lives. Painful as this experience was I always believed that this and similar, but happily, less tragic experiences with other informants taught me more about the real essence of Zuni life—of those aspects of it which most interest me—than any amount of census taking and measuring of fields—although I did that too, and do not underestimate the importance of data of this kind (Bunzel 1952:xix–xx).

Bunzel assessed why, even with these doubts, the Zuni freely gave her information for the books reprinted here.

> I think I eventually convinced them that it was to their advantage to have these rituals recorded. They would complain that the boys didn't want to learn. It takes the whole winter to learn one of these long chants and then the men who have to perform them have to come every night to the man who is the owner or keeper of a ritual and they have to learn from him. It takes hours to perform. To learn these things letter-perfect takes a long time. I convinced them it was to their advantage to have them written down and preserved. Since they complained about how the young men didn't want to bother with elaborate ceremonies I said, "You have them written down in the books and then you have them forever."
>
> I think the Zuni really did gain from recording the information. When I went back there after a number of years they had the book around. And they would bring the book, put it on the table, read from it, and they would tell me if it was right and they would tell me if anything was wrong. They were pleased, and they would read it, and they would say, "Yes. That's right" (Bunzel 1985).

Bunzel helped preserve prayers in *Zuni Ritual Poetry*. In some cases her preservation techniques had an immediate benefit:

> A woman asked me to copy down for her the prayers for offering the monthly prayer sticks, and for offering corn meal, so that she could learn them, for she knew no prayer for these occasions (Bunzel 1932a:493).

Bunzel found little resentment upon her last, brief return to the pueblo in 1938 (Bunzel 1985). And Zuni scholars and artists (see Wright 1985) use Bunzel's works today, especially *The Pueblo Potter* and *Zuni Kachinas*. Edmund Ladd (1979:492), a Zuni and professional anthropologist, has said, "Bunzel (1938:352) has captured the essence of Zuni economic attitudes." Unlike the ambiguity concerning Stevenson's ethnographic work, Zunis see Bunzel's work as valuable partly because it is presented in a usable form.

VII

Bunzel's works on Zuni religion are cited widely because of her ability to present complex matters clearly, to delineate the important characteristics of the system, to see how the parts fit together, to grasp what is most important to the Zuni, to understand that all was not to be told, nor necessarily needed to be told. She knew that she only understood a part, and that she needed to see the whole through the metaphor of the complete path. Not a romantic like Cushing, who saw Zuni life as a form of escape, or a dedicated evolutionist like Stevenson, who felt that all knowledge about Puebloan peoples needed to be saved because they would inevitably be swamped by civilization, Bunzel did not emphasize the strange and wonderful of Zuni culture. Bunzel saw herself as a social scientist. Zuni provided for her a set of facts that had to be explained in relation to other psychological, social, religious, or economic facts. Since Zuni was changing, the saving of the old knowledge—the sober recording of languages, myths, and tales, the description of ceremonies, songs, prayers, and costumes—was to Bunzel, as it was to her contemporaries, an end in itself. This end, however, was embedded in a search for what it meant to be a Zuni, and that is what keeps Bunzel's work from being just fact laid upon dry fact.

Ruth Bunzel walked many paths and each led, in her words, to "partial truths." "No matter how wise we are, we never learn the whole truth about another culture or, for that matter, about our own" (Bunzel 1952:xiv). She realized her strengths and weaknesses. Bunzel knew how to listen and this quality suited her for Zuni life. At the Daughters of the Desert conference in 1986, Margaret Hardin (1986:p.c.) felt that these personality traits "preadapted her to Zuni work." As Bunzel (1932a:480) herself reflected, "In all social relations, whether within the family group or outside, the most honored personality traits at Zuni are a pleasing address, a yielding disposition, and a generous heart. . . . A characterization intended to convey the highest praise was the following: 'Yes, __ is a nice polite man.'" Bunzel's personality lent itself to this description.

Speaking of her Zuni fieldwork, Bunzel (1985) thought that "You have to be able to stick it out and be lonely." One has to have to be able to live on the fringe of a group and survive. But these same qualities—her quietness and ability to listen and blend into the background—were partly responsible for limiting her academic opportunities.

> There was a time when I wanted to have a good stable academic job with students. It wasn't in the cards. I never had a permanent position in the department at Columbia as a professor or assistant professor. It was always year-to-year and each year wondering what you were going to do the next year. I had no stability (Bunzel 1985).

Nevertheless, it is her ability to work with the Zuni that has never been surpassed for its sensitivity and quality, its attention to the complete path.

VIII

Ruth Bunzel did not return to Zuni for many years, although she continued to correspond with Flora Zuni. She went on to other topics, especially the study of economics and culture change, and visited other cultures. She worked briefly in psychology and conducted ethnographic research in Guatemala, Mexico, and Spain. During World War II she worked in the Office of War Information with Benedict, and later helped direct the Contemporary Cultures Research Project at Columbia. She worked closely with the Chinese in New York City.

As noted above she held temporary teaching and adjunct positions—with a year-to-year rather than a tenured appointment; one woman in the department was enough for college administrators. She usually taught "extension" courses, which meant her classes were in the evening or in the summer. She retained this marginal position, partly because of the hostility of Ralph Linton, who became the department chair after Boas retired. She had been given a "small office behind Duncan Strong in 1935" (Goldfrank 1978:99) through Ruth Benedict's intervention and was able to remain in daily contact with her colleagues. But as money became scarcer during the Depression and World War II, she was unable to return to the Southwest.

In the 1950s and 1960s Bunzel worked extensively with a group of anthropologists who were protesting against the nuclear-arms proliferation of the Cold War (Mead 1964:88). While she would have liked to have returned to Zuni, she told us in 1985 that the lack of a permanent position, and the fact that she had to assist others on their projects, meant she did not have the funds nor the freedom to conduct further fieldwork at Zuni. "So much of your life is accident. You go where the money is and where you can get it to do your work" (Bunzel 1985). She also began to feel that the Zuni were being overworked, that anthropologists were overstaying their welcome there. She did not want to intrude.

Zuni, of course, continued to be one of the most widely studied societies. The anthropologists who have worked at Zuni have influenced and been influenced by the pueblo. Bunzel is one who has been influenced the most. All her subsequent work reflects her initial orientation at Zuni—her methodology, her techniques for quiet participant observation, her life with one family, her attempts to conform to proper female behavior. Bunzel's sensitivity to the political and cultural situation at the time of her fieldwork carried over to her work at Chichicastenango, Guatemala (Bunzel 1952), another community that was experiencing factionalism. Because of her work at Zuni, Bunzel was able to understand the nuances of that Mesoamerican pueblo and, as she had at Zuni, she tried to minimize her role as a divisive influence in community life. She strove for understanding on Guatemalan terms as she had tried to understand using Zuni concepts and orientations.

> The questions which I asked myself after my first brief visit to Zuni had impressed me with the alien character of Zuni life, and to which on later trips I sought the answers, were "What is it like to be a Zuni? How does it feel to live in a culture so organized? Can we ever know how it feels?" I believe that the close and often painful relationships with individual Zunis gave me some kind of answer to these questions (Bunzel 1952:xx).

Bunzel's ability to recognize and handle delicate situations, and her attempts to allay Zuni anxieties, made her a friend as well as the objective anthropologist she aimed to be. She did not visibly force herself on the Zuni; she tried to be a family member. Yet she worked hard to obtain the information she had come to collect. Bunzel walked a delicate line.

Bunzel tried to deal with problems of real interest to the Zuni, not only of interest to herself, Boas, or Benedict. In this she succeeded. Her writings in this book are attempts to understand Zuni religion and world view. While limited, as is the understanding of all outsiders, it is important because it is a framework that captures much of the beauty of Zuni life while serving as a compendium of factual information. The Zuni have contributed to this understanding by sharing their knowledge, their perspectives, and their homes with Bunzel. They did help Bunzel make Anglo-American culture better.

> It felt like a great homecoming to get back to Zuni. I never realized just how much I liked the place until I got back and got my first whiff of burning cedar, which will always mean Zuni to me. I got quite emotional over Zuni and the Southwest my first night . . . when I was enveloped in the familiar smell. I reached Zuni in the midst of a rain dance, and Zuni is always beautiful and exciting when there is a dance in progress (APS: RB to FB, August 30, 1925).

References Cited

Babcock, Barbara A. and Nancy J. Parezo

1988 *Daughters of the Desert. Woman Anthropologists and the Native American Southwest, 1880–1980*. Albuquerque: University of New Mexico Press.

Basso, Keith H.

1979 History of Ethnological Research. *Handbook of North American Indians. Vol. 9. Southwest*. Alfonso Ortiz, ed. Pp.14–21. Washington: Smithsonian Institution Press.

Benedict, Ruth

1930 Psychological Types in the Culture of the Southwest. *23rd International Congress of Americanists, Proceedings*. Pp.572–581.

1934 *Patterns of Culture*. Boston and New York: Houghton Mifflin.

1935 *Zuni Mythology*. 2 vols. Columbia University Contributions to Anthropology Vol. 21. New York: Columbia University Press.

Boas, Franz

1927 *Primitive Art*. Cambridge: Harvard University Press. [Re-issued 1955. New York: Dover Press.]

1940 Decorative Designs of Alaskan Needlecases: A Study in the History of Conventional Designs. Based on Materials in the U.S. National Museum. In Franz Boas. *Race, Language and Culture*. Pp.564–592. New York: Free Press. [Originally published in German in 1908.]

Bunzel, Ruth

1924 Letter to Franz Boas, August 24. Boas Papers. American Philosophical Society. Philadelphia, PA.

1925 Letters to Franz Boas, August 15 and August 30. Boas Papers. American Philosophical Society. Philadelphia, PA.

1926 Letter to Franz Boas, July 25. Boas Papers. American Philosophical Society. Philadelphia, PA.

1929a *The Pueblo Potter: A Study of Creative Imagination in Primitive Art*. Columbia University Contributions to Anthropology No. 8. New York: Columbia University Press. [Reprint: 1972. New York: Dover.]

1929b Psychology of the Pueblo Potter. In *Pritimive Heritage*. Margaret Mead and Nicolas Calas, eds. Pp.266–275. New York: Random House.

1932a Introduction to Zuni Ceremonials. *47th Annual Report of the Bureau of American Ethnology for 1929–1930*. Pp.467–544. Washington: Government Printing Office. [Reprinted in this volume.]

1932b Zuni Origin Myths. *47th Annual Report of the Bureau of American Ethnology for 1929–1930*. Pp.545–610. Washington: Government Printing Office. [Reprinted in this volume.]

1932c Zuni Ritual Poetry. *47th Annual Report of the Bureau of American Ethnology for 1929–1930*. Pp.611–836. Washington: Government Printing Office. [Reprinted in this volume.]

1932d The Nature of Katcinas. *47th Annual Report of the Bureau of American Ethnology for 1929–1930*. Pp.837–1006. Washington: Government Printing Office. [Reprinted as *Zuni Kachinas*. 1978. Glorieta, NM: Rio Grande Press.]

1933 Zuni Texts. *Publications of the American Ethnological Society* No. 15. New York: G. E. Stechert.

1935 Zuni. In *Handbook of American Indian Languages*. Vol. 4. Pp.388–515. New York: Columbia University Press.

1938a The Emergence. *Journal of American Folklore*. 41:288–290.

1938b The Economic Organization of Primitive Peoples. In *General Anthropology*. Franz Boas, ed. Pp.327–408. New York: D. C. Heath.

1952 Chichicastenango. *American Ethnological Society Publication* No. 22. New York: J. J. Augustin.

1953 Psychology of the Pueblo Potter. In *Primitive Heritage*. Margaret Mead and Nicolas Calas, eds. Pp.266–275. New York: Random House.

1975 Minutes of talk given to New York Women's Anthropology Caucus. Dec. 12, 1975. Taken by Constance Sutton. [Copy housed at the Wenner-Gren Foundation for Anthropological Research, New York.]

1985 Interview (with Jennifer Fox). Daughters of the Desert Oral History Project under the direction of Barbara A. Babcock and Nancy J. Parezo. New York: Wenner-Gren Foundation for Anthropological Research.

Cushing, Frank Hamilton

1883 Zuni Fetishes. *Second Annual Report of the Bureau of Ethnology for 1880–1881*. Pp.3–45. Washington: Government Printing Office.

1896 Outlines of Zuni Creation Myths. *Thirteenth Annual Report of the Bureau of American Ethnology for 1891–1892*. Pp.321–447. Washington: Government Printing Office.

1901 *Zuni Folk Tales*. New York: G. P. Putnam's Sons. [Reprint: 1931. New York: Alfred A. Knopf.]

1920 Zuni Breadstuff. *Museum of the American Indian, Heye Foundation. Indian Notes and Monographs* No. 8. New York.

Eggan, Fred

1986 Discussion and Comments. Daughters of the Desert Conference. Globe, AZ; Wenner-Gren Foundation for Anthropological Research.

Eggan, Fred and T. N. Pandey

1979 Zuni History, 1850–1970. In *Handbook of North American Indians. Vol. 9. Southwest*. Alfonso Ortiz, ed. Pp.474–481. Washington: Smithsonian Institution Press.

Fawcett, David M. and Teri McLuhan

1988 Ruth Leah Bunzel. In *Women Anthropologists: A Biographical Dictionary*. Ute Gacs, Aisa Khan, Jerri McIntyre, and Ruth Weinberg, eds. Pp.29–36. Westport, CT: Greenwood Press.

Goldfrank, Esther S.

1978 *Notes on an Undirected Life: As One Anthropologist Tells It*. Queens College Publications in Anthropology No. 3. Flushing, NY.

Green, Jessie, ed.

1979 *Zuni: Selected Writings of Frank Hamilton Cushing*. Lincoln: University of Nebraska Press.

Hardin, Margaret Ann

1983 *Gifts of Mother Earth: Ceramics in the Zuni Tradition*. Phoenix: The Heard Museum.

1986 Zuni Potters and The Pueblo Potter: The Contributions of Ruth Bunzel. Paper delivered for the Daughters of the Desert Conference. Globe, AZ: Wenner-Gren Foundation for Anthropological Research.

1986 Discussion and Comments. Daughters of the Desert Conference. Globe, AZ: Wenner-Gren Foundation for Anthropological Research.

Hoebel, E. Adamson

1954 Major Contributions of Southwestern Studies to Anthropological Theory. *American Anthropologist* 56(4):720–727.

Howard, Jane

1984 *Margaret Mead: A Life*. New York: Simon and Schuster.

Kroeber, Alfred L.

1916 Thoughts on Zuni Religion. In *Holmes Anniversary Volume: Anthropological Essays Presented to William Henry Holmes in Honor of His Seventieth Birthday*. Pp.269–277. Washington: J. W. Bryan.

1917 *Zuni Kin and Clans*. New York: Anthropological Papers of the American Museum of Natural History Vol. 18, Part 2.

Ladd, Edmund J.

1979 Zuni Economy. In *Handbook of North American Indians. Vol. 9. Southwest*. Alfonso Ortiz, ed. Pp.492–498. Washington: Smithsonian Institution Press.

Langness, L. L.

1970 Entree into the Field: Highland New Guinea. In *A Handbook of Method in Cultural Anthropology*. Raoul Narrol and Ronald Cohen, eds. New York: Columbia University Press.

Li, An-che

1937 Zuni: Some Observations and Queries. *American Anthropologist* 39(1):62–76.

Mead, Margaret

1959a Apprenticeship under Boas. In *The Anthropology of Franz Boas: Essays on the Centennial of His Birth*. Walter Goldschmidt, ed. Pp.29–45. American Anthropological Association Memoir, No. 89.

1959b *An Anthropologist at Work. The Writings of Ruth Benedict*. Boston: Houghton Mifflin. [Revised edition. 1973. New York: Avon Books.]

1965 *Anthropologists and What They Do*. New York: Franklin Watts.

1986 Field Work in Pacific Islands, 1925–1967. In *Women in the Field: Anthropological Experiences*. Peggy Golde, ed. Pp.293–331. Berkeley: University of California Press.

Mead, Margaret and Ruth Bunzel, eds.

1960 *The Golden Age of American Anthropology*. New York: George Braziller.

Newman, Stanley

1954 A Practical Zuni Orthography. Appendix to Zuni Law: A Field of Values by Watson Smith and John Roberts. *Papers of the Peabody Museum of American Archaeology and Ethnology* 43(1):163–170. Cambridge: Harvard University.

1965 Zuni Grammar. *University of New Mexico Publications in Anthropology* No. 14. Albuquerque: University of New Mexico Press.

Pandey, Triloki Nath

1972 Anthropologists at Zuni. *Proceedings of the American Philosophical Society* 116(4):321–337.

1978 Flora Zuni—A Portrait. In American Indian Intellectuals. Margot Liberty, ed. Pp.217–225. *1976 Proceedings of the American Ethnological Society*. St. Paul: West.

Parsons, Elsie Clews

1916 The Zuni A'Doshle and Suuke. *American Anthropologist* 18(3):383–347.

1917 Notes on Zuni. *Memoirs of the American Anthropological Association* 4(3–4):151–327.

1919 Increase by Magic: A Zuni Pattern. *American Anthropologist* 21(3)279–286.

1922 Winter and Summer Dance Series in Zuni in 1918. *University of California Publications in American Archaeology and Ethnology* 17(3):171–216. Berkeley: University of California Press.

1924 The Scalp Ceremony at Zuni. *Memoirs of the American Anthropological Association* No. 31.

1939 *Pueblo Indian Religion.* 2 vols. Chicago: University of Chicago Press.

Reichard, Gladys A.

1944 *Prayer: The Compulsive Word.* Seattle: University of Washington Press.

Shaul, David

1985 Personal communication.

Smith, Watson and John M. Roberts

1954 Zuni Law: A Field of Values. *Papers of the Peabody Museum of American Archaeology and Ethnology* 43(1). Cambridge: Harvard University.

Spicer, Edward H.

1948 Southwestern Chronicle: Pueblo Ethnology. *Arizona Quarterly* 4(1):78–88.

Stevenson, Matilda Coxe

1881 *The Zuni and the Zunians.* Washington: Privately Printed.

1887 The Religious Life of the Zuni Child. *Fifth Annual Report of the Bureau of Ethnology for 1883–1884.* Pp.533–555. Washington: Government Printing Office.

1888 Zuni Religion. *Science* 11(268):136–137.

1904 The Zuni Indians: Their Mythology, Esoteric Fraternities, and Ceremonies. *Twenty-third Annual Report of the Bureau of American Ethnology for 1901–1902.* Pp.1–608. Washington: Government Printing Office.

Tedlock, Dennis

1979 Zuni Religion and World View. In *Handbook of North American Indians. Vol. 9. Southwest.* Alfonso Ortiz, ed. Pp.499–508. Washington: Smithsonian Institution Press.

Wilson, Edmund

1956 *Red, Black, Blond, and Olive: Studies in Four Civilizations: Zuni, Haiti, Soviet Russia, Israel.* New York: Oxford University Press.

Wright, Barton

1985 *Kachinas of the Zuni.* Flagstaff, AZ: Northland Press.

Acknowledgments

I would like to thank Ruth Bunzel for granting Barbara Babcock and me an interview and the Wenner-Gren Foundation for providing us with the funds to save the words and reflections of this truly remarkably individual. I would also like to thank the University of New Mexico Press, especially Jeff Grathwohl and Beth Hadas, for reprinting important anthropological works on the Southwest that have been too long out of print. I hope that they will do many more. I would also like to thank Raymond H. Thompson, T. J. Fergusson, Barbara Mills, Nathalie Woodbury, and Richard Woodbury for reading the drafts of the introduction and Barbara Babcock, Margaret Hardin, Fred Eggan, and other participants of the Daughters of the Desert conference for their stimulating conversation about Bunzel. Their comments, as always, are insightful and welcome.

I had hoped to have the time to travel to Zuni and go over the introduction, to retrace Loki Pandey's steps, but unfortunately a broken-down car, university budget cuts, and a new time-consuming administrative job meant this research trip will have to wait for another occasion. As a result trying to understand the Zuni views of Bunzel has been difficult and is incomplete. Even Bunzel's own views are incomplete. Bunzel disliked speaking about herself and once she finished a project and had gone on to other matters, she no longer dwelt on it. Her persona is conspicuously absent in all her published works. However, Bunzel's writings on other cultures where she refers to her Zuni experiences, her discussions with Margaret Mead, insights drawn from the work of Triloki Pandey, her correspondence with Boas, and our extensive interview with Bunzel (Babcock and Parezo 1988) have provided data for this paper. This interview was videotaped and is now housed at the Wenner-Gren Foundation for Anthropological Research in New York City.

INTRODUCTION TO ZUÑI CEREMONIALISM

By RUTH L. BUNZEL

CONTENTS

TABLE OF SOUNDS

The following symbols have been used in the texts and the recording of native names.

Vowels:

a, e, i, o, u have their continental values. As in English, long vowels tend to be closed, short vowels to be open, but the quality is variable and not significant. o is always closed, and is distinguished from o which is open.

ä—English hat.
ai—English i.
w—English w.
y—English y.

Consonants:

p—French père.
p̄—Glottalized p; the glottalization is very slight and the sound is frequently confused with the medial.
t—French té.
t̄—Glottalized; glottalization very slight, as in the labial.
k̭—Palatalized k, unaspirated.
k̭̄—Palatalized k, glottalized.
k—Spanish boca.
k̄—Glottalized k.
m—English m.
n—English n.
ŋ—English ng (before k only).
l—English l.
ł—Voiceless l.
s—English s.
c—English sh.
ts—German Zeit, but without aspiration.
t̄s—Glottalized; with slight force of articulation almost like dz.
tc—English church.
t̄c—Glottalized with slight force of articulation.
h—More affricative than English h.
'—Glottal stop.

Length is indicated by a point following the letter; both vowels and consonants may be long. All accented syllables are lengthened, some of the length being accorded to the terminating consonant. Where not indicated the primary accent is on the first syllable; the secondary accent, in words of four or more syllables, on the penult. Compound words retain their original accents.

INTRODUCTION TO ZUÑI CEREMONIALISM

By Ruth L. Bunzel

CONDITIONS OF LIFE

The Zuñi tribe numbered in 1928 approximately 1,900 individuals, settled in the desert of western New Mexico on land which the nation had already inhabited for many centuries prior to the advent of the Spaniards in 1540. The reservation which they now hold under Government protection is a strip of land roughly following the course of the Zuñi River from its headwaters near the Continental Divide southwest to a point some miles east of the Arizona border. The general conformation of the land is a high, broad valley dropping sharply from northeast to southwest. The upper end of the valley is hemmed in by rugged mountains of red and white sandstone, cut by deep canyons densely forested. Toward the west the country lies open. The average altitude of the valley is about 6,000 feet.

The Zuñi River which drains this country is a permanent stream, which, however, varies greatly in volume of water. For the greater part of the year it is a thin trickle threading its devious way through broad, glistening mud flats. During the summer season this trickle may be transformed within a few moments into a raging torrent that inundates the mud flats and frequently overflows the containing banks. These sudden floods, caused by cloud-bursts in the eastern mountains, generally subside within a few hours, although the stream frequently runs high for two or three days during the spring freshets, when the river is said to be impassable for days at a time. The valley is traversed also by numerous arroyos filled with rushing water in times of flood, but otherwise quite dry. In all the surrounding mountains are numerous permanent springs of sweet water.

The mountains and canyons of the east, well watered by virtue of their nearness to the divide, are covered with thick forests of conifers. The arid plains of the west sustain only a meager covering of sage, greasewood, yucca, and small cacti, with occasional poplar and cottonwood trees near springs and along watercourses.

The high altitude and excessive aridity produce a healthy and invigorating climate. There are great seasonal and daily fluctuations in temperature. There are summers of blazing noons (110° F. is by no means unusual) and cool, almost chilly, nights. In winter, especially in December, the nights are bitter cold, the days, for the most part, mild and sunny.

There are two periods of precipitation—in summer from July to September, and in winter from December to March. The summer rains begin early in July, increasing in intensity as the season advances. The rainy season ends about September 15. In summer the sun rises every day in an unclouded sky of brilliant blue. By noon this blue dome begins to fill with great puffs of white cumulus clouds, increasing in density, with heavy black clouds along the southern horizon. The late afternoon is generally marked by sudden and violent showers of short duration. These showers, which are very local, can literally be seen stalking out of the southeast just before sunset. The storms increase in frequency, intensity, and duration toward the close of the rainy season. The most destructive rains occur in September.

The winter precipitation starts with light snowfalls early in December. December is a month of low temperatures and frequent snowfalls. After the New Year the temperature moderates, but the weather continues very inclement, snow and rain alternating. There is a great deal of fog and continuous downpours of cold rain.

The spring months are marked by high winds of prevailing westerly direction. These winds from the open desert are laden with fine sand and cause untold discomfort. The sand storms of May, striking the young corn, are especially destructive.

ECONOMIC AND SOCIAL LIFE

The Zuñis have been agriculturists for many centuries. Since very early prehistoric time they have raised maize, beans, and squash by a system of dry cultivation.[1] From the first Spanish settlers they obtained the seeds of wheat. This, however, could be grown only in specially favored localities which could be irrigated by hand from large, permanently flowing springs. Recently, in 1909, the waters of one fork of the Zuñi River have been impounded behind a dam built by the United States Government. From this reservoir sufficient water is drawn to irrigate a strip of land on the north bank of the river, immediately adjacent to the village. This strip, approximately 1 mile wide and 6 miles long, is well suited for the cultivation of wheat and alfalfa. Maize is still raised by old methods of dry farming on sandy fields lying at a considerable distance from the village, mainly situated on the south bank.

From the Spaniards, also, the Zuñis got their first sheep. They now own large and profitable herds. These are kept in remote parts

[1] Zuñi agricultural methods are admirably described in Cushing's Zuñi Breadstuffs, Indian Notes and Monographs, Museum of the American Indian, vol. VIII, pp. 157ff.

of the reservation. The wealthiest herders even rent land in surrounding townships. Rabbits are still hunted, primarily for sport, but the deer and antelope, once important items in Zuñi economy, have vanished from the mountains. Sheep, furthermore, are the chief source of negotiable wealth. The sale of wool in June and of lambs in October provides the herders with a considerable cash income for the purchase of luxuries of white manufacture. They have, also, horses derived from the same source and a few cattle, but the land is not suitable for cattle breeding. Cattle are not milked and are used for meat only. Some women have a few pigs and chickens. The labor of agriculture and herding is done entirely by the men.

Herding, of course, is an all-year-round occupation, at which men take turns, groups of brothers herding their sheep together and taking turns in watching them. A man with his own herd usually goes three times a year, for a month at a time, unless he is wealthy enough to pay some one to do this for him. All men who own sheep spend lambing time with their herds to see that all lambs are properly earmarked. At this time the sheep are herded at permanent camps, and the women also go out there. Lambing occurs in April and is followed immediately by shearing. Sheep dipping takes a few weeks for everyone in midsummer.

The first agricultural work of the season is early plowing and the planting of wheat in February or March. In March the irrigation ditches are cleaned. Corn must not be planted until after certain ceremonies held about the time of the vernal equinox, and frequently it is delayed until after wool-sell. The cornfields are plowed over, but the actual planting is done with the digging stick. The early summer, after the return from sheep camp and after the summer solstice ceremonies, is spent hoeing and irrigating. There is an alfalfa crop in June and another in August. There may be another in November, but this is not usually harvested. The horses are turned into the unharvested field for winter pasture. The wheat harvest begins in August and continues until all is in, which may not be until November. The wheat is cut with a sickle, threshed by horses, and winnowed by hand on primitive outdoor threshing floors.

Peaches, squash, and melons ripen in August and must be harvested before the frosts, which may occur at this altitude any time after the end of August. There is a spell of heavy rain in September which interrupts outdoor work. The first green corn is ready for eating in August, but the general corn harvest does not take place until November. This is the last agricultural work, except for a few people who do a little fall plowing. The months from November until March, free of agricultural work, are given over to the great ceremonies—the Ca'lako, the winter solstice ceremonies, society initiations, the winter katcinas, and sometimes the general tribal initiation.

The 1,900 inhabitants live, for the most part, in Zuñi proper and its immediate vicinity. There are, however, three large farming villages and one small one, which are occupied for varying periods during the summer months. Even those families that make their homes there permanently return to Zuñi after harvest time for the period of the great ceremonies in December and January.

None of the farming villages have any civil or religious organization of their own, nor are any religious ceremonies performed at any of them, except when a dance set from one of the kivas is invited to dance there during the summer.

Despite modern expansion [2] the main village still remains a unit whose physical compactness is reflected in an intricate and closely knit social organization.

There are households, kinship groups, clans, tribal and special secret societies, and cult groups. A man must belong to several of these groups, and the number to which he may potentially belong is almost unlimited. There is no exclusive membership. He is born into a certain household, and his kinship and clan affiliations are thus fixed, unless altered by adoption. At puberty he is initiated into one of the six dance groups that comprise the male tribal society. He may, through sickness, be conscripted into one of the medicine societies; if he takes a scalp he must join the warriors society; and if connected with a sacerdotal household he may be called upon to join one of the priesthoods.

These groups all have their joint activities and a great part of a man's time is spent in participation in these activities. His economic activities are all bound up with the household, a communal unit to which he has certain obligations. His ordinary social contacts are all predetermined by his family and clan affiliations. Religious participation is confined to attendance at the ceremonies of those groups with which he is identified. In fact, the only sphere in which he acts as an individual rather than as a member of a group is that of sex. A man's courtship and marriage are matters of individual choice. In the bid for attention they suffer from being entirely divorced from group activity. At Zuñi no action that is entirely personal and individual receives more than passing interest. Births, deaths, and initiations figure largely in local gossip—marriages do not. It is curious to note that among the culturally related Hopi, where a marriage is the occasion for elaborate gift exchanges between the

[2] Population movements in and out of the town are analyzed by Kroeber in his Zuñi Kin and Clan, pp. 120, 198.

clans of the bride and groom, weddings are one of the most frequent topics of conversation.

The economic unit is the household, whose nature and methods of function illustrate admirably certain very fundamental Zuñi attitudes. The household is a group of variable composition, consisting theoretically of a maternal family; that is, a woman and her husband, her daughters with their husbands and children. To this permanent population is added a fluctuating group of miscellaneous male relatives of the maternal line—the unmarried, widowed, divorced, and those rendered homeless by passing domestic storms. This group occupies a single house consisting of several connecting rooms. There is a single kitchen drawing upon a common storehouse. The household owns certain cultivated fields which can not be alienated. In addition, the various male members individually own certain fields—generally fields recently brought under cultivation—which remain their own after they have severed connection with the household. However, all fields, whether collectively or individually owned, are cultivated by the cooperative labor of the entire male population of the household. The products go into the common storeroom to become the collective property of the women of the household. The women draw on the common stores for daily food and trade the surplus for other commodities. Sheep are owned individually by men but are herded cooperatively by groups of male kindred. When the profits of the shearing are divided a man is expected out of these to provide clothing for himself, his wife and children, including children by previous marriages, and his mother and unmarried sisters, in case they are not otherwise provided for.

Personal relations within the household are characterized by the same lack of individual authority and responsibility that marks the economic arrangements. The household has no authoritative head to enforce any kind of discipline. There is no final arbiter in disputes; no open conflict. Ordinarily the female contingent of blood relatives presents a united front. A man finding himself out of harmony with the group may withdraw quietly whenever he chooses and ally himself with another group. With his departure obligations cease, and his successor fathers his children. Diffusion of authority and responsibility is especially marked in the treatment of children.

The tribe is divided into 13 matrilineal exogamous clans, varying greatly in size from the Yellowwood, consisting of two male members, and which will therefore become extinct with the present generation, to the large so-called Dogwood (Pi'tcikwe) clan, which comprises several hundreds of individuals. The kinship system follows, in the main, the Crow multiple clan system, all members of one's own clan being designated by classificatory terms. There are different terms for classificatory relatives of the father's clan. Adoption is frequent, and the usual terms are applied to adoptive relatives. The terms are stretched to include also all affinal relatives. There is no avoidance and no joking relations. There is some indication of a joking relationship between a man and women of his father's clan, especially his father's blood sister, who is also his most important ceremonial relative. A woman has important ceremonial obligations to her brother's children, especially his male children, and in most cases she is compensated for her services. The clan as such has no social or political functions, although each individual feels his closest ties to be with members of his clan, upon whom he calls for assistance in any large enterprise, such as harvest, housebuilding, initiations, etc. His closest ties, naturally, are with blood kin, especially the maternal household in which he was born.

Each male is initiated at puberty into the katcina or mask dance society, which thereby assumes the rôle of a tribal cult, in distinction to other ceremonial groups of more restricted membership. Other ceremonial groups are the 12 medicine societies composed of medicine men and those whom they have cured, the war society, the rain priesthoods, and innumerable minor cults, consisting in the main of members of maternal households to whom are intrusted the care of various objects of fetishistic power. Most men of advanced age are affiliated with several of these groups.

The real political authority of the tribe is vested in the council of priests, consisting of three members of the chief priesthood and the heads of the three other priesthoods. The head of the hierarchy is the head of the chief priesthood—the house chief (k̥a'kwemosi), p̄ekwin, who is priest of the sun and keeper of the calendar, is, as his name indicates, a sort of talking chief for the priesthood. Two bow priests, members of the war society, act as messengers and the executive arm of the priesthood. The heads of the katcina society are called on in an advisory capacity in matters relating to their province. The principal matters to come before the council for decision are the appointment of civil officers, choice of the impersonators of the gods at the annual festival, the insertion of important ceremonies, such as the tribal initiation, into the regular calendar, the discussion of what action should be taken in cases of calamity, such as earthquakes and drought, the determination of tribal policy in new contingencies—such questions as whether automobiles are fire, and should therefore be taboo during the winter solstice. The maintenance of these policies is the duty of the bow priests and the secular officers.

The priests do not act in secular affairs, being too sacred to contaminate themselves with dispute or wrangling. Crime and warfare are the concerns of the bow priests. Civil law and relations with aliens, especially the United States Government, are delegated to the secular officers appointed by the council.

The only crime that is recognized is witchcraft. An accusation of having caused death by sorcery may be brought by the relatives of the deceased. The bow priests examine the accused and review the evidence. If found guilty in former days the accused was hung by his wrists and subjected to other forms of torture until he confessed. If the confession was of such a nature as to vitiate his power by revealing its source, a common Zuñi idea, he might be released at the discretion of the bow priests, or he might be executed. Public torture and execution of witches has been stopped by Government authorities but convicted witches may be done away with secretly unless they escape to other villages.

Revelation of the secrets of the katcina cult to the uninitiated is a crime against the gods and is punishable by death by decapitation. Punishment is meted out by masked impersonators of the gods, appointed by the heads of the katcina society. No such executions have taken place within the memory of living men, but they figure prominently in folklore, and the authority and readiness of the priests so to act is never questioned in Zuñi. Flogging by masked impersonators has recently been substituted for execution. During one of the writer's visits katcinas were summoned to administer punishment to a youth found guilty of selling a mask. The accused escaped so the katcinas whipped all men in the kivas for purification.

Crimes of personal violence are rare, but such as do occur are considered matters for private adjustment, either with or without the help of the civil officers. Murder by overt means, not sorcery, bodily injury, rape, and theft are settled by property payments by the family of the guilty man to the family of the one who has been wronged. These payments are made promptly and quietly by the guilty man's relatives, since they are likely to fare worse in the hands of the officers than in those of private individuals. Adultery is not a crime. Along with stinginess and ill temper it is a frequent source of domestic infelicity and divorce, but is never regarded as a violation of rights. Sexual jealousy is no justification for violence.

The chief duties of the officers (governor, lieutenant governor, and eight tenientes) are the adjudication of civil suits, such as boundaries, water rights, inheritance, restitution for loss or injury to livestock, management of cooperative enterprises of a nonreligious character, such as road building, cleaning of irrigation ditches, execution of Government ordinances regarding registration, schooling, etc., and all manner of negotiation with outside powers. Because of the increasingly diversified contacts with whites, the office of governor is becoming more and more exacting and influential, although it still lacks prestige in native opinion. The civil officers hold office at the pleasure of the priests and may be removed by them at any time and for any cause. The office is not one that is sought, since the settlement of disputes must inevitably be a source of grievance to someone, and the thing that a Zuñi will avoid above anything else is giving offense.

In all social relations, whether within the family group or outside, the most honored personality traits are a pleasing address, a yielding disposition, and a generous heart. All the sterner virtues—initiative, ambition, an uncompromising sense of honor and justice, intense personal loyalties—not only are not admired but are heartily deplored. The woman who cleaves to her husband through misfortune and family quarrels, the man who speaks his mind where flattery would be much more comfortable, the man, above all, who thirsts for power or knowledge, who wishes to be, as they scornfully phrase it, "a leader of his people," receives nothing but censure and will very likely be persecuted for sorcery.

A characterization intended to convey the highest praise was the following: "Yes, ——— is a nice polite man. No one ever hears anything from him. He never gets into trouble. He's Badger clan and Muhekwe kiva and he always dances in the summer dances." The informant could be eloquent enough when she wished to detract.

No single fact gives a better index to Zuñi temperament than that suicide is absolutely unknown among them, and the very idea is so remote from their habits of thought that it arouses only laughter.

RELIGIOUS LIFE

In so far as the culture of any people is an integrated and harmonious whole, it shows in all its phases the same character and individuality. At Zuñi the same ceremonious collectivism that characterizes social activities is the essence also of all religious participation. The relation between man and the supernatural is as free of tragic intensity as the relation of man to man. The supernatural, conceived always as a collectivity, a multiple manifestation of the divine essence, is approached by the collective force of the people in a series of great public and esoteric rituals whose richness, variety, and beauty have attracted the attention of poets and artists of all countries. Nowhere in the New World, except in the ancient civilizations of Mexico and Yucatan, has ceremonialism been more highly developed, and nowhere, including these civilizations, has it gone so far toward taming man's frenzy. In Zuñi, as in all the pueblos, religion spreads wide. It pervades all activities, and its very pervasiveness and the rich and harmonious forms in which it is externalized compensate the student of religion for the lack of intensity of that feeling. For although the Zuñi may be called one of the most thoroughly religious peoples of the world, in all the enormous mass of rituals there is no single bit of religious feeling equal in intensity and exaltation to the usual vision quest of the North American Indian.

Man and the Universe

THE SOUL

According to Zuñi belief, man has a spiritual substance, a soul (tse'makwin, thoughts, from tse'ma, to think, ponder). This is associated with the head, the heart, and the breath. The head is the seat of skill and intelligence, but the heart is the seat of the emotions and of profound thought. "I shall take it to my heart" means I shall ponder it carefully, and remember it long. The word for life is t̂ek̂ohanan·e, literally daylight. The breath is the symbol of life. It also is the means by which spiritual substances communicate and the seat of power or mana. Inhaling is an act of ritual blessing. One inhales from all sacred objects to derive benefit from their mana. At the end of any prayer or chant all present inhale; holding their folded hand before their nostrils, in order to partake of the sacred essence of prayer.[3] The feather is the pictorial representation of the breath. Death occurs when "the heart wears out." When a person is very sick his heart is wearing out. "Medicine men can fix it up when they come to cure, and it will go for a while, but sooner or later you will have to get a new one." Getting a new heart is the first rite in society initiations.[4]

Dreams are believed to be of supernatural causation, and foretell the future if one can properly interpret them. Certain persons in particular are believed to "dream true." Dreams of the dead are believed to be visitations of the dead, and are always portents of death. Visual and auditory hallucinations are believed to be similarly caused. "Bad dreams," a term which includes hallucinations, is a disease of supernatural origin, as opposed to bodily disease, which is caused by witchcraft. There are special rituals for curing "bad dreams," to which we shall allude frequently in the following pages.

In rare instances the soul can leave the body and return to it again. This occurs during sickness and is a matter of great seriousness. A friend has reported such an experience as follows:

"When I was sick of the measles I was very sick. On the third day I didn't know anything. Maybe I fainted or maybe I really died [5] and came back. I never believed that could happen, but it really did, because when I came back the room was going round and round and there was a little light coming through the window, although there was a bright light in the room. While I was dead I dreamed I was going toward the west." The narrative goes on to describe her encounter with her dead grandfather and unknown dead women, her "aunts."

---

[3] See texts for symbolism of breath as the seat of sacred power.

[4] Texts, p. 802.

[5] The two words are the same in Zuñi (aceḵä.)

"I was so happy to see my grandfather. Since then I've never worried about dying, even when I was very sick, because I saw all these dead people and saw that they were still living the way we do." After this experience the girl was initiated into a medicine society,[6] to "save her life," because her people (i. e., the dead) had asked her for feathers.

Visual and auditory hallucinations are caused by supernaturals. They are regarded as omens of death. The most common hallucinations of this type are the apparent movement of sacred objects on an altar—especially masks.

Death is usually caused by witchcraft. The usual method of the sorcerer is to shoot foreign bodies into his victim. But other more indirect methods may be used. Sorcery, however, is never practiced openly as in Oceania. No one admits having sorcery, and everyone suspects others very vaguely. Suspicion of sorcery subjects a person to social ostracism, but a death caused by sorcery is an occasion for formal interference on the part of the authorities. There is considerable internal and comparative evidence in the body of witchcraft belief and practice to indicate that their present great development is post-Hispanic, and that the belief in less specific supernatural causation is earlier and more aboriginal.

Considerable confusion exists in the Zuñi mind concerning the fate of the soul after death. General folk belief has it that for four days after death it remains in Zuñi, causing great inconvenience, and, indeed, danger, to survivors, and on the fourth day departs for Katcina Village (kołuwala·wa)[7] in the west. However, various cult groups hold beliefs at variance with this. Dead medicine men, probably not all members of medicine societies, but those who possess the ultimate powers of "calling the bear," join the beast priests at Cipapolima in the east.[8] The name Cipapolima is undoubtedly related to the Keresan shipap^{u}, the place of emergence and the destination of the dead. The word shipap^{u} is not known at Zuñi, but wenima (Keresan wenimatse) is sometimes used esoterically in songs for Kołuwala·wa. When the priests invoke the uwanami in prayer they also call by name deceased members of their order,[9] indicating that deceased priests join the uwanami at the four oceans of the world.

Corpses are prepared for burial according to the ceremonial affiliations of the deceased. All are clothed in everyday clothing, men in white cotton shirts and trousers, women in calico dresses and black woolen blanket dresses. In addition, each wears the characteristic garment of his group: male members of societies the hand-woven

---

6 See pp. 528, 791.

7 See text of origin myth, p. 574.

8 See prayer of medicine man, pp. 804, 829, 831.

9 Stevenson, p. 175, substantiated by further information.

loin cloth which constitutes their ceremonial costume, officers of the Katcina society the white embroidered kilt and embroidered blanket of the katcinas and, possibly, masks.[10] Priests, curiously enough, are adorned for burial with the face paint and headdress of warriors.[11]

Infants were formerly buried within the houses, as was common in almost all prehistoric villages; because "they thought they would have no place to go," and so they "wanted them around the house." Most people admitted that there was some doubt whether the uninitiated, for example women, are admitted to Kołuwala·wa, although folk tales frequently allude to their going there to join their husbands.

The rôle of the dead in the religious life is described below (p. 509). At this point it need only be said that they are the bestowers of all blessings, and are identified especially with rain. If rain falls the fourth day following the death of a noted man it is usually thought of as his rain, and is a source of consolation to the bereaved. The worship of the dead is the foundation of all Zuñi ritual. The dead form part of the great spiritual essence of the universe, but they are the part which is nearest and most intimate.

THE EXTERNAL WORLD

To the Zuñi the whole world appears animate. Not only are night and day, wind, clouds, and trees possessed of personality, but even articles of human manufacture, such as houses, pots, and clothing, are alive and sentient. All matter has its inseparable spiritual essence. For the most part this spiritual aspect of things is vague and impersonal. Although all objects are called ho'i, "living person," in a figurative sense, they are not definitely anthropomorphic; they have consciousness but they do not possess human faculties. To all these beings is applied the term k̑äpin ho'i "raw person"; man, on the other hand, is a "cooked" person.

Prayers are full of description of natural phenomena in anthropomorphic guise. I quote some of the most striking:

When our sun father
Goes in to sit down at his ancient place,
And our night fathers,
Our mothers,
Night priests,
Raise their dark curtain over their ancient place. . . . . .

That our earth mother may wrap herself
In a fourfold robe of white meal;
That she may be covered with frost flowers;
That yonder on all the mossy mountains,
The forests may huddle together with the cold;

---

[10] Hodge is the authority for this statement.

[11] Stevenson describes, pp. 315–317, the burial of Naiuchi, priest of the Bow and also head of Eagle clan priesthood. However, the Onawa priesthood use the same face paint and headdress in interring their dead.

That their arms may be broken by the snow,
In order that the land may be thus,
I have made my prayer sticks into living beings.

Following wherever the roads of the rain makers come out,
May the ice blanket spread out,
May the ice blanket cover the country;
All over the land
May the flesh of our earth mother
Crack open from the cold;
That your thoughts may bend to this,
That your words may be to this end;
For this with prayers I send you forth.

When our earth mother is replete with living waters,
When spring comes,
The source of our flesh,
All the different kinds of corn,
We shall lay to rest in the ground.
With their earth mother's living waters,
They will be made into new beings.
Coming out standing into the daylight
Of their sun father,
Calling for rain,
To all sides they will stretch out their hands.
Then from wherever the rain makers stay quietly
They will send forth their misty breath;
Their massed clouds filled with water will come out to sit down with us;
Far from their homes,
With outstretched hands of water they will embrace the corn,
Stepping down to caress them with their fresh waters,
With their fine rain caressing the earth,
With their heavy rain caressing the earth,
And yonder, wherever the roads of the rain makers come forth,
Torrents will rush forth,
Silt will rush forth,
Mountains will be washed out,
Logs will be washed down,
Yonder all the mossy mountains
Will drip with water.
The clay-lined hollows of our earth mother
Will overflow with water,
From all the lakes
Will rise the cries of the children of the rain makers,
In all the lakes
There will be joyous dancing—
Desiring that it should be thus,
I send forth my prayers.

That our earth mother
May wear a fourfold green robe,
Full of moss,
Full of flowers,
Full of pollen,
That the land may be thus
I have made you into living beings.

That yonder in all our water-filled fields
The source of our flesh,
All the different kinds of corn
May stand up all about,
That, nourishing themselves with fresh water,
Clasping their children in their arms,
They may rear their young,
So that we may bring them into our houses,
Thinking of them toward whom our thoughts bend—
Desiring this,
I send you forth with prayers.

Yonder on all sides coming to the forests,
And to some fortunate one
Offering prayer meal,
Crushed shell,
Corn pollen,
We broke off the straight young shoots.
From where they had stood quietly
Holding their long life;
Holding their old age,
Holding their waters,
We made them come forth,
We brought them hither.
This many days
Yonder in our houses
With us, their children,
They stayed.
And now this day,
With our warm human hands
We took hold of them.

With eagle's wing,
And with the striped cloud wings of all the birds of summer,
With these four times wrapping our plume wands
(We make them into living beings)
With our mother, cotton woman,
Even a roughly spun cotton thread,
A soiled cotton thread,
With this four times encircling them
And tying it about their bodies
And with a water bringing hair feather,
We made our plume wands into living beings.
With the flesh of our mother,
Clay woman,
Four times clothing our plume wands with flesh,
We made them into living beings.
Holding them fast,
We made them our representatives in prayer.

From wherever my children have built their shelters,
May their roads come in safety.
May the forests
And the brush
Stretch out their water-filled arms

And shield their hearts;
May their roads come in safety,
May their roads be fulfilled.

Of this animate universe man is an integral part. The beings about him are neither friendly nor hostile. In so far as all are harmonious parts of the whole, the surrounding forces sustain and preserve humanity in the status quo.

Among these vague impersonal forces are certain clearly defined individuals and classes of beings who definitely influence human affairs. These are such beings as the sun, the earth, the corn, prey animals, and the gods of war. These are called a·′wona·wi′lona[12] "the ones who hold our roads." They, too, belong to man's world, and have no animus against man. But in as much as they may withhold their gifts, their assistance must be secured by offerings, prayers, and magical practices.

The sense of conflict as the basic principle of life does not dominate man's relation to the universe any more than it dominates man's relation to man. The Promethean theme—man's tragic and heroic struggle against the gods—has no place in Zuñi philosophic speculation. Nor have any of the other concepts of cosmic conflicts which have always absorbed the interest of Asiatic and European philosophers and mystics, the antithesis between good and evil, or between matter and spirit. There is no Satan in Zuñi ideology, and no Christ.

The world, then, is as it is, and man's plan in it is what it is. Day follows night and the cycles of the years complete themselves. In the spring the corn is planted, and if all goes well the young stalks grow to maturity and fulfill themselves. They are cut down to serve man for food, but their seeds remain against another planting. So man, too, has his days and his destined place in life. His road may be long or short, but in time it is fulfilled and he passes on to fill another rôle in the cosmic scheme. He, too, leaves his seed behind him. Man dies but mankind remains. This is the way of life; the whole literature of prayer shows no questioning of these fundamental premises. This is not resignation, the subordination of desire to a stronger force, but the sense of man's oneness with the universe. The conditions controlling human affairs are no more moral issues than those, like the blueness of the sky, to which we may well be indifferent. It is a remarkably realistic view of the universe. It is an attitude singularly free from terror, guilt, and mystery. The

[12] This term Mrs. Stevenson erroneously interprets as referring to a bisexual deity; creator and ruler of the universe. The term is never used in this sense, nor was I able to find any trace of such a concept among them. The confusion seems to be due to the fact that the missionaries have hit upon this term as the nearest equivalent to "God." The Zuñis, accordingly, always translate the term "God." When asked if a·wona·wi′lona is man or woman they say, "Both, of course," since it refers to a great class of supernaturals. The following texts show that the term is applied to any being addressed in prayer.

Zuñi feels great awe of the supernatural, and definitely fears certain beings in his pantheon—the recently dead, the Koyemci, certain "dangerous" katcinas, but this is quite different from the cosmic terror that crushes many primitive and civilized peoples.

COSMOLOGICAL BELIEFS

The cosmology of the Zuñis is extremely fragmentary. The earth is circular in shape and is surrounded on all sides by ocean. Under the earth is a system of covered waterways all connecting ultimately with the surrounding oceans. Springs and lakes, which are always regarded as sacred, are the openings to this system. On the shores of thee ncircling ocean live the Uwanami or rain makers.[13] They have villages in the four world quarters. The underground waters are the home of Kolowisi, the horned serpent.

Within the earth are the four enclosed caves which the people occupied before coming out into this world—the four wombs of earth mother. The sky (a'po'yan·e, stone cover), solid in substance, rests upon the earth like an inverted bowl. The sun has two houses, in the earth and in the sky. In the morning he "comes out standing to his sacred place"; in the evening he "goes in to sit down at his other sacred place." The sun also travels north and south, reaching his "left hand" (i. e., southernmost) sacred place at the winter solsticial rising. The change in the length of days passes unnoticed.[14]

The moon is reborn each month and in 14 days reaches maturity; after that her life wanes. These are, in general, inauspicious days. Children born while the moon is waning are unlikely to live long.

The stars are fixed in the sky cover. The most prominent feature of the night heavens is the milky way, frequently mentioned in myth and song and figuring prominently in religious art. Some of the stars and constellations are named and recognized—the morning star (Venus or Jupiter) (moyatcunłana, great star), Ursa Major (kwililekä, the seven), Orion's belt (ipi'lakä, the row), the Pleiades (k̄upa·kwe, seed stars). No observations are made of the positions of the stars and movements of the planets. All calendrical computations are made on the basis of the movements of the sun and the moon.

Clouds and rain are the attributes of all the supernaturals, especially the Uwanami and the katcinas. Wind and snow are associated with the War Gods. Windstorms during ceremonies are due to incontinence or other malfeasance on the part of participants or to sorcery on the part of some jealous or envious outsider. The whirlwind appears in folklore, but not in ritual. All natural phenomena are personalized, and tales are told of them. But they are not therefore necessarily a·wona·wi'lona.

---

[13] See p. 513.

[14] See p. 534 for more detailed account of the calendrical system.

There is little speculative interest in the origin and early history of the world, animate and inanimate, although there is great interest in the early history of mankind, and the origin of laws, customs, and rituals. Zuñi myth and ritual contain innumerable expressions of what Haeberlin calls the "idea of fertilization," [15] but to the Zuñis these are unrelated episodes—they do not view them as parts of a great cosmological concept. There are many tales of a maiden being impregnated by the sun or the rain; the sun is called "father," the earth "mother"; and the people are believed to have originated within the earth in the fourth "womb." [16] Yet the general concept of the sexuality of the universe as the source of life, which is found all about them, most fully developed among the Omaha and the Yuman tribes, and in attenuated form among the Hopi, is not known at Zuñi. Cushing records the myth of the sky cohabiting with the earth to produce life, indicating that the notion was current in that day. It has completely vanished at the present time. I have recorded Zuñi creation myths from priests and laymen, in secular and ritualistic form, and all commence the same way, nor do the Zuñis recognize in these myths the implications of profounder cosmological concepts.[17] They are not interested in cosmology or metaphysics. It is interesting in this connection to note the extreme paucity of etiological tales as compared with other North American mythologies.

There was, however, a mythic age, "when the earth was soft," during which things now impossible took place. During this time animals could become human, and humans could change into animals. During this period also the katcinas came in person to the villages. It was at this time that customs originated and took form. Then the earth hardened; things assumed their permanent form and have since remained unchanged.[18]

Ritual: The Control of the Supernatural

TECHNIQUES OF CONTROL

Man is not lord of the universe. The forests and fields have not been given him to despoil. He is equal in the world with the rabbit and the deer and the young corn plant. They must be approached circumspectly if they are to be persuaded to lay down their lives for man's pleasure or necessity. Therefore the deer is stalked ritualistically; he is enticed with sacred esoteric songs, he is killed in a prescribed manner, and when brought to the house is received as an

---

15 Haeberlin, The idea of fertilization in the culture of the Pueblo Indians. M. A. A. A., vol. III, no. 1.

16 The word ťehulikwin is used for womb, but also for any dark enclosed place. It means literally "inside space."

17 Text in ritualistic form, p. 549.

18 Many tales open, "Long ago when the earth was soft."

honored guest and sent away with rich gifts to tell others of his tribe that he was well treated in his father's house.

So, too, the great divinity, the sun, and all the lesser divinities, the katcinas, the rain makers, the beast gods, the war gods, and the ancients, must be reminded that man is dependent upon their generosity; and that they, in turn, derive sustenance and joy from man's companionship. The myth of man's beginnings opens as follows: "Indeed, it has come to pass. In this world was no one. Each day the sun came out. Each day he went in. In the morning no one gave him prayer meal. No one gave him prayer sticks. It was a lonely place. He said to his two children, 'You will go into the fourth womb. Your fathers, your mothers . . . you will bring out into the daylight of your sun father. . . .' "

For all techniques for coping with the spiritual essence of things the Zuñi have the general term t̃ewusu, "religion." This concept embraces all rituals from the casual gesture of offering meal to a dead bird to the most highly elaborated ceremony, any sanctified custom, any urgent request. The basic element seems to be a request, explicitly stated or merely implied, for aid or succor, bolstered by an action or complex of actions that is automatically effectual. Practically all the techniques employed by primitive or civilized man to influence the supernatural are known at Zuñi—fetishism, imitative magic, incantation, and formulæ figure largely in ritual while the more personal approaches of prayer (which in Zuñi, however, is largely formulistic), purification, abstinence, and sacrifice are also conspicuous. The weighting is on the side of the mechanistic techniques which are highly developed. The personal techniques appear always in their milder and more ritualized forms. Prayer is but slightly removed from formula and incantation, only very moderate forms of abstinence are practiced, and these are rigidly circumscribed; sacrifice is never more than the offering of a pinch of corn meal and a prayer stick. One of the important means of achieving rapport with the spirit world, intoxication, is unknown in Zuñi or the other pueblos. Intoxication has been important in the religions of Mexico, and the peyote cult has recently spread to all tribes of the plains and the plateau, but it has never been adopted in the pueblos, except at Taos. On the plains early Indian tribes without drugs produced the same sense of heightened and unearthly experience by means of self-torture and the most rigorous abstinence. The Zuñis use narcotic and vision-producing drugs, the Jamestown weed (datura) and the mysterious tenatsali, but for such prosaic purposes as to discover lost property or the author of sorcery. Although they employ many of the ritualistic forms used throughout North America, such as fasting and purging before ceremonies, these are used for an entirely different purpose and with different effects.

FETISHISM

A large part of Zuñi ceremony centers about the veneration of sacred objects. Some of these, like the fetishes of the rain priests, are of indescribable sanctity, and in them rests the whole welfare of the people. At the other end of the scale are little pebbles, of which almost every man possesses several, which he may have found in the mountains and to which, because of their peculiar form and color, he imputes magical properties. To all such objects are made periodic offerings of corn meal, and at stated times they are removed from their usual resting places and honored. Zuñi fetishes are themselves powerful, and offerings are made to them directly, but they are also the means of reaching still more powerful supernaturals. The important objects of this type are the fetishes (eto·we) of the priests, and their accompanying objects; masks, both tribal and personal; the altars of the medicine societies; stone images of the Beast Gods, whether owned by groups or individuals; the feathered ears of corn (mi·we) given to members of higher orders of societies at their initiation; personal fetishes or amulets of all sorts. Medicine, paint, feathers, and all other items in the regalia of the katcinas, are more or less sacred.

The eto·we of the priests correspond to the medicine bundles of other North American tribes. They consist of the eto·we proper, bundles of plugged reeds filled with seeds or water containing miniature frogs, according to Stevenson (Zuñi Indians, p. 163), pots of sacred black paint, and a miscellaneous assortment of obsidian knives and arrow points, "thunder stones," polished round stones that are rolled over the floor during their ceremonies, rattles of olivella shells and sometimes mi·we like those of society members. These objects are believed to have been brought by the Zuñi from the lowest of the four worlds where they had their origin and are called tcimiḳänapkoa, "the ones that were at the first beginning." They are kept in sealed jars in houses where they are believed to have rested since the settlement of the village. They are "fed" regularly at each meal by some woman of the house where they are kept, and are removed only for the retreats held in their honor. (See below, cult of the Uwanami, for brief account of these ceremonies. For the location of these eto·we, the membership of the priesthoods and the order of retreats, see Stevenson, Zuñi Indians, p. 163ff, and Kroeber, Zuñi Kin and Clan, p. 165ff.) All altars are called teckwin·e, a name derived from the stem teckwi- meaning sacred or taboo.

Masks are with few exceptions connected with the katcina cult. Some are, like the fetishes of the rain priests, "from the beginning" and are tribal property administered in trust by self-perpetuating cult groups. Other masks are individual property which are destroyed at the death of the owner. Like eto·we, masks are regularly fed.

The altars of the medicine societies consist of painted slat altars, a sort of reredos erected at certain of their ceremonies, stone images of the Beast Priests, tutelary gods of the medicine societies, and the same sort of miscellaneous collection of objects as are used on priests' altars. Furthermore, each member of the higher or curing orders of the medicine societies possesses a mi'le (plural miwe), an ear of corn wrapped in feathers which is his personal amulet, and is destroyed at his death. The miwe of members are placed on society altars during all ceremonies.

Some men always carry with them pieces of medicine roots or packages of red paint as amulets. Others possess collections of pebbles and sticks of black paint, from which they seek help in special emergencies, and which are honored with prayers and songs. Perfect ears of corn and ears with flattened ends are believed to have protective powers. One man sold to the writer a personal fetish, a "teckwin·e," together with the ritual and prayers connected with its use. The fetish consisted of four stones, two slender uprights about 2 inches long, one brown and one white, male and female, respectively, a curiously colored triangular stone about an inch long called the "heart" and another round stone called the "head." There was a ritual for setting them up, and prayers. The ritual was used at the winter solstice "or any time."

There also is the "Santu," a small St. Francis, inherited from early Franciscan padres, whom the Zuñis consider a Virgin, and who is besought at a special festival held in her honor, for the blessing of fertility.

The possession of a major fetish, such as eto·we or a mask, protects the house where it is kept; "it gives you something to pray for and makes the house valuable." But its possession may also be a source of danger, for if neglected or desecrated it may cause harm to its keeper. That is one of the reasons why priests endeavor to be exemplary in their conduct.

COMPULSIVE MAGIC

About each sacred object clusters a body of fixed ritual of magical purport. A large number of these magical practices might be classed as imitative magic. During the retreats of priests polished round stones are rolled across the floor to "call the thunder," for thunder is caused by the rain makers rolling the thunderstone in their ceremonial room. At many points in ceremonies tobacco smoke is blown to the six cardinal points "that the rain makers may not withhold their misty breath." There are innumerable rites of this kind. Among the most conspicuous are the presence on every altar of water from a sacred spring, "that the springs may always be full"; the sprinkling of water to induce rainfall; the blowing of smoke to produce clouds; the mixing of great bowls of yucca seeds to produce clouds; the rolling of the thunderstones (the Hopi device of stamping on boards, and the use of the "lightning stick" seem not to be employed at Zuñi); the planting of seeds in the floor of new houses to produce fertility; the conservation of ashes and sweepings in the house during the winter solstice ceremony and finally throwing them out with the prayer, "May you return as corn; may you return as meal"; the placing on winter solstice altars of ears of corn for plentiful crops; and of clay images of peaches, domestic animals, jewelry, and even money to secure increase; the presentation of dolls to pregnant women for safe delivery; the use of bear paws in medicine ceremonies "to call the bear"; and finally, the whole practice of masking in order to compel the presence of the supernaturals in their other bodies, i. e., as rain. The list might be greatly amplified. Many of these practices have been analyzed by Doctor Parsons, Increase by Magic, American Anthropologist, vol. 21, p. 203. There is a certain elasticity in these practices and new ones based on this principle may be readily introduced.

These techniques, despite their mechanistic character, belong distinctly to the realm of religion, since they require a special setting to be effective. The Zuñis use yucca root for washing the hair, and great bowls of the suds are mixed in much the same way they are on the priests' altars. But a woman does not bring rain every time she washes her hair, nor a man every time he smokes a cigarette. These everyday arts become magical techniques only when performed by special persons at stated times and places, in the presence of certain powerful fetishes and to the accompaniment of set prayers, songs, and other ritual acts. Sorcery consists largely in using these and other magical techniques outside of their legitimate settings.[19]

This brings us to another type of magical compulsion which is less apparent but perhaps more fundamental in the development of Pueblo ritual, which might be called, for lack of a better term, formulistic magic. This is the use of apparently irrelevant formulæ or actions to produce a desired result. The efficacy of the formula depends upon its absolutely correct repetition. Every word, gesture, bit of regalia is part of the charm. Hence, the great perturbation in Zuñi if a dancer appears wearing a feather from the shoulders instead of the breast of the eagle, if a single gesture before an altar is omitted, or if the words of a prayer are inverted. A very large part of Zuñi ritual is of this type; in fact all imitative magic has its secret formula

[19] A common type of love sorcery, practiced by men, is to get control of a woman's person by possessing oneself of a fragment of her clothing, a bit of the fringe of her shawl or belt, and carry it about constantly in the pocket or tied to the headband. Should this fail as a love charm, the sickness or death of the victim can be caused by exposing the fragments in a high windy place. Prayer sticks may also be used for sorcery.

to give it validity. These formulæ comprise the great mass of esoteric practice. To this category belong rituals for setting up and removing altars, prayer-stick making, all songs and dances, and most important of all, practically all of the so-called prayers.

PRAYER

Prayer in Zuñi is not a spontaneous outpouring of the heart. It is rather the repetition of a fixed formula. Only in such prayers as those accompanying individual offerings of corn meal and food is a certain amount of individual variation possible, and even here variation is restricted to the matter of abridgment or inclusiveness. The general form of the prayer, the phraseology and the nature of the request, conform strictly to types for other prayers. All more important prayers are fixed in content and form, and great importance is attached to their correct rendition. The rigidity increases in proportion to the importance of the occasion. The words of these prayers, like the fetishes themselves, are tcimik̂änapkoa, "according to the first beginning." That the desired undeviating repetition claimed for prayers is not always achieved is illustrated by a study of variants to be published in the Journal of American Folklore, which shows also the very narrow margin of variability. That a long prayer should have changed so little in the 50 agitated years since Cushing's time is really remarkable.

There are definite fixed rituals and prayers for every ceremonial occasion, and any moderately well-informed Zuñi can identify any of them even when removed from its proper setting. As a check upon informants I read all the prayers I had collected to another informant, a young woman who herself was not actively associated with any major cult, but who was generally well informed through her family connections. In every case she could identify the prayer after about five lines had been read. "It belongs to A·'ciwani—to P̂ekwin. This is what he says when he first goes in in summer"; or "It is the prayer for planting prayer sticks. Anyone can use it." The same woman, however, asked me to copy down for her the prayers for offering the monthly prayer sticks, and for offering corn meal, so that she could learn them, for she knew no prayers for these occasions: "I never learned any prayer for the prayer sticks, and so I just put them down and sprinkle corn meal without saying anything. My husband belongs to a society and knows these prayers but he would not teach me his prayers. I would have to go to my 'father' (the man who initiated her) to learn them and I would have to give him a present for teaching me." This same woman could repeat long prayers when they occurred in tales, so it was not lack of knowledge.

This brings us to another important point, namely, that not only must a prayer be repeated verbatim to be effectual, but it must have been acquired by legitimate means. It must be learned according to definite technique from someone who has the right to use it, and it must be paid for. Otherwise "maybe you can say it but it won't mean anything, or maybe you'll forget it when the time comes to say it." Hence the confusion concerning just what is and what is not "esoteric" in Pueblo ritual. Knowledge of the details of "esoteric" ceremonies is widely diffused, but the power to perform any ceremony effectively is restricted. And since there is an ill-defined feeling that in teaching prayers, "giving them away," as the Zuñis say, the teacher loses some of the power over them, men are "stingy" with their religion.[20] Therefore a man who will tell readily enough a long difficult prayer that he has learned out of curiosity, or as an investment against the time when the present owner dies, will balk at telling a simple common little prayer for offering corn meal to the sun, which everyone knows, but which nevertheless "belongs" to him in a way that the other does not. Hence the paradoxical situation that the very last person to ask for an a·ciwani prayer is one of that group. This, incidentally, is one of the reasons why Christian missionaries are ludicrous in the eyes of Zuñis. "They throw away their religion as if it weren't worth anything and expect us to believe it." Such conduct is not only ridiculous but irreverent.

There are other formulæ at Zuñi besides prayers and songs. Many ritualistic acts, such as offering corn meal or prayer sticks, are of this character. Once the writer caused considerable perturbation by sprinkling corn meal upon a Zuñi altar. "Because sprinkling corn meal is like a prayer; even if you don't say anything you are asking for good luck, and because you are strong when you go away you will take all our good luck with you to your country." Similarly no one at Zuñi would make me a prayer stick to offer with the offerings of my family at the solstice, although many connived at my acquiring prayer sticks for scientific purposes.

SINGING AND DANCING

Singing and dancing by large groups hold an important place in public and secret rituals. Many ritual acts are accompanied by song. There are special song sequences for setting up and taking down altars, for mixing medicine water or soapsuds, for bathing the head at initiations, to accompany various acts of curing. These are all special songs of the curing societies. Like prayers, they must be

[20] This was made painfully evident to the writer in the death of one of her best informants who, among other things, told her many prayers in text. During his last illness he related a dream which he believed portended death and remarked, "Yes, now I must die. I have given you all my religion and I have no way to protect myself." He died two days later. He was suspected of sorcery and his death was a source of general satisfaction. Another friend of the writer, a rain priest, who had always withheld esoteric information, remarked, "Now your friend is dead. He gave away his religion as if it were of no value, and now he is dead." He was voicing public opinion.

learned ritualistically. They are in the nature of incantations; many of them are in foreign languages or have no intelligible words. In addition to these songs of the medicine societies, there are many individually owned songs of magical power, especially songs for planting, for "dancing the corn":[21] individual medicine songs, or songs associated with personal amulets. Certain women also have grinding songs in addition to the well-known songs of the men. These esoteric songs, especially those connected with curing, are very valuable. One man paid a pair of moccasins, a blanket, and a saddle for a song to be used as a love charm. The Great Fire Society has a song for delayed parturition but only two old men of the society know it and they are "stingy" with it. It is the knowledge of songs of this kind which makes the great medicine men of the tribe.

The more patent musical literature of the tribe is the large body of dance songs. These are of many kinds, the songs of the katcinas, the songs sung by the medicine societies for such katcinas as do not sing for themselves, the songs of the medicine societies for the general winter curing ceremonies, for initiations, and for special dances. Katcina songs differ rhythmically and melodically among themselves, those, say, of Kok̄ɔkci are quite different from those of Hemucikwe, or the still more divergent Kumance, and all katcina songs are sharply differentiated from medicine songs. The songs of the various societies differ, and a man can usually classify any song he hears. With the exception of a few secret songs, all songs are songs of sequence, sung by groups, the leader holding the sequence.

Katcina songs are made new for each dance. Song making probably is usually the setting of new words to traditional melodies, according to fairly fixed patterns of structure. The dance step is a simple beating of time with the foot, the body movements being synchronized with the song rhythm. Rhythms are simple, but the melodic structure is subtle and complex. A fuller account of katcina dancing is given on page 896. Most katcinas use only rattles to accompany the song. One group uses a bundle drum, the Koyemci use a barrel drum, and one set uses the pottery drum of the medicine societies.

The dance songs of the societies are more vigorous in rhythm than those of the katcinas, and almost always employ the drum in addition to rattles. A chorus surrounding the drum sings for the dancers. The dance step also is more energetic. Sometimes choirs from the medicine societies sing for certain katcinas, and in that case the rhythm and dance step are those associated with society rather than katcina songs. The societies have song sequences for each of their ceremonies. Most of these are traditional in tune and words, but

[21] A ceremony performed by the women of each household at the winter solstice when the corn is taken out and "danced" so that it will not feel neglected during the ceremonial season.

innovations in words are introduced in specified places. These innovations, as well as those of the katcina songs, are frequently social comment. The society choirs are led by the drummer who holds the sequence. He is a permanent officer of the society, although his office is not sacred like that of the medicine chief or fire maker.

The following partial list of the song cycles of the Great Fire Society is some index of the wealth of musical endowment at Zuñi:

Chief song cycle.[22] Dance songs used in general curing ceremonies in December. This contains 6 sequences containing, respectively, 29, 15, 16, 17, 14, and 31 songs.

Thunder songs. Twenty songs for the first dancing of katcinas at New Year.

Dancing songs (for the dancing of katcinas at the New Year). Seven sequences, the number of songs not known.

Katcina songs. For dancing of katcinas at winter dance series and at Ca'lako. Number of songs not known.

Medicine water songs. Eight songs for making medicine water; no drum.

Fire-making songs. Four songs used for making New Year fire; no drum.

Purificatory songs. Four songs for purification sung at the conclusion of dancing; no drum.

Storm-cloud songs. Twenty-two songs without drum sung for rain on first night of winter solstice. Very esoteric.

Songs of blessing. Sung for increase on eleventh night of winter solstice. Number not known, "a big bunch." Esoteric.

Dawn songs. "Two big bunches" sung at closing of meetings during solstice. Very esoteric. No drum; slow rhythm.

Prayer-stick songs. Four songs for blessing prayer stick bundle before planting. Very esoteric.

A number of special songs sung at the new year meeting: a "going-out song," a "coming-in song," a song calling by name the appointees to sacred offices, a song welcoming the New Year.

This does not include the songs of the special meetings of the society used at their public dance in January and February, individual curing ceremonies, and initiations. The informant died before the list was completed. Some of these songs are used only once a year or, like initiation songs, at intervals of several years, and their content and sequence must be kept by the drummer.

With the exception of a few lullabies and children's play songs, there is no secular music at Zuñi. The only work songs, those for the grinding of corn, are sacred, since everything connected with the handling of corn is sacred activity. There are two sequences of songs for ceremonial grinding; the most popular are the Flute songs,

[22] The sequences are all named.

taken out of the dance songs of the Corn dance and retaining the characteristic ritard at the close which is found in all dance songs. These songs are sung by men accompanied by drum. Women have songs which they use during summer when drumming is taboo.

Group dancing is regarded as a pleasurable activity, pleasing alike to gods and man. Joy is pleasing to the gods and sadness is a sin against them; therefore, for the common man dancing is the most readily accessible and effective form of worship. Usually it is a boy's first voluntary participation in ritual. He dances in mask before he learns the simplest prayer—some people never learn prayers—and long before he learns to make his own prayer sticks. The dance, particularly the masked dance, is preeminently the province of the young, although many men continue to dance in old age. The origin myth of katcina dancing stresses its pleasurable side. It relates that when the people first settled in villages and increased in number they did not know how to enjoy themselves.[23] So, their priests made prayer sticks and sent them to their lost children who had been transformed into katcinas, and the katcinas came and danced for their people. But they were the dead, and so when they came someone died. Therefore the people were instructed to copy their masks and dance with them. "When you dance with them we shall come and stand before you," the katcinas promised, and also promised that it would not fail to rain. Katcina folklore abounds in tales of the devices used by katcinas to enable them to come to Itiwana to dance. There is no myth to explain the origin of unmasked dancing, but the same ideology of summoning the supernaturals in this manner is current. And during the winter solstice, when all the ritual groups are holding their ceremonies, the heads of households take six perfect ears of corn and hold them in a basket while they sing for them. This is called "dancing the corn," and is performed that the corn may not feel neglected during the ceremonial season.

The principal occasions for dancing are the series of summer and winter katcinas, the culminating ceremonies of the Ca'lako, the retreats of the medicine societies during the solstices, initiations, and the Scalp dance. Certain societies hold special ceremonies in which dancing by members and outsiders figures prominently, the winter ceremonies of the Wood Society and Big Fire Society; the Yaya, the dance of the Shuma'akwe. The so-called Corn dance and the Santu dance are other ceremonies in which dancing is conspicuous. In all these cases dancing accompanies less spectacular rites, usually extending over a longer period than the dance itself. Frequently the dance is subsidiary to these secret and potent rites. Usually it is the younger and less responsible members of the group who dance, the priests and leaders meanwhile remaining in retreat or sitting quietly behind

---

[23] See origin tale, p. 605.

their altars. Even in katcina dances, where the dance itself is the essential rite, the pattern of dancing for the priests is preserved. In summer the katcina dances are held during the season when the priesthoods are in retreat, and the katcina group always dances in front of the house where the priests are "in."

In order for any rite to be efficacious the protagonist must "have a good heart," or, to use more familiar phraseology, he must be in a state of grace. Joy and freedom from care are the chief requirements of a state of grace, second only to physical purity. Therefore the custom of dancing for the priests while they are in retreat, and of various groups visiting to dance in one another's house during synchronous periods of retreat. During a katcina dance that lasted for several days a group of "little dancers" [24] came one night to dance in the kiva. "Because the dancers could not go home to their wives, and were lonely in the kiva. Therefore these others came to dance for them so that they should not be sad."

Connected psychologically as well as ceremonially with public dancing is the practice of clowning. There are organized groups of clowns who assist at all katcina dances and amuse the populace by obscene or satirical or childish pranks. There are masked and unmasked clowns; the masked clowns, the Koyemci,[25] are the most feared of all the katcinas. The Ne'we·kwe society also are clowns, and are regarded as the most powerful medicine men, and potential witches. They are famous for love magic.

OFFERINGS

Offerings of various kinds are included in all Zuñi rituals. The principal offerings to the supernaturals are food, tobacco, prayer meal (coarse cornmeal containing ground white shell and turquoise), and prayer sticks. The usual food offering consists of a bit of food from each dish that is set out, thrown into the fire or merely dropped on the floor with a brief, perfunctory prayer. The supernaturals nourish themselves on the spiritual essence of the food. All priests and the wives of priests make such an offering before eating of any dish. Also women in houses where fetishes are kept offer food in the fire before serving a meal. These offerings are more formal at quasi-ceremonial feasts, such as the feasts accompanying house building, harvest, etc. Men during participation in ceremonies also make offerings of food in the river, where it is readily accessible to the gods. Food offerings are made especially to the ancestors (a·łacina·we) and the katcinas. On the day of the dead large quantities of food are sacrified in the river and the fire (see p. 621).

---

[24] The "little dancers" are the children of the katcinas. One or a group may come to play pranks in connection with any katcina dance. They are impersonated by young boys.

[25] For fuller accounts see p. 946, and Parsons, p. 229.

Meal is offered to the sun each morning by all men who hold any permanent or temporary sacerdotal position and by many other individuals, both men and women. Meal is sprinkled on prayer sticks when they are planted, and on masks, fetishes, and other sacred objects when they are taken out for use and when they are returned to their places. It is sprinkled upon katcinas by onlookers, and their leader sprinkles meal before them "to make their road." Handfuls of meal are thrown into the air through the kiva hatchway to welcome the new year. A bowl of corn meal stands on every society altar and everyone who enters the room to participate in the ceremony sprinkles corn meal on the altar before taking his place. In addition to the use of meal as an offering it is also used for delineation of sacred symbols. Every altar is set up upon a painting of white meal representing clouds, and from the center of this a line runs out toward the door of the room, or the foot of the ladder. This is the road of life and along it persons entering the room walk up to the altar. It is also the road by which the supernaturals enter. Colored sand paintings, similar in technique to those of the Navaho, are used in initiation ceremonies. A cross of corn meal marks the place prepared to receive a sacred object, corn meal is used to mark the walls of a house at its dedication, and marks of corn meal are made on the hatchway of the kivas to indicate the duration of a ceremony. Corn meal is rubbed on the head and face of the newborn and on the body of the dead. In short, there is no ceremonial occasion on which it is not used.

The most important and valuable gift to the gods is the prayer stick. This is a small stick, carefully smoothed and painted, to which various feathers are attached with cotton cord. The length and form of the stick, the wood of which it is made, the color of the pigment, and the feathers are all definitive of the character of the offering, and vary according to the beings to whom it is offered, the sacerdotal position of the giver, and the occasion upon which it is given.

The whole matter of the varieties and manufacture of prayer sticks is too complex to go into here. A few outstanding points can be mentioned. The wood most commonly used is the red willow. For certain occasions other shrubs are required. When wood for prayer sticks is gathered corn meal is offered to the shrub from which the twigs are cut. Only perfectly straight shoots are taken. Generally the bark is removed. There are four common prayer stick measures; from the tip of the middle finger to the base of the finger, to the center of the palm, to the wrist, to the inside of the elbow. Frequently faces are indicated by notching one side of the stick. The feathers are attached to the back of the stick and are thought of as constituting its clothing. The two upper feathers are the most important and characteristic. Usually they are from the turkey and eagle, respectively; or they may both be from the eagle. Feathers from the breast or back of the turkey are used on sticks for the ancestors and the katcinas, tail feathers of the turkey on certain sticks made by the a'ciwanii. Sticks for the sun, moon, and the Uwanami have a downy eagle feather in this position and the use of this feather entails particularly stringent taboos upon the giver. Sticks for the war gods, and for the katcina priests (the Ca'lako sticks) have an eagle tail feather in this position. The second feather is almost always one from the shoulders or back of the eagle. After this comes a duck feather, and feathers of the "summer birds," all the brightly colored birds: jay, red hawk, oriole, bluebird, humming bird, road runner, etc. Birds are snared or shot for their feathers, and the feathers are carefully kept, wrapped separately in paper and laid away in native wooden boxes with sliding covers. The feathers are attached with commercial cotton cord. The sticks are painted after the feathers are attached. The character and manufacture of the pigments are described in another place (p. 859). Most sticks are painted black, but those for the sun and moon are painted blue and yellow, respectively, and these colors have sex associations. Paired blue and yellow sticks are symbolic of fecundity.

The principal occasions upon which prayer sticks are offered by large groups of people are at the solstices. On these occasions persons of both sexes and all ages offer to the ancestors and to the sun (if male), or to the moon (if female). Furthermore, at the winter solstice all members of the katcina society make a second offering to the katcina and members of the medicine societies to the tutelary gods of their societies. At each full moon all members of societies offer to the ancestors, to the katcinas (if males) and to the tutelary gods of their societies. At the winter dances and at the end of Ca'lako each man makes a prayer stick for the katcinas, but does not himself plant it. Furthermore, a large part of the ritual of every ceremony concerns the making and offering of special types of prayer sticks by those participating. Prayer sticks are sometimes offered individually and sometimes the offerings of many persons are bundled together into a k̜ä-atcin·e which is deposited by someone delegated to plant it. Prayer sticks are buried or deposited in corn fields, in the river mud, in shrines in the mountains, in springs, in excavations in or near the village.

Prayer sticks provide the clothing of the supernaturals. Just as the supernaturals nourish themselves on the spiritual essence of food offered in the fire or the river, they clothe themselves in the feathers of prayer sticks. This is especially true of the katcinas, whose beautiful feathers form their most conspicuous ornaments. (For a treatment of this idea in folklore, see the tale of Hetsilulu, p. 1048.)

The offering of prayer sticks is one of the most important acts of Zuñi ritual and four days after making any offering of prayer sticks the giver must refrain from sexual intercourse, and from quarreling. There are additional restrictions connected with special offerings—after the offering to the sun at the winter solstice one must eat no meat or anything cooked with grease for four days.[26] The same restriction applies to the a·ciwan·i after offerings to the uwanam·i, and to p̄ekwin after his various offerings to the sun. Also to all novices, including boys initiated into the katcina society, after their initiation. (They plant prayer sticks as the final rite in the initiation.)[27] After the plantings of the Ca'lako party the members and their households must refrain from trade for four days. There is no restriction on work for wages. No one trades during the first four days of the winter solstice—many people do not trade for 10 days—and the households of priests do not trade while these priests are in retreat. The feeling about trading at these seasons seems to be that since these are periods of magical power, during which forthcoming events are preordained, if property passed out of one's hands during this time all one's wealth would soon melt away. Therefore, during these periods, necessities are purchased at the store on credit, but no payments are made.

Prayer sticks are especially male offerings. Although women frequently offer prayer sticks they never make them. Their male relatives (actual or ceremonial) make them for them. So also, although men offer food and corn meal, it is always prepared for them by the women. This division in ritual is a reflection of the general economic pattern, in which the females supply food and the males the clothing of the household. So also women furnish the food of the gods and men their clothing.

TABOO AND ABSTINENCE

The special restrictions which follow the planting of prayer sticks is part of a general feeling of taboo directed toward all things sacred. The Zuñi word for taboo is teckwi. An altar is called teckwin·e (sacred thing); a person upon whom there is any ceremonial restraint also is teckwi. It is almost impossible to reduce the list of Zuñi taboos to any sort of system. Some of them seem even more fortuitous than their magical formulæ. Some prohibitions are dictated by fear or repulsion, some are designed to preserve the power and sanctity of rituals and objects, others are rites of purification, one at least is designed to provoke the pity of the gods, the vigil of the priests

[26] Except members of the ci'wana·kwe.

[27] The restrictions on meat and grease, as well as salt and sugar, are observed after all prayer-stick plantings in other pueblos.

before the coming of the corn maids (see myth, p. 914). The following activities are all "teckwi" in Zuñi terminology:

Foods.—Members of the ci·wana·kwe society must not eat jack rabbit, nor a common purple-flowered herb. This is felt so strongly that a member of this society will not even touch a jack rabbit nor permit it to be brought into the house in which he lives. No Zuñi eats or touches meat or grease during the first four days of the winter solstice; [28] priests refrain from eating meat and grease for 10 days, and during the periods of their retreat; p̄ekwin does not eat meat and grease after offering prayer sticks to the sun; initiates do not eat meat for four days after their initiation; warriors who have taken a scalp do not eat meat, grease, salt, or any hot food for one year; mourners (especially widows and widowers) do not eat meat, salt, or hot foods for four days following a death.

Objects.—All sacred objects are taboo to all people who do not "belong" to them. The strength of this feeling varies according to the power of the fetish. No one would dare to touch one of the priest's fetishes except the chief of the priesthood, and no one will enter the room where it is kept except the chief priest and the female head of the house. This is true also of the permanent masks and society altars. When the people who keep one of the Ca'lako masks moved to a new house they called the head of the kiva whose mask they kept to transfer it, "because they were afraid to touch it." Corn fetishes, prayer sticks, ceremonial garments are all handled with great respect, and no more than necessary.[29]

Places.—The rooms where sacred things are kept are taboo to outsiders. All shrines are taboo except when visited officially. There is one War God shrine (co'łuwayällakwi) which may be visited by those who wish to pray for good luck in war or gambling. Otherwise it is not permitted for individuals to visit shrines even for purposes of prayer.[30] Rooms where retreats or ceremonies are being held, unless the ceremony is specifically public, are taboo to those not belonging to the ceremony. If any one crosses the threshold he is "caught," and must be initiated into the group, or where this is impossible (like meetings of the katcina priests), must be ceremonially whipped and make certain payments to his "father." Altars are always erected on the side of the room away from the door, "the valuable place." Strangers are always seated near the door, by the fireplace and away from the "valuable place." Mourners and warriors who have taken scalps sit "away from the fire."

---

[28] Certain exceptions to this rule are discussed on p. 623.

[29] A good friend would not unwrap her mi'le for me to look at, although she permitted me to examine it when it had been taken out for a ceremony.

[30] Mrs. Stevenson (Zuñi Indians, p. 154) gives a graphic description of the reluctance of her Zuñi guides to accompany her to ķołuwala·wa·. The writer has had similar experiences with guides who showed her the location of shrines but themselves refused to approach them.

Sex taboos.—Sex relations are forbidden between members of the same clan or the same medicine society. Relations with members of the father's clan are frowned upon. A man may not have relations with the wife of a member of his kiva or medicine society (his brother's wife, hence his sister).[31] These are primarily social taboos but the punishment for them is of the same kind as punishment for breaking of strictly religious taboos.

Sex relations are taboo during the 10 days of the winter solstice, for four days following the planting of prayer sticks, and during participation in dances or other ceremonies.[32] Warriors who have taken a scalp must refrain from sexual intercourse for one year and must go through a cermony of purification at the end of that time before they may again sleep with their wives.[33] The same rules apply to the widowed who wish to remarry.

Other tabooed activities.—Priests, and others holding temporary or permanent religious offices, must not engage in any quarrels or disputes with fellow tribesmen or outsiders. Hence, they are not appointed to civil offices. One must not quarrel for four days following planting of prayer sticks. Priests and appointees to religious office must not leave the Zuñi Valley during the terms of their office. (This is a taboo that is frequently broken to the distress of the orthodox.) This prohibition against going about may be an extension of the retreat to the daily life of those who are regarded as "working for their people all of the time." There are no taboos upon labor, except in the case of initiations, when the novice must do no work, and especially must lift no heavy weights during the four days between the ceremony at which he receives a new heart and his final initiation. No one must sleep during attendance at religious ceremonies, but there seems to be no restriction on conversation. There are certain ceremonies in which speech is forbidden to participants, especially the 24-hour vigil of the priests, while awaiting the arrival of the corn maids on the last day of the Ca'lako ceremonies. There are a number of special taboos relating to the wearing of masks—a man while wearing a mask must not speak, he must not give anything away, he must not engage in any defiling activity. A man wearing a mask or katcina body paint is teckwi to others, and must not be touched, approached, or stared at. There are also special taboos concerning death, mourning, and the scalp dance which incorporates all the purificatory rites of mourning. For four days the widow or widower (also the scalper and the woman who has touched the scalp) must not approach the fire, must not touch or be touched by anyone, must not receive anything directly from the hand of another person, must not talk, and

---

31 These are only the more important incest rules, a full discussion of which belongs to another place.

32 In many ceremonies this is extended to include touching, even accidentally, addressing, or even seeing a person of the opposite sex.

33 There is some confusion about the sexual taboos placed upon the woman who brings the scalp (see p. 674).

must sleep very little, if at all. The food and sex taboos observed at this period have already been mentioned. There are also special taboos relating to death by violence, by lightning, or away from home. There are no strictly religious taboos upon pregnant or menstruating women. There are, of course, many taboos that belong to the realm of folklore rather than that of religion.

To all of the foregoing prohibitions, as well as others not mentioned, the Zuñis apply the word teckwi, but it is obvious that they embrace many different attitudes toward the tabooed object or action. There are the taboos relating to death and mourning, sacred objects, places, and rites. In all these cases the prohibition rises out of the mingling of fear and reverence in the attitude toward the sacred. Fear is the predominant feeling actuating the rites for the dead, and the fear of the dead is extended to those intimately associated with him in life. Hence, the widow is untouchable during the period when the malice of the dead is active. Those who have killed an enemy in warfare are similarly threatened, since they have cut off a man before his time. In the taboos against touching sacred objects and trespassing on sacred places the feeling of fear is less apparent but none the less present, for sacred things are dangerous in proportion to their power. Whereas death is feared as the result of violating taboos of mourning, in the case of other violations the fear is vague and general, and the results of infringements are less clearly foreseen.

On the other hand, there are a number of personal restraints which are forms of abstinence rather than taboos. To this class belong the sex prohibitions, the prohibitions on certain kinds of foods at certain times, and the restrictions upon the activities of persons participating in ceremonies. The general purpose of all these restrictions is withdrawal. That they are not primarily purificatory is shown by the fact that in many cases they follow rather than precede the approach to the gods; as, for instance, the sexual taboos following the planting of prayer sticks. A man approaching the gods with a request cuts himself off from the world in order that he may concentrate all his thoughts upon wresting his desire from the supernatural. For this purpose all distracting activities are denied him.

Relations with women are forbidden, also trading, quarreling, moving about. The fullest expression of this spirit is the retreat which forms the basis of all important ceremonies. The retreat is practiced by many ceremonial groups, but the more important retreats are those of the priesthoods who "go in" in turn during the summer, and those of the medicine societies at the winter solstice and at initiations. The katcina priests hold retreats before the public ceremonies of the Ca'lako. Retreats are always practiced by groups. The individual retreat is not found at Zuñi. A retreat always is preceded by the making of prayer sticks. In the evening these are made into k̂a-etcin·e (see p. 500) and planted somewhere outside the village. When the emissaries return, the group "goes in" in the house where their sacred possessions are kept. The men have brought their bedding to this house, for they are to sleep there during the period of the retreat. Usually the sacred things are taken out and an altar is set up. During the retreat the room containing the sacred objects is taboo to all outsiders. The men do not leave the room (except in the case of the medicine societies, where men may go out in the day time and eat at their homes). They sleep in the house of their retreat, and their meals are served by a woman of that house, the wives of the men contributing cooked food. There are frequent sessions of song, prayer, and meditation, especially at night. Retreats usually last four or eight days. The Koyemci (see p. 946) "go in" for 14 days, and brief retreats of one night are held by priests at the solstices and at other times. Retreats frequently end with a second prayer stick planting, with the usual restrictions on conduct for the four following days, which make of this period a modified form of retreat. The main priesthoods open their summer retreats with a period of strictest retreat. In addition to the usual restrictions they forego all animal food. On the fourth day they make a second offering of prayer sticks, and, although they remain in seclusion for four days longer, the food restriction is lifted. They do not plant prayer sticks again on coming out. The minor priesthoods disband on the fourth day, although they are still under restrictions. The bow priests, although they plant prayer sticks and are "in," do not remain in their house. The "poor man" who has planted prayer sticks is in much the same position as the bow priest. Although not confined to his house he is somewhat withdrawn from life and is "sacred."

Priests live always under certain restraints, and in this restriction of activity of certain individuals may be seen the germs of a monastic life. However, it is not the sexual prohibitions that are made lifelong for the holy men of Zuñi. Celibacy as a way of life is regarded with extreme disfavor by the community. Mrs. Stevenson states (Zuñi Indians) that p̄ekwin although married is expected not to cohabit with his wife, but I could find no evidence that this is the case. He is expected to observe rigidly the long periods of sexual continence, which his elaborate ceremonies require, but continence at other times is not considered necessary or desirable.

There is, moreover, a marked difference in attitude between the Zuñi priest and the Christian or Buddhist monk. Zuñi ideology does not oppose matter and spirit as conflicting or mutually exclusive principles. The priest, therefore, does not renounce the world, the flesh, and the devil because the world and the flesh are evil. Rather he strips his life of trivial, irrelevant, and distracting matters in order to leave his mind free for his great work—the material and spiritual welfare of his people.[34]

PURIFICATION

In addition to these taboos and restrictions which may be regarded as secondarily purificatory there are also certain positive rites of purification. Among these bathing, especially bathing of the head, holds first place. Bathing of the head is obligatory before participation in any ceremony and usually at the conclusion of the ceremony. For important festivals everyone in the village bathes his head. The head of the newborn infant is bathed before he is presented to the sun. In most pueblos a name is given at this time, but not at Zuñi. Bathing of the head with name-giving forms the culminating rite of initiations; after important participations in masked ceremonies the head and body are bathed by paternal aunts. The purpose of ritual bathing after ceremonies is to make the participants safe for human contact. The ceremony at which the Koyemci are paid for their year's work by their paternal clan is called "washing." At this the head is bathed symbolically with water and corn meal. Curiously enough, the sweat bath is never used ritualistically at Zuñi, although it is used therapeutically and forms an important part of rituals of all surrounding tribes, including the Navaho and the ancient and modern peoples of Mexico. One ceremonial group (łewe'kwe) bathes in the frozen river during its ceremonies. As in other North American tribes, purges and emetics are used for ceremonial purification.

Ashes are used for purification after childbirth and at points in the ceremonies of medicine societies. Piñon gum is burned and the smoke inhaled as a rite of purification after a death in the household or as a protection against witches, whenever sorcery is suspected.

There is a special form of purification called "wiping off" (cuwaha) used in connection with war and healing. This consists of expectorating into cedar bark or corn husk (on a prayer stick in some cases of cures), waving the packet four times over the head in counterclockwise circuits and throwing it down, or, in the case of healing, taking it out toward the east to be buried.

During the initiations of boys into the katcina society property is destroyed for purification. Katcinas visit all the housetops in the village, and from each a bowl or basket is thrown down and destroyed. This also is called cuwaha.

Whipping, never used as a means of punishment, is reserved for purposes of purification. During initiations katcinas go about the village whipping everyone they meet unless they carry corn or water, "to take away the bad luck." People call upon the katcinas at other

[34] For a description of the priestly ideal, see texts, p. 666.

times to whipthem to cure them of "bad dreams" (see p. 481). The whipping of the initiates is probably also purificatory.

Ceremonial Pattern

A full ceremony at Zuñi utilizes all of the foregoing techniques. The usual ceremonial pattern is a retreat followed by a dance. Frequently the dance is public, the retreat, of course, always being secret. Sometimes, also, the dance is not performed by the same group that hold the core of the rite, but by some cooperating group or by an organized group of laymen (e. g., the dances by girls and youths during the scalp dance). The relative importance attached to the esoteric and the spectacular approaches varies among the different cults. The ceremonies of the katcina society are weighted on the side of the spectacular. In the summer katcina dances only the leaders offer prayer sticks and observe continence, and even for them there is no formal retreat. The priesthoods, on the other hand, concentrate on secret rites and dispense entirely with public dancing, unless some katcina group chooses to honor one of the priesthoods by dancing on its "middle day."

A retreat usually opens and closes with offerings of prayer sticks. Sometimes there is a public announcement of the opening of the ceremony such as the announcements by p̄ekwin of the solstices, of the opening of the scalp dance, and the beginning of the Ca'lako festival. There is some kind of set-up of sacred objects—a formal altar, fetishes, masks, medicine water, etc.—and much of the ritual of the retreat is concerned with the manipulation of these objects. Those participating in the retreat practice various forms of abstinence. Sexual continence is always required. Sometimes there are taboos on certain foods or, rarely, on all food. There is a variable amount of seclusion. At intervals throughout the retreat there are recitals of prayers and songs. The rest of the time is spent preparing paraphernalia for the final dance, if there is to be one, rehearsing, and telling tales, especially the origin myths in the ritualistic forms appropriate to the particular ceremony. A great deal of instruction in ritualistic affairs is given during these retreats.

The form which the concluding ceremonies takes is subject to unlimited variation. Each ceremony has its characteristic features, of which the most conspicuous is always group dancing. Dancing always continues with brief intervals for many hours; the emotional effect is cumulative, although there is no definite climax. The dancing itself is always reduced to its barest essentials—the rhythmic repetitions of a single body movement. Although impersonation is common there is no dramatic representation. Whenever myth is suggested it is in a highly stylized and symbolic form. Great importance is attached to correctness and uniformity in costume and regalia, which are definitive for each dance. Dancing may be continuous, like the initiation dancing of the societies, or may be broken by intervals filled with clowning, jugglery, or other rituals, like the summer katcinas, or two or more groups may dance in turn.

Dancing is always semipublic. Sometimes, for example, the last night of the winter ceremony of the medicine societies, specially privileged outsiders (that is, outside the active group) may attend. Other dances are performed in lay houses or outdoors and are free to all who wish to come, including whites.

Despite the enormous complexity of Zuñi ceremonialism the elements of which it is built and the underlying patterns are comparatively simple. The ideology is difficult of comprehension because it is monistic, abstract, and impersonal where we tend to be dualistic, concrete, and personal, but the philosophical ideas in themselves are neither abstruse nor involved. So also the complexity of ritual is more apparent than real. All ceremonies have five principal aspects—the manipulation and veneration of sacrosanct objects; offerings; purification, abstinence, and seclusion; recitation of sacred formulæ; public celebration. Each of the five approaches is itself subject to little variation. The texts recorded in the following pages illustrate how little complexity has been introduced into prayer. Prayers may be long or short, condensed or expanded, but the content, outline, and phraseology are always the same. So, too, with other techniques. The complexity of Zuñi ritual is a complexity of organization rather than content. The baffling intricacy of ceremonies like the winter dance of the Wood Society and associated groups, and the initiation of boys into the Katcina society are due chiefly to two processes in organization: The diversification of function and the piling up and telescoping of distinct ceremonies. It is characteristic of Zuñi rituals that their different parts are not necessarily performed by the same individuals or the same groups. The group that makes offerings and goes into retreat may have no control of the sacred object in whose honor the retreat is being held. Everything connected with the handling of fetishistic objects may belong to a second group, while a third group holds the sacred words of the chants, and yet a fourth group manages the public ceremonies. Each of these groups has its own organization, mode of succession, and minor rituals, so that the complete picture of any major ceremony, such as the Ca'lako, with all its ramifications, gives an impression of bewildering and baffling complexity.

It is more difficult to uncover the ceremonial pattern in ceremonies which are the products of coalescence. The winter solstice ceremonies, thought of at Zuñi as a unit, are clearly a synchronization of independent cults. In other cases the essential separateness of parts of a ceremony is somewhat obscured. The dance of the Wood Society and other groups is undoubtedly an amalgamation of at least two factors: A snow-making ceremony comprising a retreat of the keepers of the "winter fetishes," with a dance in their honor, the muaiye, combined with a war ceremony of the bow priesthood in conjunction with the warlike societies. We are here not necessarily dealing with a historical process. The ceremony is certainly now conceived as a unit and may always have been as it is at present, although in view of the complex history of Zuñi as shown archeclogically there is no reason to doubt that any ceremony may have been derived from several diverse sources. But however diverse the sources, the resulting product has been well pruned to fit the Zuñi pattern.

The public rituals constitute the most important esthetic expression of the people. Not only are they "artistic" in the superficial sense, in that they embrace the types of behavior which we arbitrarily lump together as "the arts"—ornament, poetry, music, the dance—but they provide the satisfaction of the deeper esthetic drive. Zuñi children do not mind being whipped by the Sälimop̃iya "because they are such pretty dancers." I have heard women say of the mourning ceremonies of the Ca'lako, "We all cry. It is so beautiful that our hearts hurt." I have watched the faces of old men as I read to them the texts of their prayers. Zuñi rituals have a style of their own that belongs to ritual as an art. They are ordered and formal; they are well designed; they begin in quietness and end in serenity. Their quality is gracious and benign. They have moments of splendor, but they are not gorgeous or "barbaric" or frenzied. All of Zuñi life is oriented about religious observance, and ritual has become the formal expression of Zuñi civilization. If Zuñi civilization can be said to have a style, that style is essentially the style of its rituals.

Ceremonial Organization

The basis upon which all Zuñi ceremonialism rests is the cult of a·'łacina·we, the ancients or the ancestors. In their worship all participate, regardless of age, sex, or affiliation with special cults. Nor are the a·'łacina·we ever omitted from the ceremonies devoted primarily to the worship of other beings. The special and characteristic offering to the a·'łacina·we is food. At the great public ceremony devoted to them exclusively, Grandmothers' Day [35] (Catholic All Souls Day), the outstanding feature is the sacrifice of great quantities of food in the fire and the river. They receive other offerings, too—prayer meal, smoke, and, of course, prayer sticks. The prayer stick for a·'łacina·we is a small stick painted black, the principal feather being from the back of the turkey. Offerings of food to a·'łacina·we form a

[35] See p. 621.

conspicuous part of all public ceremonies, and no prayer omits to mention them. So pervasive is this cult of the ancestors that other classes of beings (the katcinas, for instance) tend to merge their identity in them.

The a·'łacina·we are, in Zuñi terminology, a·'wona·wi'lona, "the keepers of the roads"; that is, beings who guide, protect, nourish human life. They are, therefore, as a group, beneficent beings. They are identified with the greatest of all blessings in this arid land, the clouds and the rain. In prayers they are referred to as "those who have attained the blessed place of waters," and when they return they come clothed in the rain. When, on summer afternoons, the great cumulus clouds pile up along the southern horizon, a Zuñi mother will point them out to her children, saying, "Look, there the grandfathers are coming!" However, this identification with the rain is not restricted to the a·'łacina·we, but appears also in beliefs concerning other supernaturals, especially the U'wanam·i, the so-called rain makers, and the koko or masked gods or katcinas. Even the A'hayuta and the We·'ma·we walk in the rain. Rain is an attribute of divinity, and all the divine ones come clothed in waters. The dead are, in general, the bestowers of all blessings for which the Zuñis ask—life, old age, rain, seeds, wealth, power, fecundity, health, and general happiness.[36] Despite their prevailingly beneficent character, toward individual dead persons, and especially toward the recently dead, the attitude is strongly ambivalent, mingled of tender reverence and fear. This fear is not due to the evil nature of the dead, but to the fact that so long as they remember human life they will long for their dear ones left behind in this world. Therefore they come to trouble them in dreams and day dreams, until the living man sickens of grief and dies. Therefore the recent dead must be cut off. Their road is darkened with black corn meal, and they are implored, with offerings of corn meal and prayer sticks, not to trouble the living.

There is nothing esoteric in the worship of the ancestors. In this all individuals are on an equal footing and have direct access to the supernaturals without the mediation of priests. There are no fetishes or other permanently held paraphernalia used in their worship, nor are there special places sacred to them, unless perhaps the river bank, especially the point called Wide River, where offerings of food are customarily made. No man stands in any special relationship toward them. It is quite clear that there is no ancestor worship in the restricted meaning of the word. A man prays to *the* ancestors, not to his own ancestors. Certain groups of men have special relations to certain groups among the dead—priests invoke deceased priests, medicine men deceased medicine men, impersonators of the katcinas their predecessors in office, but never their progenitors as

---

[36] See texts, p. 641.

such. Such special relationships belong in the realm of special cult activities which will be considered.

Against this background general nonesoteric religious activities have developed a large number of esoteric cults, each devoted to the worship of special supernaturals or groups of supernaturals, and each having a priesthood, a body of secret ritual, permanent possessions of fetishistic power, special places of worship, and a calendrical cycle of ceremonies. I distinguish six major cults of this type, which might be named from the supernaturals toward whom their principal ceremonies are directed: 1, the cult of the Sun; 2, the cult of the Uwanami; 3, the cult of the katcinas; 4, the cult of the priests of the katcinas (a distinct but closely related cult[37]); 5, the cult of the Gods of War; 6, the cult of the Beast Gods. The functions, activities, and personnel of these groups overlap and interweave in a bewildering intricacy that baffles analysis. The p̃ekwin who is speaker of the sun is also priest; he has certain specifically priestly functions. Some activities belong to one, some to another, of his affiliations. This is true also of the bow priests, leaders of the war cult, who as guardians of secret rites are associated with fraternities; the fraternities or medicine societies, which are devoted primarily to the worship of the Beast Gods, gods of life, medicine, and witchcraft, have one ceremony devoted entirely to the invocation of the Uwanami. Some are of distinctly warlike character; others possess masks and take part in masked rituals. However, in spite of this interlocking, there is no difficulty in assigning any major ritualistic group in Zuñi to one or the other of these cults on the basis of supernatural sanction, method, and tangible possessions.

THE CULT OF THE SUN

The sun is the source of all life. Indeed the word for life is t̃ek̃ohanan·e, daylight (t̃e, time or space; k̃ohana, white; n·e, nominal suffix). The sun is therefore "our father,"[38] in a very special sense, but not in the sense of progenitor. He is associated in worship with the moon, who is "our mother." However, life is not thought of as springing from the union of these two. The moon is "mother" by courtesy only. The animating female principle of the universe is the earth mother, but there is no cult of the earth.[39]

Each morning as the sun sends his first level beams striking across the houses his people come out to meet him with prayers and offerings. Men and women stand before their doors, facing the east,

---

[37] See p. 521.

[38] "Father" in Zuñi is a term of respect applied to all supernaturals and to all human beings who have any claim to one's respect or affection.

[39] The phallic element is not absent from the worship of the sun and moon. At the solstices adult males plant blue sticks to the sun, females yellow ones to the moon. The sticks planted in the Ca'lako homes, which are specifically for fecundity, are double; one stick is painted blue, the other yellow, and they are male and female, respectively. Like the sun prayer sticks, they are made with downy feathers of the eagle.

their hands full of corn meal which is offered to the sun, with prayers for long life. Every priest or appointee to ceremonial office and every man during the time he is engaged in any ceremony must observe this morning ritual. But many others, "poor people," never omit it, even on the most bitterly cold winter mornings.

But the great ceremonies at which the sun father is honored are in the keeping of his special priest, whose title, p̄ekwin, means, literally, speaking place. The p̄ekwin is the most revered and the most holy man in Zuñi. Even in this society which diffuses power and responsibility until both become so tenuous as to be almost indiscernible, the p̄ekwin is ultimately held responsible for the welfare of the community. He holds his power directly from the Sun Father, with whom he has a very special and intimate relationship. The p̄ekwin performs many duties in no way connected with his office as priest of the sun. He is the active member of the priestly hierarchy and the officiating priest at all ceremonies at which the priests function jointly. It is he who sets up the altars for these ceremonies and even the altar for the scalp dance; it is he who meets the priests of the katcinas when they visit Zuñi and "makes their road"; it is he who installs new priests, including bow priests, and formally appoints to office the impersonators of the katcinas.

As priest of the sun he is the keeper of the calendar. He sets the dates for the solstices, from which all other ceremonies are dated. His calculations are based on observation of the sunrise in winter and the sunset in summer. These observations are made at shrines outside of the village. When the sun rises (or sets) behind certain landmarks, the date for the solstice is at hand. However, the calendar is disarranged by the desire to have the celebration of the solstice coincide with the full moon, and the p̄ekwin is the subject of bitter criticism when the sun fails to oblige in this matter. It is at the solstices that the sun is celebrated with great public ceremonies. For some period before the p̄ekwin observes fasts and continence and makes frequent offerings of prayer sticks to the sun and moon and the ancients. In winter the public ceremonies are opened by the p̄ekwin's announcement made from the housetop at dawn. At this time he orders the people to make prayer sticks for their sun father and their moon mother.[40] For 10 days the p̄ekwin "counts days" for his sun father. Then on the tenth day all people offer their prayer sticks to the sun or moon, along with others for the ancients, and special society offerings. The solstice ceremonies continue for 10 days longer, but the part of the sun in them is finished on the tenth day.

In summer the announcement by the p̄ekwin takes place eight days before the planting, and the whole celebration is less elaborate.

[40] See texts, p. 636.

As in the winter, there are other ceremonies at this time but in different forms.[41]

The p̄ekwin has, furthermore, a great public ceremony, the ła·hewe or Corn Dance, which should be performed every fourth year in midsummer. It has not been performed for many years. This ceremony commemorates the departure of the corn maids and celebrates their return. It follows the usual ceremonial pattern of periods of retreat spent in preparation for the public ceremony of the last day. On this occasion the e′tone of the priests are exposed in public and there is dancing alternately by two groups of girls.

The writer has not seen this ceremony. It has not been held for many years, and very little is known about it save that "it belongs to p̄ekwin." Since it is so peculiarly his dance we may assume that it is connected in some way with the worship of the sun, but what this connection is, toward what blessing it is directed, and what techniques it employs are by no means clear from the only description we have, and further information is lacking.

THE CULT OF THE U′WANAM·I

The U′wanami, a term generally translated rain makers,[42] are water spirits. They live in all the waters of the earth, the four encircling oceans and the underground waters to which springs are gateways. Cumulus clouds are their houses; mist is their breath. The frogs that sing from every puddle after the drenching summer rains are their children. The ripple marks along the edge of ditches washed out by heavy rains are their footprints.

The worship of the U′wanami is enormously elaborated and is in the hands of the priesthoods, of which there are 12.[43] Each priesthood contains from two to six members. Several have women associates. Membership, in the main, is hereditary within matrilineal family groups—the family in whose house the fetish of the group is guarded. Each group operates with a fetish. These fetishes, the e′to·we, are the most sacrosanct objects of Zuñi worship. They were brought from the innermost depths of the earth at the time of the emergence and are kept in sealed jars, from which they are removed only for the few secret rites in which they are employed. In these e′to·we rest the power of the priests. (For description of e′to·we see Stevenson, p. 163ff.) Besides the e′to·we various other objects are

---

[41] See p. 537.

[42] The term rain maker is a very misleading one. In Zuñi thought all supernaturals are rain makers. The Uwanami are definitely associated with the six regions and are probably the Zuñi equivalent of the Keresan shiwana, or storm clouds. The bow priests of the Uwanami, K̥äławani, Tsik̥ahaiya, Kopctaiya are associated with thunderstorms and sudden tempests. (See texts, p. 664.)

[43] I have omitted the p̄ekwin and the bow priests who occupy the fifth and sixth places in the order of retreats, because they are not, strictly speaking, priests, but function merely ex officio. They do not possess e′to·we. (See pp. 591, 592, 660.)

included in the sacred paraphernalia of the priests—pots of sacred black paint, round stones, "thunder stones," obsidian knives, and other objects, all of which were brought from the lower world. The e'to·we themselves are each in two parts, k̥ä'etow·e, water fetish, and tcu'e'to·we, corn fetish. The rain-making function is decidedly the more important.

In addition to the objects on the altar of their retreat, the chief priesthood is said to maintain a permanent altar in the fourth underground room of their house. In addition to the usual objects on priestly altars, this altar contains two columns of rock, one of crystal and one of turquoise, a heart-shaped rock which is "the heart of the world," with arteries reaching to the four cardinal points, and various prayer sticks, including two, male and female, which are "the life of the people." All objects on the altar, including the e'to·we, are said to be petrified. This altar is the center of the world, the spot beneath the heart of k̥änastep'a when he stretched out his arms. Only the high priest himself has access to this chamber.[44]

The priests, as such, hold no public ceremonies, although their presence is necessary at many ceremonies of other groups. Their own ceremonies for the Uwanami are held in secret in the houses where their fetishes are kept.

At the winter solstice the priesthoods observe a one-night retreat. Following the planting of the prayer sticks to the sun is a taboo period of 10 days, during which many rites are celebrated. On the fifth or sixth night (depending on the phase of the moon) each priesthood goes into retreat in its ceremonial house. During the day the priests make prayer sticks for the U'wanami of the different directions. Before sunset these are deposited at a distant spring. When the messengers return from the spring the various sacred objects are removed from their jars and placed on a meal painting, along with ears of corn, clay models of peach trees, animals, even money, upon which the blessing of increase is invoked. All night prayers are chanted and songs sung. The ceremony ends at sunrise. This ceremony is repeated by all the priests in their respective houses at the two full moons following.

The great ceremonies of the priests occur after the summer solstice. At this time rain is urgently needed for the young corn plants just rising out of the ground. The rainy season starts about July 1. Should the rains be delayed beyond that date great hardship is suffered.

Four days following the summer planting of prayer sticks the priesthoods begin their great series of summer retreats which last from

---

[44] Information concerning this altar was secured from a fairly reliable informant who gained access to it and made a very remarkable painting of it. The author does not consider the information quite beyond question, but gives it for what it may be worth.

the end of June well into September; that is, throughout the whole rainy season. The four chief priesthoods, associated with the north, east,[45] south, and west, go in for eight days each. They are followed late in July by the p̄'ekwin and the Bow Priest, who go in for four days each, and later by the minor priesthoods ("darkness priests"), who also go in for four days each. As in the winter, the day preceding the retreat is spent in making prayer sticks, which are deposited in the afternoon at the same sacred spring. The altar is set up that night. Since the sole preoccupation is with rain magic, no corn or peach trees are used on the summer altar. For four days following the planting to the U'wanami, the supplicants refrain from eating meat or grease, in addition observing the usual requirements of continence and kindliness. Throughout this period they remain night and day in their ceremonial room. No outsider enters but the woman of the house who serves their meals. There are frequent sessions of prayer and song, especially during the hours between midnight and dawn. The U'wanami are invoked, and the deceased priests of the order are called upon by name. All are believed to be present. On the fourth day, at dawn, prayer sticks are offered to the ancients, and after that the minor priests are free, except for the restriction on sexual activity for four days following any offering of prayer sticks. The four principal priesthoods remain in seclusion for four days longer. At dawn on the eighth day they come out, and that same evening the set next in order goes in. (For order of retreats, see Stevenson, p. 180.)

The purpose of these retreats is to secure rain—immediate rain for the thirsting young plants. Should the days of any group fail to be blessed with rain it receives the censure of the community, and one of its members will surely be suspected of laxness in the observance of his duties.

The rain priests are, like the p̄ekwin, holy men. They are expected to keep themselves aloof from worldly affairs. In former times they did no manual labor, but lived on contributions from the people, but this is no longer the case. The priest should be gentle, humble, and kind. Above all, he is supposed to eschew quarrels.

Associated in worship with the Uwanami is Kolowisi, the horned water serpent who inhabits springs and underground waters. With the characteristic Zuñi elasticity he is variously conceived as individual and multiple. One folk tale collected by the writer describes Kolowisi's village with all the serpents engaged in masked dances as at Kołuwala·wa.

Kolowisi is the guardian of sacred springs and punishes trespassers, especially women. In an unpublished song recorded by Cushing,

[45] The usual cycle of north, west, south, east is reversed in this instance.

Kolowisi is associated with flood, although the familiar Hopi myth of Palulukong has not been recorded for Zuñi. He also figures in myths of magical impregnation. This is in harmony with his rôle in ritual where he appears at the initiation of small boys, a ceremony designed to impress the youngsters with the power of the katcinas. At this ceremony he vomits forth water and seeds which are given to the children to take home. The water is sprinkled on their corn, and the seed is used for planting.

The effigy of Kolowisi which is used at this ceremony[46] is kept by the Kolowisi priesthood, a group belonging to the Corn clan which stands ninth in the order of retreats according to Mrs. Stevenson (Zuñi Indians, pp. 167, 179). Although this group is invariably called the Kolowisi priesthood, the association with Kolowisi may well be secondary like the association of the priests of the west with the Koyemci masks, or of the twelfth priesthood with the K̮ana·kwe.

The public ceremony of Kolowisi takes place in connection with the initiation of little boys.

The effigy of Kolowisi enters the village accompanied by the initiating katcinas at sunset on the eighth day of the ceremony.[47] He spends the night in Hek̮apa·wa kiva where he is suckled by Ahe'a, the grandmother of the katcinas. The following morning the head of the serpent is thrust through the kiva wall, while the katcinas dance for him. In the afternoon he vomits water and corn, fertilizing talismans for the novices.

THE CULT OF THE KATCINAS [48]

During their search for the middle the Zuñis had to ford a stream.[49] The first group of women to cross, seeing their children transformed in midstream into frogs and water snakes, became frightened and dropped them, and they escaped into the water. The bereaved mothers mourned for their lost children, so the twin heroes were sent to see what had become of them. They found them in a house beneath the surface of Whispering Waters (hatin k̮ai'akwi). They had been transformed into the katcinas, beautiful with valuable beads and feathers and rich clothing. Here they spent their days singing and dancing in untroubled joyousness. The twin heroes reported what they had seen, and further decreed that thereafter the dead should come to this place to join the lost children.

The identification of the dead with the katcinas is not complete. When men offer prayer sticks, they offer to the ancients *and* to the

---

[46] Pictured in Stevenson, pls. XIII and XIV.

[47] For abridged description of this ceremony, see p. 975. Fuller but incomplete account in Stevenson, pp. 65–102, the portion describing the part of the Kolowisi being found on pp. 94–96, 100, and 101.

[48] Katcina is a Hopi word, which has become standardized in the literature of the pueblos. The Zuñi term is koko.

[49] Origin myth, text, p. 595.

katcinas, and their sticks are different—those of the katcinas contain, in addition to the turkey feather, that of the duck, for the katcinas travel between their village and the village of their fathers in the form of ducks. There is great confusion in regard to the destination of the dead. Those who in life are intimately associated with the Beast Gods at death join them at their home in Ci'papolima, in the east. There is some indication that the priests join the U'wanami. Only those who are intimately associated with the cult of the katcinas, that is, members of the kotikan·e (katcina society), and especially officers in this society and possessors of masks, can be sure of admission to the village of the katcinas. There seems to be no clear idea of what becomes of people without ceremonial affiliations—women and children, for instance.

The lost children pitied the loneliness of their people and came often to dance for them in their plazas and in houses prepared for their use. But after each visit they took someone with them (i. e., someone died). Therefore they decided no longer to come in person. So they instructed their people to copy their costume and headdresses and imitate their dances. Then they would be with them in spirit. (See text, p. 605.)

These dances, in which the katcinas are impersonated, are the most spectacular, perhaps the most beautiful, of all Zuñi ceremonies. Instituted according to tradition solely as a means of enjoyment, they have become the most potent of rain-making rites, for since the divine ones no longer come in the flesh, they come in their other bodies, that is, as rain. The mask is the corporeal substance of the god and in donning it the wearer, through a miracle akin to that of the Mass in Roman Catholic ritual, becomes the god.

Therefore the masks with which this cult operates are second in sacredness to the fetishes of the rain priests themselves. They are the property of individuals; they are buried with his other possessions four days after death. The possession of a mask is a blessing to the house; it guarantees the owner admission to the dance house of the gods, and is the means by which the spirit can return after death to delight his beloved ones on earth and assuage his own loneliness. Therefore, as soon as a man can afford the very considerable expense involved, he will have a mask made for himself. These masks are carefully guarded in the back rooms of houses, protected from the eyes of children. Like the fetishes of the rain priests, they receive daily offerings of food from some female member of the household. When they are to be used they are repainted by someone whose special office that is, and redecorated to represent the special god to be impersonated.

The organization which performs the rites of the katcinas is the ko'tiḵän·e or katcina society, whose membership comprises every adult male. In exceptional cases females may be initiated.[50] The initiation includes two separate ceremonies frequently separated by several years. Until the rites are completed, at about the age of 10 or 12, boys are expected to be kept ignorant of the mysteries of the cult, and to believe the dancers are indeed supernatural visitors from the village of the gods. At the first ceremony they are severely whipped by the katcina priests [51] to inspire them with awe for these creatures. There is another and more severe thrashing at the second ceremony. Whipping is the prerogative of the katcinas. It is employed by no other ceremonial group at Zuñi and as a mechanism of juvenile punishment is unknown. The American method of establishing discipline by switching is met at Zuñi with horrified contempt. The katcinas whip to instill awe for the supernatural, but also to remove sickness and contamination. The whipping of katcinas is a blessing. It is administered with the formula, "May you be blessed with seeds" (t̄o' t̄owaconan aniktciat'u). Therefore outsiders are never whipped.

The katcina society has a set of officers, the katcina chief (ko'mosona), his p̄ekwin (ko'p̄ekwin), and two bow priests, who act as hosts when the gods come to dance. They receive them, lead them into the plazas for their performances, sprinkling corn meal before them. They are the arbiters in all matters pertaining to masked rituals. The society is organized into six divisions (upa·we), associated loosely with the six directions. Each group has a house of special construction set aside for the use of the katcinas—the so-called kivas.[52] In early days these were men's clubhouses, but their use is now being abandoned, even in ceremonies, in favor of more modern and spacious dwelling houses. Membership in one or another of these six groups is determined by the choice of a ceremonial father at a boy's birth or, at the latest, at the time of the preliminary initiation. His association is lifelong, unless he is expelled for sexual transgression or severs his connection because of disagreement with the leaders. In either case he will be received gladly into another group. Each group has a number of officers—from two to six or more—who run its affairs. They decide upon the dates for dances and the particular dance to be performed; they compose new songs, decorate the masks, assemble the costumes, and rehearse with the participants. Upon them also falls the more vital task of performing the secret rituals that will insure success. They prepare and plant prayer sticks and observe

[50] "To save their life" if they suffer from hallucinations, the mental sickness caused by supernatural beings.

[51] See p. 521.

[52] Kiva is a word which has been adopted into southwest literature to denote the subterranean or semi-subterranean chambers found in all modern and prehistoric pueblos. The word is of Hopi provenience. The Zuñi term kiwitsin·e is probably derived from it.

all the ritual requirements attendant thereon. They consecrate new masks and bless all the dancers before they leave for the plaza.

The dances themselves are large group dances, performed by one or two rows of dancers in formation, frequently with solo performers. The costumes, including masks, are brilliant, picturesque, often of exquisite workmanship; the songs are varied and striking. The performances proceed with the spirit and precision of a well-trained orchestra. The dance groups in summer frequently number over 60 dancers. As many as 90 have been observed.

Each kiva group is required to dance at least three times during the year—once in the winter, once in the summer, and once in the fall, during the five days following the departure of the Ca'lako gods.[53] In addition to this they may dance at any other time they choose, except the 4 days following the close of the Ca'lako festival and the 10 days of the winter solstice. The dances of the winter series are performed indoors at night but may be repeated outdoors on the following day. The summer dances are performed outdoors and in the daytime.[54]

Eight days after the close of the winter solstice the kiva which is to inaugurate the winter series sends in two katcinas to announce the dance on the fourth night following.[55] On the appointed night society altars are set up in the six houses which fill the rôle of kivas, and society choirs are summoned to provide music for the dancers. The various groups of dancers make the rounds of these six houses. The kiva presenting the dance will perform one of about six traditional dances. This group brings seeds to be distributed among the populace. On the same night any other kiva that wishes to participate will prepare dances which may be in the traditional style or some new variant, fanciful, grotesque, or amusing. The hilarity of the occasion is increased by the presence of isolated groups of dancers, especially the "little dancers," the mischievous children of katcina village, and the attendance of masked or unmasked clowns. At the indoor dances not all participants need be masked, and where no mask is used the same magical power resides in the face and body paint. If the dance is repeated outdoors where it can be viewed by the uninitiated masks are obligatory.

In contrast to the light-hearted gaiety of the winter dances, those of summer are marked by great solemnity and intense religious devotion. At this time rain is urgently needed, and the whole religious mechanism strains to the task of compelling it.

Eight days after the summer solstice and on the "middle (i. e., fourth) day" of the retreat of the first priesthood, the gods, accom-

---

[53] See pp. 702, 941.

[54] Except the first dance of the summer series, when all-night ceremonies are held in the kiva on the night preceding the outside dancing.

[55] At least, so it used to be. At present the dance is held "when they get ready."

panied by the Koyemci[56] and officers of the katcina society, appear at sunset, marching across the plain. They come from the village of the katcinas.[57] From now on until they are sent home in November, the katcinas are believed to be present in the village, lurking in the kivas. After dancing in all the plazas the dancers retire to the home of the Katcina Chief where an altar has been set up. After all-night ceremonies they dance throughout the day in the four plazas while society choirs continue to sing in the house of their retreat and the house of the Koyemci. This first dance is a most solemn occasion. Until rain falls the participants may touch neither food nor drink, nor engage in any unnecessary conversation. They must, of course, observe sexual continence. At later dances continence is required only of the leaders who have offered prayer sticks and of the Koyemci.

After this first dance other kivas follow as they can get ready. It is considered desirable to perform these dances as rapidly as possible while rain is needed. But with characteristic Zuñi procrastination they are put off and finally performed in rapid succession in September, and the resulting deluges play havoc with the crops already ripe for the harvest.

The gods remain in the village until they are sent home in the fall. In November, after the regular series of dances is over, and it is evident that no more extra dances are to be interpolated, the gods are sent home. The Koyemci are generally the first to go. One night they will be heard singing in the yard before their house. After making the rounds of the plazas they go out toward the west, and whoever dares stick his head outdoors while they are about will surely be drawn along with them (i. e., he will die). After the Koyemci have gone the others follow within a few days.

They all return again to Zuñi with the Katcina Priests when they come for the Ca'lako ceremonies. After the Katcina Priests depart for their home the others remain to dance for five nights in the houses they have dedicated and in the plazas of the town. Certain dances are regularly performed during this time and others may be introduced. On the fifth day they depart for the east to visit the supernaturals who dwell in that quarter. On that day every man who owns a mask takes it out to the east of the village. Here he offers prayer sticks and food in one of the six holes dug by the kiva heads. Setting down the mask and making a road of meal toward the east, he sends him out. For four days the masked gods are visiting in the east, and consequently no masked dances may be performed. They return after four days, and from that time on until the beginning of

56 See p. 946.

57 Every fourth year there is a pilgrimage by the priests, officers of the Katcina Society, and the chosen impersonators of the priests of the masked gods to the home of the gods, a lake 86 miles west of Zuñi. On other years the offerings are made at Rainbow Spring, 17 miles to the southwest.

the winter solstice any of the dances performed after Ca'lako may be repeated by request, or new ones may be presented.

THE CULT OF THE KATCINA PRIESTS [58]

Intimately associated with the foregoing activities are those rites and ceremonies which form the cult of the katcina priests. This cult also employs, as its principal technique for controlling the supernatural, impersonation by means of masks. But the beings impersonated are of a different order. The masks are differently treated and the character of the rites in which they function, and the personnel and calendrical cycle are quite independent. Like all supernaturals, they are bringers of rain, but the special blessing which lies within their power to bestow is fecundity.

The katcina priests also live at Ko'łuwala·wa (katcina village) and form, indeed, the priestly hierarchy that rules that village. But they are definite individuals, with personal names and distinct personalities. There are, for instance, the Koyemci—they are the fruit of an incestuous union between brother and sister, and display the stain of their birth in their grotesque appearance and uncouth behavior. They are the sacred clowns, privileged to mock at anything, and to indulge in any obscenity.[59] On them fall the most exacting sexual restrictions. They are the most feared and the most beloved of all Zuñi impersonations. They are possessed of black magic; in their drum they have the wings of black butterflies that can make girls "crazy." [60] In the knobs of their masks is soil from the footprints of townspeople.[61] One who begrudges them anything will meet swift and terrible retribution. But everyone goes in hushed reverence and near to tears to watch them on their last night when they are under strict taboo. At this time, from sundown until midnight the following day, they touch neither food nor drink. They neither sleep nor speak, and in all that time they do not remove their masks. This truly heroic self-denial earns them the sympathetic affection of the people, an affection manifested in the generous gifts that are given them on this their last day in office.[62]

P̂autiwa, chief of the masked gods at Ko'łuwala·wa, is a truly magnificent person. His prestige is enormous. He possesses in unlimited measure the three most admired qualities—beauty, dignity, and

[58] The term is awkward, but it is a literal translation of the Zuñi term.

[59] They are, however, surpassed in obscenity by the Ne'we·kwe. The presence of white people at Zuñi is resulting in the gradual suppression of these practices. The word obscene is used advisedly since their practices are universally so regarded at Zuñi. Here the proprieties are meticulously observed. It is a society of strong repressions. Undoubtedly the great delight in the antics of the clowns springs from the sense of release in vicarious participations in the forbidden.

[60] I. e., sexually.

[61] A widely used love charm.

[62] The very deep affection that is felt for the Koyemci is by no means extended to the impersonator when he is released from office.

kindliness. In folklore he appears as the successful lover of mortal maids. Literature is full of the exploits of his illegitimate offspring, to whom he is unfailingly generous. His two brief appearances at Zuñi mark him as a prince of gods and men. The moment he appears in the plaza at the close of the solstice ceremonies, the hilarity which has prevailed subsides in an instant and is replaced by hushed reverence. The two gods who have been making merry on the housetop to the great delight of the populace suddenly pale to insignificance before the newly risen splendor of P̄autiwa's beauty and stateliness.

His p̄ekwin, K̯äklo, is very different. He is a bustling, officious, self-important individual, somewhat ridiculous in spite of his great power. In the midst of his most sacred ceremony he engages in none too gentle horseplay with the Koyemci. His speech is an incoherent jumble.

Sayataca is more austere. Like P̄autiwa, he has tremendous dignity and prestige, but he lacks P̄autiwa's charm. When he speaks—and he speaks often and at incredible length—his voice booms with authority and importance.

One might continue to enumerate the personality traits of the individual katcinas. The Sayałia, avengers and exorcisers, hideous and terrible; the Ca'lako, giant gargoyles, terrifying but not unlovely; the Sä'limop̄ia, youthful and beautiful, and impetuous with the ardor of youth; and many others.

Each of these appears at Zuñi to perform a special ceremony which he alone has the right to perform. For each of these katcinas there is a permanent mask used only in his rites. This is tribal property. It is the mask given by the Divine One himself, and has been passed down through the generations like the fetishes of the rain priests. Like them, these ancient masks are kept permanently in jars in definite houses, from which they are removed only for use and with elaborate ceremony. Furthermore, connected with each is a cult group which preserves its secret ritual, including the words of prayers and chants.

The mask of P̄autiwa is kept in a house of the Dogwood clan. The cult group in charge of his ritual comprises all who have ever impersonated the god at his appearance in the winter solstice. These men meet each year to select the impersonator. He learns the prayers and rituals from some older man of the groups and is thereafter permanently associated with this group.[63]

The masks of the Cula·witsi, Sayataca, Hututu, and the two Yamuhakto are kept in another house of the Dogwood clan. The custodians of their cult are a self-perpetuating group of four men of various clan affiliations. The impersonators of the gods are chosen by the priests and go to the cult heads to learn what they must do.

[63] Certain members of the Sun clan form a subsidiary cult group, whose function is to dress P̄autiwa.

This knowledge—that is, the power which it confers—is "given back" at the end of the year.

The Koyemci masks are kept in the house of the West priesthood. Their cult is in the keeping of four groups of men who themselves impersonate the gods. Each group holds office for a year and returns again after four years. The head of the group, who impersonates the father, is appointed by the priests and he chooses his associates, filling any vacancies which may have occurred since the last incumbency.

The six Ca'lako masks, associated with the six kivas, are kept in six different houses and each has a permanent group of wo·we,[64] who instruct the impersonators in the duties of their offices. The impersonators are chosen by the officers of the kivas and hold office for a year.

The mask of K̯ä'klo is kept in the house of the p̄ekwin of the Katcina Society. His rites are known to a group of four men, who take turns in impersonating the god. The head of this group receives from the priests a crook summoning him to appear.

The 12 Sälimop̄ia masks, two of each color, are kept in six different houses, along with other masks associated with them in the principal ceremony in which they appear, the preliminary whipping of little boys. Each kiva has a Salimop̄ia wo'le who is trustee of their ritual.

At the new year ceremony which terminates the celebration of the solstice Pautiwa comes to give his orders for the coming year. He leaves with the priests or on the roofs of the kivas the feathered sticks with which are appointed those who impersonate the gods at the great fertility ceremony of November, the so-called Ca'lako. He leaves one stick for the father of the Koyemci, one for each of Sa'yataca group, one for each of the six Ca'lako. There is also a stick for Bitsitsi, who is not a katcina, but who plays an important rôle in the ceremony of the Corn Maids which follows the Ca'lako. In this P̄autiwa himself appears.

The impersonators are chosen immediately—the impersonators of the Koyemci and the Sayataca group by the priests, two impersonators for each of the six Ca'lako by the officers of their respective kivas. Each month at the full moon they plant prayer sticks at distant shrines, visiting them in a body in fixed order. After October the plantings take place every 10 days, and as the time for the ceremony approaches, each group goes into retreat like priests, in its ceremonial house. The great public ceremony is held in the houses of prominent citizens who volunteer to provide this costly service. There should be eight houses, but in recent years the expense involved has become so great that not enough men volunteer. In that case the groups double up at the last moment. The house is newly built or completely renovated for the occasion, and the visit of the gods is the

[64] Literally servant or domesticated animal, a word that defies translation.

dedication and blessing of the new dwelling. They deposit prayer sticks under the threshold and in the roof—symbols of fertility. The sticks are double, painted blue and yellow, and they are male and female respectively. They plant seeds in the center of the floor and on the altar leave a basket of seed corn to be used by the host in his spring sowing. The burden of their prayer is that the store rooms may be filled to overflowing, and the house so full of children that they jostle one another in the doorway. (See text of Ca'lako prayer, pp. 718, 773.)

The gods depart after all-night ceremonies but during the following days each kiva presents a masked dance. They may present more than one if they so choose. These dances are performed for five nights in all the houses and on the fifth day in the plaza. On this day the Koyemci, who have remained in retreat throughout this period, are rewarded for their services by gifts from the members of their fathers' clans. Late at night, after visiting every house in the village to bestow a final blessing, they are released from their arduous duties.

The Koyemci, in addition to participating in this cycle of ceremonies, are required to attend upon the masked dancers during the summer dance series. On these appearances they play the rôle of clowns; and many of their games are of frankly phallic significance.[65] In their drum they place the wings of black butterflies, a potent love charm.

Every fourth year [66] P̄autiwa leaves a feathered staff for K̯ä'klo, by whose order is performed the preliminary whipping of the small boys. K̯ä'klo does not himself perform this rite. He comes twice at intervals of eight days to inform the priests and officers of the kivas that this is the wish of the gods. They in turn appoint the gods who administer the whipping—12 Sä'limopia, four Sa'yałia and 10 other gods. The ceremony, held the day after K̯ä'klo's final visit, is one of the most elaborate and spectacular at Zuñi. The boys are severely whipped in the plaza. They are taken into the kiva to have feathers tied in their hair as a symbol of their novitiate. The writer has never witnessed this ceremony, and can only guess at its significance on the basis of the description given by Mrs. Stevensom.[67] The point seems to be exorcism. The boys are whipped "to save their lives," and previous to this, there is general whipping and destruction of property throughout the village, "to take away bad happenings." The Sä'limopia and Sayałia appear as exorcisors during the winter solstice ceremony. And whenever any taboo of the masked god cult is broken the Sayałia appear to administer punishment and to whip

[65] See E. C. Parsons, Notes on Zuñi, pt. 2, p. 229.
[66] Due to recent disintegration this ceremony has not been held for more than six years.
[67] Twenty-third Ann. Rept. Bur. Amer. Ethn., p. 65.

all present in order to counteract the contaminating influence of the transgression. At the Ca'lako two Salimopia are present to perform this service.

The final whipping of the boys is performed by the Sayałia by order of the priests, some time during the Ca'lako festivities. This also seems to be a rite of exorcism, and is followed by general whipping to remove bad luck.

Another masked ceremony held at irregular intervals, and by express order of P̄autiwa, is the dance of the K̯ä'na·kwe or white gods. This is a group dance like the kiva dances but is performed by a special self-perpetuating cult group owning ancient masks and esoteric ritual. The beings impersonated are of a different order. They do not live at Kołuwala·wa. They are essentially hostile, and therefore must not remain overnight in the village. Their rites have no place in the regular cycle. They bring with them seeds, which are given to the priests, and large quantities of food, which they throw away to the people, so the purpose of their rite may be assumed to be fertility.

THE CULT OF THE WAR GODS

The war cult of the Pueblos, as in other tribes, is greatly in abeyance at the present time due to enforced peaceableness. Although the Pueblos probably were never aggressive warriors, intertribal warfare was once an important part of life, and was accompanied by elaborate ceremonies.

The gods of war in Zuñi are the A'hayuta, twin children of the Sun begotten of a waterfall when the Zuñis, wandering in search of the middle, were in dire need of military leadership.[68] They led the people to victory and gave them the rites of war. They are the patrons of contests of all kinds, including foot races and games of chance. In folklore the A'hayuta appear as two dirty, uncouth, cruel, and disobedient children, masking their great powers behind obscene and ridiculous exteriors. They live on the mountain tops, they are lords of the high places, and their shrines are on all the prominent mountains about Zuñi.

The cult of the A'hayuta, the gods of war, and leadership of war parties, is delegated to the Bow Priests, and several less important groups, the priests who keep pa'eton·e, a war fetish, the priests of the great shell and the scalp chief, who takes care of the scalps in the scalp house, and the men who carve and decorate the idols of the war gods.

Membership in the bow priesthood is restricted to those who have killed an enemy. No matter what the circumstances of the killing, no escape is possible from the burden of membership, for the slayer

---

68 See text of origin myth, p. 597.

must seek magical protection from the vengeance of the ghost. The bow priesthood supplies this protection. He is initiated in the course of the scalp dance, which celebrates the victory and propitiates the ghost.[69]

The bow priesthood is organized in somewhat similar fashion to the medicine societies—a circumstance which led Mrs. Stevenson to include it among them. There is a society chief and a battle chief. They have a ceremonial chamber in a house in the eastern part of the town, where certain of their ceremonial paraphernalia is kept. Pa'ettone, which is used only in war rites, is kept in another house, and has its own hereditary priesthood, members of which are not necessarily Bow Priests. The great shell also has its own priesthood. It is brought out for all war ceremonies. The Scalp Chief has a male and two female associates, who take charge of the scalp from the time it is brought into the village until it is placed in the scalp house. He plants prayer sticks each month for the scalps. At the winter solstice and at the scalp dance idols are made of the elder and younger War Gods. They are carved, respectively, by men of the Deer and Bear clans. These are hereditary offices, and each has several associates, male and female.

The Bow Priests are leaders in war and defenders and protectors of the people in times of peace. To them falls the task of policing the town, in the religious but not the civil sense. In this capacity they must wage constant warfare against the insidious inner enemy—namely, the witches—whose secret power causes sickness and death. Of this activity, too, they have recently been stripped. They are furthermore the defenders and the executive arm of the religious hierarchy. They protect their altars from desecration, carry their messages, and execute their orders. To perform these duties two bow priests are assigned to the priestly hierarchy, two to the katcina society, and two to each of the medicine societies.[70]

The great annual ceremony of the Bow Priests is held at the winter solstice. Six days after the p̄ekwin announces the solstice a man of the Deer clan and a man of the Bear clan and their associates start to make the images of the War Gods to be used at this ceremony. On the tenth night following the p̄ekwin's announcement these images, together with pa'etone, the great shell, the e'tow·e of the chief priests, and all the paraphernalia of the war cult are taken to the chief kiva. In the kiva are assembled the priests of the council, the priests of pa'ettone and the great shell, the image makers and their associates, and the full membership of the bow priesthood. At

---

69 See texts, p. 674.

70 That is, this used to be the pattern. The bow priesthood is now reduced to three members—one who has no society affiliations serves the priests, one is Bow Priest of the katcinas, and associated also with the Rattlesnake Society, the third is associated with the Hunters and the Little Fire Society, and formerly served the priests.

this time the Bow Priests sing comato·we.[71] the songs given to the Bow Priesthood at the founding of the order by A'hayuta. At dawn the ceremonies end, and later in the day the images are taken by the Bow Priests and the priests of the council to two of the mountain shrines of A'hayuta. This is the day on which everyone plants prayer sticks to the sun.

At the full moon in March the Bow Priests make prayer sticks for A'hayuta. At night they meet in their ceremonial room, where their altar is set up.[72] There are no images of the gods of war at this time. Again during the night comato·we are sung. Four days later there is a kick-stick race under the special patronage of the gods of war. After this it is safe for people to plant corn. Spring wheat is planted before this time, but corn is planted only after these ceremonies. The precise nature of the connection between the War Gods, stick racing, and planting is obscure.

There are no ceremonies for the War Gods at the summer solstice. However, the two Bow Priests who serve the priests of the council have their place in the series of summer retreats for rain. The day the p̄ekwin comes out they plant prayer sticks to the U'wanami Bow Priests. For four days they observe all the requirements of retreat, save that they do not remain in seclusion in their ceremonial room. Instead they visit each day a distant mountain shrine of A'hayuta where they offer corn meal and turquoise. They have no altar at this time—probably because all their fetishes are for war, and therefore can have no place in these purely priestly activities.[73] The bow priesthood does not convene at this time.

Formerly the bow priests held a great public dance after harvest in the fall. This was an occasion of great festivity, as always when there is dancing by the girls. Like the scalp dance, it was accompanied by sexual license. However, the dance has not been performed in 20 years, since two girls of a good family were killed by a stray shot from the housetops. The Bow Priests met in their ceremonial room, but there was no altar and no offerings of prayer sticks.

The scalp dance is held at irregular intervals, whenever an enemy is killed. Its purpose is to induct the scalper into the Bow Priesthood for his own protection, to strip the dead enemy of his power and develop his capacities as rain maker, and to celebrate fittingly with all manner of festivity the destruction of the enemy. The principal events are outlined in another place.[74]

There are other groups which have definite associations with war. The Ant society figures prominently in the ceremonies of the scalp

---

[71] The word means "spiral." It is accompanied by a circle dance. Approaching spiralwise toward a center is characteristic of war dances throughout North America. See text of origin myth, p. 597.

[72] This ceremony has never been described. The writer has not witnessed it; merely knows that it takes place.

[73] Or perhaps because of the association between A'hayuta and wind, snow, and cold weather.

[74] P. 674.

dance and the O′winahaiye. The Wood society holds a ceremony in which the Bow Priesthood participates. The Great Fire society is privileged to wear the great feather, part of the war chief's regalia. The arrow order of this society uses the body paint of the war chiefs. The Hunters' society is also a war society. The members of this, as well as those of the Cactus society, can not be inducted into the bow priesthood, because they are already warriors. Members of the Cactus society offer prayer sticks to A′hayuta. The Hunters' and Cactus societies have male members only.

All these groups, however, are devoted primarily to the worship of the Beast Gods and receive from them their sanctions and power.

THE CULT OF THE BEAST GODS

In the east at Cipapolima live the Beast Gods (we′ma·we or we′ma a·′ciwan·i). These are the beasts of prey and partake of their rapacious nature. They are the most dangerous and violent gods in the Zuñi pantheon. They are the priests of long life (onaya·naḳä a·′ci′wan·i, literally road fulfilling priests). They are the givers of medicine, not only medicinal plants, but the magic power to make them effective. They are the source also of black magic or witchcraft. Their leaders are associated with the six directions, as follows: North, Mountain Lion; west, Bear; south, Badger; east, Wolf; above, Knife-wing;[75] below, Gopher. Of all, the most powerful is the Bear. He is compelled through impersonation at curing ceremonies. The symbol of his personality is the bear paws which are drawn over the hands and have the same properties as the masks of the gods. The worship of the beast gods is conducted by 12 societies or fraternities. Membership in these societies is voluntary and is open alike to males and females.[76] All offices are held by men, and only they have the ultimate magical powers—the powers of impersonating the bear, the use of the crystal, the power to remove sickness by sucking, and the use of magical songs. Some knowledge of therapeutic plants is hereditary in certain matrilineal families. Except for midwifery, which is practiced independently, all medical practice is in the hands of these societies. They are, in fact, medical guilds, closed corporations which guard their secrets jealously. The combined body of esoteric knowledge and ritual held by these groups is enormous, and this is genuinely esoteric. To collect it one would have to be on terms of utmost intimacy with all the officers in all the societies. No knowledge is more closely guarded than this.

---

75 A mythical monster with wings of knives. Mrs. Stevenson names eagle as god of the upper regions, and shrew for below. The present list is quoted from a prayer of the Great Fire society.

76 Except the Cactus society, a war society, and Hunters which have only male members. The Cactus society cures wounds made by bullets or by any pointed object, including cactus. The Hunters have no curing rituals.

Each society in addition to practicing general medicine has a specialty—one cures sore throat, another epilepsy, another has efficacious medicine for delayed parturition, yet another cures bullet wounds, and so forth.

Initiation into the societies is a precaution taken to save one's life. If a person is desperately ill he is given by his relatives to one of the medicine societies.[77] The officials of the society come in a body to cure him. They bring with them all their ceremonial paraphernalia and lend the whole force of their ritual toward defeating the disease. If the patient recovers he is not necessarily cured. He has been granted a respite, and until he fulfills his pledge and receives a new heart and places himself under the direct protection of the Beast Gods through joining the society which cured him, his life is in jeopardy. Since initiation involves one in great expense, frequently many years elapse before it is completed.

The societies have, perhaps, the most highly developed ritual of all the cult groups. They possess elaborate altars which are kept in the houses in which they habitually meet. These consist of carved wooden tablets, stone fetishes, and various other sacred objects. These altars are set up on a meal painting at all ceremonies in which the society takes part. On the altar are also placed feathered ears of corn, the personal fetishes of members of the medicine order of the society. This fetish (mi'le) is made for the novice by his father at the time of his initiation; it remains his personal fetish until he dies, when it is dismantled and buried by members of the society. If a man is compelled to be absent from any meeting of his society he or some member of his household takes his mi'le to the society room to be placed upon the altar.

All members of medicine societies plant prayer sticks each month at the full moon. The offering includes, besides the usual sticks for the ancients and for the katcinas, sticks for the Beast Gods, made in each society according to different specifications. These sticks are planted either in cornfields or at Red Bank, a point on the river bank east [78] of town. These are offered separately by each individual.

The collective ceremonies of the medicine societies are held in the fall and winter. During the summer the cult of the Beast Gods is in abeyance. As a symbol of this, the drums of the societies must not be touched during this time, not even to beat out the rhythm for grinding songs. At the full moon in October (in some societies November), the members are summoned to their ceremonial house. They make

[77] In less serious cases an individual medicine man is called. He removes the cause of sickness and is paid for his trouble. At the winter ceremony the recovered patient has his head bathed in the society room and exchanges gifts with his "father."

[78] The Beast Gods live in the east. Therefore all ceremonies of the curing societies are oriented toward the east, in contrast to ceremonies for the ancients and the katcinas, which are oriented toward the south and west. It is interesting to note that historically the medicine cult is undoubtedly of Keresan, i. e., Eastern origin.

their prayer sticks here during the day. At sundown the altar is set up. Female members, who do not attend this meeting, send food and leave their miwe for the altar. After dark the drum is taken out and songs of the Beast Gods are sung. The gods are present in the village at this time, much the way the katcinas are present throughout the summer.

The great meetings of the societies are held at the winter solstice. On the ninth day following the P̃ekwin's announcement society members meet early in the morning at their ceremonial houses. The day is spent in prayer-stick making. The solstice prayer-stick bundles of the societies are the most elaborate and beautiful products of this highly developed art. They contain sticks for the ancients, for deceased members of the society, and for Paiyatamu,[79] gods of music, poetry, flowers and butterflies. Included in the bundle are the crook, symbol of old age, and twigs of various medicinal plants. There are no offerings to the Beast Gods at this time.

At sundown the altar is set up. Women members, if they are not planning to attend the night meeting, come bringing food and their miwe and sprinkle corn meal on the altar. Late at night, about 2 or 3 o'clock in the morning, the Ne'we·kwe visit the kiva where the priests have been waiting in silence before the altar of the Gods of War. Here they perform a rite of exorcism, without which the ceremony can not proceed. When they have left the Bow Priests start their song. As soon as their drum is heard the society people, who have also been waiting in their own houses, start their own rites. The songs sung at this time are for the U'wanami. They are among the most beautiful and sacred of all Zuñi songs, and are known only to the most learned members of the societies. The ceremony ends at daybreak. The members come home, each bringing with him his mi'le, his bundle of prayer sticks, and a bundle of several ears of corn that have rested all night on the altar. The corn is kept for spring planting and the prayer sticks are buried that afternoon, along with each man's individual offerings to the sun and the ancients. After this planting all society members except the Sa'niakakwe and the Ci'wanakwe must abstain from all animal food for four days, in addition to the usual requirement of continence. The food taboo obligatory for society members is optional with others. For them, too, it used to be obligatory and is probably related to the offering to the sun.

This ceremony is for rain and fertility. It has nothing whatever to do with curing, and in it the Beast Gods play no rôle. It is quite

79 Paiyatamu is the Keresan word payatyamu, "youth." He is associated with all things gay and youthful. He is another romantic adventurer in folklore. His prayer stick, significantly, is double, and is painted blue and yellow, the colors associated with sex. The flutes of Payatamu are played at the phallic ritual of O'lolowickya. (Parsons: Winter and Summer Dance Series.) They are important in the Corn dance.

distinct from the "going in" of the Beast Gods which immediately follows it, and is so regarded by the Zuñis themselves.

On the evening of the tenth day of the solstice, the day of the universal planting, the societies convene for their great retreat.[80] Female members sleep at home, and return in the daytime to attend to their household duties. Their attendance, even at the evening meetings, is not obligatory until the final night. Male members, however, are in retreat; they sleep and eat at their society houses, although they are permitted to visit their homes between times. This privilege is not accorded to officers of societies who observe as strict a retreat as priests. The altar is put up on the first evening, and remains in place until the conclusion of the ceremonies on the fourth morning following. The room is taboo to outsiders, with the exception of members of the household.

The days are spent making prayer sticks and preparing their costumes and regalia for the great ceremony of the last night. At night songs are sung for the Beast Gods. Each day at dawn the members go out in groups to offer corn meal and to present their miwe to the rising sun. During the evenings tales are told and instruction in the ritual is given.

On the last night all the society members, male and female, assemble in full ceremonial costume, including face and body paint. To the society house also come those who wish to be cured of chronic ailments, since curing during public ceremonies entails no obligation on the part of the patient.[81] About midnight a fresh altar is prepared. Sometimes there are demonstrations of fire eating and other tricks by qualified groups before the chief business, the invocation of the Beast Gods, is reached. The songs of the Beast Gods are sung with the accompaniment of rattle and drum, and society members dance. The dance is without formation, members rising to dance whenever they choose and leaving the floor when they are tired, usually after four or eight songs. The purpose of this dancing is to create a proper atmosphere in which to summon the Beast Gods. The participants gradually work themselves into a state of mental excitement bordering on hysteria. Finally those who are qualified to impersonate the bear [82] draw over their hands the bear paws that lie on the altar, and

[80] The Łe'we·kwe do not go in at this time. Their retreat follows six days after the close of the solstice ceremonies.

[81] The following ceremony of purification is held in Cochiti during the winter: "People may go to the giant, flint, or cikame houses. The ritual is similar. The shamans approach each person, touch him and draw out an object, usually a stone, which he is told is a sickness. An altar is erected with corn meal paths and fetishes but the rainbow arch is not used. After the sickness has been removed each person is given water "medicine" from the bowl. This is sprinkled over their bodies and they are allowed to drink some. This same formula is used in times of actual sickness. The shamans sing and pray all night while the people pray and walk around the altar sprinkling corn meal to the animal helpers and protectors. (Goldfrank, p. 72.)

[82] Only the oldest and most learned of the medicine men. They acquire power to summon the bear only after the expenditure of great effort and much property.

in so doing assume the personality of the bear, much as the wearer of a mask becomes a god. They utter the cries of animals and otherwise imitate beasts, especially the bear.

In this condition they are enabled by gazing into the crystal to see the hidden sickness in those present. When they see sickness in anyone they draw from his body the foreign substance that has caused it. Dust, stones, bits of calico, feathers, fur or the entrails of animals are extracted from the mouth and other parts of the bodies of patients. Each article as it is extracted is exhibited to the company and dropped into a bowl to be disposed of the following day. Both practitioner and patient are nude save for the breechcloth, which necessitates considerable skill in sleight-of-hand, even though clumsy tricks would pass in the prevailing state of hysterical excitement. It is general knowledge that these "cures" are accomplished by sleight-of-hand. However, such knowledge by no means decreases the respect in which these tricks are held. These practices have the sanction of powerful and greatly feared divinities and are performed directly under their control. The act itself is but a symbol of the relationship with the supernaturals. The efficacy lies not in the performance of the act itself but in the god-given power to perform it.

As the night advances the excitement increases. Groups of medicine men and women selected by the society chief visit other society houses in response to invitations previously delivered with the customary offering of corn meal. They dash through the streets simulating cries of animals. They are barefoot—practically nude, although the ground may be covered with snow or ice.[83] In the house of their hosts they give demonstrations of their curing powers.

The ceremony ends at dawn. The excitement suddenly subsides. The miwe are once more taken out to the sun. On returning to the ceremonial room there are brief concluding ceremonies in a quiet vein. Then the altar is dismantled and the members depart to eat breakfast at their homes. Meat is served for the first time in four days.

In the afternoon male members of societies offer prayer sticks to the Beast Gods.[84] For four days continence must be observed.

The Łewekwe observe their great retreat for the Beast Gods after the winter solstice ceremonies are at an end. The stick-swallowing order of the Great Fire society also has a retreat at this time. The retreat terminates in a public dance by both societies with exhibitions of sword swallowing. In connection with this there is a retreat with a public dance on the last day for mu'etowe, a snow fetish. So that the whole ceremony combines functions of curing and weather control.

---

[83] The men are naked, and temperature on a midwinter night may be below zero.

[84] At the same time all initiated males offer to the masked gods. There are also special plantings by males and females for fecundity and wealth.

We have already alluded to the attendance of the Ne'wekwe at the winter dances of the masked gods, and their summer ceremony, which is only rarely performed. This ceremony comprises a four-day retreat with prayers for rain, at which there is no singing to the drum of the songs of the Beast Gods. The retreat ends with an all-night ceremony the last night and a public dance the last day. In this ceremony, as well as in the initiation rites, importance is given to various obscene and cruel practices. The dance may be repeated by request. In this ceremony they are assisted by the Ci'wanakwe.

The other ceremonies of the medicine societies which are held at irregular intervals as occasions arise are concerned specifically with curing and initiation. Curing ceremonies are very secret. Only officers of the societies and those possessed of the required medical knowledge and magical powers are present. Prayer sticks are made and an altar is set up in the sick room and songs are sung. There is a general rite of exorcism by spitting. Since disease is generally caused by a witch injecting foreign bodies into the patient, the most obvious method of cure is to locate and remove the foreign substance. The medicine man locates the foreign substance either by use of the crystal or by partaking of a vision-producing drug.[85] The practitioner then removes it by the same sleight-of-hand that is practiced at public healing ceremonies. Or, if the patient knows who has bewitched him, or learns it under the influence of tenatsali, the Bow Priests are summoned and attempt to extract a confession from the accused. The confession strips him of his power and effects an automatic cure. In former days witches were hung. Since this practice has been ended by the United States Government authorities witch baiting has declined in importance in medical practice and greater weight is given to extracting foreign bodies.[86]

The ceremonies in the sick room are continued for four nights, provided the patient lives that long. Purely therapeutic measures, massage, sweating, blood letting, and the administration of drugs may be employed as supplement and continue beyond the period devoted to magical practices.

Should the patient recover he must eventually fulfill his pledge of membership in the society, thus placing himself permanently under the protection of the Beast Gods. The initiation ceremony is held in November, or after the winter solstice ceremonies. The retreat begins four days before the full moon, so that the final ceremony comes the night the moon is full. The initiation rites are in part public ceremonies. To the final ceremonies other societies are invited in a body, and persons of no society affiliation may attend as individuals. Frequently there are public dances outdoors, as part of the initiation

[85] Tenatsali, an unidentified plant, perhaps Jamestown weed.

[86] The extraction of foreign bodies is the usual technique employed by individual medicine men summoned to treat minor ailments.

rites. In these there is great variability among the different societies. In all, however, the core of the ceremony is the same. It is described in some detail in another place.[87]

THE CALENDAR

Between all of these independent cults is the binding element of calendrical observances. Each cult has ceremonies extending through an annual cycle, starting from the winter solstice, and returning again into the winter solstice. Their solstice ceremonies are all nicely synchronized. They are fitted into a period of 20 days, and so neatly arranged that there are no conflicts, even for a man with varied ceremonial affiliations.

The name by which the Zuñis refer to the period of the solstice is itiwana, the middle, the same name that they give, esoterically, to their village. Mrs. Stevenson and others interpret this as being a contraction of the sentence yätokä i′tiwanan te′ ′tci "the sun reaches the middle." This is unquestionably correct, but the term has a more significant connotation. It is the middle of the year, the point common to all the different cults, and is indeed the center of their whole ceremonial life. There is no doubt that the Zuñis themselves think of their rituals as being organized about this focal point. Their application of the term "middle" to it is sufficient indication.[88] The linguistic identification of concepts of time and space is characteristically Zuñian. The solstice is, therefore, the center of time, just as Zuñi itself is the center of space.

The winter solstice ceremonies start when the p̄ekwin announces from the housetop that all men shall make prayer sticks for the sun to be offered in 10 days. The date is calculated by observations of the sunrise from a petrified stump in a cornfield east of the village. When the sun rises at a particular point on the mesa to the southeast it is time for the p̄ekwin to start his own plantings. If correctly calculated, then the general prayer-stick planting will take place on the day when the sunrise reaches its most southerly limit—that is, on the 22d of December. However, the Zuñis seem never to have been able to decide on the relative merits of solar and lunar calendar, and the desire to have the observation of the solstice occur at the full moon disarranges the calculations and naturally leads to dissention among the various priests. However, the date is definitely set by the p̄ekwin and the others, whatever their views, fall into line.

---

87 See p. 791.

88 E. C. Parsons (Winter and Summer Dance Series in Zuñi in 1918, University of California Publ., v. 17, No. 3, p. 171) designates the winter dance series of the katcinas, koko a·wan itiwana, the itiwana of the masked gods. These dances follow at stated intervals after the solstice, but are not actually part of it. This indicates the Zuñi pattern that each cult must have a center, and this center must correspond to the centers of other cults. The katcinas do not figure in the solstice ceremonies proper.

The ceremonies fall into two periods of 10 nights each.[89] The first nine days are spent in preparation of great quantities of prayer sticks by all men. Images of the war gods are carved by men to whom this office belongs. The great ceremonies begin on the tenth night. On this night the new year fire is kindled in the kiva and the Bow Priests hold their ceremony for the War Gods. At the same time all the societies hold ceremonies in honor of the Uwanami.

On the following morning the images of the War Gods are taken to their shrines. The priests take the younger brother to Corn Mountain to a shrine the position of which is visible at the village. There the priests kindle a fire, and the appearance of their smoke is the signal for the beginning of the great fire taboo. For the next 10 days—that is, until dawn on the twentieth day—no fire or light must be seen outdoors, nor must any sweepings or ashes be thrown out. For the whole period priests observe continence, eat no animal food, and they and their households refrain from trade of any description. Others observe continence for eight days following the planting of prayer sticks, and refrain from animal food and trading for four days. The conservation of fire, and especially the saving of ashes and sweepings, are fertility magic, that the house may be full of corn, as it is of ashes. Throughout this period a sacred fire is kept burning in He′'iwa kiva.

The eleventh to the fourteenth nights [90] are given over to the retreats and ceremonies of the medicine societies, with the great all-night ceremony ending at dawn on the fourteenth day. On this afternoon occurs the second general planting of prayer sticks to the katcinas, the Beast Gods, and to the ancestors for wealth.

On the following day the priests again make prayer sticks for the Uwanami in preparation for their retreat the following night. This takes place on the sixteenth night. The prayers are for rain and fertility. On the altar are placed clay images of animals and objects on which blessings are invoked. The prayer sticks are planted at springs the following morning.

Also late on the sixteenth night all the kivas are visited by P̂autiwa (called on this occasion Komhałikwi, "witch god") who throws into each a ball of fine corn meal to be used during the coming year by the Ca'lako impersonators in their morning prayers. His visit takes place late at night when none can see him. The rite seems to be one of exorcism.

On some night during the 10 days of the fire taboo, generally the night of the priests' retreats, each family that owns sacred possessions of any description employs them in rites of fertility magic.[91] Clay

---

[89] In computing the dates of ceremonies only nights are counted. The pekwin's announcement is made at dawn. The following night is the first day. Taboo periods begin at sundown or late afternoon and continue through four nights, ending the fourth morning at dawn. The days are not counted.

[90] Sometimes called "the first four nights of the komosona's count." For 10 days the p̂ekwin counts days for the sun. Then he is finished and the komosona counts days for Pautiwa.

[91] Itsuma·wa, the ritualistic term for planting.

objects, similar to those used on the altars of the priests, are modeled by the women of the house. These are set out at night along with ears of corn and the sacred object, mask, rain fetish, sacred medicine, or personal fetishes such as pebbles to which are imputed magical properties. For one night the family are in retreat. They remain awake until day and repeat prayers and songs whose burden is a request for fertility of crops and flocks, and the fecundity of women. The ears of corn are set aside for spring seeding. The clay objects are later buried in the floor of the house, or thrown out on the twentieth day with the sweepings. They are the seed from which the real objects will grow.

On one of these days pregnant women, especially those who have been unfortunate with previous babies, visit the shrines at the base of the rock pillars on the west side of Corn Mountain. A woman undertaking this pilgrimage is accompanied by her husband and a priest. They deposit prayer sticks at the foot of the rock pillars and she scrapes a bit of dust from the rock and swallows it, from one side if she desires a boy, from the other if she wishes a girl. In addition to this, or instead of it, a pregnant woman may have made for her at this season a doll, similar to those sometimes given to children during the winter dances of the katcinas. The doll is made by anyone who "knows how," that is, who has the supernatural power to make it effective. It will ensure a safe delivery and a healthy child.

Meanwhile the impersonator of P̄autiwa for the final day has been chosen. On the nineteenth day the priests of the council make the crooks of appointment to be given to the impersonators of the katcina priests. Just before sunset arrive Ci'tsukä and Kwe·lele, two masked gods from the east. They bring the new year from the east. Their masks belong to the Great Fire Society and appear, along with another mask, at certain curing ceremonies of that society. I can offer no explanation of the conspicuous part they play in the celebration of the New Year. They go to the chief kiva where are assembled the priests of the council and the impersonators of P̄autiwa and the four Sai'yaƚia. They dance all night in the kiva to the songs of the Great Fire Society. Late at night the Saiyaƚia visit all the kivas "to send out the old year." It is a rite of exorcism. At dawn the new year fire is kindled. Before sunrise the katcinas, accompanied by the p̄ekwin, the chief of the Katcina Society and the guardian of the sacred fire, go out to the east carrying firebrands and a lighted torch. After brief prayers they return. The sound of their rattles as they pass is a signal to the people. The great fire taboo is now ended and from each household the men and women emerge bearing live coals from the fire, and the accumulated ashes and sweepings. Soon the fields from which night has not yet departed blossom with a hundred piles of glowing embers. The masked gods return to the kiva where they dance until day. Anyone, man, woman, or child, who desires good luck, may go to the kiva at this time to receive the blessing of the presence of the gods.

The day is one of great festivity and rejoicing. All day the gods from the east dance on the roof of the kiva, throwing food and other articles to the populace. Meanwhile the bow priests summon to the kiva the men chosen to impersonate the gods during the coming year. When they have all arrived the wands of office are distributed by the p̄ekwin.

The merrymaking continues in the plaza until sundown, when P̄autiwa appears. He visits all the kivas. On the roof of each he lays down the crook of office for the Ca'lako god to be chosen from that kiva. The bar of the hatchway he marks with four lines of corn meal, to indicate that the masked gods will visit the village. Then using a twig to represent a scalp, he performs a brief ritual symbolizing the taking of an enemy scalp. Thus he brings the new year. After visiting all the kivas he departs for the west, taking Ci'tsuk̭ä and Kwe'lele with him.

After dark each house in the village is visited by Tcakwenaok̭ä, a female masked impersonation and the special guardian of women in childbirth.[92] She is accompanied by other masked gods. As the group reaches each door live coals are thrown out of the house as a rite of purification. Tcakwenaok̭ä comes only once to bring the blessing of fecundity. The other gods return for four consecutive nights, in accordance with the promise of P̄autiwa. In early days the first dance of the winter series took place four days after the departure of the exorcising divinities (Stevenson, p. 141). Now it takes place any time the leaders wish. This closes the celebration of the solstice, unless the retreat and dance of the łewekwe which follow 10 days after the coming of P̄autiwa be considered as part of the solstice ceremonies.

Theoretically the second half of the Zuñi year repeats the ceremonial calendar of the first six months. As in December, the summer solstice is marked by a ceremonial period called i'tiwana, the middle. As in the winter, this is a synchronization of independent cults. But here the resemblance ceases. The actual ceremonies, and above all the relative weight of various elements, are quite different.

Before the summer solstice the p̄ekwin makes daily observations of the sunsets from a shrine at Ma'tsak̭ä, a ruin a few miles east of Zuñi. When the sun sets behind a certain point on the mesa to the northwest the p̄ekwin begins his plantings to the sun and to the ancestors. On the morning after his fourth planting he announces that in eight days everyone shall make prayer sticks for the sun, the moon, the ancients,

[92] In 1927 the visit of Tcakwenao'k̭ä was omitted. The man who owns her mask, a very dangerous one, and knows her ritual, was in prison for burglary. No one else dared touch the mask. (See p. 931.)

and the katcinas. The prayer sticks are offered in the afternoon of the eighth day, which should be the summer solstice, June 22. The offerings are less elaborate than those of the winter solstice, but their precise nature is not known to the writer. There is only one planting. Prayer sticks for the katcinas are offered together with the others on the eighth day. There are no offerings to the Beast Gods. The offerings are made in cornfields. For four days everyone refrains from sexual intercourse, trading, and quarreling, but there is no restriction on food.

On the day preceding the offering the societies, except the Wood Society,[93] meet in their houses. Altars are erected, but there are no images of the Beast Gods. The members remain in retreat overnight, and their prayers on this occasion, as on the night preceding the solstice in December, are directed primarily toward the rain makers. There is no four-day retreat in honor of the Beast Gods following this, and no general healing of the sick. This part of their activities is temporarily in abeyance.

On the third day following the solstice the impersonators of the Koyemci visit each house in the village and are doused with water by the female inhabitants as a suggestion to the supernatural powers to do likewise. Then they go into retreat.

On the fourth day following the general prayer stick planting the first of the chief priesthoods goes into retreat, to remain in for eight nights.

On the same day preparations are begun for the first of the summer rain dances. Every fourth year a pilgrimage is made to the village of the katcinas, a lake about 80 miles to the west. On the fourth day following the solstice the officers of the katcina society and the impersonators of all of the katcina priests, accompanied by the chief of the Hunters Society and men of the Deer and the Badger clans leave for the home of the gods. The lake is reached on the evening of the second day. Offerings of prayer sticks are made at various shrines and turtles are hunted. The party returns next morning, arriving at Zuñi the fourth day at sunset, the seventh after the solstice.

On intervening years the same party leaves at dawn on the seventh day to plant at a spring at Ojo Caliente, 17 miles southwest of Zuñi. The spring symbolizes the more distant shrine. Since the date coincides with the monthly planting of the katcina priests, the impersonators separate, some going with the others to Ojo Caliente, some taking the offerings of his fellows to the spring at which they make their regular monthly planting. Each person makes offerings for both springs.

---

[93] Stevenson, p. 150. This society does not meet with the others in the winter rites. Its rituals are especially potent for bringing cold winds and snow. For it to function at this time would be disastrous.

Returning at evening, the party from the katcina village is met on the plain by a group of katcinas from the kiva that is to present the first dance. The priests bring the gods back with them from their village. From now until they are sent home in the fall they are present, though invisible, in the village. After dancing in the four courts of the village the dancers retire to the house where they are to spend the night. Here one of the societies which has been invited to provide music has erected its altar. The gods are welcomed and throughout the night dance for the delectation of the hosts. Their presence is manifested by rain. Meanwhile the Koyemci hold similar rites in their own ceremonial house.

The dancers on this occasion abstain from food and drink until they have made the round of the plazas four times the following morning, or until rain falls.[94] Each round takes about an hour, and the outdoor dancing begins at sunrise. Dancing in the plazas continues throughout the day, while in the two houses visited by the gods the medicine societies keep up continuous singing. At sunset the dancers depart and the society people dismantle their altars and return home. With this ceremony the celebration of the summer solstice closes.

The chief priesthood remains in retreat for four more nights, and comes out on the eighth morning. The second priesthood goes in that same evening and the rest follow in regular order.

The summer solstice observances are notable in the complete absence of any ceremonies to secure the blessings of the Beast Gods or the Ahayuta. The omission of the Ahayuta is especially noteworthy. In the winter they are appealed to for protection and aid in war, but more especially for snow and cold winds. Prayer sticks are offered at all their shrines in conjunction with the dance of the Wood Society, a potent snow-making ritual. The second calendrical ceremony of the Bow Priesthood is held in March, before corn planting and in preparation therefor. The ceremony has never been observed nor described, nor, unfortunately, have the words of the prayers and songs been recorded. However, it corresponds to the summer solstice ceremonies of other cults, in being a partial repetition, with variations, of their winter observances. The writer hazards the guess, in the absence of direct evidence, that this is an appeal for snow and violent rains to swell the spring freshets and prepare the ground for the reception of seeds.

If the winter ceremonies emphasize rites having as their object medicine, war, and fecundity, the summer ceremonies are weighted

---

[94] At Acoma the summer dance of katcinas is held early in July, the public ceremonies consuming four days, from about the 10th to the 14th. These are preceded by a period of purification lasting eight days. The participants abstain from food and especially from water from nightfall preceding the dance until noon the day of the dance. (White, MS.) The date is that of the Hopi Niman. In certain Aztec ceremonies there is prohibition on drinking from nightfall until noon.

overwhelmingly on the side of rain, the most conspicuous features being the retreats of the priests and the dances of the katcinas. It is tempting to attribute this pattern difference to practical consideration. The first of July is the approximate date of the opening of the rainy season in this semiarid land. At this time the corn plants are about 10 inches high and desperately in need of rain. Two more weeks of drought and blazing heat will burn them beyond hope. Upon prompt and plentiful rains in July depends the welfare of the tribe. It is, therefore, to this end that all the magical resources of the tribe are bent. The Ahayuta, associated with wind and low temperatures, are shunned.

On the other hand, in December the conditions are reversed. The crop is already harvested and whereas it is desirable to have heavy snowfalls in the mountains to feed the spring freshets, inclement weather in the valley is a great hardship and works ruin among the flocks that form so large a part of Zuñi wealth. Therefore prayer sticks are twice offered at the mountain shrines of the Ahayuta with prayers for snow. The Uwanam:i and the katcinas receive but very meager attention, and the efforts of the tribe are focused on rites directed toward war, medicine and fecundity. At both solstices the sun father is appealed to in similar fashion for his great blessing of life.

Personal Religious Life

The vast wealth of ceremonial elaboration which we have been considering is notably weak on the side of what have been called "crisis rites." In contrast to the ceremonial recognition given to natural phenomena—the solstitial risings of the sun, the alternation of summer and winter, the perpetual dearth of rain—crises in personal life pass almost unnoticed. The ceremonies surrounding birth, puberty, marriage, and death are meager and unspectacular. There is sprinkling of ashes for purification of the newborn. On the eighth day of life the infant is presented to the sun with brief prayers, but the occasion is not one of any ceremonial importance. There are no ceremonies whatsoever at marriage, and mortuary rituals are simple and undramatic in comparison with calendrical ceremonies. Relatives are summoned at death. The body is dressed for burial, all present weep and sprinkle corn meal on the head of the deceased with brief prayers, and the corpse is interred at once. Four days later prayer sticks are planted, and the property of the deceased, including certain ceremonial possessions, is buried and additional prayer sticks may be offered to the dead after an interval of time. But there are no public demonstrations and no elaborate ceremonies of mourning.

On the other hand, initiations are always important occasions. The general initiation of all young males into the Katcina Society corresponds in some ways to puberty ceremonies of other tribes, even though it has very little relation to the physical fact of adolescence. The first "initiation" takes place at the age of from five to seven years. It corresponds to no physiological change and marks no change of status on the part of the child. The child who has been "initiated" in this preliminary ceremony has no more knowledge or responsibility than one who has not yet gone through the rite. The final ceremony at which knowledge is revealed takes place anywhere between the ages of 10 and 20, depending on the interference of schooling—in old days it probably took place between the ages of 10 and 14—and is unrelated either to physical maturity or the assumption of adult responsibilities. It is an initiation solely into the katcina cult and has nothing to do with the social status of the individual. Marriage, for instance, does not depend upon it, nor participation in other ceremonies. Although any initiated boy may, if he wishes, take part in masked dances, he does not feel any obligation to do so. It is usually many years before he assumes even the responsibility of making his own prayer sticks. Curiously enough, considering general North American custom, no notice whatever is taken of the advent of maturity in girls.

Initiations into medicine societies are more clearly ceremonial recognition of personal crises. The initiate is a patient who has been snatched from the jaws of death and his initiation into the group that saved him is the ceremonial assumption of his new status. At his initiation he gets a "new heart," and, as a symbol of the new life he has begun, receives a new name.[95] This name, however, is not usually used and does not ordinarily replace his childhood name or names. The ceremony may be delayed for years—sometimes as long as 20 years—after the cure which it affirms. Like initiation into the Katcina Society, it involves a minimum requirement of attendance, and the privilege of additional participation as the interests and ability of the individual may dictate. Children need not assume any responsibilities upon initiation.

Religious participation starts among children when, as infants on their mother's backs, they are taken to watch the katcinas dance. The summer dances outdoors are largely attended by small children of both sexes. During the morning and early afternoon they constitute the entire audience. Formerly children were not permitted to attend night dances of the katcinas where the katcinas dance unmasked, but this rule is broken among the more lax parts of the population.

Children learn early to share the interest of their elders in the more spectacular phases of religious life. They are keen observers of dances, they know songs, and give accurate and lively accounts of

[95] Contrary to custom in other pueblos, and reported information from Zuñi, naming is not a part of the initiation into the Katcina Society.

ceremonies which they attend; they are interested in sacerdotal gossip; and they orient their activities about great religious festivals. In early childhood boys and girls are especially interested in religious affairs. Sometime between the ages of 5 and 10 boys make their first direct contact with the deeper aspects of religion, on their preliminary initiation into the Katcina Society. This makes no change in a child's religious life. It is only after his final initiation, which may occur any time after the age of 10, that active participation in dances begins. Boys of 10 or 12 take part in the winter dancing but rarely in the more strenuous dancing of the summer series. At about the same age girls have their attention diverted from religious spectacles to their own adult activities.

Most adult men engage in other religious activities besides the required minimum of katcina dancing and the semiannual prayer stick plantings required of all persons. The younger men, who find exhilaration in dancing and singing, dance many times a year, either with their own groups or with others, and organize extra dances. As their knowledge of dance forms increases they may advance to formal office in one of the six dance societies. Those who display an aptitude in memorizing long prayers, if of exemplary conduct, may be appointed to impersonate one of the gods.

Membership in curing societies is not ordinarily a matter of individual choice. Once initiated into one of these groups a man may limit his activities to attendance at the regular winter meetings and initiations. Or if he has sufficient intellectual curiosity to pay high for esoteric knowledge he may, by accumulating knowledge and the supernatural power which knowledge gives him, advance to a position of influence in his society. For a successful career as a medicine man, intelligence and ambition seem more important than piety and virtue. However, although a man of questionable moral character may build up a good medical practice, he is not likely to be chosen for office in his society.

Membership in priesthoods is even less a matter of free choice than curing societies. Priesthoods are hereditary in maternal families, and to fill a vacancy the members select the least quarrelsome rather than the most intelligent of the eligible young men.

The priesthoods are the branch of religious service that carries the greatest prestige and heaviest responsibilities. Because of the heavy responsibilities the office is avoided rather than sought, and considerable difficulty is experienced in recruiting the priesthoods. As one informant said, "They have to catch the men young to make them priests. For if they are old enough to realize all that is required of them, they will refuse." She was not thinking of the taboos and restraints of the priestly life, but of the sense of responsibility for the welfare of the tribe which lies so heavily on the shoulders of the priests. The same informant continued: "Yesterday my younger brother went with his uncle to the spring for water for their altar. He was dressed in his ciwan·i costume and looked very handsome. As he went out, light rain fell, and everyone was happy that they had been blessed with rain. But my heart hurt and my eyes were full of tears to see my younger brother. He is so young and yet he has his mind on these serious things."

Another and very different type of voluntary participation is to "take the crook" for the ca'lako, that is to volunteer to entertain the gods in one's house. This involves the host in very great expense, and can be undertaken only by a man who is wealthy in his own right or who has wealthy relatives who are willing to help him. This munificence brings to the house the blessing of fecundity but is primarily a social activity in that it merely provides the background for a great tribal festival. Its rewards (to the individual) are to be measured largely in terms of social prestige. If volunteers fail, the obligation to hold the ceremony falls upon members of the religious hierarchy.

The religious activities of women are less varied and picturesque than those of men. In early adolescence a girl's interest is diverted from religious affairs. About the time she assumes adult dress—or did before the days of the American school—she falls under a system of chaperonage that hampers her movements. Especially running around to public dances is regarded as unbecoming. So if she goes to dances at all she goes to watch discreetly from the houses of relatives who live on the plaza, or gets very much dressed up and stands and giggles on the corner of some housetop with a group of equally dressed up and equally self-conscious little girls. Furthermore, about this time she assumes adult responsibilities in the household, and beyond that all her interests are absorbed in mating activities. Adult economic status comes later to boys than to girls. In the years between initiation and marriage boys give much of their attention to dancing, while girls of the same age are cooking, grinding, and caring for their sisters' babies.

After marriage they become even more domestic, and remain so throughout the period of childbearing. Not only is their time filled with domestic duties, but it is displeasing to a man to have his wife gadding about, and Zuñi women, despite their economic and social security, are careful not to displease their men. Furthermore, their avenues of participation are restricted. They are not, except in very rare cases, initiated into the Katcina society, the only democratic religious organization. Some of the priesthoods have women members, but these positions are, it seems, even harder to fill than positions for men. One of the reasons is that husbands get very restive under the long periods of continence required of their wives. A man will remain continent during his own ceremonies but seems to think it is too much to expect him to remain continent during his wife's ceremonies also. Here, again, the problem is to catch the girl young enough. Women are initiated into medicine societies on an equal basis and as frequently as men. They participate in the dances of the society, but they are debarred from holding office. They frequently practice medicine and are "given" children for their society, but they must call upon male members for assistance in cures and to perform many of the initiation rites over their children. Women never possess the ultimate medical power, that of calling the bear, and do not usually possess esoteric songs. However, their knowledge of actual therapeutics is often greater than that of men. Most societies have "mothers" who brew their medicines and jealously guard the secrets of the treatment of medicinal herbs.

Some women who are well endowed mentally exert a good deal of influence indirectly upon religious affairs. Although their activities may be restricted, knowledge is not taboo to them. There are women who know prayers and rituals better than their men folks and some men customarily consult their wives, mothers or sisters on matters of sacerdotal procedure. In the Onawa priesthood the member with the best verbal memory is a young woman, not especially intelligent in other respects. However, she has an aggressive, managing mother who, although not herself a member of the priesthood, is the head of the priestly household, and contrives to run her brothers and children. Several other women have a reputation for their knowledge of esoteric lore. One, in particular, is reputed to be the only person who knows the prayers, songs and secret rituals of Anahoho, one of the katcinas coming at the initiation ceremony.

Women are less active in religion than men, but their activity is not essentially different in kind. The richness of ceremonial tends to mask the fact that in any but a superficial sense, religious activity is limited in scope.

The religious life of an individual is exclusively a series of participations in group rituals. No avenue is left open for individual approach to the supernatural. All over North America individual mystical experience is prized. On the plains such experience is valued since it provides one with a guardian in the supernatural world, or furnishes supernatural sanction for some special exploit. Among the Pima of the Southwest, the experience itself is regarded as the highest value in life. In Zuñi the religious life is a highly developed system of techniques for producing rain and furthering the growth of crops. Certain socially valuable attitudes and modes of behavior are regarded as more favorable to this purpose, and much esthetic joy and enhancement of life are achieved through them. But these subjective values are secondary and merely incidental to the primary purposes of religious participation, which is an objective social good.

ZUÑI ORIGIN MYTHS

By RUTH L. BUNZEL

CONTENTS

ZUÑI ORIGIN MYTHS

By Ruth L. Bunzel

Three English versions of Zuñi origin myths have already been published. Cushing published his "Outlines of Zuñi Creation Myths" (Thirteenth Annual Report of the Bureau of Ethnology) in 1891. The next published version is that contained in Mrs. Stevenson's monograph, and a third recorded by Dr. Elsie Clews Parsons appeared in the Journal of American Folk-Lore in 1923 (vol. 36: 135–162). The three versions placed side by side give one of the most striking examples of the great handicap under which the science of ethnology labors. All ethnological information comes to us through the medium of another mind, and, with data so complex and subtle as those of human civilization, no matter how clear and honest that mind is, it can absorb only what is congenial to it, and must give it out again through such means of expression as it may command. The Zuñis are as much preoccupied with the origins and early history of their people as were, for instance, the ancient Hebrews, and the three accounts are what might be gathered from any people by individuals of varying interests.

Doctor Parsons, asking for "the" origin myth, got the basic account of the early history of the people which is generally current in folklore. The narration, of course, suffers in vividness and subtlety of expression from having been recorded through an interpreter. Mrs. Stevenson's version is an attempt to give a comprehensive and coherent account of Zuñi mythology in relation to ritual. The Cushing version contains endless poetic and metaphysical glossing of the basic elements, most of which explanatory matter probably originated in Cushing's own mind.

Cushing, however, hints at the true character of Zuñi mythology. There is no single origin myth but a long series of separate myths. Each ceremonial group has a myth which contains, in addition to a general synopsis of early history, the mythological sanction for its own organization and rituals. There is not, however, any collected version which is "the talk," because no mind in Zuñi encompasses all knowledge, the "midmost" group to which Cushing refers being a figment of his own imagination. These separate myths are preserved in fixed ritualistic form and are sometimes recited during ceremonies, and are transferred like any other esoteric knowledge. The "talk" of K̯äklo is a myth of this kind. It recounts in poetic form the origin of the tribe, their coming into this world, the origin of K̯äklo's ceremony, and the wanderings of the people in search of the middle. The synoptic version in "Zuñi Indians," mentions the episodes peculiar to this version. The Stevenson "origin myth," recorded in the opening pages of her monograph, is not a ritual version. Into the general outline have been introduced whatever bits of special information she had acquired. Her most intimate associations were with the Ne'we·kwe society, and many episodes of the esoteric myth of that society appear in her account.

The main outlines of the origin myths are known to all, and great delight is found in recounting them. The history myth is not fixed in form or expression and varies in comprehensiveness according to the special knowledge of the narrator. The Parsons version treats the katcina origins fully; the Stevenson version society origins. Portions or the whole general outline in brief or extended versions were told me on many occasions as I sat by Zuñi firesides. One old priest desired me to write it down in text so that I and others might read it. But although an excellent narrator he was a bad dictator. He spoke so rapidly, vividly, and with such wealth of gesture and mimicry that only a sound picture could do justice to his narration. However, the version recounted the principal events briefly without any special elaboration of any portion, and therefore added nothing to published versions.

The following text recorded from another informant is an origin myth in esoteric ritual form. It belongs to the priests—"any priesthood." It is recited for purposes of instruction during the winter retreat. It was related to me by a man who was not himself a priest but was born in the Pałto·kwe house and learned the tale from his maternal uncle. He was a member and an officer of the Great Fire society and characteristically refused to give the origin myth of his society since that was his "very own prayer." The tale related to me publicly by the chief priest of the Onawa priesthood did not contain the elaboration of priestly origins found in the following text, nor any of the striking stylistic features.

The brief text which follows, the "talk of Komosona," belongs to the same category. This is the ritual form of the tale of origin of masked dancing and the safeguards of the katcina cult. It is recited in the form given by the katcina chief at the final initiation of boys into the katcina society. It was told by the same informant. Less formal versions are, of course, current. Both this and a version of the origin of the people were introduced into an autobiography of an old woman, when speaking of her girlhood days spent with her grandfather.

TCIMIK̭ÄNA'KONA P̂E'NA·WE
first beginning according to — words

no'miłte. luk̭' u'lo'nan kwa tcu'hoł tcu'wa. hic yä'tok̭ä
truly this world not anyone who very sun

kwai''inan hic kwa'to. kwa tcu'hoł ca'mli ha'lawotinan·e
coming out very goes in not anyone early prayer meal

łe'ena'map̂ kwa tcu'hoł te'lik̭inan·e łe'ena'map̂ hic
(not) bringing not anyone prayer-stick (not) bringing very

t̂e'wu'acona. yam tcaw a·'tcia le'sanikwanan— t̂on a·'witen
place lonely his children both to thus to them saying "you fourth

t̂e'hulikwin a·'nuwa. yam a·'tatcu yam a·'tsita k̭ä'-e'to·ne
womb to shall go. your fathers your mothers water fetish

tcu'-'eton·e mu'-e'ton·e łe'-eton·e le· ti'k̭ä a·'ciwani ti'k̭ä
corn fetish ——— wood fetish all society priests society

p̂'e'kwi·we ti'k̭ä a·'pi'ła·ci'wan·i hoł yam yä'tok̭ä ta'tcu
speakers society bow priests yonder your sun father

an t̂e'k̂ohanakwi t̂on a·'wili kwa·''in·a" a·'tcia le''anikwap̂
his daylight to you with them shall come out" the two to thus to them having said

a·'tci le'skwanan, "kop ma' le' hon kwa'ton·a." "ten
the two thus saying, "how well thus we shall go in." "however

e'lek̭än·a." yam a'mitolan pi''łan wi'lolonan co''le yä'łtonan
it will be well" their rainbow bow lightning arrow laying across

pi''łana yä'łtonan i'pakuk̭ä. i'pakunan p̂a'ni·k̭äp. s'
bow on laying across he shot shooting descending so

a·'tci kwa'tok̭ä a·'witen t̂e'hulikwin a·'tci kwa'top t̂e'k̂win
the two entered fourth womb into both having entered dark place

u'le kwa yu''he·tam·e. a·'tci le'skwanan "ho'k̭ämp
inside it was. not it was (not) clear. The two thus saying "which way

hon a·'nap e'lek̭än·a" s'a·tci su'nhakwin tahn a·'k̭ä.
we having gone will be well" so the two the west to direction went.

a·'tci tcu'wai a'nikto·k̭ä. a·'tci lesanikwak̭ä. "ho'k̭ämp t̂o
The two someone met face to face the two thus to him said "which way you

i'ya'" "li·'wanem k̭älicianikwin ta'hna ho' i'ya" "kop
come" "hither west towards direction I come" "what

t̂o' le'yen a'luya" "ho' yam le'na· tun-a'luya."
you doing go about" "I my crops watching go about."

"hop t̂on a·'teaiye" "e'ła kwa hoł hon a·'team·e
"where do you live" "no not anywheres we do (not) live

li·′wan i′yamakwin ta′hna ho′n tatc-ili te′′ona yä′tok̭ä
hither above towards direction us father having the one who is sun

ci′wan·i ho′′na kwa′tok̭äp̑a hon kwatok̭ä" a·′tci le′′kwap
priest us having made come in we came in they thus saying

"ma′ ho′nkwa" an su′we le′skwanan "a′ma hon u′nace"
well is that so his younger brother thus saying come: let us see

le′′kwanan a·′tcian pi′′łan a′′unan a·′tci kwahoł o′ma·k̑usna
thus saying their bow putting down they something leaves dry

pep̑ewi ku′sna a·′tci wo′tehkunan a·′tcian pi′′łan yäłt·onan
grass dry they throwing them down their bow putting down on top

a′sosuk̭ä′k̭ä. a.′tci a′sosuk̭äp ma′ke· lo′mon kwai′′k̭a.
drilled for fire they drilling for fire coals glowing came forth.

kwai′ip a·′tci puaps a′l·ok̭ä. lo′—p̑a t̑e′k̑ohatip "at̑u′—.
having come forth they having blown on it it caught fire Aglow! Becoming bright "Ouch!

kwap t̑o′n u′hsi" le′′kwanan to′tsipo la′nik̭ä. a′wico mi′toye
what yours that thus saying crouching he fell. Moss horn is

a′wic ho′ktiye a′wico te′tc ho′′i. a′si k̭epilap̑a am papa
moss tail is moss only person. Hands webbed his elder brother

le′skawanan "iyos a′klałk̑ä" le′′kwap a′klałk̭′äp tsa′wak̭
thus saying, "Poor thing! Now put out the fire!" thus having said fire having put out young man

le′sk̭wanan. "he·— k̑otci′—. kwap t̑o′n u′hsi." "ma′
thus saying "He, ouch! What yours that?" "Well,

ho′′na ma′ke·" a·′tci le′′anik̭′äp. "kwap ma′ t̑on u′wanap̑a."
our coals," they thus to him having said "What well you have growing?"

"ma′ i·′ła hon u′wanap̑a" le′′kwap. k̭ä′wawula tun a′luya
"Well, here we have things growing," thus having said wild grass watching he goes about.

a·′tcia le′sanikwanan
To them thus to them saying:

"Ma′ si′ hon a·′wa·ce." A·′tcia ye′hkup k̭ä′liciankwin
"Well now us let go!" Them having gone before west towards

ta′hna a·′wa·k̭ä. łu′walakwin a·′te′tcik̭ä. i′sk̑on yam t̑e′hwiti-
direction they went. Village at they arrived. There their space

wanakwin i′t̑inak̭ä. i′sk̑on i′yanitaton i′tinak̭ä. isk̑on iyan-
middle in they sat down. There close to one another they sat down. There one another

tehkunapk̭ä. le′stikwanan "e·h mas a·′tci p̑ene. hinik kwahoł
they questioned. thus (they) saying: "yes well now both speak! I think some

p̑e′nan te′yułanam·e p̑e′nan te′k̑änä. | u′hson ho′ t̑on
word not over-long word will be. that us you

ai′yu′ya·k̑äp̑a" | uhs ai′yu′ya·na hon t̑e′wanan a·′tek̭än·a." |
having caused to know it that knowing we time shall live.

"hatci′" "-hatci′" le′′anak̑äp. "Ma′ i·′nami′łte. | li·′wan i′ya-
"Is it not so?" "It is so," thus it being said, "Well without doubt it is true. hither above

makwin ta′hna hon ta′tc′ili te′′ona | yä′tok̭ä | kwa k̭ä·′k̭i
towards direction us father with the one who is sun not ever

tcu'wa te'lik̯inan·e łe'ana'ma | kwa tcu'wa ha'lawo·tinan·e
who prayer stick does (not) bring not who prayer meal

łe'ana'ma | kwa tcu'wa ło·''o łe'ana'ma | łe'sna te''onak̯ä
does (not) bring no who shell does (not) bring thus because it is

| hoł yam yä'tok̯ä ta'tcu | an t̄e'k̄ohanakwi t̄on i'łu-
yonder your sun father his daylight into you standing

wakna kwai''itunonak̯ä | t̄o'n hon a·'wona-e'latek̯ä | tenat
in order that you may be the ones to go out you we on your roads have passed however

ho'łnotikoł t̄on a·p̄enuwa" | le''a·'tc'i'kwap̄a | "haiyi'
whichever way you may speak." thus they having said "Haiyi!

ma' ho'nkwa' le'sna te''onak̯ä ho''na t̄on a·'wona-e'latek̯ä. |
Well is that so? thus because it is us you on our roads have passed

A'tic hon te'wuko'liya a·'teakwin ho''na t̄on a·'wona-
Truly we poor where we live us you on our roads

e'latip hoł a'wełak̄una hon a·'p̄enuwa t̄sena. eł kwa hon
having passed somewheres deviating we shall speak far be it from us! Indeed, not we

i'yuna·wam·e tomt hon i'yatcuclen-u'likwi tomt hon i'yan-
(do not) see one another just we trampling on one another where we are inside just we on one another

tcuk̄oclen-ulikwi tomt hon i'ya'pinakwi tomt hon i'potcełnakwi
spitting where we are inside just we on one another urinating just we defiling ourselves where

tomt hon i'tapantin-u'laconankwi ho' t̄on a·'wona-e'latep̄a
just we following one another pushing where us you on our roads having passed

a'tichoł hon a'wełak̄un a·'p̄enuwa ma' u'łaticic pi'cle ci'wa·ni
surely not we deviating shall talk well rather north priest

lu'k̄on ho'łno p̄e'nap i'snok̄on te'k̯än·a. ma' a·tc a'ntecemati"
this one wherever his word being there it shall be. Well you two summon him"

a·'tcia le''ana'k̯äp a·'tci pi'clankwin ta'hna i'tiu'łak̯ä. . . .
to them thus it having been said they north towards direction stood beside. . . .

*A·'tci picle ci'wan·i o'na-e'latip "t̄on i'ya" le''kwap "e·h
They north priest on his road having passed, "You come," thus having said, "Yes.

hon i'ya ko to' t̄e'wanan te'aiye" "k̯e't̄sanici ho' t̄e'wanan
We come. How you time are living?" "Happily I time

te'akwi łom t̄on o'na-e'latek̯ä. a·tci i·'mu"—a·'tci i·'mup
when (I) live me you on my road have passed. sit down." They having sat down

i'sk̄on i'yanitehkunanapk̯ä.
there one another they questioned.

"Ma' a·'tci p̄e'ne | hinik kwa'hoł p̄e'nan te'yułanam·e
"Well both speak! I think some word not over long

p̄e'nan te'ak̄an·a | t̄e'wuna' u'hsona hom t̄on yu·''ya·k̯än·a." |
word will be. Finally that me you will make know."

"Ma' i·'na·miłte | hoł yam yä'tok̯ä ta'tcu | an t̄e'k̄o-
"Well without doubt it is true Somewhere your sun father his daylight

hanakwi t̄on i'łuwakna-kwai''itunona'k̯ä | t̄om łon o'na-
into you standing that you may be the ones to go out you we on your road

e'latek̯ä. | hołnotikoł t̄o' p̄e'nap te'k̯anä." | "Ma' i·'namiłtë |
have passed. Whichever way you speaking. it shall be." "Well, without doubt it is true.

a'tic le''na hon te'wuko'liy a·'teakwi | ho''na t̄on a·'wona-
truly thus we poor where we live us you on our roads

e'latep̄ä | hoł a'wełak̄una ho' p̄e'nuwan t̄sena. | tomt hon
having passed somewhere stepping aside I shall speak far be it. Just we

i'yatcuclen-u'likwi | tomt hon i'yantcukoclena·wankwi |
on one another trampling where we are inside just we on one another spitting where

tomt hon i'p̄ɔtcełena·wankwi | tomt hon iyahpina·wankwi |
just we ourselves defiling where just we on one another urinating where

tomt hon i'tapantin-u'laconankwi | ho''na t̄on a·'wona-
just we one another following pushing where us you on our roads

elatep̄a | hołn a'wełak̄una te'k̯än·a." | le''kwap i's̄kɔn
having passed wherever stepping aside it shall be." Thus having said there

łu'walemak̯ä. k̯äł a·'wa·k̯ä. łu'walakwin a·'winan yam te'hwi-
they arose. Hither they went village to coming their middle

tiwana i't̄inaknan i's̄kɔn i'yantehkunanapk̯ä. "e·h ma' la'k̯i-
space sitting down there one another they questioned. "Yes well, even

mante łon i'yona-e'łatenapk̯ä. ime' kwatikoł p̄e'nan te'yu-
now we one another's roads have passed. Surely somewhat word not

łanam·e p̄e'nan te'ak̯än·a. | t̄e'wuna' u'hsona hom t̄on
over long word will be. Finally that me you

yu''ya·k̯äna·wap̄ä | uhs ai'yu'ya·na ho' t̄e'wanan te'k̯an·a. |
having made know that knowing it I time shall live."

le'ciantikwak̯ä. | leciantikwap̄a, | "ma' i·'namiłte | hoł
Thus to one another they said. Thus to one another having said. "Well without doubt it is true somewhere

yam yä'tok̯ä ta'tcu | an t̄ek̄ohanakwi t̄on i'łuwakna-
your sun father his daylight into you standing

kwai'i'tunona'k̯ä | t̄o'n hon a·'wona-e'latek̯ä." | le''kwap
in order that you may be the ones to come forth you we on your roads have passed." Thus having said

"hai'yi ma'honkwa. | a'tic kwa hon le''na i'yuna·wam·e
"Haiyi! Well is that so? Truly not we thus one another see

a·'teakwi | tomt hon i'yatcuclen-u'likwi | tomt hon
where we live just we on one another trampling where we are inside just we

i'yatcuk̄oclen-u'likwi | tomt hon i'yahpina·wan kwi | tomt
on one another spitting where we are inside just we on one another urinating where just

hon i'p̄ɔtcałena·wankwi | tomt hon i'tapantin-u'laconankwi |
we ourselves defiling where just we one another following pushing where

ho' t̄on a·'wona-elatepä | hołn a'wełak̄una ho' p̄e'nuwan
us you on our roads having passed somewheres stepping aside I shall speak

t̄sena * | ma' u'łat hom su'we k̯ä'lici ci'wan·i lu'k̄ɔn
far be it! Well rather my younger brother west priest this one

ho'ɫnatikoɫ p̂e'nuwa li'ɫno te'atu le''kwap i'snok̂ɔn te'k̯än·a.

wherever he may speak 'here let it be!' thus saying there it shall be.

ma' t̂e'wuna' a·tci a'ntecemati." pi'cle ci'wan·i le''kwap

Well finally you two summon him!" North priest thus saying,

a·'tci k̯ä''liciankwin i'tiuɫak̯ä. . .

they west towards stood beside. . .

The section between asterisks to be repeated for the priests of the six directions in the following order:

k̯ä'lici ci'wan·i	west priest
a'laho ci'wan·i	south priest
t̂emak̂o ci'wan·i	east priest
i'yama ci'wan·i	above priest
ma'nila'ma ci'wan·i	below priest.

ma' i'mat hoɫko'n tcu'waiya tse''makwin a'k̯ä yam

Well it seems somewhere according to someone's thought by means of our

yä'tok̯ä ta'tcu an t̂e'k̂ohanakwi hon i'ɫuwakna kwai''itun'ona

sun father his daylight into we standing up the ones to go out

te'ak̯än·a." le''kwap a·tci tse''mak̯ä. "a'ma laɫ hon

may be." Thus having said they thought. "Come! Then we

k̯ä'k̯äli ci'wan·i a'cuwak̯äce." a·tc a·'k̯ä. a·'tci k̯ä'k̯äl

Eagle priest let us talk with." They went. They eagle

i'nkwin te''tcinan. "t̂on i'ya." "e·h." "a·'tci i·'mu." a·'tci

where he stays arriving. "You come." "Yes." "You two sit down." They

i·'muk̯ä. "a·tci p̂ene." "t̂om hon ce'me'a." "hoɫtci." "lalik

sat down. "You two speak." "You we call." "Where?" "Nearby

hon a·'tatc i ɫap̂ona k̯ä'-eto·we t̂i'nanɫa'k̂ikwi t̂om hon

we fathers the ones (we) have water fetish staying quietly where you we

a'ntecemati." "haiyi." s'a·wa·k̯ä. k̯ä'-eto·we ti'nankwi

summon." "Haiyi." So they went. Water fetish staying where

a·'te'tcik̯ä. "ma' la'k̂imante hom ton a'ntecematip̂a

they arrived. "Well, now even me you having summoned

t̂o''na ɫo' a·'wona-e'latek̯ä. ime' kwa'tikoɫi p̂e'nan

you I on your roads have passed. Surely some word

te'yuɫanam·e p̂e'nan te'ak̯än·a. t̂e'wuna' u'hsona hom

not over long word will be. Finally that me

t̂on yu''ya·k̯äp̂a uhs ai'yu'ya·na ho' t̂ewanan tek̯än·a."

you having made know that knowing it I time shall live."

le''kwap "ma' i·'namiɫte ho''na·wan a·'tatcu k̯ä'-eto·we

Thus having said "Well, without doubt it is true our fathers Water fetish,

tcu'-eto·we mu'-eto·we ɫe·'eto·we le· ti'k̯ä a·'ciwan·i yam

corn fetish ——— wood fetish all society priests their

yä'tok̯ä ta'tcu an t̂e'k̂ohanakwi i'ɫuwakna kwai''in·a.

sun father his daylight into standing up will come forth.

a·'wan o'neałan·e t̂o' te'cun·a" "ma' ho'nkwa'ati." le''kwanan
Their road you shall seek." "Well, is that so." Thus saying,

"so a·'ne." le''kwanan i'tulohk̯ä. i'mtek̯änan la'lik̯ä'kon
"now I am going." Thus saying he circled around. Coming back to his starting place a little ways off along

a·'k̯ä. i'mtek̯änan tem t̂a la'lik̯a'kon a·'k̯ä. i'mtek̯änan
he went. Coming back to his starting place yet again farther off along he went. Coming back to his starting place

lał hic la'lik̯a'kon a·'k̯ä. i'mtek̯äp kwa hoł yu''he·-
then very much farther off along he went. Having come back to his starting place not anywhere it was

tam·e. i'k̯ä. k̯ä'-eto·we t̂i'nakwin i'k̯ä. i·'mup a'nteh-
(not) clear. He came. Water fetish staying where he came. Having sat down He ques-

kunak̯ä. "si' lehoku t̂o' o'neałan kwai''inan tecuk̯än a·'k̯ä.
tioned him. "Now yonder you road going out seeking went.

ko' ko'lea t̂o' u'lohnan u'nak̯ä." "kwa hoł yu''he·tam·e."
In what manner you world saw?" "Not anywhere it was (not) clear."

"hai'yi·." "ma' ko''ma so' a·'ne." s'a·k̯a.
"Haiyi." "Well, very well so I am going." So he went.

a·'nap a·'tci tse''map. "a'ma hon yam nan-i'li te''ona cok̯äpiso
He having gone, the two thought. "Come! we our grandfather with, the one who is ——

hon a'ntecematice." a·'tci le''kwanan a·tc a·'k̯ä. a·'tci co'k̯äpis
let us summon." They thus saying they went. They ——

i'nkwin a·'tci te''tcinan "ho''na na'na ko' t̂o' t̂e'wanan
where he stays they arriving, "Our grandfather how you time

te'aiye?" "k̯e'tsanici ho' t̂e'wanan te'akwi hom t̂o' o'na-
are living?" "Happily I time when I live me you on my road

e'latek̯ä. i'me' hi'ntcoł kwa'tik p̂e'nan te'yułanam·e p̂e'nan
have passed. Surely I think some word not over long word

te'ak̯än·a. t̂e'wuna' u'hson hom t̂on yu''ya·k̯äp̂a uhs ai'yu'-
will be. Finally that me you having made know that knowing

ya·na ho' t̂e'wanan te'k̯än·a. le''kwap ma' i·'namiłte. hon
I time shall live." Thus having said "Well, without doubt it is true. We

a·'tatc i'lap̂ona k̯ä-eto·we tcu'-eto·we mu'-eto·we łe'-eto·we
fathers the ones (we) have, water fetish corn fetsih —— wood fetish

le· ti'k̯ä a·'ciwan·i yam yä'tok̯ä ta'tcu an t̂e'k̯ohanakwi
all society priests their sun father his daylight into

i'łuwakna kwai''inuwap̂a t̂o' a·'wan o'neałan te'cutun'ona'k̯a
standing being about to come forth you their road that [you] may be the one to seek

t̂om hon a'ntecemati." "honkwa'." le''kwap s'a·wa·k̯ä. a·'te'tcinan
you we summon." "Indeed?" Thus having said so they went. Arriving

i't̂inaknan i'tehkunak̯ä. "e·ma' lak̯imante hom t̂on a'ntece-
sitting down he questioned them. "Yes, well, even now me you have

matik̯ä. ime' kwa'tikoł p̂e'nan te'yułanam·e p̂enan te'k̯än·a.
summoned. Surely some word not over long word will be.]

t̂e'wuna' u'hsona hom t̂on yu''ya·k̯äp̂a uhs ai'yu'ya·na ho'
Finally that me you having let know that knowing it I

t̂e'wanan te'k̯än·a." "ma' i·'namiłte. ho''na·wan a·'tatcu ho''-
time shall live." "Well, without doubt it is true. Our fathers, our

na·wan a·'tsita k̯ä'-eto·we tcu'-eto·we mu'-eto·we łe'-eto·we
mothers, water fetish, corn fetish, —— wood fetish,

ti'k̯ä a·'ciwan·i yam yätok̯ä tatcu an t̂e'k̂ohanakwi i'łuwakna
society priests, their sun father, his daylight into standing up

kwai''ina. t̂o' a·'wan o'neałan te'cun·a. a·'tci le''kwap a'laho-
shall come forth. You their road shall seek." They thus having said south

ankwin ta'hna kwai''ik̯ä. i'tulohk̯ä. i'mtek̯'äp kwa hoł
towards direction he went out. He circled around. coming back to his starting place not anywhere

yu''he·tam·e kwi'lik̯äna·na la'likä'ko a·'k̯ä. i'mtek̯äp kwa hoł
it was not clear. The second time farther out along he went. Coming back to his starting place not anywhere

yu''he·tam·e. ha''ik̯äna·na la'lik̯ä'kon a·'k̯ä kwa hoł
it was (not) clear. The third time farther out along he went not anywhere

yu''he·tam·e. a·'witenak̯äna·na hic ai'yaton a·'k̯ä. kwa hoł
it was (not) clear. The fourth time very twice as far he went. not anywhere

yu''he·tam·e. k̯ä-eto·we t̂i'nakwin te''tcip a·'tc a'ntehkunak̯ä.
it was (not) clear. Water fetish where they were staying arriving they questioned him.

"si' ho''na na'na le'hok[u] t̂o' u'lohnan u'nak̯än a·'k̯ä.
"Now, our grandfather yonder you the world to see went.

ko' ko''lea t̂o u'lohn u'nak̯ä." a·'tci le''kwap "ma' kwa
In what manner you the world saw?" They thus having said, "Well not

hoł yu''he·tam·e." "ma' ho'nkwa'ati'." a·'tci le''kwap "ko''ma
anywhere it was (not) clear." "Well, is that so?" They thus having said, "Very well,

so a·ne." le''kwanan s'a·k̯ä.
now I am going." Thus saying so he went.

Co'k̯äpis a·'nap a·'tci tse''mak̯ä. "a'ma lał yam nan a'cu-
—— having gone, they thought, "Come! now our grandfather let

wak̯'äce a'neława te''ona." a·'tci le''kwanan a·'tc a·'k̯ä. a·'tc
us talk with hawk the one who is." They thus saying they went. They

a'nelaw i'nkwin te''tcinan. "t̂on i'ya." "e·h." "a·'tci i·'mu." "ko'
hawk where he was staying arriving. "You come." "Yes." "You two sit down." "How

t̂o' t̂e'wanan te'aiye." "k̯e'tsanici. "ma' s'a·tci p̂ene. hi'niktci
you time live?" "Happily." "Well, now you two speak. I think

kwatikoł p̂enan te'yułanam·e p̂e'nan te'ak̯an·a. t̂e'wuna' hom t̂o'
some word not over long word may be. Finally me you

yu''ya·k̯äp uhs ai'yu'ya·na ho' t̂e'wanan te''k̯än·a" "ma'
having let know that knowing it I time shall live." "Well,

i·'namiłte'. ho''na·wan a·'tatcu k̯ä-eto·we tcu'-eto·we mu'-
without doubt it is true. Our fathers water fetish, corn fetish, ——

eto·we łe'-eto·we ti'k̯ä a·'ciwan·i yam yä'tok̯ä ta'tcu an
—— wood fetish, society priests, their sun father his,

t̂e′k̂ohanakwi i′łuwakna kwai′′ina t̂o a·′wan o′neałan te′cun·a.″
daylight into standing up coming forth You their road shall seek.″

s’a·wa·k̭ä. a·′te’tcinan i′tinak̭ä. isk̂on i′tehkunak̭ä. e·h ma’
So they went. Arriving they sat down. There he questioned them. "Yes, well

la′k̭imante hom t̂on a′ntecematinapk̭ä. i′me’ kwa′tikoł p̂e′nan
even now me you have summoned. Surely some word

te′yułanam·e p̂enan te′k̭än·a. u′hson hom t̂on yu′′ya·k̭ä-
not over long word will be. That me you having let

na·wap̂a uhs ai′yu’ya·na ho’ t̂e′wanan tek̭än·a. le′′kwap̂a. "ma,
know that knowing it I time shall live." So having said "Well

i·namiłte′. ho′na·wan a·′tatcu k̭ä-eto·we tcu′-eto·we mu′-eto·we
without doubt it is true. Our fathers' water fetishes, corn fetishes, ————

łe′-eto·we ti′k̭ä a·′ciwan·i yam yätok̭ä ta′tcu an t̂e′k̂ohanakwi
wood fetishes, society priests, their sun father, his daylight, into

i′łuwakna kwai′′in·a. t̂o’ a·wan o′neałan te′cun·a.″ "ma’ ho′nkwa’-
standing up shall come forth. you their road shall seek." "Well, indeed?"

ati′.″ le′′kwanan. kwai′′ik̭ä. a′lahoa′nkwin ta′hna a·′k̭ä.
Thus saying he went out. South toward direction he went.

co′k̭äpis a·′k̭äte′a’kowa a·′k̭ä. i′mtek̭äp kwa yu′′he·tam·e.
———— where he had gone along he went. Coming back to his starting place not it is (not) clear.

kwilik̭äna·′na la′lik̭änk̂o a·′kä. i′mtek̭äp kwa hoł yu′′-
The second time further out along he went. Having come back to his starting place not anywheres it is

he·tam·e. ha′′ik̭äna·′na a·′k̭ä k̭ätuł-ulapna’kona. a·′witena-
(not) clear. The third time he went ocean encircling along. The fourth

k̭äna·na la′lik̂ona a·′k̭ä. i′mtek̭’ap kwa hoł yu′′he·tam·e.
time further out along he went. Having come back to his starting place not anywheres it is (not) clear.

k̭ä′-eto·w t̂i′nakwin i′k̭ä. "kwa hoł yu′′he·tam·e." "haiyi′." "e·h.
Water fetishes staying place he came. "Not anywheres it is (not) clear." "Haiyi!" "Yes

ko·′ma’ so a·ne." "ma’ łu’u." s’a·k̭ä.
Very well, Now I am going." "Well go." So he went.

i’sk̂on a·′tci tse′′mak̭ä. "si’ a′ma lał hon yam nan
There they thought. "Now, come! Now we our grandfather,

a′ntecematik̭äce.″ a·′tci le′′kwanan a·′tc a·′k̭ä. a·′tci
let (us) summon." They thus saying they went. They

t̂suy i′nkwin te′′tcik̭ä. "t̂on iya." "e·h. ko’ t̂o t̂e′wanan
Humming-Bird where he stays arrived. "You come." "Yes. How you time

te′aiye″ "k̭e′tsanici ho’ t̂ewanan te′akwi hom t̂on o′na- e′latek̭ä.
live?" "Happily I time when I live me you on my road have passed.

a·′tci i·′mu.″ a·′tci i·′mupma’s a·′tci p̂e′ne. hi′ntcoł
You two sit down." They having sat down, Well now, speak. I think

kwa′tik p̂e′nan te′yułanam·e p̂e′nan te′ak̭äna. t̂e′wuna’
some word not over long word may be. Finally

u′hson hon t̂on yu′′ya·k̭’äp̂a uhs ai′yu’ya·na ho’ t̂e′wanan
that us you having let know that knowing it I time

te′k̯̂än·a." "ma' i·namiłte′ hon a·′tatc i′lap̂ona k̯̂ä′-eto′we
shall live." "Well, without doubt it is true, we fathers the ones (we) have water fetishes

tcu′-eto·we mu′-eto·we łe′-eto·we ti′kä a·′ciwani yam
corn fetishes ——— wood fetishes society priests their

yä′tok̯ä ta′tcu an t̂e′k̂ohanakwi i′łuwakna kwai′′in′a.
sun father his daylight into standing up shall come forth

t̂o' o′neałan te′cutun'onakä t̂om hon a′ntecemati." "ma'
You road that (you) may be the one to seek you we summon." "Well,

honkwa'ati′" le′′kwap s'a·wa·k̯ä. a·′te'tcinan i′tehkunak̯ä.
indeed?" thus having said so they went. Arriving he questioned them.

"e·h ma' lak̯imante hom t̂on a′ntecematinapk̯ä. i′me'
"Yes well even now me you have summoned. Surely

p̂e′nan te′yułanam·e p̂e′nan te′ak̯än·a" t̂e′wuna' u′hson
word not over long word may be" Finally that

hom t̂on yu′′yak̯äp̂a uhs ai′yu'ya·na ho' t̂e′wanan te′k̯̂än·a."
me you having let know, that knowing it I time shall live."

le′′kwap̂a ma' i·′namiłte ho′′na·wan a·′tatcu k̯̂ä′-eto·we
thus having said "Well, without doubt it is true. our fathers water fetishes

tcu′-eto·we mu′-eto·we łe′-eto·we tik̯ä a·′ciwan·i yam
corn fetishes ——— wood fetishes society priests their

yä′tok̯ä tatc an t̂e′k̂ohanakwi i′luwakna kwai′′in·a. t̂o'
sun father his daylight into standing up shall come forth. You

a·′wan o′neałan te′cutun'on a′k̯ä t̂om hon a′ntecematik̯ä"
their road that you may be the one to seek you we have summoned."

le′′kwap a′lahoa′nkwin ta′hna kwai′′ik̯ä. a·′k̯ä. i′mtek̯äp
This having said, south towards direction he went out. He went. Having come back to his starting place

kwa hoł yu′′he·tam·e la′lik̯änkwin a·′k̯ä. i′mtek̯äp kwa
not anywheres it is (not) clear. Farther out he went. Coming back to his starting place not

hoł yu′′he·tam·e. lał ha′′ik̯äna·n a·k̯ä. i′mtek̯äp kwa hoł
anywheres it is (not) clear. Then the third time he went. Having come back to his starting place not anywheres

yu′′he·tam·e a·′witenak̯äna·′na a′′p̂o'yan t̂e′łakwi'ko a·′k̯ä.
it is (not) clear. The fourth time the sky touching along he went.

i′mtek̯äp kwa yu′′he·tam·e i′k̯ä. k̯̂ä-eto·w t̂i′nakwi i′nan
Coming back to his starting place not it is (not) clear. He came. Water fetishes where they stay coming

"kwa yu′′he·tam·e" "hai′yi" "e·h· ko'ma so a·′ne." "ma' łu′u"
"Not it is (not) clear." "Indeed?" "Yes. Very well, Now I am going." "Well, go."

a·k̯ä. a·′tci le′skwak̯ä "si' ko′pleatap e′lek̯äna. le·′wi
He went. They thus said: "Now and how will it be right?" So many

kwa′hoł wowa·latap̂a kwa a′wek a′łpitina'ma a·′walun'ona
some creatures winged not ground do not touch. The ones who go about

i·′natik̯ä." a·′tci le'kwanan, "a′ma hon lał yam nan
have failed." They this saying, "Come! we now our grandfather

a'cuwaḵäce tcu'mali te'a'ona tem ta lu'k̄ɔ k̄i'nawa'ḵä
let us address. Locust the one who is. Yet again this one wet because of

tse''mak t̄su'metun le'stena'' a·'tci le''kwanan a·tc a·'ḵä.
thoughts strong to be so being'' they thus saying they went.

a·'tcian na'na o'mali a·tc o'na-e'lateḵä. "t̄on i'ya" "e·h
Their grandfather locust they on his road passed. "You come?" "Yes

hon i'ya" "a·'tci i·'mu." "ko·'na t̄on t̄e'wanan a·'teaiye"
We come." "You two sit down." "How you time are living?"

"ḵe'tsanici.
"Happily.

Si' ma' la'ḵimante hom t̄on o'na-e'lateḵä. i'me' kwa'tikołi
Now well even now me you on my road have passed. Surely some

p̄e'nan te'yułanam·e p̄e'nan te'aḵän·a. t̄e'wuna' u'hsona
word not over long word may be. Finally that

hom t̄on yu''ya·ḵäp̄a uhs ai'yu'ya·na ho' t̄e'wanan te'ḵän·a.
me you having let know, that knowing it I time shall live."

le''kwap̄a "ma' i·'namiłte hon a·'tatc i'lap̄ona ḵä'-eto·we
This having said, "Well without doubt it is true. We fathers the ones (we) have, water fetishes,

tcu'-eto·we mu'-eto·we łe'-eto·we ti'ḵä a·'ciwan·i yam
corn fetishes ——— wood fetishes society priests their

yä'toḵä ta'tcu an t̄e'k̄ohanakwi i'łuwakna kwai''itun'on a'ḵä
sun father his daylight into standing up that thay may be the ones to come forth

t̄om hon o'na-e'lateḵä." "ma' ho'nkwa." le''kwap a·'wakä.
you we on your road have passed." "Well indeed?" This having said, they went.

a·'te'tcinan i't̄inaḵa. i't̄inaknan i'tehkunaḵä. "e·h. ma'
Arriving they sat down. Having sat down, he questioned them. "Yes. Well

laḵimante t̄o·'na ło a·'wona-e'lateḵä. i'me' kwatik p̄e'nan
even now you I on your roads have passed. Surely some word

te'yułanam·e p̄e'nan te'aḵän·a t̄e'wuna' u'hsona hom t̄o'
not over long word may be. Finally that me you

yu''ya·ḵäna·wap̄ u'hson ai'yu'ya·na ho' t̄e'wanan te'ḵän·a."
h aving let know, that knowing it I time shall live."

"ma' i·'namiłte hon a·'tatc i'lap̄ona ḵä-eto·we tcu'-eto·we
"Well, without doubt it is true. we fathers the ones (we) have water fetishes corn fetishes

mu'-eto·we łe'-eto·we ti'ḵä a·'ciwan·i yam yä'toḵä ta'tcu
——— wood fetishes society priests their sun father

an t̄e'k̄ohanakwi i'łuwakna kwai·''itunonaḵä t̄om hon
his daylight into standing up that they may be the ones to come forth you we

a'ntecematiḵä." ma' ho'nkwa'ati." le''kwanan o'mali te''ona
have summoned." "Well, indeed?" This saying locust the one who is

i'sk̄ɔnt i'ḵeato'ḵä. i'ḵeato·'u. t̄o'pa tekwin pi'kwe·ḵä.
right there raised himself. He rises! Another place to he passed through.

ta i'sk̄ɔn i'ḵeato·'u. t̄o'pa te'kwin pikwe·ḵä. ta i'sk̄ɔn
Again there he rises! Another place to he passed through. Again there

i'k̯eato·'u. ta to'pa te'kwin pikwe·k̯ä. i'skon i'k̯eato'u tomt
he rises! Again another place to he passed through. There he rises. Just

ko·w a·'nan t͡su'mena te'nk̯ä. t͡su'menan te'nan i'k̯wałt
a little having gone strength gave out. Strength giving out back

i'k̯ä. k̯ä'-eto·we t͡i'nankwi i'nan le'skwanan "ho' ha''ikänan
he came. Water fetishes where they stay coming thus saying: "I three times

ho' pikwe·nan a·'witenak̯äna·na ho' t͡sumena te'nk̯ä." "hai'yi·
I, passing through the fourth time I strength wore out." "Indeed?

ma'ho'nkwa'ati le'kwap s'a·k̯ä. a·'nap a·'tci tse''mak̯ä.
Is that so?" so saying now he went. He having gone, they thought.

"A'ma lał hon yam na'na ła'k̯aia tsa'wak̯i a'cuwak̯äce
"Come! Now we our grandson Reed Youth let us address.

tem ta luk̯on ho'tot͡su'mewak̯ä hoł e'letun le'stena." a·'tci
Yet again this one point strong with somewhere that it may be well so may it be." They

le''kwanan a·'tc a·'k̯ä. a·'tci ła'k̯aia tsa'wak̯ i'nkwin te''-
thus saying they went. They Reed Youth where he stays arriv-

tcinan "t͡on i'ya" "e·h. ko' t͡o' t͡e'wanan teaiye" "k̯e'tsanici ho'
ing "You come?" "Yes. How you time are living?" "Happily I

t͡e'wanan teakwi hom t͡on o'na-e'latek̯ä. a·'tci i·'mu." le''kwap
time when I live me you on my road have passed. You two sit down." Thus having said

a·'tci i·'muk̯ä. i'sk̯on i'tehkunak̯ä. "e·h ma' la'k̯ima' hom
they sat down. Then he questioned them. "Yes, well even now me

t͡on o'na-e'latek̯ä. hi'ntcol kwatik p̂e'nan te'yułanam·e
you on my road have passed. I think some word not over long

p̂e'nan te'ak̯än·a. u'hson hom t͡on yu''ya·k̯äp̂a uhs ai'yu'-
word may be. That me you having let know that knowing

ya·na ho' t͡e'wanan te'k̯än·a." le''kwap, "ma' i·'namiłte.
it I time shall live." Thus having said, "Well, without doubt it is true.

hon a·'tatc i'lap̂ona k̯ä-eto·we tcu'-eto·we mu-eto·we
We fathers the ones (we) have water fetishes Corn fetishes ———

łe-eto·we ti'k̯ä a·'ciwan·i yam yä'tok̯ä ta'tcu an t͡e'-
Wood fetishes society priests their sun father his day-

k̯ohanakwi i'łuwakna kwai''itun'onak̯ä t͡om hon o'na-e'latek̯ä."
light into standing up that they may be the ones to go forth you we on your road have passed."

"haiyi' ma' ho'nkwa'ati" le''kwap s'a·wa·kä. a·'te'-
"Haiyi! well, indeed?" thus having said so they went. arriv-

tcinan i·'muk̯ä. i'sk̯on i'tehkunak̯ä e·h ma lak̯imante hom
ing he sat down. There he questioned them. "Yes, well even now me

t͡on a'ntecematina·wap̂a t͡o''na ło' a·'wona-e'latek̯ä. i'me'
you having summoned you I on your roads have passed. Surely

kwatik p̂e'nan te'yułanam·e p̂e'nan te'ak̯än·a. u'hsona hom
some word not over long word may be. That me

t͡o yu''ya·k̯äp̂a uhs ai'yu'ya·na ho' t͡e'wanan te'k̯än·a."
you having let know that knowing it I time shall live."

"ma' i·'namiłte. ho''na·wan a·'tatcu k̭ä'-eto·we tcu'-eto·we
"Well, indeed it is true. Our fathers water fetishes corn fetishes

mu'-eto·we łe'-eto·we ti'k̭ä a·'ciwan·i yam yä'tok̭ä ta'tcu
——— wood fetishes society priests, their sun father

an t̂ek̂ohanakwi i'łuwakna kwai''itun'ona'k̭ä t̂om hon
his daylight into standing up that they may be the ones to come forth you we

a'ntecematik̭ä." le''kwap, "haiyi' ma' ho'nkwa'ati" le''kwanan.
have summoned." Thus having said, "Haiyi! Well, indeed?" thus saying

kwai''ik̭ä tcu·'mali kwai''ik̭äteakowa kwai'ik̭ä tci'mnakwe
he went out Locust where he had gone out along he went out. For the first time

pi'kwai'ik̭ä. kwi'lik̭ana·'na pi'kwai'ik̭ä. h·a'ik̭ana·na pi'kwai'ik̭ä·
he passed through. The second time he passed through. The third time he passed through·

a·'witenak̭ana·na pi'kwai'inän yam yä'tok̭ä ta'tcu an
The four thime passing through his sun father his

t̂e'k̂ohanakwi ye·'lana kwai''ik̭äk̭ä. kwai''ik̭änan i'k̂wałt
daylight into standing up he came forth. having come forth back

kwa'tok̭ä. i'k̂wałt kwa'tonan k̭ä'-eto·we t̂i'nankwin te''tcinan.
he went in. back going in water fetishes where they stayed reaching.

"t̂i'ya" le''anak̭'äp "e·h" le''kwap, "si' le'hok[u] o'neałan te'atun'ona
"You come?" thus it was said. "Yes" thus having said, "Now yonder road the one that should be

t̂o' tu'nak̭än a·'k̭ä. ko'tcilea hoł te'k̭än·a k̭e·'si" le''anak̭äp
you to see went. How somewhere may it be now" thus having said

"ma' i·'namiłte' hoł ko''lea t̂on a'ntecemana hom t̂on
"Well indeed it is so where whatever you wishing me you

a'ntecematina'pkona yam yä'tok̭ä ta'tcu an· t̂e'k̂ohanakwi
what (you) have wished our sun father his daylight into

ho' ye·lana kwai''ik̭äk̭ä k̭e·'si." le''kwap, "ha·li·' e'lahkwa."
I standing went forth now." thus having said, "Hali thanks!"

"so a·ne." "łu''u·" -le''kwap s'a·k̭ä.
"Now I go." "Go on," thus having said so he went.

A·nap s'iwokwi'k̭ä. s'iwokwi'k̭äp. i'sk̂on a·'tci a'cek̭ä
He having gone so they sat in a circle. So they having sat in a circle There the two pine tree

t̂ap e'lak̭ä. i'sk̂on si' i't̂inak̭ä. a·'witen t̂e'wana i'sk̂on
ladder set up. There now they stayed. Four days there

i't̂inak̭ä. a·'witen t̂e'wana·we le''kwap a·'witen t̂e'pikwai''ina·.
they stayed. Four days thus saying Four years passed.

i'sk̂on le· ti'k̭ä a·'ciwan·i i'yan tenap pi''lapk̭ä. t̂i'nan
there all society priests for one another song sequences told off. Sitting

e'hk̂ona e'letokna i·'hatiak̭ä. i'st lał kwi'lik̭ana·n t̂i'nan'ona
the ones in front carefully listened. There next second row the ones who were sitting

lał i'tehw i'hatiak̭ä. ist ha''ik̭ana·n t̂i'nanp̂a''ona sic a·'wa-
then with gaps heard. Those third row the ones who were sitting only here

yu'otip e'tsak̭äna lał ist a·'witenak̭än t̂i'nan yäl'ona hic
and there being clear then those fourth row sitting the ones behind very

a·'wan a'ce· lal i'tehw-e'tsak̄äna le'snap̄a co'ya tco'łoło-
for them exceedingly then with gaps being clear being thus dry grass rattling

ap a'k̄ä. i'sk̄on a·'wan t̄e'wanan i'te''tcap i'sk̄on yam
because of there their time being used up there their

eleteli·we łe'an i'yante'tcik̄änan łu'walemak̄ä. "si' kop
sacred things carrying one another reaching around they arose. "Now how

li·ł t̄e'cinak̄än·a." "ma' li·ł k̄o'lin t̄e'hulik̄an·a. le'stikleap
here place shall be named?" "Well here sulphur fume inner world shall be." Furthermore

lu·'hoti-k̄ä'pinak̄än·a." le''tikwanan, "e·ha ma' honkwa. le'sti-
dust raw it shall be." Thus having said, "Eha. Well perhaps. Thus

ci'nap e'lek̄än·a." le''tikwanan s'u'kwai'ik̄ä. u'kwai'inanan
being called shall be well." Thus saying now they came forth. Coming forth

to'pa te'an yam e'leteli·we wo·'ta-pi'lak̄änan i't̄inan
one place their sacred things putting down making a row sitting down

ła'k̄ik̄ä. i'sk̄on a·'tci k̄ä'łatsilu t̄ap e'lak̄ä. t̄ap e'la'up i'sk̄on
they stayed quietly. There the two spruce ladder set up. ladder having set up there

a·'witen t̄e'wanan i't̄inak̄ä. tem t̄a i'sk̄on le· ti'k̄ä
four days they stayed. Yet again there all society

a·'ciwan·i i'yan te'nap pi''lanapk̄ä. t̄i'nan e'hk̄ona e'letokna
priests for one another song sequences told off. Sitting the ones in front carefully

i'hatiak̄ä. ist kwi'lik̄ana·na t̄inanan'ona lał i'tehwa
listened. There second row sitting the ones then with gaps

yu''he·tonapk̄ä. lał ist ha''ik̄än'a·nan t̄i'nanpa'ona a·'wai-
they distinguished. Then those in the third row sitting the ones to them

yu'otip e'tsak̄äna lał ist t̄i'na yä'l'ona hic a·'wan top'a'
here and there it was clear then those sitting the ones behind very to them single

hoł e'tsk̄äna le'snap̄a kwa'hoł le'na· tco'łoło'a'non'akä
somewhere being clear thus being some growing things rattling the ones be cause of

i'sk̄on a·'wan t̄e'wanan i'te'tcap i'sk̄on yam e'leteli·we
there their time used up there their sacred things

łe'an i'yante'tcik̄äna i'sk̄on łu'walemak̄ä. "si' kop lił
carrying one another reaching around there they arose. "Now how here

t̄ecinak̄än·a" "ma' li·ł a'nosian t̄e'hulik̄än·a a'k̄äp kwa
place shall be called?" "Well here soot inner place shall be because not

tem hon i'yuna·wam·e." "e·ha honkwa. le'stecinap
yet we one another do not see." "Eha perhaps. Thus place being called

e'lek̄än·a." le''iyantikwanan i'sk̄on łu'walemak̄ä to'pa
will be well." Thus to one another saying there they arose another

te'kwin a·'pikwai'inan i'sk̄on yam e'leteli·we wo'ta-pi''lak̄änan
place to passing through there their sacred things putting down setting in a row

i't̄inan łak̄ik̄ä. i'sk̄on lo'k̄wimo t̄ap e'lak̄ä. lo'k̄wimo
sitting down they stayed quietly. There piñon ladder he set up. Piñon

t̄ap e'la'up isk̄on le· ti'k̄ä a·'ciwan·i le·w a·'ciwan·i
ladder having set up there all society priests all priests

i′yan tenap -pi′′lanapk̬ä. t̂i′nan e′hk′ona e′letokna i′hatiak̬ä.
for one another song sequences told off. Sitting in front the ones carefully listened.

kwi′lik̬äna·na t̂i′nanan′ona lał i′tehw a·′wan e′tsak̂äna
Second row sitting the ones then with gaps to them being clear

ha′′ik̬anan t̂i′nanpa′nona a′waiyu′otip e′tsak̂äna a·′witen-
in the third row sitting the ones to them here and there being clear fourth

ak̬äna·na t̂i′nan′ona a·′wan to′pałhoł e′tsak̂äna le′snap̂a
row sitting the ones to them singly somewhere being clear thus being

co′ya tco′łoło′anona′k̬ä. i′sk̂ɔn a·′wan t̂e′wanan i′te′tcap
dry grass rattling the ones because of. There their time used up

yam e′leteli·we łe′an i′yante′tcik̬äna łu′walemak̬ä. i′łuwaknan
their sacred things carrying one another reaching around they arose. Standing up

"Si′ kop li′ł t̂e′cinak̂än·a?" "ma′ li′ł te′pahaiyan t̂ehulik̂än·a
"Now how here place shall be called?" "Well here fog inner place shall be

a′k̂äp kɔ·′witapte li′ł e′tsak̂än·a." "e·ha′. ma′ ho′nkwa
because a little even here will be clear." "Eha. Well perhaps

le′st̂ecinap̂a e′lek̂än·a." le′′tikwanan łu′walemaknan u′kwai′ik̬ä.
thus place being called will be well." Thus saying arising they came forth.

to′pa te′kwin a·′pikwai′inan i′sk̂ɔn a·′tci yam e′leteli·we
Another place to passing through there the two their sacred things

wɔ·′ta-pi′lak̂äna i′sk̂ɔn i′t̂inak̬ä. i′t̂inakna i′sk̂ɔn a·′tci
putting down setting in a row there they sat down. Sitting down there the two

ła′niłk̂oha t̂ap e′lak̬ä. i′sk̂ɔn le· ti′k̬ä a·′ciwan·i le·w a·′ciwan·i
cottonwood ladder set up. There all society priests all priests

i′yan te′nap-pi′′lapk̬ä. t̂i′nan e′hk̂ona e′letokna yu′′he·tonapk̬ä.
for one another song sequences told off. Sitting in front the ones carefully distinguished

kwilik̬äna·na t̂i′nanan′ona lał i′tehw a·′wan e′tsak̂äna. ist
The second row sitting the ones then with gaps to them being clear. Those

ha′′ik̬äna·na t̂inanpa′ona a·′wan yu′otip e′tsak̂äna lał
third row sitting the ones to them here and there being clear then

a·′witenak̬äna·na t̂inan yä′l′on a·′wa to′pałhoł e′tsak̂äna
fourth row sitting last the ones to them single somewhere being clear

le′snap̂a kwa′hoł le′′na tcu′łoło′an′on a′k̬ä. i′sk̂ɔn a·′wan
thus being some growing things rattling because of. There their

t̂e′wanan i′te′tcap a·′wan a·′witen t̂e′wak̬ate′a yam eleteliwe
time used up their four days passed when their sacred possessions

łean iy′ante′tcik̬äna łuwalemak̬ä. i′łuwaknan "si′ kop lił
carrying one another reaching around they arose. Standing up "Now how here

te′cinak′än·a?" "ma′ lił lata te′hulik̂an·a a′k̂ap yam yä′tok̬ä
place named shall be?" "Well, here wing inner place shall be because our sun

ta′tcu an lata· hon u′napa." le′tikwanan u′kwai′ik̬ä. yam
father his wings we see." Thus saying they came forth. their

yätok̯ä tatcu an t̑ek̑ohanakwi iłuwakna kwai'ik̯ä. eleho̷ł
sun father his daylight standing came out nearly

t̑ek̑ohatin'ihap̑a ukwai'ika.
day about to break they came out.

ukwai'ina isk̑on yam e'leteli·we wo·'ta-pi''lak̯äna i't̑inan
Coming out there their sacred things putting down setting in a row sitting down

ła'k̯ik̯ä i'sk̑on a·'tci le'sanikwanan, "si ko·wi te'nala'ap̑a
they stayed quietly. There the two thus saying to them, "Now a little after a while

t̑o''na·wan ta'tcu yam t̑e'łaci'nakwi, ye·'lana kwai''ik̯äp̑a
your father his ancient place to standing coming forth

yaiyu'anikto t̑on una·wa. eł t̑on i'hapisk̯äna·'wamek̯än·a."
face to face you shall see Don't you shut your eyes!"

le''a·wanikwap. ko·wi tenala'ap yä'tokwai'ik̯ä. yä'tokwai''ip
thus to them saying a little after a while sun came forth sun coming forth

u'natik̯änapk̯ä. a·'wan t̑unan'kona k̯ä'tuponoł pa'ni·lep u'nap̑a
they saw him! Their eyes from them tear drops rolling down they saw him.

ko·wi tenala'ap t̑u'na· a·'wits'umetik̯ä. "ha'kotci'" le'tikwak̯ä.
Little after a while eyes became strong. "Ouch!" thus they said.

a'wico te'tc a·'ho'i. a'wic a·'hoktip̑a a'wic a·'mitop̑a a·'wasi
Moss only persons. Moss tailed Moss horned hands

k̯e'pilap̑a i'yunatik̯äna·we.
webbed one another they saw.

"ti·'comaha' haiyi lec hon a·'wina'k̯ä" le''tikwap i'sk̑on a·'wan
"Alas! Haiyi! thus we appear?" thus saying there their

kwa ko''leho̷ł a·'te'ona yu''he·ton te'am·ap ta·''tcic ko·'wi te'a
not what kind beings distinguishable not being meanwhile little way

pi'tcik ła'cik̯i sa'ma k̯ä'kweye. an to''sito le'sanikwanan:
dogwood old man alone is living. His spider thus to him saying

k̯äpatu'. k̯ä'k̯äłip t̑o' i'waten·a." "kopla·'ti?" "hon a·'tatc
"Put on water. Water getting warm you shall wash your head." "Why?" "We fathers

i'lap̑ona hon a·'tsit i'lap̑ona k̯ä-e'to·we tcu-e'to·we mu-e'to·we
the ones (we) have we mothers the ones (we) have ——— ——— ———

łe-e'to·we le· ti'k̯ä a·'ciwan·i yam yätok̯ä ta'tcu an
——— all society priests their sun father his

t̑e'k̑ohanakwi i'łwwakna kwai''ik̯ä. kwa ko''leho̷ł a·'ho'
daylight into standing have come forth. Not what kind persons

a·'te'ona yu''he·tam·e. t̑o' a·'wan yu''he·tonan a'can·a."
beings is not distinguishable. You them distinguishable shall make."

le'anikwap. "ko'cikat'el·ea ho'łomacko'na kwa tcuw a·'wunam·e.
Thus to him saying "Certainly not! far off where not anyone does not see them.

t̑i'nan łak̯i'kona hoł a·'wan a·'yu'ya·naticukwa" le''kwap.
Staying quietly where somewhere them one can not get to know them." thus saying

"eł le'skwana'ma. te'nat e'lek̯än·a kwa t̑o' sa'ma te'acukwa
"Don't thus say. However it shall be well. Not you alone shall not be.

te′nat hon a·′nuwa,” le′kwap k̑ä′k̑äłip i′watek̯ä. i′watep
However we shall go,” thus saying Water getting warm he washed his head. Having washed his head

ta·′tcic a·′tci le′skwanan, “a′ma lał hon yam ta′tcu o′na-
meanwhile the two thus saying, “Come on. There we our father road

e′latece pi′tcik łacik̯ona luk̑on tem ta tse′′ma a′nikwatu
let us pass. Dogwood old man the one this one yet again thinking he must know

le′stena ak̑ap ho′′na·wan a·′tatcu k̑ä-e′to·we tcu-e′to·we
probably because our fathers ——— ———

mu-e′to·we łe-e′to·we kwa ko′′lehoł a·′ho′ a·′te′ona yu′′he·-
——— ——— not what kind persons beings distin-

tonan te′am·e” a·′tci le′′kwanan a·tc a·′k̯ä.
guishable is not.” The two thus saying the two went.

a·′tci te′′tcik̯ä. a·′tci ye·′makup “u′k̑wahtci′ s′a·tc iya′”
The two arrived. The two having climbed up “Now indeed! Now the two come!”

an to′′sito le′′kwanan an tu′knan i′tcupatcunan ye′mak̯ä.
His spider thus saying his toe crawling along climbed up.

la′cokt he′k̯äpana i′tcupatcuk̯ä. a·′tci kwa′tok̯ä. a·′tci
Ear back part she crawled along. The two entered. The two

kwa′top “t̑on i′ya” le′kwap “e·h. ho′′na ta′tcu ko′ t̑on
having entered “You come!” thus having said “Yes. Our father, how you

t̑e′wanan te′aiye.” “k̑etsanici ho′ t̑e′wanan te′akwi hom
time live?” “Happily I time living when my

t̑on o′na-e′latek̯ä. a·′tci i·′mu.” a·′tci i·′muk̯ä. “ma′ s′a·′tci
you road have passed. Both sit down.” The two sat down. “Well, now both

p̑e′ne. hiniktci kwa′tikoł p̑e′nan teyułanam·e p̑e′nan te′ak̯än·a.
speak. I think some kind word not too long word shall be.

tewuna′ u′hsona hom t̑on yu′′ya·k̑äp̑a uhs ai′yu′ya·na ho′
Finally that me you make know that knowing I

t̑ewanan te′k̑än·a.” “ma′ i·namiłte′. hon a·′tatc i′lap̑ona
time shall live.” “Well indeed it is so. We fathers having the ones

k̑ä-e′to·we tcu-e′to·we mu-e′to·we łe-e′to·we le· ti′k̯ä a·′ciwan·i
——— ——— ——— ——— all society priests

yam yä′tok̯ä ta′tcu an t̑e′k̑ohanakwi i′łuwakna kwai′′ina′
their sun father his daylight into standing coming out

kwa ko′′lehoł a·′ho′ a·′te′ona yu′he·to te′′am·ep̑a a′k̯ä t̑om
not what kind persons beings distinguishable not being therefore you

hon o′na-e′latek̯ä.” “haiyi′ ma′ honkwa′ati. ko′cikat′e′l·ea.
we road have passed.” “haiyi. Well perhaps so. Certainly not.

ho′łomackona kwa tcu′wa u′nam·e. t̑i′nan ła′k̑i′kona hon
From far off where not someone does not see. Staying where they are quiet we

tcuw a·′wanaiyu′ya·nacukwa.” le′kwanan, “ma′ e′te t̑om hon
someone can not know them.” Thus saying, “Well but you we

a′kcihk̯ä.” a·′tci le′kwap s′a·′wa·k̯ä.
have chosen.” the two thus saying now they went.

a·′te′tcinan “hom a·′tatcu hom a·′tsita ko′′na t̑on t̑e′wanan
Arriving my fathers my mothers how you time

a·′teaiye?” “k̑e′tsanici ho′′na·wan ta′tcu ho′′na·wan tca′′le.
are living?” “Happily our father our child

i'tinak̯ä. le''tikwap i·'muk̯ä. i·'munan i'sk̂ɔn i'tehkuna'k̯ä.
be seated," thus having said he sat down. Sitting down there he questioned them.

"e'm·a la'k̂iman·te hom t̂on a'ntecematina·wap̂a t̂o''na ło'
"Well yes even now me you having wished for you I

a·'wona-e'latek̯ä. hi'ntcoł kwa'tik p̂e'nan te'yułanam·e p̂enan
roads have passed. I think some kind of word not too long word

te'ak̯än·a. t̂e'wuna' u'hson hom t̂on yu''ya·k̂äna·wap̂a
shall be. Finally that me you having made know

u'hs ai'yu'ya·na ho' t̂e'wanan te'k̂än·a. le''kwap ma'
that knowing I time shall live." Thus having said "Well

i·'namiłte ho''na·wan a·'tatcu ho''na·wan a·'tsita k̂ä'-eto·we
indeed it is true our fathers our mothers ———

tcu-eto·we mu-eto·we łe-eto·we yam yä'tok̯ä ta'tcu an
——— ——— ——— their sun father his

t̂e'k̂ohanakwi kwai''ipte kwa ko'leahoł lukni a·'ho' a·'te'ona
daylight into having come forth even though not what kind these persons beings

k̯es kwa yu'he·tonan te'amap̂a t̂om hon a'ntecematinapk̯ä."
now not distinguishable not being you we have wished for."

le''ank̂äp "haiyi' ma ho' i'tetcut'u. ko'cikat'el·ea. ho'łomac'kona
Thus being said "Haiyi! Well I let (me) try Certainly not. From far off

kwa tcu'wa a·'wunam·e. t̂i'nan ła'k̂i'kona ko''le· a·'ho'i
not someone sees them. Staying quietly where what kind persons

a·'te'ona a·'wan aiyu'ya·natina'cukwa. ma ho' i'tetcuna
beings them one can not get to know. "Well I shall try"

le''kwanan wɔ·'tał-pi''lan ye'liawełak̯ä. an to''sito
thus saying laying in a row he stood beside them. To him spider

le'skwanan li·ł ał-pa'łtona k̂ä'-eton·e lał ist an
thus saying, "Here lying at the end ——— then those it

i'pito·we tcu'-eto·we lał ist al'ona łe'-eton·e lał ist
touching ——— then those lying the ones ——— then those

i'pito·we mu'-eto·we" le''anikwap le'skwak̯ä "ma lu'k̯ä
touching ——— thus to him having said thus he said "Well this

k̂ä'-eton·e lał luk̯ an i'pito·we t̂em·ła tcu'-eto·we lał
——— Then this it touching all ——— Then

luk̯ łe'-eton·e lał luk̯ an i'pito·we t̂em·ła mu-eto·we
this ——— Then this it touching all ———

le''kwap "halihi·' elahkwa'." ko' ko'lea lu'kni a·'wa yä'tcu
Thus having said "Halihi! Thanks!" How which one these their month

pi''lan te'k̂än·a? le''kwap lu'k̯ä ta'yamtco luk̯ o'nan-u'lak̯äkwam·e
sequence shall be?" thus having said, "This branches broken (January) this on the road no snow lying (February)

luk̯ łi'tekwak̯ä tsa'n'ona luk̯ łi'tekwak̯ä ła'n'ona luk̯ yä'tcun
this sandstorm small the one (March) this sandstorm (April) large the one this month (May)

kwa ci'am·e lu'k̯ä i'kohpu luk̯ t̂a'yamtco luk̯ o'nan-u'lak̯ä-
not named this turn about (June) this branches broken (July) this on the road no snow (August)

kwam·e luk̯ łi'tekwak̯ä tsa'n'ona luk̯ łi'tekwak̯a ła'n'ona
lying this sandstorms (September) small the ones this sandstorms (October) large the ones

luk̯ yätcu kwa ci′am·e luk̯ i′k̂ohpu. le·′wi luk̯ä yätcu
this month not (November) named this turn about (December) So many this months

pi′′lan·e.” “halihi′. elahkwa′ ho′′na·wan ta′tcu kwa t̂o’
sequence.” “Halihi! Thanks our father not you

tewukoli’yamek̯äna. e·t kwa t̂o’ e′leteli·we tse’mak-t̂eła-
poor shall (not) be. But not you sacred things thoughts touching

k̂wam·ek̯ä’en·te hoł k̯ä·k̯i i′tiwanan yu’he·ton yo·’ap̂a t̂om
even if not somewhere sometime the middle distinguishable becoming your

tse’makwin ak̯ä luknia·wan kwahoł haito i′k̯eatok̯än·a
thoughts because of these their something ordained shall rise.

kwahoł tomt t̂o’ wɔ· teamek̯än·a.” le’anakna’ yätok̯ä
Something just you servant shall not be.” Thus having been said Sun

ukna’k̯ä “luk̯ t̂om eletelin tek̯äna.” le’na teatip a·′teak̯ä.
was given him “this your sacred thing shall be.” Thus having happened they lived.

a·′witen t̂e′wana·we a·′witen t̂e′wana′we le’kwap a·′witen
Four days four days thus saying four

t̂e′pikwai’ina i′sk̂ɔn a·′teak̯ä—n a·′wan t̂e′wanan i′te’tcan’ihap
years there living their time used up about to be

tu′nunutik̯ä. a·′tci le′skwanan “tcu′wap t̂a imetcik̯ä?” “ma
it rumbled. The two thus saying “Who also remains behind?” “Well

i·me e·t hon t̂e′młoł le′stena” le’kwap t̂a tu′nutnutik̯ä. t̂a
I don't know but we all so I thought,” thus having said again it rumbled. Again

tu′nunutip “ma i′mat tem t̂a tcu′hoł i′metci′k̯äci?” le′′kwa-
having rumbled “Well apparently yet again someone remained behind?” thus say-

nan a·tc a·′k̯ä. yam u′kawi’ik̯ä tekwin a·′tci te′′tcip
ing the two went. Their coming out place the two arriving

a·′tci e′laiye. a′mpisat̂ap tsi′polo·we. a·′tci le′skwanan
the two stand. Mischief maker and Mexicans. The two thus saying

“haiyi·′ temc t̂a t̂on i′metcik̯ä?” “e·.” “tem t̂ac kwa′hoł
“Haiyi? Yet also you remained behind?” “Yes.” “Yet again something

a′k̯ä e′letun’ona t̂on ho′′i?” a·′tci le’kwap “ma le′snap̂a.
because of to be well the one you person?” the two thus having said “Well thus being.

e· li·ł k̯ä′-eto·we t̂e′k̂ohana ya′hna·wapte kwa t̂o′wa
Yes, here —— daylight issued even though not corn

k̂ɔkc an k̯ä′hkwin a′k̯ä a·′ho’ a·′team·e. k̯äwawuli·a·w
good its juice with persons are not. Wild grasses

a′k̯ä te’tc a·′ho’i. tem t̂a hoł i′tiwanan·e t̂on o′na-e′latena·-
with only persons. Yet also somewhere the middle you road having

wap̂a hom ak̂ e′lek̯än·a. hoł ho’ e′ma’an·a u′lohna
passed me with shall be well. somewhere people will be many country

t̂enan·a kwa e′letun te′am·e. le′sna te′onak̯ä ho’ kwai′′ik̯ä.”
will give out not to be well is not. this being the one because of I came forth.”

le'kwap "haiyi'. ma honkwa'ati. si ta·'tci t̑o·'o kwap a'k̯ä

Thus having said, "Haiyi! Well, perhaps it is so. No meawhile you, what with

t̑om e'letun'ona t̑o' ho'i?" le''anikwap "ma i·'nami'łte. hoł

your to be well the one you person?" Thus to him having said, "Well, indeed it is true. Somewhere

i'tiwanan e'latenak̯k̑äp̑a homan t̑o'waconan a'k̯ä tem t̑a

the middle having come upon my seed with yet also

e'lek̯an·a. a'k̑äp k̯ä'-eto·we kwa t̑o'waconan·e k̑okcak̯ä

shall be well. Because —— not seed good with

a·'ho' a·'team·e. k̯ä'wawulaw a'k̯ä te''tci. hom t̑o'waconan·e

persons are (not). Wild grasses with only. My seed (of corn)

no·''anoti·we." le'kwap a·'tci il-a·'k̯ä. k̯ä-eto·we t̑i'nakwin

bean clans." Thus having said the two with he went. —— staying place

a·'te'tcinan i't̑inak̯äp i'sk̑on a'ntehkunak̯ä. "si a'ma' ko'plea

arriving having sat down there he questioned him. "Now come on how

t̑om a'k̯ä e'lek̯än·a?" "ma luk̯ä hom t̑o'waconan łu'ptsikwa,"

you with shall be well?" "Well this my seed of corn yellow,"

le''kwanan łu'ptsikwa mi''le u'nak̯äk̯ä. "si yam ho''i hom

thus saying yellow ear of corn he showed. "Now your person to me

u'tsi" le''kwap wi'hat̑san u'k̯ä. wi'hat̑san u'tsip i'mat kohoł

give," thus having said baby he gave. Baby having given apparently some thing

a'lewuk̯ä. we'tik̯ä. ko·'wi t̑e'wap a'cek̯ä. a'cep

he did to her. She became sick. A little time she died. Having died

le'skwa "si p̑a'lona·we. ak̑oknan p̑a'lo·k̯ä. a·'witen t̑ewap

thus he says "Now bury her." Digging a hole he buried her. Four days past

a·'tcia le'sanikwak̯ä "a'ma si tun-te'hace. yam u'kwai'ik̯ä

to the two thus to them he said, "Come on, now go see her. Their coming out

te'kwin a·tc a·'k̯ä. a·'tci te''tcip t̑sa'na so'pi'lak̯e'a. a·tci

place to the two went. The two having arrived the little one sand is scooping up. The two

te''tcip ci'kwitco'ya k̯e'tsana. a·tc u'nan a·tc a·'k̯ä a·'tci

having arrived she smiles she is happy. The two seeing the two went. The two

t̑i'nankwin te''tcinan "he· hi'to! honkwat t̑on a'k̯ä e'letun'ona

where they were staying arriving "Listen! Perhaps you with to be well the one

tem ho''i kwa he'kw a'cenamk̯ä." "ma łe'sna te'k̑än·a a'tcia

yet person not really did not die." "Well thus it shall be," to the two

le'anikwak̯ä.

thus to them he said.

i'sk̑on yam e'leteli·we i·'łean i'yantetcik̯änan k̯äł a·'wa·k̯ä.

There their sacred things picking up one another reaching around hither they went.

k̯a·k̑äna tci'mik̯äk̯a a'wicok̯aia le'anak̑änankwi a·'wik̯ä.

Sometime being the first beginning moss spring thus where it is called they came.

i'sk̑on yam e'leteli·we wo'ta-pi'lana isk̑on i·'t̑inak̯ä. a·'witen

There their sacred things putting down setting in a row there they sat down. Four

t̂ewana le'anak̂äp a·'witen te'pikwai'ina· i'sk̂on a·'tci
days thus it being said four years there the two

wɔ'k̂ocok̯ä. a·'tci a'wan a'wicokti'we a·'wan a'wiconmito·we
washed them. The two their moss tails their moss horns

le· a·'tci wɔ'tuk̯ä. "tcukwe·' le'nap t̂on a·'tcikwanak̂än·a."
all the two took away. "Behold. thus being you sweet shall be."

i'sk̂on a·'teak̯ä—.
There they stayed.

a·wan t̂ewanan i'te'tcap k̯äł a·wak̯ä. yam e'leteli·we
Their time used up hither they went. Their sacred things

łean i'yante'tcik̂äna itiwan·a te'cuna k̯äłhokw a·'wona'k̯ä.
carrying one another reaching around the middle seeking off yonder roads went.

k̯ä·k̯ä tcimik̂ak̯ä a'wełuyan k̂aiakwi a·'wik̯ä. isk̂on
Sometime the first beginning cumulus cloud spring to they came. There

yam e'leteli·we wɔ'·ta-pi'lana i·'tinan ła'k̂ikna i'sk̂on
their sacred things putting down setting in a row sitting down staying quietly there

a·'witen t̂e'wana·we i·'t̂inak̯ä. a·'witen t̂e'wana·we le''kwap
four days they sat down. Four days thus saying

a·'witen t̂e'pikwai'ina·. i'sk̂on i·'tinak̯ä. i'sk̂ɔ·n yam
four years. There they sat down. There their

t̂e'wanan pi''lanapk̯ä. k̂ä-etowe a·'wan a·'witen t̂e'ƚina·we
time they told off. ——— their four nights

a·'witen yä'to·we k̂ä't̂sana ƚi'ton-t̂e'łakwi a·wan t̂e'wanan
four days fine rain rain touching their time

t̂e'wak̯ä. łe'-eto·we mu'-eto·we a·wan t̂ewana yo·'ap̂a
time passed. ——— ——— their days becoming

a·'wite yäto·we a·'witen t̂e'ƚina·we u'pina t̂e'wak̯ä. a·'wan
four days four nights snow time passed. Their

t̂e'wanan i'te'tcap̂a i'sk̂on a·'teak̯ä.
time used up there they stayed

a·'wan t̂e'wanan i'te'tcap łu'walemak̯ä. yam e'leteli·we
Their time used up they arose. Their sacred things

łean i'yante'tcik̂äna kałok[u] a·'wona'k̯ä. k̯ä·'k̂ä
carrying one another reaching around off yonder roads went. Sometime

tci'mik̂ak̯ä ci'pololon k̂aia le'anak̂änkwi o'neał i·'k̂änapk̯ä.
first beginning mist spring thus called to road they brought.

i'sk̂on i·'t̂inan ła'k̂ikna yam e'leteli·we wo'ta-pi'lana
There sitting down staying quietly their sacred things putting down setting in a row

i''t̂inan ła'k̂ikna. i'sk̂on i'yan t̂e'wanan pi''lanapk̯ä. i'yan
sitting down staying quietly. There one another time they counted up. For one another

k̂ä'cimak̯ä u'lohn u'natinapk̯ä k̂ä'-eto·w a·wa a·'witen
waters with world they beheld ——— their four

yä'to·we a·'witen t̂e'ƚina·we k̂ä'łana ƚi'ton-t̂e'łakwi a·'wan
days four nights heavy rain rain touching their

t̂e'wanan te'ak̯ä. a·'wan t̂e'wanan i'te'tcap̂a łe'-etowe
time was. Their time used up ———

mu'-eton·e a·'wan t̂e'wanan yo·'ap̂a a·'wite yä'to·we
——— their time becoming four days

a·'witen t̂e'ƚi'na·we u'pinan-t̂e'łakwi a·'wan u'lohnan te'ak̮ä.
four nights snow touching their world was.

a·'wan t̂e'wanan i'te'tcap̂a i'sk̂ɔn a·'teak̮ä.
Their time used up there they stayed.

a·'wan t̂e'm·ła t̂e'wak̮ä tea'ana yam e'leteli·we łean
Their all time passed when it was their sacred things carrying

i'yante'tcik̂äna k̮äłhok^u a·'wona'k̮ä. a·'wona'k̮ä. t̂am-e'lan
one another reaching around hither roads went. Roads went. Tree standing

k̮ai'akwi a·'wik̮ä. i'sk̂ɔn i't̂inan łak̂ikna yam e'leteli·we
spring to they came. There sitting down staying quietly their sacred things

wɔ'ta-api'lana i·'t̂inan łak̂ik̮ä. i'sk̂ɔn i'yan t̂ewanan unatik̂äk̮ä.
putting down setting in a row sitting down they stayed quietly There one another time made see.

k̮ä'-eto·w a·'wan t̂e'wanana a·'wite yä'to·we a·'witen
——— their time four days four

t̂e'ƚina·we k̂ät̂sana ƚiton-t̂ełakwi a·'wan t̂ewanan a·'k̮ä.
nights fine rain rain touching their time went.

a·'wan t̂e'wanan i'te'tcap̂a łe'-eton·e mu'-eto·we a·'wan
Their time used up ——— ——— their

t̂ewanan yo·'ap̂a a·'wite yäto·we a·'witen t̂e'ƚina·we u'pinan-
time becoming four days four nights snow

t̂e'łakwi a·'wan u'lohnan te'ak̮ä. a·'wan t̂e'wanan i'te'tcap̂a
touching their world. was. Their time used up

i'skɔn a·'teak̮ä—.
there they stayed.

a·'wan t̂e'm·ła t̂e'wana te'a'ana yam e'leteliwe łean
Their all time when it was their sacred things carrying

i'yante'tcik̂äna i'sk̂ɔn ƚu'walemaknan k̮ä'ł a·'wa·k̮ä. k̮ä·k̂ä
one another reaching around there arising hither they came. Sometime

tci'mik̮äk̮ä upuilimakwi a·'wik̮ä. i'sk̂ɔn a·'winan yam
First beginning ——— to they came. There coming their

e'leteli·we wɔ'ta-pi'lanan i't̂inan ła'k̂iknan i'sk̂ɔn i'yat̂su-
sacred things putting down setting in a row sitting down staying quietly there one another

manapk̮'ä. i'sk̂ɔn yam t̂o'waconan t̂e·m·ła i't̂sumanapk̮ä.
they contested. There their seed of corn all they planted.

i'sk̂ɔn i'yan k̮ä'cimak̮ä i'yan t̂e'wanan u'natina'k̮ä. k̮ä'-
There one another waters with one another time was beheld. ———

eto·w a·'wa a·'witen yä'to·we k̮ä'łana ƚi'ton-t̂ełakwi
——— their four days heavy rain rain touching

i'sk̂ɔn a·'wan a·'t̂owa ho'i ya·'k̂änapk̮ä. kwaƚi·'tam·e a·'p̂ali.
there their corn plants persons became finished. There was no rain; they were bitter

i'sk̂ɔn a·'tci le'skwak̮ä "si tcu'wakon tse''makwinak̮ä
There the two thus said, "Now, who the one thoughts with

ho''na·wan a·'t̂owa yä'litina?" a·'tci le''kwana ko'ko k̂wi'n·e
our corn plants will become palatable?" The two thus saying crow black

6066°—32——37

a'ntecematik̯ä. luk̂ɔn i'na a·'wan a·'t̂owa a·'cukłip̂a
they summoned. This one coming their corn plants pecking

a·'wisikwatik̯ä. a·'wisikwatip̂a s'u'hson a'k̯ä yo'nawilap a·'teak̯ä.
they became good to eat. Having become good to eat now that one with becoming with them they lived.

i'sk̂ɔn a·'wan t̂e'wanan i·'te'tcap i'sk̂ɔn łu'walemak̯ä.
There their time used up. There they arose.

yam e'leteliwe i'yante'tcik̯äna k̯ał a·wa·k̯ä. k̯ä·k̯ä tci'-
Their sacred things one another reaching around hither they went. Sometime first

mik̯äk̯ä k̯e'at̂'inakwi a·'wik̯ä. i'sk̂ɔn yam e'leteliwe
beginning cornstalk sitting to they came. There their sacred things

wɔ'ta-pi'lak̯äna i'sk̂ɔn a·'witen t̂e'wanan i·'tinak̯ä. a·'witen
putting down setting in a row there four days they sat down. Four

t̂e'wana le''kwap a·'witen t̂e'pikwai'ina. i'sk̂ɔn yam t̂o'waconan
days thus said four years. There their seed of corn

t̂e'mła i·t̂sumanapk̯ä. i'sk̂ɔn i'yan k̯ä'cim a'k̯ä i'yan
all they planted. There one another waters with one another

t̂e'wanan u'natina'k̯ä. .k̯ä'-eto·w a·'wite yä'to·we a·'witen
time was beheld. ——— four days four

t̂e'łina·we k̯ä'łana łi'ton-t̂e'łakwi łe'-eto·we mu'-eto·we a·'wite
nights heavy rain rain touching ——— ——— four

yä'to·we a·'witen t̂e'łina·we u'pinan-t̂e'łakwi a·'wan u'lohnan
days four nights snow touching their world

te'ak̯ä. a·'wan t̂e'wanan i'te'tcik̯ä. a·'wan a·'t̂owa ho'i-ya·'-
was. Their time was used up. Their corn plants persons

k̯änapk̯ä. ho'i-ya·'k̯äna·wap a·'ło'o. i'sk̂ɔn a·'tci le'skwanan
were finished. persons being finished they were hard. There the two thus saying,

"si tcu'wap tse''makwin a'k̯ä ho''na·wan a·'t̂owa a·'wicak̯ä-
"Now who thoughts with our corn plants shall become

tin·a?" "ma la'cip̂owa." a·'tci le'kwanan a·'tci mu'hukw
soft?" "Well, soft feather bundle." the two thus saying the two owl

a'ntecematik̯ä. mu'hukw i'k̯ä. i'nan a·'wan a·'t̂owa
summoned. Owl came. Coming their corn plants

a·'cukłip̂a a·wicak̯atik̯ä.
pecking they became soft.

i'sk̯ɔn łu'walemakunti'ahna a·'tci le'skwak̯ä "si ama lał
There about to arise the two thus said, "Now come on there

hon t̂o'wa ci'wan a'cuwak̯äce. a·'tci le'kwanan a·'tc a·k̯ä.
we corn priest let us speak with." The two thus saying the two went.

a·'tci t̂o'wa ci'wan an i'nkwin te'tcinan "ko'na t̂on t̂e'wanan
The two corn priest his staying place arriving "How you time

a·'teaiye." "k̯e'tsanici hon t̂e'wanan a·'teakwi ho'na t̂on a·'wona-
are living?" "Happily we time living when us you roads

e'latek̯ä a·'tci i·'mu." a·'tci i·'muk̯ä. i'sk̂ɔn i'yantehkunanapk̯ä.
have passed. Both sit down." The two sat down. There one another they questioned.

"ma a·'tci p̂ene. hi'nik kwa'tik p̂e'nan te'yułanam·e p̂enan
"Well both speak out. I think some-kind word not too long word

te'k̯än.a. t̂e'wuna' u'hsona hom t̂on yu'ya·k̯äp̂a uhs
will be. Finally that me you making know that

ai'yu'ya·na ho' t̑e'wana te'ak̯an·a." "ma i·namiłte. t̑e'wan
knowing I time shall live." "Well without doubt it is true. To-morrow

yä'ton·e hon łu'wale'kona li·łno hon i'tiwanan te'cun a·ne.
day we standing the ones right here we the middle seeking go.

kwa hoł hon i'tiwanan e'latena'ma ho'na·wan tca'we a·'wok̯
Not anywhere we the middle do not come upon. Our children, women

a·'te'ona a·'yu'te'tcik̯ä. a·'k̑oye'a. le'sna te''onak̯ä t̑om hon
beings have gotten tired. They are crying. Thus being because of you we

o'na-e'latek̯ä. t̑ewa yä'ton t̑om tcawatci t̑un e'hkwik̯än·a.
road have passed. To-morrow day your children both looking shall go ahead.

ho'nkwat hoł a·'tci i'tiwanan e'latep̑a i'sk̑on ho'na·wan
Perhaps somewhere the two the middle coming upon there our

a·'tatcu ho''na·wan a·'tsita k̯ä-eto·we tcu'-eto·we mu'-eto·we
fathers our mothers ——— ——— ———

łe'-eto·we le· ti'k̯ä a·'ciwan·i yu'łak̯itip̑a ho''na·wan tca'we
——— all society priests coming to rest our children

yu''te'tcinana·wa. ak̯äp son i'tiwanan e'laten-i·'natik̯äk̯ä."
shall rest. Because now we the middle to come upon have failed.

"haiyi'. ma honkwa'. yu'he·to p̑enan a'k̯ä ho'na t̑on a·'wona-
"Haiyi! Well perhaps. Plain word with us you roads

e'latek̯ä. ma te'nat le'sna te'k̑än·a." le'kwap s'a·tc a·'k̯ä.
have passed. Well, however thus it shall be." Thus having said now the two went.

t̑e'wap ca'mli łu'walemakuntiahnan mi'le yaminakna t̑a
Next day early being about to arise ear of corn being broken and

mo'le wo'tik̯ä. t̑o'wa ci'wan·i a·tci yelak̯ä. a·tci le'skwak̯ä
egg he put down. Corn priest(s) both stood up. The two said,

"si hom tca·'we ha'me li·wan a'lahoankwin ta'hna t̑on
"Now my children some this way to the south direction you

a·'wa·nuwa. lu'k̯ä t̑on wo'tihna·wa." le''tikwap̑a mi'l-
shall go. This you shall take." Thus saying ear of corn

am· mi'ton·e lał mu'la mo'le. lał mi'l an co'walin·e lał
its horn and then macaw egg. Then ear its butt and then

k̑wa'laci mo'le k̯äłem a·'wa·tun'ona wo'tihnapk̯ä. lał alaho-
raven egg hither to come the ones they took. Then south

ankwin a·'wa·tun'ona mi'l am miton tap mu'la mo'le.
to to go the ones ear its horn and macaw egg.

"si hom tca'we li·'wan a'lahoankwin ta'hna t̑on a·'wa·nuwa.
"Now my children this way south to direction you shall go.

ten k̯äk̯i hoł hon i'tiwana e'latenapk̯ä tea k̯ä·k̑omastapte
Yet sometime somewhere we the middle have come upon when after a long time even

hon i'yona-e'latena·wa." le'tikwanan k̯äł a·'wa·k̯ä.
we one another's roads shall pass." Thus saying hither they went.

Ko'łuwalawatun te'kwin a·'wik̯ä. e''lactok̯ yu''te'tcip am
Katcina village to be place to they came. Girl getting tired her

pa'pa le'skwak̯a, "a'ma wan i·mu. ho' t̑una ye·'makut'u.
elder brother thus said, "Come on, wait, sit down. I looking let me climb up.

ko′’kona hon a·′wa·tun te′kwin te′linak̭än·a.” le’kwap
How it is we about to go place it shall appear.” Thus saying

an ik̭in i·mup am pa′pa te′pok̭äłakwi ye·′mak̭ä. ye·′maknan
his younger sister sitting down her elder brother hill to climbed up. Climbing up

k̭ä′łem t̑un-e′la·yäla’k̭ä. “e·ha! ho′nkwa le′’em·i hon a·′wa·tun
hither looking standing he was above. “Eha! Perhaps on this side we about to go

te′kwi. ho′nkwa le’ te′lin·a. le’kwanan p̑a′ni·k̭ä. p̑a′niup
place. Perhaps thus it appears.” Thus saying he descended. Descending

ta·′htcic an i′k̭ina sɔ′kwai′’ik̭änan yä′liułanan yu’te’tcik̭äp̑an
meanwhile his younger sister sand scooping cut lying down on it being tired

a′lap̑a p̑i′’nan i′nan an cu′lihte k̭e′atop i′te·h k̭e′atop
sleeping wind coming her grass apron rising blew rising

le’nat a′co tcu′alap p̑a′ni·nan u′natik̭änan ko′kwiyutceti-
thus vulva lying asleep he descending beholding feeling desire

k̭änan yam i′k̭ina ye·′maknan yam i′kin co′hap yam
his sister climbing on his younger sister having intercourse his

i′k̭in o′kwinan “hiyaha′” le′’kwan’iyahnan “wa′tsela wa′tsela”
younger sister waking “Hiyaha” thus about to say “Watsela watsela,” (she said)

am pa′pa “ha hwai′” le’kwanan i′muna p̑i′laknan sa′kwin
Her elder brother “Hahwai!” thus saying sitting arising foot

a′k̭ä t̑omt t̑si′na’up k̭ä′piyäłan yo·′k̭ä. a·tci p̑en a′l·u’ya.
with just drawing river course became. The two speaking go about.

am pa′pa ko·′yemcinama p̑e′yep an i′k̭ina ko′mok̭ätsik̭
Her elder brother koyemci like speaking his younger sister komokatsik̭

p̑e′yep a·′ho’ a·wi·k̭ä.
speaking people came.

“he he. ya′sek ho′’na·wan tcawa·tci t̑op a·ho′’i
“He he alas our children both other persons

yo·′k̭ä.” le′’tikwap am pa′pa p̑e′nan “lał a·′wiwahi’ ten
became.” Thus saying her elder brother speaking, “There cross over however

e′lek̭än·ai′.” le′’kwap a·′te’tcinan u′kwatok̭ä. k̭ä′winana
it will be well,” thus saying they arriving they entered river in

u′kwatop a·′wan a·′t̑sana ha′me mi′k̭aiał a·′wiap ha′me
having entered their children some water snakes coming, others

e′to·w a·′wi·ap ha′me tak̭ a·′wi·ap ha′me te′wac a·′wiap
turtles becoming, others frogs coming, others lizzards coming,

yam a·′tsita a·′wuteclena·wap a·′k̭onan a·′yaknacna·wap
their mothers having bitten crying out dropping them

k̭ä′wiankwin u′kwatelap t̑opak̭än a·′łaci te’tci i′t̑inan-
river into entering other side old people only sitting down

yälak̭äp. ho’ i′tiwihak̭ip a·tci le′skwanan “si wan yu′luk̭iti.
above people divided in half the two thus saying, “Now, wait stay here.”

a·′tci le′’kwap ha′me yu′łak̭itip. a·′tci le′skwak̭ä si t̑on
The two thus saying, some waiting quietly, the two thus said, “Now you

u′kwatop t̑o′’na·wan tca′we kwa′hoł wɔ·′weat̑an a·′wiyan·a.
having entered your children some creatures dangerous will become.

t̂o' a·'wuteclana·wap̂a k̂onan·te eł i'yakna'ma. t̂o'p̂ak̭ä
You having bitten crying out although don't drop them. Other side

t̂on u'kwai'ip t̂o''na·wan tca'we yam ko'n ho'i te'akona
you coming out your children their kind person which they were

kwa a·'wiyo·na'map̂a tci'mi t̂on kwi'hokwaiina'wa." le'a·wanti-
not not becoming then first you will throw in." Thus to them

kwap u'kwatełk̭ä. a·'wan tca'we t̂op̂ a·'ho' a·wiyo·na' a·'wu-
saying they went in one by one. Their children other persons becoming having

teclana·wap̂a a·'k̂onan·te a·'wiwa'hik̭ä. a·'wan tca'we i'kwałt
bitten them crying out although they crossed over. Their children back

yam ko'n ho''i te'akona a·'ho' a·'wiyo·ap̂a. "hanah·a·' honkwa'
their kind person that they were persons becoming. "Hanaa! Perhaps!

le'nap e'lek̭anaŋ·k̭ä." le'tikwana' i'sk̂ɔn t̂em·ł a·wiwa'hik̭ä.
thus it would have been well." Thus saying there all were on the other side.

i'sk̂ɔn yam e'leteli·we wɔ'ta-pi'lak̭äna i·'t̂inan ła'k̭ik̭ä.
There their sacred things putting down setting in a row sitting down stayed quietly.

i·'t̂inan ła'k̭ikna a·'witen t̂e'wana·we le''kwap a·'witen
Sitting down staying quietly four days thus saying four

te'pikwai'ina i·'t̂inak̭ä. isk̂on kona t̂e'łina·we t̂omt
years they stayed. There each night just

te'na·we'anak̭ä e'lute a·'teaiye. a·'wan t̂em·ła t̂e'wap a·'tci
singing loud with joyfully they lived. Their all time passed the two

le'skwanan "si a'ma lał hon ne''we·'kwe a'cuwak̭äce."
thus saying, "Now come on there we Ne'we·kwe let us speak to."

le'' a·tc i'kwana a·'tci ne''we·kwe t̂inankwin a·k̭ä. a·'tci
Thus the two saying the two Ne'we kwe staying where they went. The two

te''tcinan "ko' t̂on t̂e'wanan a·'teaiye." "k̭e'tsanici. t̂onc i·'ya.
arriving, "How you time are living?" "Happily you come?

i·'t̂inak̭ä." a·tci i·'mup i'sk̂ɔn a·tci a'ntehkunak̭ä. "si ma a·tci
Be seated." The two sitting down there the two he questioned. "Well now both

p̂e'ne. hi'nik kwatikoł p̂enan te'yułanam·e p̂e'nan te'k̭än·a.
speak out. I think some kind word not too long work will be.

t̂e'wuna' u'hson hom t̂on yu''ya·k̭äp̂a uhs ai·'yu'ya·na ho'
Finally that me you making know that knowing I

t̂e'wanan te'ak̭äna. ma i·nami'łte. t̂e'wan yä'ton hon łu'wal-
time shall live." "Well, indeed it is true. To-morrow day we shall

akun·a hon a·'tatc i'lap̂ona hon a·'tsit i'lapona k̭a'-eto·we
arise we fathers the ones (we) have we mothers the ones (we) have ———

tcu'-eto·we mu'-eto·we łe'-eto·we le· ti·'k̭ä a·'ciwan'i li·ł
——— ——— ——— all society priests here

i'tiwanan te'cuna a·'wa·ne. kwa hoł i'tiwanan e'latena'ma
the middle seeking go. Not anywhere the Middle not coming upon

ho''na tca'we a·'wok̭' a·'te'ona a·'yu'te'tci·k̭ä a·'k̂oye k̭e·si.
our children women beings are tired they cry now.

lesna te''onak̭ä t̂o'na hon o'na-e'latek̭ä. t̂e'wan yäton·e t̂on
Thus being because of you we road have passed. To-morrow day you

t̂un e'hkwik̯än·a. honkwat hoł t̂on i'tiwan·a e'latep̂a i'sk̂on
looking shall go ahead. Perhaps somewhere you the middle coming upon there

ho''na·wan tca'we yu''te'tcinahna·wa." a·'tci le'kwap "hana'
our children shall rest." The two thus saying, "Hana'

t̂omte kwa hon yai'yu'ya·nam·e. kwa'tikoł a'k̯ä hoł hon
just not we have no knowledge. Somehow because of somewhere we

te'nin a'cap̂a kwa e'letun te'am·e." a·tcia le''kwap̂a "ma t̂a
wrong doing not to be well it is not." To the two thus saying, "Well and

te'ałati t̂a tenas t̂o''na hon a'kcihk̯ä." a·'tci le''kwap "ma
no matter. And however you we have chosen." The two thus saying "Well

honkwa'ati." "e· so a·ne." "łu''no." a·tci kwai''ik̯ä.
perhaps it is so." "Yes; I go." "Go ahead." The two went out.

a·'te'tcinan "si ama lał hon yam tca'we a·'wacuwak̂äce."
Arriving, "Now come on there we our children let us speak to."

le''kwanan s'a·tc a·'k̯ä. k̂änakwin kwa'top ko'ko t̂i'mp̂ot̂iye.
thus saying now the two went. lake into entering katcinas staying it is full.

"si wan. yu'łak̂äti. ho''na·wan a·'tatcu a·tc i·'k̯ä." le''tikwap
"Now wait. Stay quiet! our fathers both have come," thus saying

ko'ko łu'walan-la'nik̯ä. łu'walan-la'nip a·tcia lesanikwa "si
katcinas suddenly stood still. Suddenly standing still to the two thus to them he said, "Now

ho''na·wan a·'tatc a·'tci lak̯iman·te ho''na t̂on a·'wona-
our fathers two now even us you roads

elatek̯ä. ime' kwatikoł p̂enan teyułanam·e p̂e'nan te'ak̂än·a.
have passed. I think some kind word not too long word will be.

u'hson ho''na t̂on a·'yu'ya·k̂äp̂a uhs ai'yu'ya·na hon
That us you making know, that knowing we

t̂e'wanan a·'tek̂än·a" le'kwap̂a "ma i·'namiłte. t̂e'wan yä'ton·e
time shall live." thus saying, "Well indeed it is true. Tomorrow day

hons łu'walemakun·a a'k̯ä to''na hon a·'wacuwak̯än i'ya."
we now shall arise, therefore you we to speak with come.'

"ma honkwa'ati. t̂on k̂e'tsanic a·'wa·t'u. ho''na·wan
"Well, perhaps it is so. You happily may (you) go. Our

a·'łacinawona t̂on ya'tinep̂a eł i'tse'menamt'u. kwa hon
parents the ones you telling them, 'Don't worry.' Not we

a·'yałakwai'namk̯a. i'camałti te'atunon a'k̯ä hon i·'t̂inak̯ä.
were not destroyed. Forever to stay the one because of we stopped.

t̂omt to'pnint a'ntewak̯ä t̂ehw e'tciye. le'sna te'onak̯ä
Just only once passing the night space remains. Thus being because of

le'witea hon i·'t̂inak̯ä. ho'n u'lohnan ła'cana k̂ä'cim e'tcihana
nearby we stopped. Our world getting old, waters giving out

t̂o'waconan e'tcihana kwa tcu'wa t̂on yam tci'mik̂äk̯ätekwi
seeds giving out not anyone you your first beginning place

te''tcicukwa. hoł k̂ä'cim e'tcihana t̂o'waconan e'tcihana
could not reach. Some time waters giving out seeds giving out

t̂on te'lik̯inan i'k̂äna·wa. le'hoł yam tci'mik̂äk̯ä te'kwi hon
you prayer stick shall send. Yonder our first beginning place we

a'ḵa a'cuwa-t̂ełakunakna·wa a'ḵä kwa ḵäcim i·natinam·e
with it speaking shall be bent over therefore not waters without fail

te'ḵän·a. le'na te'atunonaḵä le'witea hon i·'t̂inan-łaḵiḵä."
shall be. Thus being the one because of nearby we stopping stay quietly."

a·tcia le'anaḵäp "ma honkwa'ati." "e·. hom ta'tcona hom
To the two thus having said, "Well perhaps it is so." "Yes. My father the one my

tsi'tona t̂o' a'tinap̂a eł tse''menamtʻu. kwa hon a·'yała-
mother the one you telling don't worry. Not we are not

kwai'ina'ma." le''tikwanan yam a·'łacinan a·'wan t̂sume-
destroyed." Thus saying their parents to them strong

p̂ena·w a·'ḵänapḵä. "son a·'ne ho'n tca'we. ḵetsanici t̂on
words they sent. "Now we go, our children. Happily you

t̂e'wanan a·'teatʻu." "le'snap̂a le'santik t̂on a·wa·tʻu." a·tcia
time may (you) live." "Thus just the same you may (you) go." To the two

le''anaḵäp a·tc kwai''iḵä. a·'tci te''tcinan a·'tci ya'tineḵä.
thus having spoken the two went out. The two arriving the two told them.

"si ho''na tca'we li·ł t̂o''na·wan tcaw i·'t̂inaḵä. a·'yałakwai'ḵä
"Now our children here your children stay. They have been destroyed

t̂on le''tikwap̂a eł·a'. a·'wots a·'te'ona a·'tsawaḵ a·'ho'
you thus saying No! Men beings youths persons

a·'ya·na a·'woḵ a·'te'ona e'wactoḵ a·'ho' a·'ya·na i'ḵetsana
completing women beings maidens persons completing happy

e'lute a·'teaiye. to''na·wan ts'ume p̂ena· a·wi·ḵäna·we. eł
joyously they live. To you strong words they send. Don't

t̂on i'tse'menamtʻu" le'a·wanaḵäp "haiyi'. honkwa."
you worry," thus to them saying, "Haiyi! Perhaps."

s'a·'want̂ewaḵä. t̂e'wap ca'mli łu'walemaḵä. yam e'leteli·we
So they passed the night. Next day early they arose. their sacred things

łe'an i'yante'tciḵäna ḵał a·wa·ḵä. ha'nłipinḵakwin a·'wi'ḵä.
carrying one another reaching around hither they went. ——— ——— they came.

ta·'htcic ne'we·kw a·tci a·tci t̂un-e'hkwiye. a''ḵälikwin a·tc i'yap
Meanwhile Ne'we kwe both the two looking were ahead. Rock in water to they coming

e'wactoḵ a·'tci e'he· k̂o'cap. a·'tci ai'naḵä. a·tci ai'nap
girls two blanket dresses washing. Them they killed. Them having killed

a·'tci mo't̂sihḵäp a·'tci a'nk̂ohaḵä. a·'tci ank̂ohap a·tci
them having scalped the two they found out. Them having found out the two

yam ḵäpin ho'iwaḵä a·'tci ci'pololon i'p̂ehana la·k ḵä'-
their raw person because of the two mist wrapping themselves there ———

eto·we t̂i'nakwin a·'tci te''tciḵä. "hana. uhkwahtci'. hon
——— staying where the two arrived. "Alas! So now indeed! we

t̂eninacḵä." le'kwap i·nak̂wan t̂ewana yo·'ḵä. i'sk̂on yam
wrong have done." Thus having said enemy his time became. There their

ḵä'cima iyan t̂e'wanan u'natiḵä. ḵä-'eto·w a·wa a·'wite
water one another's time beheld. ——— their four

yä'to·we a·'witen t̂e'łina·we k̯äłana łi'to t̂e'wak̯ä. i'sk̂ɔn
days, four nights heavy rain rain time passed. There

a'mekuliya hoł k̯ä'we p̂a'ni·una u'mo ye·'läna a'haiyut
rock cave somewhere water falling foam standing ———

a·'tci ye'tsak̯äk̯äk̯ä. a·'tci k̯ä-eto·w t̂i'nakwin i'k̯ä.
the two appeared. The two ——— staying where they came.

ta·'htcic i'sk̂ɔn a·'witen t̂e'hulikwi u'nasinte u'hep̂o'lolo
Meanwhile there four inner place in whirlwind wrapped-in-wool

k̯ailuh tsa'wak̯i ha'łtuŋkä ɔ·'loma cu'tuiŋk̯ä t̂e'k̂ohanakwi
youth ——— ——— ——— daylight into

i·'t̂inakna kwai''ina. i'sk̂ɔn co'mato te'na·pi'la'uwuk̯ä.
sitting down coming out. There spiral song sequence he taught them.

i'snak̂ɔnte su'sk̯i łat-a'l·up̂a te'pehan u'kna'k̯ä. i'sk̂ɔn
Right there coyote hunting went about pottery drum was given to him. There

co'matok̯äna'k̯ä.
the spiral dance was danced.

le'snahoł a·'teap a·'tci le'skwak̯ä "si hom su'we i'tiwana-
Thus sometime being the two thus said: "Now me younger brothers, the Middle

kwi kwas a'nt̂ewanam·e t̂e'hwaiye. yam tca'we le· we·ma·
to not now not over night is distant. Our children this many beast

a·'ciwan·i kwa'hoł wɔ·w a·'latap̂a hon ha'p̂ok̯än·a lu'k̯ä
priests some kind creatures winged we shall assemble this

t̂e'łinan·e." a'tc a·'k̯ä la·k[u] co'mk̯äkwekwi a·tc te''tcik̯ä.
night." The two went Yonder ——— they arrived.

i'sk̂ɔn a·'tci we'ma· t̂e'm·ła ha'p̂ok̯äk̯ä. ho'ktitaca ai'nce
There the two beasts all assembled. Mountain lion bear

yu'nawik̂o te'pi to'naci su'sk̯i ła'nak̂o ya'ci k̯ä'k̯äli pi'pi
wolf wildcat badger coyote fox squirrel eagle buzzard

co'k̯äpiso a'neława cu'tsina k̂wa'laci muhukwi le'sna t̂emł
——— hawk bald headed eagle raven owl thus all

a·tc ha'p̂ok̯äk̯ä. ta·'htcic ya'ci kwa'hoł wo·w a·'latap̂a
the two assembled. Meanwhile squirrel some creatures winged

a'kciye. ta·'htcic muhukwi we'ma·w i'nkwin a'kciye.
is with. Meanwhile owl beasts where they stay is with.

"si hom tca'we yam yäto'k̯ä ta'tcu an t̂e'k̂ohanan·e t̂on
"Now my children your sun father his daylight you

i'cematin·a· ho'k̯antikoł i'k̂olowate yä'tokwai'ip̂a yam yä·'tok̯ä
will scramble. On whichever side the ball is hidden when the sun rises your sun

ta'tcu an t̂e'k̂ohanan·e t̂on o'k̯äna·wa." a·'tci le'kwap "ma
father his daylight you will win." The two thus having said "Well

ho'nkwa'ati'" i'sk̂ɔn s'a·tc a·nap i'teh-p̂iyahk̯ä. we'ma·
perhaps it is so." There now the two having gone they threw it down. Beasts

a·'wan la'nik̯ä. i'k̂olonapk̯ä. i'k̂olok̯'äp kwa'hoł wɔ·w a·'latap̂a
theirs it fell. They hide the ball. They hiding the ball something creatures winged

a·'weletcełk̯ä. kwa t̂a'pna·wam·e. a·'wite te'tc a'kcicna'k̯ä. kwa
came one by one. Not they did (not) take it. Four only it was withdrawn. Not

t̂a′pna·wam·e le′snate t̂e′k̂ohatin’ihap ta·htcic yä′ci a′klan a′la-
they did (not) take it. Thus even daylight about to come meanwhile squirrel by the fire lying

pi′łaiye. le′sna hoł a·′weletco kwa t̂a′pna·wam·e. k̭ä′k̭äli le′s-
was by the fireplace. Thus somewhere they came one by one not they did (not) take it. Eagle thus

kwanan "lakw a′la-pi′łan a·t‘u." pi′pi e′lemaknan a·tci te′′tcinan
saying "Over there lying by the fire the one go!" Buzzard rising the two arriving

le′sanikwak̭ä "t̂oc ala?" "eł·a. kwa ho’ a′łna’ma." "ticomaha′.
thus to him said, "Do you sleep?" "No. Not I do (not) sleep." "Alas!

ko’ma t̂o’ a·t‘u." le’kwap "ana′ kwa ho’ a·′cukwa." le′’kwap
Very well you go!" thus having said "Oh dear, not I won't go." Thus having said

te′’tcinan "kwahe kwa a′ntecemana’ma." le′’kwap tcu′watikoł
arriving "Not at all not he does not wish to." Thus having said Someone

a·′k̭ä. t̂a kwa t̂a′pna’ma. k̭e·′si t̂e′k̂ohatin’iha. "lakw
went Again not he did (not) take it. Now daylight is about to come. "Over there.

a′la-piłan a·′t‘u." le′tikwap t̂a pip a·′k̭ä. "ti′comaha′.
lying by the fire go!" Thus having said again buzzard went. "Alas!

tsa′wak̭i t̂o’ a·′t‘u." "ana′ kwa ho’ yu′’aniktam·e" le′’kwap
Young man you go!" "Oh dear, not I do not feel like it." thus having said

t̂a a·′k̭ä. "kwa a′ntecemana’ma." le′’kwap t̂a tcu′watikoł
again he went. "Not he does not want to." Thus having said again someone

a·′k̭ä. t̂a kwa t̂a′pnamk̭ä. k̭e·′si t̂e′k̂ohatin’iha. an to′sito
went. Again not he did (not) take it. Now daylight was about to come To him spider

le′skwanan "lak̭ i·′yap t̂o se′waht‘u." le′’kwap t̂a le′stikwak̭ä
thus saying "Now coming you consent." Thus having said again thus saying

"lakw a′lap-piłon a·′t‘u." le′’tikwup t̂a tcu′watikoł a·′k̭ä.
"Over there lying by the fire the one go." Thus having said again someone went.

te′’tcinan le′sanikwak̭ä "ti′coma tsa′wak̭i! t̂o’ a·′t‘u." "ma
Arriving thus to him he said, "alas young man! you go." "Well

ho’ a·′nuwa." le′’kwanan p̂i′lak̭ä. p̂ilakup an to′sito le′skwanan
I shall go." thus saying he arose. Having arisen to him spider thus saying

"u′hsi t̂am i′łea’u." lehoł t̂am ko′ni i′łeak̭ä. i′łea’up a·tc
"That stick pick up." This much stick short he picked up. Having picked it up the two

a·′k̭ä k̭e′sic yä′tokwai’in’iha. a·′tci te′’tcinan an to′sito
went. Now sun is about out to come. The two arriving to him spider

le′skwanan la′k̭änhoł i′mon a·′tcia ya′k·toha. le′’kwap
thus saying "On the far side sitting ones the two strike. Thus having said

k̭umtc′! a·′tci i′tehk̭ä. a·′tci i′tehnan a·′tci a′’uk̭ä. le′snoł
——— The two he threw down. The two throwing down the two he laid out. Thus

e′lap ho′ktitaca le′skwanan "s’hanat. he′kwat t̂a′pinuwanholi′."
standing mountain lion thus saying "Now hurry. See whether you can not take it."

le′’kwap. an to′sito le′skwanan. "ma’ e′łapa kwa ho’
Thus having said to him spider thus saying, "'Oh no. Not I

ta'pcukwa le'anikwa." "ma' e'łap̄a kwa ho' ta'pcukwa.
won't take it,' thus say." "Well no, not I won't take it.

he'kwat u'laphołi. kop ma le ho' t̄a'pin·a. kwa u'lam·e."
See if it isn't there at all. How indeed I shall take it Not (ball) is not inside."

"ma kwa ten u'lam·e. le·'wi łom tcaw ha'p̄onaiye
"Well not however it is not inside. So many my children are gathered

tcu'watikoł łe'ona t̄o' hi·'ninci yat̄enan t̄o t̄a'pin·a."
whoever holding it the one you the right one grabbing you will take it."

"i'ya'." i'sk̄ɔn an to'sito p̄e'nan "kwa li·ł t̄i'nan tcu'hoł
"All right." There to him spider speaking, "Not here sitting who

łe'am·e. i'sno ɔt-a'l·un'ona łe'aiye." le''kwap. a·'k̯ä. mu'hukw'
is not holding it. That one dancing going about the one he is holding it." Thus having said he went Owl

a's·an ya'ktohap lo'mo·n kwai''ip a·'k̯ä. te''ticnan
on the hand striking shining coming out he went. Arriving

t̄o'ma·tin a'hnan a·'wil a·'k̯ä. kwa'hoł wɔ·'we a·'latap̄a
hollow sticks taking with them he went. Something creatures winged

i·k̄olonapk̯ä. to'sito p̄a'ni·nan t̄oma· t̄em·ł u'he p̄ile·k̯ä.
they hid the ball. Spider coming down hollow sticks all web strung.

u'lin p̄i'k̯aiak̯ä. le'sna we'ma· a·'witełk̯ä. kwa'tikoł t̄om·e
Ball she tied. Thus beasts came one by one. Whichever stick

ya't̄ena·wap le'k̄on a'nahap. a'stem·ła te'tc a'kcicna·we.
touching there pulling away ten only they withdrew.

yä'to kwai'ik̯ä. yä'tokwai''inan ho'łomac i'mik̯eatup s'a·tc·
Sun rose. Sun having risen far having ascended now the two

i·'k̯ä. a·'tci le'skwanan "si le·wi hom tca'we t̄oms yam
came. The two thus saying "Now all my children you now your

yä'tok̯ä ta'tcu an t̄e'k̄ohanan o'k̯änapk̯ä. t̄o'no we'ma·we
sun father his daylight have won. You, beasts,

yam yä'tok̯ä ta'tcu an t̄e'k̄ohanan·e t̄on i'tosok̯ä. t̄on
you sun father his daylight you have lost. You

yä'tonil·i t̄on yatelan·a. yä'to kwatona t̄e'łinana t̄on
all day you will sleep. Sun setting by night you

ła'ta-a·'wal·un·a. t̄o·'o mu'hukwi e·t t̄o kwa wow
hunting will go about. You owl but you not creatures

a·'latap̄anankwi a'kcitun'ona te'amek̯ä le'snate t̄o' yam
winged with to be with the one were not therefore you your

yä'tok̯ä ta'tcu an t̄e'k̄ohanan·e t̄o' tosok̯ä t̄o' t̄o'miyacna.
sun father his daylight you have lost. You made a mistake.

yä'tona t̄o' łat-a'l·una i'yamakwin u'lohn i'lap̄ona t̄om
By day you to hunt going about above world the one who has you

a'nk̄ohak̯än·a. p̄a'ni·na yam a'witelin tsi'ta a'ntehaktceł'na
will find. Coming down his earth mother removing a bit from her

t̄om ak̯' ya·'k̯äna·wap̄a hoł li·ła le''hatina t̄o' t̄e'k̄ohanan
you with it having finished wherever here thus thinking you daylight

pa'łtona ho''i te'k̂än·a." a·'tci le''a·wanikwanan a·tc
ending person will be." The two thus to them saying the two

a·'wantewak̭ä. we'ma· wɔ'ptsick̭ä.
they passed the night. Beasts separated.

a·tc a·'k̭ä. k̂ä'-eto·w t̂i'nakwin a·tc te''tcik̭ä. i'sk̂on
The two went ——— staying place the two arrived. There

łu'walemak̭ä. yam e'leteliwe łe'an i'yante'tcik̭äna łu'wale-
they arose. Their sacred things carrying one another reaching around they arose

mak̭ä. łe'-eto·we le'skwak̭ä. "si hom a·'suwe ta·'tcic li·'wan
——— thus said, "Now my younger brothers meanwhile this way

p̂i'clankwin ta'hna ho' o'neał a·'k̂än·a hoł k̭ä·k̂i i'tiwan·a
the north to direction I road shall make go. Somewhere sometime the Middle

yu'he·toti·k̭äte'a k̂ä·k̂i le·'hatina t̂o'n ho' a·'wona-e'laten·a."
has become plain when sometime thus thinking you I roads shall pass,"

le'kwanan p̂i'clankwin ta'hna a·'k̭ä.
thus having said the north to direction he went.

ta·'htcic tcuw o'k̭ä a·'wunatik̂än "nai'yaha' hopek luk̭n
Meanwhile some woman beholding them "Naiyaha! where indeed these

a·wa·ne." le''kwap
are going? thus having said

naiya he·ni naiya.
naiya he·ni naiya.

tomt mopina'k̭ä. k̂o'hana i't̂sinap̂a a·'wa·ne. ta·'htcic k̂ä'-
Just it hailed. White striped they go. Meanwhile ———

eto·we k̭ał a·wa·k̭ä he'cot̂ayälakwin a·'wik̭ä. a·'wiyap kwa
this way went. House Mountain to they came. Having come not

a·'pikwai'ik̭änaknam·k̭ä. i·'łakna'k̭ä. ho''i ła'na i'tulaco'ya.
they would not let them pass. There was fighting person large walks back and forth.

lesn i'łakna'k̭ä. le'snate su'nhak̭ä. Su'nhap i'kwałt ha'n-
Thus there was fighting. Even thus evening came. Evening having come back

łipink̭äkwin a·'te'tcik̭ä. t̂e'wap t̂a a·'wa·k̭ä. łi·ton-p̂ɔ't̂i
Hanłipinkä to they came. Next day again they went rain thick

i'łakna'k̭ä. su'nhap t̂a i'kwałt a·'wa·k̭ä. t̂e'wap ca'mli
there was fighting. In the evening again back they went. Next day early

ha''ik̭äna·na t̂a a·'wa·k̭ä. t̂a i'łakna'k̭ä. ho''i łana i'tu'łeletco
the third time again they went. Again there was fighting. Giant walked back and forth

toms co'psik̭ätean te'an·te kwa a'cena'ma. yä'ton·e kwa·top
just arrows sticking in even not she did not die. Sun having set

i'kwałt a·'wa·k̭ä. t̂e'wap ca'mli a·'wa·k̭ä. a·'te'tcip i'łakna'k̭ä.
back they went. Next day early they went. Having come there was fighting

kwa ya'nt̂ewusuna'wam·e ho''iłana i'tulaco'ya tomt pokokon
not They did not yield. Giant walked back and forth just shot

te'an·te kwa ya'nt̂ewusuna'ma. a'haiyute a·'tci le'skwanan
even being not she did not yield. Ahaiyute the two thus saying,

"t̂i'comaha' ko'plea te''onak̯ä kwa luk̯ ho'n a·'pikwai'i-
"Alas how because of not these us do not let us

k̯äna·wam·e? hołkon i'k̯enak̯än·a? i'sno i'tulaco'yen'ona
pass? Wherever may his heart be? That one the one who walks back and forth

i'kenatun tea'kona hon haiyałucapte kwa ya'nt̂ewusuna'ma.
heart where it should be all over where it is we striking even though not he does not yield.

i'mat kwa hon ha'ntikwa'na'ma. t̂e'wuna' a'ma łu
It seems not we do not overcome him. Finally come on go

yam tatc i'nkwin ye·'makce. i·'natinam·e luk̂on
your father where he stays climb up. Without doubt this one

ai'yu'ya·na" le''kwap an su'we yä'tok̯a i'nkwin ye·'mak̯ä.
knows." Having thus said his younger brother sun where he stays climbed up.

e'lehoł i'tiwap te''tcik̯ä "t̂o i·'ya?" "e·. ho' i·'ya."
Nearly noon he arrived. "You come?" "Yes. I come."

"mas p̂e'ne hi'nik kwa'tikoł p̂e'nan te'yułanam·e p̂e'nan
"Well now speak out. I think some kind word not too long word

te'ak̯än·a. t̂e'wuna' u'hsona hom t̂o' yu''ya·k̯äp̂a uhs
will be. Finally that me you having made know that

ai'yu'ya·na ho' t̂e'wanan te'k̯än·a." le''kwap "ma i·namiłte.
knowing it I time shall live." Thus having said, "Well without doubt it is true.

ho''na·wan a·'tatcu ho''na·wan a·'tsita k̯ä'-eto·we tcu'-eto·we
Our fathers our mothers ——— ———

mu'to·we łe'-eto·we le· ti·'k̯ä a·'ciwan·i t̂e'k̂ohana ya'hnapte
——— ——— all society priests daylight into having emerged even

li·ł i'tiwanan te'cun a·'wonap̂a luk̂no kwa a·'pikwai'ik̯ä-
here the middle seeking roads going these not they will not let

na·wam·e. i'sno i'tulaco'yen'ona hołkon i'k̯e·nak̯än·a? te'ałt i'k̯en-
them pass. That one walking back and forth the one wherever her heart may be? In vain heart

tun tea'kona hon haiyołucapte tomt co'ptsik̯atean tean·te kwa
where it should be are over where it is we shooting even though just arrows sticking in even being not

ya'ntewusuna'ma." "haiyi'. tek̯aiał t̂on o'tsi. kwa hoł
she does not yield." "Haiyi! For nothing you men. Not anywhere

łu'ninan i'k̯e·nam·e. i'teała·we i's̆k̂on t̂on haiyałuce'a. an
body in her heart is not. It is vain there you go on shooting. Her

tci''monan i'k̯enaiye. le'kwanan lu'k̯ä t̂om t̂ap lu'k̯ä t̂om
rattle in heart is. Thus having said "This yours and this your

pa'pona." le''kwanan kwi'li łi''akwa łe'an u'k̯ä. "tenat t̂on
brother's." Thus having said two turquoise rabbit sticks he gave him. "However you

ai'yaknahap̂a yam a'nikwanan a'k̯ä ho' yam i'nasnak̯ä
letting it go my wisdom with I my weapons

wo'tan·a." "haiyi'. ma honkwa'ati. ko'ma so' a·ne." "łu a·'ce."
shall take." "Haiyi! Well perhaps it is so. Very well, now I go." "Go on, go."

"k̯e'tsanici t̂o' a·'t'u." le''anik̂äp p̂a'ni·k̯ä. Am pa'pa
"Happily you may (you) go." Thus being said he descended. His elder brother

le'sanikwanan "si ko'tcilea t̂om a'tinak̯ä?" "ma i'namiłte.
thus to him saying, "Now how is it to you did he tell?" "Well indeed it is true.

yo'se· hon to'lonan hai'yałuce'a kwa i'sk̂'ɔn i'k̯enam·e.
In vain we body on keep on shooting not there heart is not.

an tci''mon i'k̯enaiye. luk̯ a'k̯ä. ya'łakwai'in·a."
Her rattle heart is. This with she will be destroyed."

le''kwanan yam pa'pa t̂o'p̂a łe'an u'k̯ä. yam pa'pa
Thus having said his elder brother one rabbit stick he gave. His elder brother

łe'an u'tsip "si hanat ko'ma t̂o·'o." le''kwap an su'we
rabbit stick having given "Now hurry. Very well you," thus having said his younger brother

i'tokwan a'wełanan ya'ktonan ya'k̯täp ts'i—kwe! yä'tok̯
to the right went around throwing it having thrown it tsikwe! sun

i'nkwin łe'an ye·mak̯ä łe'an ye·'makup yä'tok̯ä a'hk̯ä.
where he stays rabbit stick ascended rabbit stick having ascended sun took it.

"si a'matcic t̂o·'o" le''kwap am pa'pa we'cik̯än a'wełanan
"Now go on you." thus having said his elder brother to the left going around

i'pakuk̯ä. i'pakunan k̂ɔ—t̂sa! an łe'an·e an tci''mon
threw it. Having thrown it Crack! his rabbit stick her rattle

ya'ktap t̂u—n! yutulak̯ä. yu'tulak̂äp a·wan ho''i ła'na
struck t'uun! they ran away. Running away their giant

a'cek̯ä. a'cep yu'tulak̯ä. i'tapant̂in-a·k̯ä łu'walakwin
died. Having died they ran away. Following them he went village to

a·'te'tcinan u'kwatełna a·'wa·k̯ä. "luk̯ hom k̯ä'kwen·e·."
arriving going in here and there they went. "This my house."

ta·'htci "luk̯ ho'ma." le''tikwanan co'łatsena a·'wa·ne ho'ti·koł
Meanwhile "This mine." Thus saying arrows sticking in they go. Wherever

a·'te'tcinan u'kwatop o'k̯atsik̯ ła'ci le'hoł a'ktsik̯ t̂sa'na
reaching going in old woman old this much boy small

k̯ä'tsik t̂sa'na u'p̂e. a·'wan t̂e'hwitiwa he'pik̯äk̂ap i'map
girl small are inside. Their middle space urine vessel standing

k̯änait u'tea· wɔ'p̂ap a·'wan no'a'akona pi'tsem u'le
——— flowers putting in their noses in cotton wool

wɔ·p̂ap wɔpkwatonaiye. a·'wunatik̯än·a "ati—! hapupe'!"
putting in pot they are bending over. Beholding them. "Ati! Ghosts!"

le''tikwap a·'tci le'sa·wanikwanan "eł t̂on kon a·'wale-
thus having said the two thus to them saying "Don't you something

wuna·wamet'u! t̂a hi'nik luknio kwahoł ai'yu'ya·nap̂a
do anything to them. Also I think these something know.

t̂e'wuna' le'n a'tanitina lukn a·'ho'i" le''kwanan. a·'tci
Finally thus in danger these are alive," thus having said the two

kwa'tok̯ä. a·'tci kwa'tonan a·'tci ya'ntekunak̯ä. "t̂ac t̂on
entered. The two entering the two questioned them. "And do you

kwa'hoł ai'yu'ya·nap̂a t̂e'wuna' le'n a'tanitina kwa t̂on
something know? Finally thus in danger not you

a·'yałakwai'ina'ma." "ma hon e'letelin ilap̂a." "haiyi'· ma
are not destroyed." "Well we sacred thing have." "Haiyi'. Well

ko'ma	t̂a'pna·we.	hon	a·'wa·nuwa.	hoł	yam	a·'tatcu	yam
very well	take it.	We	shall go.	Somewhere	your	fathers	your

a·'tsita	k̭ä'-eto·we	tcu'-eto·we	mu'-eto·we	łe'-eto·we	t̂on
mothers	———	———	———	———	you

a·'wona-e'latena·wap̂a	t̂o''na·wan	hi·'nina	t̂e'wanan	te'ap̂a	
roads having passed	your	the same	time	being	

kwa	hoł	tomt	t̂on	wɔ·w	te'am·ek̂än·a.	te'ała	t̂a luk̭
not	somewhere	just	you	slaves	shall not be.	No matter	and this one

le·w	a'ktsik	t̂sa'na	luk̭ä	yam	tatc	i'la·wa.	te'ał	luk̭
such	boy	little	this	their	father	they will have.	No matter	this

le·'wi	k̭ä'tsik̭	t̂sa'na	luk̭	hon	tsit	i'l'a·wa."	"le''anak̭äp
so	girl	little	this	we	mother	shall have."	"Thus having been said

yam	e'letelin·e	t̂apna·wap	s'a·wa·k̭ä.	k̭ä'-eto·we	t̂i'nakwin
their	sacred thing	picking up	now they went.	———	where they were staying

a·'te'tcinan	i'sk̂on	le'sa·wana'k̭ä	"si	t̂e'wanan	a'cna·we'."
arriving	there	thus to them was said,	"Now	time	make!"

"hɔ'l·o.	kwa	hon	a·k̭e·la'cukwa.	t̂em	t̂o''na·wan	t̂e'wanan
"No.	Not	we	first won't be.	Still	your	time

i'te'tcik̭ätea	hon	t̂e'wanan	yä'łtona·wa"	le''anak̭äp̂a	i'sk̂ɔ
has been used up when	we	time	shall lay on top,"	thus having been said	there

k̭ä·'-eto·w	i'kwanik̂änapk̭ä.	k̭ä'-eto·w	a·'wan	t̂e'wanan
———	they worked.	———	their	time

yo·''ap	a·'witen	yä'to·we	a·'witen	t̂e'łina·we	k̭ä'tsana
becoming	four	days	four	nights	fine rain

ł̂i'ton-te'łakwi	k̭ä'-eto·w	a·wan	t̂ewanan	te'ak̭ä.	a·'wan
rain touching	———	their	time	was.	Their

t̂e'wanan	i'te'tcap	a·'t̂san	a·'tci	yam	hotil·i	i'kwanik̂änapk̭ä.
time	used up	children	both	their	grandmother with	worked.

a·'wan	t̂e'wanan	yo·''ap̂a	a·'witen	ya'to·we	a·'witen
Their	time	becoming	four	days	four

t̂e'lina·we	k̭ä'łana	ł̂i'ton-t̂e'łakwi	a·'wan	t̂e'wanan	te'ap̂a
nights	heavy rain	rain touching	their	time	was.

i'sk̂ɔn	k̭oli	a·'cuwana'k̭ä.	k̭äwaian	akwe	yo·'k̭ä.	i'sk̂on
There	sulphur fumes	were wiped off from them	river	course	became.	There

le'sa·wana'k̭ä	"ha'lihi'	e'lahkwa.	ho'nkwic	hi'nina	t̂o''na·wan
thus to them was said	"Halihi!	Thanks.	Perhaps	the same	your

hai'tocnan·e.	kwakona	t̂o''na·wan	a'notak̂än·a?"	"ma	hon
ceremony.	What one	your	clan may be?"	"Well	we

t̂o'wa	łu'ptsikwa·w	anotaiye."	le'tikwap̂a	"haiyi·!	e·t	t̂on
corn	yellow theirs	(our) clan is."	Thus having said,	"Haiyi!	But	you

t̂o'wa	łu'ptsikwa·wan	a'notak̭ä'en·tę	t̂on	k̂olin	a'k̭ä	a·'wi-
corn	yellow theirs	(your) clan was even though	you	sulphur fumes	because of	the

k̂witik̂ona'k̭ä	t̂on	t̂o'wa	k̂wi'nakwa·wa	a'notak̂än·a.
ones who became black, therefore	you	corn	black theirs	your clan shall be."

le'a·wana'k̭ä.
Thus to them said.

i'sk̂on łu'walemak̭ä. yam e'leteli·we łe'an i'yante'tcik̭äna
There they arose. Their sacred things carrying one another reaching around

k̭ałhokᵘ a·wona'k̭ä. k̭ä·k̂ä tci'mik̭äk̭ä ha'lona i'tiwanakwi
hither roads came. Sometime the first beginning ant hill middle to

o'neał i'k̂änapk̭ä. i'sk̂on a·'patc a·'wan i'satona nom
road they made come There Navajo their helper bug

ci'lowa u'natik̭änapk̭ä. "si a·'ma wa'n·i te'ałt le'si hon
red they beheld. "Now come, wait! in vain so far we

i'tiwan·an te'cun a·'wona'k̭ä. kwa hoł luk̭ä hon u'na·wam·ek̭ä."
the middle seeking roads have been going. Not anywhere this we have not seen."

le·'tikwana yam nan a'ntecematinapk̭ä k̂änastepi. luk̂on
Thus having said their grandfather they summoned K̂'änastepi. this one

i'k̭ä. "ko''na t̂on t̂e'wanan a·'teaiye." "k̭e'tsanici hon t̂e'wanan
came. "How you time live?" "Happily we time

a·'teakwi ho''na t̂o a·'wona-e'latek̭ä. i'it̂nak̭ä." le'anak̭äp̂a
living when us you roads have passed. Be seated." Thus said

i·muk̭ä. i'sk̂on i·tehk̂unak̭ä. "e· ma lak̭iman·te hom t̂on
he sat down. There he questioned them. "Yes now, even now me you

a'ntecematinapk̭ä. ime' kwatik p̂e'nan te'yułanam·e p̂e'nan
have summoned. Apparently some kind word not too long word

te'k̂än·a. t̂e'wuna' u'hson hom t̂on yu''ya·k̂äna·wap̂a uhs
will be. Finally that me you having made know that

ai'yu'ya·na ho' t̂e'wanan te'k̂än·a." "ma i·namiłte. ho''na·wan
knowing I time shall live." "Well, indeed, it is true. our

a·'tatcu ho''na'wan a·'tsita k̭ä-eto·we tcu'-eto·we mu'-eto·we
fathers, our mothers, ——— ——— ———

łe-eto·we le· tik̭ä a·'ciwan·i t̂e'k̂ohanan ya'hnap̂e'en li·ł
——— all society priests daylight into emerging even tho here

i'tiwanan te'cuna a·wonaiye. t̂o' a·'wan i'tiwanan te'cun·a.
the middle seeking road go. You for them the middle shall seek.

k̭e·sic e'letap̂a t̂om tse''makwin a'k̭ä t̂o'man i'k̭ena'a
This now being well, your thoughts because of your heart at

ho''na·wan a·'tatcu k̭ä'-eto·we tcu'-eto·we mu'-eto·we łe'-eto·we
our fathers ——— ——— ——— ———

le· ti'k̭ä a·'ciwan·i i't̂inan i'łak̭ik̂äp̂a a·'t̂apana tse''mak-
all society priests sitting down coming to rest following them thoughts

t̂e'łakwi hon t̂e'wanan a·'tek̭än·a." le''anak̭äp t̂e'wankwin
touching we time shall live." Thus said east toward

t̂un i'p̂oak̭ä. we'cik̭ä hic a's·i tsa'łinaiye. i'tohkwa a's·i
looking he sat down. Left all arm is stretched straight. To the right arm

to'tsip̂oaiye. pi'clankwin t̂un i'p̂oana i'tsałip̂a hic an
stands bent over. To the north looking sitting down stretching out his arms very his

hi·'nin a's·i i'tiułapk̭ä. "a'ma hon pi'clankwin ta'hn a·'wiwa'-
the same arms stood against (the sky). "Come we to the north direction let (us)

hice. li·'wan ho' it̂ohk ko·w a's·i to'tsip̂oaiye." le''kwap
cross over. On this side I to the right a little arm stands bent over." Thus having said

a·′wiwa′hik̭ä. i′t̄inak̭ä. i′p̄oana le′si te′kwin a′s·i u′łek̭ä
they crossed over. They sat down. Sitting down all sides arms he reached out

an a′s·i hi·′nina. "li·′ła i′tiwanici." le′kwap̄a i′sk̄ɔn an
his hands were the same. "Here is the middle," thus having said there his

a·′tatcu an a·′tsita k̄ä′-eto·we tcu′-eto·we mu′-eto·we
fathers, his mothers, ——— ——— ———

łe′-eto·we le· ti′k̭ä a·′ciwan·i ti′k̭ä p̄e′kwi·we ti′k̭ä a·′pi′-
——— all society priests, society speakers, society bow

ła·ciwan·i a·′wan tca′we yułak̄iti′k̭ä.
priests, their children came to rest.

le′n i′nɔ·te te′atik̭ä.
Thus long ago it happened.

Talk Concerning the First Beginning

Yes, indeed. In this world there was no one at all. Always the sun came up; always he went in. No one in the morning gave him sacred meal; no one gave him prayer sticks; it was very lonely. He said to his two children:[96] "You will go into the fourth womb. Your fathers, your mothers, k̄äeto·we, tcu-eto·we, mu-eto·we, łe·-eto-we, all the society priests, society p̄ekwins, society bow priests, you will bring out yonder into the light of your sun father." Thus he said to them. They said, "But how shall we go in?" "That will be all right." Laying their lightning arrow across their rainbow bow, they drew it. Drawing it and shooting down, they entered.

When they entered the fourth womb it was dark inside. They could not distinguish anything. They said, "Which way will it be best to go?" They went toward the west. They met someone face to face. They said, "Whence come you?" "I come from over this way to the west." "What are you doing going around?" "I am going around to look at my crops. Where do you live?" "No, we do not live any place. There above our father the Sun, priest, made us come in. We have come in," they said. "Indeed," the younger brother said. "Come, let us see," he said. They laid down their bow. Putting underneath some dry brush and some dry grass that was lying about, and putting the bow on top, they kindled fire by hand. When they had kindled the fire, light came out from the coals. As it came out, they blew on it and it caught fire. Aglow! It is growing light. "Ouch! What have you there?" he said. He fell down crouching. He had a slimy horn, slimy tail, he was slimy all over, with webbed hands. The elder brother said, "Poor thing! Put out the light." Saying thus, he put out the light. The youth said, "Oh dear, what have you there?" "Why, we have fire," they said. "Well, what

[96] Watusti and Yanaluha, called k̄äeto′w′ a·wan′ aᵘwati′ a·tci (rain fetish's two mouths).

(crops) do you have coming up?" "Yes, here are our things coming up." Thus he said. He was going around looking after wild grasses.

He said to them, "Well, now, let us go." They went toward the west, the two leading. There the people were sitting close together. They questioned one another. Thus they said, "Well, now, you two, speak. I think there is something to say. It will not be too long a talk. If you let us know that we shall always remember it." "That is so, that is so," they said. "Yes, indeed, it is true. There above is our father, Sun. No one ever gives him prayer sticks; no one ever gives him sacred meal; no one ever gives him shells. Because it is thus we have come to you, in order that you may go out standing yonder into the daylight of your sun father. Now you will say which way (you decide)." Thus the two said. "Hayi! Yes, indeed. Because it is thus you have passed us on our roads. Now that you have passed us on our roads here where we stay miserably, far be it from us to speak against it. We can not see one another. Here inside where we just trample on one another, where we just spit on one another, where we just urinate on one another, where we just befoul one another, where we just follow one another about, you have passed us on our roads. None of us can speak against it. But rather, as the priest of the north says, so let it be. Now you two call him." Thus they said to the two, and they came up close toward the north side

They met the north priest on his road. "You have come," he said. "Yes, we have come. How have you lived these many days?" "Here where I live happily you have passed me on my road. Sit down." When they were seated he questioned them. "Now speak. I think there is something to say. It will not be too long a talk. So now, that you will let me know." "Yes, indeed, it is so. In order that you may go out standing there into the daylight of your sun father we have passed you on your road. However you say, so shall it be." "Yes, indeed, now that you have passed us on our road here where we live thus wretchedly, far be it from me to talk against it. Now that you have come to us here inside where we just trample on one another, where we just spit on one another, where we just urinate on one another, where we just befoul one another, where we just follow one another about, how should I speak against it?" so he said. Then they arose. They came back. Coming to the village where they were sitting in the middle place, there they questioned one another. "Yes, even now we have met on our roads. Indeed there is something to say; it will not be too long a talk. When you let me know that, I shall always remember it," thus they said to one another. When they had spoken thus, "Yes, indeed. In order that you may go out standing into the daylight of your sun father, we have passed you on your road," thus they said. "Hayi! Yes, indeed. Now that you have passed us on our road here where we cannot see one another, where we just trample on one another, where we just urinate on one another, where we just befoul one another, where we just follow one another around, far be it from me to speak against it. But rather let it be as my younger brother, the priest of the west shall say. When he says, 'Let it be thus,' that way it shall be. So now, you two call him." Thus said the priest of the north and they went and stood close against the west side.[97] . . . .

"Well, perhaps by means of the thoughts of someone somewhere it may be that we shall go out standing into the daylight of our sun father." Thus he said. The two thought. "Come, let us go over there to talk with eagle priest." They went. They came to where eagle was staying. "You have come." "Yes." "Sit down." They sat down. "Speak!" "We want you." "Where?" "Near by, to where our fathers, k̃ä-eto·we, tcu-eto·we, stay quietly, we summon you." "Haiyi!" So they went. They came to where k̃ä-eto·we stayed. "Well, even now when you summoned me, I have passed you on your roads. Surely there is something to say; it will not be too long a talk. So now if you let me know that I shall always remember it," thus he said. "Yes, indeed, it is so. Our fathers, k̃ä-eto·we, tcu-eto·we, mu-eto·we, łe-eto·we, all the society priests shall go out standing into the daylight of their sun father. You will look for their road." "Very well," he said, "I am going," he said. He went around. Coming back to his starting place he went a little farther out. Coming back to his starting place again he went still farther out. Coming back to his starting place he went way far out. Coming back to his starting place, nothing was visible. He came. To where k̃ä-eto·we stayed he came. After he sat down they questioned him. "Now you went yonder looking for the road going out. What did you see in the world?" "Nothing was visible." "Haiyi!" "Very well, I am going now." So he went.

When he had gone the two thought. "Come, let us summon our grandson, cok̃äpiso,"[97a] thus they said. They went. They came to where cok̃äpiso stayed. "Our grandson, how have you lived these days?" "Where I live happily you have passed me on my road. I think perhaps there is something to say; it will not be too long a talk. So now when you let me know that, I shall always remember it," thus he said. "Yes, indeed, it is so. Our fathers, k̃ä-eto·we, tcu-eto·we, mu-eto·we, łe-eto·we, all the society priests are about to come out standing into the daylight of their sun father. We summon you that you may be the one to look for their road." "Indeed?" Thus he said. They went. When they got there, they questioned

[97] The foregoing paragraph repeated for the six directions as indicated in text.

[97a] An unidentified bird.

them where they were sitting. "Even now you have summoned me. Surely there is something to say; it will not be too long a talk. So now when you let me know that, I shall always remember it." "Yes, indeed, it is so. When our fathers, our mothers, k̦ä-eto·we, tcu-eto·we, mu-eto·we, łe-eto·we, the society priests, go forth standing into the daylight of their sun father, you will look for their road." Thus the two said. He went out to the south. He went around. Coming back to the same place, nothing was visible. A second time he went, farther out. Coming back to the same place, nothing was visible. A third time still farther out he went. Nothing was visible. A fourth time he went, way far, but nothing was visible. When he came to where k̦ä-eto·we were staying, the two questioned him. "Now, our grandson, way off yonder you have gone to see the world. What did you see in the world?" Thus the two asked him. "Well, nothing was visible." "Well indeed?" the two said. "Very well, I am going now." Saying this, he went.

When cok̦äpiso had gone the two thought. "Come, let us go and talk to our grandson chicken hawk." Thus they said. They went. They reached where chicken hawk stayed. "You have come." "Yes." "Sit down." "How have you lived these days?" "Happily. Well now, speak. I think there is something to say; it will not be too long a talk. So now, when you let me know it, I shall always remember that." "Yes, indeed, it is so. When our fathers, k̦ä-eto·we, tcu-eto·we, mu-eto·we, łe-eto·we, the society priests, go out standing into the sunlight of their sun father, you will look for their road." So they went. When they got there they sat down. There he questioned them. "Yes, even now you summoned me. Perhaps there is something to say; it will not be too long a talk. When you let me know that, I shall always remember it." Thus he said. "Yes, indeed, it is so. When our fathers, k̦ä-eto·we, tcu-eto·we, mu-eto·we, łe-eto·we, the society priests, go out standing into the daylight of their sun father, you will look for their road." "Is that so?" Saying this, he went out. He went to the south. He went where cok̦äpiso had been. Coming back to his starting place, nothing was visible. A second time he went, farther out. He came back to his starting place, nothing was visible. He went a third time, along the shore of the encircling ocean. A fourth time farther out he went. He came back to his starting place. Nothing was visible. To where k̦ä-eto·we stayed he came. "Nothing is visible." "Haiyi!" "Yes, so I am going." "Well, go." So he went.

Then the two thought. "Come on, let us summon our grandson," thus they said. They went. They came to where humming bird was staying. "You have come?" "Yes, how have you lived these days?" "Where I live happily these days you have passed me on my road. Sit down." When they had sat down: "Well, now, speak. I think there is something to say; it will not be too long a talk. So now if you let me know that, I shall always remember it." "Yes, indeed, it is so. When our fathers, k̯ä-eto·we, tcu-eto·we, mu-eto·we, łe-eto·we, the society priests, go out standing into the daylight of their sun father, you shall be the one to look for their road; for that we have summoned you." "Is that so?" Saying this, they went. When they got there, he questioned them. "Well, even now you summoned me. Surely there is something to say. It will not be too long a talk. So now when you let me know that I shall always remember it." Thus he said. "Yes, indeed, it is so. When our fathers, k̯ä-eto·we, tcu-eto·we, mu-eto·we, łe-eto·we, the society priests, go out into the daylight of their sun father, that you shall be the one to look for their road, for that we have summoned you." Thus the two said. He went out toward the south. He went on. Coming back to his starting place, nothing was visible. Farther out he went. Coming back to the same place, nothing was visible. Then for the third time he went. Coming back to the same place, nothing was visible. For the fourth time he went close along the edge of the sky. Coming back to the same place, nothing was visible. He came. Coming where k̯ä-eto·we were staying, "Nothing is visible." "Hayi!" "Yes. Well, I am going now." "Very well, go." He went.

The two said, "What had we better do now? That many different kinds of feathered creatures, the ones who go about without ever touching the ground, have failed." Thus the two said. "Come, let us talk with our grandson, locust. Perhaps that one will have a strong spirit because he is like water." [98] Thus they said. They went. Their grandson, locust, they met. "You have come." "Yes, we have come." "Sit down. How have you lived these days?" "Happily." "Well, even now you have passed me on my road. Surely there is something to say; it will not be too long a talk. So now when you let me know that, that I shall always remember." Thus he said. "Yes, indeed, it is so. In order that our fathers, k̯ä-eto·we, tcu-eto·we, mu-eto·we, łe-eto·we, the society priests, may go out standing into the daylight of their sun father, we have come to you." "Is that so?" Saying this, they went. When they arrived they sat down. Where they were sitting, he questioned them. "Well, just now you came to me. Surely there is something to say; it will not be too long a talk. So now if you let me know that, that I shall always remember." "Yes, indeed. In order that our fathers, k̯ä-eto·we, tcu-eto·we, mu-eto·we, łe-eto·we, the society priests, may go out standing into the daylight of their sun father, we have summoned you." "Indeed?" Saying this, locust rose right up. He goes up. He went through into another world. And again

[98] That is, like water, he can go through anything solid.

he goes right up. He went through into another world. And again he goes right up. Again he went through into another world. He goes right up. When he had just gone a little way his strength gave out, he came back to where k̲ä-eto·we were staying and said, "Three times I went through and the fourth time my strength gave out." "Hayi! Indeed?" Saying this, he went.

When he had gone the two thought. "Come, let us speak with our grandson, Reed Youth. For perhaps that one with his strong point will be all right." Saying this, they went. They came to where Reed Youth stayed. "You have come?" "Yes; how have you lived these days." "Where I stay happily you have passed me on my road. Sit down." Thus he said. They sat down. Then he questioned them. "Yes. Well, even now you have passed me on my road. I think there is something to say; it will not be too long a talk. When you let me know that, that I shall always remember." Thus he said. "Yes, indeed, in order that our fathers, k̲ä-eto·we, tcu-eto·we, mu-eto·we, łe-eto·we, the society priests, may go out standing into the daylight of their sun father, we have come to you." "Hayi! Is that so?" Having spoken thus, they went. When they arrived they sat down. There he questioned them. "Yes, even now that you have summoned me I have passed you on your roads. Surely there is something to say; it will not be too long a talk. When you let me know that, that I shall always remember." "Yes, indeed, it is so. In order that our fathers, k̲ä-eto·we, tcu-eto·we, mu-eto·we, łe-eto·we, the society priests, may go forth standing into the daylight of their sun father, we have summoned you." Thus they said. "Hayi! Is that so?" Saying this, he went out. Where Locust had gone out he went out. The first time he passed through, the second time he passed through, the third time he passed through. Having passed through the fourth time and come forth standing into the daylight of his sun father, he went back in. Coming back in he came to where k̲'ä-eto·we were staying. "You have come?" Thus they said. "Yes," he said. "Far off to see what road there may be you have gone. How may it be there now?" Thus they said. "Yes, indeed, it is so. There it is as you wanted it. As you wished of me, I went forth standing into the daylight of my sun father now." Thus he said. "Halihi! Thank you!" "Now I am going." "Go." Saying this, he went.

After he had gone they were sitting around. Now as they were sitting around, there the two set up a pine tree for a ladder. They stayed there. For four days they stayed there. Four days, they say, but it was four years. There all the different society priests sang their song sequences for one another. The ones sitting in the first row listened carefully. Those sitting next on the second row heard all but a little. Those sitting on the third row heard here and there.

Those sitting last on the fourth row heard just a little bit now and then. It was thus because of the rustling of the dry weeds.

When their days there were at an end, gathering together their sacred things they arose. "Now what shall be the name of this place?" "Well, here it shall be sulphur-smell-inside-world; and furthermore, it shall be raw-dust world." Thus they said. "Very well. Perhaps if we call it thus it will be all right." Saying this, they came forth.

After they had come forth, setting down their sacred things in a row at another place, they stayed there quietly. There the two set up a spruce tree as a ladder. When the ladder was up they stayed there for four days. And there again the society priests sang their song sequences for one another. Those sitting on the first row listened carefully. Those sitting there on the second row heard all but a little. Those sitting there on the third row heard here and there. Those sitting last distinguished a single word now and then. It was thus because of the rustling of some plants. When their days there were at an end, gathering together their sacred things there they arose. "Now what shall it be called here?" "Well, here it shall be called soot-inside-world, because we still can not recognize one another." "Yes, perhaps if it is called thus it will be all right." Saying this to one another, they arose.

Passing through to another place, and putting down their sacred things in a row, they stayed there quietly. There the two set up a piñon tree as a ladder. When the piñon tree was put up, there all the society priests and all the priests went through their song sequences for one another. Those sitting in front listened carefully. Those sitting on the second row heard all but a little. Those sitting behind on the third row heard here and there. Those sitting on the fourth row distinguished only a single word now and then. This was because of the rustling of the weeds.

When their days there were at an end, gathering together their sacred things they arose. Having arisen, "Now what shall it be called here?" "Well, here it shall be fog-inside-world, because here just a little bit is visible." "Very well, perhaps if it is called thus it will be all right." Saying this, rising, they came forth.

Passing through to another place, there the two set down their sacred things in a row, and there they sat down. Having sat down, the two set up a cottonwood tree as a ladder. Then all the society priests and all the priests went through their song sequences for one another. Those sitting first heard everything clearly. Those sitting on the second row heard all but a little. Those sitting on the third row heard here and there. Those sitting last on the fourth row distinguished a single word now and then. It was thus because of the rustling of some plants.

When their days there were at an end, after they had been there, when their four days were passed, gathering together their sacred possessions, they arose. When they arose, "Now what shall it be called here?" "Well, here it shall be wing-inner-world, because we see our sun father's wings." Thus they said. They came forth.

Into the daylight of their sun father they came forth standing. Just at early dawn they came forth. After they had come forth there they set down their sacred possessions in a row. The two said, "Now after a little while when your sun father comes forth standing to his sacred place you will see him face to face. Do not close your eyes." Thus he said to them. After a little while the sun came out. When he came out they looked at him. From their eyes the tears rolled down. After they had looked at him, in a little while their eyes became strong. "Alas!" Thus they said. They were covered all over with slime. With slimy tails and slimy horns, with webbed fingers, they saw one another. "Oh dear! is this what we look like?" Thus they said.

Then they could not tell which was which of their sacred possessions. Meanwhile, near by an old man of the Dogwood clan lived alone. Spider said to him, "Put on water. When it gets hot, wash your hair." "Why?" "Our father, our mothers, k̥ä-eto·we, tcu-eto·we, mu-eto·we, łe′-eto·we, all the society priests, into the daylight of their sun father have come forth standing. They can not tell which is which. You will make this plain to them." Thus she said. "Indeed? Impossible. From afar no one can see them. Where they stay quietly no one can recognize them." Thus he said. "Do not say that. Nevertheless it will be all right. You will not be alone. Now we shall go." Thus she said. When the water was warm he washed his hair.

Meanwhile, while he was washing his hair, the two said, "Come let us go to meet our father, the old man of the Dogwood clan. I think he knows in his thoughts; because among our fathers, k̥ä-eto·we, tcu-eto·we, mu-eto·we, łe-eto·we, we can not tell which is which." Thus they said. They went. They got there. As they were climbing up, "Now indeed! They are coming." Thus Spider said to him. She climbed up his body from his toe. She clung behind his ear. The two entered. "You have come," thus he said. "Yes. Our father, how have you lived these days?" "As I live happily you pass me on my road. Sit down." They sat down. "Well, now, speak. I think some word that is not too long, your word will be. Now, if you let me know that, remembering it, I shall live." "Indeed it is so. Our fathers, k̥ä-eto·we, tcu-eto·we, mu-eto·we, łe-eto·we, all the society priests, into the daylight of their sun father have risen and come out. It is not plain which is which. Therefore we have passed you on your road." "Haiyi, is that so? Impossible! From afar no one can see them. Where they stay quietly no one can recognize them." Thus he said. "Yes, but we have chosen you." Thus the two said. They went. When they came there, "My fathers, my mothers, how have you lived these days?" "Happily, our father, our child. Be seated." Thus they said. He sat down. Then he questioned them. "Yes, now indeed, since you have sent for me, I have passed you on your road. I think some word that is not too long your word will be. Now if you let me know that, remembering it, I shall always live."

Thus he said. "Indeed, it is so. Even though our fathers, our mothers, k̯ä-eto·we, tcu-eto·we, mu-eto·we, łe-eto·we, have come out standing into the daylight of their sun father, it is not plain which of these is which. Therefore we have sent for you." Thus they said. "Haiyi. Well, let me try." "Impossible. From afar no one can see them. Where they stay quietly no one can tell which is which." "Well, let me try." Thus he said. Where they lay in a row he stood beside them. Spider said to him, "Here, the one that lies here at the end is k̯'ä-eto·we and these next ones touching it are tcu-eto·we, and this next one is łe-eto·we, and these next ones touching it are mu-eto·we." Thus she said. He said, "Now this is k̯ä-eto·we, and these all touching it are tcu-eto·we, and this one is łe-eto·we, and all these touching it are mu-eto·we." Thus he said. "Halihi! Thank you. How shall be the cycle of the months for them?" Thus he said: "This one Branches-broken-down. This one No-snow-on-the-road. This one Little-sand-storms. This one Great-sand-storms. This the Month-without-a-name. This one Turn-about. This one Branches-broken-down. This one No-snow-on-the-road. This one Little-sand-storms. This one Great-sand-storms. This the Month-without-a-name. This one Turn-about. Thus shall be all the cycle of the months." "Halihi! Thank you. Our father, you shall not be poor. Even though you have no sacred possessions toward which your thoughts bend, whenever Itiwana is revealed to us, because of your thought, the ceremonies of all these shall come around in order. You shall not be a slave." This they said. They gave him the sun. "This shall be your sacred possession." Thus they said. When this had happened thus they lived.

Four days—four days they say, but it was four years—there they stayed. When their days were at an end, the earth rumbled. The two said, "Who was left behind?" "I do not know, but it seems we are all here." Thus they said. Again the earth rumbled. "Well, does it not seem that some one is still left behind?" Thus, the two said. They went. Coming to the place where they had come out, there they stood. To the mischief-maker and the Mexicans they said, "Haiyi! Are you still left behind?" "Yes." "Now what are you still good for?" Thus they said. "Well, it is this way. Even though k̄ä-eto·we have issued forth into the daylight, the people do not live on the living waters of good corn; on wild grasses only they live. Whenever you come to the middle you will do well to have me. When the people are many and the land is all used up, it will not be well. Because this is so I have come out." Thus he said. "Haiyi! Is that so? So that's what you are. Now what are you good for?" Thus they said. "Indeed, it is so. When you come to the middle, it will be well to have my seeds. Because k̂'ä-eto·we do not live on the good seeds of the corn, but on wild grasses only. Mine are the seeds of the corn and all the clans of beans." Thus he said. The two took him with them. They came to where k̄ä-eto·we were staying. They sat down. Then they questioned him. "Now let us see what you are good for." "Well, this is my seed of the yellow corn." Thus he said. He showed an ear of yellow corn. "Now give me one of your people." Thus he said. They gave him a baby. When they gave him the baby it seems he did something to her. She became sick. After a short time she died. When she had died he said, "Now bury her." They dug a hole and buried her. After four days he said to the two, "Come now. Go and see her." The two went to where they had come out. When they got there the little one was playing in the dirt. When they came, she laughed. She was happy. They saw her and went back. They came to where the people were staying. "Listen! Perhaps it will be all right for you to come. She is still alive. She has not really died." "Well, thus it shall always be." Thus he said.

Gathering together all their sacred possessions, they came hither. To the place called since the first beginning, Moss Spring, they came. There they set down their sacred possessions in a row. There they stayed. Four days they say, but it was four years. There the two washed them. They took from all of them their slimy tails, their slimy horns. "Now, behold! Thus you will be sweet." There they stayed.

When their days were at an end they came hither. Gathering together all their sacred possessions, seeking Itiwana, yonder their roads went. To the place called since the first beginning Massed-cloud Spring, they came. There they set down their sacred possessions in a row. There they stayed quietly. Four days they stayed. Four days they say, but it was four years. There they stayed. There they counted up the days. For k̄ä-eto·we, four nights and four days. With fine rain caressing the earth, they passed their days. The days were made for łe-eto·we, mu-eto·we. For four days and four nights it snowed. When their days were at an end there they stayed.

When their days were at an end they arose. Gathering together all their sacred possessions, hither their roads went. To the place called since the first beginning Mist Spring their road came. There they sat down quietly. Setting out their sacred possessions in a row, they sat down quietly. There they counted up the days for one another. They watched the world for one another's waters. For k̦ä-eto·we, four days and four nights, with heavy rain caressing the earth they passed their days. When their days were at an end the days were made for łe-eto·we and mu-eto·we. Four days and four nights with falling snow the world was filled. When their days were at an end, there they stayed.

When all their days were passed, gathering together all their sacred possessions, hither their road went. To Standing-wood Spring they came. There they sat down quietly. Setting out their sacred possessions in a row, they stayed quietly. There they watched one another's days. For k̦ä-eto·we, four days and four nights with fine rain caressing the earth, they passed their days. When all their days were at an end, the days were made for łe-eto′we and mu-eto·we. For four days and four nights, with falling snow, the world was filled. When all their days were at an end, there they stayed.

When all their days were passed, gathering together their sacred possessions, and arising, hither they came. To the place called since the first beginning Upuilima they came. When they came there, setting down their sacred possessions in a row, they stayed quietly. There they strove to outdo one another. There they planted all their seeds. There they watched one another's days for rain. For k̦ä-eto·we, four days with heavy rain caressing the earth. There their corn matured. It was not palatable, it was bitter. Then the two said, "Now by whose will will our corn become fit to eat?" Thus they said. They summoned raven. He came and pecked at their corn, and it became good to eat. "It is fortunate that you have come." With this then, they lived.

When their days were at an end they arose. Gathering together their sacred possessions, they came hither. To the place called since the first beginning, Cornstalk-place they came. There they set down their sacred possessions in a row. There they stayed four days. Four days they say, but it was four years. There they planted all their seeds. There they watched one another's days for rain. During k̦ä-eto·we's four days and four nights, heavy rain fell. During łe-eto·we's and mu-eto·we's four days and four nights, the world was filled with falling snow. Their days were at an end. Their corn matured. When it was mature it was hard. Then the two said, "By whose will will our corn become soft? Well, owl." Thus they said. They summoned owl. Owl came. When he came he pecked at their corn and it became soft.

Then, when they were about to arise, the two said, "Come, let us go talk to the corn priest." Thus they said. They went. They came to where the corn priest stayed. "How have you lived these days?" "As we are living happily you have passed us on our road. Sit down." They sat down. There they questioned one another. "Well, speak. I think some word that is not too long, your word will be. Now, if you let me know that, remembering it, I shall always live." "Indeed, it is so. To-morrow, when we arise, we shall set out to seek Itiwana. Nowhere have we found the middle. Our children, our women, are tired. They are crying. Therefore we have come to you. To-morrow your two children will look ahead. Perhaps if they find the middle when our fathers, our mothers, k̂ä-eto·we, tcu-eto·we, mu-eto·we, łe-eto·we, all the society priests, come to rest, there our children will rest themselves. Because we have failed to find the middle." "Haiyi! Is that so? With plain words you have passed us on our road. Very well, then, thus it shall be." Thus he said. The two went.

Next morning when they were about to set out they put down a split ear of corn and eggs. They made the corn priest stand up. They said, "Now, my children, some of you will go yonder to the south. You will take these." Thus he said (indicating) the tip of the ear and the macaw egg. And then the ones that were to come this way took the base of the ear and the raven egg. Those that were to go to the south took the tip of the ear and the macaw egg. "Now, my children, yonder to the south you will go. If at any time you come to Itiwana, then some time we shall meet one another." Thus they said. They came hither.

They came to the place that was to be Katcina village. The girl got tired. Her brother said, "Wait, sit down for a while. Let me climb up and look about to see what kind of a place we are going to." Thus he said. His sister sat down. Her brother climbed the hill. When he had climbed up, he stood looking this way. "Eha! Maybe the place where we are going lies in this direction. Maybe it is this kind of a place." Thus he said and came down. Meanwhile his sister had scooped out the sand. She rested against the side of the hill. As she lay sleeping the wind came and raised her apron of grass. It blew up and she lay with her vulva exposed. As he came down he saw her. He desired her. He lay down upon his sister and copulated with her. His sister awoke. "Oh, dear, oh, dear," she was about to say (but she said,) "Watsela, watsela." Her brother said, "Ah!" He sat up. With his foot he drew a line. It became a stream of water. The two went about talking. The brother talked like Koyemci. His sister talked like Komak̂atsik̂. The people came.

"Oh alas, alas! Our children have become different beings." Thus they said. The brother speaking: "Now it will be all right for you to cross here." Thus he said. They came and went in. They entered the river. Some of their children turned into water snakes.

Some of them turned into turtles. Some of them turned into frogs. Some of them turned into lizards(?). They bit their mothers. Their mothers cried out and dropped them. They fell into the river. Only the old people reached the other side. They sat down on the bank. They were half of the people. The two said, "Now wait. Rest here." Thus they said. Some of them sat down to rest. The two said (to the others), "Now you go in. Your children will turn into some kind of dangerous animals and will bite you. But even though you cry out, do not let them go. If, when you come out on the other side, your children do not again become the kind of creatures they are now, then you will throw them into the water." Thus they said to them. They entered the water. Their children became different creatures and bit them. Even though they cried out, they crossed over. Then their children once more became the kind of creatures they had been. "Alas! Perhaps had we done that it would have been all right." Now all had crossed over.

There setting down their sacred possessions in a row, they stayed quietly. They stayed there quietly for four days. Thus they say but they stayed for four years. There each night they lived gaily with loud singing. When all their time was passed, the two said, "Come, let us go and talk to Ne'we·kwe." Thus they said. They went to where the Ne'we·kwe were staying. They came there. "How have you passed these days?" "Happily. You have come? Be seated." They sat down. Then they questioned them. "Now speak. I think some word that is not too long your word will be. If you let me know that, remembering it I shall always live." "Indeed it is so. To-morrow we shall arise. Our fathers, our mothers, k̜ä-eto·we, tcu-eto·we, mu-eto·we, łe-eto·we, all the society priests, are going to seek the middle. But nowhere have we come to the middle. Our children and our women are tired. They are crying now. Therefore we have passed you on your road. To-morrow you will look ahead. If perhaps somewhere you come to Itiwana there our children will rest." Thus they said. "Alas! but we are just foolish people. If we make some mistake it will not be right." Thus he said. "Well, that is of no importance. It can't be helped. We have chosen you." Thus they said. "Well indeed?" "Yes. Now we are going." "Go ahead." The two went out.

They came (to where the people were staying). "Come, let us go and speak to our children." Thus they said. They went. They entered the lake. It was full of katcinas. "Now stand still a moment. Our two fathers have come." Thus they said. The katcinas suddenly stopped dancing. When they stopped dancing they said to the two, "Now our two fathers, now indeed you have passed us on our road. I think some word that is not too long your word will be. If you will let us know that we shall always remember it." Thus he said. "Indeed it is so. To-morrow we shall arise. Therefore we have come to speak to you." "Well indeed? May you go happily. You will tell our parents, 'Do not worry.' We have not perished. In order to remain thus forever we stay here. To Itiwana but one day's travel remains. Therefore we stay near by. When our world grows old and the waters are exhausted and the seeds are exhausted, none of you will go back to the place of your first beginning. Whenever the waters are exhausted and the seeds are exhausted you will send us prayer sticks. Yonder at the place of our first beginning with them we shall bend over to speak to them. Thus there will not fail to be waters. Therefore we shall stay quietly near by." Thus they said to them. "Well indeed?" "Yes. You will tell my father, my mother, 'Do not worry.' We have not perished." Thus they said. They sent strong words to their parents. "Now we are going. Our children, may you always live happily." "Even thus may you also go." Thus they said to the two. They went out. They arrived. They told them. "Now our children, here your children have stopped. 'They have perished,' you have said. But no. The male children have become youths, and the females have become maidens. They are happy. They live joyously. They have sent you strong words. 'Do not worry,' they said." "Haiyi! Perhaps it is so."

They stayed overnight. Next morning they arose. Gathering together all their sacred possessions, they came hither. They came to Hanłipiŋka. Meanwhile the two Ne'we·kwe looked ahead. They came to Rock-in-the-river. There two girls were washing a woolen dress. They killed them. After they had killed them they scalped them. Then someone found them out. When they were found out, because they were raw people, they wrapped themselves in mist. There to where k̦ä-eto·we were staying they came. "Alack, alas! We have done wrong!" Thus they said. Then they set the days for the enemy. There they watched one another's days for rain. k̦ä-eto·we's four days and four nights passed with the falling of heavy rain. There where a waterfall issued from a cave the foam arose. There the two Ahaiyute appeared. They came to where k̦ä-eto·we were staying. Meanwhile, from the fourth innerworld, Unasinte,[99] Uhepololo,[1] Kailuhtsawak̦i, Hattuŋka, Oloma, Catunka, came out to sit down in the daylight. There they gave them the comatowe song cycle.[2] Meanwhile, right there, Coyote was going about hunting. He gave them their pottery drum. They sang comatowe.

After this had happened, the two said, "Now, my younger brother, Itiwana is less than one day distant. We shall gather together our

[99] Whirlwind.

[1] "Wool rolled up."

[2] "Spiral," a song sequence and dance occurring as the last rite of the scalp dance. Comatowe is also sung at the winter solstice.

children, all the beast priests, and the winged creatures, this night." They went. They came yonder to Comk̯äkwe. There they gathered together all the beasts, mountain lion, bear, wolf, wild cat, badger, coyote, fox, squirrel; eagle, buzzard, cokapiso, chicken hawk, bald-headed eagle, raven, owl. All these they gathered together. Now squirrel was among the winged creatures, and owl was among the beasts. "Now my children, you will contest together for your sun father's daylight. Whichever side has the ball, when the sun rises, they shall win their sun father's daylight." Thus the two said. "Indeed?" They went there. They threw up the ball. It fell on the side of the beasts. They hid it. After they had hidden it, the birds came one by one but they could not take it. Each time they paid four straws. They could not take it.

At this time it was early dawn. Meanwhile Squirrel was lying by the fireplace. Thus they came one by one but they could not take it. Eagle said, "Let that one lying there by the fireplace go." They came to him and said, "Are you asleep?" "No. I am not asleep." "Oh dear! Now you go!" Thus they said. "Oh no, I don't want to go," he said. He came back. "The lazy one does not wish to." Thus they said. Someone else went. Again they could not take it. Now it was growing light. "Let that one lying by the fireplace go." Thus they said. Again Buzzard went. "Alas, my boy, you go." "Oh, no, I don't feel like it." Thus he said. Again he went back. "He does not want to," he said. Again some one else went. Again they did not take it. Now it was growing light. Spider said to him, "Next time they come agree to go." Thus she said. Then again they said, "Let that one lying by the fireplace go." Thus they said; and again someone went. When he came there he said, "Alas, my boy, you go." "All right, I shall go." Thus he said and arose. As he arose Spider said to him, "Take that stick." He took up a stick, so short. Taking it, he went. Now the sun was about to rise. They came there. Spider said to him, "Hit those two sitting on the farther side." Thus she said. Bang! He knocked them down. He laid them down. Then, mountain lion, who was standing right there, said, "Hurry up, go after it. See whether you can take it." Thus he said. Spider said to him, "Say to him, 'Oh, no, I don't want to take it.' So she said." "Oh, no, I don't want to take it. Perhaps there is nothing inside. How should I take it? There is nothing in there." "That is right. There is nothing in there. All my children are gathered together. One of them is holding it. If you touch the right one, you will take it." "All right." Now Spider is speaking: "No one who is sitting here has it. That one who goes about dancing, he is holding it." Thus she said. He went. He hit Owl on the hand. The white ball came out. He went. He took up the hollow sticks and took them away with him. Now the birds hid the ball. Spider came down. Over all the sticks she spun her web. She fastened the ball with her web. Now the animals came one by one. Whenever they touched a stick, she pulled (the ball) away. Each time they paid ten straws. The sun rose. After sunrise, he was sitting high in the sky. Then the two came. They said, "Now, all my children, you have won your sun father's daylight, and you, beasts, have lost your sun father's daylight. All day you will sleep. After sunset, at night, you will go about hunting. But you, owl, you have not stayed among the winged creatures. Therefore you have lost your sun father's daylight. You have made a mistake. If by daylight, you go about hunting, the one who has his home above will find you out. He will come down on you. He will scrape off the dirt from his earth mother and put it upon you. Then thinking, 'Let it be here,' you will come to the end of your life. This kind of creature you shall be." Thus they said. They stayed there overnight. The animals all scattered.

The two went. They came to where k̯ä-eto·we were staying. Then they arose. Gathering together all their sacred possessions, they arose. Łe-eto·we said, "Now, my younger brothers, hither to the north I shall take my road. Whenever I think that Itiwana has been revealed to you, then I shall come to you." Thus he said, and went to the north. Now some woman, seeing them, said, "Oh dear! Whither are these going?" Thus she said:

Naiye heni aiye
Naiye heni aiye.

In white stripes of hail they went.

Meanwhile k̯ä-eto·we came hither. They came to House Mountain. When they came there they would not let them pass through. They fought together. A giant went back and forth before them. Thus they fought together. Thus evening came. In the evening they came back to Hanłipiŋka. Next day they went again. In heavy rain they fought together. In the evening they went back again. Next morning they went again for the third time. Again they fought together. The giant went back and forth in front. Even though she had arrows sticking in her body she did not die. At sunset they went back again. Next morning they went. They came there, and they fought together. Still they would not surrender. The giant went back and forth in front. Although she was wounded with arrows, she would not surrender. Ahaiyute said, "Alas, why is it that these people will not let us pass? Wherever may her heart be, that one that goes back and forth? Where her heart should be we have struck her, yet she does not surrender. It seems we can not overcome her. So finally go up to where your father stays. Without doubt he knows." Thus he said. His younger brother climbed up to where the sun was.

It was nearly noon when he arrived. "You have come?" "Yes, I have come." "Very well, speak. I think some word that is not too long your word will be. So if you let me know that, I shall always remember it." Thus he said. "Indeed, it is so. Our fathers, our mothers, k̯ä-eto·we, tcu-eto·we, mu-eto·we, łe-eto·we, all the society priests, have issued forth into the daylight. Here they go about seeking Itiwana. These people will not let them pass. Where does she have her heart, that one who goes back and forth before them? In vain have we struck her where her heart should be. Even though the arrows stick in her body, she does not surrender." "Haiyi! For nothing are you men! She does not have her heart in her body. In vain have you struck her there. Her heart is in her rattle." Thus he said. "This is for you and this is for your elder brother." Thus he said, and gave him two turquoise rabbit sticks. "Now, when you let these go with my wisdom I shall take back my weapons." "Haiyi! Is that so? Very well, I am going now." "Go ahead. May you go happily." Thus he said. He came down. His elder brother said to him, "Now, what did he tell you?" "Indeed, it is so. In vain do we shoot at her body. Not there is her heart; but in her rattle is her heart. With these shall we destroy her." Thus he said, and gave his brother one of the rabbit sticks. When he had given his brother the rabbit stick, "Now go ahead, you." Thus he said. The younger brother went about to the right. He threw it and missed. Whiz! The rabbit stick went up to the sun. As the rabbit stick came up the sun took it. "Now go ahead, you try." Thus he said. The elder brother went around to the left. He threw it. As he threw it, zip! His rabbit stick struck his rattle. Tu---n! They ran away. As they started to run away, their giant died. Then they all ran away. The others ran after them. They came to a village. They went into the houses. "This is my house;" "This is my house;" and "This is mine." Thus they said. They went shooting arrows into the roof. Wherever they first came, they went in. An old woman and a little boy this big and a little girl were inside.

In the center of their room was standing a jar of urine. They stuffed their nostrils with k̯änaite flowers and with cotton wool. Then they thrust their noses into the jar. The people could see them. "Oh, dear! These are ghosts!" Thus they said. Then the two said to them, "Do not harm them, for I think they know something. So even though it is dangerous they are still alive." Thus they said. The two entered. As they came in they questioned them. "And now do you know something? Therefore, even though it is dangerous, you have not perished." "Well, we have a sacred object." "Indeed! Very well, take them. We shall go. Your fathers, your mothers, k̯ä-eto·we, tcu-eto·we, mu-eto·we, łe-eto·we, you will pass on their roads. If your days are the same as theirs you will not be slaves. It does not matter that he is only a little boy. Even so, he will be our father. It does not matter that she is a little girl, she will be our mother." Thus he said. Taking their sacred object they went. They came to where k̠ä-eto·we were staying. There they said to them, "Now make your days." "Oh, no! We shall not be first. When all your days are at an end, then we shall add on our days." Thus they said. Then they worked for k̠ä-eto·we. K̠ä-eto·we's days were made. Four days and four nights, with fine rain falling, were the days of k̠ä-eto·we. When their days were at an end, the two children and their grandmother worked. Their days were made. Four days and four nights, with heavy rain falling, were their days. Then they removed the evil smell. They made flowing canyons. Then they said, "Halihi! Thank you! Just the same is your ceremony. What may your clan be?" "Well, we are of the Yellow Corn clan." Thus they said. "Haiyi! Even though your eton·e is of the Yellow Corn clan, because of your bad smell, you have become black. Therefore you shall be the Black Corn clan." Thus they said to them.

Then they arose. Gathering together all their sacred possessions, they came hither, to the place called, since the first beginning, Halona-Itiwana, their road came. There they saw the Navaho helper, little red bug. "Here! Wait! All this time we have been searching in vain for Itiwana. Nowhere have we seen anything like this." Thus they said. They summoned their grandchild, water bug. He came. "How have you lived these many days?" "Where we have been living happily you have passed us on our road. Be seated." Thus they said. He sat down. Then he questioned them. "Now, indeed, even now, you have sent for me. I think some word that is not too long your word will be. So now, if you will let me know that, I shall always remember it." "Indeed, it is so. Our fathers, our mothers, k̠ä-eto·we, tcu-eto·we, mu-eto·we, łe-eto·we, all the society priests, having issued forth into the daylight, go about seeking the middle. You will look for the middle for them. This is well. Because of your thoughts, at your heart, our fathers, k̠ä-eto·we, tcu-eto·we, mu-eto·we, łe-eto·we, will sit down quietly. Following after those, toward whom our thoughts bend, we shall pass our days." Thus they said. He sat down facing the east. To the left he stretched out his arm. To the right he stretched out his arm, but it was a little bent. He sat down facing the north. He stretched out his arms on both sides. They were just the same. Both arms touched the horizon. "Come, let us cross over to the north. For on this side my right arm is a little bent." Thus he said. They crossed (the river). They rested. He sat down. To all directions he stretched out his arms. Everywhere it was the same. "Right here is the middle." Thus he said. There his fathers, his mothers, k̄ä-eto·we, tcu-eto·we, mu-eto·we, łe-eto·we, all the society priests, the society p̄ekwins, the society bow priests, and all their children came to rest.

Thus it happened long ago.

Komosona an p̂enan·e

inɔ·te t̂o′wa yä′la łu′wala yäłtap a·′wunan a·′wehkwi hic ha′p̂ok̭ä ha′p’onan le·′ep i′yantehkunacna’k̭ä. kopleat̂ap hon e′lutea te′k̭̂än·a-a·′wots a·′te’ona k̭es em·a i′htohnaiye a·′wok̭ a·′te’ona k̭es e′m·a i′htohnaiye kwa hon e′lutea a·′natun te′akona yu′’he·tam·e. le′’tikwap a·′wan p̂e′kwin le′skwanan kwac yu′’he·tam·e le′’kwap e′ła kwa yu′’he·tam·e hai′yi tek̭̂aiał t̂on a·′wotsi a′k̭ä la′lik hon to′pin·te hon tci′mik̭̂änapk̭ä. i′mat le’kon a·′wan te′lik̭inan i′tiułak̭̂än·a a′k̭ä la′lik ho′’na·wan t̂e′apk̂una. i′t̂inan ła′k̭̂ikä. le’kwap au′h·ito le’tikwanan te′lik̭ina· ya·′k̭̂änapk̭ä. te′lik̭inan ya·′k̭̂änan ha′tin k̭̂aia′kwin te′lik̭inan a·′k̭̂änapk̭ä. a·′wan te′lik̭inan te’tcip i′sk̂ɔn i′yantse’manapk̭ä. si tcu′watik̭äp i′tiwan·akwi t̂e′k̂ohanan yam a·′tatcu yam a·′tsita yam tca′we a·′wan t̂e′wanan pi′’lak̭̂än·a le′’anak̭äp kok’wa·ciwan·i le′stikwanan ma a′k̭ä lu′k̭ä hon tatc i′l·ap̂a le′’anaknan k̭ä′klo ci′wan·i a′ntecema′tinapk̭ä. yam a·′tatcu ha′p̂onakwin i·yap i′sk̂ɔn te′lik̭inan a′k̭ä ya′t̂ena-t̂sumek̭̂änak̭̂äp a·′teak̭ä—.

te′lakwai’ik̭ä. ƚi′tekwak̭ä t̂san’ona yä′tcu i·mup s’isk̂ɔn i′yantece-man i′wokwi’k̭ä. k̭ä′klo ci′wan·i le′skwanan kople′a i′tiwan·akwi t̂e′k̂ohanan a·′tatcu a·′tsita tca′we ho’ a·′wona-e′latek̭än·a le’kwap an a·′nana mo′’lanhakto a·′ci·wan·i i′seto·nan k̭ał a·′wa·k̭ä. tcim t̂e′k̂ohatip e′lehoł ya′to kwai’ip t̂o′wa yä′lakwin a·′wi·k̭ä. T̂o′wa yä′lakwin a·′wi·nan a·′wulohk̭ä—. ho′łtikoł k̭̂ä′kwekwin a·′ye·mak̭ä. i′sk̂ɔn a·′ho’ anhap̂op i′sk̂ɔn p̂e′yek̭ä. ko’lehoł te′atun’ona lak̭t̂ap a·′witen t̂e′wana hom tca′w a·tc i·′yan·a. t̂o′’na·wan a·′tci t̂e′wanan pi′’la’un·a. le′’kwap i′sk̂ɔn a·′p̂eyek̭ä a·′ho’ le′stikwanan ma ho′nkwa. i′sk’ɔn ko’lehoł teatun’ona i′yanhetocnan a·′wa·k̭ä. a·wa·nap a·′ho’ a·′teak̭ä—.

a·′witen t̂e′wap kok̂wa·tc i·k̭’ä. a·′wan k̭̂äkwe’koa a·tc a·′wan t̂e′wanan pi′’lak̭ä. lak̭t̂ap a·′witen t̂e′wana· hon a·′wi·yan·a. ha′’i t̂e′wanan yä′ton·e t̂on kwa·hoł ye′lek̭enapk̭ät̂ap a·′witen t̂e′wanan yä′tonan hon a·wi′yan·a. t̂e′ƚi·nan k̂ɔ′kci t̂o′’na·wan t̂e′wanan te′k̭̂än·a le’k̭̂wanan s’a·tc a·′k̭ä.

a·′witenak̭äna·na yä′to kwai′’ip o′k̭anan i′towacenapk̭ä. su′nhap a·tc i·′k̭ä he′cik̭̂änak̭ä a·′tci p̂en-a′l·uk̭ä. ya′ton kwa′ton s’a·tc a·′k̭ä. a·tci koko ya′niktohap s’a·′wik̭ä. ɔ′ti·-a·′wal·uk̭ä. i′te’tci-k̭änapk̭ä t̂a ha′m·e a·′wik̭ä. t̂a u′hson ɔ′ti·-a·′wal·uk̭ä. t̂a ham·

The Talk of the Katcina Chief

Long ago, when the village stood on the top of Corn Mountain, those whose roads go ahead all met together. When they had gathered together they questioned one another: "How shall we enjoy ourselves? Now the men are greatly increasing in number and the women are greatly increasing in number. It is not yet clear with what pleasures we shall pass our time." (5) Thus they said to one another. Their p̄ekwin said, "Is it not clear?" Thus he said. "No, it is not clear." "Indeed, in vain you are men! Yonder once we had our first beginning. Perhaps there we shall set down prayer sticks for them because there our children stay quietly." Thus he said. "Hear! hear!" they said. They made prayer sticks. (10) When they had finished their prayer sticks, to Whispering Spring they sent their prayer sticks. When their prayer sticks arrived there, there they (the divine ones) thought it over among themselves. "Now which of you will count up the days at Itiwana for our daylight fathers, our mothers, our children?" Thus they said. The priests of the katcinas said: "Well, this one, because he is our father." Thus they said. They sent for k̭ä'klo priest. (15) When he came to where his fathers were gathered together they laid hold of him fast with their prayer stick. They waited.

It was spring. At the new moon of the month of little sand storms (March) there, desiring one another, they sat down together in council. K̭ä'klo priest said, "How shall I come to our daylight fathers, our mothers, our children, at Itiwana?" Thus he said. His grandfathers, Molanhakto,[3] priests, set him on their backs. They came hither. (20) Just at dawn, shortly before sunrise, they came to Corn Mountain. At Corn Mountain they went about in the streets. Then somewhere they climbed up to a house. There where the people were gathered together he spoke. How it would be (he told them). "This day and four more days, and then my two children will come. They will count the days for you." (25) Thus he said. The people spoke. They said, "Well, is that so?" After he had gone the people waited.

After four days the two katcinas came.[4] At all their houses they counted the days for them. "Four days from this day we shall come. On the third (30) day you will have made everything ready and then on the fourth day we shall come. May you all pass a good night." Saying this, the two went.

Four times the sun rose and the women folks cooked. In the evening the two came. "Make haste!" they went about saying. The sun went in. (35) They went. Then meeting them the others came. They went about, dancing. They finished. Then others came.

[3] The Koyemci, esoteric name.

[4] The announcers who come four days before ko'uptconawe.

a·′wik̯ä. t̄a u′hson a·′wa·nap t̄a ham. a·′wik̯ä. u′hson a·wa·nihap i′te’tcik̯ä. s’a·wa·k̯ä.

le′snahoł a·wi·tela kɔ·′wihoł t̄e′wap tcu′watikoł a′cep kɔ·′wihoł t̄e′wap t̄a a·′wik̯ä. t̄a a·′wa·nap t̄a tcu′watikoł a′cep le′snak̄ɔn a·′wi·tełnan ho’ i′yona te’tci a·′witela.

le′snahoł a·′teap et łu′walona e′lute a·′teapte kwa e′lam·e. lu′kniak̄ɔn·te le′stikwanan si hom tca′we kwa hi′nik le′’nate hon a·′witelap e′lecukwa. le′’tikwana ho′’na t̄on el a·′wuna-p̄an·a. kwa hon le· a·wina’ma le’tikwanan yam co′’yan·e yam u′lin·e a·tc a′nimuna·wap a·′ho’i a·tci u′napk̯ä a·′tci u′nap̄ap t̄on e′le a·tci u′nap̄an·a a′k̯ä t̄on a·′tci a′nteliana a·′ho’ a·′ya·k̯̄äna·wa. t̄on a′k̯a yɔ·′tip̄ap tomt hon a·′winan t̄o′’na·wa łu-e′hkwik̯̄än·a. le′’natap honkwat e′lek̯’än·a. a′k̯äp to′’na ho′’i yo′nate′’tci hon a·′wi·telap kwa e′lam·e. le′’iyanaknan i′sk̄ɔn a·′ya·k̯̄änapk̯ä pa′tcin u′lin·e a·′ho’ a·′ya·’ap łu′walan ɔ·′tipk̯ä. mo′łana·wap łu′walan i·′k̯̄etsana kwa tcuhoł a′cena’ma. lesnahoł a·′teaiye. le′sna’kona y·ɔ′tip̄ap kwa tcu′hoł a′cena’ma a·′teak̯ä—.

te′htsitip ko[1]′uptconak̯̄äp t̄e′łap ɔ′ti-a·′walup tcuwa ma′k̯i yam a′ktsik i′l·i te′maiyaiye. ɔ·′tipk̯ä. Ya′łakwai’ik̯ä.

kɔ·′wihoł t̄e′wap te′kwanan a·′t̄san i′k̄ocena·wap t̄o′p̄a tsa′wak̯ i′snok̄onhoł a·′nap a·′t̄sana i′k̄ocena·wap a′ktsik le′skwanan i′sno tsa′wak̯ a·nan te′cukhok t̄ełap ko′k̄we’le te′ak̯ä. kwa ho′nkwa ko′k̄w a·′witelena’ma le′’kwap a·′t̄san i·′hatianan yam k̯̄ä′kwin a·′te′’tci·łnan yam a·′łacina·we ya′tinan honkwa kwa kokw a·′witelena’ma le′’tikwap tcu′wap le′skwa k̯̄aiyu’ani le′skwe’a. le′’tikwap te′lok̯änap̄a! kwa le′sna te′am·e a·′wantehacan·a le′’awa-naknan a·′wan a·′tatcu i·′yatina·wap p̄e′na· te′’tci.

u′pa·wa’kona kokw i′kwana kwahoł wɔ·w a′t̄an·i a·′ho’ a·′ya·’a. ye′lek̯̄äp a·′wik̯ä. te′cun a·′wal·uk̯ä. łu′walan t̄em·ła kwa′hoł a′wana’me. i·natik̯ä ta·′htcic an a·′łacina·we lakhoł a·′witen t̄e′li’ta p̄ɔ′tcip̄a i′k̄oloye. to·mt i′tok̯ena.wa. kwa hoł yu’he·tamap ko′łu-wala·kwin p̄enan a·k̯äk̯ä. ko′łuwala·kwin p̄e′nan te′’tcip i′sk̄ɔn łu′walemak̯ä. sai′yał’at̄ap te′mtemci k̄o′hana ko′yemci ko′ko t̄e′m·ła k̯äł a·′wa·k̯ä. te′cuna a·′wal·uk̯ä. ki′witsiwa’kona p̄e′nan

Then those went about, dancing. Then others came. When those had gone still others came. When those were about to go they made an end of it. They went.

Thus they came in groups. After a short time someone died. Then after a few (40) days they came again. Again after they had gone someone died. Thus whenever they came, they took someone with them when they went.

Thus they lived. And although the people of the village enjoyed themselves, yet it was not right. Then these (the katcinas) said, "Now, my children, I think it should not be thus. If we keep on coming it will not be right." Thus they said. "You will look at us well. We do not always (45) look like this." Thus they said. Then the two set down their face mask and their helmet mask. The people looked at them. As they looked at them—"You will look at them well so that you can copy them. You will make them and give them life. When you dance with them we shall come and stand before you. If we do thus perhaps it will be all right, because if we take someone with us when we (50) come it is not right." Thus they said to one another. Then they made them. When they brought to life the chin mask and the helmet mask, the people of the village danced in them. They made them right, and the people of the village were happy. No one died. Thus they live. When they danced thus no one died. Thus they lived.

In the winter they had ko'uptconawa. At night they went about, dancing. Some young woman (55) was watching the dance with her little boy. They danced. It was all over.

A few days later the children were playing outdoors. A young man went by where the children were playing. The little boy said, "See that young man going by there? The other night he was a katcina maiden. Perhaps the masked gods do not really come." Thus he said. The children heard him. When they came to their houses, (60) they told their elders. "Perhaps the masked gods do' not really come." Thus they said. "Who said so?" "K̄ai'yuani says so." Thus they said. "Keep quiet! Don't do that. They will punish you." Thus they said to them. Their fathers told one another. They talked only of that.

In the kivas they worked on their masks. They made some dangerous monsters. (65) When they were ready they came. They went around searching. In all the village they could not find him. Meanwhile his parents were hiding him way back in the dust in the fourth inner room. They just brought him food. When they did not see him they sent word to the village of the katcinas. When their message came to the village of the katcinas they arose. The

kwa′tełk̭̄äna·wan i′te’tcap kwa hoł tcu·′wa. an k̭̄äkwin a·′te’tcik̭ä. an k̭̄äkwin a·′te’tcinan p̄e′na kwa·tok̭̄äna·wap kwa tcu·′wa. ho′łomackon a·′k̭ä. ko′yemci a·′p̄ani·nan kwa yu·’he·tam·e. le′’tikwe’a. le′’tikwap sai′yaħi’a a·′witen te′an i′łapatci t̄si′nan·e i′łuwak̭ä. ham a·tci t̄e′wankwin t̄u′na ye·′la’up ham a·′tci su′nhakwin t̄u′na ye·′la’up te′ponulapk̭ä. i′mtek̭änan ʙuix! le′’tikwap a′wek i′helotik̭ä kwi′lik̭̄änan te′ponulapk̭ä i′mtek̭änan ʙuix! le′’tikwap an k̭ä′kwen o′k̄ok̭ä. ha’ik̭anan te′ponu′lapk̭ä. i′mtek̭änan ʙuix! le′’tikwap an k̭̄ä′kwen e′lehoł i′tehłakun o′k̄ok̭ä. a·′witenak̭änan te′ponulapk̭ä. i′mtek̭änan ʙuix! le′’tikwap an k̭̄ä′kwen o′k̄ok̭ä i′tehłakun o′k̄op la′khok[u] a·′witen t̄e′li’tan p̄o′’ule ko·′yemci le’stikwanan la′k·we k̭ihe p̄o’ule′! le′’tikwanan a′nakwai’ik̭̄änapk̭ä. ko′k̄w’ a·′witełna ya′ktocnapk̭ä. i·′t̄enap te′mtemci k̄o′hana i·′k̭änan a′lu’ya hu· hu· te′mtemci·’. hu·′. na′na hanat ya′kto halasap s’on a·′wa·nuwa. ko·′yemci le′’anak̭äp te′mtemci i′k̭äne’u i′k̭änan a′l·u’ya hic k̭äk̭̄hoł tenala’ap e′lakwin te′’tcinan hak̭̄ämpinan yat̄enan huk̄we′ a′ptsik̭ä! wic a′ptsinan i·′teh-k̭̄e′atok̭ä. la′nip a′hnan t̄a i′teh-k̭̄e′atok̭ä. la′nip a′hnan t̄a i′teh-k̭̄e′atok̭ä. la′nip t̄a i′teh-k̭̄e′atok̭ap la′nip ko·′yem·ci tikwa·wak̭ä. ko′łuwala·kwin a·′te’tcinan u′kwatok̭ä.

ta·′htcic t̄o′wa yä′lan k̭̄aiyu’ani an łu′nin mo′łam·e p̄alok̭ä. le′’na te′atip ko′tik̭än i′tehyak̭ä a′k̭ä hoł tcu·′wa ko·′wi tsam ła′na ko′puana’k̭ä lu′k̭ä p̄enan ko′mosona yam tcaw a·′wamp̄eye’a. hoł tcu·′wa t̄o′miyacnan p̄e′nap a′ntehacan·a. a′k̭ä lu′k̭ä p̄e′na· i′panaiye. yai′yu’ya·na t̄on a·′tek̭än′a.

le’n i′no·te te′atik̭ä.

sayałia and white temtemci and the koyemci and (70) all the katcinas came hither. They went about searching. They called into all the kivas. When they had been to all of them and found no one there they came to his house. They called in. "He's not here. He has gone far away." The koyemci came down. "We can't find him," they said. When they had said this the sayałia stood on four cross marks (on the roof). Two of them (75) stood facing the east, the other two stood facing the west. They turned around. When they had made a complete circuit they called, "Bu——ix!" The earth shook. The second time they turned about. When they had made a complete circuit, "Bu——ix!" they said. The walls of the house cracked. They turned around the third time. When they had made a complete circuit, "Bu——ix!" they said. (80) The house cracked nearly to the ground. The fourth time they turned around. When they had made a complete circuit, "Bu——ix!" they said. The walls cracked all the way down to the ground; there in the fourth room he was sitting. The koyemci said, "Look in there, our little friend is sitting within!" Thus they said. They pulled him out. The katcinas came. They struck him. When they were finished the white temtemci walked around angrily. "Hoo—tem-tem-ci tem-tem-ci hoo—!" "Grandfather hurry! Hit him hard! (85) We want to go!" Thus said the koyemci. Temtemci was angry. He was running around angrily. A long time afterwards he came to where the boy was standing. He seized his forelock. Hu̹kwe! He cut him. He cut his head off at the neck and threw it up. It fell. He picked it up and again threw it up. It fell. He picked it up and again threw it up. It fell. Again he threw it up. It fell. Then the koyemci used it as a kick stick. They came to the village of the katcinas. (90) Near by on an ant hill they set it down. Then they went in.

Meanwhile at Corn Mountain they buried K̹aiyu'ani's headless body. By doing thus they made the Katcina society valuable. Therefore, to any little boy who is initiated into the Katcina society the katcina chief tells this story. Whoever forgets and talks of this will be punished. Therefore these words are not to be told. (95) You will be mindful of it.

This happened long ago.

ZUÑI RITUAL POETRY

By RUTH L. BUNZEL

CONTENTS

* The items marked with an asterisk are presented in text with interlinear and free translation; the others text and free translation only.

ZUÑI RITUAL POETRY

By Ruth L. Bunzel

INTRODUCTION

The Nature and Function of Prayer

Spoken prayer in Zuñi is called t̃ewusu p̃ena·we, "prayer talk." This includes personal prayers, all the set prayers of rituals, chants, the origin myth in its ritual forms, the "talk" of komosono and other set speeches. It is also used for urgent requests. (t̃ewusu p̃eye'a—"he speaks prayers, i. e., begs, implores.")

Prayer is never the spontaneous outpouring of the overburdened soul; it is more nearly a repetition of magical formulae. A good deal has already been said (p. 493) about the rôle of prayer in the ritual. The prayers constitute the very heart of a ceremony. Like fetishes, they are sacred and powerful in themselves. Their possession is a source of power; their loss or impairment a great danger. Zuñis will describe esoteric ceremonies fully and vividly, but there are two thing which they are equally reluctant to do—to exhibit sacred objects or to repeat the words of a prayer. There is much less reticence about songs, except for a few special, secret songs. Prayer frequently forms part of set rituals. Then whether publicly declaimed or muttered so as to be inaudible to profane ears, the efficacy of the prayer depends in no small measure on its correct rendition. The prayers for individual use, such as accompany offerings of prayer meal, food, or prayer sticks, requests for medical service, etc., are also fixed in form and content, although they are individually varied in degree of elaboration. "Some men who are smart talk a long time, but some are just like babies." There are certain other occasions on which men can display their skill in handling the poetic medium—when they are visited in their houses by the katcinas; when they are called upon to take part in the games of the Koyemci; when they are appointed to office; or otherwise signaled out for honor or blessing by the supernaturals. In such cases one must improvise quickly and handle correctly the ritual vocabulary, rhythms, characteristic long periods, and, above all, speak without any hesitation or fumbling and for as long as possible. There is no time limit, no admonitions to be brief and to the point.

The set prayers must be formally learned—they are not just picked up. The most formal instruction is that connected with the transmission of the prayers of the Ca'lako. Each kiva has a Ca'lako wo'le, who, among his other duties, keeps the prayers. Immediately after the winter solstice the Ca'lako appointees come to him to be taught the necessary prayers. The wo'le meets with them for the four nights following each planting of prayer sticks, and as often besides as may be necessary. The Saiyataca party, whose ritual is the most elaborate, meets every night. Most of this time is given to the "long talk," the litany that is declaimed in the house of the host on the night of their final ceremonies. There are many other prayers that accompany all their activities—prayers for the making and planting of prayer sticks, for getting their mask from the people who keep it and returning it, for various stages in dressing and in their progress toward the village, for the dedication of the house, for blessing the food, for thanking the singers and the hosts, for going away. However, the "long talk" and the "morning talk" are chanted aloud in unison and must be letter perfect. The method of instruction is for the wo'le to intone the prayer, the pupils joining in as they can. One-half of the chant is taken each night. The phraseology of the prayers is so stereotyped that the principal difficulty in learning a long prayer is to keep the sequence. For this purpose certain cult groups have special mnemonic devices. The K̂äklo "talk" recorded in text by Mrs. Stevenson is such a record. It is an outline naming in order the various personages called and the places visited, it being assumed that the performer can fill in the outline from his knowledge of the poetic forms. It takes the men appointed to impersonate the gods all of the year to learn their prayers. As the time for the ceremony approaches great concern is felt, and sometimes the ceremony is postponed because the men are not ready. On the night after the ceremony the men go once again to the wo'le and give the prayer back. They recite it for him. At the close he inhales, and they do not, and so he takes from them the spirit of the prayer.

The instruction in prayers that are not publicly performed is less formal. Boys learn the a, b, c's of religious participation, including elementary prayers, from their fathers. After initiation into a medicine society a man goes at once to his ceremonial father to learn to make the prayer sticks of the society, and at the same time learn prayers for the making and offering of prayer sticks. He makes some payment to his father for this information—a shirt or a headband or a few pieces of turquoise. Women do not make their own prayer sticks, but they go similarly to their "fathers" to learn the required prayers. So every additional bit of knowledge is acquired. As more esoteric information is sought, the expense for instruction increases greatly. A certain old man in one of the priesthoods knew a particular prayer and the order of events in a rarely performed ceremony. He refused to teach these things to anyone. When he was very old and his death was expected his colleagues wished to learn this prayer from him. He was finally persuaded to teach them for a consideration. The woman member of the priesthood contributed a woman's shawl, the men things of greater value, to his fee. He taught the prayer but withheld the other information, and finally died without communicating it. Sometimes a man who is apt and curious and wealthy may collect prayers, the way men in other societies accumulate oil paintings or other works of art, and eventually turn them to profit. The cost of most information is not so excessive that a poor man can not, with the practice of a little thrift, acquire whatever he wishes to know.[1] He can, if he wishes, and if he has friends, learn the prayers of the Ne'we·kwe without actually joining their society. His ceremonial affiliations restrict his right to use these prayers, but many men go to expense to learn prayers they have no intention of using. The Saiyataca texts recorded in the following pages and many others were given me by a man who had never impersonated Saiyataca and never expected to. They were verified after the informant's death by the Saiyataca wo'le, who wondered how and why the informant had learned them. I myself heard the actual chant twice after recording the text and know it to be correct.

Zuñi Poetic Style

As might be expected, prayers are highly formalized in content and mode of expression. Nearly all prayers are requests accompanying offerings. They have three sections, which always appear in the same order: A statement of the occasion, a description of the offering, and the request. In long and important prayers the statement of the occasion is a synoptic review of ritual acts leading up to the present moment of a ceremony. Thus, Saiyataca's chant begins with a description of the winter solstice ceremony when the appointment was made and follows the Saiyataca party through all the minor ceremonies of the year, even enumerating the various shrines at which prayer sticks were offered. The prayers over novices at their initiation ceremony begin with a formal description of their illness and cure. In prayers which do not mark the culmination of long ceremonies the statement of the occasion may be no more than a statement of the time of day or the season of the year, and some veiled allusion to the special deities who are being invoked.

[1] In Zuñi a "poor man" is one who has no special knowledge or position in the ceremonial system. A "valuable" man has knowledge and prestige. "Knowledge" (anikwanan·e) is the word for supernatural power.

There is always a formal request for all the regular blessings—long life, old age, rain, seeds, fecundity, riches, power, and "strong spirit." This formal request closes the prayer. Any special request, such as those for summer storms and winter snows, safety in war, rescue from disease, precede this. Requests that are strictly personal never figure in prayer. One prays always for "all good fortune," never for special and particular benefit. The only exceptions are in the case of prayers in sickness and the prayer of a widower to his dead wife with the request that she should not pursue him.

Zuñi prayers are distinctly matter of fact. They deal with external events and conditions rather than inner states. Outside of the request, their content is limited to two fields: Natural phenomena, such as sunrise, sunset, dawn, night, the change of seasons, the phases of the moon, rainstorms, snowfall, the growth of corn; and ritual acts, especially the making of prayer sticks, setting up of altars, and transfer of authority. Rituals of a more intimate and personal character, such as fasting and abstinence, are never mentioned. In their prayers Zuñis do not humble themselves before the supernatural; they bargain with it.

There are regular stereotyped phrases for all things commonly alluded to in prayer. The sun always "comes out standing to his sacred place," "night priests draw their dark curtain," the corn plants "stretch out their hands to all directions calling for rain," the meal painting on an altar is always "our house of massed clouds," prayer sticks are "clothed in our grandfather, turkey's, robe of cloud." Events are always described in terms of these stereotypes, which are often highly imaginative and poetic.[2] These fixed metaphors are the outstanding feature of Zuñi poetic style. There are not very many of them; they are used over and over again, the same imagery appearing repeatedly in one prayer. A prayer recorded by Cushing more than 50 years ago contains all of the same stereotypes and no turns of expression different from those in use to-day. A comparison of Cushing's texts [3] with mine shows a rigidity of style in oral tradition.

The sentence structure is that of continued narrative in the hands of a particularly able story-teller. Zuñi is a language that is very sensitive to skillful handling. Oratory is a recognized art, and prayer is one of the occasions on which oratory is used. The best prayers run to long periods—the longer the better, since clarity of expression is not necessary, nor particularly desirable.

Zuñi, like Latin, is a highly inflected language and can handle effectively involved sentences that can not be managed intelligibly in

---

[2] Some of the most striking passages have been quoted. (See pp. 483–486.)

[3] Unfortunately Cushing has published only short texts which do not do justice to Zuñi style. One long text which he recorded is to be published in the Journal of American Folk-Lore with a parallel modern version.

English. These features, which are difficult enough of translation in prose, are emphasized in the poetry. The long period is a characteristic feature. The typical Zuñi word order is subject, object, verb; the verb always holding the final position. The usual method of expressing temporal or causal subordination is by means of participial or gerundive clauses, fully inflected, preceding the principal proposition. These participial clauses are impossible in English. In the translation it has been necessary, therefore, to break up the original sentences. Thereby an important and effective stylistic feature is unavoidably lost. But the reader should think of the Zuñi sentences rolling on like the periods of a Ciceronian oration to their final close.

Another difficulty of translation, which will be alluded to frequently in the following pages, is the impossibility of translating the word plays with which the texts abound. To quote one example: The root łea- means, in its intransitive inflection, to wear or hold in the hand; in its transitive inflection, to clothe or to give into the hand. There the sentence li·ł ho' ťo' teliḵinan a·łea'u means both, "I here hand you these prayer sticks," or "I clothe you with these prayer sticks." Folk tales and religious beliefs utilize this double entendre. It is believed, for instance, that when people neglect to plant prayer sticks to the gods their clothing wears out. The passage where the word cipololon·e is used with the double meaning of "smoke" and "mist" is a striking example. The suppliant offers smoke of the sacred cigarette to the rain makers. They are conceived as taking the cigarette and smoking in turn. They "send forth their smoky breath," i. e., mist or fog.

Word play is used with still greater subtlety in the description of the prayer-stick offering. Many Zuñi roots are neutral; i. e., can be inflected to form both nouns and verbs.[4] ikwi- is to tie something about something else; ikwin·e, literally a tying about, is the usual word for belt. To say, therefore, "I tie the cotton about it," is precisely the same as to say "I belt him with a cotton belt." So the whole image of the making of the prayer stick or the dressing of an idol is built up linguistically. It is very difficult to tell how much is word play, how much metaphor, and how much is actual personification. The Zuñi finds these ambiguities intriguing.

This leads us to the third form of word play, the deliberate use of ambiguity, both verbal and grammatical. There are passages where subject and object are deliberately confounded, although there are excellent means for avoiding such ambiguity. These sentences are perfectly grammatical and can be correctly interpreted in two ways.

[4] This is not, strictly speaking, true in precisely these terms. As a matter of fact these stems are probably verbal, but a complete demonstration of their character would take us into linguistic subtleties beyond the scope of this paper.

The use of obsolete or special words has occasioned some difficulty. The expression k̹acima t̃apela for ladder is one case. Tapela, the Zuñis say, is an "old word" for ladder. T̃apelan·e, however, was a load of wood tied up as it used to be in the days when wood was brought on foot. Wood is no longer brought in this way, but the word, fixed in metaphor, has survived. There are a number of similar examples. In such cases the old translation has been retained.

It has been impossible, of course, to render the original rhythm. One characteristic feature, however, has been retained, namely, its irregularity, the unsymmetrical alternation of long and short lines. Cushing, in his commendable desire to render Zuñi verse into vivid and intelligible English verse, committed the inexcusable blunder of reducing the Zuñi line to regular short-line rhymed English stanzas. If one were to choose a familiar English verse form it should be the line of Milton or, better still, the free verse of the King James version of the psalms. I have tried to retain the sense in the original of the fluidity and variety of the verse form. In reading the translations one must be mindful of Zuñi methods of declamation. The short lines are declaimed slowly and with marked emphasis, the long lines are spoken rapidly, unaccented syllables are slurred or elided, and the word accents pile up on each other. The two types of line are like the booming of the surf and the rushing of the brook.

Zuñi poetry has no feminine endings.[5] The heavy accent with noticeable lengthening on the final syllable can not be transferred to English. The translation therefore suffers greatly from loss of sonority and vigor. In the original every line is like the declaration of a creed—an effect which no translation can adequately render. It is interesting to note that although the natural cadence of Zuñi is trochaic, the poetic rhythm is predominantly iambic. The principal word accent in Zuñi is invariably on the first syllable, with a secondary accent, in words of four or more syllables, on the penult. The final syllable is always unaccented, yet the important poetic stress is always on the final syllable of the line, which gives the verse a curious syncopated quality, very difficult of reproduction. The final syllable is usually distinguished by prolongation and a high falling tone.

[5] Every line ends in a vowel. Most Zuñi words terminate in vowels, but words ending in consonants—for example, the participles in -nan and -ap take special forms -na or -nana and -ap̃'a when occurring finally; -a is the most usual vocalic ending, but there is no true rhyming.

I. PRAYERS TO THE ANCIENTS

An Offering of Food to the Ancestors

The offering of food to the dead forms an important part of Zuñi household ritual. Cushing states that a bit of food is offered in the fire at each meal by all partaking, and that no child is weaned until he is able to make this offering with a suitable prayer. At the present time the practice is by no means universal. It is made, with very little ceremony, by priests and the female heads of their houses. The female heads of houses holding ceremonial objects make offerings to these objects before serving food. Each appointee to ceremonial office makes offerings at nightfall in the river, about a mile west of Zuñi. The food thus offered is carried by the river to the supernaturals at the village of the masked gods. Offerings of food are conspicuous at any ceremonial meal, and each man holding ceremonial office receives a package to be offered later in the river. With offerings in the house no prayer is spoken—at most only a few words are mumbled: "Eat; may our roads be fulfilled," or "May we be blessed with life." With outdoor offerings, long prayers are spoken. Offerings, whether of food, corn meal, or prayer sticks, are never made specifically to one's own ancestors, but to *the* ancestors.

After the crops are harvested in fall ghosts' day or grandmothers' day is announced by the sakisti (sacristan of the ancient mission church).[2] On this day large quantities of food are prepared, only products of that year's harvest being used, a lamb of that spring's lambing, bread made of new wheat and corn, and anything else that has been raised. The melons are gone by that time, but some are always saved for the grandmothers. Before eating the evening meal women make their offerings in the fire, a few ears of corn, a dish of lamb stew, a loaf of bread, a roll of paper bread. After dark the men take even greater quantities to the river. The following prayer is used, probably, with this special offering.

This day my children,	lu'k̯ä yä'ton·e
	hom tca'we
For their fathers,	yam a·'tatcu
Their ancestors,	yam a·'łacina·we

[2] In 1927 it fell on November 9. For the probable Catholic origin of the feast in All Souls' Day, see Parsons All Souls' Day at Zũni, Acoma, and Laguna; Journal of American Folk Lore 30:495.

For you who have attained the far-off place of waters,[3]
This day
My children
Have prepared food for your rite.

Now our sun father
Has gone in to sit down at his sacred place.[4]
Taking the food my children have prepared at their fireplaces
(I have come out.)
Those who hold our roads,[5]
The night priests,[6]
Coming out rising to their sacred place
Will pass us on our roads.
This night
I add to your hearts.
With your supernatural wisdom
You will add to your hearts.
Let none of you be missing
But all add to your hearts.
Thus on all sides you will talk together.
From where you stay quietly
Your little wind-blown clouds,
Your fine wisps of cloud,
Your massed clouds you will send forth to sit down with us;
With your fine rain caressing the earth,
With all your waters
You will pass to us on our roads.
With your great pile of waters,
With your fine rain caressing the earth,
With your heavy rain caressing the earth,
You will pass to us on our roads.
My fathers,
Add to your hearts.
Your waters,
Your seeds,
Your long life,[7]
Your old age
You will grant to us.

le'hokᵘ ḵä'cima t̄e'wa o'ḵäna'kowa

lu'ḵä yä'ton·e
hom tca'we
t̄o''na·wan hai'to
i'ton ya·'ḵänapḵä.
ho'na·wan yä'toḵä ta'tcu
yam t̄e'łacinakwi
i·'mina kwa'toḵäp̄a
hom tca'we
yam a'klinawa i'to ya·'ḵänapkowa
i·'łeana
hon a·'wona·wi'lona
t̄e'łiaḵa a·'ciwani
yam t̄e'łacinakwi
i·'łuwakna kwai'ina
ho'n a·'wona-elatena·wa.
lu'ḵä t̄e'łinan·e
to''na ho' a·wiḵe·na telia'u.
yam a'nikwanan a'ḵä
i'ḵe·na i·'telian·a.
eł tcu'hoł i'metcam·e
i'ḵe·n i·'teliana.
le'si te'kwi t̄on ya'cu t̄ełaḵäna

yam t̄i'nan ła'ḵi'kowa
yam pi'tcinan·e
su'lahaiyan·e
yam a'wełuyan ya·na i·muna kwai'i ḵäna
yam ḵä't̄sana łiton-t̄ełakwi

yam ḵä'cimaḵ·ä
ho'na t̄on a·'wona-e'latena:
yam ḵä'cima pu'ckwin·e
yam ḵät̄sana łiton-t̄ełakwi

yam ḵä'łana łiton-t̄ełakwi

ho'na t̄on a·'wona-ełatena·wa
hom a·'tatcu
i'ke·n i·'teliana
yam ḵä'cima
yam t̄o'wacona·
yam o'naya·nakä
yam ła'ciaḵa
t̄o ya'niktciana·wa

[3] That is, the dead.

[4] The sun has two resting places: One above, to which he "comes out standing" at sunrise; one below the world, to which he "goes in to sit down" at sunset.

[5] A·wonawil'ona—used of any supernaturals who influence human affairs. This is not a special deity, as Mrs. Stevenson believes.

[6] That is the night itself, anthropomorphically envisaged.

[7] Onaya·naḵä—literally "road fulfilling."

Therefore I have added to your hearts.	a'k͙·ä t̃o'na ho' a·'wik͙e·na teliak͙ä.
To the end, my fathers,	te'wuna' hom a·'tatcu
My children:	hom tca'we
You will protect us.	ho'na t̃on a·'te'yan·a
All my ladder descending children [8]	le·'wi łe'tsilon p̃a'ni·nan hom tca'we
Will finish their roads;	te'mła a·'wona-ya·''ana
They will grow old.	a·'łacin·a
You will bless us with life.	ho''na t̃on t̃ek̃ohanan ya'nik-tcia·nawa.

The Preparation of Prayer Sticks at the Winter Solstice

Twice during the winter solstice ceremony each adult male makes prayer sticks. The first time he makes for himself offerings to the sun, and to the ancestors. For the grown women of the family he makes offerings for the moon and the ancestors; children offer to the ancestors. If he is a member of a society he makes the special offering appropriate to his rank in the society. These solstice offerings are quite different from monthly society offerings.

The offerings of each family are deposited in an excavation in the family field, generally the cornfield, despite the fact that these are at greater distances from the village. After the offerings are made everyone is supposed to abstain from animal food, in addition to the usual requirement of sexual continence. Abstinence from meat is required because of the offering to the sun, which employs only downy feathers, which are especially potent and carry with them the pledge of abstinence. Among the younger people only those who belong to societies fast from meat. The others would consider it wrong to do so. "While we were away at school we ate meat, and it is a bad thing to break one's custom."

On the fourth day each initiated male offers to the katcinas, and each male society member offers to the beast gods. These offerings are made in the cornfield or in the fields to the east of the village. That night, after dark, special offerings are made in the corrals for the increase of horses, cattle, and sheep, for clothing and ornaments, and for medicine. Each man uses a different kind of stick and guards this secret knowledge jealously.

There are prayers to be said at each stage of the process of prayer-stick making. Prayers are always offered to the trees before cutting the sticks. Corn meal is offered to the "lucky" tree. This is not cut, but another is taken. The rest of the prayers are generally

[8] That is, human, the inhabitants of Zuñi.

omitted until the stick is finished. Then the following brief prayer is spoken over it before it is set aside until the time comes to plant it:

This many are the days
Since our moon mother
Yonder in the west[9]
Appeared, still small;
When but a short space yet remained
Till she was fully grown,
Then out daylight father,[10]
Pekwin of the Dogwood clan,
For his sun father
Told off the days.
This many days we have waited.
We have come to the appointed time.
My children,
All my children,
Will make plume wands.
My child,
My father,[11] sun,

My mother, moon,
All my children will clothe you with prayer plumes.[12]
When you have arrayed yourselves in these,
With your waters,
Your seeds
You will bless all my children.
All your good fortune
You will grant to them all.
To this end, my father,
My mother:
May I finish my road;
May I grow old;
May you bless me with life.

le'si t̂e'wanan·e
hon ya'onak̭ä tsit i'lap̂ona
li·'wan k̂älician kwin ta''na
kɔ·'wi t̂sana ye'tsak̂äna
ho''i ya·'k̭ätun te'kwi
kɔ·'w a'nte'we'tcikwi

hon t̂e'k̂ohanan tatc i'lap̂ a·'te'ona
pi'tcik a'nota p̂e'kwin ci'wan·i
yam yä'tok̭ä ta'tcu
an t̂e'wanan pi''lana
le'si t̂e'wanan·e
hon t̂e'wanan a·'teak̭ä
hai'tokwin te'tcik̭ä
hom tca'we
te'mła hom tca'we
te'lik̭ina·we a·'ya·k̂äna·wa
hom tca'le
hom ta'tcu
yä'tok̭ä
hom tsi'ta ya'onan·e
hom tcawe
te'mła te'lik̭ina·we t̂o''na łe'ana·wa
t̂on i·'łeana

yam k̂ä'cima
yam t̂o'waconan·e
hom tca'we te'mła t̂o' ya'nhaitena
yam kwa'hoł te'mła ha'lowilin·e
te'mła t̂o' ya'nhaitena
t̂e'wuna' hom ta'tcu
hom tsi'ta
ho' o'na ya·tu
ła'citu
hom t̂e'k̂ohanan a'niktciatu.

An Offering of Prayer Sticks at the Winter Solstice

This many are the days
Since at the new year
For those who are our fathers,
K̂ä'eto·we,[13]

le'si t̂e'wanan·e
i'tiwan·a
hon a·'tatc i'lap̂ona
K̂ä-eto·we

[9] The new moon, first appearing at sunset in the west.

[10] Our human father. Father is a courtesy term applied to all supernaturals, all men who hold high office.

[11] "My father, my child," the most intimate form of address, used only in relations of implying intense affection. "My father, my child," and "my mother, my child," are sometimes used as great endearments between husband and wife.

[12] A common play upon words a'łea'u means either to give into one's hand or to clothe one. Likewise i'łea'u (reflexive) means either to take in one's hand or to clothe oneself.

[13] Literally "the water object in the dish," the rain-bringing fetish of the priests. (M. C. Stevenson, 23d Ann. Rept. Bur. Amer. Ethnology, p. 163.)

Tcu'eto·we,[14]
The days [15] were made.
From all the wooded places
Breaking off the young straight shoots
Of the male willow, female willow,
In our hands we held them fast.
With them we gave our plume wands human form.
With the striped cloud wing
The one who is our father,
Male turkey,
We gave our plume wands human form.[16]
With the flesh of our mother,
Cotton woman,
Even a poorly made cotton thread,
With this four times encircling the plume wands,
And tying it about their bodies,
We finished our plume wands.
Having finished our plume wands

And offering our fathers their plume wands
We make their days.[17]
Anxiously awaiting their days.
We have passed the days.
After a little while
Your massed clouds,
Your rains,
We shall desire.
We have given you plume wands.
That with your waters,
Your seeds,
Your riches,[18]
Your long life,
Your old age,
You may bless us—
For this I have given you plume wands.
To this end, my fathers,
May our roads reach to dawn lake;[19]
May our roads be fulfilled;
May we grow old;

tcu-e'to·we
a·'wan t̄e'wanan yo·k̯ä
le·wi t̄akwił-p̄ɔ·'t̄i
pi'lɔtsi pi'lok̯ä
a·'k̯̄äwułkwiʿna

yam a'sin a'k̯ä
a·'wiyat̄ena-t̄su'mek̯̄äna
te'lik̯ina a·'ho' a·'ya·k̯̄äna
yam nan i'lap̄ a·'te'ona
ton ɔts an ła'pihaiyan la'tan·e

a'k̯ä te'lik̯ina· a·'ho' a·'ya·k̯̄äna
yam tsit i'lap̄ a·'te'ona
pi'tsem o'k̯ä
an ci''nan·e
kɔ·'t̄i pi''lenapte
ak̯' a·'witela'ma
te'likina pa'nulapna i'kwiyante''-tcina
te'likina a·'ya·k̯̄äk̯ä.
te'likina· a·'ya·k̯̄äna
yam a·'tatcu
te'lik̯inan a·'łeana

a·'wan t̄e'wanan yo·''ap̄a
a·'wan t̄e'wanan a'nt̄sumeʿna
hon t̄e'wanan a·'teaiye.
kɔ·'wi te'la'ap̄a
a'wełuya·we
łi'to·we
a'ntecemana·wa.
t̄o''na te'lik̯inan a·'łeak̯ä.
yam k̯̄ä'cima
yam t̄o'waconan·e
yam u'tena·we
yam o'naya·nak̯ä
yam ła'ciak̯ä
hom t̄on a'niktciana'
a'k̯ä t̄o''na te'likinan ho' a·'łeak̯ä.

t̄e'wuna' hom a·'tatcu
t̄e'luaian k̯̄äiakwi te''tcina
hon a·'wona-ya·'tu
hon a·'łacitu

[14] The other half of the priestly fetish. This is the corn fetish.

[15] The retreat of the priests.

[16] Fashioned like human beings. The stick is the body, the feathers, the robes, the cotton cord is the belt, the paint is the flesh. This is the order of processes in the making of prayer sticks.

[17] "To make days" is to observe the taboo period.

[18] Clothing and ornaments, which constitute personal property, hence wealth.

[19] The water that lies on the easternmost rim of the world. This is where the sun comes out, and stands, therefore, as the symbol of fulfillment.

To where the road of our sun father goes
May our roads reach;
May our roads be fulfilled;
May we grow old;
May we be blessed with life.

yam yä'toḳa ta'tcu
an o'nan·e
o'neałan te''tcina
hon a·'wona ya·'tu
hon a·'łacitu
hon t̄e'k̄ohanan ya'niktcia'tu.

A Monthly Offering of Prayer Sticks

At each full moon (in some societies at the new moon) each member of a society offers prayer sticks. In addition to special offerings prescribed by the society there are two to four short black sticks for the ancestors and, for males, one similar black stick, with the addition of a duck feather, for the katcinas. The sticks are buried in the cornfield or at Red Earth, a point on the river bank east of the town. The prayer sticks are deposited with the following prayer, which was secured from one of the headmen of the Wood Society.

This many are the days
Since our moon mother,
Yonder in the west
Appeared still small.
When she became fully grown
Seeking yonder along the river courses
The ones who are our fathers,
Male willow,
Female willow,
Four times cutting the straight young shoots,
To my house
I brought my road.
This day,
With my warm human hands
I took hold of them.
I gave my plume wands human form.
With the striped cloud tail
Of the one who is my grandfather,
The male turkey,
With eagle's thin cloud tail,
With the striped cloud wings
And massed cloud tails
Of all the birds of summer,
With these four times I gave my plume wands human form.
With the flesh of the one who is my mother,
Cotton woman,
Even a poorly made cotton thread,
Four times encircling them and tying it about their bodies,
I gave the plume wands human form.
With the flesh of the one who is our mother,
Black paint woman,
Four times covering them with flesh,
I gave my plume wands human form.

In a short time the plume wands were ready.
Taking the plume wands,
I made my road go forth.
Yonder with prayers
We took our road.
Thinking, "Let it be here,"
Our earth mother
We passed upon her road.
Our fathers,
There on your earth mother,
There where you are waiting your plume wands
We have passed you on your roads.
There where you are all gathered together in beauty
Now that you are to receive your plume wands,
You are gathered together.

This day I give you plume wands.
By means of your supernatural wisdom
You will clothe yourself with the plume wands.
Wherever you abide permanently,
At the place of the first beginning,
Touching one another with your plume wands,
You will bend down to talk together.
From where you abide permanently,
Your little wind-blown cloud,

Your thin wisps of cloud,
Your hanging stripes of cloud,
Your massed up clouds, replete with living waters,
You will send forth to stay with us.
They will come out standing on all sides.
With your fine rain caressing the earth,
With your weapons, the lightning,
With your rumbling thunder,
Your great crashes of thunder,
With your fine rain caressing the earth,
Your heavy rain caressing the earth,
With your great pile of waters here at Itiwana,[20]
With these you will pass us on our roads.
In order that you may come to us thus
I have given you plume wands.

My fathers,
When you have taken your plume wands,
With your waters,
Your seeds,
Your riches,
Your power,
Your strong spirit,
Will all your good fortune whereof you are possessed,
Me you will bless.

Corn meal is then sprinkled on the prayer sticks with the following prayer:

This day, my fathers,
I have given you plume wands.
The source of our water of life.
The source of our flesh,
Flesh of the white corn
Prayer meal
I give to you.
Taking your plume wand,
Your prayer meal,
With your waters,
Your seeds,
Your riches,
Your long life,
Your old age,
With all your good fortune
You will bless us.
This is all.

MONTHLY OFFERING OF PRAYER STICKS

le′si t̑e′wanane
this much time

hon	ya′onak̯ä	tsit	i′lap̑ona
we	moon	mother	the one we have

li′wan	k̯̑älician′kwin	ta′‘na
hither	to the west	direction

ko′wi	t̑sa′na	ye′tsak̯̑äna
a little	small	becoming visible

ho′’i	ya·′k̯̑äk̯a	te′a’ana
person	finished	when she was

la′lhok^u	le·′wi	k̯̑ä′piyałana·na		tapana
yonder	all	river	along	following

hom	a·′tatcu	i′lap̑ona
we	fathers	the ones we have

pi′lɔtsi	pi′lok̯ä
male willow	female willow

a·′wi	tela’ma
four	times

[20] The Middle, the ceremonial name for Zuñi.

a'k̲ewułkwi'nakna
breaking off the young shoots

yam hecot̂akwi
our house to

hon o'neał i'k̲änapk̲ä
we road made come

lu'k̲ä yä'ton·e
this day

yam a's·in k̲äłnak̲ä
my hand warm with

ho' a·'wiyat̂ek̲ä
I took hold of them

te'lik̲ina a·'ho' a·'ya·k̲äk̲ä
prayer sticks persons (I) finished

yam na'nili te'ona
our grandfather the one who is

ton ɔts an ła'pihaiyan la'tan·e
turkey male his hanging cloud wing

k̲äk̲äl an su'lahaiyan la'tan·e
eagle his cirrus cloud wing

la'łhok^u ɔ't̂o'ik̲aiak̲ä wɔ·'we
yonder summer birds

a·'wan łapihaiyan la'tan·e
their hanging cloud wing

a'wełuyan k̲äten·e
cumulus cloud tail

a'·k̲·ä a'witela'ma
with them four times

te'lik̲ina a·'ho' a·'ya·k̲äk̲ä
prayer sticks persons (I) finished

yam tsit i'lap̂a te'ona
our mother having the one who is

p̂i'tsem o'k̲ä an ci''nan·e
cotton woman her flesh

kɔ·'t̂i p̂i''lenapte
rough cotton cord even though it is

a'witela'ma
four times

pa'nulap i'kwiyan-te''t̂cina
winding around tying it reaching around

te'lik̲ina a·'·ho' a·'ya·k̲äk̲ä
prayer sticks persons (I) finished

yam tsit i'lap̂a ·'te''ona
our mother having the ones

ha'kwin o'k̲' an ci''nane
black paint woman her flesh

a'witela'ma ci'n i'yante't̂cina
four times flesh reaching all over

te'lik̲ina a'ho' a·'ya·k̲äna
prayer sticks persons finishing

we'tsim te'la'apa
after a little while

yam te'likinan e'lete'akä
my prayer stick (I) made ready

te'likinan i·'łeana
prayer stick taking

o'neałan kwai''ikäna
road making go out

le'hoku ťe'wus akä
yonder prayers with

hon o'neał a'känapkä
we road made go

hoł li·'ła le''hatina
somewhere here thinking

yam a'witelin tsi'tana
our earth mother at

hon o'na-e'latena
we on her road passing

ho''na·wan a·'tatcu
our fathers

yam a'witelin tsi'tana
our earth mother

ťom te'likinan co'kya·kwi
your prayer stick waiting where

ťo'na hon a·'wona-e'latenapkä
you we on your roads passed

ťon te'mła ha'pona ko'kci
you all gathered beautifully

yam te'likinan i·'łeanaptun te'a
your prayer stick about to take where

ťe'mła ťon ha'ponaiye
all you are gathered

lu'kä yä'ton·e
this day

ťo''na hon te'likina a·'łea'u.
to you we prayer sticks give

yam a'nikwananak·ä
your knowledge with

te'likinan i·'łea'u.
prayer stick take

hoł yam ťi'nan-ła'kikwi
somewhere your staying quietly place

yam tci'mikänapkä te'kwi
your first beginning place

te'likinan a'kä
prayer stick with

ťo ya'cuwa ťełakuna
you speaking will bend over

yam ťi'nan ła'ki'kowa
your staying quietly wherever

yam pi'tcinan·e
your wind cloud

yam su'lahaiyan·e
your cirrus cloud

yam ła'pihai'yan·e
your black striped cloud

yam a'wełuyan k̓ä'ʿkwi· ya·'na'a
your cumulus cloud with living water replete

i·'muna kwa''ik̓än·a.
sitting down will make come forth

le'si te'kwin i·'łuwakna kwai'ina
on all sides standing coming out

yam k̓ät̄sana ƚiton-t̄ełakuna
your fine drops rain bending down

yam sa'wanik̓ä
your weapon

wi'lolonan·e
lightning

ku'lulunan·e
thunder

yam ła't̄satsa t̄i'nana
your crashes of thunder

yam k̓ä't̄sana ƚi'ton-t̄ełakwi
your fine drops rain bending down

yam k̓ä'łana ƚi'ton-t̄ełakwi
your large drops rain bending down

li·'ła i'tiwanakwi
here Itiwana at

yam k̓ä'cima puckwai'ina
your waters the larger portion

a'k̓·a ho'na t̄on a·'wona-e'latena·.
with this us you on our roads will pass.

a·'wona-e'latenapt̄unak·ä
On our roads in order that you may pass

t̄o'na ho' te'lik̓inan a·'łeak̓ä
to you I prayer sticks have given

hom a·'tatcu
my fathers

yam te'likinan i·'łeana
your prayer stick taking,

yam k̓ä'cima
your waters,

yam t̄o'waconan·e
your seeds,

yam u'tenan·e
your clothing,

yam sa'wanik̓ä
your weapon,

yam tse''makwin t̄su'me
your mind, strong

yam kwa'hoł te'mła te'n·i ha'lowilin·e
your something all every bit good luck

hom t̑o a'niktciana.
to me you will grant.

k̭ä'wai'anak̭a t̑e'wusu
Prayer meal with prayer.

lu'k̭ä yä'tone
This day

hom a·'tatcu
my fathers

te'likinan t̑o'na ho' a·'łeak̭ä.
prayer stick to you I gave

yam a'k̭·ä a·'k̭ä'k̑ona
your with it that which waters you

yam a'k̭·ä a·'ci'nona
your with it that which is (your) flesh.

t̑owa k̑ohana
corn white

ha'lawo·tinan·e
prayer meal

t̑o''na ho' ha'lawo·tinan a·'łea'u.
to you I prayer meal give.

te'likinan·e.
prayer stick.

halawo·tinan·e
Prayer meal

i·'łeana
taking

yam k̭ä'cima
your waters,

yam t̑o'waconan·e
your seeds,

u'tcnan·e
clothing,

o'naya·nak̭ä
long life,

ła'ciak̭ä
old age,

yam kwa'hoł te'mła te'n·i ha'lowilin·e
your something all every bit good luck

t̑on ho'n a'niktcian·a.
you to us will give.

le·wi.
That is all.

Prayers to Dead Wife, with Offerings of Prayer Meal and Prayer Sticks

When a man's wife dies for four days he observes the most stringent taboos. He remains continent; he abstains from eating meat, grease, and salt. He sits alone, away from the fire, and must not be touched. He should not speak or be spoken to. Each morning at dawn he drinks an emetic and goes out on the eastern road to offer black corn meal to the dead spouse. He holds the black meal in the left hand, passes it four times over his head, and throws it away as rite of exorcism. Then, using the right hand, he scatters white meal, and prays. These taboos are the same as those offered by a warrior who has taken a scalp, and are directed to the same ends, the removal of contamination and the propitiation of the ghost. The ghost, who is lonely, will try to visit her husband in dreams. To prevent this he uses black corn meal, "to make the road dark" or "to forget."

After the four days he plants prayer sticks and resumes normal life. For 12 months he should remain continent, lest the dead wife become jealous. During this period he is "dangerous." At the end of this period he has intercourse with a stranger to whom he gives a gift, the instrument for removing the contamination. She throws this away. Next day both plant prayer sticks. If he desires to shorten the period, he gets some man with esoteric knowledge to make him especially potent prayer sticks—two or four sets—planted at intervals of four days, which are offered to the dead wife with the following prayer. These same rites are observed also by a widow and a warrior who has taken a scalp.

This is the only example which has come to my knowledge of any offering made to an individual, and even in this the ancestors are included. This prayer is also used with offerings of prayer sticks to the dead, on the fourth day after death, the day in which the spirit is believed to reach the land of the dead.[21]

My fathers,	hom a·'tatcu
Our sun father,	ho''na·wan yä'tok̭ä ta'tcu
Our mothers,	ho'na·wan a·tsita
Dawn	t̄e'luwaiak̭ä
As you arise and come out to your sacred place,	hoł yam t̄e'łaci'nakwi
	i'łuwakna kwai''ina
I pass you on your road.	ho' t̄o'n o'na-e'latena
The source of our flesh,	yam a'k̭ä ci''na ya·'na
White corn,	t̄o'wa k̄o'hana

[21] Two versions follow, one dictated by a man, the other taken from the autobiography of a woman, in the account of the death of her first husband.

Prayer meal,
Shell,
Pollen,
I offer to you.
Our sun father,
To you I offer prayer meal.
To you we offer it.
To you we offer pollen.
According to the words of my prayer
Even so may it be.
There shall be no deviation.
Sincerely
From my heart I send forth my prayers.
To you prayer meal,
Shell I offer.
Pollen I offer.
According to the words of my prayer

Even so may it be.
Now this day,
My ancestors,
You have attained the far-off place of waters.[22]
This day,
Carrying plume wands,
Plume wands which I have prepared for your use.
I pass you on your roads.
I offer you plume wands.
When you have taken my plume wands,
All your good fortune whereof you are possessed
You will grant to me.
And furthermore
You, my mother,[23]
Verily, in the daylight
With thoughts embracing,
We passed our days
Now you have attained the far-off place of waters.
I give you plume wands,

ha'lawo·tinan·e
ło·''o
o'nean·e
t̃o'na ho' a·'łea'u
ho''na·wa yä'tok̯ä tatc i'lap̃ona
t̃o''na ło ha'lawo·tinan a·'łea'u
t̃o''na hon a·'łea'u.
t̃o''na ho' o'nean a·'łea'u
ho'łno ho' t̃e'wusu p̃e'yena'kowa
i'snok̃o t̃e'k̯̃än·a.
kwa a'weła'kowa kwa te'amek̯̃än·a
hi'yawołucna
yam i'k̯e·na ho' t̃ewusu p̃e'nan k̯̃wai''ik̯̃äna
t̃o''na ha'lawo·tinan·e
ło·''o a·'łea'u
o'nean a·'łea'u
ho'łno'kona ho' t̃e'wusu ho' p̃eyena'·kowa
i'snok̯on te'k̯̃än·a.
ma' lu'k̯a yä'ton·e
hom a·'łacina·we
le'hok[u] t̃on k̯̃ä'cima łe''wok̯'änapk̯ä.
lu'k̯ä yä'ton·e
t̃o''na·wan hai'to
yam te'lik̯inan ye'lete'u'kowa
te'lik̯inan i'leana
t̃o''na ło a·'wona-e'latena·.
t̃o'n te'likinan a·'lea'upa
ho''na·wan te'likinan i'leana

yam kwahoł t̃e'ni ha'lowilin i'lap̃ a·'te'ona
hom t̃on a'nhaitena·wa.
le'stikleap̃a
t̃om ho' tsi't·i'li
e'pac t̃e'k̃ohanana
i·'tsemak-t̃e'łakwi
hon t̃e'wanan te'ak̯ä.
le'hok[u] t̃o' k̯̃äcima t̃e''wok̯ä.

t̃o'man hai'to

[22] The dead, whose abiding place is a lake.

[23] A term of endearment used for one's wife or child in moments of great tenderness. Often "my mother, my child."

Plume wands which I have prepared for your use.
Drawing your plume wands to you,
And sharing my plume wands,

Indeed, under no conditions shall you take anyone away. [24]

Among all the corn priests' ladder descending children,
All the little boys,
The little girls,
And those whose roads go ahead,
Was one, perhaps even a valuable man,
Who, his heart becoming angry because of something,
Injured you with his power.[25]

That one only you will think to drag down.

All of your good fortune whatsoever

May you grant to us.
Preserving us along a safe road,
May our roads be fulfilled.

ło yam te'likinan e'lete'u'kowa
t̄om ho' te'likinan a'nhaitepa
te'likinan a'nułana
ho'man te'likinan a'k̯' i·'yanhaitena
iłte'lekwante
tcu'waiyatik ho'łi
t̄o a'hawak̯̄äna'm·ana
le· t̄o'wa ci'wan an łe'tsilon p̄a'ni·nan tca'we
kɔ·w a'ktsik ła'na
kɔ·'wi k̯ätsik ła'na
a·'won-eʻ'kwinte
hoł tcu'wa t̄e'ʻyak̯' ho''i te'an·te

kwa'tikoł a'k̯ä
i'k̯e·n i·'samatina
yam sa'wanik̯' a'k̯ä
t̄om a'nat̄suma' kona
lu'k̯äk̄on te''tci
a'naʻ-u'łanak̯ä
t̄om tse''makwi te'k̯̄'än·a
yam kwahoł te'mła t̄e'ni ha'lowilin·e
ho''na t̄o' ya'nhaitena
o'neała k̄ɔ'kci 'kona
hon a·'te'ʻ·ya
t̄on a·'wona-ya·'k̯̄änaptu.

[24] The dead are lonely without the living and try to draw them away. The wife longs for her living husband, the mother for her children. Therefore these individuals stand in grave danger of death.

[25] The sorcerer whose ill will caused the fatal illness.

II. PRAYERS TO THE SUN

Prayer at Sunrise

Now this day,
My sun father,
Now that you have come out standing to your sacred place,
That from which we draw the water of life,
Prayer meal,
Here I give to you.
Your long life,
Your old age,
Your waters,
Your seeds,
Your riches,
Your power,
Your strong spirit,
All these to me may you grant.

lu'k̭ä yä'ton·e
hom yä'tok̭ä ta'tcu
yam t̆e'łacinakwi
t̆o' ye·'lana kwai''ik̭̆äp̆a
yam k̭̆'ä''kwi-ya·'na te''ona

ha'la wo·tinan·e
li·'ła t̆om ho' łe'a'up̆a
yam o'naya·nak̭ä
yam ła'ciak̭ä
yam k̭̆ä'cima
yam t̆o'waconan·e
yam u'tenan·e
yam sa'wanik̭ä
yam tse''makwin t̆su'me
te'm·ła hom t̆o' a'niktcian·a.

Presenting an Infant to the Sun

On the eighth day of life an infant's head is washed by his "aunts"—that is, women of his father's clan, his most important ceremonial relatives. Corn meal is placed in his hand and he is taken outdoors, facing the east, at the moment of sunrise. Corn meal is sprinkled to the rising sun with the following prayer, spoken by the paternal grandmother:

Now this is the day.
Our child,
Into the daylight
You will go out standing.
Preparing for your day,
We have passed our days.
When all your days were at an end,
When eight days were past,
Our sun father
Went in to sit down at his sacred place.
And our night fathers
Having come out standing to their sacred place,
Passing a blessed night
We came to day.
Now this day
Our fathers,
Dawn priests,
Have come out standing to their sacred place.

k̭esi t̆e'wanan·e
ho''na·wan t̆e'apk̆unan·e
t̆e'k̆ohanankwi
t̆o' ye·'lana kwai''ik̭̆än·a
t̆om t̆e'wanan yo''ap̆a
hon t̆e'wanan a·'teak̭ä·
t̆om le'na t̆e'wanan i·'te'tcap̆a
ha'elek̭ä t̆e'wak̭ä te'a'ana
hon yä'tok̭ä tatc i'lap̆ona
yam t̆e'łacinakwi i·'muna kwa'tok̭̆äp̆a
ho'na t̆e'łiak̭ä a·'tatc i'lap̆ona
yam t̆e'łacinakwi
i'łuwakna kwai''ik̭̆äna
t̆e'łinan k̭̆ɔ'kci
hon a·'wantewak̭ä
lu'k̭ä yä'ton·e
ho''na·wan a·'tatcu
t̆e'luwaiak̭ä a·'ciwan·i
yam t̆e'łacinakwi

Our sun father
Having come out standing to his sacred place,
Our child,
It is your day.
This day,
The flesh of the white corn,
Prayer meal,
To our sun father
This prayer meal we offer.
May your road be fulfilled
Reaching to the road of your sun father,
When your road is fulfilled
In your thoughts (may we live)
May we be the ones whom your thoughts will embrace,
For this, on this day
To our sun father.
We offer prayer meal.
To this end:
May you help us all to finish our roads.

i·łuwakna kwai′′ik̭̄äp̄a
ho′′na yä′tok̭ä ta′tcu
yam t̄e′łacinakwi
ye·′lana kwai′′ik̭̄äp̄a
ho′′na·wan t̄e′apk̄unan·e
t̄om t̄e′wanan te·′ak̭ä.
lu·k̭ä yä′ton·e
t̄o′wa k̄o′han an ci′′nan·e
ha′lawo·tinan·e
yam yä′tok̭ä ta′tcu
hon ha′lawo·tinan łe·ana·wa·
yam yätok̭ä ta′tcu
o′neała te′′tcina
t̄o′ o′na-ya·′an·a
t̄o′ o′na ya·′′ap̄a
t̄om tse′′makwin a′k̭ä
to′ma·nan tse′′makwin-te′łakwi
yam hon a·′teatun′on ak̭ä
lu′k̭ä yä′ton·e
yam yä′tok̭ä ta′tcu
yam ha′lawo·tinan łe′ana
t̄e′wuna′ ho′′na t̄o′ temłate a·′wona-ya·′k̭̄äna.

The P̄ekwin Sets the Date for the Summer Solstice

Before the summer solstice the p̄ekwin makes daily observations of the sunset from a shrine east of the village. When the sun sets behind a certain point in the mesa he begins to count days with offerings of prayer sticks. There are six such offerings according to Mrs. Stevenson.[1] At dawn of the morning following the last offering he announces from the highest housetop in Zuñi that the summer solstice will take place after eight days.

Now that those who hold our roads,
Dawn ancients,
Youths,
Matrons,
Maidens,
Over their sacred place,
Have raised their curtain.
Here, on the corn priests' housetop
I stand up.
My fathers,
My sun father,
We have made your days.
Divine ones,
Remember your days.

hon a·′wona·wi′lona
t̄e′luwaiak̭ä a·′łaci
a·′tsawaki
a·′mak̭i
e′wactok̭i
yam t̄e′łacinakwi
a·lani k̭̄e′atok̭ä te′kwi
li·′ła t̄o′wa ci′wani
an te′ala ho′ ye·′la′u.
hom a·′tatcu
hom yä′tok̭ä ta′tcu
t̄o′man t̄e′wanan yo′′ap̄a
k̭̄ä′pin a·′ho′i
yam t̄e′wanan ai′yu′ya·nap̄a

[1] Twenty-third Ann. Rept. Bur. Amer. Ethn., p. 148.

When this many days, eight days, are past,
On the ninth day.
All together
We shall reach your appointed time.
This many days anxiously waiting
You shall pass the days.
I think it is this many days, eight days,
And then on the ninth day.
You will grant that all of us finish our roads.

le'si t̄e'wana ha''elek̯a t̄e'wanan·e
te·nalek̯ä yä'ton·e
k̯e'si t̄e'mɫamo
to''na·wan hai'tokwin te''tcina
le'si t̄e'wanan a'nt̄sume'na
t̄on t̄e'wanan a·'t̄ek̯'än·a
hi'ntcoɫ le'si t̄e'wanan ha'elek̯ä t̄e'wanan·e
tenalek̯a yä'ton·e
t̄e'mɫa ho''na t̄on a·'wona-ya·'k̯ä-na·wa.

Prayer of the Fire Keeper at the Winter Solstice

The keeper of the New Year fire is appointed by the priests on the ninth day following the p̄ekwin's announcement of the solstice. This is the day on which all people cut prayer sticks. During the day he collects wood from houses in the village and in the evening builds the New Year fire in he''iwa kiva. On this evening the images of the gods of war are taken to the kiva for their all-night ceremony. The fire keeper must be a man of the Badger clan or a child of that clan. He is called tsu'pal-i'lona (the one who has the blood pudding; the fire is his tsu'palon·e, or blood pudding). During the ensuing ten days he must observe continence and eat no meat or other animal food. He sleeps and eats at his own house, but returns to the kiva to tend the fire, which must be kept burning throughout the period. He visits every house in the village to get wood for his fire.

At sundown on the ninth day of the second period [2] he comes to the kiva. Here p̄ekwin has made a meal painting and set up an altar. When all the priests have arrived p̄ekwin goes to summon the impersonators of P̄a'utiwa and the four Sa'yaɫia. They come unmasked, their masks having been taken to the kiva earlier in the day.

At sunset Ci'tsuk̯a and Kwe'lele, gods from the east, enter the village from the east. They dance for a few minutes on the roof of the kiva and then go in. After brief prayers they go to the house of the Great Fire Society to eat. The masks belong to this society, and the impersonators must be chosen from the Great God order of the society.

Late at night they are again summoned to the kiva. Here are the priests, the impersonators of P̄a'utiwa and the Sa'yaɫia, men of the Dogwood and Sun clans who dress P̄a'utiwa, and singers from He'iwa kiva. With Ci'tsuk̯a and Kwe'lele go the headmen of the Great Fire Society and a group of singers from that society. The two choirs sing alternately and Kwe'lele and Ci'tsuk̯a dance. The fire keeper sits all night beside the fireplace, within a circle of meal across which he must not step.

[2] See p. 535.

At the first sign of dawn P̃a'utiwa dresses. When he is ready the chief of the Great Fire Society kindles fire with the ancient drill which Kwe'lele carries. As soon as the fire appears Kwe'lele lights his torch. The fire keeper takes a brand from his fire and, accompanied by Kwe'lele with his torch, p̃ekwin, Ko'mosona, P̃a'utiwa, and the four Sa'yaħia, goes out to the east. At a point well beyond the last house they pause. The fire keeper lays down his brand, and Kwe'lele extinguishes his torch. All pray and sprinkle meal. Then the party returns to the kiva.

This is the sign to the village that the fire taboo is ended, and immediately everyone hastens to take out their fire and sweepings. When they return to the kiva the fire keeper and p̃ekwin pray. Then the people go to their houses to take out the fire from their hearths. They return immediately, and the masked gods dance until daylight. At this time anyone may enter the kiva to receive the blessings of the gods.

The following prayer is spoken by the fire keeper when he returns from the east in the morning. It was dictated by a member of the Great Fire Society.

This many are the days
Since the sun, who is our father,
Stood yonder beside his left hand sacred place.[3]

Then our fathers
Having prepared plume wands for the rite of their ancestors,
And having breathed their prayers upon the plume wands,
With their sacred cigarette,
Their prayer meal
My fathers
Laid hold of me.
When the sun who is our father
Had yet a little space to go
To go in to sit down at his sacred place,
Our two fathers,
The ones who hold the high places,[4]
Once more assuming human form.
With their sacred possessions,
With their house chiefs,
Their p̃ekwins,
Their bow priests,
With all of these,
They made their roads come in,

ma' lesi t̃e'wanan·e
hon yä'tok̯ä tatc i'lap̃ a·'te'ona
li·'wan yam we'cik̯änem t̃e'łacinakwi
i'tiułak̯ä te'a'ana
yam a·'łacinawe
a·'wan hai'to te'lik̯inan ye'lete'una
te'lik̯inan t̃e'wus a'nułakna

k̯ä'cima po'n·e
ha'lawo·tinan a'k̯ä
hom a·'tatcu
hom ya't̃ena-t̃sumek̯äna·wap̃a
hon yä'tok̯ä tatc i'lap̃ a·'te'ona
yam t̃e'ła cinakwi
i·'muna kwa'tok̯ätunte'kwi
kɔ·w a'nt̃e'wetcikwi
hon a·'tcia tatc i'lap̃a
te'alan i'lon a·'tci
a·'tci tci'm'on ho''i-ya·'k̯äna
yam e'leteli·we
yam k̯ä'kwa·mosi
yam p̃e'kwi·we
yam a·'p̃i'ła·ci'wan·i
i·'te'tcinici
a·'tc o'neałan kwa'tok̯äna

[3] i. e. the north, therefore the winter solstice.
[4] The War Gods whose shrines are on mountain tops.

And sat down quietly.
Then the one who is my daylight father
Laid hold of me.
Presenting me yonder to all the directions,
He seated me,
Giving me the world.
After a blessed night
We came to day.
Next day
Saying, "Let it be now,"
Our two fathers
Yonder passed their elder brothers on their roads.[5]
As they counted up the days for us
Eagerly awaiting their days
We passed the days.
When all of their days were past,
Then our two fathers,
K̯ä'wułia P̄a'utiwa
We passed at their middle day.
Yesterday
When our sun father
Had yet a little space to go
To go in to sit down at his sacred place,
Yonder our fathers of all directions,
Water bringing birds,[6]
P̄ekwin, priest,
From where he stays quietly
Making his road come forth,
Making his road come hither,
Thinking, "Let it be here,"
Fashioned his fathers massed cloud house,[7]
Spread out their mist blanket,
Sent forth their life-giving road,
Prepared their spring.
Then our two fathers,
K̯a'wułia
P̄a'utiwa
To his house chiefs,
His p̄ekwins,
To his bow priests,
To all of these,

a·'tc i'miła'k̄uk̯ä.
ho' t̄e'k̄ohanan tatc i'li te''ona
ho'ma ya't̄ek̯ä
la'łhokᵘ le'si te'kwi
hom e'lulatena
hom a'nim·ła'k̄una
hom 'u'lo'n u'tsip̄k̯ä
t̄e'łinan k̄ɔ'kci
hon a·'wan t̄e'wak̯ä
t̄e'wa yä'on·e
hoł k̯ä·'k̯i ke·si' le''anak̯äp̄a
hon a·'tcia tatc i'lap̄ a·'te''ona
le'hokᵘ a·'tcia a·'papa
a·'wona-e'latena
a·tc ho''na·wan t̄e'wan pi''lup̄a
a·'tcia t̄e'wanan a'nt̄sume'na
hon t̄e'wanan a·'teak̯ä te'a'ana
ło'kwa le· t̄e'wak̯ä te'a'ana
hon a·'tcia tatc i'lap̄ a·'te'ona
k̯ä'wułia p̄a'utiwa
hon a·'tcia i'tiwanan e'latenapk̯ä
t̄e'cukwa yä'tone
ho'n yä'tok̯ä tatc i'lap a·'te'ona
yam t̄e'łacinakwi
i·'muna kwa'tok̯ätun te'kwi
kɔ·w a'nt̄e'wetcikwi
la'łkokᵘ le'si te'kwi
hon a·'tatc i'lap̄ona
k̯ä'cima wɔ·'we p̄e'kwin a·'ciwan·i
yam t̄i'nan ła'k̯i'kona
o'neała kwai''ik̯äna
o'neał i'k̯äna
hoł li·'ła le''hatina
yam a·'tatcu
a·'wan a'wełuyan k̯ä'kwen ya·'k̯äna
a·'wan ci'pololon p̄e'wuna
a·'wan o'naya·nak̯ä o'neałan a·'k̯äna
a·'wan k̄ä'nakwe·nan ye'lete'u-napk̯ä te'kwi
hon a·'tcia tatc i'lap̄ a·'te'ona
k̯ä'wułia
p̄a'utiwa
yam k̯ä'kwa·mo'si
yam p̄e'kwi·we
yam a·'pi'ła·ci'wan·i
i·'te'tcinici

[5] The idols are taken to the mountain shrines.

[6] The birds who sing before the rain. They are believed to be messengers of the supernaturals, sent to announce the rain. Hence p̄ekwin, the speaker of the priests and announcer of ceremonies, is called figuratively "water birds."

[7] The meal painting on the altar.

Made his road come in.
They sat down quietly.
Yonder toward the east,
To our two fathers
White masked god,[8]
Black masked god,[9]
To where they were made ready
The prayers reached;
Carrying their waters,
Carrying their seeds,
Making their road come hither,
Going along one road,
They sat down quietly.
After a blessed night,
With our children we came to day.
When the ones who are our fathers,
Dawn old men,
Dawn youths,
Dawn boys,
Dawn old women,
Dawn matrons,
Dawn maidens,
Dawn girls,
Had risen standing to their sacred place,
Saying, "Let it be now,"
Four times
Drawing up our grandmother,[10]
And making her arise,
Making her go ahead
Yonder toward the east
With prayers
We made our roads go forth.
How the world will be,
How the days will be,
We desired to know.
Perhaps if we are lucky
Our earth mother
Will wrap herself in a fourfold robe
Of white meal,
Full of frost flowers;
A floor of ice will spread over the world,
The forests,
Because of the cold will lean to one side,
Their arms will break beneath the weight of snow.
When the days are thus
The flesh of our earth mother
Will crack with cold.
Then in the spring when she is replete with living waters

o'neała kwa'tok̭̃äna
i't̃inan i'łak̭̃ik̭̃äp̃a
li·'wan te'luwankwin ta''na
hon a·'tatc i'lap̃a
ko'ko k̃o'hana
ko'ko k̃wi'n·e
k̭es hoł a·'wan ya·'nici
t̃e'wusu p̃e'nan i'tiułak̭̃äp̃a
yam k̭̃ä'cima łe'ap̃a
yam t̃o'waconan łe'ap̃a
o'neał i'k̭̃äna
to'pint o'neał a·'nap̃a
i'tinan-ła'k̭̃ikna
t̃e'łinan k̃ɔ'kci
hon tca'wilap̃ a·'want̃ewak̭ä
hon a·'tatc i'lap̃ona
t̃e'luwai ak̭' a·'wiɔts a·'łaci
t̃e'luwaiak̭' a·'tsawak̭i
t̃e'luwaiak̭' a·'waktsik̭i
t̃e'luwaiak̭' a·wok̭' a·'łaci
t̃e'luwaiak̭' a·'mak̭i
t̃e'luwaiak̭' e'wactok̭i
t̃e'luwaiak̭' a·'k̭ätsik̭i
yam t̃e'łacinakwi
i·'łuwakna k̭̃e'atok̭̃äp̃a
hoł k̭ä·k̭̃i k̭e·si le''anak̭̃äp̃a
yam hot i'li te''ona
a·'witela'ma
a'na'-e'lamak̭̃äna
an o'neał e''kwikona
le'hok[u] te'luwankwin ta''na
t̃e'wus a'kä
hon o'neał a·'k̭̃änap̃a
ho'łko'n u'lo'nan te'atun'ona
hołko'n t̃e'wanan te'atun'ona
a'ntecemana
ho'nkwe·t hon a·'halowilap̃a
hon a·'witelin tsit i'lap a·'te'ona
a·'wite i'yałto
o'p̃ana k̃ohana
tse'nak-u'tea-p̃ɔ t̃i
kɔ·'wi łem p̃e u'lo'na
t̃a'kwił-p̃ɔ·t̃i
yam i't̃sumanan ak̭ä
kɔ·'wi łuwał o'nana
kɔ·w a·'wasi-ya'mtcona
hoł t̃e'wanan te'ap̃a
hon a·'witelin tsit i'lap̃ a·'te'ona
kɔ·wi ci''nan o'k̭̃oclena
k̭̃ä''kwi-ya·'na te'lakwai'ik̭̃äna

[8] Citsuk̭ä.
[9] Kwelele.
[10] The fire.

Our mothers,
All different kinds of corn
In their earth mother
We shall lay to rest.
With their earth mother's living waters
They will be made into new beings;
Into their sun father's daylight

They will come out standing;
Yonder to all directions
They will stretch out their hands calling for rain.
Then with their fresh waters
(The rain makers) will pass us on our roads.
Clasping their young ones in their arms
They will rear their children.
Gathering them into our houses,

Following these toward whom our thoughts bend,
With our thoughts following them,
Thus we shall always live.
That this may be
Eagerly we have awaited your day.
Now that all their days are at an end,
Eagerly waiting until another day shall come,
We shall pass our days.
Indeed it is so.
Far off someone will be my father,

The divine one,
He of the Badger clan.
Asking for his life-giving breath
His breath of old age,
His breath of waters,
His breath of seeds,
His breath of fecundity,
His breath of all good fortune,

Asking for his breath.
And into my warm body
Drawing his breath,
I shall add to your breath.
Do not despise the breath of your fathers,
But into your bodies
Draw his breath.

yam a·'tsita
t̄o'wa temłanana
yam a·'witelin tsit'tana
hon t̄i'nan kwatok̯äna·wa
yam a·'witelin tsit an k̯ä''kwin äk̯a
tci'm'on ho''i-ya·'k̯äna
yam yä'tok̯ä ta'tcu
an t̄e'k̯ohanankwi
i·'łuwakna kwai''ina
la'łhok^{u} le'si te'kwi
k̯a·'cima ce'man a's ta'k̯äna·wap̄a

yam k̯ä'cima tcim'on ak̯ä
ho'n a·'wona-e'latena·wap̄a

t̄e'apk̯unan i·'k̯eckuna

tca'lona ya·'k̯äna·wap̄a
yam he'cot̄akwi
a·'wana'-u'łana
a·'tapana
tse''mak-t̄e'lakwi
tse''mak yä'lu
hon t̄e'wanan te'atun'ona'k̯ä
a'ntsume'na
hon t̄e'wanan a·'teak̯ä te'kwi
k̯es a·wan t̄e'wanan i·'te'tcikwi

lak^{u} t̄o'pa t̄e'watun te'kwi
a'ntsume'na
hon t̄e'wanan a·'tek̯än·a.
no'mił·te
ho'łomackona tcu'waiya ho' tatc i'lik̯än·a
k̯ä'pin ho''i
to'nac a'notan i'li te''ona
an o'naya·'nak̯ä p̄i''nan·e
an ła'ciak̯ä p̄i''nan·e
an k̯ä'cima p̄i''nan·e
an t̄o'waconan p̄i''nan·e
an t̄e'apk̯unan p̄i''nan·e
an kwa'hoł te'mła p̄i''nan i'li te''ona
p̄i''nan ai'ncemana
yam t̄ehuł k̯ä'łnakwi
p̄i''nan a'na'-kwa'tok̯äna
t̄o''na·wan an p̄i''nan te'liana·wap̄a
eł yam a·'tatcu
a·'wan p̄i''nan ya'tcitunam·e
yam ce'łnakwi
p̄i''nan a'na'kwatok̯äna

That yonder to where the life-giving road of your sun father comes out
Your roads may reach;
That you may finish your roads;
For this I add to your breath.
To this end, my fathers,
My children,
May all of you be blessed with light.

hoł yam yä'tok̥ä ta'tcu
an o'naya·'nak̥ä o'neała kwai''inakwi
o'neała te''tcina
yam i·'yona-ya·'k̥änaptun'on a·k̥ä t̃o''na·wan ło p̃i''nan te'liana·we. [11]
te'wuna' hom a·'tatcu
hom tca'we
a'nsamo t̃o'n t̃e'k̃ohanan ya'niktciat'u.

[11] Plural verb with singular subject, due possibly to rhythmic requirements. The correct form would be telia'u. Byron does this, too, and Blake.

III. PRAYERS TO THE UWANAMMI

Four days after the summer solstice the priesthoods begin their series of retreats to pray for rain. Each set in turn goes in at the house where their sacred bundle is kept. The four chief priesthoods associated with the four cardinal points go in for eight days each. They are followed by the p̄ekwin, who goes in for four days. He is followed by the bow priest, who observes a 4-day retreat, although he does not stay in his house. After these the minor priesthoods, "the darkness people," follow in fixed order. They go in for four days each. The last come out about the first week in September, which is near the end of the rainy season.

Retreats always start in the evening, generally after sunset, and nights only are counted. They end at sunrise on the fourth or eighth morning following. The day before the retreat begins is spent by the priests in making prayer sticks. These are tied together in the afternoon, and shortly before sunset the chief priest accompanied by an associate leaves to plant them in a distant spring. They return late at night. They go immediately into the inner room set aside for their retreat, where the other members have already assembled. The chief priest sets up his altar—a meal painting, one or more feather-wrapped corn fetishes, pots of black paint that have been brought from the underworld, stone knives, thunder stones, and finally the sacred bundle itself.

The first of the two prayers below is said with the offering of corn meal when gathering willow sticks, the second on setting the sacred bundle on the altar. They were dictated by a former member of the priesthood of the water serpent, and have been verified by a priest of the priesthood of the south.

Prayer of a Priest on Going Into Retreat

This day
Desiring the waters of our fathers,
The ones who first had being,[1]
In our house
Having prepared prayer meal,
Shells,
Corn pollen,
Hither with prayers
We made our road come forth.
This way we directed our roads.
Yonder on all sides our fathers,
Priests of the mossy mountains,
All those whose sacred places are round about,
Creatures of the open spaces
You of the wooded places,
We have passed you on your roads.
This day
Prayer meal,
Shell,
Corn pollen
We offer to you, my fathers.
Offering these to you,
Four times we offer them to you.

[1] The priestly bundles.

You of the forest,
You of the brush,
All you who in divine wisdom,
Stand here quietly,
Carrying your waters
You will go before
Thus to Itiwana
Our roads will go.
The water filled rooms of your daylight children
Your road will enter.
Sitting down quietly,
After a blessed night
With us, your children,
You will come to day.
To-morrow
When he who holds our roads,
Our sun father,
Coming out to stand at his sacred place
Passes our roads,
Then we shall pass one another on our roads.
The divine ones
From wherever they abide permanently
Will make their roads come forth.
They will come.
And where they sit down quietly
All of us shall pass one another on our roads.
For our fathers,
Our mothers,
Those who first had being,
And also for our fathers,
Rain maker priests,
Rain maker p̂ekwins,
Rain maker bow priests
For their rite
We shall give our plume wands human form.
We have given our plume wands human form,
With the massed cloud wing
Of the one who is our grandfather,
The male turkey,
With eagle's thin cloud wings,
And with the striped cloud wings
And massed cloud tails
Of all the birds of summer;
And with the flesh of the one who is our mother
Cotton woman,
Even a rough cotton thread,
A soiled cotton thread
With this four times encircling our plume wands
And tying it about their bodies,
We have given our plume wands human form.
Then also with the flesh of our mother,
Black paint woman,
Covering them with flesh,
We have prepared our plume wands.
When our plume wands were ready,
Saying, "Let it be now."
Taking our plume wands,
Our plume wands which had been finished,
Rising, we came out of our house.
With prayers we made our roads come forth.
At the place called since the first beginning
Rock wedge,[2]
Where our fathers,
Rain maker priests,
In their rain-filled inner rooms [3]
Were all gathered together in beauty
To receive their plume wands,
There we passed them, on their roads,
Passing them on their roads
There we gave our fathers plume wands,
Our fathers,
By means of their divine wisdom
Laid hold of their plume wands.
On all sides
They will talk together, touching one another with the plume wands,[4]
Yonder at the north encircling ocean
You will hold discourse together touching each other with them.
And then also
Yonder at the west encircling ocean,
You will hold discourse together,
Touching one another with them,
And then also yonder toward the south,

---

[2] A shrine in the mountains southwest of Zuñi, used by the priests and by personators of the masked gods.

[3] Inside the spring. Springs are the homes of the rain makers.

[4] The prayer sticks constitute the means of communication.

You will hold discourse together,
Touching one another with them;
Then also yonder toward the east,
You will hold discourse together, touching one another with them.
Then also above
You will hold discourse together, touching one another with them;
And then also in the fourth womb,[5]
You will hold discourse together, touching one another with them.
You will encircle the world with your discourses.
My fathers,
Grasping your plume wands,
You will see your plume wands.
You will see whether they have been finished with precious paint,[6]
Or else are unfinished.
With your spittle,
With your flesh,
With your divine wisdom,
They will be made over afresh into human beings;
They will be strong.
From wherever you abide permanently
You will make your roads come forth.
Your little wind blown clouds,
Your thin wisps of clouds,
Your great masses of clouds
Replete with living waters,
You will send forth to stay with us.
Your fine rain caressing the earth,
Your heavy rain caressing the earth,
Here at Itiwana,
The abiding place of our fathers,
Our mothers,
The ones who first had being,
With your great pile of waters
You will come together.
When you have come together
Our mothers,
Our children,
All the different kinds of corn,
Nourishing themselves with their father's waters
Tenderly will bring forth their young.
Clasping their children [7]
All will finish their roads.
Then our children,
Our ladder-descending children,
Will gather you in.
Into all their houses.
You will make your roads enter.
To stay there quietly.
Then also tenderly
Their young will multiply
Multiplying our young,
Those toward whom our thoughts are bent,
You will live.
You will not think to hurry to some other place.[8]
Indeed, this shall not be.
But always in their houses
You will remain at rest.
In order that our children's thoughts may be bent to this,
For this you are our father,
You are our mother;
For this you who first had being,
Perpetuating your rite of the first beginning
Sit here quietly.
Holding all your country,
Holding all your people,
You sit here quietly.
Even as you sit here quietly,
Even as you listen to us,
We pray to you.
With your words,
Divine ones,
With your words
You hold all your people.
Do not let any one fall from your grasp [9]
When he has gone but a little ways!
In order that this may not be,
Our father,
Our mother,
The one who first haa being,
Even as you listen to us
We pray to you.
Our father,
Our mother,
The one who first had being,
Keeping your days,
Your days that have already been made,

[5] The fourth underground world, the place of origin of the people.

[6] Paint which has been brought from the underworld. It is the property of the priests. A tiny bit added to ordinary black paint makes the prayer stick "finished" (telikinan ya·na) as distinct from the "unfinished" or "worthless" prayer stick (telikinan cimato).

[7] The young ears, wrapped in their leaves.

[8] When the spirit of the corn leaves the country the ears in the storerooms shrivel up and waste away.

[9] That is, die before he reaches the full number of his days.

We pass our days.
Whenever your days are at an end,
Then we shall fulfill our thoughts.
Our mother,
The one who first had being,
To wherever you abide permanently,
To your fourth inner room,
You will make your road go in.
Then again, holding your country,
Holding your people,
You will sit down quietly for us,
Therefore as children to one another
We shall always remain.
My child,
My mother,
According to my words,
Even so may it be.
Do not let go of your people;
Let not your thoughts be thus.
Let no difficulty befall any of our daylight children,
Our ladder descending children,
When they have gone but a little ways on their road!
That this may not be
I commission[10] you with my prayers.
Because of my words
You will sit down quietly.
This many are the days,
And when your days are at an end,
You will sit down quietly.
Although we say we have fulfilled your thoughts
No! we have not yet fulfilled your thoughts.
Our office never lapses.
When we come to another day,[11]
Then again eagerly awaiting your rite
We shall pass our days,
For the winter eagerly waiting
We shall pass our days.
This is all.
Thus with plain words,
My father,
My mother,
My child,
Thus you sit down quietly.[12]

CI′WANI A·′NI
Priest his

lu′k̭ä yä′ton·e
This day

hon a·′tatc i′lap̂ona
we fathers the ones (we) have

tci·′mik̭änapkowa
the ones that first had being

a·′wan k̭ä′cim a′ntecemana
their waters desiring

yam he′cot̂an·e
our house

ha′lawo·tinan·e
prayer meal

ło·′′o o′nea· ye′leteʼuna
shell pollen having prepared

k̭ä′łhok[u] t̂e′wus a′k̭ä
hither prayer with

hon o′neała kwai′′ik̭äna
we roads making come forth

k̭ä′łhok[u] o′neał a·′k̭äk̭ä.
hither roads made go.

---

10 Literally, "I set you up outside the door," used of appointing an object or person to any ceremonial or civil office.

11 The next period of retreat. The rite is handed down in a self-perpetuating group through the generations.

12 The last part of the prayer refers to the bundle on the altar rather than the prayer stick offering.

ło'k̄wa le'wi tea ho''nan a·'tatcu
Yonder all places our fathers

a'wico yä'la a·'ciwan·i
moss mountain priests

le· t̄e'łacin u'lapnapkowa
all sacred place the ones that are around.

te'wuli a·'te'ona
open space the ones who are.

t̄a'kwił-p̄ɔ·'t̄i
forests

t̄o''na hon a·'wona-e'latek̯ä
you we on your roads passed

lu'k̯ä yä'ton·e
this day

ha'lawo·tinan·e
prayer meal

ło·''o
shell

o'nea·we
pollen

hom a·'tatcu
my fathers

t̄o''na hon a'łea'u.
to you we give.

t̄o''na hon a·'łeana
to you we having given

a·'witela'ma hon t̄o'n a·'łeak̯ä.
four times we to you gave.

le'wi t̄a'kwił-p̄ɔ·'t̄i
all forests

ła'kwił-p̄ɔ·'t̄i
brush

yam a'nikwanan a'k̯ä
their knowledge with

yam łu'wa-ła'k̄i'kowa
their staying quietly where it is

yam k̯ä'cim i·łeana
their waters holding

t̄on o'neał e'ʻk̄una·wap̄a
you road leading

la'lik i'tiwanakwi
nearby Itiwana to

hon o'neała te''tcik̯än·a
we roads shall make reach

t̄e'k̄ohanan yam tca'we
daylight your children

a·'wan k̯ä'cim t̄e'li'tokwi
their water inner room in

t̄on o'neał kwa'tok̯äna
you road will make go in

t̄on i·′t̄inan-ła′k̄ik̄äna
you will sit down quietly

t̄e′łinan k̄ɔ′kci
night good

ho′′na tcawi′lap̄a t̄on a·′want̄e′wan·a
us children having you will come to day

t̄e′wan yä′ton·e
to-morrow

ho′n a·′wona·wi′lona
us the one who holds (our) roads

ho′′nawan yä′tok̄ä ta′tcu
our sun father

yam t̄e′łacinakwi ye·′lana kwai′′ik̄äna
his ancient place standing coming out

ho′n a·′wona-e′latep̄a
us on (our) roads passing

hon i′yona-e′latena·wap̄a
we one another on (our) roads passing.

k̄ä′pin a·′ho′i
raw persons

hoł yam t̄i′nan ła′k̄ikona
where their staying quietly (where it is)

o′neała kwai′′ik̄äna
road making come forth

o′neał i′k̄äna
road making come

i′t̄inan ła′k̄ik̄ä te′kwi
they sat down quietly when

te′mła hon i′yona-e′latena
all we one another meeting

yam a·′tatcu
our fathers,

yam a·′tsita
our mothers,

tci′mik̄änapkowa
the ones that first had being,

le′stiklea yam a·′tatcu
furthermore our fathers,

u′wanam a·′ciwan·i
rain-maker priests,

u′wanam p̄e′kwi·we
rain-maker pekwins,

u′wanam a·′p̄i′ła·ci′wan·i
rain-maker bow priests,

a·′wan hai′to
their rite

hon te′lik̄ina· a·′ho′-a·′ya·k̄äna·wa.
we prayer sticks into human beings fashioned.

hon te′lik̄inan a·′ho′-a·′ya·k̄äna
we prayer stick into human beings fashioning

yam nan i'li te''ona
our grandfather the one who is

ton ɔts an a'wełuyan la'tan·e
turkey male his cumulus cloud wing,

k̯ä'k̯äl an su'lahaiyan la'tan·e
eagle his cirrus cloud wing,

la'łhoku ɔ'lo'ik̯aiak̯ä wɔ·'we
yonder summer birds

a·'wan ła'pihanan la'tan·e
their rain cloud wing,

a'wełuyan k̯ä'ten·e
cumulus cloud tail.

yamtsit i'lap̄a te''ona
our mother the one who is

pi'tsem ok̯' an ci''nan kɔ·ti pi'lenapte
cotton woman, her flesh rough cord, even

pi''le ci'k̯änapte
cord dark, even

ak̯' a·'wit·ela'ma
with it four times

te'lik̯ina pa'nulapna i'kwiyante''tcina
prayer stick encircling belting all around.

hon te'likina· a·ho'-a·'ya·k̯änapk̯ä
we prayer stick into human beings fashioned

tem ta yam tsit i'lap'a te''ona
and also our mother having the one who is

ha'k̄win o'k̯a
black paint woman.

an ci''nan a'k̯ä
her flesh with

ma'c i'yante'tcina.
flesh reaching all over.

hon te'lik̯inan ye'lete'unapk̯ä.
we prayer stick made ready.

te'lik̯inan ye'lete'una.
prayer stick making ready

k̯ä'k̯i k̯e'si le''anak̯äp̄a
whenever now this saying

yam te'lik̯inan ya·'k̯äkowa
our prayer stick which we had finished

te'lik̯inan i'łeana
prayer stick taking

yam he'cot̄anan ye·'lana kwai''ik̯äna
our house standing coming out

le'hoku t̄e'wus a'k̯ä
yonder prayers with

hon o'neał kwai''ik̯äna
we road making come forth

k̭ä·'k̂ä tcimik̂äk̭ä
wherever ther first beginning

a'łap̂atsi le''anak̂äna
rock wedge called

ho''na·wan a·'tatcu
our fathers

u'wanam a·'ciwan·i
rain-maker priests

yam te'likinan i'łeanaptun te'a
their prayer stick where they were to take them

yam k̂ä'cima t̂e'li'tona
their water inner room (in)

te'm·ła ha'p̂ona k̂ɔ'kcikwi
all gathered together beautifully where

hon a·'wona-e'latenapk̭ä.
we on their roads passed them.

hon a·'wona-e'latena
we on their roads passing them

i'sk̂ɔn yam a·'tatcu
there (to) our fathers

hon te'lik̭inan a·'łeanapk̭ä
we prayer sticks gave to them

ho''na·wan a·'tatcu
our fathers

yam a'nikwanan a'k̭ä
their knowledge with

yam te'lik̭inan ya't̂ena i'łeana
their prayer stick grasping taking

le'si te'kwi
to all directions

te'lik̭inan a'k̭ä
prayer stick with

t̂on ya'cuwa t̂e'łakuna·wa.
you talking together will touch.

li·'wan pi'cle k̭ä'tuł-u'lapnakwi
yonder north ocean where it surrounds

t̂on a'kä ya'cuwa t̂e'łakuna·wa.
you with it talking together will touch.

tem ta le'stiklea
and also furthermore

li·'wan k̭älicankwin ta''na k̭ä'tuł-u'lapnakwi
yonder to the west direction ocean surrounding at

t̂on a'kä ya'cuwa t̂e'łakuna
you with it talking together will touch

temta li·'wan a'lahoankwin ta''na
and also yonder to the south direction

t̂on a'k̭ä ya'cuwa t̂e'łakuna
you with it talking together will bend down

tem ta li·'wan t̂e'luwankwin ta''na
and also yonder to the east direction

t̂on a'k̯ä ya'cuwa t̂e'łakuna·wa.
you with it talking together will bend down.

tem ta iyamakwin ta''na
and also above direction

t̂on a'k̯ä ya'cuwa t̂e'łakuna·wa.
you with it talking together will bend over.

tem ta a·'witen t̂e'hulikwi
and also fourth womb in

tem ta t̂on a'k̯ä ya'cuwa t̂e'łakuna·wa.
and also you with it talking together will bend over.

ya'cu i'tulo'k̯äna·wa.
talking you will send around.

hom a·'tatcu
my fathers

yam t̂on te'lik̯ina ya't̂en·a·
your you prayer stick grasping

yam t̂on te'likinan u'natik̯äna'wa
your you prayer stick will see

ho'lontapt a·'ya·k̯äna
whether finished

t̂a''t̂cat kwa a·'ya·namep̂a
or else not finished

yam pi'k̯än·e
your spittle

yam ci''nan·e
your flesh

yam a'nikwanan a'k̯ä
your knowledge with

tci'm'on a·'ho'-a·'yak̯änak̯ä
new into human beings having fashioned them

t̂su'mek̯än·a.
they will be strong.

hoł yam t̂i'nan ła'k̂i'kowa
wherever your staying quietly where it is

t̂on o'neała kwai''ik̯'äna
you roads making come forth

yam pi''tcinan·e
your wind cloud

yam su'lahaiyan·e
your cirrus cloud

yam a'wełuyan·e
your cumulus cloud

k̯ä''kwi ya·'na
living water filled with

i·'muna kwai''ik̯äna
sitting down making come forth

yam k̯ä't̂sana ƚi'ton-t̂e'łakuna
your small drops rain touching (the earth)

yam k̯ä'łana ƚi'ton-t̂e'łakuna
your large drops rain touching (the earth)

i'tiwanakwi.
at Itiwana.

yam a·'tatcu
Your fathers,

yam a·'tsita
your mothers,

tci'mik̂änapkowa
the ones that first had being,

t̂i'nan-ła'k̂ikwi
sitting quietly where

yam k̂ä'cima pu'ckwe·na
your waters, the greater pile

t̂on a'k̂' i'yona-e'latena·wa.
you with it, will pass each other on your roads.

e'latena·wap̂a
having passed

ho''na·wan a·'tsita
our mothers

ho''na·wan tca'we
our children

t̂o'wa te'm·łanana
corn all kinds

yam a·'tatcu
their fathers

a·'wan k̂ä'cima i'k̂ä'kuna
their waters drinking in

e'letokna i't̂eapk̂uk̂äna·wa
carefully will bring forth young

ko·'wi tca'l i'k̂eckuna
somewhat child clasping in (their) arms

te'm·ła a·'wona-ya·''ana
all their roads will become finished

ho''na·wan tca'we
our children

łe'tsilon p̂a'ni·nan ho''na·wan tca'we
ladder descending our children

t̂o''na a·'wana'-u'łana
you drawing toward them

t̂on a·'wan he'cot̂akwi
you their houses to

o'neała kwatok̂än·a
roads will make enter

i't̂inan ła'k̂ikna
sitting down quietly

tem ta e'letokna
and also carefully

t̂e'apk̂unan ci'wuna a·'teap̂a
young multiplying when they are

i'skon tse''mak t̂e'łakwi
that thoughts bending toward

t̂e′apk̂una ci′wuna
young multiplying

t̂on a·′teap̂a
you being thus

kwa hołte′kwi tse′′mak i′k̂äcetik̂äna
not somewhere thoughts to hurry away

t̂on a·′team·ek̂äna
you shall (not) be

a·′wan he′cot̂a′kowa
their houses where they are

t̂on yu′′łak̂′ a·′teap̂a
you resting being

ho′′na·wan tca′we
our children

i′skɔn tse′′mak-t̂e′łakwi
there thoughts bending toward

t̂a·′teaptun′on a′k̂ä
in order that they may be thus

t̂om hon tatc i′lap̂a
you we father having

t̂om hon tsit i′lap̂a
you we mother having

tci′mik̂ä′kowa
the one that first had being

yam ko′′nhoł tci′mik̂ä′kowa te′lia‘na
you matters first beginning according to following

li·t t̂o′ i′m·-łak̂iye
here you stay quietly

le· yam u′lo‘nan ya′kna
all your world holding,

le· yam ho′′i ya′kna
all your people holding,

t̂o′ i′m·-łak̂iye
you stay quietly

t̂o′ i′m·-łak̂inte
you stay quietly even as

ho′′na t̂o ya′nhatiawan·te
to us you listen even as

hon t̂e′wus a·′p̂eye′a.
we prayers talk.

t̂o′man p̂e′naw a′kä
your words with

k̂ä′pin a·′ho′i
raw persons

to′′na·wan p̂enaw ak̂ä
your words with

le· yam a·′ho′i yaknap̂a
all your people holding

eł kɔ·w a·′nap̂a
let not a little having gone

tcu'waihoł ya'kna p̄i'ya'na
someone holding let fall

eł te'ametun'on a'k̯ä
let it not be thus for this

ho''na·wan ta'tcu
our father,

ho''na·wan tsi'ta
our mother,

tci'mik̯ä'kowa
the one that first had being

ho''na t̄o' a'nhatiawan·te
to us you listening even as

hon t̄e'wus a·'p̄eye'a
we prayers speak.

ho''na·wan ta'tcu
Our father,

ho''na·wan tsi'ta
our mother,

tci'mik̯ä'kowa
the one that first had being

t̄om t̄e'wanan yo·'kowa
your day which has become

hon t̄e'wanan i'lap̄a
we day having

hon t̄e'wanan a·'teaiye
we day live

hoł t̄om t̄e'wanan i'te'tcap̄a
when your day when it is used up

hon a'k̯ä tse''makwi· mo'la·n·a
we with it thoughts fulfill

ho''na·wan tsi'ta
our mother

tci'mik̯ä'kowa
the one that first had being

hoł yam i'm·-łak̯ikwi
where your sitting quietly where

a·'witen t̄e'li'to
fourth inner room

t̄o' o'neała kwatok̯än·a
you road will make enter

tem ta yam u'lo'nan ya't̄ena
and also your world grasping

yam ho''i ya't̄ena
your people grasping

to' i'mi-ła'k̄una
you will sit down quietly

hon a'k̯ä
we for this

ho'n tca'wili t̄e'wanan te'k̄än·a.
us children having time will live

hom tca''le
my child,

hom tsi'ta
my mother,

ho'man p̄enana·'kowa
my words according to

i'snok̄on te'k̄än·a
there will it be

e'ł yam ho''i ya'kna'na
do not your people let go

et t̄om tse''makwi te'am·ek̄än·a.
let not your thoughts let it not be

ho''na·wan t̄e'k̄ohanan tca'we
our daylight children

łe'tsilon p̄a'ni·nan tca'we
ladder descending children

eł tcu'wantikhoł
do not someone

eł ko·w a·nap̄a
do not a little having gone

tcu'wantikhołi
someone

kwa'tikhoł a'k̄ä
something because of

eł te'nin a'cnam·etun'on a'k̄ä
do not difficult do not make it for this

t̄om ho' t̄e'wusu a'nuła'u.
you I prayer set forth.

ho'man p̄e'nan a'k̄ä
my word with

t̄o' i'mi-ła'k̄un·a
you will sit down quietly

le'si t̄e'wanan·e
this many days

t̄oms t̄e·'wanan i'te'tcik̄a te'a
you now days come to an end when

t̄o i'mi-ła'kun·a
you will sit down quietly

e·t hon tse''makwi mo'ła·na·we hon le''tikwap̄a
but we thoughts fulfill we saying

e'ła· kwa hon tse''makwi mo'la·na·wam·e
no! kwa we thoughts we do not fulfill

eł kwa la'ninam·e hon a·'ho'i.
never not falling down we people.

t̄o'p̄a t̄e'watun te'kwi hai'to a'nt̄sume'na
another day to be when ceremony eagerly

tem ta hon t̄e'wanan a·'tek̄än·a.
and also we time shall live

te''tsinan·e a'nt̄sume'na
winter eagerly

a·'ho' t̂e'wanan a·'tek̭än·a
people time shall live

le·'wi
all

le· p̂e'nan a'k̭ä
this many words with

hom ta'tcu
my father

hom tsi'ta
my mother

hom tca''le
my child

t̂o' les i'mi-łak̂u
you thus sit down quietly

Prayer of a Priest During His Summer Retreat

This many are the days,
Since those who are our fathers,
Those who are our mothers,
The ones who first had being
K̭ä'etoew·
Tcu'eto·we
Had kept for them their days.
This many days,
Anxiously waiting,
We passed our days.
When all these days were past,
Now we have come to the appointed time.
Our fathers,
Our mothers,
In your fourth inner room
You stay quietly.
This day we have reached the appointed time.
Our fathers,
Our ancestors,
Yonder, you who were priests when you were alive,
We have reached your appointed time.[13]
This day
Your day has been made.
The one who is my father,
The one who is my mother,
Four times I shall hold you fast.

le'si t̂e'wanan·e
hon a·'tatc i'lap̂ona
hon a·'tsit i'lap̂ona
tci·'mi k̂änapkowa
k̂ä-e'to·we
tcu-e'to·we
a·' wan t̂e'wana yo·''ap̂a
le'si t̂e'wanan·e
a'nt̂sume'na
hon t̂e'wanan a·'teak̭ä.
hon t̂e'wanan a·'teak̭ä te'kwi
k̭es le'na hai'tokwin te''tcik̭ä

ho''na·wan a·'tatcu
ho''na·wan a·'tsita
yam a·'witen t̂e'li'tona
t̂on t̂i'nan ła'k̂ik̭ä
lu'k̭ä yä'ton·e
hai'tokwin te''tcik̭ä
ho''na·wan a·'tatcu
ho''na·wan a·'łaci'na·we
la'łhok[u] t̂on a·'ciwan·i
k̭ä'k̂ä a·'ho' a·'teakowa
t̂o'na·wan hai'tokwin te''tcik̭ä.

lu'k̭ä yä'tone
t̂o''na·wan t̂e'wanan yo·'k̭ä
yam tatc-i'li te''ona
yam tsit-i'li te''ona
a·'witela'ma
ya't̂ena-t̂su'mek̂än·a.

---

[13] In the songs used during the retreat all the deceased members of the priesthood as far back as tradition goes are invoked by name—a notable exception to the taboo on the use of the names of the dead. The dead priests who abide with the rain makers are believed to be present in spirit. The sense of continuity is stronger in the priestly rituals than in other Zuñi rites.

This day
With the flesh of the white corn,
Prayer meal, commissioned with our prayer,
This day with prayer meal
Four times we shall spread out the mist blanket.[14]
We shall fashion the house of massed clouds,
We shall fashion the life-giving road,
Four times we shall fashion your spring.
This day,
My father,
My mother,
Four times I shall set you down quietly.
Four times you will sit down quietly.
Holding all your world,
Holding all your people,
Perpetuating your rite had since the first beginning,
You will sit down quietly among us.
When you have sat down,
At your back,
At your feet,
We shall sit down beside you.
Desiring your waters,
Keeping your days for this
We shall pass our days.
Our fathers,
Rain maker priests,
Rain maker p̄ekwins,
From wherever you abide permanently
You will make your roads come forth.
To the one whom you call father,
To the one whom you call mother,
Four times with all your waters

To us your mother,
Your fathers,
You will come.
In order that you may thus come to us,
Our father,

lu'k̭ä yä'ton·e
t̄o'wa k̄o'han an ci''nan·e
ha'lawo·tinan·e
t̄e'wusu ya'nułana
lu'k̭ä yä'ton·e
a·'witela'ma
ci'pololon p̄e'wuna
a'wełuya k̭ä'kwen ya·'k̭äna

o'naya·'nak̭ä o'neałan ya·'k̭äna

a·'witela'ma k̭ä'nakwe·nan ya·'k̭äna
lu'k̭ä yä'ton·e
hom ta'tcu
hom tsi'ta
a·'witela'ma t̄om ho' a'nim-ła'k̄una.
a·'witela'ma t̄o' i·'m-iła'k̄una

le· yam 'u'loʻnan ya't̄ena
le· yam ho''i ya't̄ena
yam ko'nhoł tci'mik̭ä'kowa te'liaʻna
t̄o' i·'miła'k̄una

t̄o' i'miła'kuk̄a
t̄o'man ma'si'a
t̄o'man sa'kwi'a
i·'miyawełana
t̄o'man k̭ä'cim a'ntecemana
t̄o'man t̄e'wanan i'lap̄a
hon t̄e'wanan a·'tek̭än·a
ho''na·wan a·'tatcu
u'wanam a·'ciwan·i
u'wanam p̄e'kwi·we
hoł-yam t̄i'nan ła'k̭i'kowa

t̄on o'neała kwai''ik̭än·a.

yam tatc-i'lap̄ona
yam tsit-i'lap̄ona
yam k̭ä'cim a'k̭ä
a·'witela'ma
yam tsi'ta
yam a·'tatcu
ho''na t̄on a·'wona-e'latena·wa.
ho''na t̄on a·'wona-e'latenaptun'on a'k̭ä
ho''na·wan ta'tcu

[14] The meal painting on the altar.

Our mother,
Perpetuating your rite had since the first beginning,
This one[15] sits quietly here.
Your day is made.
Keeping your days we pass our days.
Our mothers,
The ones who first had being
Keeping your days,
We pass our days.
That all our fathers,
Our mothers,
Our children,
That all these may be filled with the water of life,
Anxiously awaiting the making of your days,
We have passed our days.
Our children,
All the different kinds of corn,
All over their earth mother
Stand poor at the borders of our land.
With their hands a little burnt,
With their heads a little brown,
They stand at the borders of our land.
So that these may be watered with fresh water
We keep your days.
That all our children
May nourish themselves with fresh water
Carefully they will rear their young.
And when our daylight children
Have nourished themselves with fresh water
We shall live happily
All our days.
This is all.
Thus speaking plain words
I set you down quietly.

ho''nawan tsi'ta
yam ko''nhoł tci'mik̭ä'kowa te'lia'na
li·ł lu'k̭' i'm-iła'k̄uk̭ä
to''na·wan t̄e'wanan yo·k̭ä
t̄o''na·wan t̄e'wanan i'lap̄ hon t̄e'wanan a·'teaiye.
ho''na·wan a·'tsita
tci'mik̭äna'kowa'
t̄o''na·wan t̄e'wanan i'lap̄a
hon t̄e'wanan a·'teaiye.
yam le· a·'tatcu
yam a·'tsita
yam tca'we
le· k̭ä'cim a·'k̭ä'kunakwi

t̄o''na·wa t̄e'wanan yo·''kowa
a'nt̄sume'na
hon t̄e'wanan a·'teaiye.
ho''na·wan tca'we
t̄o'wa te'młana·wa
yam a'witelintsi'ta' a·na'kowa
te'wuko'liya łu'waneł-pa'łtoye.

ko·w a·'wasi-tca'pina
ko·w a·'wotsimowa-so'sona
łu'waneł-pa'łtoye.

łu'k̭niak̄on k̭äcima tci'm'ona
a·k̭ä'k̄unakwi
hon t̄e'wanan i'lap̄a.
le·wi ho''na·wan tca'we
k̭ä'cima tci'm'ona
i·'k̭ä'k̄unaptun'ona
e'letokna t̄e'apk̄unan o'na-ya'k̭än·a.
ho''na·wan t̄e'k̄ohanan tca'we
k̭ä'cima i·'k̭ä'kuna

t̄e'wanan k̭e' t̄sanici
hon t̄e'wanan a·'tek̭äna.
le·'wi
le yu''he·to p̄e'nan kwai''ina
t̄om ło' a'nim-ła'k̄u.

The P̄ekwin Goes Into Retreat

The retreat of the p̄ekwin follows next after the priests of the four directions. He is priest of the sun, and is associated, according to Mrs. Stevenson, with the zenith. This association, however, does not seem firmly fixed.

[15] The sacred bundle.

The p̄ekwin has no eton·e or priestly bundle. He has pots of black paint brought from the underworld and undoubtedly other ceremonial paraphernalia. But his altar lacks the water and seed-filled reeds which constitute the most sacred and potent possessions of the other priests. He is thought to be so pure in heart that he has no need of magic to make his prayers effective. Therefore, before going into retreat he plants his prayer sticks not at a spring, but in his cornfield. He does not bring back a jug of the sacred water of some spring to place on his altar. For the first part of his retreat "he tries himself." He sits down before an altar consisting only of his paint pots on a painting of meal. It lacks even the bowl of medicine water. As soon as the first rain falls he may mix his medicine in the fresh rain water. If no rain falls, he must continue until the end without even this frail aid to prayer. He is tested at each retreat, and it is always a point of special note whether or not his days are blessed with rain.

The following prayer is recited at the beginning of his retreat. The first part is spoken outside when he plants his prayer sticks, the latter half after he returns to his home.[16]

This many are the days,
Since the new year,
The cycle of the months of our fathers,
The ones that first had being.
This many days
We have awaited our time.
It has come to summer.
My fathers,
My mothers,
The ones that first had being,
Your day goes on.
Not long ago,
At the middle of the year [17]
I made my fathers' days.[18]
This many were the days of the rain makers of all directions.
And now that my fathers' days are at an end,
Yonder, wherever the roads of the rain makers come forth,[19]
Where people pray to finish their roads,
There you stand at the borders of our land,
Male willow, female willow.
Four times breaking off the straight young shoots,

le'si t̄e'wanan·e
i'tiwana
yam a·'tatcu
tci'mi·k̄änapkowa
a·'wan yä'tcu pi'lan·e
le'si t̄e'wanan hon t̄e'wanan a·'teak̄ä.
ɔ'loik̄änakwin te''tcik̄ä
hom a·'tatcu
hom a·'tsita
tci'mik̄änapkona
to'na·wan t̄e'wanan a·'ne
ło'kwa le'tea i'tiwanak̄ä tea
yam a·'tatcu
a·'wan ho t̄e'wanan a'cana
lałhok^{u} le·'wi u'wanam·i
le'si t̄e'wanan·e
yam a·'tatcu
a·'wan t̄e'wanan i'te'tcik̄ätea
la'łhok^{u} u'wanam·i
a·wan o'neała kwai''i'kowa
ho' o'na-ya·'k̄ana'kwi

t̄on łuwalan-pa'łtoye

pilo'tsi pilo'k̄ä te'ona
a'witela'ma a'k̄ewułkwi'na'kowa

---

[16] Dictated by a man formerly associated with the priesthood of the Water Serpent.

[17] The summer solstice. The pekwin plants several times at this time. After that he must keep count of the days and see that each priesthood goes in on schedule time.

[18] The retreats of the four chief priesthoods.

[19] At springs and along watercourses.

To my house
I brought my road.
Sitting down quietly,
Throughout a blessed night
With our children [20] we came to day.
This day, my fathers,
You who here were p̂ekwins,
You who used to take care of the world,
You who used to be chiefs of the downy feather,[21]
And furthermore, my sun father,
My child,
This day,
When you came out standing to your sacred place,
This day
In my house
For your rite
I fashioned plume wands in human form.
With the striped cloud wing of my father,
Male turkey,
With the striped cloud wing of oriole, p̂ekwin priest,[22]
And blue jay, p̂ekwin priest,
And the wings of all the different birds of summer,
With these four times
I gave my plume wands human form.
With the flesh of my mother,
My grandmother,
Yucca fiber,
Cotton woman,
Even a soiled cotton thread,
With these I gave my plume wands human form.
With the flesh of the one who is my mother,

hom hecot̂akwi
o'neał i'k̯äna
i·'t̂inan ła'k̯ikna
t̂e'łinan k̂o'kci
ho'n tca'wilap a·'want̂e'wak̯ä

lu'k̯ä yä'ton·e
hom a·'tatcu
li·'łno t̂on p̂e'kwi·w a·'teakowa
to'n u'lo'na i'lap̂ a·'tea'kowa
k̯ahaiya te'kwi t̂on a·'mos a·'teakowa
le'stiklea hom yä'tok̯ä ta'tcu
hom tca''le
lu'k̯ä yä'ton·e
yam t̂e'łacinakwi
t̂o' ye·'lana kwai'ik̯äk̯ä te'a'ana
lu'k̯ä yä'ton·e
yam he'cot̂an·e
t̂o'na·wan haito
ho' te'lik̯ina a·'ho' a·'ya·k̯äna

yam ta'tcili te'ona

ton ɔ'tsi an ła'pihanan la'tan·e
o'nołik̯ä p̂e'kwin ci'wan·i
an ła'pihanan la'tan·e
mai'ya p̂e'kwin ci'wan·i
la'łhok^u ɔ'lo'ik̯aiak̯a wo·'we
a·'wa' la'tan·e t̂em·ła
a'k̯·ä a'witela'ma
te'lik̯ina a·'ho' a·'ya·k̯äk̯ä

yam tsi'ta
yam ho'ta
ho'yalaciwi
p̂it̂sem o'k̯ä
a·'tcian ci''nan p̂i'le ci'k̯änapte
a'k̯·a te'lik̯inan ho'i ya·'k̯änapk̯ä.

yam tsi't i'li te''ona

---

[20] The willow sticks.

[21] Prayer sticks offered to the sun, the moon, and the rain makers are made with downy feathers of the eagle. After planting these sticks the suppliant must refrain from animal food for four days. The downy feather is considered the p̂ekwin's because he always plants to the sun. The other priests use it when rain is urgently needed and thereafter must abstain from animal food. Prayer sticks to the ancestors, deceased members of societies or priesthoods, and the katci·nas are made with turkey feathers. It is as guardian of the calendar that the p̂ekwin "takes care of the world."

[22] The bird associated with the north. The birds of the six directions are the p̂ekwins or heralds of the directions. The p̂ekwin, who is the herald of the sun, is frequently referred to as, "all the birds of summer, p̂ekwins." The feather of the blue jay is the feather of the priests which they are entitled to wear in the hair on ceremonial occasions.

The one who first had being,
Black paint woman,
With her flesh making the flesh of my plume wands,
I gave them human form,
Saying, "Let it be now."
Taking my plume wands,
The plume wands which had been prepared,
I made my road come forth.
I made my road go forth.
Somewhere in my water-filled fields [23]
I passed my earth mother on her road.
My fathers,
My ancestors,
You who used to be p̄ekwins,
You who used the downy feather,
You who used to take charge of the world,
And furthermore my child,
My father,
Sun,
My child, my mother, moon,
My fathers,
Divine ones,
This day
I give you plume wands.
Taking your plume wands,
There where you abide permanently,
Clasping them in your arms,
Caressing them,
With your supernatural wisdom,
You will distribute them amongst you.
After a little while
To my house
My road will reach.
Making your days, I shall pass the days.

tci'mik̯ä'kowa
ha'kwin o'kä an ci''nan a'k̯ä
te'lik̯inan a·ci'nan ya·'k̯äna

ho'i ya·'k̯änapk̯ä te'a
k̯ä·'k̯i k̯esi' le''anak̯äp̄a
yam te'lik̯inan e'lete'u'kowa
te'lik̯inan i·'łeana

ho' o'neała kwai''ik̯äna
o'neał a·'k̯äna
hoł yam k̯ä'cima te'atci'nakwi

yam a·'witeli·n tsi'ta ho' o'na-e'latek̯ä
hom a·'tatcu
hom a·'łacina·we
t̄on p̄e'kwiwe a·'tea'kowa
k̯a'haiyatekwi t̄on u'lo'nan i'lap̄ a·'tea'kowa

le'stiklea hom tca''le
hom ta'tcu
yätok̯ä
hom tca''le hom tsi'ta ya'onan·e
hom a·'tatcu
k̯ä'pin a·'ho'i
lu'k̯ä yä'ton·e
t̄o''na ho' te'lik̯inan a·'łea'u
te'lik̯inan i·'łeana
yam t̄i'nan ła'k̯ikwi

t̄on a·'k̯eckuna t̄e'łak̯una

yam a'nikwanan a'k·ä
t̄on te'lik̯inan i·'yanhaitena

we'tsim te'nala'ana
yam hecot̄akwi
ho' o'neała te'tcik̯äna
t̄o'na·wan t̄e'wanan a'cna
hon t̄e'wanan a·'tek̯än·a.

[He deposits the plume wands, then he returns to his ceremonial house, sets up his altar, which consists of dishes of sacred black paint and bowls of prayer meal. The prayer continues:]

This day, my fathers,

luk̯a yä'ton·e
hom a·'tactu

---

[23] He plants in his cornfield, not at a sacred spring.

You who are my child, sun,
You who are my mother, moon,
This day
I have passed you on your roads.
This day, upon the flesh of the white corn,
Prayer meal,
Breathing my prayers
Four times I have spread out your mist blanket;
I have fashioned your cloud house;
I have fashioned your road.
Now that this is at an end
Your days are made.
After a little while
From where you abide permanently
You will make your road come forth.
Yonder from the south,
Where, they say, is the abiding place of summer,
My fathers,
Send forth your quick breath.[24]

Send forth your massed clouds to stay with us,
Stretch out your watery hands,
Let us embrace!
To Itiwana you will come
With all your people,
Hiding behind your watery shield [25]
With all your people;
With your fine rain caressing the earth,
With your heavy rain caressing the earth,
Carrying your weapons,
Your lightning,
(Come to us!)
Raise the sound of your thunders!
At Itiwana
With your great pile of waters
May you pass me on my road.
That this may be
I have made your days.
When your days are at an end,

Meeting me with all your waters,
May you stay with us,

t̄om ho' tca'' ili yä'tok̭ä
t̄om ho' tsi't ili ya'onan·e
lu'k̭ä yä'ton·e
hom t̄on o'na-e'latekä.
lu'k̭ä yä'ton·e
t̄o'wa k̄o'han an ci''nan·e
ha'lawo·tinan·e
t̄e'wus a'nułana
a'witela'ma ho' ci'pololon p̄e'wuk̭ä

ho' a'wełuyan k̭ä'kwen ya·'k̭äk̭ä.
t̄o'na ho' o'neała ya·'k̭äk̭ä
i'te'tcik̭a te'a
t̄o'na·wan t̄e'wanan yo·'k̭ä.
we'tsim te'nala'ana
hoł yam t̄c·'nan ła'k̭i'kowa

t̄on o'neała kwai''ik̭äna.

li·'wan a'lahoa'nkwin ta'ʻna
hoł ɔ'lo'ik̭'äna·wa le'anak̭änkwi

hom a·'tatcu
yam k̭a'hai ya'nkakuna ĸwai''i-k̭äna
yam a'wełuyan imuna kwai''ik̭äna

yam k̭ä'cima astaʻnap̄a
ho'n i·'wiyat̄en-t̄su'mek̭än·a
i'tiwana'kowa
yam ho' i'lap'a
yam k̭ä''alan·e yai'yal·ana

yam ho' i'lap'a
yam k̭ä'tsana łi'ton-t̄e'łakwi

yam k̭ä'łana łi'ton-t̄e'łakwi

yam sa'wanik̭a łe'ana.
yam wi'lolonan·e
ku'lulunan·e
te'hato·nan k̭e'ato'u
i'tiwanakwi
yam k̭ä'cima pu'ckwe·na
t̄on a'k·ä hom o'na-e'latenapt̄un'-onak̭ä
t̄o'na·wan t̄e'wanan yo·k̭ä
t̄o'na·wan t̄e'wanan i'te'tcitun-te'kwi
yam k̭ä'cim a'k̭·ä
hom t̄on o'na-e'latena łon a·'te-k̭än·a.

[24] The sudden showers of summer, which at Zuñi always come from the southeast.
[25] The rain makers cover themselves with clouds as a warrior with his shield.

Do not cause people to speak ill of your days,[26]
But with waters caressing the earth
Let your days be filled.
With your waters
You will pass me on my road.
Those which all my ladder descending children
Have sown with magical rites,
All the different kinds of corn,
Yonder all over their earth mother,
They stand poor at the borders of our land.
With their hands a little burnt,
With their heads brown,
They stand poor at the borders of our land.
That these may be nourished with fresh water,
Thus runs the thought of my prayer.
When the time of my days is at an end,
Though I say "my days are at an end,"
No—it is not so.
Waiting anxiously until another day comes
We shall pass the days.
My fathers,
Now I have fulfilled your thoughts.

This is all.

eł t̃on yam t̃e'wanan ci'łk̯äna·'wamek̯än·a
yam t̃e'wanan·e
k̯ä'cima-t̃e'łakwi
hon t̃e'wanan a·'tek̯än·a.
yam k̯ä'cim ak̯·ä
hom t̃on o'na-e'latena·'wap̃a
le· łe'tsilon p̃a'ni·nan hom tca·we

la'łhok^{u} a·'wan it̃sumana·we
t̃o'wa t̃e'm·łana
yam a'witelin tsi'tana'kowa
te'wuko'liya łu'walan-pa'łtoye

ko·w a·'wasi·we tca'pina
a·'wotsimo'wa so'sona
te'wuko'liya łuwalan pa'łtoye.

lu'kniak̯o k̃ä'cim a·k̃äʻk̃unakwin

li·łno hom t̃e'wusu tse'makwi·a·naiye
hom t̃e'wanan·e
t̃e'wanan i·'te'tcap̃a
t̃e'wanan i·'te'tcik̯ä le'kwap̃a

e'ła
t̃opa t̃e'watun te'kwi a'nt̃sumeʻna

hon t̃e'wanan a·'tek̃än·a.
hom a·'tatcu
to''na·wan ho' tse''makwi· mo'ła·k̯ä ke·'si
le·wi.

The Bow Priest in Retreat in Summer

On the day the p̃ekwin comes out of retreat in summer the bow priest begins to count days. He is not a rain priest. He has no altar; he has no rain-making fetish; his sacred possessions are associated rather with war. Therefore, instead of remaining in meditation and prayer in his ceremonial house, he makes offerings at the various shrines of the gods of war on mountain tops around Zuñi. The first day he goes to the north, to Twin Mountains; the second day to the west—the place actually visited is a shrine to the south on a knoll near the road to the Salt Lake. The third day he goes to the south, Face Mountain, a shrine southeast of Zuñi; the fourth day to the east, a knoll near the Black Rock road. At each of these shrines he offers corn meal and turquoise with prayers for rain and fertility. He offers these in his capacity of priest rather than as warrior.

[26] The p̃ekwin is severely criticized should it fail to rain during the days of his retreat. Criticism does not fall so heavily on other priests should they fail.

This many days,
Making the days of my two fathers,
The ones who hold the high places,[27]
Keeping their days,
I have lived.
My fathers,
Rain maker priests,
Rain maker p̄ekwins
And you, far off at the fourth rim of the encircling ocean,
You who are our fathers, rain maker bow priests,
Tsik̯ähiya,[28] K̯äławani,[28]
From wherever you abide permanently
Send forth your misty breath;
Your little wind blown clouds,
Your thin wisps of cloud,
Your black streaks of cloud,
Your masses of clouds replete with living waters,
You will send forth to stay with us.
With your fine rain caressing the earth,
With your heavy rain caressing the earth,
With your great pile of waters here at Itiwana
You will pass us on our roads.
Desiring this, my fathers,

I have made your days.
When you pass me on my road
All my ladder descending children
Will refresh themselves with your living waters.
That the crowns of their heads may sometimes be wet with dew,
In order that this may be
You, my fathers, yonder on all sides,

le'si t̄e'wanan·e
yam a·'tcia tatc i'li te''ona
te'alan i'lona
a·'tcian t̄e'wanan a'cna
a·'tcian t̄e'wanan i'li ho' t̄e'wanan te'aiye
hom a·'tatcu
u'wanam a·'ciwan·i
u'wanam·i p̄e'kwi·we.
la'łhok^{u} a·'witen i·'yałto k̯ä'tuł u'lapna'kowa
t̄o''na hon a·'tatc i'li u'wanam a·'p̄i'ła·ci'wan·i
tsi'k̯ähaiya k̯ä'ławan·i
hoł yam t̄i'nan ła'k̯i'kowa
yam ci'pololon·e ya'nhakuna kwai''ik̯äna
yam p̄i'tcinan·e
yam su'lahaiyan·e
yam ła'pihaiyan·e
yam a'wełuyan k̯ä'kwi ya·'na

i·'muna kwai''ik̯'äna
yam k̯ä't̄san łi'ton t̄e'łakwi

yam k̯ä'łana łiton t̄e'łakwi

i'tiwanakwi yam k̯ä'cima p̄u'c-kwe·n a'k̯ä
hom t̄on o'na-e'latena·wa
lu'k̯' a'ntecemana
hom a·'tatcu
t̄o''na·wan ho' t̄e'wanan a'ck̯ä
hom t̄on o'na-e'latena·wap̄a
le·wi hom łe'tsilon p̄ani·nan tca'we
a'k̯a k̯ä'cima k̯ä'kwik̯äna

ko·w a·'wɔt̄simowa k̯ä'łaiya hoł t̄e'wanan a·'teatun'ona

t̄em t̄a la'łhok^{u} le'si te'kwi hom a·'tatcu

[27] Or "those who guard the housetops"—the twin gods of war.

[28] Supernaturals associated in their dual capacity of warriors and rain makers with sudden thunderstorms. They live in springs and have long streaming hair. (Tsik̯ahaiya means "quick moving hair.") A dirigible which flew over Zuñi some years ago was identified with K̯äławan·i, who looks "like an icicle" when he appears to mortals. K̯äławani is sometimes impersonated in mask with a tablet headdress and long flowing hair reaching to his knees. The third supernatural usually mentioned with Tsik̯ahaiya and K̯äławani is Kupictaiya (cf. Keres Kopictaiya), called by Mrs. Stevenson lightning makers. There is some confusion in the minds of the Zuñi as to whether these are individuals or classes of supernaturals. The latter is more in keeping with Zuñi ideology.

You who dwell in high places,
For this you live at sacred places
Round about on all the mossy mountains.
My fathers,
To all your ladder descending children
You will grant your power.[29]
In order that my children may have strong hearts
It is now your day.
From wherever you stay permanently
Your massed clouds filled with living water, may you send forth.
Making your road come forth from where you stay permanently,
With your rain caressing the earth,
With your terrible lightning,
Make your thunders resound!

At Itiwana may you pass me on my road.
When you have passed me on my road,
My mothers,
My children,
All the different kinds of corn,
Nourishing themselves with their fathers' waters,
Tenderly will bring forth their young.
When they have finished their roads,
When they are old,
My children,
My ladder descending children,
Will bring in their children,
All the different kinds of corn,
Into their houses.
That they may always be the ones toward whom our thoughts bend,
For this all my children carefully have reared their young.
All my children
Will make their roads come into their houses.
Staying there permanently,
Your young increasing,
You will always remain.

te'alan i'lap̂ona
le·w a'wico yä'la'kowa
t̂o'n t̂e'łacin u'lapna a·'teaîye

hom a·'tatcu
le· łe'tsilon p̂a'ni·nan yam tca'we

t̂on sa'wanik̯ä ya'nhaitena·wa.
a'k̯a hom tca'we sa'wanik̯' a·'wik̯e·na a·'teatun'on a'k̯ä
t̂o''na·wan li·ł t̂e'wana·we.
hoł yam t̂i'nan ła'k̯i'kowa

a'wełuyan k̯ä''kwi ya·'na i·'muna kwai''ik̯äna
yam t̂i'nan ła'k̯i'kowa o'neała kwai''ik̯äna
yam łi'ton t̂e'łakuna
yam sa'wanik̯ä wi'lolonan·e
yam ku'lulunan·e
t̂e'**ha**·t̂onan k̯e'ato'u
i'tiwanakwi hom t̂on o'na-e'latena·wa
hom t̂on o'na-e'latena·'wap̂a

hom a·'tsita
hom tca'we
t̂o'wa t̂e'młana'na
yam a·'tatcu
a·'wan k̯ä'cim i·'k̯ä'kuna
e'letokna t̂e'apk̂unan o'na· ya·'k̂äna·wa
a·'wona· ya·''ap̂a

a·'łacia·p̂a
hom tca'we
łe'tsilon p̂a'ni·nan hom tca'we
yam tca'we t̂o'wa te'młana'na

yam he'cot̂akwin a·'wana'-u'łana
i'sk̂ɔn tse''mak t̂e'łakwi hoł yam t̂e'wanan a·'teatun'on a'k̯ä

hom tca'we e'letokna t̂on t̂e'apk̂unan o'na·ya·'k̯änapk̯ä
le·w hom tca'we
a·'wan he'cot̂a'kowa o'neała kwa'tok̯äna
t̂on i't̂inan ła'k̯i'kna
t̂e'apk̂unan ci'wuna t̂on t̂ewanan a·'teap̂a

[29] Or weapons.

That the thoughts of my ladder descending children
May bend to this,
That this may be,
My fathers,
Thus runs the thought of my prayer.
Thus all my children
May always be well provided with seeds.
Desiring this,
I watch over our daylight fathers,
The ones who here have in their keeping
The rites of our fathers,[30]
Those who first had being,
Our daylight fathers,
Who perpetuate the rites which they hold in their keeping,
The rites of those who first had being;
Sitting down among my daylight fathers
Watching over my fathers—
That one am I.
My fathers,
You know me well.
Do not let me be a poor person.[31]

My fathers,
You who hold the high places, your representative am I.
I have a bandoleer,[32]
I have an armlet; [33]
Because of this
I am my father's mouth.[34]

All my ladder descending children,
All of them I hold in my hands,
May no one fall from my grasp
After going but a little ways—

Those yonder toward the east,
In all the villages that stand against the place of the rising sun,

hom ɫe'tsilon p̄a'ni·nan tca'we

i'skɔn tse''mak-t̄e'ɫakwi a·'teatun-'on a'k̯ä
hom a·'tatcu
li·'ɫno hom t̄e'wusu tse''makwi a·'naiye
hom le'na tca'we
a'k̯' i'ceɫte'ma t̄o'waconan a·n e'la k̯äna
luk̯' a'ntecemana
li·'ɫno yam a·'tatcu
tci'mik̯änapkowa

ho''na·wan a·'tatcu
ko''lea i·mos i'lap̄ a·'te'ona
t̄ek̄ohanana yam a·'tatcu
tci'mik̯änapkowa
ko''leholɫ i'mɔs i'lap̄a·'te'ona i·'yantelia'na
t̄e'k̄ohanan yam a·'tatcu
a·'wan i'maweɫa

yam a·'tatcu
a·'wai yu'patci ho' ho''i
hom a·'tatcu
hom to'n an'ai'yu'ya·nap̄a
eɫ kwa'hoɫ te'wuko'liya ho''i te'am·e
yam a·'tatcu
te'alan i'lap̄ona ya'ntelia'na ho' a'k̯ä ho''i.
ho' yä'tonan i'li
ho' pa'sikwin i'li
le'sna te''onak̯ä
yan a·'tatcu
a·'wan ho' a'watin·e.
le· ɫe'tsilon p̄a'ni·nan yam tca'we
te'mɫa ho' a·'yaknaiye.
kwa ko·w a·'nap̄a.
yam tcu'waya eɫ ya'kna p̄i'ya'na te'ametun'on a'k̯ä
lehok^{u} t̄e'luwaiyankwin ta''na
ɫu'wala· u'ɫa te'mɫa
yä'tokwai'inankwin te''tcinan

[30] The priests who possess sacred bundles. The bow priests are their messengers and the guardians of their secret rites.

[31] A person with no ceremonial prerogatives.

[32] A bandoleer embroidered with shells and containing hair from the scalps which he has taken since his installation as bow priest. It is a dangerous object which the warrior hangs by the door to protect the house. It is too dangerous to be brought into back rooms. Its contaminating influence must be kept especially from seeds and water.

[33] An arm band embroidered in shell, part of the warrior's regalia.

[34] The twin deities who led the people out from the underworld are called "the mouth of the sacred bundles" (K̯ä'eto·we a wan a^{u}watin·e). These individuals, while distinct from the twin gods of war, are not unrelated. See origin myth, p. 549.

Even to all those villages
That stand against the place of the setting sun,
Even every little bug,
Even every dirty little bug,
Let me hold them all fast in my hands,
Let none of them fall from my grasp—
In order that this may be,
My fathers,
I ask you for life.
May my children's roads all be fulfilled;
May they grow old;
May their roads reach all the way to dawn lake;
May their roads be fulfilled;
In order that your thoughts may bend to this,
Your days are made.
Now your days are at an end.
Whatever I have wished
I have spoken
All our prayers which we have completed for each other;
Thus I have fulfilled our thoughts.
Eagerly awaiting until it shall be another day,
Until the winter,
I shall now pass my time.
My fathers,
Your waters,
Your seeds,
Your riches,
Your power,
Your strong spirit,
All this you will grant us;
May my road be fulfilled,
May I grow old,
Even until I go with strong hands grasping a bent stick,[35]
Thus may I grow old.

yä'ton kwa'telenankwin te''tcinan
le łuwala·u'ła te'mła

kwa ko·wi no'me t̄sa'napte
nom a'ntcimo'apte
te'mła a·'wiyat̄en-t̄su'mek̯äna

eł kwa tcu'wa ya'kna p̄i'ya'na te'ametun'on a'k̯ä

hom a·'tatcu
to''na ho' t̄e'k̄ohanan yai'ncemana
hom tca'we te'mła a·'wona ya·''an·a
a·'łaci'an·a
t̄e'luwaiyan k̯aiakwi o'neała te''tcikwi te'mła a·'wona· ya·''-an·a.
i'sk̄ɔn tse''mak-t̄e'łakwi yam t̄e'-wanan teatun'onak̯ä
t̄o''na·wan t̄e'wanan te'ak̯ä
t̄o''na·wan t̄e'wanan i·te''tcik̯ä
hołko'n a'ntecemana
p̄e'nan kwai''ina
yam hon i·'yant̄ewusu p̄ena· ya·'-k̯änapkowa
ho' tse''makwin mo'ła·k̯ä.
t̄o'p̄a t̄e'watun te'kwi

te''tsinan·e a'nt̄sume'na
hos t̄e'wanan te'k̯än·a
hom a·'tatcu
yam k̯ä'cima
yam t̄o'waconan·e
yam u'tenan·e
yam sa'wanik̯ä
yam tse''makwin t̄su'me
te'mła homs ton a'niktciana·wa.
ho' o'naya·'an·a
ho' ła'ci'an·a
t̄a'p̄owan łe'a t̄su'me ho' ła'ci'an·a.

[35] That is, leaning on a cane, a common symbol for long life and old age. At the winter solstice the feather offerings of society members all contain bent prayer sticks as a prayer for old age.

IV. PRAYERS OF THE WAR CULT

The Bow Priest Makes Prayer Sticks at the Winter Solstice

My two fathers,
You who dwell in high places [1]
Ma'ase·wi [2]
Uyuye·wi
For you it is the new year.
Since it is the new year,
All the beings that dwell in mossy mountains,
The beings who dwell in shady places,
The forest beings,
The brush beings,
Oak being
Willow being [3]
Red willow being [3]
łaniłkowa being [3]
Cottonwood being
Taking the straight young shoots of all these,
These we shall make into prayer plumes.
For my fathers,
The divine ones,
I have destined these prayer plumes.
When my fathers
The divine ones
Take hold of their prayer plumes,
When they clothe themselves with their prayer plumes,
Then all to my children
Long life,
Old age,
All good fortune whatsoever,
You will grant;
So that I may raise corn,
So that I may raise beans,
So that I may raise wheat,
So that I may raise squash,
So that with all good fortune I may be blessed.

hom a·'tatc a·'tci·
te'alan i'lon a·'tci
ma''ase·wi
u'yuye·wi
to'na i'tiwanan te''tci
i'tiwanan te''tcina
le·w a'wico yä'la'kowa a·'te'ona
te'łula'kowa te''wa i'lap̑ a·'te'ona
t̑akwił p̑ɔ·'t̑i
łakwił p̑ɔ·t̑i
a'si a·'te'ona
i'pina a·'te'ona
ła'l·atu a·'te'ona
ła'niłkowa a·'te'ona
p̑o·la a·'te'ona
te'mła a·'k̭̑äwułkwi'na
u''sona te'lik̭ina·we
a·'ya·k̭̑äna·wa.
yam a·'tatcu
k̭̑ä'pin a·'ho'i.
te'lik̭inan a·'wanhai'tek̭ä.
hom a·'tatcu
k̭̑äpin a·'ho'i
te'lik̭inan a·'yat̑ena
te'lik̭inan i·'łeana
le·'w hom tca'we
o'na ya·'nak̭ä
ła'ciak̭ä
kwa'hoł yam te'n·i ha'lowilin·e
te'mła hom t̑on a'nhaitena·wa
a'k̭' ho'o mi'ya'un·a
no'k̭ä'un·a
k̭äiya'un·a
ho' mɔ'la'un·a
kwa'hoł te'mła hom t̑on a'nik-tciana·wa.

[1] The gods of war, whose shrines are on mountain tops. The phrase might also be rendered as "those who guard the housetops."

[2] The Keresan name for the elder of the two gods of war. His Zuñi name, which is esoteric, is Matsailema. According to Mrs. Stevenson he is the younger brother. Both this name and that of Uyuye.wi were unknown to the interpreter to whom the prayer was read, but her father, who carves the image of the younger brother, knew the names.

[3] The identifications are uncertain.

Prayers Before Going on a War Party

Before going on the warpath the bow priests are summoned to their ceremonial house. The chief bow priest addresses them:

Now this many days
Because of the thoughts of the enemy

Our thoughts have been troubled;
Our appetite has failed.
This very day
That by which they live,
Turquoise,[4]
To my fathers I have offered
At all their abiding places.
Yonder into the enemy's country
We shall take the warpath.

Because of the enemy,
Because of their thoughts,
We wish in vain see one another,[5]
We can not see him of whom we think.
Because it is thus,
To be avenged
We have made up our minds.
My children,
You shall set your minds to be men.
You shall think to provide yourselves with good weapons.
Then, perhaps, we shall have the good fortune,
To get that which we wish,
That for which we ask—
Namely that with the enemies' flocks,
Their clothing,
Their precious stones,
Their good shell beads,
That with these our houses may obtain hearts,
For this we have sent forth our prayers.
Waiting anxiously until the appointed time shall come,
Cleansing our hearts,
Cleansing our thoughts,
Thus shall we live.
Indeed we shall not be alone.
Because yonder all about
Abide our fathers.

ma' le'si t̄e'wanan·e
a·'winakwe
a'wan tse''makwin a'k̫ä
te'tse'mak-p̄onołkwiʻna
k̫ä'p i'kwiłin i·'natina
yam a·'teon a'k̫ä
tci'mte yä'ton·e
yam a·'tatcu
t̄i'na·-te'mła
ho' ło·''o a·'łeak̫ä.
lehok^{u} i'nak̄wan 'uloʻnakwi
sa'munan a'k̫ä
hon le'hoł o'neał a·'k̫̄äna·wa.
a'k̫̄äp a·'winak̄wa·wa tse''makwin a'k̫ä
i·'yuna·wet̄iyaʻna
hon a'ntse'man a'ni·nena·we.

le'sna te''onak̫ä
a'suk̫äna'k̫ä
ho' tse''makwi ya·'k̫̄äk̫ä
hom tca'we
t̄on ɔ'ts̄in tse''makuna·wa
t̄on i'nasnan k̄ɔ'kc a'ntse'nana·wa

ho'nkwe·k hon a·'halowili

hoł ko'n a'ntecemana
p̄ena· ya·''k ona
a·'winak̄w a·'wan wɔ·'we

a·'wan u'tena·we
a·'wan a''cona·we.
a·'wan ło·' a·'k̄ɔk·ci
a'k̫ä ho''na·wan he'cot̄a i'k̫e·nap-tun'onak̫ä
hon p̄e'nan kwai''ik̫änapk̫ä

hoł hai't̄okwin te''tcituntekwi a'n-t̄sumeʻna
i'k̫e·n i·'k̄ɔkcuna
tse''mak i·'k̄ɔkcuna
hon t̄e'wanan a·'tek̫än·a.
a'tic hon a·'sam a·'tek̫äna tse'na
a'k̫ä la'łhok^{u} ho''na·wan a·'tatcu
t̄i'na· u'lapnaiye.

[4] Turquoise, above all else, the gift to the gods of war.
[5] Some of our number have died.

Spreading word about among them,
You will think to give them good turquoise.
To this end, my children,
Through all the time set aside for them,

Eagerly you will await their day.
After a good night
May you come to day.
And to-morrow
After a good day may you come to evening.
And as each day comes,
Eagerly may you wait their day.

May your thought not be vacillating.
Indeed, though I call myself poor,
Far off I shall have someone for my father.
For there is one who by virtue of the dry bow [6]
Holds us all as his children.
His representative am I.

Asking for life from him
I shall add to your breath.
And furthermore,
Emerging into the daylight
Yonder on all the mossy mountains
All about they have set their sacred places,[7]
The ones who hold the high places,
Ahayuta yellow,[8]
Blue,
Red,
White,
Many colored,
The dark one,
These were bow priests.

Holding us as their children
They abide in all their sacred places round about.
To all these places
Sending forth my prayer to them,

la'ʻnok̄ɔ.
a·'wan p̄enan i'tulohana
ło''o k̄ɔkci a·'łeatun'ona
t̄on a'ntse'mana·wa
t̄e'wuna' hom tca'we
le'k̄ɔn hai'to

a'nt̄sumeʻna
hon t̄e'wanan a·'tek̭än·a
t̄e'łinan k̄ɔ'kci
t̄on a·'want̄ewatu.
t̄e'wan yä'ton·e
yä'ton k̄ɔ'kci
t̄on su·'nhak̭äna·wa
i'sk̭än t̄e'wanan a·'tun te'kwi
a'nt̄sumeʻna
t̄on t̄e'wanan a·'tek̭än·a
eł i'k̭e'łuʻna
t̄o'na·'wan tse'makwi teaʻmetu
t̄a·'tcic te'wuko'liya lekwanante
ho'łomacko'na
tcu'waya ho' tatc i'lik̭än·a
pi'łan k̄u'sn'ak̭ä

ho' tca'wili te''ona
lu'k̭ak̄ɔ a'ntelia'na
yam ho''i te''ona
t̄e'k̄ohanan ai'ncemana
t̄o''na'wan ho' p̄i''nan te'liun·a
le'stikleap̄a
t̄e'k̄ohanan yaʻnak̭äp̄a
la'łhok^{u} a'wico yäla'kona
t̄e'łacin u'lapk̭änapk̭ä

te'alan i'lap̄ona
a'haiyuta łu'ptsina
łi'an·a
a'hon·a
k̄ohan·a
i't̄op̄anaʻna
ci'k̭an·a
lu'knok̄ɔ
pi'łaciwan·ik̭äk̭ä
ho''na tca'wilap̄a
t̄e'łacin u'lapna
a·'teaiye
laʻnok̄ɔ
yam t̄e'wusu p̄e'nan te''tcik̭äna

[6] Pi'łan k̄usna, dry bow, used metaphorically for the war chief. The supernaturals, in this case the war gods, exert power through their human representatives.

[7] At the time of the emergence.

[8] The war gods, as inhabitants of their six shrines, associated with the six directions.

I ask for their life-giving breath,
Their breath of old age,
Their breath of riches,
Their breath of waters,
Their breath of seeds,
Their breath of fecundity,
Their breath of power,
Their breath of strong spirit,
Their breath of all good fortune of which they are possessed—
Asking for their breath,
And into my warm body drawing their breath,
I shall add to your breath.
To this end, my children:
May you be belssed with life.

a·'wan o'naya·nak̭a p̄i''nan·e
ła'ciak̭ä p̄i''nan·e
u'tenan p̄i''nan·e
k̭̄ä'cima p̄i''nan·e
t̄o'waconan p̄i''nan·e
t̄e'apk̄unan p̄i''nan·e
a·'wan sa'wanik̭ä p̄i''nan·e
tse''makwin t̄su'me p̄i''nan·e
kwa'hoł te'mła p̄i''nan i'lap̄ a·'te'ona
p̄i''nan yai'ncemana
yam te'huł k̭'ä'łnakwi
p̄i''nan a'lit̄o·na
to''na·wan ho' p̄i''nan te'li'una
t̄e'wuna' hom tca'we
t̄o' t̄e'k̄ohanan ya'niktcia'tu.

The date for starting is set. Any man who wishes to join the party tells the bow priests, and the destination is determined according to the size of the party. During the interval offerings are made by the bow priests at the various shrines referred to in the preceding prayer. The night before they leave all volunteers meet at the ceremonial house of the bow priests. Each man deposits prayer meal, corn pollen, and some precious material—shell, turquoise, red paint, or iridescent black paint—in each of four corn husks. These are immediately taken to four distant shrines, by the elder and younger brother bow priests, the war chief, and the society chief of the bow priesthood. On reaching the shrine the emissary says:

How are you this evening?
(He answers himself, speaking in the person of the god:)
Happy. Have you come? Sit down.
Now, indeed, you have passed us on our roads.
Indeed, words not too long your words will be.
If you let us know what they are,
Always we shall remember them.
Is it not so?
THE MAN: Indeed it is so.
As you know,
To all your different abiding places
I have gone about,
With words of taking our road into the enemy's country.
To-morrow upon that
The sun will arise.
THE GOD: Is that so?
That must not be.
We can not part with you.

— ko' t̄on su·nhak̭̄änapk̭ä—
— k̭̄e'tsanici· t̄onc a·'wia· i·'t̄inak̭̄ä
ma' la'k̭̄ämante
ło'na t̄o' a·'wona-e'latek̭ä
i'me' kwa'tik p̄e'na te'yu'lanam·e
p̄e'nan te'ak̭̄än·a
t̄e'wuna' u''son ho''na t̄o ai'yu'ya·k̭̄äp̄a
u'son ai'yu'ya·na
hon t̄e'wanan a·'tek̭̄än·a hatci'—
— ma'i·'na mi'łte
e'pac le'hok[u] i'nak̄w an u'lo'nakwi
o'neał a·'k̭̄äna'k̭ä
p̄e'naw ak̭ä
li·łno t̄on t̄i'na-te'mła
ho' a'luk̭ä.
t̄e'wan yä'ton·e
u''son a'k̭ä yä'to kwai''in·a.—
—haiyi'
kwa le'sna te'acukwa
t̄om hon i'tcemana·we—

THE MAN: Nevertheless there is no choice.
To do that very thing I have made up my mind.
And furthermore,
Thinking to bring you fine shell,
Prayer meal,
Corn pollen,
Red paint,
Sparkling paint,
Eager for this I have passed my days.

Now this day
We have reached the appointed time.
Therefore we have passed you on your road.
THE GOD: Is that so?
Nevertheless, in spite of your speaking thus,
We can not part with you.
We have your plume wands,
We have your shells,
We have your prayer meal.

THE MAN: Yes, that is why I have spoken words
Of going to the enemy's country.

Because on account of the enemy's thoughts
Our children have been destroyed.
Our flocks have been destroyed.
Because of the enemy's thoughts,
We wish to see our relatives,

And thinking of them we fail in it.
THE GOD: Is that so?
Very well, although we cherish you,

You think thus.
Our elder brothers yonder,
The ones who abide in different places,
Do they also know it?
THE MAN: Yes, certainly.

At all their abiding places,
I have bent down to speak to them.

—ma' e·te

t̄a tenat hoł ko'lea te'atun'ona ho' tse'makwi ya·'k̄ăk̯ä
le's tikleap̄a
ło·''o k̄ɔ'kci
ha'lawo·tinan·e
o'nean·e
a'hokona
t̄su'hap̄a te''ona
t̄on a·'łeatun'ona
lon a'ntse'man t̄e'wanan a·'teak̯ä te'kwi
lu'k̯ä yä'ton·e
k̯es hai'tokwin te''tcik̯ä

a'k̯ä t̄o''na łon a·'wona-e'latek̯ä.—

—haiyi'
ma' e·t t̄o le'sna p̄eyepte

t̄om hon i'tcemana·we.
t̄o'man łon te'likinan a·'łeaiye
t̄o'man hon ło·' a·'łeaiye
t̄o'man hon ha'la wo·tinan a·'łeaiye.—
—ma' le'sna te''onak̯ä

hoł i'nak̄w an u'lo'nakwi a·nak̯ä
ho' p̄e'nan kwai''ik̄äk̯ä.
a'k̄'äp a·'winak̄w a·wan tse''makwin a'k̯ä
ho''na·wan tca te'cukwai''ina·we
ho''na·wan wɔ· te'cukwai''ina·we
a·'winak̄w a·'wan tse''makwin a'k̯ä
yam i'yanik̯inan·e
u'nak̯äni·ya'nan
hon a'ntse'man a'ni·na·we.—
—haiyi'
ma' i'mat tom hon i'tcemana·-wapte
t̄o' lesna tse'ma
la'łhok[u] hon a·'papa
t̄i'na·wan'ona

ai'yu'ya·napci—
—e·h
ma' le'hap̄a
le· t̄i'ma·-te'mła
ho' ya'cu wa te'łakuk̯ä.—

THE GOD: Well, the one who is my elder brother,
The one who stays at Long House Top,
Does he know?
THE MAN: Yes, at a time when he knows it I pass you on your road.
THE GOD: The one at Echo's abiding place, does he know?
THE MAN: Yes, even when he knows, I have passed you on your road.
THE GOD: The one who stays Where the rainbow bends over,
Does he know?
THE MAN: At a time when he knows,
I have passed you on your road.
THE GOD: Those yonder, where all talk together,
Do they know?
THE MAN: Yes, when they already know,
I have passed you on your road.
THE GOD: Very well. Now, perhaps, you have taken thought for your good weapons?
THE MAN: Yes, I have taken thought.
THE GOD: Very well,
Our father, our child,
You shall set your mind to be a man.
Truly you shall not be alone.
Perhaps all your fathers,
In all their different abiding places,
Are in agreement.
THE MAN: Now this night,
My prayer meal,
My shell,
My corn pollen,
My sparkling paint,
My red paint,
My water roll,[9]
You have taken.
If you let me know how the world will be
How the days will be
That I shall always remember.

—ma' co' pap i'li te''ona
te'alan ta'cana i'n'ona ai'yu'ya·naci.—
—e·h. ai'yu'ya·nakwi t̄om ho' o'na-e'latek̯ä.
—te'cimik̯ i'm'ona ai'yu'yanaci.—
—e'h. ai'yu'ya·nakwinte t̄om ho' o'na-e'latek̯ä.—
—a'mitolan te'p̄o'ulan te''onac
ai'yu'ya·na—
—ai'yu'ya·n·kwi
t̄om ho' o'na-e'latek̯ä.—
—la'łhoku le·w an ya'cuwa i'p̄it̄o
ai'yu'ya·nap̄aci.
—ma' ai'yu'ya·nakwi
t̄o' ło a·'wona-e'latek̯ä.—
—ma' honkwa'ati'
ma' i·me' t̄o inasnan k̄ɔ'kci a'ntse'mak̯ä—
—ma' ho' a'ntse'mak̯ä—
—ma' ho'nkwa'ati'
ho''na·wan ta'tcu
ho''na·wan tca''le
t̄o' ɔ'tsin tse''makuna
a'tic t̄o' sa'm·a te'k̯̄änan tse'na
i'me' le·wi t̄ona a·'tatcu
t̄i'na-te'mła
ya'nselionaye.—
—ma' lu'k̯ä t̄e'łinan·e
ho'man ha'lawo·tinan·e
ho'man ło''o
ho'man o'nean·e
ho'man t̄su'hap̄a
ho'man a'hoko
ho'man k̯̄ä'cima p̄o'n·e
t̄on i·'łeana
hoł ko'n u'lo'nan te'atun'ona
ko'n hoł t̄e'wanan te'atun'ona
hom ton yu'ya·k̯̄äna·wap̄a
u''s ai'yu·'ya·na
ho' t̄e'wanan tek̯äna.

[9] The cigarette.

He goes off a little way, and sitting down waits for an omen. The four messengers return at the same time to the ceremonial house and report what they have seen. Plans are made according to the divinations.

Prayers of the Scalp Dance

Whenever an enemy is killed the slayer, if not already a member of the bow priesthood or one of the other two warrior societies, the Hunters (Saniak̲äkwe) or the Cactus Society (K̄ocikwe), must immediately join the bow priesthood to protect himself from the malevolence of the slain enemy. The initiation takes place in the course of the scalp dance which is held to celebrate the victory.

The purpose of the scalp dance is twofold. First, to purify the scalper from the contaminating contact with the dead and make him safe for human association and by placing him under the protection of the war gods, through membership in their cult, the bow priesthood, save him from pursuit by the ghost; the second purpose is to propitiate the dead enemy, strip him of his power for evil, and turn to good account his potentialities as a rain maker. This propitiation of the scalp is primarily the office of the scalp chief, who also retains guardianship of the scalps reposing in the scalp house.

Accompanying these important secret rites of purification and propitiation are the great public festivities. Throughout the twelve days of the ceremony unrestrained merrymaking accompanied by sexual license is indulged in by young and old of both sexes. These three strands run side by side, all culminating in the great ceremonies of the final day.

The order of events in this long and elaborate ritual has been described in the accounts by Mrs. Stevenson [10] and Doctor Parsons [11] with varying emphasis on the different aspects, according to the affiliation of the informants.

For convenience in reading the following prayers the events may be briefly summarized.

The returning war party camps overnight outside the village. At dawn four men chosen to announce their return ride toward the village uttering their war cry. They are met by the scalp chief, who inquires concerning the exploits of the war party.

During the day the scalp chief secretes the scalp at a distance from the village in a diminutive shelter of brush. The scalper and his "elder brother," the member of the bow priesthood who has "caught" the novice, take turns in watching over it. Toward evening they go through a sham conflict and take the scalp, bringing it to a place on the plain where p̄ekwin has prepared an altar. Here they are met

---

[10] Twenty-third Ann. Rept. Bur. Amer. Ethn., p. 578.

[11] Scalp Ceremonial at Zuñi.

by men and women appointed to take part in the coming ceremonies, the priests, the scalp chief, the bow priesthood, the Ant Society, the guardians of war bundles, and the male populace. There is ceremonial smoking by all present. Prayer sticks are planted by the scalper in a near-by ant hill, and many songs are sung and prayers offered. Finally the scalp is placed on the foot of the aunt of the scalper, who kicks it four times. Encircling the village four times, in counterclockwise circuit, the party goes in. The scalp is set upon a tall pole in the plaza amid general rejoicings, and the period of festivity is announced first by p̄ekwin and then by the bow priest.

The scalper goes into retreat in the ceremonial house of the bow priests. For four days he eats no meat or grease or any hot food. He sits away from the fire, sleeps little, does not speak, and is untouchable. He drinks emetics and goes out each morning to pray for deliverance from the scalp. He must also observe the sexual taboos placed upon the widowed.[12] The woman who brought in the scalp must also observe all these taboos. The days are spent in preparation for the final ceremonies.

On the fifth day the scalp is washed by two men appointed for this purpose. Thus is the enemy received into the company of the rain makers who live in the scalp house. Meanwhile the public festivities have begun. There are public dances each day, two selected groups performing on alternate days, while at night young and old of both sexes dance about the scalp pole.

About the sixth day a man of the Deer clan and a man of the Bear clan start work on the images of the gods of war. On the twelfth night these and all their paraphernalia are taken into the house of the bow priests. Here, in an all-night ceremony, the novice is finally taken into their company to share their supernatural prerogatives, including the special protection of the gods of war.

The following day is the "great dance." The images of the gods of war, the various war bundles, and the chief priestly bundles are set up on an altar in the plaza, behind which sit all the high officials of the Zuñi hierarchy. Throughout the day various dancers take turns in dancing before this altar. Toward evening the bow priests sing the songs given them at the institution of their society by the gods of war.

After this the altar is demolished and the meal painting obliterated. The sacred bundles are returned to the houses where they are kept. The images of the gods of war are taken to their houses by members of the bow priesthood, and next day carried to appropriate shrines (not the ones that are visited during the winter solstice). Late at night the scalp is removed from the pole by the scalp chief and deposited by him in the scalp house, with special prayers for protection in his dangerous office.

---

12 See p. 632.

The following prayers represent but the least fragment of this complex ritual. They deal almost entirely with the office of scalp chief; that is, the propitiation of the scalp. They were dictated by an old man, a son of a former scalp chief, now deceased.

At dawn the scalp chief meets four men who announce the return of the war party: [13]

Now, neglecting your children,	ma' t̄on yam tca'-tek̭äłacna
Neglecting your wives,	o'ye-tek̭äłacna
Yonder into the country of the enemy	lehok^{u} i'nak̄w anu'lo'nakwi
You made your road go forth.	ton o'neał a·'k̄änapk̭ä.
Perhaps one of the enemy,	i'me' i'nakwe te''ona
Even one who thought himself virile,	ɔ'tsina ya'ntse'ma'ente
Under a shower of arrows,	i'nakwe te''ona
A shower of war clubs,	ko·'wi co'-łi'tekwanel·a
	ko·'wi t̄a-łi'tekwanel·a
With bloody head,	ko·'wi ce'mk̭aia
One of the enemy,	i'nakwe te''ona
Reached the end of his life.	t̄e'k̄ohanan pa'łtop̄a
Our fathers,	hon a·'tatc i'lap̄ona
Beast bow priests,	we·'ma· a·'p̄i'ła·ciwan·i
Took from the enemy,	i'nakwe te''ona
His water-filled covering.[13a]	k̭ä'cima p̄o''yan ai'yonapk̭ä
Now you will tell us of that,	t̄e'wuna' u'son ho''na t̄on ai'yu'ya-k̭äna·wa
And knowing that we shall live.	u'son ai'yu'ya·na
	hon t̄e'wanan a·'tek̭än·a
Is it not so?	hatci'

The four announcers reply:

Indeed it is so.	ma' i·na mi'łte
Neglecting our children,	hon yam tca'-tek̭äłacna
Neglecting our wives,	yam o'ye-tek̭äłacna
Yonder into the enemy's country	le'hok^{u} i'nak̄wan u'lo'nakwi
We made our road go forth.	hon o'neał a·'k̭änapk̭ä
Indeed it is so.	ma'i·'na mi'łte
We started out.	łon u'kwe·k̭ä.
We went.	hon a·'wa·k̭ä.
Yonder at Rock Cave we arrived.	lakw a'mekuliakwi hon a·'te'tcina.
There we spent the night.	hon i'sk̄ɔn a·'want̄ewak̭ä
Early next day we arose.	t̄e'wap ca'mli
	hon łu'walemakna
We went on.	hon a·'wa·k̭ä
At Ox-Eye-Place	k̭änaituna·kwi

[13] Twenty-third Ann Rept. Bur. Amer. Ethn., p 579.

[13a] K̭acima po''yan·e, the scalp. The usual ceremonial appellation .

We arrived.
There we spent the night.
Next day we went on.

Yonder at Cattail Spring we arrived.
There, when we arrived at their camp site,
We attacked them.
There this one,
(And one of the enemy)
Fought together. . . . .

hon a·'te'tcina
i'skon hon a·'want̑ewak̯ä
t̑e'wap hon a·'wak̯ä
lak^{u} to''olelak̑änakwi hon a·'te'tcina
i'sk̑on t̑i'nakwi
hon a·'te'tcina
i'sk̑on hon ya'nte'unapk̯ä
i'skon lu'k̯on i·wiyałtok̯ä. . . . .

(The account breaks off here. The informant lacked imagination to continue the narrative of the exploits of the war party.)

In the evening the scalp is brought into the village.[14] At the close of the ceremonies on the plain the scalp chief deposits in an excavation between two mounds of bread which he collected earlier in the day at the houses of the priests. The offering is specifically to the slain Navaho.

This day
Into the corn priests' [15] country,
You will make your road enter.
With the fruit of the corn priests' labor
You will add to your heart.[16]
So that if any of the corn priests' ladder descending children
Should by mistake cut off your road,[17]
No evil consequence [18] may come to him because of it.
And furthermore,
You who are my grandfather,
Male turkey,[19]
Weakening the enemies' hearts,

You will remain here always.
So that your children,
Their breath drifting hither only,
When they attain their house,
They will make their roads come in.[20]
Longing for them
You will live.
To this end, add to your hearts.

lu'k̯ä yä'ton·e
t̑o'wa ci'wan an u'lo'nakwi
t̑o' o'neała kwa'tok̑än·a
t̑o'waci'wan·an yu'mokwe·nan a'k̯ä

t̑o' i'wik̯e·na te'liana a'k̯ä
le t̑o'wa ci'wan an łe'tsilon p̑ani·nan tca'we
hoł tcu'wa t̑o'miyacna
t̑o'man o'neał aptsip̑a
kwa ak̯' i·'yatonan te'am·ek̑äna

le'stikleap̑a
t̑om ho' nan i'li ho'tolo'waci

a·'winakwe
a·'wik̯e·na ła'tapik̑äna
t̑o' i'miła'k̑una.
a'k̯ä to''na·wan tca'we
k̑ä'łem te''tci
ai'yupi'la'na yam he'cot'a o'k̯anapk̯a te'kwi
o'neała kwa'tok̑äna
i·'ya'hawak̑äna
ton a·'tek̑än·a
t̑ewuna' i'k̯e·na te'liana·we.

[14] See Twenty-third Ann. Rept. Bur. Amer. Ethn., p. 581.
[15] The priests, hence Zuñi.
[16] He offers bread cooked in the houses of the priests.
[17] Cross their road while they encircle the village.
[18] i'yatonan·e, literally, an exchange, especially bad dreams or hallucinations—the usual means whereby supernaturals punish the breaches of mortals—provided, always, proper precautions are not taken.
[19] Wing feathers of the male turkey, which had lain on the meal painting, are deposited in the hole with the food. Turkey feathers are used on prayer sticks for the dead.
[20] May more of the enemy be killed and brought in thus.

After the scalp has been set up in the plaza the p̄ekwin addresses the people:

Now this day
This many of the children of the corn priests,
Neglecting their children,
Neglecting their wives,
Went out yonder into the enemy's country.
Then suddenly, one of the enemy,
Even one who stayed quietly in his hut,
Even one who thought himself a man,
In a shower of arrows,
In a shower of stones,
In a shower of war clubs,
With bloody head,
The enemy
Reached the end of his life.
The ones who are our fathers,
Beast bow priests,
With their claws,
Tore from the enemy
His water-filled covering.
Into the country of the corn priests
The enemy made his road enter.
Four times encircling the town,

The corn priests water-filled court

He made his road enter,
In the corn priests' water-filled court
Setting him up,
When his days are made,
Eagerly you shall await his time.

When all the enemy's days are passed,
When those who are our fathers,
Rain maker priests,
With their fresh waters
Have sprinkled the enemy,[21]

Whenever his day is made,
Tirelessly unwearied

You shall pass the time.
For indeed, the enemy,

ma' lu'k̯ä yä'ton·e
le· t̄o'wa ci'wan an tca'we

yam tca'-tek̯äłacna
o'y-tek̯äłacna
lehokᵘ i'nak̄wan 'u'loʿnakwi

k̯e'ct̄ce·t i'nakwe te''ona
yam ha'cot̄cina
yu'łak̄ i'młak̄äpte
i'nakwe te''ona
ɔ'tsina ya'ntse'mante
kɔ·wi co'-łi'tekwanel·a
kɔ·'w a'-łitekwanel·a
kɔ·wi t̄a-łitekwanel·a
kɔ·'wi ce'mk̄aia
i'nakwe te''ona
t̄e'k̄ohanan pa'łtoup̄a
hon a·'tatc i'lap̄ona
we·'ma a'pi'ła·ciwan·i
yam sa'wanik̄ a'k̯ä
i'nakwe te''ona
k̯ä'cima p̄o''yan ai'yona·wap̄a
i'nakwa te''ona
t̄o'wa ci'wan an uloʿnakwi
o'neała kwa'tok̄äna
a·'witela'ma
o'neał u'lapk̄äna
t̄o'wa ci'wan an k̄ä'cima t̄eʿwi·tokwi
o'neała kwa'tok̄äna
t̄o'wa ci'wan an k̄ä'cima t̄e'ʿ wita

ye'liato'up̄a
a'n t̄e'wanan yo''ap̄a
an t̄e'wanan a'nt̄sumeʿna
t̄on t̄e'wanan a·'tek̄än·a.
hoł i'nak̄w an te'mła t̄e'wak̯ä te'a'ana
hon a·'tatc i'lap̄ona
u'wanam a·'ciwani
yam k̄ä'cima tci'm'on ak̯ä
i'nakwe te''ona
k̄ä'łina·wap̄a
hoł yam t̄e'wana yo''ap̄a
pu'a'aconici
o'ntia'ułunici
t̄on t̄e'wanan a·'tek̄äna
he'kt̄ce·t i'nakwe te''ona

[21] The washing of the scalp on the fifth day.

Even though he was without value,
Notwithstanding he was a being of this kind—
Yet he was a water being;
He was a seed being.
Desiring the enemy's waters

Desiring his seeds
Desiring his wealth
Eagerly you shall await his day.

Whenever his days are made,
Throughout the days,
Throughout the nights,
Tirelessly, unwearied,

You shall live.
Indeed, even though you ache from singing,
Even though you fain would sleep,
In order to win the enemy's waters,

His seeds,
His wealth,
His power,
His strong spirit,
To win these.
Throughout the nights
Throughout the days,
Tirelessly, unwearied

You shall live.
Then indeed, if we are lucky,
To some little corner
Where the dust lies thick,
(You will steal away.)
In order to procreate sturdy[22] men
And sturdy women,

Tirelessly you will live.

To procreate strong males,
To procreate sturdy females,
To be the ones toward your thoughts may bend,
Eager for this,
You will keep the days.
For indeed, the enemy,
Even though on rubbish[23]

kwa'mastapt̂ a'k̯ä
ho''i ya·'k̯ätapte

k̯äcim ho''i te'a'k̯a
t̂o'waconan ho''i te'a'k̯ä
i'nakwe te''ona
an k̯ä'cim a'ntecemana
an t̂o'waconan a'ntecemana
an u'tenan a'ntecemana
a'nt̂sumeʻna
t̂on t̂e'wanan a·'tek̯äna.
hoɫ yam an t̂e'wanan yo''ap̂a
yä'to·we
t̂e'ɫina·we
pu'a'aconici
o'ntia'uɫunici
t̂on a·'tek̯än·a
he'kt̂ce·t te'neap̂-u'apte

a'liak̯' a'liteapte
i'nakwe te''ona
an k̯ä'cima
an t̂o'waconan·e
an u'tenan·e
an sa'wanik̯ä
an tse''makwin t̂su'me
o'k̯änakwi
t̂e'lina·we
yä'to·we
pu'a'aconici
o'ntia'uɫunici
t̂on a·'tek̯än·a.
ho'nkwe·t hon a·'halowilap̂a
kɔ·'wi p̂o'tceyo ya'hona
kɔ·'w he'cok̂op̂a t̂sa'na

ɔ'tsi ya'sute
o'k̯ä ya'sute
i'ʻtoʻtun'on a'k̯ä
pu'a'aconici
t̂on a·'tek̯äna
hoɫ ɔ'tsia iʻtohap̂a
o'k̯ä ya'sut̂ iʻtohap̂a
i'sk̂ɔn tse''mak- t̂e'ɫakwı yam a·'-teatun'ona'k̯ä
a'nt̂sumeʻna
t̂on t̂e'wanan a·'tek̯äna.
he'kt̂ce·t i'nakwe te''ona
kwa'hamackon a'k̯ä

[22] Children conceived at this time are under the special protection of the gods of war, and are therefore especially strong.

[23] The Navajos have no cultivated crops.

He lived and grew to maturity,
By virtue of the corn priests' rain prayers
(He becomes valuable;)
Indeed, the enemy,
Though in his life
He was a person given to falsehood,

He has become one to fortell
How the world will be,
How the days will be.
That during his time,
We may have good days,
Beautiful days,

Hoping for this,
We shall keep his days.
Indeed, if we are lucky,
During the enemy's time
Fine rain caressing the earth,
Heavy rain caressing the earth,
(We shall win.)
When the enemy's days are in progress,
The enemy's waters,
We shall win,
His seeds we shall win,
His riches we shall win,
His power,
His strong spirit,
His long life,
His old age,
In order to win these,

Tirelessly, unwearied,
We shall pass his days.
Now, indeed, the enemy,
Even one who thought himself a man,
In a shower of arrows,
In a shower of war clubs,
With bloody head,
The enemy,
Reaching the end of his life,
Added to the flesh of our earth mother.
Beast bow priests,
With their claws,
Tore from the enemy
His water-filled covering.

ho''i ya·''ente
t̄o'wa ci'wan an k̭̄ä'cima p̄e'yen a'k̭ä

he'kt̄e·t i'nakwe te''ona
t̄e'k̄ohanana
kwa'hoł yo'sek̭änak̭ä
ho''i te'k̭ä'ente
ko'n u'lo'nan te'atun'ona
ko'na t̄e'wana te'atun'ona
ho''i yo·k̭ä
hoł an t̄e'wanan·a
yä'ton k̄ɔ'kci
yä'ton tso'ya
t̄e'wanan te'atun'ona
u''son a'nt̄sume'na
hon t̄e'wanan a·'tek̭̄än·a.
ho'nkwe·t hon a·'halowilap̄a
hoł i'nak̄wan t̄e'wanana
kɔ·'wi k̭̄ä't̄sana łi'ton-t̄e'łakwi
kɔ·'wi k̭̄äłan łi'ton-t̄e'łakwi

hoł an t̄e'wanan te'ap̄a

i'nakwe te''ona
hon an k̭̄äcim o'k̭̄äna·wa
hon an t̄o'waconan o'k̭̄äna·wa
hon an u'tenan o'k̭̄äna·we
an sa'wanik̭ä
an tse''makwin t̄su'me
an o'naya·nak̭ä
an ła'ciak̭ä
o'k̭̄änak̭̄äk̭ä
pu'a'aconici
o'nta'ułunici
hon t̄e'wanan a·'tek̭̄än·a
he'kt̄ce·t i'nakwe te''ona
ɔ'tsina ya'ntse'ma'ente

ko·'wi co'-łi'tekwanel·a
ko·'wi t̄a-łi'telwanel·a
ko·'wi ce'mk̭̄äia
i'nakwe te''ona
t̄e'k̄ohanan pa'łto·na
ho''na·wan a'witelin tsi'ta
ci''na te'lia'up̄a
we·ma· a·'pi'ła·ci'wan·i
yam sa'wanik̭' a'k̭ä
i'nakwe te''ona
an k̭̄ä'cima p̄o''yan ai'yona·wap̄a

Then the enemy
Into the corn priests' country
Made his road enter.
Now shout!
O- - - - - - - - - - -.
Again—
O- - - - - - - - - - - -.
Again—
O- - - - - - - - - - - -.
Once more—
O- - - - - - - - - - - -.
P̑u-hu hu
Huh hu
We- - - - - - - - - - - -.

i'nakwe te''ona
t̑o'wa ci'wan an u'lo'nakwi
o'neała kwa'tok̯äk̯ä
t̑e'wuna' we'ana·we'
o ———
te'ya
o ———
te'ya
o ———
ałnate
o ———
p'u hu hum hu hum we———

The elder brother bow priest addresses the people in the same vein. Then the scalp chief offers to the scalp a handful of bread saved from his earlier offering.

Now, this day
That you have been set up
In the corn priests' rain-filled court,
All the children of the corn priest
Will be dancing for you.
All the children of the corn priest
Will pass you on your road.
They will add to your heart.
Should anyone by mistake touch you
May no evil consequence befall him because of it.
With this fruit of the corn priests' labor
Add to your heart.
Your long life,
Your old age,
Your waters,
Your seeds.
Grant them.
To cleanse the thoughts
Of whoever has angry thoughts,
For this you will stand up here.

ma' lu'k̯ä yä'ton·e
t̑o'wa ci'wan an äk̑cima t̑e''wito'a
t̑o' ye'liato'una
le· t̑o'wa ci'wan an tca'we
t̑o'ma ta'łna a·'tek̑äna
le· t̑o'wa ci'wan an tca'we
t̑om o'na-e'latena·wa
t̑om i'ke·na te'liana·wa
hoł tcu'wa t̑omiyacna
t̑om a'łpitina
kwa i·'yatonan te'amek̑än·a
t̑o'wa ci'wan an yu'mo·kwe·nan a'k̯ä
i'k̯e·n i·'teliana.
yam o'naya·'nak̯a
yam ła'ciak̯ä
yam k̑ä'cima
yam t̑o'waconan·e
t̑o' ya'nhaiten·a
hoł tcu'wa tse''makwi· sa'mu tea'-kowa
hon tse''makwi· k̑ɔ'kcunakwi
t̑o e'latok̑än·a.

After four days the scalp is washed at any spring outside the town or in the river. Care is taken that the water used for the washing does not flow back into the river to bring death to those who drink of it. The scalp washer bites the scalp to get the power of the beast gods. "He acts like an animal," and therefore he does not need, in order to save his life, to observe the taboos generally required by contaminating contact with the dead. Prayer sticks are planted before the ceremony. At the conclusion the bowl is broken and cast away

6066°—32——44

and offerings of food are thrown about on the ground. During the ceremony of washing, the choir sings new songs made for the occasion and the scalp washer prays:

Now this day
Our sun father,
Having come out standing
To his sacred place,
A little space yet remains
Ere he goes in to sit down at his other sacred place.
Now four times raising our niece,[24]

And making her stand up,
Her road going first,
Hither with prayers,
We have made our road come forth.
Here, near by, our fathers,

Rain maker bow priests,
Where your watery road comes forth,
Where you are waiting,
We have passed you on your road.
We have offered you plume wands.
Taking your plume wands,
With them you will take firm hold
Of the enemy's water-filled covering.

With your fresh water
You will sprinkle him.
Then again, if your hands go first,
Our hands following,
We shall meet no evil consequence.[25]
You who are our fathers,
Rain maker bow priests,
K̭äławan-i,
Tsik̭ähaya,
K̄upictaya
Beast bow priests,
By virtue of your thoughts
The enemy
Reached the end of his life.
When with your clear water
You have sprinkled the enemy,

ma' lu'k̭ä yä ton·e
hon yä'tok̭ä tatc i'lap̄ a·'te'ona
yam t̄e'łacinakwi
ye·'lana kwai''ik̭äna
yam t̄o'pak̭ä t̄e'łacinakwi
i·muna kwa'tok̭atun te'kwi
kɔ·w a'nte'wetcikwi
yam e'ye te''ona
a·'witela'ma
a'na'-e'lemak̭äna
yam o'neał e''kwikona
k̭ä'łhok[u] t̄e'wus a'k̭ä
hon o'neał a·'k̭änapk̭ä
ło·'kwi le·'wi te'a'a
hon a·'tatc i'lap̄ona
u'wanam a·'pi'ła·ci'wan·i
yam k̭äcim o'neał kwai''ina

co'kya·kwi t̄on a·'wona-e'latena

t̄on te'lek̭inan a·'łeak̭äp̄a
te'lik̭inan i·'łeana
i'nakwe te''ona
an k̭ä'cima p̄o''yan·e
ya't̄ena-t̄su'mek̭äna
yam k̭ä'cima tci'm'on a'k̭ä
t̄on k̭ä'łin·a
t̄em t̄a t̄o''na·wan a'si· e''kwi'kona
hon a·'was-yä'lu'kona
kwa i·'yatonan te'amek̭äna
t̄on hon a·'tatc i'lap̄a
u'wanam a·'pi'ła·ci'wan·i
k̭ä'ławan·i
tsi'k̭ahaiya
ku·'pictaiya
we·ma· a·'pi'ła·ci'wan·i
t̄o''na·wan tse''makwin a'k̭ä
hoł i'nakwe t̄e'k̄ohanan pa'łto·k̭ä.

yam k̭ä'cim a'k̭ä
i'nakwe te''ona
t̄on k̭ä'lina·wap̄a

[24] Brothers' daughter; i. e., the scalp. The rite of head washing is always performed by the paternal aunt. No explanation is given for inversion of sex.

[25] That is, from contact with the scalp.

When into the corn priests' country
He has brought his road,
When in the corn priests' water-filled court
He has been set up,
All the corn priests' children
With the song sequences of the fathers,
Will be dancing for him.
And whenever all his days are past,

Then a good day,
A beautiful day,
A day filled with great shouting,
With great laughter,
A good day,
With us, your children,
You will pass.
Thus the corn priests' children
Winning your power,
Winning your strong spirit,
Will come to evening.
To this end, my fathers,
Now let us take hold of our niece.

t̄o'wa ci'wan an u'lo'nakwi
o'neał a·'k̭äna
t̄o'wa ci'wan an k̭ä'cima t̄e''witona

ye'liato'up̄a
t̄o'wa ci'wan an tca'we
yam a·'tatcu
a·'wan i'piclenan te'na-pi''lan a'k̭ä
ta'łna a·'tek̭än·a
hoł an k̭ä·'k̭ä te'mła t̄e'wak̭a tea''-ana
yä'ton t̄ɔ'kci
yä'ton tso''ya
kɔ·'wi we'ana ła'na
kɔ·'wi ci'kwi ła'na
yä'ton t̄ɔ'kci
ho''na ton tca'wilap̄a
t̄e'wanan a·'tek̭än·a
a'k̭a t̄o'wa ci'wan an tca'we sa'wa-nik̭' ok̭änak̭äna
tse''makwin t̄sum o'k̭änak̭ana
su·'nhak̭äna·wa
t̄e'wuna' hom a·'tatcu
yam e'ye te''ona
hon ya't̄enapce k̭e·si.

After the dancing of the last day the scalp chief takes down the scalp. He and his associates remain in hiding on the outskirts of the village until midnight. Then they proceed singing to the scalp house. Each has under his tongue several grains of black corn to prevent pursuit by the ghost.[26] The scalp chief places the scalp in the jar in the scalp house and prays:

Now this many are the days
Since the enemy
Reached the end of his life.
Our fathers,
Those who hold the high places,
Beast bow priests,
Tore from the enemy
His water-filled covering.
Into the corn priests' country,
They made his road enter.
And in the corn priests' water-filled court
Standing him up,
They made his days.
This many are the days.
And when the set number of days had all been counted up,

ma' le'si t̄e'wanan·e
i'nakwe te''ona
t̄e't̄ohanan pa'łtop̄a
hon a·'tatc i'lap̄ona
te'alan i'lap̄ona
we·ma· a·'pi'ła·ciwan·i
i'nak̄w an k̭ä'cim p̄o''yan ai'yo-na·wap̄a
t̄o'wa ci'wan an u'lo'nakwi
o'neała kwa'tok̭äna
t̄o'wa ci'wan an k̭ä'cima te'wito

ye·'liato·na
t̄e'wanan a'cap̄a
le'si t̄e'wanan·e
an t̄e'wanan ai'yälenan a·'tea'k̭a te'a'ana

[26] Compare with use of black corn to bring forgetfulness of dead relatives.

Way back, when all these days had past,
The ones who are our fathers,
Rain maker priests,
With their clear water
Took firm hold of him.[27]
Again in the corn priests' court
Setting him up, they made his days.
This many days
The corn priests' children
With their fathers' song sequences

Have consumed in dancing.
Then yesterday,
When the number of their days was at an end,
Those who are our fathers,
The two who hold the high places,[28]
With their elder brothers' plume wands,
Their prayer feathers,
Their shells,
In these wrapping themselves they renewed their human form.[29]
Holding their world,
Holding their people fast,
Sitting down quietly,
With us their children
After a blessed night [30]
They came to day.
This very day
When he who is our sun father,
Coming out standing to his sacred place
Passed us on our roads,
Saying, let it be now,
Those who are our fathers,
The ones that first had being,[31]
Came out standing
Into the daylight of their sun father.
Near by, in the corn priests' court,
Our two fathers,
The ones who hold the high places,
With all their sacred things

łok̄wan te'mła t̄e'wak̯ä te'a'ana

hon a·'tatc i'lap̄ona
u'wanam a·'ciwan·i
yam k̯̄ä'cim a'kä
ya't̄ena-t̄su'mek̯äna·wap̄a
t̄o'wa ci'wan an t̄e''wito'a
ye'liat̄o·na' t̄e'wanan a'cap̄a

le'si t̄e'wanan·e
t̄o'wa ci'wan an tca'we
yam a·'tatcu
a·wan i'piclenan tena·-pi''lan a'k̯ä
ta'łna a·'teak̯a te'a'ana
t̄e'cukwa yä'ton·e
k̯es an t̄e'wanan i·'te'tcap̄a

hon a·'tcia tatc i'lap̄a
te'alan i'lon a·'tci
yam a'papon te'lik̯inan·e

a·'wa la'cowan·e
a·'wan ło' ak̯ä
a·tc i·'p̄a'una tci'm'on ho'i-ya·'-k̯̄äna
yam u'lo'nan ya't̄ena
yam ho''i ya't̄ena-t̄su'mek̯äna
a·tc i'me-ła'k̄una
t̄e'łinan k̄ɔ'kci
ho' tca'wilap a·'want̄ewak̯ä

tci'mte yä'ton·e
hon yä'tok̯ä tatc i'lap̄ a·'te'ona
yam t̄e'łacinakwi
ye·'lana kwai''ik̯äp̄a
hon a·wona-e'latep̄a
hot k̯ä·'k̯̄i k̯e·si' le''anak̯äp̄a
hon a·'tatc i'lap̄ona
tci'mik̯änapkona
yam yä'tok̯ä ta'tcu
an t̄e'k̄ohanankwi
i·'łuwakna kwai''ina
la'lik t̄o'wa ci'wan an t̄eli'tokwi
hon a·'tcia tatc i'lap̄ a·'te'ona
te'alan i'lon a·'tci
yam e'leteli·we a·'wili

[27] The washing of the scalp.
[28] The gods of war. The allusion is to the making of the images.
[29] The completion of the images.
[30] In the house of the bow priests.
[31] The sacred war bundles, and the bundle of the chief priesthood.

Made their roads enter.
Yonder from all sides,
Those who are our fathers,
All the water bringing birds,
P̄ekwins, priests,[32]
Made their roads come forth.
They made their roads come hither.
With his hand,
With his heart
His fathers' cloud house he fashioned,[33]
Their mist blanket he spread out,
Their life-giving road he sent forth,
Their perfect spring he prepared;
Then our two fathers,
Those who hold the high places,
With their house chiefs,[34]
Their p̄ekwins,
Holding all their sacred things
Sitting down quietly
Throughout a blessed day,
With us, their children, they came to evening.
When the one who is our sun father
Had gone in to sit down at his sacred place,
And our night fathers,
Our night mothers,
Night priests,
Slowly rising to their sacred place,

Had passed us on our roads,
We passed you on your road.
You, Navaho priests,[35] have died.
Truly during your lives
You dealt falsely,
Although that was your nature in life,

o'neała kwa'tok̭äp̄a
la'lhok^{u} le'si tekwi
hon a·'atc ilap̄ona
k̭äcima wɔ·'we p̄e'kwi· a·'ciwan·i

o'neała kwai''ilek̭äna
o'neał i'k̭äna

yam a'sin a'k̭ä
yam i'k̭e·nan a'k̭ä
yam a·'tatc'on a·'wan a'wełuyan
k̭ä'kwe ya·'k̭äna
ci'pololon p̄ewuna

o'naya·'nak̭' o'nealan a·'k̭äna
k̭ä'nakwe·nan ya·'na ye'lete'una
hon a·'tcia tatc i'lap̄a
te'alan i'lon a·'tci
yam k̭ä'wa·mosi
yam p̄e'kwi·we
yam e'leteli·we a·'wili
a·tc i'me-ła'k̄una
yä'ton k̄ɔ'kci
hon tca'wilapa su·'nhak̭änapk̭ä

hon yä'tok̭ä tatc i'lap̄ona
yam t̄e'łacinakwi
i·'muna kwa'tok̭äp̄a
hon t̄e'łiak̭' a·'tatc i'lap̄ona
hon t̄e'łiak̭' a·'tsit i'lap̄ona
t̄e'łiak̭' a·'ciwan·i
yam t̄e'łacinakwi
kɔ·w i·'łuwakna ye·'makna
hon a·'wona-e'latena·wap̄a
t̄o''na łon a·'wona-e'latenapk̭ä
t̄on pa'tcu ci'wan·i ya'ce·napk̭ä
k̭e·'stce·t t̄ek̄ohanana
kwa'hoł yo'sek̭änak̭ä
t̄on a·'ho' a·'tek̭ä'ente

[32] There is only one p̄ekwin, but he is the representative or human counterpart of all the summer birds. The translation is unavoidably awkward.

[33] The meal painting on the altar.

[34] k̭'äk̄'wa·mosi, the first priesthood of the hierarchy.

[35] The inmates of the scalp house.

Recently, by virtue of the corn priests water-bringing words,
You have passed one another on your road.
When you reveal to us [36]
How the days will be,
How the world will be,
Knowing that,
We shall pass our days.
To this end, my nieces,[37]
Add to your hearts.
So that your people you may waft hither only,
So that you may speed them hither,
On this do not fail to fix your thoughts.[38]
This is all.

t̄o'wa ci'wan an k̥ä'cima p̄e'yen a'k̥ä
t̄on i·'yona-e'latenapk̥ä

ko''nhoł t̄ewanan te'atun'ona
ko''nhołu'lo'nan te'atun'ona
ho''na t̄on ai'yu'ya·k̥äna·wap̄a.
u's ai'yu'ya·na
hon t̄e'wanan a·'tek̥äna
t̄e'wuna' hom a·'weye.
i'ke·n i·'teliana
k̥äł te''tci
ai'yupila'na
i'ya'hawak̥an·a

eł t̄on te'ałt i'yantse''manamtu k̥e·si
le·wi.

He deposits the scalp in the scalp house, replaces the cover and comes back to the village. On his way back he mounts to four housetops, leaving on each a grain of black corn "to make his road dark." At his own house the ladder has been turned upside down. As soon as he has mounted it, it is righted so that the ghost can not follow him up. He comes into the house without speaking, hangs up his blanket and goes right out. Standing on the housetop facing the east, holding in his hands what yet remains of the black corn, he prays:

This many are the days
Since our children
Neglecting their little ones,
Neglecting their wives,
Yonder into the enemy's country
Made their road go forth.
Presently, even where the enemy
Stayed peacefully in their huts

Our fathers,
The ones who hold the high places,
Having commanded the enemy to be as women,
In a shower of arrows,
A shower of war clubs,
With bloody head,
The enemy reached the end of his life.
Our fathers,
Beast bow priests,

ma' le'si t̄e'wanan·e
ho''na·wan t̄e'apk̄una·we
yam tca'-t̄ek̥äłacna
yam o'y-tek̥äłacna
le'hok[u] i'nakwe an u'lo'nakwi
o'neał a·'k̥änapkä
k̥e'ct̄ce·t i'nakwe te''ona
hoł yam ha'cotcina yu'łak̥i t̄i'nan ła'k̥äpte
hon a·'tatc i'lap̄ona
te'alan i'lap̄ona
o'k̥änakwe ya'nhe·tocna·wap̄a
i'nakwe te''ona
ko·'wi co'-łi'tekwanel·a
ko·'wi t̄a-łi'tekwanel·a
ko·'wi ce'mk̥aia
i'nakwe te''ona
t̄e'k̄ohanan pa'łtop̄a
hon a·'tatc i'lap̄ona
we·ma· a·'pi'ła·ci'wan·i

---

[36] The scalp chief hopes for some omen at this time.

[37] The scalps.

[38] May we kill more of the enemy and imprison them here to serve our ends.

With their claws,[39]
Tearing from him his rain filled covering,
Commanded him to be the one to count those who have their homes above—

All little sparkling stars.[40]

The enemy,
Having added to the flesh of our mother earth,[41]

Hither into the corn priests' country,
He made his road go.
When his road came here to Itiwana,
Our two mothers,
Taking hold of him fast,
The country of the corn priests,
Four times successively encircling

Into the corn priests' rain filled court
Making their roads come in,
There they set him up.
His days were made.
When we had lived eagerly awaiting his days,
The rain maker priests,
With their fresh water,

Took firm hold of the enemy.
Then the days were made
For those who hold the high places.
Through all these days,
Mindful of their days,
You came to the time.
Then yesterday,
Our two fathers,
Those who hold the high places,
Once more assuming human form,
After a blessed night
With us their children
They came to day.
This day [42]
When he who is our sun father

yam sa'wanik̯' a'k̯ä
k̯ä'cima p̄o''yan ai'yo·na

li'wan i'yamakwi
t̄e''wilap̄ a·'te'ona
tsu'hap̄a mo'yatcu·we
a·'wiyälena
ho''i te'atun'ona
a'nhe·tocnak̯äp̄a
i'nakwe te''ona
ho''na·wan tsi'ta
a'witelin·e
ci''na te'liana
k̯ä'łhok[u] t̄o'wa ci'wan an u'lo'nakwi
o'neał a·'k̯äk̯ä
li·ła i'tiwanakwi
o'neał i'k̯äp̄a
hon a·'tcia tsit i'lap̄ a·'te'ona
a·tci ya't̄ena-t̄sumek̯äna
t̄o'wa ci'wan an u'lo'nakna
a·'witen i·'yäłto
o'neał u'lapk̯äna
t̄o'wa ci'wan an k̯ä'ci'ma t̄e''wit-i'tiwanakwi
o'neał kwa'tok̯äna
ye'liat̄o'up̄a
an t̄e'wanan yo·'ap̄a
an t̄e'wanan a'nt̄sume'na
hon a·'teak̯a te'kwi
u'wanam a·'ciwan·i
yam k̯ä'cima tci'm'on a'k̯ä
i'nakwe te''ona
ya't̄ena-t̄su'mek̯äna·wap̄a
te'alan i'lap̄ona
a·'wan t̄e'wanan yo·''ap̄a
le'si t̄e'wanan·e
yam t̄e'wanan a'na' yu''ya·na
t̄on a·'teak̯ä tekwi
t̄e'cukwa yä'ton·e
hon a·'tcia tatc i'lap̄ a·'te'ona
te'alan i'lon a·'tci
a·'tci tci'm'on ho''i-ya·'k̯äna
t̄e'łinan k̄ɔ·kci

hon tca'wilap̄ a·'want̄ewak̯ä
lu'k̯ä yä'ton·e
hon yä'tok̯ä tatc i'lap̄ a·'te'ona

39 Sa'wanika, any weapon, and abstractly, power.

40 The fallen enemy is left face upward and commanded to count the stars; that is, taunted to do the impossible.

41 His blood fertilizes the earth. Wherever an enemy falls is formed an ant hill—a symbol, probably, of fecundity. Therefore prayer sticks are planted in ant hills, and the Ant Society figures prominently in scalp-dance ceremonies.

42 By this time it is nearly day. The images of the war gods are taken to appropriate shrines, where they replace older ones which are removed and placed on a pile of similar ones behind the shrine.

Has come out standing to his sacred place,
Saying, let it be now,
Our two fathers,
The ones who hold the high places,
Yonder will pass their elder brothers on their roads.
Wherever they pass the divine ones on their roads
Taking their places,
They will sit down quietly.
Yonder on all the mossy mountain tops,
All about they will have their sacred places.
All the forests
All the brush
Being made representatives in prayer
That all the corn priests' children
May hold fast to life;
That this may be so,
The divine ones,
Taking one another's places,
Sit down quietly.
Holding all their world,
Holding all their people fast,
They will sit down quietly.
And then also these others,[43]
Asking in prayer for life for their children
They will add to our breath,
Seeking our relatives,
Our elders,
Near-by in all their houses
Wherever they lie sleeping,
These they will hold fast.

And also our children,
Those who watch over the ones through which we prosper,[44]
Those who for the sake of their children,
For the sake of their flocks
Yonder on all sides
Wander over their earth mother,
Who even on the bare ground stand at the edges of our land—

yam t̄e'łacinakwi
ye·'lana kwai''ik̯äp̄a
hoł k̯ä·k̄i k̯e·si'le''anak̯äp̄a
hon a·tcia tatc i'lap̄ a·'te''ona
te'alan i'lon a·'tci
le'hoku yam a·'p̄ap̄a
a·tc a·'wona-e'latek̯än'a
hoł k̄ä'pin a·'ho'i
i·'yona-e'latena
i·'yäli'na
i·'t̄inan ła'k̄ikna
la'łhoku le·w a'wico yäla k̄ätsowa-'kona
t̄e'łacin u'lapk̯äna

t̄akwił-p̄ɔ·ti
łakwił-p̄ɔ· i
t̄e wus ya'nułana·wap̄a

t̄o'wa ci'wan an t̄e'apk̄una·we
ya'kna t̄su'me
hoł a·'teatun'onak̯ä
k̄ä'pin a·'ho'i
i'yäli'nan i·'t̄inan ła'k̄ikna

le·w yam u'lo'nan ya't̄ena
le· yam ho''i ya't̄ena-t̄su'mek̯äna
i·'t̄inan i·ła'k̄ik̯äp̄a
t̄em t̄a lu'knia'konte
t̄e'wusu t̄e'k̄ohanan yai'ncemana
yam tca'we
ho''na· wan p̄i''nan te'liana·wa
ho''na·wan i''yaniki'na·we
ho''na·wan a·'łacina·we
la'lik yam he'cot̄a·wa'kona
ya't̄elan a·'ne ta'pana
lu'kniak̄o
a·'wiyat̄en-t̄su'mek̯äna
t̄em t̄a ho''na·wan tca'we
yam a'k̯' el a·'te'ona

yam tca'wak̯' a·'ni

yam wɔ·'wak̯' a·'ni
la'łhoku le'si te'kwi
yam a'witelin tsi'tana'kona
a'wek pa'łtocon'ona

[43] The old images that are laid aside.
[44] The herders of sheep.

All these also they will hold fast.	lu'k̭niak̑o te'mła a·'wiyaten-t̑su'mek̭äna
I have sent forth my prayers.	ho' t̑e'wusu p̑e'nan kwai''ik̭äk̭ä
Our children,	ho''na·wan tca'we
Even those who have erected their shelters	hoł te'li·-pa'łto'konatapte
At the edge of the wilderness,	yam he'cot̑a ya·'k̭änapk̭ä te'a'kona
May their roads come in safely,	o'neał kwa'tona k̭ɔ'kci
May the forests	le· t̑akwił-p̑ɔ·'t̑i
And the brush	ła'kwił-p̑ɔ·'ti
Stretch out their water-filled arms	a·'wan k̭ä'cima a's-taʻnanak̭a
To shield their hearts;	a·'wik̭e·n ai'yala
May their roads come in safely;	o'neał kwaton·a
May their roads all be fulfilled,	a·'wona-ya·'an·a
May it not somehow become difficult for them	eł kɔ·w a·'nap̑a
When they have gone but a little ways,	kwa'tikoł a'k̭ä
	te'n·i yo·'na'mana
May all the little boys,	k̭ɔ·w a·'waktsik̭ a·'łana
All the little girls,	kɔ·w a·'k̭ätsik a·'łana
And those whose roads are ahead,	a·'won-a·'weʻkwinte
May they have powerful hearts,	sa'wanik̭' a·'wik̭e·na
Strong spirits;	tse''makwin t̑sum i'lap̑a
On roads reaching to Dawn Lake	t̑e'luwaiyan k̭aiakwi o'neała te''-tcina
May you grow old;	t̑on a·'łacitu
May your roads be fulfilled;	t̑on a·'wona-ya·'tu
May you be blessed with life.	t̑o'n t̑e'k̑ohanan ya'niktciatu'
	hoł yam yä'tok̭ä ta'tcu
Where the life-giving road of your sun father comes out,	an o'naya·nak̭ä o'neałan kwai''-inakwi
May your roads reach;	o'neała· te'tcina
May your roads be fulfilled.	t̑on a·'wona-ya·'tunt̑iyoʻna

Taking out the black corn, he passes it around four times in front of him. Reentering the house, he repeats the prayer, still holding the corn in his hand. At the end, he again passes it around counter-clockwise before him, as a rite of exorcism, and sets it aside to be planted in spring. Then his aunts wash his head and bathe him. The following day he deposits prayer sticks at amitolan t̑ep̑o'ulikwi (where the rainbow bends over), a shrine to the gods of war, located in the canyon southwest of Zuñi. The prayer is similar.

V. PRAYERS AND CHANTS OF THE PRIESTS OF THE MASKED GODS. I

The Coming of K̭äklo

In former times the preliminary initiation of small children took place every fourth year. In these years the chief of the cult group in charge of the K̭äklo ritual received from the priests at the winter solstice a prayer stick commanding his participation.

The ceremony is held in March or April. Eight days before the actual whipping of the children K̭äklo appears to announce the approaching ceremony and command those concerned to prepare for it. In each kiva he intones a long chant describing in great detail the mythological sanction of the coming ceremony.[1] After visiting all the kivas he departs.

After eight days he comes again. Again he visits each kiva, repeating his chant. At dawn he is ready to depart. As he leaves, the gods who perform the initiation ceremonies appear and enter the village.

The following prayer is spoken by the impersonator of K̭äklo at some time during his preparations for his ceremony, probably at the moment of taking out the mask before his second appearance.

This many are the days
Since the moon who is our mother
Yonder in the west a small thing
First became visible.
When she reached maturity
Then the one who is my father,
K̭äklo, p̂ekwin priest,
Perpetuating his rite had since the first beginning—
Yonder from his perfect mountain
Made his road come forth.
He made his road come hither.
Into Itiwana his road entered,
There, wherever the roads of his children come forth
He made his road enter.
His words came forth.

le'si t̂e'wanan·e
hon ya'onak̭ä tsit i'lap̂ a·'te'ona
li·wan k̭ä'liciankwin ta''na kɔ·'wi tsa'na ye'tsak̭̂äna
ho''i-ya·'k̭̂äk̭ä te''a'ana
hon tatc i'lap̂ a·'te'ona
k̭ä'klo p̂e'kwin ci'wan·i
yam yä'lan ya·'na'a
yam ko''nhoł tci'mik̭'ä'kona te'-lia'na
o'neała kwai''ik̭̂äna
o'neał i'k̭̂äna
i'tiwanakwi o'neała kwa'tok̭̂äna
la'łhok^u yam t̂e'apk̂unan o'neała·kwai''ina'kowa
o'neała· kwa'tok̭̂äna
yam p̂e'nan kwai''ina

---

[1] The text recorded by Mrs. Stevenson (Twenty-third Ann. Rept. Bur. Amer. Ethn., p. 80) is incomplete. This is a telescopic version, a mnemonic device consisting merely of a list of place names at which events and ceremonies described in the fuller version take place. The complete chant, which is intoned in very rapid rhythm, takes about six hours to perform—it is longer even than the sayataca chant. It is in the keeping of a cult group of four men who take turns in impersonating the god.

All the ladder descending children of the corn priest
Desire the breath of their fathers,
Priests of the masked gods;

Since somehow it was not clear to which clan they belonged,
K̭äklo, p̄ekwin priest,
Made his road come hither.
To all the ladder descending children of the corn priests (he came)
In order that their children may have someone whom they call their second father,
That they may have one whom they call their second mother,
Now that they have sent for us
For this we have passed you on your roads.
I have told off the sequence of your days,
Anxiously awaiting your time,
I have told off the sequence of your days.
Seemingly now all the eight days are past,
It is the ninth night,
Now all of us
Shall pass you on your roads.
We shall pass a blessed night together,
And to-morrow,
When our sun father
Has come forth standing to his sacred place,
Throughout a blessed day,
We shall come to evening.
When our children
Into the corn priest's court have brought their roads,
Our fathers,
Priests of the masked gods,
With their powerful weapons
Four times will strike our young ones,
In order that this may be
We have passed you on your roads.
This is all.
Thus with plain words
We have passed you on your road.
To-morrow

le· łe'tsilon p̄a'ni·nan t̄o'wa ci'wa an tca'we
yam a·'tatcu
kok̄wa·'ciwani
a·'wan p̄i''nan a'ntecemana
eł kwa' ho'łno a'notan te'ona yu''hetam·e a·'teakwi
ä'k̭lo p̄e'kwin ci'wan·i
o'neałan i'k̭äp̄a
le· łe'tsilon p̄a'ni·nan t̄o'wa ci'wan an t̄e'apk̄una i·meʻ
kwi'lik̭än a·'na ta'tcu le''tikwatun'-on a'k̭ä

kwi'lik̭än a·'na tsi'ta le''tikwatun' on ak̭ä
ho'n a'ntecematina'pk̭ä te'kwi
t̄o''na hon a·'wona-e'latek̭ä.

t̄o''na·wan ho' yä'lenan pi''la

t̄on t̄e'wanan a'nt̄sumeʻna
t̄o''na·wan ho' yä'lenan pi''la

hi'ntcoł le'si t̄ewanan ha''elek̭a te'wan te'nalek̭ä t̄e'na t̄e'łinan·e

k̭es te'młamo
t̄o''na hon a·'wona-e'latena·wa.
t̄e'łinan k̭o'kci hon a·'want̄ewana

t̄e'wap yä'ton·e
ho''na·wan yä'tok̭ä ta'tcu
yam t̄e'łacinakwi ye·'lana kwai''-ik̭äk̭a
yä'ton k̭o·'kci hon su'nhak̭'äna·wa

ho''na·wan tca'we
t̄o'wa ci'wan an t̄e'ʻwitokwi o'neała kwa'tok̄ä'na·wap̄a
hon a·'tatc i'lap̄ona
kok̭wa·'ciwan·i
yam sa'wanik̭' a'k̭ä
ho''na·wan t̄e'apk̄una·we
a·'witela'ma sa'wa·nik̭' a·'łapanana te'atun'on a'k̭ä
t̄o''na hon a·'wona·e'latek̭ä.
le·wi.
le· yu''he·to p̄e'nan a'k̭ä
t̄o''na hon a·'wona-e'latek̭ä.
t̄e'wan yä'not·e

Our young ones
The plume wands of their fathers,
Priests of the masked gods
They will fashion into human form.

When to our fathers,
Priests of the masked gods,
We have given these plume wands,
Then making their days,
Keeping their sacred days,
We shall pass our days.
And so, our fathers,
Your long life,
Your old age,
Your power,
Your strong spirit,
You will give to us,
So that we may be people blessed in all things.
Yonder toward the place of dawn
We shall give our fathers prayer meal.
Anxiously waiting we shall pass our days.
When all their days are at an end
With our clear water
We shall bind our children fast,

So that their roads may reach to dawn lake
So that our young ones' roads may be fulfilled.

yam t̄e'apk̄una·we
yam a·'tatcu
kok̄wa·'ciwan·i
a·wan te'lik̭ina t̄on a·'ho'-a·'ya·-k̄äna·wa
yam a·'tatcu
kok̄wa·'ciwan·i
hon te'lik̭inan a·'łeana
a·'wan t̄e'wanan a'cana
a·'wan t̄e'wanan i'lap̄a
hon t̄e'wanan a·'tek̄än'a
t̄en ho''na·wan a·'tatcu
yam o'naya·'nak̭ä
yam ła'ciak̭ä
yam sa'wanik̭ä
yam tse''makwin t̄su'me
ho''na ya'nhaitena·wap̄a
a'k̭ä kwahoł te'mła hon a'niktcia a·'ho'a·'tek̭än·a
li'wan t̄e'luwankwin ta''na
yam a·'tatcu
ha'lawo·'tinan hon a·'wan hai'tena
ant̄sume'na hon t̄e'wanan a·'tek̭'-än·a.
a·'wan t̄e'wanan i·'te'tcap̄a
yam tca'we
yam k̄ä'cima k̄o'kci hon a·'wiya-t̄ena t̄su'mek̄äna·wap̄a
a'k̭ä t̄e'luwaian k̄ai'akwi o'neała te''tcina
ho''na·wan t̄e'apk̄una·we
t̄on a·'wona-ya·''an·a.

Prayer of the Impersonator of P̄a'utiwa

P̄autiwa is the katcina chief at Katcina village. It is he who determines the order of masked rituals and dances, and sends forth masked beings to dance for his daylight children at Zuñi. The great masked ceremonies are held expressly by his order. They can only be held when he commands them at the new year. In folklore he appears frequently in the rôle of the divine lover of mortal maidens.

He appears three times annually at Zuñi—twice during the winter solstice, and at the mola·wia which closes the great masked festival of the late fall. He comes, therefore, at the beginning and end of the year. He is one of the most beautiful of all Zuñi impersonations. The mask is turquoise blue, elaborately adorned with the most precious feathers, in particular the priceless tail feathers of the macaw. He is fully clothed in rich clothing, including four embroidered white cotton blankets and innumerable strings of the finest turquoise. His gait is slow and stately. He always goes sprinkling corn meal before him. It is altogether an impersonation of the greatest splendor and solemnity.[2]

[2] See pl 1, and Twenty-third Ann. Rept. Bur. Amer. Ethn., pl. XXVIII.

The winter solstice ceremonies and P̄autiwa's part in them are described on pp. 535 and 908.

After P̄autiwa has visited all the kivas he goes out toward the west. After undressing, at a point on the river, he is met by men of the Sun clan who escort him to the house of the house chief. Here are assembled all priests of the council, and members of the Dogwood clan. On entering, the impersonator of P̄autiwa offers a long prayer recounting the duties of his office and invoking a blessing on the people. The house chief replies, thanking him, and then asks him what he has seen in his rounds of the village. He then relates what omens have been observed in the four excavations. The following prayer recited when he enters the ceremonial room, was dictated by a member of the Dogwood clan:

Now this many are the days
Since there yet remained a little space
Ere our sun father
Stood close beside his left hand sacred place,
When our daylight fathei of the Dogwood clan,
P̄ekwin, priest,
For his fathers,
The ones that first had being—
K̯äeto·we,
Tcu'eto·we,
Mu'eto·we
Mu'eto·we Łe'eto·we
All the society priests,
For them he counted up the days.
When we had lived through the full number of his days,
And when all the days were past,
He thought of those said to be the bearers of messages
To all the different directions,
The forest beings,
The brush beings.
When for their sun father,
Their moon mother,
Our daylight children
Had counted up the days
And when we come to the middle division of the days,[3]
Our children,
Whoever of them thought to grow old,
Taking prayer meal,
Taking shell,
Taking corn pollen,

ma' le'si t̄e'wanan·e
hon yä'tok̯ä tatc i'lap̄ a·'te'ona
yam we'cik̯änem t̄e'łaci·nakwi
i'tiułat̄untekwi kow a'nt̄e'wetci kwi
hon t̄ek̄ohanan tatc i'lap̄ a·'te'ona
pi'tcik a'nota p̄e'kwin ci'wan·i
yam a·'tatcu
tci'mik̯änapkowa
k̯ä'eto·we
tcu''e'to·we
mu·''e'to·we
łe·''e'towe
le· ti'k̯a a·'ciwan·i
a·'wan t̄e'wanan pi''lap̄a
an hon te'wanan ai·yalena a·'teak̯ä tekwi
łok̄w an te'mła t̄ewak̯ä tea
lałhok[u] le'si te'kwi
ya'cu'itulo'k̯änapt̄un'ona
le''anak̯äp̄ t̄akwił p̄o·'t̄i
ła'kwił p̄o·'t̄i
yam yä'tok̯ä ta'tcu
yam yä'onak̯ä tsi'ta
yam t̄e'k̄ohanan tca'we
a·'wan t̄ewanan pi'lap̄ łok̄wan i'ti'ihak̯ik̯ä te'a'ana
ho''na·wan tca'we
hoł tcu'wa ła'cina tse''ma'kona
ha'lawotinan i·'łeana
ło' i·'łeana
o'nean i·'łeana

[3] The fifth day of the pekwin's count. This is the traditional day for gathering willow sticks for making prayer sticks. As a matter of fact, sticks are brought in at any time.

Yonder toward all directions
One by one they made their roads go forth.
Yonder finding those who have been granted domain
On all the mossy mountains,
Along the slopes of the mountains,
In all the shady places,
The forests,
The brush,
And at the feet of some lucky one

Offering prayer meal,
Shell,
Corn pollen,

Among their slender finger tips
They looked about.
Breaking off the young green shoots of some lucky one,
And drawing them toward him [4]
Even from where they abide quietly,
Holding their long life,
Holding their old age,
He brought them hither.
Now this many days
In our houses,
With us, their children,
They have stayed.
Then, when all their days were past,
With their warm human hands,
They took firm hold of them.
For their ancestors,
Their children,
The ones who have attained the far off place of waters,[5]
For their sun father,
For their moon mother,
For their need
We prepared plume wands.
With the massed cloud robe
Of the one who is our grandfather,
Male turkey,

lałhok^u le′si te′kwi
o′neała· kwai′ilenapk̭ä.

lałhok^u a·′wico yä′la′kona

t̑e′letc i′tiwa′kona
t̑e′łula′kona
ulo‘na ya′niktcia′kona
t̑a′kwi-łp̑ɔ·′t̑i
ła′kwi-łp̑ɔ·t̑i
hoł tcuw ha′lowi′li′kona
an sa′kwia
ha′lawo·tinan·e
ło′·′o
o′nean·e
a·′łeakna
a′sin k̭ä′tsowakwinte
i·′yun′ulapnap·k̭ä.
hoł tcuw ha′lowili ′kona
a·′k̭äwułkwi‘nakna
a·′wana′ułak̭äp̑a.
hoł yam łu′wa·ła′k̭i′konante

yam o′naya·′nak̭ä łe′ap̑a
yam ła′ciak̭ä łe′ap̑a
o′neał i′k̭äna
le′si t̑e′wanan·e
ho′na·wan he′cota′kona
ho′na tca′wilap̑a
t̑e′wanan a·′teak̭ä
k̭es an te′mła t̑ewak̭a tea′ana

yam a′sin k̭äłnak̭ä
a·′wiyat̑enat̑su′mek̭äna
yam a·′łacina·we
yam tca′we
le′hok^u k̭äcima t̑e·‘wok̭änapk̭ä

yam yä′tok̭ä ta′tcu
yam yä′onak̭ä tsi′ta
a·′wan hai′to
hon te′likina· ye′lete′unapk̭ä.
yam nanili te′ona
ton ots an a′wełuyan p̑a′in·e

[4] Changes from singular to plural, from first to third person, are frequent in Zuñi prayers which make little effort toward coherence or clarity of expression. Indeed, obscurity is a prized feature of the style of the men "who know how to pray." Lucidity is characterized as childish.

[5] The dead. Sticks are offered to the ancestors, the sun, and the moon.

With eagle's thin cloud wing,
And with the striped cloud wings
And massed cloud tails
Of all the birds of summer,
With these four times wrapping our plume wands,
We gave them human form.
With the flesh of our grandfather,
Giant yucca
Even a roughly made cord,
Even a dirty cord,
With this four times encircling the plume wands
We tied it about their bodies;
With water-bringing hanging feathers,
We made them into living beings.
With the flesh of our two mothers,
Black paint woman,
Clay woman,

We clothed our plume wands with flesh;
Giving them flesh, we gave them human form.
Then our two fathers,
The ones who hold the high places,[6]
Wrapping themselves in their elder brothers' plume wands,
Their elder brothers' prayer feathers,
Their elder brothers' shell beads,
They became living beings;
Holding all their world,
Holding all their people fast,
The two sat down quietly.
Then while yet a little space remained
Ere our sun father
Went in to sit down at his sacred place,
Yonder from all directions,
Our fathers, water birds,
P̄ekwin priests,
By means of their supernatural wisdom
Made their roads come in.[7]
Having brought their roads hither
Thinking, "Let it be here,"

k̯äk̯äl an su'lahaiyan la'tan·e
lałhokᵘ ɔ'lo'ik̯aiak̯ä wɔ'we
a·'wan ła'pihanan la'tan·e
a·'wan a'wełuyan k̯äten·e
a'k̯' a·'witela'ma
te'lik̯ina a·'p̄a'una
a·'ho' a·'ya·'k̯äna
yam na'n ili te'ona
ho'yala'ciwu
kɔ·'t̄i pi''lenapte
pi''le ci'k̯änapte
a'k̯a a·'witela'ma pa'nulap i'kwiyan te''tci·na

k̯äcima la'cowa

te'lik̯inan ho'i ya·'k̯äna·wap̄a
yam tsi'tili te''ona
ha'kwin o'k̯ä
he'teł o'k̯ä
a·'tcian ci''nan a'k̯ä
ak̯' a·'witela'ma te'lik̯inan ma''ci'nan i·'yante'tcina
te'lik̯inan i·'ciana
ho'i ya·'k̯äp̄a
hon a·'tcia tatc i'lap̄ a·'te'ona
t̄e'alan i'lon a·'tci
yam a·'papon a·'wan te'lïkinan ak̯ä
yam a·'papon a·'wan la'cowan ak̯ä

yam a·'papon a·'wan ło·'ak̯ä
a·'tc i·'p̄a'un ho''i ya·'k̯'äna
le· yam u'lo'nan ya't̄ena
le· yam ho'i ya't̄ena t̄sumek̯äna
a·tc i'miła'k̯up̄a
hon yä'tok̯ä tatc ilap̄ a·'te'ona
yam t̄e'łaci·nakwi
i·'muna kwa'tok̯at̄un·tekwi

kɔ·w an'te'we'tcikwi
lałhokᵘ le'si te'kwi
hon a·'tatc i'lap̄ona
k̯ä'cima wɔ'we p̄e'kwiw a·'ciwan·i
yam a'nikwanan ak̯ä
o'neała kwai''ik̯äna
o'neał i'k̯äna
hoł li·'ła le''hatina

[6] The images of the gods of war are carved and set up in the houses of the image makers. See pp. 526, 535.

[7] The pekwin makes the altar painting in He'iwa kiva. The pekwin is here conceived plurally as representative of the summer-bringing birds.

His fathers' massed cloud house he fashioned,
Their mist blanket he spread out,
Their life-giving road he fashioned,
Their perfect spring he prepared.

When all was ready our two fathers,
The ones who hold the high places,
And their house chiefs,
Their p̄ekwins,
Their bow priests,
All with their sacred possessions,[8]
Made their roads come in.
Perpetuating their rite handed down since the first beginning,
The two sat down quietly.
Listening for this,
All the society priests
Kept to their houses.[9]
And to wherever they staid in,
Along a single road
The divine ones came to them.
Sitting down quietly
Throughout a blessed night
With us, their children, they came to day.
Next day,
Saying, "Let it be now,"
Our two fathers,
The ones who hold the high places,
Met their elder brothers,[10]

Changing places with them
The divine ones sat down quietly,
And counted the days for us.
When all our days were passed in anticipation,
And when we came to the middle division of the days,
The ones who are our fathers
Those of the Dogwood clan

yam a·'tatcona·wa
a'wełuyan k̭ä'kwen ya·k̭äna
ci'pololon p̄e'wuna
o'na·ya·'nak̭ä o'neałan ya·'k̭'äna
k̭ä'nakwai'in·e ya·'na ye'lete'uk̭ä te'kwi
hon a·'tcia tatc i'lap a·'te'ona
te'alan i'lon a·'tci
yam k̭ä'k̄wa·mos·i
yam p̄e'kwi·we
yam a·'pi'ła·ciwan·i
yam e'leteli·we a·'wili
a·tc o'neała kwa'tok̭äna
yam ko· tci·'mik̭ä'kowa te'lia'na

a·tc a'miła'k̄upa
lek̄o yu·''hatia'na
le· ti'k̭ä a·'ciwan·i
hoł yam he'cotak̭änapk̭ä tea'kona

t̄o'pint̄ o'neała' a·na
k̭ä'pin a·'ho'i
i·t̄inan ła'k̭ikna
t̄e'łinan k̄ɔ'kci
ho'n tcawilap̄ a·'want̄ewak̭ä.

t̄e'wap̄ yä'ton·e
hoł k̭ä·'k̭i k̭e·'si le''anak̭äp̄a
hon a·'tcia tatc i'lap̄ a·'teo'na
te'alan i'lon a·'tci
yam a·'papa
a·tc a·'wona-e'latena
k̭ä'pin a·'ho'i
i·'yali'na i·t̄inan-ła'k̭ikna
ho'na·wan t̄e'wanan pi''lana·wap̄a
hon a·'want̄ewanan ant̄sume'na a·'teak̭a te'a'ana
łok̭w a·'wan i'tiwi·'hak̭ik̭a te'a'ana

hon a·'tatc i'lap̄ona
pi''tcik a'not a'nilap̄ a·'te'ona

[8] The war gods come into the kiva, followed by the various sacred war bundles, and parts of the rain-making bundles of the chief priesthoods.

[9] The priests wait in the kiva until they are visited by the Ne'we·kwe. Then they start their ceremonies, and, on hearing their drum, the other societies that have been waiting start their own ceremonies.

[10] The war gods are taken out to their shrines, where they are set up to replace the images of previous years.

Desiring one another sat down in council.
Among all our ladder descending children
We looked about.
Toward whoever was trustworthy
Our fathers, who once had been thus,[11]
Bent their thoughts,
Their thoughts following,
The living ones chose me
To be the one to keep their prayers.
Yonder from all sides,
From wherever they abide permanently
The divine ones made their roads come forth.
They made their roads come hither,
Their roads went first,
The others followed at their backs.
Into my house
The divine ones made their road enter.
After they had sat down quietly
We in the daylight
Met one another.
The divine ones' prayers leading,
Our words following,
With prayer meal
We held one another fast.
That I might be the one to represent our father,
K̄äwułia, P̄autiwa,[12]
My daylight father,
He of the Dogwood clan who holds this rite,
For this with prayer meal
He held me fast.
Now that this many days
Eagerly we have lived.
Yesterday the appointed time arrived,

i·'yanteceman i·'wokwikna
le· yam łe'tsilon p̄a·'ni·nan tca'we
hon a·'wun-ulapnapk̯a
hoł tcuw hi'yawołucna
yam a·'tatc a·'tekwi
tse''mak te'łakwi
ts·e''mak yä'lu
t̄e'wus p̄en ili te'at̄un'ona
hon a'nawana'k̯äp̄a
k̯ä'pin a·'ho'i
lałhok^{u} le'si te'kw·i
yam t̄i'nan ła'k̯i'kona
o'neała kwai''ik̯äna
o'neał i'k̯äna
o'neał e'ʻk̯una·wap̄a
a·'wa ma'sikwi e'layä'lu
k̯ä'pin a·'ho'i
ho'man he'cot̄akwi
o'neał i'k̯äna
i·it̄nan ła'k̯ik̯ä te'a'ana
t̄e'k̄ohanana
hon i·'yona-e'latena
k̯äpin a·'ho'i
a·'wan t̄e'wusu p̄e'nan e'ʻkwi'kona
yam p̄e'nan yä'luna
ha'lawo·tinan a'k̯ä
hon i·'wiyat̄en-t̄su'mek̯äk̯ä
yam tatcili te''ona
k̯äwułia p̄a'utiwa
a'ntelia'na
ho' ho'i te'at̄un'on a'k̯ä
ho' t̄e'k̄ohanan tatc i'li te'a'ona
pi'tcik a'not'an ilap̄ te'a'ona
ha'lawo·tinan a'k̯ä
hom ya't̄ena-t̄su'mek̯äk̯ä
le'si t̄e'wanan·e
a'nt̄sume'ʻna
hon t̄e'wanan a·'teak̯ä te'a'ana
t̄e'cukwa yä'ton·e
k̯es le'n hai'tokwin te'tcip̄a

---

11 The selection is made by members of the cult group; that is, by former impersonators of the god. The choice is inspired by deceased impersonators.

12 In prayers, he is always referred to under the double name. No explanation of the first part could be elicited. The dual form of the verb and the pronoun is used.

When all my fathers,
Passed me on my road,
Yonder from all sides
The divine ones made their roads come forth.
They made their roads come hither
Whenever it was that they first took hold of our plume wands,
In the brush,
The straight green shoots of some lucky one
Drawing toward them,
They held them fast.
Holding in our hands
Plume wands ordained for our two fathers,
K̯äwułia,
P̄autiwa,
Thus we came to evening.
With the massed cloud robe
Of him who is our grandfather,
Male turkey,
With eagle's thin cloud wing,
With the striped cloud wings
And massed cloud tails
Of all the birds of summer,

With these four times wrapping our plume wands
We gave them human form;
With the one who is our grandfather,
Giant yucca,
Even a roughly made thread,
Even a dirty thread,
With this four times encircling them,
We tied it about their bodies;
With our mothers,
Black paint woman,
Clay woman,
With their flesh four times we clothed our plume wands all over with flesh,
Putting flesh on our plume wands
We gave them human form.
Then when yet a little space remained
Ere our sun father went in

homa le'n a·'tatcu
hom o'na-e'latena·wap̄a
la'łhokᵘ le'si tekwi
k̯ä'pin a·'ho'i
o'neała kwai'ik̯äna
o'neał i'k̯äna

hoł k̯e·'la yam te'likinan ya't̄ena
t̄su'mek̯änapk̯ä te'a'ana
ła'kwil p̄ɔ·'t̄i
hoł tcuw ha'lowili'kona
a·'k̯äwułkwiʻnakna
a·'wana-uła'kona
a·'wiyat̄en-t̄su'mek̯äna
yam a·'tcia tatc ilap̄ a·'te'ona
k̯äwułia
p̄a'utiwa
a·'tcian hai'to
hon te'lik̯inan łe'ap̄a
su'nhak̯änapk̯a
yam nan i'li te''ona
ton ots an a'wełuyan p̄a''in·e

k̯ä'k̯äl an su'lahaiyan la'tan·e
la'łhokᵘ ɔ'lo'ik̯aiak̯ä wɔ'we
a·'wan ła'pihanan la'tan·e
a'wełuyan k̯ä'ten·e
a'k̯' a·'witela'ma
te'lik̯ina a·'p̄a'una

a·'ho' a·'ya·'k̯äna
yam nan i'li te''ona

ho'yalaciwa
kɔ't̄i pi''lenapte
pi''le ci'k̯änapte
a·'witela'ma pa'nulapnan i'kwian te''tcina

yam tsit i'li te''ona
ha'kwin o'k̯ä
he'teł ok̯' a·'tcian ci''nan·e
ak̯' a·'witela'ma te'lik̯inan ma' ci'nana

i·'yante'tcina te'lik̯inan i·'ci·'nana
ho''i ya·'k̯äna·wap̄a
hon yä'tok̯a tatc i'lap̄ a·'te'ona

yam t̄e'łaci'nakwi

To sit down at his ancient place
For our two fathers

We made the bundle of wood [13]
The bundle of sticks,[13]
The bundle of twigs—[13]
That which is generally called the water terrace.
Then perpetuating their rite had since the first beginning,
The two assumed human form.
Holding all their world
Holding all their people fast,
With us their children
They came to day.
When he who is our sun father,
Coming out standing to his ancient place
Passed us on our roads,
Saying, "Let it be now,"
The divine ones leading

We following at their backs,
Yonder to the south,
With prayers we made our road go forth.
Reaching the place
Whence my fathers make the world over anew,[14]
Representing my father,
K̯äwuɫia P̂autiwa,

I assumed his person.[15]
Carrying his waters,
His seeds,
And carrying my fathers' perfect [16] plume wands,
I made my road come hither.
I offered my fathers plume wands,

Praying to know how the world would be,
I offered my fathers plume wands.

Drawing my plume wands to them
How the days will be.

i·'muna kwa'tot̂un te'kwi
kow a'nte'we'tcikwi
hon a·'tcia tatc i'lap̂ a·'te'ona
i·'yaniɫ po·k̯'i
ɫa'ɫ po·'k̯'i
tseɫ po'k̯'i
e'tsak̯ä k̂ä''etcin le'anik̂än'ona

yam ko· tci'mik̯'a'kona te'lia'na

a·tc ho''i ya·'k̯'äna
le· yam u'lo'nan ya't̂ena
le· yam ho''i ya' t̂ena-t̂su'mek̂'äna
a·tc ho'na tcawil a'ntewak̯ä.

hon yä'tok̯a tatc i'lap̂ a·'teona
yam t̂e'ɫaci'nakwi ye·'lana kwai·''ik̂ana
ho'n a·'wona-elatep̂a
hoɫ k̯ä'k̂i k̯esi le'anik̂äp̂a
k̂äpin a·'ho'i
o'neaɫ e''kuna·wap̂a
a·'wa ma'sikwi e'layälu
le'hok[u] a'laho'ankwin ta''na
t̂e'wus a'k̯ä
o'neaɫ kwai''ik̂änapk̯ä.
hoɫ yam a·'tatcu
a·'wan tcim'ona u'lo'na ya·'nakwi
o'neaɫa te'tcik̂äna
yam tatc ili te''ona
k̂äwuɫia
p̂a'utiwa
a'ntelia'na ho''i ya·'k̂äna
an k̂ä'cima
an t̂o'wa conan·e
yam a·'tatc a·'wan te'lik̯inan ya·'na i·'ɫeana
o'neaɫ i'k̂äna
yam a·'tatcu
ho' te'lik̯inan a·'ɫe'up̂a
ko'n hoɫ u'lo'nan te'at̂un'ona t̂e'wusu p̂enan kwai''ik̂äna
yam a·'tatcu
ho' te'likinan a·'ɫeap̂a
homan te'likinan a'nuɫa'a
hoɫ ko'na t̂e'wanan te'at̂un'ona

[13] These are three esoteric names for a large bundle of prayer sticks, the common name of which is K̯ä'etcine, "water steps," so called from the fact that it is arranged like a terraced house, with the longer sticks in the center. With characteristic Zuñi double entendre it might mean also the steps by which the rain gods descend from heaven.

[14] Pautiwa comes from the land of summer. Therefore he clothes himself and comes in from the south.

[15] He puts on the mask, thereby assuming the form and personality of the god. This power to change one's personality resides in the mask which is the body of the god.

[16] The teɫna·we or staves of office made by the priests and "finished" with their sacred paint.

They revealed to me.
Knowing that,
I prayed that throughout the country of the Corn priests
Our earth mother might be wrapped
In four layers of green blanket,
That the land might be full of moss,
Full of flowers
Full of corn pollen—

Sending forth prayers that it might be thus,
I offered my fathers' plume wands.
Four times I made my road encircle
The land of the Corn priests
Then yonder, wherever the water roads of my kiva children come out,
I laid down plume wands.
Then far off to his own country
My father

Made his road go forth
Carrying my fathers' plume wands,

Carrying his prayer meal,
I made his road go forth.
Far off at the place of the first beginning
Touching them with my plume wands,
With all the others he will hold discourse.
Our fathers will take hold of our plume wands.
Then in that way
Their long life,
Their old age,
They will grant to us.
That our roads may reach to where the life-giving road of our sun father comes out,
That we may finish our roads—
This they will grant us.
This day in accordance with whatever you wished,
Whatever you wished when you appointed me,
I have fulfilled your thoughts.
With thoughts in harmony
May we live together.

hom t̄u'nak̯ana·wap̄a
u's ai'yu'ya·na
t̄o'wa ci'wan an u'lo'na'a

a·'witen i·'yałto
hon a'witelin tsit i'lap̄ a·'te'ona
p̄a''i łi'ana
ko·w a'wicona p̄o't̄i

ko·w u'tea p̄o't̄i
ko·w o'nea p̄o't̄i
u'lo'nan te'at̄un'ona
t̄e'wusu p̄e'nan kwai·''ik̯äna
yam a·'tatcu
ho' te'lik̯inan a·'łeak̯ä.
a·'witen i·'yälto t̄owaci'wan an u'lo'na'a
ho' o'neał ulapk̯äna
la'łhok[u] le·'wi yam u'pa tca'we
a·'wan k̯ä'cim o'neał kwai''ina'kona
te'lik̯inan wo't̄a łat̄una

le'hok[u] yam u'lo'nakwi
ho' tatc ili te''ona
o'neał a·'k̯äp̄a.
yam tatc i'li te''ona
ho' te'lik̯inan łe'ana
ha'lawo·tinan łe'ana
ho' an o'neałan a'·k̯äp̄a
homan te'lik̯inan a'k̯ä
lehok[u] yam tci'mik̯äk̯ä te'kwi
ak̯' ya'cuwa t̄e'łat̄up̄a
hon a·'tatc i'lap̄ona
homan te'likinan ya't̄ena-t̄su'mek̯äna
la'k̯änkonte
yam o'na·ya·'nak̯ä
yam ła'ciak̯ä
ho'na ya'nhaitena·wap̄a
hoł yam yä'tok̯ä ta'tcu

yam o'na·ya·'nak̯a o'neała kwai'''inakwi o'neał te'tcina
hon a·'wona ya't̄un'ona
ho'na yanhaitena·wa.
lu'k̯ä yä'ton·e
hołko'n ya'ntecemana
hoł t̄on ko'n a'ntecemana'
hoł ton a'nułanapkona
ho' tse''makwin mo'ła·k̯ä k̯e·'si.
t̄o'pint i·'tse'mat̄una
hon t̄e'wanan a·'tek̯än·a

For even while I call myself poor,
Somewhere far off
Is one who is my father.
Beseeching the breath of the divine one,
K̯äwuɫia P̄autiwa,

His life giving breath,
His breath of old age
His breath of waters,
His breath of seeds,
His breath of riches,
His breath of fecundity,
His breath of power,
His breath of strong spirit,
His breath of all good fortune whatsoever,
Asking for his breath
And into my warm body drawing his breath,
I add to your breath
That happily you may always live.

To this end, my fathers,
My children:
May you be blessed with light.

ta·′tcic tewuko′liya le′kwanante
ho′ɫomackona tcu′wa tatc i′lik̯an·a
k̯ä′pin ho′i

k̯ä′wuɫia
p̄a′utiwa
an o′na·ya·′nak̯ä p̄i′′nan·e
an ɫa′ciak̯ä p̄i′′nan·e
an k̯äcima p̄i′′nan·e
an t̄o′wa conan p̄i′′nan·e
a·n u′tenan p̄i′′nan·e
an t̄e′apk̄unan p̄i′′nan·e
an sa′wanik̯ä p̄i′′nan·e
an tse′makwin t̄sume p̄i′′nan·e
kwahoɫ t̄emɫa p̄i′′nan ho′′i te′′ona p̄i′′nan ai′ncemana

yam ce′ɫnakwi
p̄i′′nan a′naʿkwa′tok̯äna
t̄o′na ho′ p̄i′′nan te′liup̄a
a′k̯ä k̯e′tsanici
t̄on t̄ewanan a·′tek̯änʿa.
t̄ewuna′ hom a·′tatcu
hom tca′we
t̄o′ t̄e′k̄ohanan ya′niktcia′tu

VI. PRAYERS AND CHANTS OF THE PRIESTS OF THE MASKED GODS. II

Prayers and Chants of the Ca'lako Ceremonies

During the taboo period of the winter solstice [1] ceremony the priests select men who are to impersonate the priests of the masked gods during the coming year. They are notified of their appointment, and on the final day of the winter solstice are summoned to Hei''wa kiva to receive their staves of office—the feathered staves which the impersonator of P̄autiwa left there the night before.

The men who are chosen must be known to be above reproach—men of pure heart and kindly disposition, who will not neglect any of the taboos attaching to their office and who will be diligent in their prayers.

Their duties begin the evening of the day on which they receive their sticks of office. Every day at sunrise they must offer meal to the sun with prayers for their people. They must go out of the village toward the east for their prayer. Many Zuñis pray each morning, but on priests and impersonators of the gods this observance is obligatory. Every evening after dark they sacrifice food in the river to the west of the village.

On their first evening following their appointment they start their nightly meetings with the trustees of their ritual to learn the long prayers and complicated rites connected with their office. These nightly meetings continue throughout the year until their days are fulfilled in November. The 10 Koyemci meet in the house of their father, the impersonators of the priests of the masked gods—Cula·witsi Sayataca, Hututu, the two Yamuhato meet in the house of the impersonator of Sayataca. The little boy Cula·witsi and his ceremonial father are required to attend only the four nights following the planting at the new moon. The Ca'lako impersonators meet formally only on these four nights each month, but hold informal meetings in between. The first prayer that is learned is the one that accompanies the monthly offerings of prayer sticks.

At each full moon all the impersonators plant together at springs in the mountains south of Zuñi.

On these days they gather early in the morning in their ceremonial houses to make their prayer sticks. Long prayers are recited at the conclusion of their work. Then after a feast they leave for the shrines, which lie to the south at a distance of 4 to 8 miles. The prayer sticks are deposited beside the spring in regular order, and

[1] See p. 535.

long prayers are offered. The impersonators of Sayataca recite the prayer, the others joining in according to the extent of their knowledge. Toward sunset the party approaches the village, marching in regular order across the plains, singing songs of the masked dancers.

Throughout the year each group of impersonators must work for the household which is to entertain them at the great public festival. From midsummer on every day is spent in labor for their hosts. They do all the work of the fields and build the new home in which the gods are to be received.

On the morning of the tenth planting, which takes place early in October, the impersonators of Sayataca and Molanhakto receive from the priest the two day counts—cotton strings containing 49 knots. One knot is untied each morning until the day of the great public ceremony. During this period there are plantings at intervals of 10 days at rock shrines to the southwest of the village.

The public ceremonies start on the fortieth day,[2] with the arrival of the Koyemci in the evening. They come masked, visiting each of the four plazas to announce the coming of the gods in eight days. They then go into retreat in the house of their father, where they remain in seclusion, with the exception of appearances in the plaza, until the festival is concluded fifteen days later.

Four days after the appearance of the Koyemci the Sayataca party come in in the evening and go into retreat in the house of the impersonator of Sayataca. On the same night the Ca'lako impersonators go into retreat in their respective houses.

On the eighth day there is another planting of prayer sticks with elaborate ceremonies at which the gods are summoned from the village of the masked gods.

After they are clothed and masked they approach the village. The giant Ca'lako gods wait on the south bank of the river but the priests of the masked gods—Cula·witsi, Sayataca, Hututu, two Yamuhakto, and two Salimop̄ia—enter the village in mid afternoon. After planting prayer sticks in six excavations in the streets of the village they repair to the house where they are to be entertained for the night. This is always a new or at least a renovated house, and the visit of the gods is a blessing, a dedication. Prayer sticks are planted inside the threshold (formerly under the outside ladder) and in a decorated box suspended from the center of the ceiling. The walls of the house are marked with corn meal. In all excavations in the center of the floor seeds of all kinds are deposited. Similar rites are performed later in the evening by the six Ca'lako and the Koyemci in the houses where they are to be entertained.

[2] That is, if the ceremony is not postponed. However, almost without exception, a postponement of 10 days is necessary.

After the blessing of the house the gods are seated by the p̄ekwin, their masks raised. Reed cigarettes are brought and each god smokes with the person seated opposite him, exchanging with him the customary terms of relationship. Then the host (in the Sayataca house, the village chief serves as host) questions the gods concerning the circumstance of their coming. In the long recital that follows he reviews all the events leading up to the present moment, and invokes upon the house all the blessings of the gods, especially the blessing of fecundity.

This litany chanted in unison by the four leaders (Cula·witsi is not required to learn it) takes about six hours to perform. It is chanted in loud tones and very slowly in monotone, except for the last syllable of each line, which is higher in pitch, heavily accented, and prolonged.

The chants of the Ca'lako, which omit the recital of the 29 springs visited by the gods on their way to Zuñi and curtail other portions, take from one to two hours to perform.

All are finished at about 11 o'clock at night, when an elaborate feast is served in all the houses. After this all the masked personages dance until day in the house of their hosts.

At the first sign of approaching dawn Sayataca ascends to the roof of the house where he has spent the night, and facing the east, unties the last knot in his counting string while he intones another prayer. Returning to the house, he repeats the prayer. He then thanks the members of the society choir who furnished the music during the night. The dancing continues until sunrise, when the heads of all impersonators are washed by the women of the house where they were entertained, as a symbol of their permanent association with these houses.

At about noon, after planting prayer sticks and performing magical ceremonies in a field on the south of the river, the Ca'lako gods and the Sayataca group depart for their home in the west. This closes their year, and the impersonators of the Sayataca group and the six Ca'lako are now free after the exacting period of service.

The Koyemci, however, are not yet free. Throughout the year their duties have been heavier. They hold nightly meetings and participate in the monthly plantings of the other impersonators. Furthermore, at all of the dances of the summer series (six in all, lasting from one to eight days) they must come out and "play," observing all the usual taboos from the evening preceding the dance until the final departure. They may appear also in winter, and if they do must observe the same restrictions. If any extra dances are inserted into the calendar in the summer and fall, as frequently happens, the Koyemci are required to attend.

For five nights following the departure of the Ca'lako gods, dancers from each of the six kivas are supposed to visit all the houses which have entertained the gods. Some of them dance in the plaza during the day. Throughout this period the Koyemci remain in strict retreat in the house where they were entertained. At night they dance in their house; during the day they "play" in the plaza and attend any dancers who appear there. These are days of great festivity.

On the fifth evening they eat early and sparingly, and from this time on food and drink are taboo until the following night. Speech also is forbidden them, nor may they appear unmasked. After they enter upon this period the character of their dancing changes, becoming more solemn. They do not indulge in their usual obscenity. On the following morning they come out early and are taken to be washed in the house of the village chief. Here the women give them gifts of food. On coming out, they are taken by men of their fathers' clans to the houses of their fathers' sisters. Here they receive gifts from all members of the fathers' clan. Each impersonator will receive as many as thirty slaughtered sheep, as many baskets of corn or wheat flour, bread, melons, and miscellaneous gifts of clothing, frequently of great value. The gifts are brought to the plaza, where they remain until night. Meanwhile the Koyemci attend upon the various dancers until later at night.

At nightfall the last of the dancers, the Molawia, have departed. Then the Koyemci, in pairs, visit every house in the village to invoke upon it the blessings of the gods. At each house they receive gifts of food from the female inhabitants. Returning to the plaza, they take their prayer sticks out to plant. They return to the house of their father late at night, and removing their masks for the first time all day give them to their father to return to the house where they are kept. When he comes back he thanks his children for their year of work and sets them free. Then for the first time since the preceding evening they drink, and after eating and bathing return to their homes. Their retreat, fifteen days, is the longest in Zuñi ritual.

The following prayers are only a fragment of the whole ritual. In addition to those recorded there are long series of prayers spoken at the time of appointment to office, for making prayer sticks, for offering corn meal to the sun (different in summer and winter) and food to the ancestors, for untying the knots of the day count, for each stage of dressing for the public ceremony, and for each offering of prayer sticks. In addition, the host and officials of the Katcina society have many long prayers.

Each of the six Ca'lako impersonations has a different chant, and that of the Koyemci is again different.

Prayer of the Impersonators of the Masked Gods With Monthly Offering of Prayer Sticks

And now indeed it is so.
At the New Year
Our fathers
Four times prepared their precious plume wands.
With their plume wands they took hold of me.[1]
This many days
Anxiously we have awaited our time.
When the moon, who is our mother
Yonder in the west
As a small thing appeared,[2]
Carrying our fathers' precious plume wand,
With our own poor plume wand
Fastened to our fathers' plume wand,
At the place called since the first beginning
Snow hanging, or where snow hangs,
To our fathers,
Priests of the masked gods,
Cula·witsi, ƥekwin priest,
Sayataca, bow priest,
Hututu, bow priest,
Yamuhakto, bow priests,
To all the masked gods,
(Our plume wands we gave.)
Where they were to receive their plume wands,
All happily gathered together,
There we passed them on their roads.
This day
We shall give you plume wands.
Keeping your days,
Throughout the cycle of your months,
Throughout the summer,
Anxiously we shall await your time.
Our fathers,
Yonder toward the south
Wherever your roads come out,
We have given you plume wands.

i·'na no'miłte
i'tiwan·a
hon a·'tatc i'laƥona
a·'witela'ma
te'lik̭inan ya·'na ye'lete'una
te'lik̭inan a'k̭ä hom ya'ƭena-ƭsu'mek̮äk̭ä
le'si ƭe'wanan·e
ƭe'wanan a'nƭsume'na
hon ƭe'wanan a·'teak̭ä.
hon ya'onak̭ä tsiƭ i'laƥ a·'te'ona
li·'wan k̮ä'lici'a'nkwin ta'ʻna
ko·wi'ła'na ye'tsak̮äk̭a te'a'ana
yam a·'tatcu
a·'wan te'lik̭inan ya·'na'a
yam te'lik̭inan ci'maƭo
yam a·'tatcu a·'wan te'lik̭inan ya·na a'mpatcuna
te'lik̭inan i·'łeana
k̭ä·'k̮ä tci'mik̮äk̭ä
'u'hana'a 'uhanaiye le'anak̭ä

yam a·'tatcu
koƙwa·'ciwan·i
cu'la·witsi ƥe'kwin ci'wan·i
sai'yataca ƥi'łaci'wan·i
hu·'tutu ƥi''łaci'wan·i
ya'muhakto a·'ƥi'ła·ci'wan·i
ko'ko te'mła

yam te'lik̭inan i·łeanaptun te'a

te'mła ha'ƥona ƙo'kcikwi
ƭo''na hon a·'wona-e'latenapk̭ä.

lu'k̭ä yä'ton·e
ƭo''na hon te'likina a·'łeana·wa.
ƭo''na·wan ƭe'wanan a'cna
ƭo''na yä'tcu pi'lan·e

ɔ'lo'ik̭änan·e
a'nƭsume'na hon ƭe'wanan a·'te-k̮än·a.
hon a·'tatc i'laƥona
li'wan a'laho'a'nk·win ta'ʻna
ƭo''na·wan o'neała· kwai''inapkowa
ƭo''na hon te'lik̭ina a·'łeanapk̭ä.

[1] The appointment of the impersonator at the winter solstice.

[2] The new moon. The first planting may be at the new moon or at the full moon, depending upon how quickly the appointments of the Ca'lako impersonators and the nine Koyemci are made.

When your springs were at an end,
Our fathers,
In their rain-filled room
Met together.
The flesh of their mother, cotton woman,
Four times counting up,
They gave their day counts human form.[3]
Of our two fathers,
Sayataca, bow priest,
Molanhaktu, house chief,
They had need.
The two passed their fathers on their roads.
With the flesh of their mother,
Cotton woman,
Four times counted up, and given human form,
With this they took hold of them.
From where our fathers stay,
Carrying the day count
They made their roads go forth.
To their own houses
Their roads reached.
A little later
,
Carrying their fathers' day count
With their plume wands fastened together,
They made their roads go forth.
Yonder we took our way.
At the place called since the first beginning.
Aiyayak̯ä,[4]
Our fathers,
Rain makers,
Our fathers,
Priests of the masked gods,
Where they were all gathered together,
We passed them on their roads.
Giving them our fathers' plume wands,

Giving them their day count,
This many days
The days of their counting string,
Anxiously we have awaited our time.

t̂o''na·wa k̯̂ä'nakwe·na i·'te'tcapa
hon a·'tatc i'lap̂ona
yam k̯̂ä'cima t̂e'li'tona
t̂e'młamo i·'yona-e'latena
yam tsit i'lap̂ a·'te'ona
pi'tsem o'k̯ä an ci''nan·e
a·'witela'ma
i·'yälenan ho''i ya·'k̯äna.
hon a·'tcia tact i'lap̂ona
sai'yataca p̂i''łaci'wan·i
mo'lanhakto k̯̂äkwemos·i
a·tci a'ntecematinak̯̂äp̂a
yam a·'tatcu
a·'tc a·'wona-e'latek̯ä.
yam tsit i'lap̂ a·'te'ona
pi'tsem o'k̯' an ci·'nan·e
a·'witela'ma ya'lenan yam ho''i ya·'k̯̂änapkowa
a·'tcia ya't̂enapk̯ä.
yam a·'tatcu t̂i'na'a
ya'lenan i·'łeana
o'neał kwai''ik̯̂äna
yam he'cot̂akwi
o'neała te''tcik̯̂äna
we'tsim te'la'ap̂a
yam a·'tatcu
a·'wa yä'lenana
yam te'lik̯inan a'mpatcu'kowa
i·'łeana
o'neała kwai''ik̯̂äna
le'hok[u] hon a·'wona·k̯̂ä.
k̯ä·k̯ä tci'mik̯'äk̯ä

a·'yayak̯ä
yam a·'tatcu
u'wanam·i
ho''na·wan a·'tatcu
kok̂wa·'ciwan·i
te'mła ha'p̂ona'kwi

hon a·'wona-e'latenapk̯ä.
yam a·'tatcu

te'lik̯inan a·'łeana
yä'lenan a·'łeana
le'si t̂e'wanane
a·'wa yä'lenan pi''lan·e
a'nt̂sume'na
hon t̂e'wanan a·'teak̯ä.

[3] Kohaito, "setting the day for the gods." The presentation of the day count with its 49 knots theoretically fixes the date of the festival. Kohaito may take place at the new moon or the full moon of October.

[4] The place used to be Halon Kwaton. See below.

When all their days were past,
When their day-count was at an end
Again we prepared plume wands.
Carrying our plume wands
At the place called since the first beginning
Rock Face,
We passed our fathers on their roads.
Meeting our fathers,

We gave them plume wands.
Keeping their days
Anxiously waiting
We passed our days.

This many are the days.
And when their days were at an end,
Over there, following your springs,
We gave you plume wands.
When all your days are past,
Our fathers,
Priests of the masked gods
Bow priests of the masked gods
Cula·witsi p̄ekwin priest,
Sayataca bow priest,
Hututu bow priest,
Yamuhaktu bow priests,
Ca'lako bow priests,
All the masked gods
There from your home set with mountains,
Bringing your waters,
Bringing your seeds,
Bringing all your good fortune,

Our fathers,
You will make your roads come forth.
"Yes,[5] now every one of us will come forth.
Our fathers at Itiwana,
We shall pass on their roads.
Let no one be left behind.
All the men,

a·'wan te'młat̄e'wap̄a
a·'wan yä'lenan i·'te'tcap̄a

tem t̄a te'lik̭inan ye'lete'una
te'likina i·'łeana
k̭ä·'k̄ä tci'mik̄ä k̭ä

p̄a'nitan i·'ma
yam a·'tatcu
hon a·'wona-e'latenapkä.
hon a·'wona-elatena
yam a·'tatcu
te'likinan a·'łeana
t̄e'wanan a'cna
a·'wan t̄e'wanan a'nt̄sume'na
hon t̄e'wanan a·'teak̭ä.
a·'wan t̄e'wanan i·'te'tcap̄a
le'si t̄e'wanan·e
a·'wan t̄e'wanan i·'te'tcap̄a
la·'khoku t̄o''na k̄änakwe·nan ta'pana
t̄o''na hon te'lik̭inan a·'łeanapk̭ä.
a·'wan te'mła t̄e'wak̭ä te'a'ana
ho'na·wan a·'tatcu
kok̄wa·'ciwan·i
kok̄wa·'p̄i'ła·ci'wan·i
cu'la·witsi p̄e'kwin ci'wan·i
sai'yataca p̄i''łaci'wan·i
hu·'tutu p̄i''łaci'wan·i
ya'muhaktu p̄i''łaci'wan·i
ca'lak̄o a·'p̄i'ła·ci'han·i
ko'ko te'mła
hoł yam yä'lan ya·'na'a

yam k̄äcim i·'łeana
yam t̄o'waconan i·'łeana
yam kwa'hoł te'ni ha'lowi'lin i·'łeana
hon a·'tatc i'lap̄ona
o'neał kwai''ik̄äna

e·' ma' k̭es te'młamo

i'tiwanakwi yam a·'tatcu
hon a·'wona-e'latenan kwai''ina
eł kwa tcu'hoł i'metcam·e
a·'wɔts a·te''ona

[5] From this point to the end the speaker quotes from the Ca'lako chant. The frequent changes of tense throughout the prayer make it impossible to fix it in the calendar. The Zuñi use of tense is not the same as ours.

Those with snow upon their heads,
With moss upon their faces,
With bony knees,
No longer upright, but bent over canes,
Now all of us
Shall pass our fathers on their roads.
And the women,
With snow upon their heads,
Even those who are with child,
Carrying one on the back,
With another on the cradle board,
Leading one by the hand,
With yet another going before,
Even all of us
Shall pass you on your roads.
Indeed, it is so
The thoughts of our fathers,
Who at the New Year
With their precious plume wands
Appointed us
Their thoughts we now fulfill.

This is all.
Thus with plain words we have passed you on your roads.
Now we fulfill the thoughts of our fathers.
Always with one thought
We shall live together.
This is all.
Thus with plain words we have passed you on your roads.
For whatever our fathers desired
When at the New Year

They sent forth their sacred words,
We have now fulfilled their thoughts.
To this end: My fathers,
My mothers,
My children,
Always with one thought
May we live together.
With your waters,
Your seeds,
Your riches,
Your power,
Your strong spirit,
All your good fortune,
With all this may you bless us."

u'tcina ha'ktop̄a
p̄o'hetci a'wiconap̄a
o'ci k̯ep yä'lupna
e'lemakna i·'natina t̄a'p̄owan sa'tili
k̯es te'młamo
hon a·'tatcu
hon a·'wona-e'latena·wa.
a·'wok̯' a'te'ona
u'tcinan haktop̄a
ya'nine·nante
t̄op̄ i·'setona
t̄op̄a łe'mana yä'łto i'k̄eck̄una
t̄op̄ i·'p̄iyana
t̄op̄a e''kuk̄äna
k̯es te'młamo
t̄o''na hon a·'wona-e'latenapk̯ä.
no'miłte
i'tiwana
te'likinan ya·'n a'k̯ä
ho'n a'nułanapkowa
yam a·'tatcu
hons a·'wan tse''makwin mo'ła·na·wa.
le·'wi.
le· yu·''he·to p̄e'nan a'k̯ä
t̄o''na hon a·'wona-e'latenapk̯ä.
yam a·'tatcu
a·'wan hon tse·'makwi mo'ła·na·we.
t̄opint i·'tse'makuna
hon t̄e'wanan a·'tek̄än·a.
le·'wi
le· yu·''he·to p̄e'nan a'k̯ä
t̄o''na hon a·'wona-e'latenapk̯ä.
i'tiwana
yam a·'tatcu
ko''n a'ntecemana
t̄e'wusu p̄e'nan kwai''ik̄änapkowa

hon tse''makwin mo'ła·na·we

te'wuna' hom a·'tatcu
hom a·'tsita
hom tca'we
t̄o'pint i·'tse'makuna
hons t̄e'wanan a·'tek̄än·a.
yam k̄ä'cima
yam t̄o'waconan·e
yam u'tenan·e
yam sa'wanik̯ä
yam tse''makwin t̄su'me
yam kwahoł teni ha'lowilin·e
temła ho'na t̄o ya'niktciatu.

Sayataca's Night Chant

And now indeed it has come to pass.
When the sun who is our father
Had yet a little ways to go to reach his left-hand altar,[3]
Our daylight father,
P̂ekwin of the Dogwood clan,
Desired the waters, the seeds
Of his fathers,
Priests of the masked gods.
Then our fathers,[4]
Sharing one another's desire, sat down together
In the rain-filled room
Of those that first came into being.[5]
Yonder following all the springs,
They sought those ordained to bring long life to man,[6]
Those that stand upright,
But (like the waters of the world),
Springing from one root, are joined together fast.[7]
At the feet of some fortunate one [8]
Offering prayer meal,
Turquoise, corn pollen,
Breaking the straight young shoots,
With their warm human hands
They held them fast.
Taking the massed cloud robe of their grandfather, turkey man,
Eagle's mist garment,
The thin cloud wings and massed cloud tails
Of all the birds of summer,
With these four times clothing their plume wands,
They made the plume wands into living beings.
With the flesh of their mother,
Cotton woman,
Even a thread badly made,
A soiled cotton thread,[9]
Four times encircling their wand they made their belts;[10]
With rain-bringing prayer feathers
They made them into living beings.
With the flesh of their two mothers,
Black paint woman,
Clay woman,
Clothing their plume wands with flesh,
They made them into living beings.
When they said, "Let it be now,"
The ones who are our fathers
Commissioned with prayers
The prayer wands that they had fashioned.
When the sun who is our father,
Had gone in to sit down at his ancient place,[11]
Then over toward the south,
Whence the earth is clothed anew,[12]
Our father, K̪äwułia P̂autiwa,[13]
Perpetuating what had been since the first beginning
Again assumed human form.[14]
Carrying his fathers' finished [15] plume wands
He made his road come hither.
Wherever he thought, "Let it be here,"
Into his fathers' rain-filled room,
He made his road to enter.
And when our sun father,
Had yet a little ways to go
To go in to sit down at his ancient place,
Yonder from all sides

---

[3] I. e., the south, therefore, at the winter solstice.
[4] The priests.
[5] E'to·we, the fetishes of the priests.
[6] The red willow, the wood most commonly used for prayer sticks.
[7] According to Zuñi cosmology, springs are outlets of a system of underground waters. By analogy, a shrub whose shoots are joined to a common rootstock is used to bring rain.
[8] This one is not cut.
[9] That is, so long as it is cotton.
[10] A characteristic word play, literally, "they brought it around to be tied" or "they reached their belts."
[11] Sunset.
[12] The south wind and the summer birds bring summer from the south.
[13] Mrs. Stevenson calls him komosona (head of the masked god cult) of Kołuwalawa. He is described as "the highest chief." None of the gods can come to Zuñi save by his order. The plans are made at the New Year, when he leaves the crooks for all the dancers.
[14] The impersonator dons the mask and becomes the god, and inversely the god assumes human form. As a matter of fact, in the evening the impersonator comes unmasked, the mask having previously been taken to the kiva.
[15] Finished with the special paint used by priests, which was brought from the underworld at the time of the emergence.

Rain-bringing birds,[16]
P̄ekwin, priest
From where he stays quietly,
Made his road come forth.
Making his road come hither,
Into his fathers' rain-filled room,
He made his road to enter.
With his wings,
His fathers' cloud house [17] he fashioned,
Their bed of mist [17] he spread out,
Their life-giving road [18] of meal he sent forth
Their precious spring [19] he prepared.
When all was ready,
Our father, K̹äwułia P̄autiwa
Reaching his house chiefs,[20]
His p̄ekwin
His bow priests,
He made his road to go in.
Following one road,
Sitting down quietly,
A blessed night
The divine ones
With us, their children, came to day.

Next day, when our sun father
Had come out standing to his sacred place,[21]
Saying, "Let it be now."
Over there to the south,
Whence the earth is clothed anew,
Our father, K̹äwułia P̄autiwa,
Perpetuating what had been since the first beginning,
Again assumed human form.
Carrying his waters,
Carrying his seeds,
Carrying his fathers' precious plume wands,
He made his road come forth.
He made his road come hither.
The country of the Corn priests,
Four times he made his road encircle.[22]
Yonder wherever all his kiva children's rain-filled roads come out [23]
His precious plume wands
He laid down.
Then turning he went back to his own country.
My father picked up the prayer plume,
And with the precious prayer plume
Me he appointed.[24]
The moon, who is our mother,
Yonder in the west waxed large;
And when standing fully grown against the eastern sky,[25]
She made her days,
For my fathers,
Rain maker priests,
Priests of the masked gods.
I fashioned prayer plumes into living beings.
My own common [26] prayer plume,
I fastened to the precious prayer plume of my fathers.
At the place since the first beginning called cotton hanging,
I brought my fathers [27] prayer plumes.
Drawing my prayer plumes toward them,

[16] An esoteric designation for the p̄ekwin.

[17] The meal painting on the altar.

[18] A line of meal reaching from the altar to the ladder, along which impersonators walk.

[19] The bowl of medicine water placed on the altar.

[20] The chief priesthood.

[21] Sunrise. P̄autiwa enters the village just after sunset. In fact, by the time he has visited all the kivas it is quite dark. However, the ceremonies on the plain, where he dresses, begin shortly after noon.

[22] P̄autiwa in coming in at this time encircles the village four times in narrowing circles, symbolic of the search for the middle.

[23] At the hatchways of all the kivas; P̄autiwa does not enter the kivas. He leaves the plume wands on the roofs. The description is of the leaving of the crooks for the six Ca'lako impersonations. The crooks for the Sayataca group and the Koyemci are brought to He'iwa kiva by the impersonator of P̄autiwa when he comes unmasked for the night ceremonies of the New Year. They have already been distributed before his afternoon appearance with the Ca'lako crooks.

[24] The "Ca'lako crook" left by P̄autiwa is taken by one of the kiva officials who is waiting in the kiva to receive it. He takes it home. Next evening members are summoned to his home for the ceremony of installation. The "crook" contains one long and two short sticks. The long stick and one short one are given to the man who volunteers to entertain the gods. The short stick is planted at the first full moon of the New Year. The long one is kept in the house until the last day of the Ca'lako festival, when it is given to the father of the Koyemci, who plants it with his own prayer sticks that night. The other short stick is given to the impersonator and is planted by him at the first full moon, as described in the folloinwg passage.

[25] At the full moon.

[26] Painted with common paint.

[27] His ancestors, the deceased impersonators of Sayataca, and the katcinas.

They spoke to those inside the place of our first beginning.[28]
Yonder following all the springs,
On all the mossy mountains,
In all the wooded places,
At the encircling ocean,
With my prayer plumes,
With my sacred meal,
With my sacred words,
They talked to those within.
Winter,
Summer,
Through the cycle of the months,
Though my prayer plumes were but poor ones,
There toward the south,
Wherever my fathers' roads come out[29]
I continued to give them prayer plumes.

And when the cycle of months was at an end
My fathers [30] made their rain roads come in
To their fathers,
Their mothers,
Those that first came into being.
Sharing one another's desire, they sat down together.
With the flesh of their mother,
Cotton woman,
Even a cord badly made,
A soiled cotton cord,
With this four times
They made the day counts [31] into living beings.
Saying, "Let it be now,"
They sent for me.
I came to my fathers,
Where they were waiting for me.
With their day count
They took hold of me fast.
Carrying their day count
I came back to my house.
Saying, "Let it be now,"
And carrying the prayer plumes which I had prepared,
Yonder to the south
With prayers, I made my road go forth.
To the place ever since the first beginning called "Ants go in," [32]
My road reached.
There where my fathers' water-filled roads come out,
I gave them plume wands;
I gave them prayer feathers;
There I asked for light for you.
That you may finish your roads,
That you may grow old,
That you may have corn,
That you may have beans,
That you may have squash,
That you may have wheat,
That you may kill game,
That you may be blessed with riches,
For all this I asked.

Then over toward the west [33]
Where the road of my fathers comes in,
I gave them plume wands.

And now, when all of their days were past,
Over toward the west,

---

[28] The rain makers.

[29] At various springs in the mountains south of Zuñi. At the present time these are visited in the following order: Uhanaa (snow hanging), January; Ałapatsi (rock wedge), February; At̂sinakwi (painted rock), March; Picuk̭aia (poison water weed spring), April; K̭änuła (mesa wall spring, lit., water against something), May; Toloknana, two plantings, in June and July; K̭äte·tci (evil smelling water), August; Opump̑ia (sack of meal hanging), September; Ayayakya (bluebird), October (ko haito). The matter, however, is not so simple, and there are always arguments as to the dates and places of planting. The first planting need not be at the full moon. If the New Year is at the full moon the first planting may be immediately after or delayed a month. If it takes place the end of January there is disagreement concerning the advisability of planting twice at Toloknana and as to whether the last planting at Ayayakya should be made at the full moon or the first quarter. The final decision rests with the personator of Sayataca. No matter when the plantings are made, it is always necessary at the end to postpone the festival because the houses are not ready. This is done after consultation with the P̑ekwin, so that the dates may not conflict with his dates for the winter solstice.

[30] The priests.

[31] A cotton string containing 49 knots. Starting with the following morning, one knot is untied each morning, the last being untied at daybreak the morning the gods go out after their night of dancing in the houses. One such string is given to the Sayataca impersonator, one to the father of the Koyemci.

[32] Halon Kwaton, at the foot of Corn Mountain. M. C. Stevenson records ko haito as being made at this place. In 1927 and in preceding years this ceremony took place at Ayayakya, on the opposite side of the valley.

[33] The plantings to the west are at intervals of 10 days. They are not at springs.

Where the gray mountain stands,[34]
And the blue mountain,
Where rain always falls,
Where seeds are renewed,
Where life is renewed,
Where no one ever falls down,[35]
At the abiding place
Of those who are our children,[36]
There I met them on their roads.

There where the one who is my father
Had prepared my seat
Four times my father[37] sprinkled prayer meal.
On the crown of my head
Four times he sprinkled prayer meal.
And after he had sprinkled prayer meal on his rain seat,
Following him,
My prayer meal
Four times I sprinkled.
My father's rain seat
I stood beside.
My father took hold of me.
Presenting me to all the directions,[38] he made me sit down.
When I had sat down,
My father
Took his grandson,
Reed youth.
Within his body,
He bored a hole going through him.
Four times drawing toward him his bag of native tobacco,
Into the palm of his hand
He measured out the tobacco.
Within his body
He placed mist.[39]
He took his grandmother[40] by the hand,
And made her sit down in the doorway.[41]
Having made her sit in the doorway,
Four times inhaling, he drew the mist through.
With the mist
He added to the hearts[42]
Of the rain maker priests of all directions.
It is well;
Praying that the rain makers
Might not withhold their misty breath,
With his prayers
He added to their hearts.
He handed it to me.
Four times inhaling,
Into my body
I made the mist pass through.
Then with the mist,
I added to the hearts of my fathers of all the directions.
When this was at an end,
We greeted one another with terms of kinship:
Father,[43]
Son; elder brother, younger brother; uncle, nephew; grandfather, grandson; ancestor, descendant.
With this many words we greeted one another.
When all this was at an end,
My father questioned me:
"Yes, now indeed
You have passed us on our roads.
Surely you will have something to say, some words that are not too long."
Thus he spoke to me.
"Yes, indeed it is so.
Back at the New Year,
All my fathers
Desiring something,
With their precious prayer plume
Appointed me.
Yonder toward the south,
At all the places where the roads of the rain makers come out,

[34] Ko'łuwalawa, katcina village. Actually the impersonator is dressed, with elaborate ceremonies, at Ak̓ohana t̓i'nakwi, a shrine about 2 miles southwest of Zuñi. Here two mounds of corn meal are made to represent the mountains at Kołwala·wa. Komosona, chief of the katcina cult, officiates as the "father."

[35] I. e., dies.

[36] The katcinas.

[37] Sayatca, the god, represented by komosona

[38] Holding his shoulder and moving him gently to the north, west, south, east, up, and then seating him.

[39] Cipololon'e, a common word play. Cipololon·e means both mist and smoke, ceremonially. The ordinary word for smoke is łik̓aian·e. The significance of the rite suffers in translation.

[40] Fire. In ritual smoking the cigarette is lighted with live coal from the fireplace.

[41] At the end of the cigarette.

[42] The common terms for offerings to supernaturals, used especially of offerings of smoke and food.

[43] Stevenson and Parsons give different translations. (See p. 762.)

I have continued to offer you prayer plumes.
Now that the cycle of your months is at an end,
Now that the counted number of your days has been told off
Now that this many days
Anxiously we have awaited your day,
Now this day,
We have reached the appointed time.
Now I have passed you on your roads."
Thus I spoke to them.

When I had spoken thus,
Hurriedly, without delay,
My father took hold of me.
From the very soles of my feet
Even to the crown of my head
He clothed me all over with all things needful.
When all this was at an end,
Then also with that which is called my belt,
His prayer meal,
He covered my navel.
With his bundle that covered it all over.
He took hold of me,
His bundle reached all around my body.
When all this was at an end,
Then also the different kinds of seeds four times he placed over my navel.[44]
All different kinds of seeds his bundle contained:
The seeds of the yellow corn,
The seeds of the blue corn,
The seeds of the red corn,
The seeds of the white corn,
The seeds of the speckled corn,
The seeds of the black corn,
And also that by means of which you may have firm flesh,
Namely, the seeds of the sweet corn;
And also those which will be your sweet tasting delicacies,
Namely, all the clans of beans—
The yellow beans,
The blue beans,
The red beans,
The white beans,
The spotted beans,
The black beans,
The large beans,
The small beans,
The little gray beans,
The round beans,
The string beans;
Then also those that are called the ancient round things—[45]
The striped squash,
The crooked-neck squash,
The watermelons,
The sweet melons,
And also those which you will use to dip up your clear water,
Namely, the gourds;
And then also the seeds of the piñon tree,
The seeds of the juniper tree,
The seeds of the oak tree,
The seeds of the peach tree,
The seeds of the black wood shrub,
The seeds of the first flowering shrub,
The seeds of the k̯apuli [46] shrub
The seeds of the large yucca,
The seeds of the small yucca,
The seeds of the branched cactus,
The seeds of the brown cactus,
The seeds of the small cactus;
And then also the seeds of all the wild grasses—
The evil smelling weeds,[47]
The little grass,
Tecukta,
Kucutsi,
O'co,
Apitalu,
Sutok̯a,
Mololok̯a,
P̄iculiya
Small p̄iculiya,
Hamato
Mitalik̄o;
And then also the seeds of those that stand in their doorways,[48]
Namely the cat-tails,
The tall flags,

[44] Every masked dancer carries a package of seeds in his belt. It is his "heart." At the close of any dance the priest who thanks the dancers takes some of the seeds to plant. Those carried by Sayataca are planted in the floor of the house he dedicates. (See p. 873.)
[45] Native squashes.
[46] An unidentified shrub sometimes used for prayer sticks.
[47] None of these have been identified. Many are food plants.
[48] The doorways of the rain makers, the springs.

The water weeds,
The water cress,
The round-leafed weed;
Across my navel
His bundle reached.
And then also, the yellow clothing bundle [49] of the priest of the north,
The blue clothing bundle of the priest of the west,
The red clothing bundle of the priest of the south,
The white clothing bundle of the priest of the east,
The many colored bundle of the priest of the above,
The dark colored bundle of the priest of the below;
Across my navel
His bundle reached.
When all this was at an end,
My father spoke to me:
"Thus you will go.
Your daylight fathers,
Your daylight mothers,
Your daylight children
You will pass on their roads.
And wherever you come to rest,
We shall come to you.[50]
Assuredly none of us shall be left behind—
All the men,
Those with snow upon their heads,
With moss on their faces,
With skinny knees, no longer upright, and leaning on canes,
Even all of these;
And furthermore the women,
Even those who are with child,
Carrying one child on the back,
Holding another on a cradle board,
Leading one by the hand,
With yet another going before,
Even all of us,
Our daylight fathers,
Our daylight mothers,
Our children,
We shall pass on their roads."
Thus my father said.
Having spoken thus,
He took hold of me.
Presenting me to all the directions he made me arise.
With his prayer meal
Four times he sprinkled his water-filled ladder.
After him,
Four times I sprinkled my prayer meal.
Taking four steps,
Four times striding forward,
Standing, I came out.

[Having come out standing,
Yonder to all directions I looked;[51]
I looked toward the north,
I looked toward the west,
I looked toward the south,
I looked toward the east.
Hither, toward the place of dawn,
I saw four roads going side by side.
Along the middle road,
Four times my prayer meal I sprinkled.
There I made the sound of the water-filled breath of the priest of the north.[52]
Taking four steps,
Four times striding forward,
To the place known since the first beginning as Great Lake,[53]
My road came.
Where my father's road comes out
I stood in the doorway.
That which formed my belt,
My prayer meal,
Four times sprinkling inside,
I opened their curtain of scum.[54]
After that,
Four times sprinkling prayer meal inside
Standing I came in.
When I came in standing,

---

49 U'tenan he'k̄un·e. A word of esoteric meaning; utenan·e is clothing and ornaments, any movable wealth. It is not the ordinary word for clothing. P̑ekwin possesses hek̄une instead of e'tone. In the Corn dance the leaders carry hek̄une on their heads. P̑ekwin makes it, and no one knows what it contains inside the rich wrappings. U'tenan hek̄une seems to be a symbol of wealth.

50 The gods who are believed to be present in spirit on this night.

51 At this point in the prayer the chief wo'le rises and whirls a rhombus, symbolizing the breath of the rain makers.

52 The north wind. Wind brings rain.

53 One of the springs at which the a·'ciwi stopped on their journey in search of the middle place.

54 In this case he actually enters the spring. The term, "to open the scum," is, however, used esoterically to refer to the entrance of any impersonator into a kiva or other ceremonial room.

My father [55]
Hurrying without delay
Where he had prepared his rain seat,
His prayer meal
Four times he sprinkled.
On the top of my head
His prayer meal
Four times he sprinkled.
After him
Four times sprinkling my prayer meal,
My father's rain seat
I stood beside.
As I stood up beside it
My father took hold of me,
Yonder to all the directions presenting me,
He made me sit down.
Having seated me
The one who is my father
Took the water bringing cigarettes which he had prepared.
Four times drawing it toward him,
He took his grandmother by the hand
And made her sit down in the doorway,
Four times inhaling, he drew the mist through.
With the mist
He added to the hearts of fathers,
Rain maker priests.
Thus it is well;
In order that the rain makers may not withhold their misty breath.
With mist he added to their hearts.
When all this was at an end,
My father handed it to me.
Four times inhaling, I drew the mist through.
Into my body drawing the misty breath,
With the mist
I added to the hearts of my fathers.
This is well;
In order that the rain makers may not withhold their misty breath,
With mist I added to their hearts.
When all this was at an end,
We greeted one another with terms of kinship:
Father,
Son; elder brother, younger brother; uncle, nephew; grandfather, grandson; ancestor, descendant.
With these words we greeted one another.
When all this was at an end
My father questioned me:
"Yes, now at this time
You have passed us on our roads.
Surely you will have something to say, some word that is not too long,
If you let us know that,
I shall know it for all time."
Thus my father spoke.
When he had spoken thus, (I answered)
"Yes, indeed it is so.
Yonder to the south,
Following wherever your roads come out,
I have been bringing you prayer sticks,
I have been bringing you prayer feathers.
Now this day,
Having reached the appointed time,
I have passed you on your roads."
"Is that so. With plain words you have come to us.
We are clothed with your prayer sticks;
We hold your prayer meal;
With your prayer plumes in our hair we are sitting in here waiting.
Here where we are just standing around,
Where we are just sitting on our haunches,
You have come to us.
When the sun who is our father
Has yet a little ways to go,
Before he goes in to sit down at his sacred place,
Nearby your daylight fathers,
Your daylight mothers,
Your children,
You will pass on their roads.
Wherever you come to rest,
All together we shall come to you.
All the men,
Those with snow upon their heads, with moss upon their faces,
With skinny knees,
No longer upright but leaning on canes;
And the women,
Even those who are with child,
Carrying one upon the back,
Holding another on the cradle board,

[55] The inhabitants of the spring, differently interpreted as rain makers, some special, unnamed class of beings living in springs, or simply ałacina'we, the ancestors.

Leading one by the hand,
With yet another going before.
Yes, with all of these,
Your daylight fathers,
Your daylight mothers,
Your children,
You will pass on their roads.
And wherever you come to rest
We shall come to you."
Thus my father spoke.
When he had spoken thus,
He took hold of me.
Yonder to all the directions
Presenting me
He made me arise.
After he had made me arise
With his prayer meal
His water-filled ladder
He sprinkled.
After him sprinkling my prayer meal
Standing, I came out.] [56]

* * *

Coming out standing
Yonder to all directions I looked.
I looked to the north,
I looked to the west,
I looked to the south,
I looked to the east,
Hither toward Itiwana [57] I saw four roads going side by side.
Along the middle road,
My prayer meal
Four times I sprinkled before me.
Then I made the sound of the rain-filled breath of the rain maker priest of the below.

Taking four steps,
Four times striding forward,
Where descends the watery road.
Of my daylight fathers,[58]
My daylight mothers,
I stood.
Then I consecrated [59] the place
Where my father's watery road descends.
That none of his children might fall from the ladder,[60]
Having still one rung left to go,
Having still two rungs left to go,
Having still three rungs left to go,
Having still four rungs left to go;
In order that none of his children should fall down
I consecrated the place where his watery road descends.
When all this was at an end
The one who is my father
On the crown of my head
Four times sprinkled prayer meal.
On his watery wood pile [61]

---

56 The bracketed portion is repeated unchanged, except for two words, for the other 28 springs visited by the A'ciwi during their migrations. In addition to substituting the names of the springs, the different winds are invoked in the following order: West, south, east, above, below, north, west, etc. The springs are visited in the following order which is not that of the ca'lako (see p. 771): 2. te'wuł i'ti-wa pik̯aia le'anak̯änakwi, the place called water cress in the valley; 3, he'i patcikwi, cliff dwelling; 4, ha'nłipink̯akwi, place of stealing; 5, k̯äna pa'łtokwi, last spring; 6, k̯ä'na i'tiwakwi, middle spring; 7, t̑o'pa pi'k̯aiakwi, the other watercress spring; 8, ko'lowisi k̯akwekwi, Kolowisi's home; 9, p̑atsik̯änakwi, dripping spring; 10, p̑o'cowakwi, grass bending over; 11, lw·k̯anakwi, ashes spring; 12, to'seluna k̯a'nakwi, cat tail spring; 13, a'miltolan k̯a'iakwi, rainbow spring; 14, k̯äpkwenakwi, water flowing out (Ojo Caliente); 15, wa'tsita'nakwi, dog's corner; 16, ca'lak̑onakwi, ca'lako place; 17, u'hanakwi, snow hanging place; 18, a'łapatsikwi, rock wedge place; 19, a't̑sinakwi, pictograph place; 20, pi'·cuk̯aiakwi, poison water weed spring; 21, k̯ä'nuła·kwi, mesa wall spring; 22, to'loknanakwi (no translation); 23, k̯ä'·tetcikwi, evil smelling water; 24, o'p̑ump̑iakwi, where the sack of flour hangs; 25, a'yayak̯akwi, bluebird place; 26, ha'lon kwa'tonankwi, where ants go in; 27, t̑o'wa yä'lakwi, Corn Mountain (substitute "toward Itiwan·a" for "toward the east"); 28, matasak̯a hepatina le'ana k̯anakwi, the place called matsak̯a hepatina; 29, k̑o'lin k̯ai'akwi e'tsak̯a hepatinakwi, sulphur spring, commonly called hepatina.

57 The middle; i. e., Zuñi. The word in common use is ci'wina·kwi.

58 The outer ladder. Sayataca still enters through the roof. None of the prayers make any mention of the planting of prayer sticks in the six permanent excavations in the street of the village. In 1927 these were visited in the following order: T̑ek̯ałnawa, o'na·wa, pa'łtowa, tsi'a'a·wa, hek̯äpawa, te''witoła'na. Their house was in the large plaza. In these excavations Cu'la·witsi, Sa'yataca and Hu'·tutu deposit telikina t̑sume (strong prayer sticks) to the Uwanami of the six regions. They are colored with the appropriate colors.

59 He deposits a double prayer stick just inside the threshold of the door, where every one passes. This was formerly planted under the ladder. Like those placed in the roof, these are colored blue and yellow and are male and female, respectively.

60 That is, die before their time.

61 K̑äcima t̑apela is an archaic expression for a load of firewood made by laying short sticks across two long poles.

Four times he threw prayer meal upward.
Then after him,
My prayer meal
Sprinkling before me,
Where my father's water-filled road ascends
I made my road ascend.
The one who is my father
Four times sprinkled prayer meal before him.
After him
Four times sprinkling prayer meal before me,
Standing, I came in.
As standing I came in
I could scarcely see all my fathers,
So full was his house.

Then my father's rain-filled room
I rooted at the north,[62]
I rooted at the west,
I rooted at the south,
I rooted at the east,
I rooted above,
Then in the middle of my father's roof,[63]
With two plume wands joined together,
I consecrated his roof.
This is well;
In order that my father's offspring may increase,
I consecrated the center of his roof.
And then also, the center of my father's floor,
With seeds of all kinds,
I consecrated the center of his floor.[64]
This is well;
In order that my father's fourth room
May be bursting with corn,
That even in his doorway,
The shelled corn may be scattered before the door,
The beans may be scattered before the door,
That his house may be full of little boys,
And little girls,
And people grown to maturity;
That in his house
Children may jostle one another in the doorway,
In order that it may be thus,
I have consecrated the rain-filled room
Of my daylight father,
My daylight mother.

When all this was at an end,
The one who is my father [65]
Four times sprinkled prayer meal
Where he had prepared my seat.
Following him,
Four times sprinkling prayer meal before me,
Where my father had prepared my seat,
I stood beside it.
My father took hold of me.
Presenting me to all the directions, he made me sit down.
After my father had seated me,
The rain invoking cigarette which he had prepared
My father drew toward him.
He took his grandmother by the hand
And made her sit in the doorway.
Having seated her in the doorway,
Four times inhaling he made the mist pass through;
Into his body
He drew the misty breath.
With the mist he added to the hearts of his fathers.
This is well:
That the rain makers may not withhold their misty breath,
With mist
He added to the hearts of his fathers.
He handed it to me.
Four times inhaling I made the mist pass through;

---

[62] Consecrating the walls of the house. Each of the impersonators makes one stroke downward on each wall, using for this purpose whatever he is carrying. Cula·witsi uses his torch, Sayataca, Hututu, the two Yaumhakto use their tełna·we, the Sälimopia their yucca. This is not done above and below.

[63] In the decorated box made to receive them. The box is called teckwin·e, the word used for any permanent or temporary altar or sacred place. The sticks are painted blue and yellow; the blue one is male, the yellow female. The female has a face painted on one side. They are deposited with the face toward the east. They are called wihawe, "babies." This term is used for prayer sticks in the excavations visited by P͡a'utiwa at the New Year, from which he foretells the future, and for the dolls given at the winter solstice ceremonies to barren or unlucky women to insure conception or safe delivery.

[64] The seeds are deposited in a permanent excavation carefully concealed. Sometimes at the winter solstice articles of clay are deposited in this excavation.

[65] P͡ekwin seats the personators in the Sayataca house, and they smoke with the priests. (See M. C. Stevenson.)

Into my warm body
I drew the misty breath.
With mist I added to the hearts of my fathers.
This is well:
That the rain makers may not withhold their misty breath,
With mist I added to their hearts.
When all this was at an end,
We greeted one another with terms of kinship:
Father,
Son, elder brother, younger brother; uncle, nephew; grandfather, grandson; ancestor, descendant.
With this many words we greeted one another.

When all this was at an end,
My daylight father questioned me:[66]
"Yes, now indeed
You have passed us on our roads,
The one whom all our fathers,
Desiring something,
Appointed at the New Year.
Yonder to the south
Wherever emerge the precious roads of our fathers,
Rain maker priests,
Rain maker P̣ekwins,
Rain maker bow priests.
With your prayer plumes—poorly made though they were,
You have asked for light for us.
Now this day, the appointed time has come."
Thus my father said to me.

Now our fathers,
Cula·witsi, p̣ekwin priest,[67]
Sayataca, bow priest,[68]
Hututu, bow priest,
The two Yamuhakto, bow priests,
Perpetuating their rite,
Have once more assumed human form.
Their seeds,
Their riches,
Their fecundity,
The seeds of the yellow corn,
The seeds of the blue corn,
The seeds of the red corn,
The seeds of the white corn,
The seeds of the speckled corn,
The seeds of the black corn,
The seeds of the sweet corn,
All the clans of beans,
All the ancient round things,
The seeds of all the different trees,
The seeds of all the wild weeds,
I carry over my navel.
Those which we brought,
These seeds we now leave here
In the rain-filled rooms
Of our daylight fathers,
Our daylight mothers.

When in the spring,
Your earth mother is enriched with living waters,
Then in all your water-filled fields,
These, with which you will renew yourselves,
Your mothers,
All the different kinds of corn,
Within your earth mother
You will lay down.
With our earth mother's living waters,
They will once more become living beings.
Into the daylight of our sun father
They will come out standing.
They will stand holding out their hands to all the directions,
Calling for water.
And from somewhere,
Our fathers with their fresh water
Will come to them.
Their fresh waters
They will drink in.
They will clasp their children in their arms;
Their young will finish their roads.
Into your house,
You will bring them,
To be your beloved ones.
In order that you may live thus,
In the rain-filled rooms
Of our daylight fathers,

---

66 P̣ekwin speaks.

67 The cula'witsi personator, usually a boy 10 to 13 years of age, is always referred to as pekwin ts̈ana, the little sun priest.

68 Sayataca is never called ḵ'ä'kawam·osi, house chief, as Mrs. Stevenson reports. The koyemci are the ḵ'ä'kwa·mosi. In prayers their father is always called mo'lan haktu ḵä'kwemosi ci'wani.

Our daylight mothers,
Our daylight children,
The seeds which we brought tied about our waists
We leave here now.
This is well;
That going but a little ways from their house
Our fathers may meet their children;[69]
That going about, as they say,
With your water-filled breath
(You may meet) antelope,
Mountain goats.
Does,
Bucks,
Jack rabbits,
Cottontails,
Wood rats,
Small game—even little bugs;
So that thus going out from your houses,
With the flesh of these
You may satisfy your hunger.
This is well;
In order that my daylight fathers' rain-filled rooms,
May be filled with all kinds of clothing,
That their house may have a heart,[70]
That even in his doorway
The shelled corn may be spilled before his door,
That beans may be spilled before his door,
That wheat may be spilled outside the door,
(That the house may be full of) little boys,
And little girls,
And men and women grown to maturity,
That in his house
Children may jostle one another in the doorway,
In order that it may be thus,
With two plume wands joined together,
I have consecrated the center of his roof.
Praying for whatever you wished,
Through the winter,
Through the summer,
Throughout the cycle of the months,
I have prayed for light for you.
Now this day,
I have fulfilled their thoughts.
Perpetuating the rite of our father,
Sayataca, bow priest,
And giving him human form [71]
I have passed you on your roads.
My divine father's life-giving [72] breath,
His breath of old age,
His breath of waters,
His breath of seeds,
His breath of riches,
His breath of fecundity,[73]
His breath of power,
His breath of strong spirit,
His breath of all good fortune whatsoever,
Asking for his breath,
And into my warm body
Drawing his breath,
I add to your breath now.
Let no one despise the breath of his fathers,
But into your bodies,
Draw their breath.
That yonder to where the road of our sun father comes out,
Your roads may reach;
That clasping hands,
Holding one another fast,
You may finish your roads,
To this end, I add to your breath now.
Verily, so long as we enjoy the light of day
May we greet one another with love; [74]
Verily, so long as we enjoy the light of day
May we wish one another well,
Verily may we pray for one another.
To this end, my fathers,
My mothers,
My children:

---

69 Game animals.

70 An empty house "has no heart." The heart of the house is anything which has been used by human beings.

71 The syntax of this passage is obscure. The reference is to the complete identification of the god with the impersonator.

72 O'naya·naḳa, literally, road finishing.

73 T͡e'apḱunan·e, a word difficult to render into English. It includes children, domesticated animals, and game.

74 I'yaniḳinawa, literally, "call one another by terms of relationship." The impersonator remains a "child" of the house he has dedicated and calls the host and hostess father and mother.

May you be blessed with light;
May your roads be fulfilled;
May you grow old;
May you be blessed in the chase;
To where the life-giving road of your sun father comes out
May your roads reach;
May your roads all be fulfilled.

Sai'yataca an p̂e'na ta'cana
Sai'yataca his talk long

e·'ma' no'miłte
yes now indeed it is so

hon yä'tok̭ä tatc i'lap̂ a·'te'ona [75]
we sun father having the ones

li·'wanem yam we'cik̭änem t̂e'łaci'nakwi
hither his left ancient place

i'tiułat̂untekwin kow an't̂e'we'tcikwi
when he should stand against it a little space yet remained for him (when)

hon t̂e'k̂ohanan tatc i'lap̂ a·'teona
we daylight father having the ones

pi''tcik a'nota p̂e'kwin ci'wan·i
Dogwood clan speaker priest

yam a·'tatcu
his fathers

kok̂w a·'ciwan·i
masked god priests

a·'wan k̭äcima
their waters

a·'wan t̂o'waconan·e
their seeds

a'ntecemana
desiring

yam a·'tatcu
their fathers

tci'mik̭äna'pkowa
the ones who first had being

a·'wan k̭ä'cima t̂e'li'tona
their water inner room in

i'yanteceman i·'wo'kwikna
one another desiring sitting down in a circle

la'lkoku k̭ä'nakwe·na· tapana
yonder springs following

t̂o'pinte ła'kwimon a'k·ä
one root with

i·'p̂iyat̂sumep̂a
holding one another fast

ho''i o'na·ya·k̭änak̭ä
person prolonging life for

ya'nuła'a
appointed

[75] A reciprocal relationship is implied; hence the obscurity of the grammatical construction. Freely translated "our sun father" or "the sun, who is our father."

łu′wanan’ona
the ones that stand

hoł tcuw ha′lowili’kona
whoever the one who is lucky

a·′wan sa′kwia
their feet

ha′lawo·tinan·e
prayer meal

ło·′’o o′nean·e a·′łeakna
shell pollen giving to them

a·′k̭ewułkwi·nakna
the young shoots breaking off

yam a′sin k̭ä′łnak·ä
his hand warm with

a·′wiyaten-t̄su′mek̭äna.
them they held fast

yam na′nili te′’ona
his grandfather [having] the one who is

ton ots an a′wełuyan p̄a’i·n·e
turkey male his cumulus cloud robe

k̭ä·′k̭äl an ci′pololon u′tcun·e
eagle his mist garment

lalhok^{u} o′lo’ik̭aiak̭ä wo′we
yonder summer birds

a·′wan ła′pihanan la′tan·e
their hanging cloud wing

a·′wan a′wełuyan k̭ä·′ten·e
their cumulus cloud tail

a′k̭’ a′witela’ma
with them four times

te′lik̭inan a·′p̄a’una
prayer stick clothing

a·′ho·’ a·′ya·k̭äna
persons having finished them

yam tsitili te’ona
his mother having the one who is

p̄itsem o′kä
cotton woman

k̄o′t̄i p̄i′’lenapte
rough string even though it is

p̄i’le ci′k̭änapte
string soiled even though it is

a′witela’ma
four times

pa′nulap i′kwiyante’tcina
winding around reaching around its waist

k̭’äcima la′cowa
water hair feather

ho’i ya·′k̭äna·wap̄a
person having finished it

yam tsitil·i te’ona
his mother [with] the one who is

ha′kwin o′k̭ä
black paint woman

he′teł o′k̭ä
clay woman

a·tcian ci’nanak̭ä
their flesh with

te′lik̭inan ci’nana
prayer stick giving flesh

ho’i ya·′k̭äp̂a
person having finished it

k̭ä·′k̭i ke·′si le’anik̭äp̂a
whenever now thus saying

hon a·′tatc i′lap̂ a·′te’ona
we fathers having the ones

yam te′lik̭inan ya·′k̭äkona
his prayer stick the one he had finished

t̂ewusu ya′nułana
prayer appointed

hon yätok̭ä tatc i′lap̂· a·′te’ona
we sun father having the ones

yam t̂e′łacinakwi
his ancient place

i·′muna kwa′tok̭äp̂a
sitting down having gone in

hon a·′tcia tatc i′lap̂ a·′te’ona
we two fathers having the ones

k̭ä′wułia p̂a′utiwa
k̭ä′wułia p̂a′utiwa

li·′wan a′lahoankwin ta′‘na
hither to the south direction

hoł yam tcim’on u′lo‘nana ya·′na’a
wherever their new world becoming made

yam ko’ tci′mik̭ä’kowa te′lia‘na
his rite according to the first beginning perpetuating

ho’i ya·′k̭äna
person having made (himself)

yam a·′tatcu a·′wan te’lik̭inan ya·n i·′łeana
his fathers their prayer stick finished taking

a·tc o′neał i′k̭’äna
the two road making come

hoł li·′ła le·′hatina
wherever here thinking

yam a·′tatcu a·′wan k̭ä′cima t̂e′li’tonankwi
their fathers their water inner room (into)

a·tc o′neała kwa′tok̭’äp̂a
the two road having made come in

hon yä′tok̭ä tatc i′lap̂ a′te’ona
we sun father having the ones

yam t̂e'łacinakwi

his ancient place

i·'muna kwa'tot̂untekwi kow a'nteʻwe'tcikwi.

sitting down when he should go in little space yet remained for him

la'łhok[u] le'si tekwi

yonder all directions

k̭ä'cima wo'we p̂ekwiw a·'ciwan·i

water birds speakers priests

hoł yam t̂i'nan ła'kik̂ana

wherever their staying quietly places (where)

o'neał kwai'i k̭'äna

road making come out

o'neał i'k̭'äna

road making come

yam a·'tatcu a·'wan k̭ä'cima t̂eli'tonankwi

their fathers their water inner room (into)

o'neała kwa'tok̭äna

road making come in

yam la'tan ak·ä

their wing with

yam a·'tatcana·wa

their fathers'

a'wełuyan k̭ä'kwen ya·'k̭äna

cumulus cloud house having made

ci'pololon p̂e'wuna

mist blanket having spread out

o'naya·'nak̭ä o'neałan a·'k̭äna

life-giving road sending out

k̭ä'nakwai'inan ya·'na ye'lete'uk̭ätekwi

spring complete he had made ready when

hon a·'tcia tatc i'lap̂ona

we both fathers the ones [we] have

k̭ä'wułia p̂a'utiwa

---

yam k̭ä'kwa·mos·i

their house chiefs

yam p̂e'kwi·we

their speakers

yam a·'pi'ła·ci'wani

their bow-priests

a·'tci te''tcin o'neała kwatok̭äna

they reaching [their] road brought in

t̂o'pint o'nealana·'na

one road along

k̭ä'pin a·'ho'i

raw persons

i't̂inan-ła'k̭ikna

sitting down quietly

t̂e'łinan k̂o'kci

night good

ho’ tca′wilap̄ a·′wan t̄ewak̯ä
us children having they came to day

t̄e′wap̄ yä′ton·e hom yä′tok̯ä tatc i′lap̄ a·′te’ona
next day we sun father having the ones

yam t̄e′łacinakwi
his ancient place

ye·′lana kwai′’ik̯äpa
standing having come out

hoł k̯ä·′k̯i k̯e·′si le′’anak̯äp̄a
whenever now having said

li·′wan a′lahoankwin ta′‘na
hither to the south direction

hon a·′tcia tatc i′lap̄ a·′te’ona
we two fathers having the ones

k̯ä′wułia p̄a′utiwa

---

yam tcim’on u′lo‘nan ya·′nakwi
his new world where it became made

yam ko’ tci′mik̯ä’kowa telia‘na
his rite according to the first beginning perpetuating

tci′m’on ho’i ya·′k̯äna
new person having made

yam k̯ä′cima i·′łeana
their waters taking

yam t̄o′waconan i·′łeana
their seeds taking

yam a·′tatcon a·wan te′lik̯ina ya·na i·′leana
their fathers’ their prayer stick complete taking

a·tc o′neała kwai’ik̯äna
the two road making come out

a·tc o′neał i′k̯äna
the two road making come

t̄o′wa ci′wan an u′lo‘na’a
Corn priest his country

a′witela’ma o′neał u′lapk̯äna
four times road encircling it

lalhoku le· yam up̄a· tcawe
yonder that many their kiva children

a·′wan k̯ä′cim o′neała kwai′’ina’kona
their water roads they come out where

te′lik̯ina· ya·na
prayer sticks complete

wo·′tała′k̯una
laying down

le′hoku yam u′lo‘nakwi
yonder their country

a·tci tu′nik̄o‘pup̄a
the two having turned around

hon tatc i′lap̄ a·′te’ona
we father having the ones

te'lik̂inan a'n'ułana
prayer stick drawing toward him

telik̂ina ya·'n ak̂·a
prayer stick complete with

hom a'nułak̂äp̄a
me having appointed

hon ya'onak̂ä tsit i'lap̄ a·'te'ona
we moon mother having the ones

li·'wan k̂äliciankwin ta''na
hither to the west direction

ko'wiłana ye'tsak̂äna
still small appearing

te'luankwin t̄a'na
to the east direction

i'tiułana
standing against

ho'i ya·'k̂änak̂a t̄e'wanan a'cap̄a
person finishing day having made

yam a·'tatcu
(for) my fathers

u'wanam a·'ciwan·i
rain maker priests

kok̄wa·ciwan·i
masked god priests

ho' te'lik̂ina ho'i ya·'k̂äk̂ä.
I prayer sticks person finished

yam te'lik̂inan ci'matana
my prayer stick poor (to)

yam a·'tatc a·'wan te'likin ya·'na a'mpatcuna
my fathers their prayer stick complete fastening to it

k̂ä·k̂i tci'mik̂'äkä
sometime the first beginning

u''hana le'anik̂'äna
cotton hanging so-called

yam a·'tatcu
my fathers

ho' te'likinan a·'łe'upa
I prayer stick having given to them

ho'man te'likinan a'n-ułana
my prayer stick drawing toward them

hoł yam tci'mik̂äkätekwi
somewhere their they had (their) first beginning where

ya'cuwa t̄ełakuna·wap̄a
talking together bending over

lałhok^u k̂änakwe·na t̄a'apana
yonder springs following

a'wico yäla'kona
mossy mountains along

t̄ak̄wiłp̄ot̄ina'kona
wooded places along

k̯ä′tuł-ulapna’kona
encircling oceans along

ho′man te′likinan ak·ä
my prayer stick with

ho′man ha′lawo·tinan ak·ä
my prayer meal with

ho′man t̃e′wusu p̃e′nan ak·ä
my prayers words with

ya′cuwa t̃ełakuna·wap̃a
talking together bending over

te‘tsinane
winter

o′lo’ik̯’änan·e
summer

yä′tcu p̃i’lan·e
month sequence

te′lik̯i′nan k̃o′t̃i’a′lewunante
prayer stick badly made even

li′wan a′lakoan′kwin ta′‘na
hither to the south direction

yam a·′tatcona·wa
my fathers’

a·′wan o′neała kwai′’ina’kona
their roads they come out wherever

ho’ te′likinan a·′łean te′ak̯ä.
I prayer stick giving to them (I) have lived.

k̯es le’na yätcu p̃i’lan i′te’tcik̯a te′a’ana
now all month sequence came to the end when

hon a·′tatc i′lap̃ona
we fathers the ones we have

yam a·′tatcu
their fathers

yam a·′tsita
their mothers

tci′mik̯änapkowa
the ones that first had being

a·′wan k̯äcima o′neałan kwa′tona
their water road coming in

i′yante′ceman i′wo‘kwikna
desiring one another sitting down in a circle

yam tsi′tili te′’ona
their mother (having) the one

p̃i′tsem o′k̯a
cotton woman

k̃o′ti p̃i’lenapte
rough cord even though it is

p̃i’le ci′k̯änapte
cord dark even though it is

a'k̭ awite'la'ma
with it four times

yä'lenan a·'tci ho''i ya·'k̂äna'wap̂a
count two having made into persons

hoł k̭ä·'k̂i k̭e·si' le''anak̂äp̂a
whenever now having said

hom a'ntecematinak̂äp̂a
me having summoned

yam a·'tatcu
my fathers

ho' a·'wona-e'latek̭ä
I on their roads passed

yä'lenanak̭·ä
with the count

hom ya't̂ena-t̂su'mek̂äna·wap̂a
me having grasped strongly

yä'lenan i·'łeana
the count taking

yam he'cot̂akwi
my house to

o'neała te''tcik̂äna
road making reach

hoł k̭ä·'k̂i k̭e·si' le'anak̂äp̂a
whenever now having said

yam te'lik̭inan ye'lete'u'kona i·'łeana
my prayer stick the one I had prepared taking

li·'wan a'lahoank̂win ta'ʻna
hither to the south direction

ho' t̂e'wus ak·ä ho' o'neała·'k̭'äk̭ä
I prayers with I my road go made

k̭ä·'k̂ä tci'mik̂äk̭ä
somewhere the first beginning

ha'lon kwa'ton le'anak̭'äkwi
ant going in where it is so called

o'neała te''tcik̂äna
road reaching

yam a·'tatcu
my fathers

a·'wan k̂ä'cim o'neała kwai''ina
their water road coming out

ho' te'lik̭inan a·'łeana
I prayer stick giving to them

ho' la'cowan a·'łeana
I prayer feathers giving to them

i'sk̂on t̂o'na·wan ho' t̂e'k̂ohanan ce'mak̭a.
there for you I light asked.

t̂on a·'wona-ya·'t̂un'ona
(that) you may be the ones whose roads may be fulfilled

t̂on a·'łacit̂un'ona
(that) you may be the ones to grow old

t̂on mi′yapt̂un’ona
(that) you may be the ones to have growing corn

t̂on no·′k̭änaptun’ona
(that) you may be the ones to have beans

t̂on mo·′lenapt̂un’ona
(that) you may be the ones to have squash

t̂on k̭äyanapt̂un’ona
(that) you may be the ones to have wheat

t̂on kwa ai′nanapt̂un’ona
(that) you something may be the ones to kill

t̂on u′tenan ya′niktcia’tun’ona
(that) you clothing may be the ones to be blessed (with)

ho’ yai′ncemak̭ä.
I for this asked.

li·′wan k̭älician′kwin ta′‘na
hither to the west direction

yam a·′tatcu
my fathers

a·′wan o′neał i′nakwi
their road where it comes

ho’ te′lik̭inan a·′łeak̭a.
I prayer sticks gave to them.

k̭es le′’n a·wan te′mła t̂e′wak̭a te′a’ana
Now so much their all time has passed when

li′wan k̭ä′licia′nkwin ta′‘na
hither to the west direction

yä′lan lo′k̭än ima
mountain gray standing

yä′lan łi’ana
mountain blue

k̭ä′cima te′łakwi
water where it lies

t̂o′waconan ci′wuna
seeds renewing

t̂eapk̂unan ci′wuna
children renewing

kwa e′ła la′ninam·e
none falls down

ho’ tca′wilap̂a
I children having

t̂i′nan ła′k̂ikwi
where they stay quietly

ho’ a·′wona-e′latek̭ä.
I on their roads passed them.

i′sk̂on ho’ ta′tcili te’ona
there my father having the one

yam k̯äcima p̄ai′yan e′lete′uk̯ätekwi
his water seat where it was prepared

yam ha′lawo·tinane
his prayer meal

a′witela′ma
four times

o′t̄a‘wite-yäłtona
sprinkling on top

ho′man o′tsimowa
my crown

yam ha′lawo·tinan·e
his prayer meal

o′ta‘wite-yä′łtona
sprinkling on top

yam k̯ä′cima p̄ai′yan a′łkwi
his water seat where it lay

ha′lawo·tinan o′ta‘wite-yä′ltop̄a
prayer meal sprinkling on top

i′ste yä′lu
him following

yam ha′lawo·tinan·e
my prayer meal

ho′ o′ta‘wite-yä′łtona
I sprinkling on top

yam ta′tc′on a·ni
my father's his

k̯ä′cima p̄ai′yan a′łkwi
rain seat where it lay

ho′ ye′li′uła′k̯ä.
I stood beside it.

ho′ma ta′tcu te′a′ona
my father the one who is

homa ya′t̄ek̯a
me grasped

łałhok[u] le′si te′kwi ta′‘k̯äna ho′m an′imła′k̄uk̯a.
yonder to all directions presenting me he made sit down quietly

ho′ i′miłak̄up̄a
I having sat down quietly

ho′ma ta′tcu te′a′ona
my father the one who is

yam na′nił·i te′′ona
his grandson (having) the one who is

ła′k̯aia tsa′wak̯′ te′′ona
read youth the one who is

an ce′łna′a
his inside

pu′su a′npikwai′i a′nhaitek̯ä
hole piercing him he gave to him

yam se′wekc wo·′p̄un a′witela′ma a‘n-ułana
his tobacco sack four times drawing toward him

yam a′stecokta
his palm of the hand

se′wekc wo·′łk̭äp̄owan i′yanhai·′tek̭ä.
tobacco measuring out he gave them to him

anc·e′łna’a
his inside

ci′pololon u′tcuna
smoke having put in

yam hot a′si′-a‘nak̭ä.
his grandmother he took by the hand.

a′nim-k̄osk̄uk̭ä.
he seated her in the doorway

a′nim-k̄osk̄una
having seated her in the doorway

a′witela’ma ci′pololon cu′lulutina a′na‘pikwai′’ik̭äk̭ä.
four times smoke sucking he made it pass through.

la′łhok^{u} le′si te′kwi
yonder on all sides

u′wanam a·′ciwan·i
rain maker priests

ci′pololon a′k·ä a·′wik̭e·na te′liak̭ä.
with the smoke (their) hearts he added to.

k̭e′sic e′letap̄a
now indeed it is well

u′wanam·ik̭ a·′te’ona
rain maker beings

yam ci′pololon ya′nhak̄unan kwai′’ina i·witceman
their smoke breath coming out withholding

a·′teamet̄un’ona
that they may not be

p̄e′nan kwai’ik̭äna
word sending out

a·wik̭e·na-te′liana
their hearts adding to

ho′ma łeak̄äk̭ä.
to me he handed it.

yam ce′łnakwi
my inside

a′witela’ma
four times

ci′pololon cu′lulutin pi′kwai’ina an′haitek̭a
smoke sucking passing through I gave him

la′łhok^{u} le′si te′kwi
yonder on all sides

.yam a·′tatcu
my fathers

ho’ ci′pololon a·′wik̭e·na te′liak̭ä.
I smoke their hearts I added to.

lu′k̭äk̄on i′te’tcap̄a
this being at an end

i′sk̃on hon i′yanik̃ik̭ä.
there we greeted one another.

ta′tcumo
father

ta′le pa′pa su′we k̭ä′k̭ä k̃ä′se na′na to′cle a′le
son elder brother younger brother uncle nephew grandfather grandson great grandfather

u′wak̭ä
great grandson

le’ n a′k̭·ä hon i′yanik̃ik̭ä
with these we greeted one another

luk̭ak̃on le’n i′te’tcap̃a
this all being at an end

ho’ tatcili te’ona
my father [with] the one who is

i′teʻkunak̭ä
questioned

e′ma’ la′k̃ima
yes now at this time

ho’n a·′wona-elatek̭ä.
us (you) have passed on our roads.

i′me’ kwa′hol p̃e′nan te′yułanam·e p̃e′nan te′ak̃äna
perhaps some word not too long word may be

le’ hom i′yantikwak̭ä.
thus to me they said

e′ma’ i·′namiłte
yes now indeed it is so

hoł i′tiwana
sometime at the middle of the year

ho′ma le’n a·′tatcu
my this many fathers

ko’n a′ntecemana
something desiring

te′lik̭inan ya·′nak̭ä
prayer stick complete with

hom a′nułana·wap̃a
me having appointed

li·′wan a′lahoankwin ta′ʻna
hither to the south direction

u′wanam a·′wan o′neała kwai′’ina ta′pana
rain makers their roads coming out following

t̃o’n ho’ te′lik̭ina łe′an te′ak̭ä te′kwi
to you I prayer sticks giving have lived when

k̭es le′’na t̃o’na·wa yä′tcu p̃i′’lan i′te’tcap̃a
now this much your month sequence being at an end

t̃o’na·wan yä′lenan p̃i′’lak̃äp̃a
your count having been counted up

le′si t̃e′wanan·e
this many days

a′nt̃sumeʻna
eagerly

hon t̑e'wanan a·'teak̭ätekwi
we time have lived when

lu'k̭ä yä'ton·e
this day

kes le'n hai'tokwin te''tcik̭a
now this much the appointed time has come

t̑o''na ło a·'wona-e'latek̭ä.
you I have passed on your roads.

lec ho' i'yantikwak̭ä.
thus I to them said.

lec ho' i'yantikwap̑a
thus I having said to them

ho'ma ta'tcu te'a'ona
my father the one who is

a'nanam·e i'k̭äcetik̭äna ho'ma ya't̑ek̭a
without delay hurrying me he grasped

sa'kwikwi we'kwikwinte
(from) feet even the soles of my feet

o'tsi'mowakwinte
even to the crown of my head

kwa'hoł łean i'yante'tcina hom łe''ek̭ä.
some clothing covering all over me he dressed

u'ᶜsona le'n i'te'tcap̑a
that all being at an end

tem t̑a ho' a'k·ä a'nikwitunona le''anak̭äp̑a
then also with it that I might have my belt as it is said

yam ha'lawo·tinan·e
his prayer meal

ho'man k̭ä'mulukwia
my navel

p̑e'han i'yante'tcina
bundle covering all over

ho'ma ya't̑ek̭a
me he took hold of

hom o'pik̑un i'yante'tcik̭äk̭ä.
my abdomen covered completely

lu'k̭ak̑on le'n i'te'tcap̑a
this all being at an end

tem t̑a t̑owaconan te'młа a'witela'ma ho'ma k̭ämulukwia
then also seeds all four times my navel

t̑o'waconan p̑e'han i'te'tcik̭äk̭ä;
seed bundle he fitted on

łu'ptsikwa t̑o'waconan·e
yellow seeds

łi·'akwa t̑o'waconan te''ona
blue seed the one that is

ci'lowa t̑o'waconan te''ona
red seed the one that is

k̃o'hakwa t̃o'waconan te''ona
white seed the one that is

ku'tcutcukwi t̃o'waconan te''ona
speckled seed the one that is

k̃wi'nikwa t̃o'waconan te''ona
black seed the one that is

tem t̃a t̃on a'ka ci'na pik̭ä a·'teat̃un'ona le'anak̭äp co't̃sito
and also you with it flesh firm the one that may be so-called sweet corn

t̃o'waconan te''ona
seed the one that is

tem t̃a t̃on a'kä ye'pna k̃o'kci a·'teat̃un'ona le'anak̭äp
and also you with delicacies good the ones that may be so-called

no· a'n·oti temła
bean clans all

no· łu'ptsina te''ona
bean yellow the one that is

no· łi'ana te'a'ona
bean blue the one that is

no· ci'lowa te'a'ona
bean red the one that is

no· k̃o'hana te'a'ona
bean white the one that is

no· ci'he te'a'ona
bean spotted the one that is

no· k̃wi'ne te'a'ona
bean black the one that is

no· ła'na te'a'ona
bean large the one that is

no· t̃sa'na te'a'ona
bean small the one that is

t̃sik̭apuli te'a'ona
little grey bean the one that is

nok̭ämuliya te'a'ona
bean round (pea) the one that is

ła'pihak̭ä te'a'ona
string bean the one that is

tem t̃a t̃o'wa k̭a'moliya le''anak̭äp̃a
and also ancient round fruits thus called

mo'teała te''ona
striped squash the one that is

mo'k̭isi te''ona
crooked-neck squash the one that is

mo'laknan te''ona
watermelon the one that is

me'luna te''ona
cantaloupe the one that is

tem t̃a a'k̭ä k̭ä'cima k̃o'kci ton ya'nawilap̃a a·'teat̃unona
and also that with which water clear you to use for this the ones that will be

le''anak̯äp̂a co'p̂a te'a'ona
so-called gourd the one that is

tem t̂a he''cot̂atan an k̂ukwin·e
and also piñon tree its seed

a'sut̂atan an k̂ukwin·e
juniper tree its seed

t̂a'wi t̂a'tan an k̂ukwin·e
oak tree its seed

mo·'tcikwa t̂atan an k̂ukwin·e
peach tree its seed

t̂ak̂win łatan an k̂ukwin·e
blackwood brush its seed

k̯e'la ci'wuna łatan an k̂ukwin·e
first flowering brush its seed

k̯äpuli łatan an k̂ukwin·e
——— brush its seed

ho'k̯äp ho'ton an k̂ukwin·e
giant yucca its seed

hot̂san ho'ton an k̂ukwin·e
small yucca its seed

me'tan an k̂ukwin·e
cactus its seed

cu'lep̂ an k̂ukwin·e
brown cactus its seed

ut̂sipana me'tan an k̂ukwin·e
small cactus its seed

tem t̂a k̯äwawula· temła le''anak̯äp̂a
and also wild grasses all so-called

k̯ä'tetci te'a'ona
grass evil-smelling the one that is

k̯ä't̂sana te'a'ona
small grass the one that is

tecuk te'a'ona

ku'cutsi te'a'ona

o'co te'a'ona

a'piłalu te'a'ona

su'łtok̯a te'a'ona

mo'lolok̯ä te'ona

p̂i'culiya te''ona

p̂i'culiya t̂san'ona

ha'mato te''ona

mi'talik te''ona

tem t̂a li'ł yam a'wena'kona t̂o'waconan
and also here your doorways in seeds

u'lato k̂o'skwi·'kona le'anak̯äp o'welu te''ona
the ones that are scattered in the doorway so-called cattail the one

tonoli te''ona [78]

to'selu te''ona [78]

p̄i'k̭'aia te''ona [78]

ha'p̄itsulia te''ona [78]
watercress the one that is

homan k̭ä'mulukwia
my navel

p̄e'han iyante'tcik̭äk̭ä
bundle he covered all over

tem t̄a pi'cle ci'wan an u'tenan he'k̄un łu'ptsikwa
and also north priest his clothing bundle yellow

k̭ä'lici ci'wan an u'tenan he'k̄un łi'ana
west priest his clothing bundle blue

a'laho ci'wan an u'tenan he'k̄un a'hona
south priest his clothing bundle red

te'mak̄oha ci'wan an u'tenan he'k̄un k̄o'hana
east priest his clothing bundle white

i'yama ci'wan an u'tenan he'k̄un tsi'lip̄ana
above priest his clothing bundle many colored

ma'nilama ci'wan an u'tenan he'k̄un ci'k̭äna
below priest his clothing bundle dark

ho'ma k̭ä'mulukwia
my navel

p̄e'han i'yante'tcik̭äna
bundle covering all over

lu'k̭ak̄on le'n i'te'tcap̄a
this all being at an end

le'na t̄o' o'na·k̭äna
thus you will make your road go forth

t̄e'k̄ohanan yam a·'tatcu
daylight your fathers

t̄ek̄ohanan yam a·'tsita
daylight your mothers

t̄e'k̄ohanan yam tca'we
daylight your children

t̄o' a·'wona-e'latena
you will pass them on their roads

ho' t̄o' yu·'łak̄uk̭ä te'a'ana
somewhere you have come to rest where

t̄om hon o'na-e'latena·wa
you we shall pass on your road

a'tichon t̄i'nan-e'tcik̭änan t̄se'na
on no account will any stay behind

a·'wots a·'te'ona
men the ones who are

u'tcinan ha'ktop̄a
snow carrying on the head

[78] Unidentified aquatic plants.

po'hetci	a'wiconap̂a			
cheeks	covered with moss			
o'ci	k̭e'pyälupna	e'lemak-i·'natina	t̂apowan	satili
knees	skinny with	unable to stand	cane	helping
kes	te'młate			
now	even all			
le'stiklea	o'k̭änan	a·'te'ona		
furthermore	womankind	the ones who are		
ya'nine·nante				
even those with child				
t̂op	i·'seto·na			
one	carrying on the back			
t̂opa	łemayäłto	i'k̭'eck̂una		
another	on the cradle	clasping		
t̂op	i·'p̂iyana			
another	holding by the hand			
t̂op	e''k̂uk̭'äna			
another	sending ahead			
k̭es	te'młate			
now	even all			
yam	t̂e'k̂ohanan	a·'tatcu		
our	daylight	fathers		
yam	t̂e'k̂ohanan	a·'tsita		
our	daylight	mothers		
yam	tca'we			
our	children			
hon	a·'wona-elatenapt̂un'ona	te'ak̭än·a		
we	the ones who shall pass them on their roads	shall be		
ho'm	ta'tcili	te''ona		
my	father (having)	the one who is		
le'ciantikwak̭ä				
thus he said to me.				
le'ciantikwana				
thus having said				

ho'ma	ya't̂ek̭a				
me	he grasped				
lałhok^u	le'si	te'kwi	ho'ma	ta'k̂una	e'lemak̭äk̭a.
yonder	to all sides		me	presenting	he made me arise.
yam	ha'lawo·tinan·e				
his	prayer meal				
yam	k̭äcima	t̂apelakwi			
his	water	woodpile			
a'witela'ma	o'ta'wite'yä'łtok̭ä.				
four times	he sprinkled meal on it.				
i'ste	yä'lu				
him	following				

yam ha'lawo·tinan·e
my prayer meal

ho' o'ta'wite'-yä'łtoḳä.
I sprinkled meal on it.

a'witenaḳän te'tcunan a'la'nana
four times step taking

a'witenaḳän ye'letelupnana
four times striding forward

ho' ye·'lana kwai''iḳäḳä.[79]
I standing came out.

ho ye·'lana kwai''i ḳäna
I standing having come out

la'łhok[u] le'si te'kwin ho' t̑unatiḳä.
yonder to all sides I looked

ho' pi'cle t̑u'natiḳä.
I north looked.

ho' ḳä'lici t̑u'natiḳä.
I west looked.

ho' a'laho t̑unatiḳä.
I south looked.

ho' te'mak̑o t̑unatiḳä.
I east looked.

ḳäłhok[u] t̑e'luanḳwin ta''na
yonder to the east direction

a·'witena·na o'neała wo·'ḳäp̑a
fourfold roads parallel

ho' unatiḳäḳä.
I saw.

i'tiw o'neała'kona
middle road along

yam ha'lawo·tinan o'ta'wite'-yä'łtona i'sk̑o ho' pi'cle ci'wan
my prayer meal sprinkling on it there I north priest

an ḳäcima ya'n hakunan ho' tehatoḳä.
his water breath I sounded

a'witenaḳän tetcun a'la'nana
four times step taking

a'witenaḳän ye'letelupnana
four times striding forward

ḳä·'ḳä tci'miḳäḳä
sometime the first beginning

ḳä'tułanakwi le''anaḳäkwi
great lake where it is named

ho' o'neał i'ḳäḳä
I road brought

---

[79] The following section is repeated for the 29 sacred springs visited by the Zuñis in their migrations.

hom a·'tatcu
my father

a·'wan o'nealan kwai'ina'a
their road coming out

ho' ye·'lik̄osk̄uk̯ä.
I stood in the doorway.

yam a'k̯a anikwian'ona
my by means of which I am belted

yam ha'lawo·tinan·e
my prayer meal

ho' a'witela'ma o'taʻwite-ʻkwa'tok̯äna
I four times sprinkling in

ho' a·wan a'wic a'łtik̯ä.
I their scum opened

i'ste yä'lu
after that

yam ha'lawo·tinan o'taʻwite-ʻkwatok̯äna
my prayer meal sprinkling in

ho' ye·'lana kwa'tok̯äk̯ä.
I standing came in.

ho' ye·'lana kwa'tok̯äp̄a
I standing having come in

ho'ma ta'tcu te'a'ona
my father the one who is

a'nanam· i'k̯äcetik̯äna
without delay hastening

yam k̯ä'cima p̄a'iyan ye'lete'uk̯a te'kwi
his rain seat he got ready when

yam ha'lawo·tinan·e
his prayer meal

a'witela'ma o'taʻwiteʻ-yä'łtona
four times sprinkling on it

ho'man o'tsimowa
my crown

yam ha'lawo·tinan·e
his prayer meal

a'witela'ma o'taʻwiteʻ-yäłtona
four times sprinkling on it

i'ste yälu
him after

yam ha'lawo·tinan·e
my prayer meal

o'taʻwiteʻ-yä'łtona
sprinkling on it

yam ta'tcu te''ona
my father the one who is

an k̯ä'cima p̄aiyanana
his water seat

ho' ye'le-ułak̯a
I stood beside

ho' ye'le-uławp̄a
I having stood beside it

ho'ma ta'tcu te'ona
my father the one who is

ho'ma ya't̄ek̯ä
me grasped

la'łhoku le'si te'kwi
yonder to all directions

hom e'lulatena
me presenting

hom a'nimła'k̄uk̯ä
me he seated quietly

ho' i'miła'k̄up̄a
I having sat down quietly

ho'ma ta'tcu te''ona
my father the one who is

yam k̯ä'cima p̄o'n·e ye'leteu'k̄ona
his water roll which he had made ready

a'witela'ma
four times

a''n'ułana
drawing toward him

yam hot as·ana'k̯a.
his grandmother taking by the hand

a'nim-k̄o'sk̄uk̯ä.
he seated her in the doorway

a'witela'ma ci'pololon cululutinan a'na'pikwai'ik̯äna
four times smoke sucking he drew it through

yam a·'tatcu
his fathers

u'wanam a·'ciwan·i
rain maker priests

ci·'pololon a'kä a·'wik̯e·na te'liak̯ä
smoke with (their) hearts he added to

k̯e'sic e'letap̄a
now indeed it is well

u'wanamik̄ a·te'ona
rain maker beings

eł yam ci'pololon ya'nhak̄una kwai'inan i'witcemana
their smoke breath coming out withholding in

a·'team·et̄un'onak̯ä
order that they may not be thus

ci'polonak̯·ä a·'wik̯e·na te'liak̯ä.
with smoke their hearts he added to

lu'k̯ak̄on i'te'tcap̄a
this being at an end

ho'ma ta'tcu te'a'ona
my father the one who is

ho'ma łeak̯äk̯ä
to me handed it

a'witela'ma ci·'pololon cululutinan a'na'pikwai'ina
four times smoke sucking drawing it through

yam ce'łnakwi ci'pololon yanhakuna kwatok̂äna
my body smoke breath taking in

yam a·'tatcu
my fathers

ci·'pololon a'k̂ä
smoke with

ho' a·wik̂ena-te'liak̂ä
I their hearts added to

k̂e'sic e'letap̄a
now indeed this is well

u'wanamik̂' a·'te'ona
rain maker beings

yam ci'pololon ya'nhak̄una kwai''inan eł i'witcemana
their smoke breath coming out not withholding

a·'team·et̄u'n'onak·ä
that they may not be thus

ho' ci'pololonak·ä a·'wik̂e·na te'liak̂ä
I smoke with their heart added to

lu'k̂ak̄on le'n i'te'tcap̄a
this all being at an end

hon i'sk̄on i'yanik̂ik̂ä.
we then greeted one another

ta'tcumo
father

ta'le pa'pa su'we k̂ä'k̂ä k̄ä'se na'na to'cle a'li
son elder brother younger brother uncle nephew grandfather grandson great grandfather

u'wak̂a le'n hon i·'yanik̂ik̂ä.
great grandson thus we greeted one another

lu'k̂äk̄on le'n i'te'tcap̄a
this all being at and end

ho'ma ta'tcu te'ona
my father the one who is

i'te'kuna'k̂ä.
inquired

e'ma' la'k̄imante
yes now at this very time

ho'na t'a·'wona-e'latek̂ä.
us you have passed on our roads

i'me' kwa'tikoł p̄e'nan te'yułanam·e p̄e'nan te'ak̂äna.
perhaps some kind of word not too long (your) word will be

u''son ho'na t'ai'yu·'ya·k̂äp̄a
that us you having let know

u''son ai'yu·'ya·na
that knowing

hon t̄e'wanan a·'tek̂äna—
we (our) time shall live

ho'ma ta'tcu te'a'ona
my father the one who is

le'ciantikwaḵ̂ä
thus he said

le'ciantikwap̂a
thus having spoken

—e·'ma' i·'nami'łte
yes now indeed it is so

li·'wan a'lahoan'kwin ta'ʻna
hither to the south direction

t̂o'na·wan o'neała kwai''ina ta'pana
your roads coming out following

t̂o'n ho' te'liḵ̂ina a·'łean te'aḵ̂atea
to you I prayer sticks giving have lived when

t̂o'na ho' la'cowan a·'łean te'aḵ̂atea
to you I prayer feathers giving have lived when

lu'ḵ̂a yä'ton·e ḵ̂es bhai'tokwin te''tcip̂a
this day now the appointed time having arrived

to'na ho' a·'wona-e'lateḵ̂ä.
you I on your roads have passed.

ma' honkwa yu·'he'to p̂e'nan ho'na t̂o' a·'wona-e'lateḵ̂ä.
Is that so (with) plain words us you have passed on your roads

t̂o'man te'liḵ̂inan hon a·'łeaye.
your prayer stick we hold them

t̂o'man ha'lawotinan hon a·'łeaye.
your prayer meal we hold

t̂o'man la'cowa·we hon a·'lacowap̂a t̂inan'uliye.
(with) your prayer feathers we feathered sit inside

ma' t̂omt hon łu'wan'u'laconankwi
now just we stand around waiting where

ḵ̂es t̂omt mo't̂sokta t̂i'na'u'likwi
now just crouched on our buttocks where we sit inside

ho'na t̂a·wona-elateḵ̂ä.
us you on our roads have passed

hon yä't̂oḵ̂ä tatc i'lap̂ a·'teona
we sun father having the ones who are

yam t̂e'łacinakwi
his ancient place

i·'muna kwa'toḵ̂ät̂un tekwi
sitting down when he should go in

kow a'nteʻwetci kwi
a little space yet remained for him

lalik t̂e'k̂ohanan yam a·'tatcu
near by daylight your fathers

t̂e'k̂ohanan yam a·'tsita
daylight your mothers

yam tca'we t̂o' a·'wona-e'laten·a
your children you on their roads will pass

t̂o' yu'łak̂uḵ̂ä te'a'ana
you have come to rest when

k̂es a'nsamo
now together

t̂om hon o'na-e'latena·wa.
you we shall pass on your roads.

a·'wots a·'te'ona u'tcinan ha'ktop̂a po'hetci a'wicona
men beings snow carrying on the head cheeks mossy

ɔ'cik̂ep ya'lupna
with knees skinny

e'lemak i·'natina t̂ap̂owan sa'tili
unable to arise (with) cane helping

o'k̂änan a·'te'ona
womankind beings

ya'nine·nante
even those with child

t̂op i·'setona
one carrying on the back

t̂op̂'a ɬe'mayä'ɬto i'k̂eck̂una
another on the cradle board clasping

t̂op i'p̂iyana
another holding by the hand

t̂op e''k̂uk̂äna
another sending ahead

k̂es temɬate
now even all of these

la'lik yam te'k̂ohanan a·'tatcu
near by your daylight fathers

yam t̂e'k̂ohanan a·'tsita
your daylight mothers

yam tca'we
your children

t̂on a·'wona-e'latena
you their roads will pass on

hoɬ t̂o yu'ɬak̂uk̂ä te'a'ana
somewhere you have come to rest when

t̂om hon o'na-e'latena·wa—
you we shall pass on your road

ho'ma ta'tcu tea'ana
my father the one who is

le'ciantikwak̂ä.
thus he said

le'ciantikwana
when he had spoken thus

i'sk̂on ho'ma ya't̂ek̂ä.
there me he grasped

laɬhok^{u} le'si te'kwi
yonder to all sides

ho'ma ta''k̂äna
me presenting

hom a'na'-e'lemak̯äk̯ä.
he pulled me up

hom a'na'e'lemak̄äna
me having pulled up

yam ha'lawo·tinan·e
his prayer meal

yam k̯ä'cima t̄a'pelakwi
his water woodpile

o'ta'wite'-yä'łtona
sprinkling on it

i'ste yä'lu
after him

ho' yam ha'lawo·tinan o'ta'wite'yäłtona
I my prayer meal sprinkling on it

ho' ye·'lana kwai·'ik̯äk̯ä.
I standing came out.

* * * * * * *

ho' ye·'lana kwai'ik̄äna
I standing having come out

la'łhok[u] le'si te'kwin ho' t̄u'natik̯ä
yonder to all directions I looked

ho' pi'cle t̄unatik̯ä
I north looked

ho' k̯älici t̄unatik̯ä
I west looked

ho' a'laho t̄u'natik̯ä
I south looked

ho' te'mak̄oha t̄u'natik̯ä
I east looked

k̯ä'łok[u] i'tiwanakwi a'witena·na o'neał wo·'k̯äpa' ho' u'natik̄äk̯ä.
hither Itiwana to fourfold road parallel I saw

i·'tiwan o'neała'kona
the middle road along

yam ha'lawo·tinan·e
my prayer meal

a'witela'ma o'ta'wite'-e'k̄una
four times sprinkling before me

i'sk̄on ho' manila'ma u'wanam ci'wan an k̯ä'cima ya'nhak̄una
there I below rain maker priest his water breath

ho' te'hatok̯ä
I sounded

a'witenak̯än te'tcu a'la'mana
four times step taking

a'witenak̯än ye'łetelupnana
four times striding forward

yam t̄e'k̄ohanan ta'tcili te''ona
my daylight father [having] the one who

yam t̄e'k̄ohanan tsi'tili te''ona
my daylight mother [having] the one who is

an k̯ä'cima o'neał p̄a'ni'nankwi
their water road descends where

ho' ye'li-ułana
I stood beside it

i'sk̄on yam ta'tcili te''ona
there my father with the one who is

an k̯ä'cima o'neałan p̄a'ni·nan ho' an e'lete'uk̯ä,
his water road descending I for him made it ready

eł an t̄eapk̄una·we
that not his children

t̄opacoł t̄a'myäłan e'tci
just one rung remaining

k̄wi'licoł t̄a'myäłan e'tci
just two rungs remaining

ha'icoł t̄a'myäłan e'tci
just three rungs remaining

a'witencoł t̄a'myäłan e'tci
just four rungs remaining

eł an t̄eapkunan p̄u'lahin p̄a'ni·na a·'teamet̄un'onak̯ä
[not] his children falling down that they might not be thus

an k̯ä'cima o'neała p̄a'ni·nan ho' an e'lete'uk̯ä
his water road descending I for him prepared it

lu'k̯a le'n i'te'tcap̄a
this all being at an end

ho'ma ta'tcu te'a'ona
my father the one who is

ho'man o'tsimona'a
my crown

hom ha'lawo·tinan a'witela'ma o'ta'wite'-yäłtonk̯'äna
me prayer meal four times sprinkling on it

yam k̯ä'cima t̄a'pelakwi
his water woodpile

ha'lawo·tinan a'witela'ma o'ta'wite'-ye'mak̄äna
prayer meal four times sprinkling upward

i'ste yä'lu
after him

yam ha'lawo·tinan·e
my prayer meal

o'ta'wite'-e'k̄una
sprinkling before me

yam ta'tcili te'ona
my father [having] the one who is

an k̯ä'cima o'neała ye'maknakwi
his water road where it ascends

ho' o'neał ye'mak̯äk̯ä
I road made ascend

6066°—32——48

ho′ma ta′tcu te′a’ona
my father the one who is

yam ha′ḷawo·tinan·e
his prayer meal

a′witela’ma o′taʻwite-ʻe′ʻk̑up̑a
four times sprinkling before him

i’ste ya·′lu
after him

yam ha′lawo·tinan·e
my prayer meal

ho’ otaʻwiteʻ-e′ʻk̑una
I sprinkled before me

ho’ ye·′lana kwa′tok̯äkä
I standing came in

ho’ ye·′lana kwatok̯äp̑a
I standing having come in

hom a·′tatcu kwa les i′yunite’tcinam·e
my fathers [not] all I was hardly able to see

t̑i′nanp̑o′t̑i ho’ a·wunatik̯äk̯ä
sitting crowded I saw them

i′sk̑on yam ta′tcili te’ona
them my father [having] the one who is

an k̯ä′cima t̑e′li’to’a
his water inner room

ho’ pi′cle ła′kwimok̯ä
I north rooted

ho’ k̯ä·′lici ła′kwimok̯ä
I west rooted

ho’ a′laho ła′kwimok̯ä
I south rooted

ho’ temak̑o ła′kwimok̯ä
I east rooted

ho’ i′yama ła′kwimok̯ä
I above rooted

yam tatc an t̑ap̑oi′tiwana’a
my father his ceiling middle

te′lik̯inan i′patciak̯ä
prayer sticks fastened together with

ho’ an t̑ap̑o’ i′tiwanan an e′lete’uk̯a
I his ceiling middle for him I prepared

k̯e′sic e′letap̑a
now indeed this is well

ho′ma ta′tcu te′a’ona
my father the one who is

an t̑eapk̯unan ci′wuna teat̑un’onak̯·ä
his offspring renewing that it might be thus

ho’ an t̑ap̑o’ i′tiwanan an e′lete’uk̯a
I his the middle of his ceiling for him (I) prepared

tem t̑a yam ta′tcili teona
and also my father with the one who is

an te'witiwana'a
his middle of the floor

t̂o'waconan te'mł ak·ä
seeds all with

ho' an te''witiwanan an e'lete'uk̂a
I his floor the middle for him prepared

k̂esic e'letap̂a
now this is well

ho' ta'tcili te''ona
my father with the one who is

an a'witen t̂eli'tokwinte
his fourth inner room even there

t̂o'wacona· wo·'p̂akwi u'kwai'in·a
seeds where they are stored coming

an a'wenakwin·te
his doorway even there

tcu p̂e'wik̂oskwi
corn spread before the door

no· p̂e'wik̂oskwi
beans spread before the door

kow a·'waktsik̂' a·'łana
half grown boys

kow a·'k̂ätsik̂' a·'łana
half grown girls

a·'wonan a·'we'kwin·te
even those whose roads go ahead

k̂es an he'cot̂ana
now his house in

t̂e'apk̂unan u'łton kwai''ilena te'at̂un'onak̂·ä
children jostling one another as they go out that it may be thus

yam t̂e'k̂ohanan ta'tcu
my daylight father

yam t̂e'k̂ohanan tsi'ta
my daylight mother

ho' a·'tcian k̂ä'cima t̂e'li'tona an e'lete'uk̂ä.
I their water inner room for him I prepared

lu'k̂ä le'n i'tetcap̂a
this all being at an end

ho'ma ta'tcu te'a'ona
my father the one who is

yam k̂ä'cima p̂ai'yan e'lete'uk̂ätekwi
his water seat where he had prepared it

yam ha'lawo·tinan·e
his prayer meal

o'ta'wite-yä'łtop̂a
sprinkling on it

i'ste yä'lu
after him

yam ha'lawo·tinan·e.
my prayer meal

o'taʻwiteʻ-eʻk̄una
sprinkling on it

yam ta'ctona k̯ä'cima p̄ai'yan a'łkwi
my father's water seat where it lay

ho' ye'li'ułap̄a
I stood beside it

ho'ma ta'tcu te'a'ona
my father the one who is

ho'ma ya't̄ek̯ä.
me grasped

la'łhoku le'si te'kwi hom taʻk̯än ani'młak̄uk̯ä
yonder to all sides me presenting he seated me

ho'ma ta'tcu te'a'ona
my father the one who is

hom a'nimłak̄up̄a
me having seated quietly

yam k̯ä'cima p̄o'n·e ye'lete'u'kona
his water roll the one he had prepared

a'ʻn'ułana
drawing toward him

yam hot a's'anaʻk̯ä
his grandmother taking him by the hand

a'nimk̄osk̄uk̯ä
he seated her in the doorway

a'nimk̄osk̄una
having seated her in the doorway

a'witela'ma ci'pololon cu'lulutinan anaʻpikwai'ik̯äna
four times smoke sucking drawing it through

yam ce'łnakwi
his body

ci'pololon ya'nhak̄una kwa'tok̯'äna
smoke breath taking in

yam a·'tatcu
his fathers

ci'pololonak̯·ä a·'wik̯e·na te'liana
smoke with their hearts adding to

k̯e'sic e'letap̄a
now indeed this is well

u'wanamik̯' a·'te'ona
rain maker beings

eł yam ci'pololon yanhak̄una kwai''inan i·'witcemana
[that not] their smoke breath coming out withholding

a·'team·et̄un'onak·ä
that they might not be thus

yam a·'tatcu
his fathers

ci'pololonak·ä a·wik̯e·na te'liak̯ä.
with smoke their hearts he added to

ho'ma łeak̭äk̭ä.
to me he handed it.

a'witela'ma ci'pololon cu'lulutina a'naʻpikwai'ina
four times smoke sucking passing through

yam t̑ehuł k̭̑äłnakwi
my body cavity warm (in)

ho' ci'pololon ya'nhak̑una kwa'tok̭̑äna
I smoke breath took in

yam a·'tatcu
my fathers

ho' ci'pololon a·'wik̭e·na te'liak̭ä.
I smoke their hearts added to

k̭e'sic e'letap̑a
now indeed this is well

u'wanamik̭' a·'te'ona
rain maker beings

eł yam ci'pololon ya'nhak̑una kwai''inan i·'witcemana
(that not) their smoke breath coming out withholding

a·'team·e un'onak̭ä
that they might not be thus

ci'pololonak̭·ä ho' a·'wik̭e·na te'liak̭ä.
smoke with I their hearts added to

lu'k̭ak̑on i'te'tcap̑a
this being at an end

hon i'yanik̭ik̭ä.
we greeted one another.

ta'tcumo
father

ta'le pa'pa su'we k̭ä'k̭ä k̭̑ä''se na'na to'cle a'li
son elder brother younger brother uncle nephew grandfather grandson great grandfather

u'wak̭a
great grandson

le'n hon i'yanik̭inapk̭ä.
thus we greeted one another

lu'k̭ä le'n i'te'tcap̑a
this all being at an end

hom t̑ek̑ohanan tat̑cili te'ona
my daylight father [having] the one who is

i·'teʻkunak̭ä
questioned [me]

e·ʻ ma' la'k̭̑äma
yes now at this time

ło'na t'a·wona-e'latek̭ä
us you on our roads have passed

hoł i'tiwana'a
sometime at the middle of the year

t̑o'ma le'n a·'tatcu
your this many fathers

ko'n a'ntecemana
something desiring

t̃om a′nułanapkona
you the one they appointed

li·′wan a′lahoa′nkwin ta′‘na
hither to the south direction

yam a·′tatcu
your fathers

u′wanam a·′ciwan·i
rain maker priests

u′wanami p̃ekwi·we
rain maker speakers

u′wanam a·′pi’ła·ci′wan·i
rain maker bow priests

a·′wan k̭ä′cima o′neała kwai’ina te‘yapte
their water roads coming out valuable even there

te′lik̭inan k̃o·t̃ia′lewunante
prayer sticks badly made even

ho’na·wan t̃o t̃ek̃ohanan ceman te′ak̭ä tekwi
for us you daylight asking have lived when

k̭es lu′k̭ä yä′ton·e hai′tokwin te′tcik̭ä—
now this day the appointed time has arrived

ho’ tatcili te’ona le′ciantikwak̭ä.
I father having the one thus he said.

yam ta′tcili te’ona
my father the one

cu′la·witsi p̃e′kwin ci′wan·i
cu′la·witsi speaker priest

sai′yataca pi’łaci′wan·i
long horn bow priest

hu·′tutu pi’łaci′wan·i
hu·′tutu bow priest

ya′muhakt a·′pi’ła·ci′wan·i
stick carriers bow priests

ya′ntelia‘na ho′’i ya·k̃äna
impersonating making persons

a·′wan t̃o′waconan·e
their seeds

a·′wan u′tenan·e
their clothing

a·′wen t̃e′apk̃unan·e
their offspring

t̃o′waconan łu′ptsikwa te′a’ona
seeds the yellow ones

t̃o′waconan łi′’akwa te′’ona
seed the blue one

t̃o′waconan ci′loakwa te′’ona
seed the red one

t̃o′waconan k̃o′hakwa te′’ona
seed the white one

t̃o′waconan ku′tcutcukwi te′’ona
seed the speckled one

k̄win·akwa t̄o′waconan te′’ona
black seed the one that is

co′t̄sito t̄o′waconan te′’ona
sweet corn seed the one that is

no· a′noti te′mła
bean clans all

t̄owa k̭ä′maliya te′’ona
ancient round fruit the one

t̄a·k̭wiłp̄ot̄ an k̄ukwi′·we
forest trees their seeds

k̭ä′wula te′mła
wild grasses all

yam k̭ämulukwia
my navel

t̄o′waconan ha′tap̄iya.
seeds carrying around my waist

yam ik̭’ona
my the ones I brought

yam t̄e′k̄ohanan ta′tcu
my daylight father

yam t̄e′k̄ohanan tsi′ta
my daylight mother

an k̭ä′cima t̄e′li·’tona
their water inner room

hon t̄o′waconan a′łak̄una·we k̭e·si.
we seeds leave now.

hon a·′witelin tsi′tili a·′te’ona
we earth mother [having] the ones

k̭ä′ʻkwi ya·′nap̄ te′lakwai’ik̭äp̄a
replete with living water when it is spring

yam̦ k̭ä′cima te′atcina’kona
your water fields all over

yam ak̭ä ci′’nat̄un’ona
that with which you may have flesh

yam a·′tsita
your mothers

t̄o′wa te′młanana
corn all kinds

yam a·′witelin tsi′tana
your earth mother in

t̄on t̄i′nana kwa′tok̭äna·wap̄a
you when you have laid them down inside

yam a·′witelin tsit an k̭äʻkwin ak̭·ä
their earth mother her living water with

tci·′m’on ho′’i ya·′k̭äna
anew persons making themselves

yam yä′tok̭a ta′tcu
their sun father

an t̑e'k̑ohanankwi
his daylight

i'łuwakna kwai''ina
arising coming out

la'łhoku le'si te'kwi
yonder to all sides

k̯ä'cima ceman a'sta'k̯äna·wap̑a
water asking their hands stretching out

ho'k̯änti'hoł̑i
from somewhere

k̯ä'cima tci'm'on ak̯ä
water fresh with

a·'wona-e'latenak̯äp̑a
on their roads having passed them

k̯ä'cima tci'm'ona
water fresh

i'k̯ä''k̑una
drinking in

tca'l i'k̯eck̑una·wap̑a
their children clasping

t̑e'apk̑unan o'naya·k̯äna·wap̑a
their offspring to the end of their roads having brought

yam he'cot̑akwi
your houses to

a·'wana'n-ułana
taking them in

a·'tapana
following them

tse''mak-t̑e'łakwi t̑on t̑e'wanan a·'teat̑an'onak̯·ä
whither your thoughts bend you your time that you may live for this

yam t̑e'k̯ohanan a·'tatcu
our daylight fathers

yam t̑e'k̑ohanan a·'tsita
our daylight mothers

yam t̑e'k̑ohanan tea'we
our daylight children

a·'wan k̯ä'cima t̑e'li'tona
their water inner room

yam t̑o'waconan ha'tap̑i i'k̯'ona
our seed (bundle) the one I brought tied about my waist

hon wo·'tała'k̑unapk̯ä k̯e·si.
we set them down quietly now

k̯e'sic e'letap̑a
now indeed it is well

yam hecot̑ana
your house

ko·'wi ye·'lana kwai''ik̯äna
a little ways standing going out

yam a·′tatcu
your fathers

a·′wan t̑e′apk̑unan·e
their offspring

t̑om k̭ä′cima p̑i′′nan a′kä a·′wulacon′ona le′anak̭äp̑a
your water breath with the ones that wait around so called

k̭ä′cima co′′wita
water deer

ha′liku te′′ona
mountain goat the one who is

ma′′wi te′ona
doe the one that is

o′holi te′′ona
buck the one that is

p̑o′k̭ä te′′ona
jack rabbit the one that is

o·′kcik̑ te′′ona
cottontail the one that is

k̑o′tci te′′ona
wood rat the one that is

i·′sk̭än kwa kowi no′me t̑sa′napte
then some small bug even the little ones

yam he′cot̑ana
your house

ye·′lana kwai′′ik̭äna
standing going out

a·′wan ci′nan a′k̭a
their flesh with

t̑on yu·′′yackwa′tea a·′teatun′onak̭ä
you well nourished that you may be thus

k̭e′sic e′letap̑a
now indeed this is well

hon t̑ek̑ohanan tatc i′lap̑ a·′te′ona
we daylight father having the ones

an k̭ä′cima t̑e′li′tona
his water inner room

u′tenan te′młananak̭·ä
clothing all kinds with

an he′cot̑a i′k̭e·nat̑un′ona
his house that it may have a heart

kow an a′wenakwinte
a little in his doorway even

tcu p̑e′wik̑oskwi
corn spread before the door

no· p̑e′wik̑io′skwi
beans spread before the door

k̭ä p̑e′wik̑o′skwi
wheat spread before the door

k̑u′ p̑e′wik̑o′skwi
nuts spread before the door

kow a·'waktsik̭ a·'łana
half-grown boys

kow a·'k̭ätsik̭ a·'łana
half grown girls

a·'wona·'weʻkwinte
even those whose roads go first

an he'cot̑ana
his house in

t̑eapk̑unan u'łton kwai''ilen teat̑un'onak·ä
his offspring jostling one another going out that it may be thus

an t̑ap̑owan i'tiwanana
his ceiling middle

te·'lik̭inan i'patcak̭·ä
prayer sticks fastened together with

ho' an e'lete'uk̭ä·
I for him prepared it

hoł ko'n a'ntecemana
sometime something desiring

t̑e'wusu p̑e'na ya·''kona
prayer words the ones that are finished

t̑e'ʻtsinan·e
winter

o'lo'ik̭änan·e
summer

yä'tcu p̑i'lan·e
the sequence of months

t̑o'na·wan ho' t̑e'k̑ohanan ce'man te'ak̭ä te'kwi
for you I daylight asking have lived when

lu'k̭ä yä'ton·e
this day

k̭es ho' tse''makwin mo'ła·kä k̭e·'si
now I thought have straightened now

yam ta'tcili te''ona
our father [having] the one who is

sai'yataca pi'łaci'wan·i
long horn bow priest

a'ntelia'na ho''i yä·k̑äna
impersonating a person having made himself

t̑o'n ho' a·'wona-e'latek̭ä
you I on your roads have passed

yam ta'tcili te''ona
your father [having] the one who is

k̑ä'pin ho''i
raw person

an o'naya·'nak̭ä p̑i''nan·e
his life-giving breath

an ła'ciak̭ä p̑i''nan·e
his old age breath

an k̭ä'cima p̑i''nane
his water breath

an t̑o'waconan p̑i''nan·e
his seed breath

an u'tenan p̑i''nan·e
his clothing breath

an t̑e'apk̑unan p̑i''nan·e
his offspring breath

an sa'wanik̭ä p̑i''nan·e
his power breath

an tse'makwin t̑sume p̑i''nan·e
his spirit strong breath

an kwahoł te'ni ha'lowilin p̑i''nan i'li te''ona
his everything good luck breath the one he has

p̑i''nan ai'ncemana
breath asking for

yam t̑e'huł k̭ä'łnakwi
my body cavity warm in

ho' p̑i''na ya'nhak̑una kwa'tok̭äna
I breath breath taking in

t̑o'na·wan ho' p̑i''nan te'liun·a k̭e·'si'
your I breath shall add to now

eł tcuwa t̑on yam a·'tatca·wa
let no one you your fathers'

p̑i''na ya'tcitanam·k̑ona
breath despise

yam ce'łnakwi
your body (in)

p̑i''nan a'na'kwa'to'k̭äna
breath drawing in

hoł yam yä'tok̭ä ta'tcu
somewhere you sun father

ceu o'neał kwai''inakwi
his road where it come out

o'neała te''tcina
(your) road reaching

i·'p̑iyat̑sumep̑a
holding hands strongly

i'yakna ło·'o
grasping one another tight

yam a·'wona ya·'t̑un'onak̭·ä
that your roads may be finished

t̑o''na·wan ło' p̑i''nan te'liun·a k̭e·'si
for you I breath shall add to now

e'pac t̑e'k̑ohanana
verily in the daylight

hon i'yanik̭inap̑a
we greeting one another

e'pac t̑e'k̑ohanana
verily in the daylight

hon i'yona ya·'k̭ana·wet̂i'ya'na
we (for one another) would that we might finish our roads

e'pac t̂ewusuk̭e·na·we
verily we shall pray (for this)

tewuna' hom a·'tatcu
finally my fathers

hom a·'tsita
my mothers

hom tca'we
my children

t̂o'na t̂e'k̂ohanan ya'niktcia't'u
to you life may it be given

t̂o'n a·'wona ya·t'u
your roads may they be fulfilled

t̂on a·'łacit'u
you may grow old

t̂o'na kwa ai'nak̭ä ya'niktciat'u
to you some killing may it be given

hoł yam yä'tok̭ä ta'tcu
somewhere your sun father

an o'naya·'nak̭ä o'neałan kwai'inakwi
his life giving road where it comes out

o'neał u'ła
(your) road stretching

t̂o''n a·wonaya·'t̂unt̂i'ya'na.
your roads may be fulfilled [would that].

Sayataca's Morning Chant[79]

And now indeed it has come to pass.
This past day,
I stood beside the water-filled ladder
Of my daylight fathers,
My daylight mothers,
My daylight children.
8 We who had stood there,
In the rain-filled room
Of our daylight fathers,
Staying quietly we came to day.
12 Now our dawn fathers,
Dawn old men,
Dawn youths,
15 Dawn boys,
Dawn old women,
Dawn matrons,
Dawn maidens,
Dawn girls,

no'miłtakwa
t̂e'cukwa yä'ton·e
yam t̂e'k̂ohanan a·'tatcu
yam t̂e'k̂ohanan a·'tsita
yam t̂e'k̂ohanan tca'we
a·'wan k̭ä'cima t̂a'pela
hon i·'łuwa-yu'łak̭ä.
hon i·łuwa-yu'ła'kona
yam t̂e'k̂ohanan a·'tatcu
a·'wan k̭äcima t̂e'li'to'kona
hon t̂i'nan ła'k̭i t̂e'wak̭änapk̭ä
hon t̂e'luwaiak̭' a·'tatc i'lap̂ona
t̂e'luwaiak̭' a·'łaci
t̂e'luwaiak̭' a·'tsawak̭i
t̂e'luwaiak̭' a·'waktsik̭i
t̂e'luwaiak̭' a·'wak̭' a·'łaci
t̂e'luwaiak̭' a·'mak̭i
t̂e'luwaiak̭' e'wactok̭i
t̂e'luwaiak̭' a·'k̭ätsik̭i

[79] At the first sign of dawn Sayataca with pekwin ascends to the roof of the house and unties the last knot in the counting string, as a sign that his year is ended. He chants the following prayer, stretching out the string at the end of each line. The prayer is afterwards repeated in the house.

Rising, standing at their sacred place,
Have come to meet us now.
My children,[80]
There in the rain-filled rooms
Of your daylight fathers,
Your daylight mothers
You have stayed throughout the night.
Finally, my children,
Make haste now,
Get ready now.
Yesterday our daylight fathers,[81]
Whoever of them wished to grow old,
Working on plume wands came to evening;
Working on prayer feathers they came to evening.
And furthermore our mothers,[82]
Whoever of them wished to grow old,
In order to add to the hearts of their ancestors,
Their children,[83]
Sitting weary by the fireplaces,
They came to evening.
With aching knees,
With sweat running down their faces,
With burned fingers,
Sitting wearily they came to evening.
And whoever else wished to grow old,
Preparing prayer meal [84]
They gave it to us.
Taking only that,
The plume wands they gave us,

yam t̑e'łaci·nakwi
i·łuwakna k̭e'atokna ho'n a·'wona-elatenapk̭ä k̭e·'si
hom tca'we
lałhok^{u} yam t̑e'k̑ohanan a·'tatcu
yam t̑e'k̑ohanan a·'tsita
a·'wan k̭ä'cima t̑eli'to'kona
t̑on t̑i'nan ła'k̭i t̑ewak̭änapk̭ä k̭e·si.
t̑e'wuna' tca'we
he'cik̭äna·we k̭e·si
ye'lete'ena·we k̭e·si.
ho'na·wan t̑e·'k̑ohanan a·'tatcu
hoł tcuwa łacina tse'makona

te'lik̭inan łeap̑a su'nhak̭änapk̭ä

la'cowan łeap̑a su'nahak̭änapk̭ä.

le'stiklea ho·na·wan a·'tsita
hoł tcuwa łacina tse'makona

yam a·'łacina·we
yam tca'we
a·wik̭ena telianakwi
yam a'klik̭äna'a
t̑i'na yu·'te'tcina su'nhak̭änapk̭ä.
ko·w o'ci łu'tsisona
ko·w ha'kwiłna kwai''ina

ko·w a'simoyałtco tca'pina
t̑i'na yu·''te'tcina su'nhak̭änapk̭ä.

hoł tcuwa ła'cina tse'makona

yam ha'lawo·tinan ye'lete'u'kona
hon a·'łea'up̑a.
u''si te''tci łe'ap̑a
ho' te'lik̭inan a·'łea'kona

---

[80] The other impersonators, including the Ca'lako, but not the Koyemci, who do not leave for six days. As a matter of fact, the dancing continues in all the houses until broad daylight. In Mrs. Stevenson's day this prayer closed the ceremonies.

[81] The priests and the men of the house and their close relatives (in 1927 several members of the clan of the house) make prayer sticks for all members of the Sayataca party.

[82] The women who cook for the feast, the women of the house, their blood relatives, members of their clan.

[83] Before the food is eaten in the night each of the seven impersonators takes a bit from each dish. All go out together and bury the food at Wide River, as an offering to a·łacina·we. (See M. C. Stevenson for a different account.) The food was not buried under the ladder in 1927.

[84] The gods are sprinkled with meal by all observers during their progress around the village in the afternoon of their entrance.

The food [85] which they cooked for us, and gave us to take along.
Taking only that,
We shall make our roads descend.[86]
With the song cycles of our fathers,[87] yonder,
Life-giving priests,
Life-giving p̂ekwins,
Life-giving bow priests,

We danced the night away.
Now at last, my children,
Hasten now,
Get ready now.
At the new year
All my fathers
With their precious plume wand
Appointed me.
There to the south
Following where come out the roads of my fathers,
Rain-makers, priests,

Even with my own poorly made plume wands,
I continued to give my fathers plume wands.
And when all the cycle of their months was at an end,
At the place called since the first beginning Ayayak̭a [88]
Meeting my fathers,

I gave them plume wands.
Their day count having been counted up,
There to the west,
Where my fathers' road comes in,
I continued to give them plume wands.
When all these days were past,

The one who is my father
Took hold of me;
Where he had laid a seat
Four times he sprinkled prayer meal upon it.

ho' i'tona'kona a·'hanełan'kona

u'ʻsi te'tci łe'ap̂a
hon o'neała p̂a'ni·k̂äna·wa
lałhokᵘ yam a·'tatcu

o'na·ya·'nak̭a a·'ciwan·i
o'na·ya·'nak̭a p̂e'kwi·we
o'na·ya·'nak̭ä a·'pi'ła·ciwan·i
a·'wan pi'clenan tena'pi'la na'k·ä
hon i'tałna t̂e'wak̂änapk̭ä.
t̂e'wuna' tca'we
he'cik̂äna·we k̭e·'si
ye'lete'ena·we k̭e·'si
hoł i'tiwana
homa le·w a·'tatcu
te'likina ya·'n a'k̭ä
hom a'nułana·wap̂a
li·'wan a'laho'ankwin ta'ʻna
yam a·'tatcu
u'wanam a·'ciwan·i
a·'wan k̂ä'cima o'neała· kwai''nai ta'pana
te'lik̭ina kɔ·'t̂i a'lewunante
yam a·'tatcu
ho' te'lik̭in a·'łea'u teak̭ä.

k̭es le·'na a·'wan ya'tcupi'la i·'te'tcik̭ä tea'ana
k̭ä·'k̂a tci'mik̂äk̭ä
ai'yaya·k̭ä le''anik̂änankwi
ho' yam a·'tatcu
a·'wona-elatena.
ho' te'lik̭inan a·'łeap̂a
a·'wa yä'lenan pi'lak̂äp̂a

li·'wan k̂älici'ankwin ta'ʻna
yam a·'tatcu
a·'wan o'neał i'nakwi
ho' te'lik̭inan a·'łean teak̭ä.
k̭es le'na a·'wan t̂e'mła t̂e'wak̭ä te'a'ana
ho'ma ta'tcu te''ona
ho'ma ya't̂ek̭ä
yam k̂äcima p̂ai'yan a'łkwi
a·'witela'ma
ha'lawo·tinan a·'witela'ma o'taʻ-witeʻ-yä'łtona

[85] The bowls of food from which the offerings are made during the night are immediately taken by the girls of the house to the houses of the impersonators, as a gift from the house. This is also done in the morning, when other gifts are also taken, a butchered sheep, piece of calico, and sometimes blankets.

[86] That is, go out. When they come in they "climb up" (the ladder).

[87] The choir of the medicine society that sang for them.

[88] The spring at which kohaito was made in 1927.

The top of my head
Four times he sprinkled.
Where his seat was laid
He took hold of me.
Presenting me to all the directions,
He made me sit down.
Taking his grandson,
Reed youth,
Within his body,
Four times he bored a hole going through.
Four times drawing toward him his bag of native tobacco.
He put his hand in.
Into the palm of his hand
Four times he measured out tobacco.
Into his body,
Four times he stuffed the mist.
He took his grandmother by the hand,
Four times inhaling he drew the mist through;
Into his body
He drew the misty breath,
Yonder on all sides
With mist he added to the hearts of his fathers.
He handed it to me.
Four times inhaling I made the mist pass through.
Into my body
I drew the mist.
Yonder on all sides.
With mist I added to the hearts of my fathers.

This is well:

That the rain makers may not withhold their misty breath,

With mist I added to their hearts.

When all this was at an end,
Then we greeted one another with terms of kinship:
Father, son; elder brother, younger brother; uncle, nephew; grandfather, grandson, ancestor, descendant.

ho'man ɔ'tsimowa'a
a·'witela'ma o'ta'wite'-yä'łtona
yam k̭̄ä'cima p̄ai'yanana
ho'ma ya't̄ek̭a
la'łhoku le'si te'kwi hom ta''k̭'äna hom a'nimłak̄uk̭ä
yam nan i'li te''ona
ła'k̭̄aia tsa'wak̭ te''ona
ai'ncełna'a
a·'witela'ma pu'suw a'mp̄ikwai'ina an'haitek̭ä
yam se'wekc wɔ'p̄on a·'witela'ma a''nułak̭ä
a'skwatona
yam a'stecokta'a
a·'witela'ma se'wekc wɔ'łak̭̄äp̄a i·'yanhaitek̭ä
ai'ncełna'a
a·'witela'ma ci'pololon u'tcuna
yam hot a'sana'k̭ä

a·'witela'ma ci'pololon cu'lulutina a'na'p̄ikwai'ik̭̄äk̭ä
yam ce'łnakwi
ci'pololon ya'nhekuna kwa'tok̭̄äk̭ä
lathoku lesi te'kwi yam a·'tatcu
ci'pololon a'kä a·'wike·na te'liak̭ä

ho'me łe'ak̭̄äkä
a·witela'ma ci'pololon cu'lulutina a'na'p̄ikwai'ik̭̄äk̭ä
yam cełnakwi
ho' ci'pololon a'letok̭ä
la'łhoku le'si te'kwi
yam a·'tatcu
ho' ci'pololon le'si te'kwi a·'wik̭e·na te'liak̭ä
k̭e'sic e'letap̄a
u'wanamik̭' a·'t̄e'ona
eł yam ci'pololon ya'nhakunan kwai''inan i·'witcemana a·'te-am·e t̄un'onak̭ä
ho' ci'pololon ak̭ä a·'wik̭e·na te'li-ak̭ä.
lu'k̭ak̄on le'n i·'te'tcap̄a
i'sk̄on hon i·'yanik̭̄ik̭ä

ta'tcu ta'le pa'pa su'we k̭ä'k̭ä k̭̄ä'se na'na to'cle a'li u'wak̭a

With this many words we greeted one another.
When all this was at an end
My father questioned me:

"Indeed now it seems you will have something to say, some word that is not too long
So finally, if you let me know it,

I shall know it for all time."

Thus my fathers spoke.

"Yes indeed it is so.
There to the south,
Following where my fathers' watery roads come forth

I have been asking for light for you.

Yesterday we reached the appointed time.
Perpetuating the rite of the one who is our father,
Sayataca, bow priest,
And once more giving him human form
I came out standing.
I looked to the north,
I looked to the west,
I looked to the south,
I looked to the east,
Hither, toward the place of dawn,
I saw four road going side by side.

Along the middle road.
Four times I sprinkled prayer meal.

Then I made the sound of the water-filled breath of the rainmaker priest of the north.
Taking four steps,
Four times striding forward,
The water filled woodpile
Of my daylight father
I stood beside.
My father
Four times sprinkled my head with prayer meal.

le'n hon i·'yanik̯ik̯ä

lu'k̯ak̄on i·'te'tcap̄a
ho' tatc i'li te'ona
i'te'kunak̯ä
e'm·a' i'mat kwa'hoł p̄e'na· te'yu·łanam·e p̄e'nan te'ak̄äna

t̄e'wuna' u''son hom t̄o' yu''ya·k̄äp̄a
u'hs ai'yu·ya·na
ho' t̄e'wanan te'k̄än·a
ho'm a·'tatcu a·'te'ona
le'ciantikwak̯ä
ma' i·'na miłte
li·'wan a'laho'ankwin ta''na
yam a·'tatcu
a·'wan k̄ä'cima o'neała kwai''ina tap̄ana
t̄o'na·wan ak̯' ho' t̄e'k̄ohanan ce'man te'ak̯ä
t̄e'cukwa yä'ton·e
k̯es hai'tokwin te''tcip̄a
yam tatc i'li te''ona

sai'yataca pi''łaci'wan·i te''ona
a'ntelia'na ho' ho'i-ya·k̄äna

ho' ye·'lana kwai''ik̄äk̯ä
ho' pi'cle t̄u'natik̯ä
ho' k̄älici t̄u'natik̯ä
ho a'laho t̄u'natik̯ä
ho t̄e'mak̄o t̄u'natik̯ä
k̄äłhok[u] t̄eluwankwin ta''na
a·'witena·na o'neała wo'k̄äp̄a ho' u'nat̄ik̯äk̯ä.
i'tiw o'neałkowa
yam ha'lawo·tinan·e
ho' a·'witela'ma o'ta'wite'-yä'łtok̯ä
i'sk̄on pi'cle u'wanam ci'wan an k̄ä'cima ya'nhakunan ho' te'ha·tok̯ä
a·'witela'ma te'tcunan ala'nana
a·'witela'ma ye'letelupna'na
yam t̄e'k̄ohanan tatci'li te''ona
an k̄ä'cima t̄a'pelakwi
ho ye'li u'łak̯ä
hom ta'tcu te''ona
yam ha'lawo·tinan·e
a·'witela'ma
ho'man o'tsimowa'a

His rain filled woodpile,
He sprinkled with meal.

After him,
I sprinkled my prayer meal on it.

This night
The thoughts of all my fathers,
Whatever they wished
When they appointed me with their precious plume wand,
I have fulfilled.
The breath of my father,
Sayataca, bow priest,
His life-giving breath
His breath of old age
His breath of waters,
His breath of fecundity,
His breath of seeds,
His breath of riches,
His breath of power,
His breath of strong spirit,
His breath of all good fortune whatsoever,—
Asking for his breath,
And into my body
Drawing his breath.
I add to your breath now.
And furthermore, the yellow clothing bundle of the priest of the north,
The blue clothing bundle of the priest of the west,
The red clothing bundle of the priest of the south,
The white clothing bundle of the priest of the east,
The many colored clothing bundle of the priest of the above,
The dark colored clothing bundle of the priest of the below,
All kinds of good fortune whatsoever,—
Asking for the breath of these,
And into my warm body
Inhaling their breath,
I add to your breath.
To this end, my children:
May you be blessed with light;
May your roads be fulfilled;
May you grow old;
Yonder to where the road of your sun father comes out,

o'ta'wite' yä'łtok̯ä
yam k̑äcima t̑a'pelakwi
yam ha'lawo·tinan·e
o'ta'wite'-yä'łtok̯ä
i'ste yä'lu
yam ha'lawo·tinan·e
ho' o'ta'wite' yä'łtok̯ä
lu'k̯ä t̑e'łinan·e
hom le'n a·'tatcu
hołko'n a'ntecemana
te'lik̯inan ya·nak̯ä
hom a'nułanapkowa
ho tse'makwi· mo'ła' k̯e·'si
yam tatc i'li te''ona
sai'yataca pi'łaciwan·i te''ona
an o'na·ya·'nak̯ä p̑i''nan·e
an ła'ciak̯a p̑i'nan·e
an k̑ä'cima p̑i''nan·e
an t̑e'apk̑unan p̑i''nan·e
an t̑o'waconan p̑i''nan·e
an u'tenan p̑i''nan·e
an sa'wanik̯a p̑i''nan·e
an tse''makwin t̑su'me p̑i''nan·e
kwa'hoł t̑e'mła te'n·i ha'lowilin p̑i''nan i'li te''ona
p̑i''nan ai'ncemana
yam ce'łnakwi
p̑i''nan a'letona
t̑o''na·wan ho' p̑i''nan te'liana·wa
le'stiklea pi'cle ci'wan an u'ten-he'konan łuptsina

k̯älici ci'wan an u'ten he'konan łi''ana
a'laho ci'wan an u'ten he'konan a'hona
t̑e'mak̑o ci'wanan u'ten he'konan k̑o'hana
i'yama ci'wan an u'ten he'konan t̑si·'lipana
ma'nila'ma ci'wan an u'ten-he'konan cik̯äna
kwa'hoł t̑e'mła te'n·i ha'lowilin te''ona
p̑i''nan yai'ncemana
yam t̑e'huł k̯äłnakwi
p̑i''nan ya'nhakunan kwa'tok̑äna
t̑o'na·wan ho' p̑i''nan te'liuna
t̑e'wuna' tca'we
t̑o'na t̑e'k̑ohanan ya'niktciatu
t̑o'n a·'wonaya·'tu
t̑on a·'łacitu
hoł yam yä'tok̯ä tatcu
an o'neała kwai''inakwi

6066°—32——49

May your roads reach
Together may your roads be fulfilled.

o'neała te''tcina
a'nsam·o
t̄o'n a·'wonaya·t̄untiyo'na.

NIGHT CHANT OF HEK̯ÄPA·KWE CA'LAKO

Host:[92] Father!
Ca'lako: Son!
Host: Elder brother!
Ca'lako: Younger brother!
Host: Uncle!
Ca'lako: Nephew!
Host: Grandfather!
Ca'lako: Grandson!
Host: Great-grandfather!
Ca'lako: Great-grandson!
Host:
This night
The ones who are our fathers
Masked god priests,
All the masked gods.
At their precious mountain,
Their precious lake,
Perpetuating what has been since the first beginning,
Have assumed human form.
Carrying your waters,
Carrying your seeds,
Making your roads come forth.
Making your roads come hither,
You have passed us on our roads
This night.
We see you,
From the soles of your feet
Even to the crowns of your heads,
Clothed in all fine things
You have passed us on our roads.
Looking at you
We know you have passed us on our roads.
Surely because you have something to say, some word that is not too long,
You have passed us on our roads.
If you let us know that

ta'tcumo
ta'lemo
pa'pamo
su'wemo
k̯ä'k̯ämo
k̄ä'semo
na'namo
a'lemo
to'clemo
u'wak̯ämo

lu'k̯ä t̄e'łinan·e
hon a·'tatc i'lap̄ona
kok̄wa·'ciwan·i
ko'ko te'mła
yam yä'la ya·'na
yam k̄ä'watulin ya·'na
yam ko''nhoł tci'mik̄ä'kona te'li-a'na
ho''i ya·'k̄äna
yam k̄ä'cim i·'łeana
yam t̄o'waconan i·'łeana
o'neał kwai''ik̄äna
o'neał i'k̄äna
ho''na t̄on a·'wona-e'latenapk̯ä.
lu'k̯ä t̄ełinan·e
t̄o''na hon u'natik̄änap·k̯ä
we'kwikwinte
o'tsimowakwi te''tcina
kwa'hoł te'mła łe'a i·'yante'tcina
ho''na t̄on a·'wona-e'latenapk̯ä.
t̄o''na hon a·'wunatik̄äna·wap̄a
ho''na t̄ona·'wona-e'latenapk̯ä.

i'me' hintcoł kwahoł p̄e'nan teyułanam·e p̄e'nan te''onak̯ä

ho''na t̄on a·'wona-e'latenapk̯ä.
u''son ho''na t̄on ai'yu·'ya·k̄äna·-wap̄a

[92] The host sits opposite the impersonator, and together they smoke a cigarette of native tobacco, and passing the cigarette back and forth, exchange terms of relationship. There are certain peculiarities in the terms used. Talemo: tale, brother's son, any male whose father belongs to my clan, hence, "my son," man speaking. There is no term for son. tca'le, "child" is use in describing a relationship; tsawak̯: "youth," in referring to a person. This is not a term of relationship. Alemo: used only in this connection. Ordinarily nana is used reciprocally for grandfather, grandson. Toclemo, uwak̯ämo used only in this connection. There are no equivalents. Possibly these, and alemo, are obsolete terms. They do not always appear in the same order in the texts. (See pp. 713, 732.) The vocative suffix, too, is used only thus. A man, in receiving a present, always in receiving a gift of tobacco, will say tatcumo or papamo, to which the answer is talemo or suwemo. To a woman he sometimes says kawumo (elder sister) or kukumo (father's sister). She answers hanimo (younger brother or sister) or ta'lemo (brother's son).

Thinking of that, we shall always live,
Is it not so?
Guests: It is so.
Ca'lako:
Now, indeed, it has come to pass.
At the New Year
All my fathers [93]
Prepared precious plume wands.
When they were ready
With sacred words,
They commissioned them,
When our sun father
Had gone in to sit down at his ancient place,
After a blessed night
They came to day.
Next day
When our sun father

Coming out standing to his ancient place,
Passed us on our roads,
Then our fathers
Four times drew toward them
The plume wands commissioned with their prayers.
The one who is our father,
K̭äwulia P̄autiwa,
With their plume wands.
Four times they held fast.
Saying, "Let it be now."
Carrying his fathers' plume wands,
He made his road come forth.
Over to the south
He made his road go.
Thinking, "Let it be here,"
Perpetuating what has been since the first beginning,
Once more he assumed human form.
Carrying his father's plume wands
He made his road come forth.
Into Itiwana
He made his road enter.
Four times he made his road go round,
Then into Itiwana

u''si tse''makuna
hon t̄e'wanan a·'tek̭än·a.
hatci'.
hatci'.

e'ma no'·miłtakwa
i'tiwana
le· hon a·'tatc i'lap̄ona
te'lik̭ina· ya·'na ye'lete'unapk̭ä.
ye'lete'una
t̄ewusu ya'nułana·wap̄a

ho''na·wan yä'tok̭ä ta'tcu
yam t̄e'łacinakwi
i·'muna kwa'tok̭äp̄a
t̄e'łinan k̄ɔ'kci
a·'wan t̄ewak̭ä.
t̄e'wap̄ yä'tone
hon yä'tok̭ä tatc ilap̄ a·'te'ona
yam t̄e'łacinakwi
ye·'lana kwai''ik̭äna
ho'n a·'wona-e'latap̄a
hon a·'tatc i'lap̄ona
yam te'lik̭inan t̄e'wus ya'nułanapkowa
a'witela'ma a'nułana

yam tatc ilap̄ a·'te'ona
k̭ä'wulia p̄a'ut̄iwa
te'lip̄inanak·ä
a'witela'ma ya't̄en-at̄su'mek̭änapk̭ä
k̭ä·'k̭i k̭e·'si le'anak̭'äp̄a
yam a·'tatcu
a·'wan te'likinan i·'łeana
o'neałan kwai'ik̭äna
li·'wan a'lahoa'nkwin ta''na
o'neał a·'k̭äk̭ä.
hoł li·'ła le'hatina
yam ko'nhoł tci'mik̭äkowa te'-lia'na
tci'm'on ho''i ya·'k̭äna
yam a·'tatcu
a·'wan te'lik̭inan ya·'na i·'łeana
o'neałan kwai·'ik̭äna
i'tiwanakwi
o'neał kwa'tok̭äna
a'witela'ma o'neał u'lapk̭äna

i'tiwanakwi

[93] The priests of the council: The three priests of the north, the head priests of the east, west, and south, and the p̂ekwin.

He made his road enter
Wherever his children's roads come out,[94]
His precious plume wands
He laid down.
After he had laid them down,
To his own country
He made his road go forth.
Then our fathers [95]
Drawing toward them their plume wands,
To their own houses
Made their roads return.
Now this many days
Eagerly they have awaited the time.
Among all their ladder descending children [96]
They looked about.
And though we were ignorant
(They sent for us [97])
Then those who are our fathers
Passed us on their roads.
When they passed us on their roads
Our fathers drew toward them
Their father's plume wand.
Drawing it toward them
They handed it to us
That we might be the ones to impersonate our father,
Ca'lako, bow priest;
For this with their plume wand
They held us fast.
Carrying their plume wand
We made our roads come forth.
To our houses,
Our roads reached.
This many are the days
We have eagerly awaited the time

When the moon who is our mother,

o'nealan kwa'tok̭äna
lałhokᵘ yam t̄eapk̄una a·'wan
o'neała· kwai·'inapkowa
te'likina· ya·'na wo·'tałak̄uk̭ä.
wo·'tała'k̄una
yam u'loʻnakwi

o'neał a·'k̭äp̄a
hon a·'tatc i'laop̄na
yam te'likinan aʻn-ułuna

yam he'co t̄akwi
o'neałan te''tcik̭äna
le'si t̄ewanane
a'nt̄sumeʻna t̄ewanan a·'teap̄ä

le· łe'tsilon p̄a'ni·nan tca'we

a·'wun-u'lapnapk̭ä
t̄e'kwante te'atip̄a

hon a·'tatc i'lap̄ona
ho'na a·'wona-elatek̭ä
ho'na a·'wona-elatep̄a
hon a·'tatc i'lap̄ona
yam a·'tatcu
a·'wan te'lik̭inan a'ʻn-ułanapk̭ä
a'ʻn-ułana
ho'na łe'ak̭änapk̭ä.
yam tatc'ili te'ona
ca'lako pi''łaci'wan·i
a'ntelia'na hon ho'i teat̄un'onak̭·ä
te'lik̭inan a'k·ä ho'na ya'tena-t̄su-mek̭änap̄k̭ä.
te'lik̭inan i·'łeana
o'neała kwai''ik̭äna
yam he'cot̄akwi
o'neała te''tcik̭äna
le'si t̄e'wanan·e
a'nt̄sumeʻna
hon t̄e'wanan a·'teak̭ä.
hon ya'onak̭a tsit i'lap̄ a·'te'ona

[94] At the entrances to the kivas.
[95] The dance directors or w·we of the kivas.
[96] Human children.
[97] The two impersonators, elder and younger brother. They take turns in wearing the mask. Both intone the prayer.

Yonder in the west,
Had grown to maturity.[98]
Carrying our fathers' precious [99] plume wand,
To which we had fastened our own common [1] plume wand,
Carrying these plume wands,
Yonder to the south,
We made our roads go.
At the place called since the first beginning
Snow hanging,
We met our fathers on their roads.
Where their watery roads come forth [2]
We stood in the doorway.
There we gave our fathers plume wands,
We gave them prayer feathers,
We gave them rain-bringing cigarettes,
We gave them prayer meal.
Making their days,
Throughout the sequence of their months
Eagerly we awaited our time.

Whenever the time came,
Yonder to the south,
Throughout the sequence of the months of summer,

Wherever the roads of our fathers come out,
We gave them plume wands.
When all their springs were at an end,
Our fathers,
For that which was soon to be
Met all together in their water-filled room.
With the flesh of their mother,

li·'wan ḵä'lici a'nkwin ta''na
ho''i ya·'ḵäḵa tea'ana
yam a·'tatcu
a·'wan te'liḵinan ya·'na
yam te'liḵinan ci'mato a'mpatcu'kowa
te'likinan i·'łeana
lehoku a·'lahoa'nkwin ta''na
hon o'neała a·'ḵänapḵä.
ḵä·'ḵä tci'miḵäḵä
u·'hana'a le'anak̄äna

yam a·'tatcu
hon a·'wona-e'latenapḵä.
a·'wan ḵä'cim o'neałan kwai''ina
hon i·'łuwan i'k̄oskwiḵä
isk̄ɔn yam a·'tatcu
hon te'liḵinan a·'łeana
la'cowa a·'łeana
ḵä'cima p̄o'ne a·'łeana

ha'lawo·tinan a·'łeana
a·'wan t̄e'wanan a'cna
a·'wan ya'tcu p̄i'lana

a·'wan t̄e'wanan a'nt̄sume'na
hon t̄e'wanan a·'teaḵä.
a·'teaḵätekwin li'wan a'laho'a'nkwin ta''na
yätcu p̄i''lan·e
ɔ'lo'iḵ'anan·e
yam a·'tatcu
a·'wan o'neała kwai''ina'kowa

hon te'liḵinan a·'łeanapḵä
a·'wan ḵä'nakwai'ina i·'te'tcap̄a

hon a·'tatc i'lap̄ona
ḵe'sti te'at̄un'onak·ä
yam ḵä'cima t̄e'li'tokwi
te'młamo i·'yona-e'latenapḵä.
yam tsit i'lap̄ a·'te'ona

[98] The 10 plantings at the springs to the south are generally at the full moon. If the moon is waxing at the New Year there may be 11 plantings (two at toloknana in midsummer). The first and last plantings may be when the moon is 6 days old. See p. 712, note.

[99] Literally "finished," i. e., with the paint brought by the priests from the underworld. This is part of the sacred paraphernalia of the priests and forms part of their altars at seasons of retreat. A tiny bit is scraped off and mixed with other paint.

[1] Painted with ordinary paint.

[2] At springs

Cotton woman,
Even a roughly made cotton thread,
A soiled cotton thread,
And with beads,
Even if only a single bead
Borrowed somewheres from among all the village branches,[3]
And with the pollen of their fathers,
Their mothers,
Their children,
The different kinds of corn,
And with turquoise,
Keeping it in their hearts,
They gave their day count human form.
Then our fathers,
Sayataca, bow priest,
Molanhakto,[4] house chief priest,

Passed their fathers on their road.
The day count to which they had given human form,
Four times drawing toward them,
With their day count
They took firm hold of their fathers.
Carrying the day count,
They made their roads come forth.
To their houses
Their roads reached.
Saying, "Let it be now,'
Carrying the plume wands which they had prepared,
Carrying their father's day count,

They made their roads go forth.
There to the south,
We made our roads go.
At the place called since the first beginning
Ants-go-in [5]
We passed our fathers on their roads.

p̄i'tsem o'ḳä
an ci'nan·e
p̄i'le ko'tinapte
p̄i'le ci'ḳänapte
la'łhok^{u} le·w łu'walan ya'tciwe
hoł yam t̄o'p̄acołi
ło''o i·'lopi'kowa

yam a·'tatcu

yam a·'tsita
yam tca'we
t̄o'wa a·'wan o'neaw a'kä
ło·'o ak·ä
i·'wiḳena·wa
yälanan ho'i ya·'ḳäḳatea'ana

hon a·'tcia ta'tcili a·'te'ona
sai'yataca p̄i''łaci'wan·i
mo'lanha'kto ḳä'kwemos·i ci'wan·i
yam a·'tatcu
a·tc a·'wona-e'lateḳa
yam yä'lenan ho''i ya·'ḳänapkowa
a'witela'ma a·'ʻnaułana
yam a·'tcia ta'tci·li te''ona
yä'lenan a'k·ä
a·'tcia t̄su'me yä't̄enapḳä.
yä'lenan i·'łeana
o'neała kwai'iḳäna
yam he'cot̄akwi
o'neała te'tciḳäna
ḳä·ḳi ke·'si' le'anaḳäp̄a
yam te'liḳinan ye'lete'ukowa i·'łeana
yam a·'tatcu
a·'wan yä'lenan i·'łeana
o'neała kwai''iḳäna
lehok^{u} a'laho'a'nkwin ta'ʻna
hon o'neał a·'ḳänapḳä.
ḳa·'ḳä tci'miḳäḳä

ha'lon kwa'tona
yam a·'tatcu
hon a·'wona-e'latenapḳä.

[3] Zuñi is the center, the trunk of the tree, the other pueblos are the branches. The Zuñis do not classify the Hopis with the "village people," as they call the eastern pueblos.

[4] "Carrying squash (round things) on the head," the father of the Koyemci. The name is characteristically ambiguous, referring both to the knobs on the mask and the squash seeds in the knobs. All the Koyemci are called Molanhaktu in songs and prayers. Koyemci is merely a nickname. They are distinguished by name, Molanhaktu a wan atcu, molanhaktu a wan pekwin, molanhaktu ocotsi, etc.

[5] The ceremony no longer takes place at this spring, which is at the foot of Corn Mountain, and at the base of the Ḳäkima, but at Ayayakya, on the west side of Ḳäkima Canyon. (See p. 712 for the names of the springs visited.)

There we gave them our father's plume wands;
There with our father's day count
We counted the sequence of the days.
This many days,
Anxiously we have awaited the time.
Yonder to the west [6]
We gave our fathers plume wands.

When the number of their days was at an end
For that which was soon to be
We again prepared plume wands.
When our plume wands were ready,
There to the west,
At the place called since the first beginning
Village of the masked gods,[7]
Where the gray mountain stands,
And the blue mountain,
Where their altar stands above,
Where their altar lies beneath,
Where our fathers abide,
We met them on their roads.
Where their water filled doorway opens outward,
We stood in the doorway.
There where our fathers' road comes out,
At their water-filled woodpile,
Four times we sprinkled prayer meal inside.

Four times stepping down
Standing we came in.
Coming in standing,
There our fathers,
(Our ancestors) rain old men,
We passed on their roads.
(Our ancestors) rain old women
We passed on their roads.
We saw them.
Not one of them was missing;

i'sk̂ɔn yam a·'tatcu
hon te'lik̭inan a·'łeana
yam a·'tatcu
a·wa yä'lenan isk̂ɔn a'kä
hon yälenan p̂i'lenapk̭a.
le'si t̂e'wanan·e
a'nt̂sume'na
hon t̂e'wanan a·'teak̭ä.
li·'wan k̂ä'lici'a'nkwin ta''na
yam a·'tatcu
hon te'likinan a·'łeana
a·'wan yä'lenan i·'te'tcap̂ k̭e'sti te'atun'onak̭ä

t̂em t̂a te'lik̭ina· ye'lete'uk̭ä.
te'lik̭ina ye'lete'una

li·'wan k̂ä'lici'a'nkwin ta''na
k̭ä·'k̂ä tci'mik̂äkä

ko'łuwala·wa
yä'lan lɔ'k̂äna
yä'lan łi''ana
t̂e'łaci·na yä'łto
t̂e'łacina pa'li
yam a·'tatcu
t̂i'nan łak̂ikwi
hon a·'wona-elatek̭ä.
a·'wan k̂ä'cima a'we'nan kwai''ina
hon ye'li-k̂oskuna
i'sk̂ɔn yam a·'tatcu
a·'wan o'neałan kwai''ina
a·'wan k̂ä'cima t̂a'pela'a
yam ha'lawo·tinan·e
a·'witela'ma o'ta'wite' kwa'to-k̂äk̭ä
a·'witela'ma we'p̂iyałto
ho' ye·'lana kwa'tok̂äk̭ä
ho' ye·'lana kwa'tok̂äna
i'sk̂ɔn yam a·'tatcu
k̂ä'cim a·'wɔts a·'łaci
hon a·wona'elatek̭ä
k̂ä'cim a·'wok̭' a·'łaci
hon a·'wona-e'latena
hon a·'wunatik̂äk̭ä
eł kwa tcu'wa i'metcam·e

[6] The plantings to the west (i. e., southwest) are at intervals of 10 days. They are not at springs. They are at the following places: Panitaime, anelawan tekyapoa, suskan acoktan·e (suma'cokta), akohana tinakwi. The last planting, at ak̭ohana t̂inakwi, is on the fortieth day, the day the Koyemci enter.

[7] The ceremony takes place at Ca'lako house, an inclosure on the west side of the hill surmounted by white rocks. The Ca'lako wo'le of each kiva impersonates the "father."

At the blessed place where they were all gathered together,
We saw them.
Then with our prayer meal
Four times we sprinkled the tops of their heads.

This we did to all.
When this was at an end,
The one who is our father,
Overhearing us,
Prepared rain seats for us.

His prayer meal
Four times he sprinkled upon us.

Following him
Our father's rain seats
We stood beside.
Then the one who is our father
Took hold of us.
Presenting us to all the directions he made us sit down.
We sat quietly;
We waited for his words.
Our father four times drew toward him
The rain cigarette which he had prepared.
Taking his grandmother by the hand,
He made her sit in the doorway.
Four times the mist passed through.

With the mist,
We added to the hearts of our fathers,
Our beloved ones of all the directions,
Asking for the waters
Of our fathers of all the directions

When all this was at an end,
Into our bodies
We drew the misty breath.
Drawing in our breath
With the terms of kinship
We greeted one another:
Father, son; elder brother, younger brother; uncle, nephew; grandfather, grandson; great-grandfather, great-grandson,
Thus we greeted one another.

t̄e'mła ha'p̄ona k̄ɔ'kcikwi

hon a·'wunatk̬ik̄ää
i'sk̄ɔn yam ha'lawo·tinan·e
a·'witela'ma a·'wan ɔ'tsimowa'kowa
a·'witela'ma ɔ'ta'wite' ła'kuna
lu'k̬äk̄on i·'te'tcik̬ä
lu'k̬äk̄on i·'te'tcap̄a
ho''no tatc i'li te''ona
tomt ha'tian ha'nłina
yam k̄ä'cima p̄ai'yan e'lete'uk̬ä te'kwi
yam ha'lawo·tinan·e
a·'witela'ma ho'na o''ta'wite'-u'łak̬ä
i'ste yä'lu
yam ta'tcona p̄aiyan a'łkwi
ho'no ye'li-u'łak̬ä
hon tatc i'li te''ona
ho'no ya' t̄ek̬ä.
le'se te'kwi ta''k̄äna ho'no a'nimła'k̄uk̬ä.
hon i'mełak̄uk̬ä.
hon se'wekc i·'cokyak̬ä.
hon tatc i'li te''ona

yam k̄ä'cima p̄o'ne e'lete'u'kowa
a·'witila'ma a''n-u'łak̬ä
yam hot̄ as·a''nak̬ä

a'mim k̬o'sk̬uk̬ä
a·'witela'ma ci'pololon a'na'pikwai'ik̬ä
la'łhok^u le'si te'kwi
yam tse'mak-t̄e'łakwi'kowa
yam a·'tatcu
ci'pololon a'kä
a·'wik̬e·na te'lia·na
la'łhok^u le'si te'kwi
yam a·'tatcu k̄ä'cima yai'ncemana
lu'k̬ak̄on i·'te'tcap̄a
yam t̄e'hułkwi ci'pololon ya'nhakun kwatok̄äk̬ä
ya'nhakuna kwa'tok̄äna
yam hon a'kä i·'yanik̬inap̄ona
i'sk̄ɔn hon a'k̬ä i·'yanik̬inapk̬ä.
ta'tcu ta'le pa'pa su'we k̬ä'k̬ä k̄ä'se na'na to'cle a'le u'wak̬amo hon a'k̄'i'yanik̬inapk̬äo

When all this was at an end,
The one who is my father
Questioned me:
"Yes, now, even now,
You have passed us on our roads.
Surely because of some words of our fathers,
Spoken at the New Year,
Because of some words of importance, some word that is not too long,
You have passed us on our roads.
So finally, if you let us know that,

Thinking always of that,
We shall pass our days."
Thus our father spoke to us, did he not? [8]
—Even so.—

"Yes, indeed it is true.
This many days
Throughout the winter,
Throughout the summer,
There to the south,
We brought you plume wands,
Wherever your roads come out,
Though our plume wands were but poorly made,
We brought you plume wands,
We brought you prayer feathers,
We brought you rain cigarettes.
When all this was at an end,
Now for that which is soon to be
We have passed you on your roads."
Thus we said to our father, did we not?
—Even so.—
When we had spoken thus
(Our father spoke.)
"Indeed, these are your days.
Now that we have remembered your days
You have come to us,
My two children."
Saying this,
Our father took hold of us.

From the soles of our feet
To the crowns of our heads,

lu'k̭at̆on i·'te'tcap̆a
hom tatc i'li te''ona
li'łt̆on i'te'kunak̭ä:
e·h ma' la'k̭äma
ho''na t̆on a·'wona-e'latek̭ä
i'me' la'lik i'tiwana hon a·'tatc i'lap̆ona

ime' a·'wan hi'ntcoł kwa'hoł p̆e'nan teyułanam·e p̆e'nan te''ona'ka
ho''na t̆on a·'wona-e'latek̭ä
t̆e'wuna' u'son ho'na t̆on ai'yu·'ya·k̭äna
u's i·'tse'makuna
hon t̆e'wanan a·'tek̭än·a
hon tatc i'li te''ona
hatc ho''na le'anikwana
hatci'
ma' no'milte
le'si t̆e'wanane
t̆e''tsinan·e
ɔ'lo'ik̭änan·e
li·'wan a'laho'a'nkwin ta''na
t̆o'na hon te'lik̭ina· a·'łeak̭ä.
t̆o''na·wan o'neała· kwai·'na'kowa
ko'ti te'lik̭inan a'lewunant·e

t̆o''na hon te'lik̭ina· a·'łeak̭ä.
t̆o''na hon la'cow a·'leak̭ä
t̆o''na hon k̭ä'cima p̆o'n·e· a·'łeak̭ä.
k̭es le'na i·'te'tcap̆a
k̭e'sti te'atun'onak̭ä
t̆o''na hon a·'wona-e'latek̭ä.
yam tatc i'li te''ona
hatc hon le'anikwak̭ä.
hatci'
hon le'anikwak̭a
e·ha
ma' t̆o'na ho'n t̆e'wanan t̆o'a'ni
hon t̆e'wanan ai'yu·ya·na a·'teakwi

ho'na ton a·'wona-e'latek̭ä
hom tca'w a·tci
hom tatc i'li te''ona
ho'na le'anikwana
ho'na ya't̆ek̭ä
we'kwikwinte
ɔ'tsimowakwinte

[8] The impersonator turns to his alternate for corroboration. He answers, "Hatci'."

Clothing us with all things needful,
He made us ready.
When he had made us ready
Four times
With our cover of thin clouds [9] he fitted us.
When he had reached the end, (he spoke):
"This is all.
With plain words
You have passed us on our road.
When our sun father
Has gone in to sit down at his ancient place,
And when our night fathers,
Our mothers,
Over their ancient place,
Have raised their dark curtain,
All together
Our daylight fathers,
Our mothers,
Our children,
We shall pass on their roads."

Thus our father spoke to us,
Did he not?
—Even so.—
"Yonder, our daylight fathers,
Our children,
All of us shall pass on their roads."

Thus our father said to us.

Now that we four times have gone ahead
Our fathers,
Even those with snow upon their heads,
With moss upon their faces,
No longer upright but leaning on canes,
Even all of them
Will pass us on our roads.
And furthermore the women,
Even those who are with child,
Holding another on the cradle,
With another going before

kwa'hoł t̄e'mła łe'a i·'yante'tcina
ho''na an e'lete'uk̯ä
ho''na an e'lete'una
a·'witela'ma
ho''na su'lahaiyan p̄o'yan i·'yante'tcik̯ä
i·'yante'tcik̄'äna

le·'wi
yu·''he·to p̄e'nan a'k̯ä
ho''na t̄on a·'wona-e'latek̯ä
hon yä'tok̯ä tatc i'lap̄a te''ona
yam t̄e'łaci·nakwi
i·'muna kwa'tok̄äp̄a
hon t̄e'łiak̯' a·'tatc i'lap̄ona
a·'tsit̄ i'lap̄ona
yam t̄e'łaci·nakwi
ko·w a'lan k̄eatok̯ä te'a
k̯es t̄e'młamo
t̄e'k̄ohanan yam a·'tatcu
yam a·'tsita
yam tca'we
k̯es t̄e'młamo hona ·'wona-e'latenat̄un'ona teak̯äna
hon tatc i'li t̄e''ona
hatc ho'na le'anikwak̯ä.
hatci'
le'hok[u] yam t̄e'k̄ohanan a·'tatcu
hom tcawe
t̄e'mła hon a·'wona-e'latenat̄un'ona te'ak̄än·a
hon tatc i'li te''ona
ho'na le'anikwap̄a
a·'witela'ma
hon o'neał e'·k̄uk̯ä tea'ana
ho''na·wan a·'tatcu
kow u'tcinan ha'ktop̄a

po'hetci a'wiconap̄a
e'lemaknan i·'natina
t̄ap̄owan sati'li
k̯es t̄e'młamo
ho'n a·'wona-e'latena·wa.
a·'wok̯' a·'teo'na
ya'nine·nante
t̄o'p̄a łe'mana yälto i·'k̄eckuna
t̄op̄ e''k̄uk̯ä

[9] The buckskin caps worn by the Ca'lako impersonators. They are the same as those worn by war chiefs. In the war dance the scalp is called k̄äcima p̂o'yane (water cover).

Leading one by the hand
Even all of them
Will come out to meet their fathers
Their mothers
Their children.

Thus speaking to us,
Our father took hold of us.

Presenting us to all the directions

He made us arise.
On our heads
Four times he sprinkled prayer meal,

On his rain-filled woodpile
He sprinkled prayer meal for us.

After him,
We sprinkled our prayer meal.
Then the one who is our father
His water-filled woodpile
He sprinkled for us.
Four times sprinkling prayer meal going out,
Stepping up four times,
We came out standing.
Yonder toward all directions we looked.
Hither toward Halona Itiwana,[10]
We saw four roads going side by side.
Along the middle path sprinkling prayer meal before us,
Hither we took our way.
At the places,[11] called since the first beginning
Great lake,
Hanłipinkya,
Cliff house,
Last spring,
Middle spring,
Water-cress spring,
Kolowisi's house,

t̄op i·p̄iyana
ḳes t̄e'młamo
yam a·'tatcu
yam a·'tsita
yam tca'we
hon a·'wona-e'latenan kwai''ina
hon tatc i·'li te''ona
ho''na le'anikwana
ho''na ya' t̄eḳä
la'łhokᵘ le'si te'kwi
ho'na ta''k̄äna
hon ana'-e'lemak̄äḳä
yam ha'lawo·tinan·e
ho'n ɔ'tsimowa'kowa
a·'wi·tela'ma
o'ta'wite' yä'łtona
yam ha'lawo·tinan·e
yam k̄ä'cima t̄a'pelakwi
ho''nan ɔ'ta'wite' u'laḳä
i'ste yä'lu
yam ha'lawotinan ɔt'a'wite' u'łana
hon tatc i'li te'ɔona
yam k̄ä'cima t̄a'pelakwi
ho''nan ɔ'ta'wite' kwai''ik̄äkä
t̄em t̄a yam ha'lawo·tinan a·'wite-la'ma ɔ'ta'wite' kwai''ik̄äna
a·'witela'ma we'pi yä'łto
hon ye·'lana kwai''ik̄äna
la·lhokᵘ le'si te'kwi hon t̄unatiḳä

k̄ä'łhokᵘ ha'lona i'tiwanakwi
a·'witena·'na hon o'neała u'natiḳä-napḳä.
i'tiwa o'nakowa yam ha'lawo·tinan ɔ'ta'wite' e''k̄una
k̄äł hon a·'wona·k̄äp̄a
ḳä·'k̄i tci'mik̄äḳä

k̄ä'tułana
ha'nłipinḳä
he''ip̄atciwa
k̄ä'napa'łto
k̄ä'na'i'tiwa
p̄i'k̄aia
ko'lo·wisi k̄ä'kwe'a

[10] The places at which they stopped, after leaving Kołuwala'wa in their wanderings in search of the center of the world. There are 29; two, k̄äpkwenakwi (water coming out, Ojo Caliente) and watsita'nakwi (dog place), are omitted from the present version. They follow Rainbow Spring. The emergence myth (and Sayataca's talk) give the last three springs as t̄owa yallakwi (Corn Mountain), matsakya hepatina, k̄olink̄aiakwi etsakya hepatina (sulphur spring, commonly called hepatina). The present account gives the three places where the impersonators deposit plumes on their way in: White rocks; Where the masked dancers come out (Grease Hill); Hepatina.

[11] Cushing translates this "The middle ant hill of the world." It is a bracketing of two names by which Zuñi is known. Halonawa in a more restricted sense refers to the ruin on the south bank of the river.

The other Water-cress spring,
Dripping spring,
Bending grass,
Ashes spring,
Cat tail spring,
Rainbow spring,
Ca'lako place,
Snow hanging,
Rock wedge,
Painted rock,
Poison weed spring,
Mesa wall spring,
Toloknana,
Evil smelling water,
Sack of flour hanging,
Bluebird place,
Where ants go in,
White rocks sitting,
Where the masked dancers come out,
Sulphur spring, otherwise called hepatina,
(At all these places),
We passed our fathers on their roads.
Wherever their rain-filled doorways open outward,
Where their roads come out,
Four times we gave them prayer meal.
Yonder toward all directions we looked,
Hither, toward Halona Itiwana,
Our daylight fathers' fourfold road we saw.

And now, at last, it seems,
Here we shall take our road,
Thus we said to one another.
Along the middle road four times sprinkling prayer meal before us
Hither we took our way.
Our daylight fathers'
Our daylight mothers' watery roads coming out,
We saw.
Sprinkling prayer meal
Where come forth the watery roads
Of our daylight fathers,
We sat down in the doorway,[12]
Four times rising
We came in.

t̑o'p̑a p̑i'k̯aia
k̯ä't̑sik̯äna
p̑o'cowa
lu·'k̯äna
to'soluna k̯aia
a'mitolank̯äna
ca'lakona.
u'hana'a
a''łapatsi'a
a''t̑sina·wa
p̑i'cuk'aia
k̯ä'nuła
to'loknana
k̯ä'tetci'a
o'p̑ump̑i'ya
ai'yaya·k̯ä
ha'lonkwa'ton
a'k̑ohana t̑inawa.
ko'm kwai'ik̯ate'a

k̑o'lin k̯aia e'tsak̯äna he'patina

yam a·'tatcu
hon a·'wona-e'latenapk̯ä.
a·'wan k̯ä'cim a'wenan kwai''ina'a
yam ha'lawo·tinan a·'witela'ma
o'neała kwai''ina
hon a·'wanhaitek̯ä

la'łhoku le'si te'kwi hon t̑u'natik̯ä

k̯ä'łhoku ha'lona i'tiwanakwi
t̑e'k̑ohanan yam a·'tatcu
a·'wan o'neała a·'witena·na a·'wan o'neała hon u'natik̯äk̯ä
i'me' honkwa
t̑a li·'łno hon a·'wana·'k̯än·a
le'con i·'yantikwana
yam ha'lawo·tinan i'tiwa o'nakowa a·'witela'ma ɔ'taʻwiteʻ e'ʻkuna
k̯äł hon a·'wona·k̯ä
t̑e'k̑ohanan yam a·'tatcu
yam a·'tsita
a·'wan k̯ä'cima o'neałan kwai''ina
hon u'natik̯änapk̯ä.
yam ha'lawo·tinan·e
yam t̑e'k̑ohanan a·'tatcu
a·'wan k̯ä'cima o'neała kwai''ina
hon i·'t̑ina k̑o'skwik̯ä
a·'witela'ma
hon i·'łuwakna kwatona

[12] The mask, borne aloft on a pole, with embroidered blankets held out by hoops concealing the bearer, is set down outside, while the two impersonators bless the house. When they are finished the mask is brought in and set down beside the altar while the prayer is chanted.

The water-filled room of our daylight fathers,
Our daylight mothers,
Our daylight children,

Four times we rooted all about: [13]

The north root,
The west root,
The south root,
The east root,
The upper root,
The lower root—
This we brought to an end.
When this was at an end,[14]
Our daylight father,
To where his rain seat had been spread
Four times he threw out prayer meal.
Our daylight father took hold of us;

Presenting us to all directions
He made us sit down.
We sat down quietly
We waited for his words.
Our daylight father
Four times drew toward him his water roll.
Taking his grandmother by the hand
He made her sit in the doorway.
Four times into his body
He drew the mist.
With mist he added to the hearts of his fathers.
That so long as we enjoy the light of day we may greet one another as kindred
We now greeted one another.
Fathers,[15]
Sons;
Elder brother, younger brother; uncle, nephew; grandfather, grandson; great-grandfather, great-grandson.
With this many words we greeted one another.

yam t̃e'k̃ohanan a·'tatcu

yam t̃e'k̃ohanan a·'tsita
yam t̃e'k̃ohanan tca'we
a·'wan k̭äcima t̃e'li'tona
a·'witela'ma hon ła'kwimona
i·'yante'tcik̭änapk̭ä
hon pi'cle ła'kwimona
hon k̭älici ła'kwimona
hon a'laho ła'kwimona
hon t̃e'mak̃o ła'kwimona
hon i'yama ła'wimona
hon ma'nila'ma ła'kwimona
lu'k̭ak̃on i·'te'tcik̭ä
i·'te'tcap̃a
hon t̃e'k̃ohanan tatci'li te''ona
yam k̭ä'cima p̃ai'yan e'lete'ak̭ä-tekwi
yam ha'lawo·tinan a·'witela'ma ho'n ɔ'ta'wite' u'łak̭ä
hon t̃e'k̃ohanan tatc i'li te''ona
ho''na ya't̃ek̭ä
le'si te'kwin ta''k̭äna
ho''na a'nimła'k̭uk̭ä
hon i'miła'k̭uk̭ä
hon se'wekc i·'cokya·k̭ä
hon t̃e'k̃onanan tatc i'lite''ona
yam k̭ä'cima p̃on·e
a·'witela'ma a''na'ułak̭ä
yam hot as·a''nak̭a

a'nimk̃o'sk̃uk̭ä.
a·'witela'ma ci'pololon yam t̃e'-hułkwi a'na'kwatok̭ä
yam a·'tatcu
ci'pololon a'kä a·'wik̭e·na te'liak̭a
t̃e'k̃ohanan yam a'k̭ä i·'yanik̭ina-p̃ona

hon a·'yanik̭inapk̭ä.
ta'tcuwe
ta'lewe
pa'pamo su'wemo k̭ä'k̭ämo k̭ä'-semo na'namo a'limo to'clemo u'wak̭ämo hon a'k̭a i·'yanikina

[13] The marking of the walls with corn meal. The roof and floor are not marked.

[14] The text makes no mention of the deposit of plume wands in the roof and of seeds in the floor. This, presumably, is an omission, since the rite is performed as in the Sayataca house, and is fully described in the Sayataca chant.

[15] For the first two terms, plurals are used tatcuwe, talewe (the regular plural of tatcu is a·'tatcu). Tale is the usual word for brother's son, or any male "child" of one's clan. This explains its use instead of the expected tcal'e.

Then we made an end of this.
Now that this is at an end,
The ones who are our fathers
From their abode set with mountains,
Set with lakes,
Making their roads come forth,
Making their roads come hither,
They have passed you on your roads.
This night,
Bringing all their good fortune,
They have passed you on your roads.
Their seeds of corn: the yellow ones,
The blue ones,
The red ones,
The white ones,
The speckled ones,
The black ones,
The sweet corn seeds;
All the different clans of beans,
The yellow beans,
The blue beans,
The red beans,
The white beans,
The many colored beans,
The black beans,
The string beans,
The small beans,
The little spotted beans,
All the different tiny beans;
With all these seeds bundled about our waists,
We have passed you on your roads.
And then also the seeds of all the forest trees:
The seeds of the piñon tree,
The seeds of the oak tree,
The seeds of the first-flowering shrub,
The seeds of all the small shrubs;
And then all the ancient round ones:
The striped squash,
The crooked-neck squash,
The watermelons,
The sweet melons,
The gourds;
The seeds of the large yucca,
The seeds of the small yucca,
The seeds of the cactus,

lu'k̥ak̄on i·'te'tcik̥ä
i·'te'tcap̄a
hon a·'tatc i'lap̄ona
yam yä'la ya·na

yam k̥ä'wutuli ya·'na
o'neała kwai''k̥äna
o'neał i·'k̥äna
t̄o''na a·'wona-e'latenapk̥ä

luk̥ä t̄e'łinan·e
yam kwa'hoł t̄e'mła te'n·i ha'lowilin i·'łeana
t̄o''na a·'wona-elatenapk̥ä.
yam t̄o'waconan łuptsikwa te''ona

łi''akwa te''ona
ci'lowakwa te''ona
k̄o'hakwa te''ona
ku'tcutcukwi te''ona
k̄wi'nakwa te''ona
co'tsito te''ona
nɔ· a'ntoti t̄e'mla
nɔ· łu'ptsina
nɔ· łi''ana
nɔ· ci'lowa
nɔ· k̄o'hakwa
nɔ· i'topana'nan'ona
nɔ· k̥win·a
ła'piyak̥ä
nɔ· t̄sa'na
nɔ· ci'he· te''ona
t̄si'k̥äp̄uli t̄e'mła
t̄o'waconan i·'hatap̄iyana

t̄o·'na hon a·'wona-e'latenapk̥ä
t̄em t̄a t̄a'kwił p̄ɔ't̄i a·'wan k̄u'kwin·e
he''cot̄a't̄an an k̄u'kwin·e
t̄a'wi t̄a'tan an k̄u'kwin·e
k̥e·'la ci'wuna ła't̄san an k̄u'kwin·e

t̄a''kwi ła't̄san an k̄u'kwin·e
t̄em t̄a t̄o'wa k̥ämoliya

mɔ'teała
mɔ'k̥isi
mɔ'laknana
me'lu·na
co'p̄a
ho'k̥ap ho'tan an k̄u'kwin·e
ho't̄san ho'tan an k̄u'kwin·e
me·'tan an k̄u'kwin·e

All of these.
With these tied about our waists,
Provided with this bundle over our navels,
We have passed you on your roads.
For you we leave these seeds.
This is all.
Thus with plain words
We have passed you on your roads.
Here for you we leave these seeds.

When in the spring,
Your earth mother is wet,
In your earth mother
You will bury these seeds.
Carefully they will bring forth their young.
Bringing them back,
Toward this your thoughts will bend.
And henceforth, as kindred,
Talking kindly to one another,
We shall always live.[16]
And now indeed it has come to pass.
The thoughts of our fathers,
Who at the New Year
With precious plume wands appointed us—
Their thoughts we now have fulfilled.
Always with one thought
We shall live.
This is all.
Thus with plain words
We have passed you on your roads.
This our father's waters,

His seeds,
His riches,
His power,
His strong spirit,
All his good fortune whatsoever,

We shall give to you.
To the end, my fathers,
My children,
Verily, so long as we enjoy the light of day,
We shall greet one another as kindred.

le·wi
i·'hatap̂i'yana
k̯̂a'mulukwia p̂e'han i·'yante'tci

t̂o'na hon a·'wona-e'latenapk̯ä.
t̂o''na t̂o'waconan hon a·łak̂una
le·'wi
le·wi yu''he·to p̂e'nanakä
t̂o''na hon a·'wona'e'latenapk̯a.
t̂o'na·wan li·'łno t̂o'waconan a·'łak̂una
hon a'witelin tsit i'lap̂ a·'te''ona
t̂e'k̂ina t̂e'lakwai''ina
yam a'witelin tsi'tana
t̂oñ t̂owaconan a·'paluna·wa
e'letokna t̂eapk̂una·wa

a·wana' 'u'łana
i'sk̂ɔn tse''mak-t̂e'łakwi

i'· 'yanik̯inap̂a
ya'cuwa k̂ɔkci
hon a·'tek̯äna
no' miłte

hoł i'tiwana'a
hon a·'tatc i·lap̂ona
te'lik̯inan ya·'na a·'k̯ä
ho''na a'nułanapkowa
a·'wan son tse''makwin mo'łak̯ä.

t̂o'pint i·'tse'makuna
hon t̂e'wanan a·'tek̯än·a
le·wi
le· yu·''he·to p̂e'nan a'k̯ä
t̂o''na hon a·'wona-e'latenapk̯ä.
lu'k̯ä hon tatci'li
lu'k̯ä an k̯̂ä'cima
an t̂o'waconan·e
an u'tenan·e
an sa'wanik̯a
an tse''makwin t̂su'me
an kwa'hoł t̂e'mła te'n·i ha'lowilin·e
t̂o''na hon ya'nhaiten·a.
t̂e'wuna' hom a·'tatcu
hom tca'we
e'pac hon t̂e'k̂ohanan hon i·'yanik̯inap̂a

16 A passage of double meaning. It refers to the relationship between man and corn and the speaker and the household which has welcomed him.

Verily, we shall pray that our roads may be fulfilled.
To where your sun father's road comes out
May your roads reach.
May your roads be fulfilled.

e'pac ho'n a·'wonaya·''antia'na
hon t̄e'wusak̄en·a·
hoł yam yä'tok̯ä ta'tcu
an o'neał kwai''ina
o'neała te''tcina
te'mła t̄on a·wonaya·t't̄u·

Washing the Head of Ca'lako Impersonator

The female head of the house washes the head of the Ca'lako impersonator at the close of the all-night ceremonies, at about 8 o'clock in the morning. The other women present sprinkle water on his head.

This day,
My two children,
With our clear water
We shall hold you fast.
My child,
In order that your road may be fulfilled,
Reaching yonder to where the road of our sun father comes out,
For this with our clear water,
We hold you fast.
Somehow because of the thoughts of our fathers,
The ones who appointed you with their plume wand,
Throughout the winter,
Throughout the summer,
Yonder to the south
Wherever the roads of our fathers come out,
With your plume wands
You have asked continually for life for us.
This day
You have fulfilled their thoughts.
With our waters
We hold you fast.
Our child,
Always talking together kindly,
So long as we still can see one another,
That thus our roads may be fulfilled
For this, with our waters
We have bound you fast.

lu'k̯ä yä'ton·e
homtca'wa·tci[17]
yam k̯ä'cima k̄o'kci
t̄o'n a'k̯ä hon ya't̄ena-t̄su'mek̯äna
hom tca'le
hoł yam yä'tok̯ä ta'tcu
an o'neał kwai''inakwi o'neał te''tcina
t̄o' o'naya·'tun'ona'k̯ä
yam k̯ä'cima k̯o'kcak̯ä
tom hon ya't̄ena-t̄su'mek̯ä.
hoł yam a·'tatcu
a·'wan tse''makwin a'kä
a·'wan te'lik̯inan a'k̯ä
t̄om a'nułana'kowa
t̄e''tsinan·e
o'lo'ik̯'änan·e
li·'wan a'laho'a'nkwin ta''na
yam a·'tatcu
a·'wan o'neała· kwai''ina'kowa
yam te'lik̯inan a'k̯ä
ho'na·wan t̄o' t̄e'k̄ohanan ce'mante'a'k̯ä
lu'k̯ä yä'ton·e
t̄o' tse''makwi· mo'la·'up̄a
yam k̯ä'cim a'k̯ä
t̄om ho' ya't̄ena-t̄sumek̯ä.
ho'na·wan tca'le
i'cełte'ma ya'cuwak̯o' kci
te'mła i·'yunap̄a'te
yam hon a·'wonaya·'tun'on a'k̯ä
yam k̯ä'cim a'k̯ä
t̄om hon ya't̄ena t̄su'mek̯änapk̯ä

[17] The dual, used in the first sentence, should be used consistently to the end, because the prayer is supposedly addressed to the two impersonators. After the first sentence, the singular is used.

The thoughts of your fathers
You have fulfilled.

Do not forget your house.
Here in your own house
You will go about happily.
Always talking together kindly
We shall pass our days.
Our child,
Your road will be fulfilled;
Your road will reach all the way to Dawn Lake.
May your road be fulfilled;
May you grow old;
May you be blessed with life.

yam a·'tatcu
a·'wan t̄o' tse''makwi· mo'ła·k̯ä
eł yam he'cot̄an·e
t̄o an t̄o'miyona'ma
li·łonhoł yam he'cot̄a'kowa
k̯e'tsanici to a'luna.
i'cełtema
ya'cuwa k̄o'kci hon a·'tek̄än·a
ho'na·wan tca'le
t̄o' o'naya·''ana
t̄e'luwaiyan k̯äi'akwi o'neała te''·tcina
t̄o' o'naya·'t'u
t̄o' łacit'u
t̄om t̄e'k̄ohanan a'niktciat'u.

"Washing" the Koyemci

The Koyemci are actually bathed in the house of the priests, and each receives a gift of food from each of the women who participate in the ceremony, the wives and daughters of priests of the council. Later at the houses of their "aunts" they are also "washed." Here the rite is entirely symbolic. Corn meal is sprinkled on the head and gifts are presented. This, too, is called "washing." Ritual washing of the head is always the function of the paternal aunt.

The wives of the priests:
This day, my fathers,

Mo'lanhakto, priests
You have passed us on our roads.
With our clear water
We hold you fast.
My children,
May your roads reach to Dawn Lake,
May your roads be fulfilled;
May you grow old.
In order that you may grow old,
With our clear water
We have bound you fast.

lu'k̯ä yä'ton·e
hom a·'tatcu
mo'lanhakt̄ a·'ciwan·i
ho·'na t̄on a·'wona-e'latenapk̯ä
yam k̯ä'cima k̄o'kci
a'k̯a t̄o''na hon a·'wiyat̄ena t̄su'me
hom tca'we
t̄e'luwaiyan k̯ai'akwi o'neała te·'tcinan
t̄on a·'wona-ya·''an·a
t̄on a·'łacian·a
t̄on a·łacitun'on a'k̯ä
yam k̯ä'cima k̯o'kci
t̄o''na hon a·wiyat̄en t̄su'mek̯änapk̯ä.

In the ancestral house of his father, meal is sprinkled on his head by his paternal aunt and all the women of his father's clan with the following prayer. The two women's prayers are characteristically brief.

My father,
This day,
With our clear water
We have held you fast.
May your road reach to Dawn Lake

May your road be fulfilled,
May you grow old.

hom ta'tcu
lu'k̯ä yä'ton·e
yam k̯ä'cimak̯ä
t̄om hon ya't̄ena-t̄su'mek̯änapk̄ä.
t̄e'luwaiyan k̯ai'akwi o'neała te''·tcinan
t̄o' o'na-ya·'ana
t̄o' ła'ci'an·a.

6066°—32——50

His father's brother hands him a bundle of prayer sticks made for him by male members of the clan.

The uncle:
This many are the days
Since our fathers,
Priests of the masked gods,
Cula·witsi, p̂ekwin, priest
Sayataca, bow priest,
Hututu, bow priest,
Yamuhaktu, bow priests,
Ca'lako, bow priests,
All the masked gods
Made their roads come hither.
Wherever perfect plume wands had been left for them,
They made their roads ascend.
Sitting down quietly they came to day.
Next day,
Laying down all their gifts—
Their seeds,
Their riches,
All that they had brought tied about their waists—
Back to their own country
They took their way.
Leaving their children[18] to stay quietly
They took their way.
And wherever plume wands had been left for them
Their children
With their words issuing forth,
With their sighing breath,
Stayed in our houses.
All their days being past
This day
For the one who is our father,
Molanhakto,

We have prepared plume wands.
Our children,
Whoever of them wished to grow old,
Upon the plume wands which they had prepared
Breathed their sacred words.
Here to our house

le'si t̂e'wanan·e
ho''na·wan a·'tatcu
kok̂wa·'ciwan·i
cu'la·witsi p̂e'kwin ci'wan·i
sai'yataca p̂i''łaci'wan·i
hututu p̂i''łaci'wan·i
ya'muhakt a·'p̂i'ła·ci'wan·i
ca'lako p̂i''łaci'wan·i
kɔ'ko te'mła
o'neał i'k̭äna
yam te'lik̭inan ya·na wɔ'tałak̭i'-kowa
o'neał ye'mak̭äna
i·'t̂inan ła'k̂inan a·'want̂ewak̭ä.

t̂e'wap̂ yä'ton·e
yam kwahoł temła
yam t̂o'waconan·e
yam u'tenan·e
a·'hatap̂iya a·'wi·'kowa
wɔ·'tała'k̂una
yam 'ulo'nakwi o'neał a·'k̭äna

yam t̂e'apk̂una·we
t̂i'nan łak̂una.
o'neał a·'k̭äna·wap̂a
a·'wan t̂e'apk̂una·we
hoł yam te'likinan wɔ·'tałak̭i te'a'kowa
yam p̂e'nan kwai''inan ak̭ä
yam he'ciatinan a'k̭ä
he'cot̂a'an a·'teak̭ä.
a·'wan te'mła t̂e'wap̂a
lu'kä yä'ton·e
yam tatc i'li te''ona
mo'lanhakto
an hai'to
hon te'lik̭ina· ye'lete'unapk̭a.
ho''na·wan tca'we
hoł tcu·'wa ła'cina tse''makowa

te'likina ye'leteukowa

t̂e'wusu ya'nułana
ho''na·wan he'cot̂akwi

[18] The katcinas, who remained behind to dance in all the Ca'lako houses.

With these we pass you on your road.
This day with these our plume wands
We hold you fast.
With these plume wands
We hold one another fast.
Whenever our father,
Saying let it be now,
Makes his road go forth,
Then also reinforcing with your words,
The prayers which we have laid upon our plume wands,
To our fathers
You will give the plume wands.
Our fathers' day has been made.

Their waters eagerly awaiting
We pass our days.
My child,
Verily at the new year,
Our fathers appointed you with their plume wand,
The perfect plume wand which they had prepared.
This many days
Anxiously awaiting your time
We have passed our days.
Throughout the cycle of our fathers' months,
Throughout the summer,
Yonder toward the south,
Wherever the roads of our fathers come forth,
Even with your poorly made plume wands
You have been asking for life for us.
Now this day,
We have reached the appointed time.
Holding this plume wand,
Anxiously you will pass the day.
When our sun father
Has gone in to sit down at his sacred place

hon a'ka a·'wona-e'latenapkowa

lu'k̯ä yä'ton·e
te'lik̯inan a'kä
t̄om ło ya't̄ena-t̄su'mek̯äk̯ä.
te'likinan a'k̯a
hon i·'wiyat̄en-t̄sumek̯äk̯ä.
hoł k̯ä'k̯i k̯e·si' le''anik̯äp̄a
yam tatc i'li te''ona
an o'neał a·'k̯äna
tem t̄a ho'łno ko'n hon te'likinan t̄e'wusu a'nułanapk̯a te'a'kowa
i'snok̯ɔn p̄e'na· yälto

yam a·'tatcu
t̄o' te'lik̯inan a·'łea'u
ho''na·wan a·'tatcu
a·'wan t̄e'wana yo·'ap̄a
a·wan k̯ä'cim ant̄sumeʻna
hon t̄e'wanan a·'tek̯äna
hom tca''le
no'miłte hoł i'tiwan·a
ho''na·wan a·'tatcu
te'lik̯inan ya·'na ye'lete'unapkowa
te'lik̯inan a'k̯ä
i·'yanułana
le'si t̄e'wanan·e
a'ntsumeʻna hon t̄e'wanan a·'teak̯ä

yam a·'tatcu
a·wa yä'tcu pi''lan·e
ɔ'lo'ik̯änan·e
li·'wan a'laho'a'nakwin taʻna
yam a·'tatcu
a·'wan o'neała kwai''ina'kowa
kɔ·'ti te'lik̯inan a'lewuna

ho''na·wan t̄on ak̯ä t̄e'k̯ohanan ce'mana a·'teakowa
luk̯ä yä'tone
k̯es le'n hai'tokwin te''tcik̯ä
lu'k̯ä te'likinan i·'łeana
t̄o a'nt̄sumeʻna yä'ton t̄e'k̯äna.
hon yä'tok̯ä tatc ilap̄ona
yam t̄e'lacinakwi
i·'muna kwatok̯äp̄a

Saying, Let it be now,
You will make your fathers' road go forth.
Then again reinforcing with your own words
The prayers which we have laid upon these plume wands,
To your fathers
Give these plume wands.
With them you shall ask for life for us.

k̭ä'k̄i k̭e·si' le'anik̄äp̄a
yam a·'tatcu
a·'wan o'neał a·'k̄än·a
tem t̄a
te'lik̭inan hon t̄e'wusu a'nułanapk̭ä te'a'kowa
i'snɔkɔn p̄e'nan yä'łtona
yam a·'tatcu
t̄o te'lik̭inan a·'łea'u
a'k̭ä ho''na·wan t̄o' t̄ek̄ohanan ce'man·a.

The Koyemci takes the prayer sticks and thanks the giver, invoking on those present all the blessings of the gods. The prayer sticks are planted with his own at night.

Dismissal of the Koyemci

The Koyemci remain all day in the plaza in attendance on the various sets of dancers. At nightfall the last of the dancers, the Molawia, have departed. Then the Koyemci in pairs visit every house in the village, to invoke upon it the blessings of the gods. At each house they receive gifts of food from the female inhabitants. Returning to the plaza, they take their prayer sticks out to plant. They return to the house of their father late at night, and removing their masks for the first time all day give them to their father to return to the house where they are kept. When he comes back, he thanks his children for their year of work, and sets them free. Then for the first time since the preceding evening they drink, and after eating and bathing, return to their homes. Their retreat, fifteen days, is the longest in Zuñi ritual. The following is the prayer of the father of the Koyemci, setting them free.

This many are the days,
My children,
Since with their plume wand they appointed us.
Throughout the winter,
And the summer
Anxiously we have awaited our time.
Hither toward the south
We have given our fathers plume wands.

For all our ladder descending children
We have been asking for life.

le'si t̄e'wan·e
hom tca'we
te'lik̭inan a'k̭ä
ho''na ya'nulak̭ä
t̄e'tsinan·e
ɔ'lo'ik̭'änan·e
a'nt̄sume'na
hon t̄e'wanan a·'teak̭ä
yam a·'tatcu
a·'wan te'lik̭inan·e
li·'wan a'laho'a'nkwin ta''na
hon te'likinan a·'łeak̭ä
le· yam łe'ts·'lon p̄a'ni·nan tca'we
hon a·'wan t̄e'k̄ohanan ce'mana a·'teak̭ä

Now we have reached the appointed time.
This night
We have fulfilled the thoughts of our fathers.

Always with one thought
We shall live.
My children,
This night
Your children,
Your families,
Happily you will pass on their roads.

Happily we shall always live.
Even though we say we have fulfilled their thoughts
No indeed
Anxiously awaiting until we shall again come to our appointed time
We shall live henceforth.
My children,
Thus I have finished my words for you.
To this end, my children:
May you now go happily to your children.

Asking for life from my fathers
Yonder on all sides,

Asking for my fathers' life-giving breath,
Their breath of old age,
And into my warm body,
Drawing their breath,
I add to your breath.
To this end, my children
May your roads be fulfilled;
May you grow old;
May you be blessed with life.

hai'tokwin te''tcik̯ä

luk̯ä t̑e'łinan·e
yam a·'tatcu
hon a·'wan tse''makwin mo'ła·napk̯ä.
topint i'tse'makuna
hon t̑e'wanan a·'tek̯än·a
hom tca'we
lu'k̯ä t̑e'łinan·e
yam tca'we
yam i·'yanik̯inan·e
k̯e'tsanici
t̑on a·'wona-e'latena·wa.
k̯e'tsanici hon t̑e'wanan a·'tek̯'än·a
e·te hon tse''makwi· mo'ła·na·we le'kwapte
e'la·
hoł k̯ä··k̯i hai'tokwink̯ te''tcitun te'kwi
ant̑sumeʻna
hon t̑e'wanan a·'tek̯än·a.
hom tca'we
le· t̑o''na·wan ho' p̑e'nan ya·'-k̯äk̯ä
te'wuna' hom tca'we
k̯e'tsanici
yam tca'we
toms a·'wona-e'laten·wa
la'łhok^{u} le'si tekwi yam a·'tatcu
t̑e'k̑ohanan yai'ncemana
yam a·'tatcu
a·'wan o'na ya·'nak̯ä p̑i''nan·e
a·'wan ła'ciak̯ä p̑i''nan·e yai'nacemana
yam t̑e'huł k̯ä'łnakwi
p̑i''nan anaʻkwatok̯äna
t̑o''na·wan ho' p̑i''nan te'lia'ana
te'wuna' hom tcawe
ton a·'wona ya'·tu
t̑on a·'łacitu
t̑o''na t̑e'k̑ohanan ya'niktcia'tu.

VII. PRAYERS OF THE MEDICINE CULT

The Great Fire Society Chief Sets Up His Altar

The Great Fire Society convenes for the first time in November at the full moon. Before sunset the male members assemble at their ceremonial house. The women bring food to the house and leave their sacred corn fetishes to be placed on the altar. The tablet altar has been set up against the west wall of the room. At sunset the choir begins to sing very softly a set of eight songs known as "For Pouring in the Water." At the beginning of the fourth song two men go out to offer food in the river. The society p̄ekwin rises and makes the meal painting and sets up the corn fetishes. At the fifth song the society chief takes the bowl for the medicine water, at the sixth he mixes the medicine, at the seventh he puts in sacred colored pebbles, during the eighth he "smokes" the altar. The following prayer is spoken in a low voice by the society chief while performing these rites.

The procedure is followed whenever the society altar is set up. It is followed by a rite of exorcism which leads into the main body of the ceremony. It is about the same for all societies. The peculiar style of the following prayer may be due to the fact that it is accompanied by song.

This many are the days
Since our moon mother
Yonder in the west,
As a small thing became visible.
Now yonder in the west,
Standing fully grown against the sky
She makes her days.
Our spring children,[1]
Whoever wished to grow old,
Carrying prayer meal,
Carrying shells,
Yonder, with prayers,
One by one they made their roads go forth.
Yonder they met those
Who since the first beginning
Have been given the world,[2]
The forests,
The brush.
At the feet of some lucky one
Offering prayer meal,
Shell,
Among their finger tips,
They looked about.
Breaking off the young shoots
Of some fortunate one,
And drawing them toward them,
These very ones who stayed there quietly,
Bearing their long life,
Bearing their old age,
He brought back.
Into the rain filled rooms
Of his daylight fathers,[3]
His mothers,
His children,
He made their roads come in.
This many days the divine ones[4]

[1] Members of the society, who have drunk from the sacred "spring"; the bowl of medicine water that stands on the altar.

[2] The shrubs whose wood is used for prayer sticks.

[3] That is, human. The ceremonial room of the society.

[4] K̄äpin a·'ho'i, literally "raw persons," as distinct from the "daylight people" "who are cooked" through having been born on a bed of warm sand.

Have remained with us their children.
Now this very day
For the rite of our fathers,
Beast priests,[5]
We have prepared plume wands.
When yet a little space remained,
Ere our sun father
Went in to sit down at his sacred place[6]
Coming to my earth mother,
Have I offered plume wands to my fathers,
And returned to my house.
Then yonder from all sides
Those who are my fathers,
The divine ones,[7]
With none among them lacking,
Will make their roads come forth,
Hither they will come.
Then having made my fathers' massed cloud house,[8]
Having spread out their mist blanket,
Having sent forth their life giving road,
Having laid down their rainbow bow,
Having laid down their lightning arrow,
I shall sit down quietly.
I shall set down my white shell bowl.[9]
Then from afar on all sides
You, my fathers,
Will come.

Yonder from the north,
The rain maker priests,[10]
Bringing their waters,
Will make their roads come hither.
Where lies my white shell bowl,
Four times they will make their road come in.

Yonder from the west
The rain maker priests,
Bringing their waters,
Will make their roads come hither.
Where lies my white shell bowl,
Four times they will make their road come in.

Yonder from the south,
The rain maker priests,
Bringing their waters,
Will make their roads come hither.
Where lies my white shell bowl,
Four times they will make their road come in.

Yonder from the east
The rain maker priests,
Bringing their waters,
Will make their roads come hither.
Where lies my white shell bowl.
Four times they will make their roads come in.

Yonder from the above
The rain maker priests,
Bringing their waters,
Will make their roads come hither.
Where lies my white shell bowl,
Four times they will make their roads come in.

Yonder from below
The rain maker priests,
Bringing their waters,
Will make their roads come in.
Where lies my white shell bowl,
Four times they will make their roads come in.

When you have all sat down quietly
Our young ones[11]
Will refresh themselves with your waters.
Then to dawn lake reaching,
Their roads will be fulfilled.

And furthermore, yonder in the north,
You who are my father,
Mountain lion,[12]

[5] We·'ma a·'ciwan·i, the special protectors of the medicine societies and the source of life, medicine power, and witchcraft.

[6] Late afternoon, the usual hour for making offerings of prayer sticks.

[7] The beast gods, who are present in spirit throughout the ceremonies.

[8] The meal painting on the altar; the "house" is the terraced outline, the "blanket" the filling of fine meal, the "road" the line of meal, generally crossed at four points, leading from the altar to the door at the farther end of the room.

[9] For mixing the medicine water.

[10] U'wanam·i—during this invocation he pours the water with a gourd, four gourds of water.

[11] T̂e'apk̂una·we—children, also domesticated and game animals. The word is used as a general term for fecundity. Here specifically the members of the society.

[12] He now invokes in turn the beast gods of the six directions, meanwhile adding pulverized roots with medicinal properties.

You are life-giving society chief;
Bringing your medicine,
You will make your road come hither.
Where lies my white shell bowl,
Four times making your road come in,
Watch over my spring.
When you sit down quietly
We shall be one person.[13]

And, furthermore, yonder in the west
You who are my father, bear,
You are life-giving society chief;
Bringing your medicine,
You will make your road come hither.
Where lies my white shell bowl,
Four times making your road come in,
Watch over my spring.
When you sit down quietly
We shall be one person.

And, furthermore, yonder in the south
You who are my father, badger,
You are life-giving society chief;
Bringing your medicine,
You will make your road come hither.
Where lies my white shell bowl,
Four times making your road come in,
Watch over my spring.
When you sit down quietly
We shall be one person.

And, furthermore, yonder in the east
You who are my father, wolf,
You are life-giving society chief;
Bringing your medicine,
You will make your road come hither.
Where lies my white shell bowl,
Four times making your road come in,
Watch over my spring.
When you sit down quietly,
We shall be one person.

And furthermore, yonder above
You who are my father, knife-wing,
You are life-giving society chief.
Bringing your medicine,
You will make your road come hither.
Where lies my white shell bowl,
Four times making your road come in,
Watch over my spring.
When you sit down quietly
We shall be one person.

And furthermore, yonder below
You who are my father, gopher,
You are life-giving society chief.
Bringing your medicine,
You will make your road come hither.
Where lies my white shell bowl,
Four times making your road come in,
Watch over my spring.
When you sit down quietly
We shall be one person.

And furthermore, yonder in the north
On all the mossy mountains,
On the tops of the mountains,
And along their slopes,
Where the ravines open out,
You hold the world in your keeping;
Ancient yellow stone,[14]
You will make your road come hither
Where lies my white shell bowl,
Four times making your road come in,
You will sit down quietly.
Then with your living waters
Our young ones will nourish themselves;
Reaching to Dawn Lake
Their roads will be fulfilled.

And furthermore, yonder in the west
On all the mossy mountains,
On the tops of the mountains,
And along their slopes,
Wherever the ravines open out,
You hold the world in your keeping;
Ancient blue stone,
You will make your road come hither
Where lies my white shell bowl,
Four times making your road come in
You will sit down quietly.
Then with your living waters
Our young ones will nourish themselves;
Reaching to Dawn Lake
Their roads will be fulfilled.

[13] During the final ceremony of the societies at the winter solstice when the sick are cured the identification is felt to be complete for those who have esoteric knowledge. At that time there is a complete change of personality; the shamans rush about uttering the cries of animals. They are very much feared. It is especially the prerogative of the bear to give this power of magical impersonation.

[14] He adds small round pebbles believed to have been brought from the underworld at the time of emergence. As a matter of fact any curiously shaped or colored pebble that may be picked up is believed to have magical properties. A collection of these forms part of every shaman's equipment. There are prayers and simple rituals for each one.

And furthermore, yonder in the south
On all the mossy mountains,
On the tops of the mountains,
And along their slopes,
Wherever the ravines open out,
You hold the world in your keeping;
Ancient red stone,
You will make your road come hither,
Where lies my white shell bowl,
Four times making your road come in
You will sit down quietly.
Then with your living waters
Our young ones will nourish themselves;
Reaching to Dawn Lake
Their roads will be fulfilled.

And furthermore, yonder in the east
On all the mossy mountains,
On the tops of the mountains,
And along their slopes,
Wherever the ravines open out,
You hold the world in your keeping;
Ancient white stone,
You will make your road come hither.
Where lies my white shell bowl,
Four times making your road come in
You will sit down quietly.
Then with your living waters
Our young ones will nourish themselves;
Reaching to Dawn Lake
Their roads will be fulfilled.

And furthermore, yonder above
On all the mossy mountains,
On the tops of the mountains,
And along their slopes,
Wherever the ravines open out,
You hold the world in your keeping;
Ancient many colored stone,
You will make your road come hither.
Where lies my white shell bowl,
Four times making your road come in
You will sit down quietly.
Then with your living waters
Our young ones will nourish themselves;
Reaching to Dawn Lake
Their roads will be fulfilled.

And furthermore, yonder below,
On all the mossy mountains,
On the tops of the mountains,
And along their slopes,
Wherever ravines open out,
You hold the world in your keeping;
Ancient dark stone,
You will make your road come hither.
Where lies my white shell bowl,
Four times making your road come in
You will sit down quietly.
Then with your living waters
Our young ones will nourish themselves;
Reaching to Dawn Lake
Their roads will be fulfilled.[15]

k̯ä'linon'ak̯ä t̂e'wusu
pouring in water for prayer

ma' le'si t̂e'wanan·e
now this many days

hon ya'onak̯ä tsit i'lap̂ a·'teona
we moon mother having the ones

li·'wan k̯älicianwkin ta''na
yonder the west to direction

kɔ·'wi ła'na ye'tsak̯̂äna
somewhat large becoming visible

li·'wan t̂e'luwankwin ta''na
yonder to the east direction

i'tiułana ho''i ya·'k̯änak̯ä t̂e'wanan a'cap̂a
standing against (the horizon) person finishing day making

ho''na·wan k̯̂ä'nakwe·nan tca'we
our spring children

hoł tcu'wa ła'cina tse''makona
whoever growing old the ones who think

[15] This is followed by the rite of "smoking" the altar. The prayer for this was withheld from me.

ha'lawotinan i·'łeana
prayer meal taking

ło·' i·'łeana
shell taking

le'hok^u t̂e'wus a'k̯ä
yonder prayer with

o'neała kwai''ilenapk̯ä
roads made go out severally

hoł tci'mik̯ana'k̯äp̂a
somewhere at the First Beginning

ulo'na ya'niktci·a'kona
world those who were given

ła'kwił-p̂o·'t̂i
the brush

t̂a'kwił-p̂o·'t̂i
the forest

a·'wona-e'latena
on their roads passing them

hoł tcu'wa ha'lowili'kona
whoever the lucky one

an sa'kwi'a
his feet (at)

ha'lawotinan·e
prayer meal

ło·''o
shell

a·'łeakna
giving

a'si k̯ätsowakwin·te
finger tips even there

i'yun u'lapnapk̯ä
they looked about among them

hoł tcu'wa ha'lowili'kona
whoever the one who is lucky

a·'k̯äwułkwi'nakna
the young shoots pulling

a·'wana' u'ła·k̯'äp̂a
drawing them toward them

hoł yam łu'wała'k̂i'konate
wherever their staying quietly even where it is

yam o'naya·'nak̯ä łe'ap̂a
their long life holding

yam ła'ciak̯ä łe'ap̂a
their old age holding

o'neał i'k̯äna
road making come

yam t̂e'k̂ohanan a·'tatcu
their daylight fathers

yam a·'tsita
their mothers

yam tca′we

their children

a·′wan k̭ä′cima t̃e′li’tokwi

their water inner room (to)

o′neała kwa′tok̭äna

road making enter

le′si t̃e′wanan·e

this many days

k̭ä′pin a·′ho’i

raw persons

ho’ tca′wilap̃a

us children having

t̃e′wanan a·′teak̭ä te′kwi

days they lived when

tci′mte yä′ton·e

even this day

we·′ma· a·′ciwan·i

beast priests

a·′wan hai′to

for them ordained

hon te′likinan ye′lete’unapk̭ä.

we prayer sticks prepared.

hon yä′tok̭ä tatc i′lap̃ a·′te’ona

we sun father having the ones

yam t̃e′łacinakwi

his sacred place

i·′muna kwa′tok̭ätun te′kwi

sitting down about to go in when it is

ko·w a′nt̃e‘wetcikwi

a little space remained for him when

ho′man a·′witelin tsit o′na-e′latena

my earth mother on her road passing

yam a·′tatcu

my fathers

te′lik̭inan a·′łeana

prayer stick giving to them

yam he′cot̃akwi

my house to

o′neał i′k̭äna

road making come

la′łhok[u] le′si te′kwi

yonder this many places

t̃o′’na ho’ a·tatc i′lap̃a

you I fathers having

k̭ä’pin a·′ho’i

raw persons

eł kwa tcu′ i′metcam·e

do not someone be (not) missing

o'neała kwai''ik̯äna
road making come forth

yam a·'tatcu
my fathers

a·'wan a'wełuyan k̯ä'kwe ya·'k̯äna
their cloud house finishing

a·'wan ci'pololon p̄e'wuna
their mist blanket spread out

o'naya·nak̯a o'neałan a·'k̯äna
life giving road making go

a·'wan a'mitolan pi''łan a''una
their rainbow bow putting down

a·'wan wi'lolonan co'l a''una
their lightning arrow putting down

ho' i·'miłak̄una
I sitting down quietly

yam k̄o'hakwa sa'l a'nimła'k̄una
my white shell bowl setting down quietly

la'ł hoku le'si te'kwi
yonder so many places

t̄o'n hon a·'tatc i'li.
you we fathers have.

‖⁝ li·'wan piclankwin ta''na
yonder to the north direction

u'wanam a·'ciwan·i
rain maker priests

yam k̯ä'cim i·'łeana
your waters carrying

o'neał i'k̯äna
road making come

yam k̄o'hakwa sa'l a'la
your white shell bowl lying

a·'witela'ma
four times

o'neałan kwa'tok̯äna. ⁝‖
road will make come in.

The foregoing section is repeated as follows:

li·'wan k̯ä'liciankwin ta''na . . .
yonder to the west direction

li·'wan a'lahoankwin ta''na . . .
yonder to the south direction

li·'wan t̄e'luwankwin ta''na . . .
yonder to the east direction

li·'wan i'yamakwin ta''na . . .
yonder to the above direction

li·'wan ma'nik̯äkwin ta''na . . .
yonder to the below direction

t̂on i'tînan-ła'k̂ik̯äp̂a
you having sat down quietly

t̂o''na·wan k̯äcima
your waters

ho''na·wan t̂e'apk̂una·we
our children

i·'k̯ä'kuna
drinking in

t̂e'luwaian k̯ai'akwi
dawn lake to

o'neał te''tcina
road reaching

a·'wona ya·''an·a.
their roads will be fulfilled.

le'st·kleap̂a
furthermore

||:li·'wan pi'clankwin ta''na
yonder to the north direction

t̂om ho' tatc i'li
you I father have

ho'ktita'cana
mountain lion (tail long)

o'naya·nak̯ä
life giving

t̂o' ti'k̯ämo'siye
you are society chief

yam a'kwan i'łeana
your medicine carrying

t̂o' o'neał i'k̯äna
you road will make come

yam k̂o'hakwa sa'l a'la
your white shell bowl lying

a·'witela'ma
four times

o'nealan kwa'tok̯än·a
road will make come in

homan k̯ä'nakwai''in·e
my spring

yai'yupatci
watching

t̂o' i·miła'k̂una
you sitting down quietly

hon to'pint̂ ho''i.:||
we one person.

The foregoing section is repeated as follows:

li·'wan k̯älicianka̯win ta''na
yonder to the west direction

t̂om ho' tatc i'li
you I father have

ai'nce . . . .
bear

li·'wan a'lahoankwin ta''na
yonder to the south direction

t̑om ho' tatc i'li
you I father have

to'naci . . .
badger

li·'wan t̑e'luwankwin ta''na
yonder to the east direction

t̑om ho' tatc i'li
you I father have

yu'nawik̭o . . .
wolf

li·'wan i'yamakwin ta''na
yonder to the above direction

t̑om ho' tatc i'li
you I father have

a'tciala'tap̑a . . .
knife wing

li·'wan ma'nik̭äkwin ta''na
yonder to the below direction

t̑om ho' tatc i'li
you I father have

k̭ä'lutsi . . .
gopher

|| li·'wan pi'clankwin ta''na
yonder to the north direction

a'wico yä'la'kona
moss mountain along

yä'la k̭ätsowa'kona
mountain point along

te'letc i'tiwa'kona
slope middle along

a'kwe· kwai''ina'kona
ravine opening along

t̑on 'u'lo'n i'lap̑a
you world having

a'łaci łu'ptsina
ancient stone yellow

o'nealan i'k̭äna
road making come

yam k̑ohakwa sa'l a'łkwi
your white shell bowl where it lies

a·'witela'ma
four times

o'neała kwa'tok̭äna
road making enter

t̂on i′t̂inan-iła′k̂ik̭äp̂a
you having sat down quietly

t̂o′′na·wan k̭ä′‘kwin·e
your living water

ho′n t̂e′apk̂unan·e
our child

i·′k̭ä‘kuna
drinking in

t̂e′luwaian k̭ai′akwi
dawn lake to

o′neał te′′tcina
road reaching

a·′wona ya·′′ana.‖
their roads will be fulfilled.

The foregoing section is repeated for the six directions as above, naming for each direction a stone of appropriate color, as follows:

. . . a′łaci łi′ana . . .
ancient stone blue

. . . a′łaci a′hona . . .
ancient stone red

. . . a′łaci k̂ohana . . .
ancient stone white

. . . a′łaci i′to‘panana . . .
ancient stone many colored

. . . a′łaci cik̭ana . . .
ancient stone dark

le′stikleap̂a
furthermore

Summoning a Shaman

When anyone is sick and it is decided to call a shaman to cure him, the family decide whether or not they consider the case sufficiently serious to warrant summoning one of the societies to come as an organization to perform its curing ritual. This is done only when they believe death is threatened and it is felt that the full power of the society is needed to save the patient's life. In such cases the patient is given to the society, and the family undertakes to see that he is initiated within a reasonable time. This is a last resort, since the expense of initiation is very great.

In less serious cases a shaman is summoned to practice as an individual. In such a case the shaman may ask assistance of some colleague who owns an especially potent song or medicine, but the society as a whole does not participate, nor is the patient initiated. However, at the following New Year he goes to the house of the society with which his doctor is affiliated and his head is washed at their altar, and he becomes their "child." Each year at the winter solstice his society father, the shaman, makes a prayer stick for him to plant.

Before the physician is summoned the patient's relatives decide what they will offer him for his services. The gift is held ready. Then the patient's father or some other mature male relative prepares prayer meal, which he wraps in a corn husk. Into this he puts some bit of the gift for the physician—a thread from a robe, or a bit of the fringe if it is a shawl. This is for the Beast Gods, their "clothing." With this he goes to the house of the shaman. The two men sit down, remove their headbands and moccasins, clasping hands over the package of meal. The patient's father repeats the following prayer, to which the shaman replies in like spirit:[16]

This day,	lu'k̯ä yä'ton·e
	ho''nan t̄e'apk̄unan·e
Because of the ill will of the foolish ones,[17]	yu''ya·nam a·'wan tse''makwin a'k̯ä
Our child wears out his spirit.	tse''mek t̄e'n·a hon a·'teaiye.
Among all our fathers,	le· yam a·'tatcu
Life-giving priests,[18]	o'na·ya·'nak̯' a·'ciwan·i
Life-giving p̄ekwins,	o'na·ya·'nak̯ä p̄e'kwi'we
Life-giving bow priests,	o'na·ya·'nak̯ä a·'p̄i'ła·ciwan·i
We have looked about.	hon a·'wun'u'lapnapk̯ä
When all unexpectedly,	te'kwant te'at̄ip̄a
The divine ones chose you	k̯ä'pin a·'ho'i
	t̄om a'naw·ana·wapk̯äte'a
We, in the daylight	t̄e'k̄ohanana
Also chose you.	t̄om hon u'naw·an·a
Now that we have let you know of it,	t̄om hon yu·''ya·k̯äna·wap̄a
Yonder in their house,[19]	hoł yam he'cot̄an·e
The divine ones have passed you on your road,	k̯ä'pin a·'ho'i t̄om o'na-e'latenapk̯ä.
With the roads of the divine ones going ahead,	k̯ä'pin a·'ho' a·'wan o'neałan-e''kwi'kowa
Into our house	ho''na·wa he'cot̄akwi
You will make your road enter.	t̄o o'neał kwa'tok̄äna
Having sat down quietly,	t̄on i·'t̄inan ła'k̯ik̯äp̄a
This day,	lu'k̯ä yä'ton·e
With the flesh of the white corn,	t̄o'wa k̄ohan an ci''nan·e
Prayer meal,	ha'lawo·tinan ło·''o te'a'ona
With ground shell,	
We have taken firm hold of our fathers,	hon yam a·'tatcu
Life-giving priests;	o'na·ya·'nak̯a a·'ciwan·i
With prayer meal held in the hollow of the left hand[20]	a·'wan we'cik̯a a'stecokta ha'lawo·tinan a'k̯ä

16 Dictated by one of the headmen of the Wood Society.

17 The witch, whose ill will has caused the sickness.

18 Society chiefs. The choice of a shaman is believed to be inspired by the Beast Gods.

19 The ceremonial house of the society.

20 The left hand is used in all curing rituals. Also in the rites of the scalp dance.

We held one another fast.
With prayer meal,
With riches,
With shell,
With these we hold one another fast.
The ones who are our fathers,
Life-giving priests,
Will hold our child,
Our child who has been bewitched

Because the heart of someone became angry.
Our fathers,
Life-giving priests,
Beast priests,
With your hands,
With your breath,
Hold him fast.
The power of the two hearted one,
The one who has bewitched our child,
The foolish one,
His power[21] they will cause to stand out
In the daylight of our sun father.
Then our child's breath will become well.
His spirit will become well.
Desiring this
With prayer meal,
With shell,
We have held one another fast.
Taking his prayer meal,
You will make your road go out.[22]
Yonder, with prayers, you will direct your road.
Somewhere on your earth mother,
Your fathers,
The divine ones,
You will pass on their roads.

hons i·'wiyat̂ena-t̂su'mek̭äk̭ä
ha'lawo·tinan·e
u'tenan·e
ło·''o
hon a'k̭ä i·'wiyat̂ena-t̂su'mek̭äk̭ä.

ho''na·wan t̂e'apk̂unan·e
hon a·'tatc i'lap̂ona
o'na·yanak̭' a·'ciwan·i
hoł tcu'wa kwa'hoł a'k̭a i'k̭e·n i·'samutina
ho''na·wan t̂e'apk̂una a'nat̂suma-'kowa
hon a·'tatc i'lap̂ona
o'na· ya·nak̭' a·'ciwan·i
we·ma· a·'ciwan·i
yam a'sin a'k̭ä
yam ya'nhakunan a'k̭ä
ya't̂ena t̂su'mek̭ä
hoł tcu'wa kwil i'k̭e'na
ho''nan t̂e'apk̂unan a'nat̂sum·a'-kowa
yu''ya·nam·e an sa'wanik̭ä
yam yä'tok̭ä ta'tcu
an t̂e'k̂ohanankwi łu'wanakwai''-ik̂äna
ho''na·wan t̂e'apk̂unan an ya'nha-kunan i·'k̂ɔkcuk̂än·a.
an tse''makwi i·'k̂ɔkcuk̂än·a.
lu'k̭ä a'ntecemana
ha'lawo·tinan a'k̭ä
ło·' a'k̭ä
hon i·'wiyat̂ena-t̂su'mak̂äk̭ä
luk̭' an ha'lawo·tinan i·'łeana
o'neała kwai''ik̂äna.
le'hok[u] t̂e'wus a'k̭ä
t̂on o'neał a·'k̂äna
hoł yam a·'witelin tsi'tana
yam a·'tatcu
k̂ä'pin a·'ho'i
t̂on a·'wona-e'laten·a

[21] Sawanikä, weapons, also, abstractly, power. There is a double meaning to these lines. The shaman will actually remove from the patient's body foreign matter which the witch has injected, and which is the direct cause of the sickness. Also, by revealing the means the witch has employed, he strips him of his power. For this reason torture formerly was used to extract confessions from those suspected of witchcraft. If a witch once reveals the source of his power he becomes helpless. Any prayer or ritual loses its potency when it is told, the power passing to the new owner. See pp. 493–494.

[22] The prayer meal which the medicine man receives is offered to the spirits at a point east of the village.

Then once more taking my prayer meal,
My riches,
My shell,
Those on which I have breathed my prayers,
Even thus will be your words upon them.
To those who once were alive,[23]
To those who used to be with us,
And furthermore, our fathers,
The beast priests,
The life-giving priests,
To them you will give the prayer meal,
The shell,
The riches.
Our fathers will take the prayer meal,
The shell,
The riches.
When you have given it to them,
And when they have accepted it,
Anxiously they will await evening.
When our sun father
Has gone in to sit down at his sacred place,
Somewhere the divine ones will pass you on your road.
They will come to their child;
The divine ones will come to their child.
Our fathers,
Life-giving priests,
Life-giving p̄ekwins,
Life-giving bow priests,
Perpetuating their rite from the first beginning,
Sitting down quietly among us,
Will look over their child,

Our child, whose spirit failed,
Because of some evil thing.

Beast priests,
With your hands,
With your breath,

t̄em t̄a hołno ha'lawo·tinan·e

u'tenan·e
ło·''o
ho' t̄ewusu ya'nułak̯a te'a'kowa

i'snok̄on p̄e'nan t̄o' yam a·'tatcu li·'łno te'k̯̄än·a.
a·'ho' a·'tea'kowa
ho'n i'li a·'tea'kowa
le'stiklea yam a·'tatcu
we·ma· a·'ciwan·i
o'na·ya·'nak̯ä a·'ciwan·i
ha'lawo·tinan·e
ło·''o
u'tenan·e
t̄o' a·'łea'up̄a
ho''na·wan a·'tatcu
ha'lawo·tinan·e
ło·''o
u'tenan i·łeana
t̄o' a·'łea'up̄a i·'łeana

a'nt̄sume'na su'nhak̯̄äna·wa
ho''na·wan yä'tok̯ä ta'tcu
yam t̄e'tacinukwi i·'muna kwat̄o-k̯̄äp̄a
k̯̄ä'pin a·'ho'i
hoł t̄om o'na-e'latena·wa.
yam t̄e'apk̄unan·e
k̄äpin a·'ho'i
yam t̄e'apk̄unan o'na-e'latena·wa
ho''na·wan a·'tatcu
o'na·ya·'nak̯ä a·'ciwan·i
o'na·ya·'nak̯a p̄e'kwi·we
o'na·ya·'nak̯a a·'pi'ła·ci·'wan·i
yam ko'lehoł tci'mik̯̄ä'kowa te'lia'na
i·'t̄inan ła'k̄iknan
yam t̄e'apk̄unan·e
un-u'lapna·wa.
ho''na·wan t̄eapk̄unan kwa'hoł a'k̯ä tse''makwin i·'nat̄ina te'a'kowa
we·ma· a·'ciwan·i
yam a'sin a'k̯ä
yam ya'nhakunan a'k̯ä

[23] Deceased shamans, united in death with their protectors and patrons, the Beast Gods. Only those members of medicine societies who have shamanistic powers, that is, the power to invoke and impersonate the bear, are so honored in death.

The power of the foolish one
You will make stand forth.
Then our child's spirit will become well,
His breath will become well.
Then that you may be the ones whom his spirit will embrace,
There at your house [24]
With your clear water
You will bind your child fast.

In order that it may be thus
We give you our child.

yu''ya·nam an sa'wanik̭ä
t̑on łu'wana kwai''ik̭äna·wa
ho''nan t̑e'apk̑unan an tse''mak-wi·'k̑ɔkcuk̭'äna
an ya'nhakunan i·'k̑ɔkcuk̑äp̑a.
i'sk̑ɔn tse''mak t̑e'łakwi yam a·'teatun'on ak̭ä
hoł yam he'cot̑akwi
yam t̑e'apk̑unan·e
yam k̭äcima k̑ɔ'kc a'k̭ä
t̑o' ya't̑ena t̑s·u'mek̭äna'tun'on ak̭ä
t̑om ho'n t̑e'apkunan a'niktci·a'u.

The Society Father Summons the Novice for His Initiation

If the patient has been given to the society he is expected to complete his initiation as soon as economic obligations permit. Should he fail in this he is troubled with bad dreams as a warning of the fate that will overtake him. Initiation is in no sense a propitiatory rite; it is, rather, an access to power. The preliminary ceremonies held at his sick bed secured him a stay, but in order finally to triumph over the disease, the patient must place himself under the protection of the Beast Gods and receive from them a new heart. Should he not do this, he will be troubled in spirit until he sickens and dies. Worry is the most serious of all illnesses, it is the sickness of the spirit caused by supernatural agencies.

Frequently many years elapse before a man is in a position to meet the expenses of intitation. Whenever he is ready his family notify the society father, who is the man who received him as a patient. At the first fall meeting of the society the date for the initiation is set at the full moon of the month at which that society customarily initiates.

Four days before the full moon the ceremonial father goes after sunset to the house of the novice to notify him that the initiation ceremonies are about to begin. Here the boy's family are assembled and waiting for him. After formal greetings are exchanged, the man sits down, removes his head band and moccasins and prays.[24a]

[24] The house of the society. Had the man been offering the child for initiation into the society he would say instead of "at your house," "in your spring."

[24a] Dictated by a member of the Great Fire Society, a man who has initiated many children into his society.

This many are the days
Since some evil thing
Made our child sick.
His breath failed.
Because of this from among all our fathers,
Life-giving priests,
Life-giving p̄ekwins,
Life-giving bow priests;
All the society priests,
Society p̄ekwins,
Society bow priests,
Unexpectedly
The divine ones chose me.

Their daylight children
Revealed themselves to you,
And choosing me,
You let me know.
Taking prayer meal,
Far off to the east,
With prayers, I made my road go forth.
Where our fathers' road comes in [25]

I passed them on their road.
Standing facing them,
I offered them prayer meal.
The divine ones' road preceded;

Their road preceding,
Following them
Hither with prayers.
We brought our roads
Into their daylight children's rain-filled rooms,[26]
The divine ones brought their road.

They sat down quietly
And we of the daylight
Met one another.
Our prayer meal,
Shells,[27]
Riches,
On which I had breathed our prayers,

le'si t̄e'wanan·e
ho''na·wan t̄e'apk̄unan·e
i'mat kwa'tik we'aḵäḵä
ya'nhakun i·'natina
yam a·'te'on a'ḵä le· yam a·'tatcu

o'na ya·'naḵä a'ciwan·i
o'naya·'naḵä p̄e'kwi·we
o'na ya·'naḵä a·'p̄i'ła·ci'wan·i
le· ti'ḵä a·'ciwan·i
ti'ḵä p̄e'kwi·we
ti'ḵä a·'p̄i'ła·ci'wan·i
te'kwant te'atip̄a
ḵ̄ä'pin a·'ho'i
yam a'nawana·'wap̄a
t̄e'k̄ohanan an tca'we
t̄om ya'nłitona
hom a'nawana
hom yu'ya·ḵ̄äna·wap̄a
ha'lawo·tinan i·'łeana
le'hoku t̄e'luwankwin ta'ʻna
t̄e'wus a'ḵä
ho' o'neał kwai''iḵ̄äḵä
yam a·'tatcu
a·'wan o'neał i'nakwi
a·'wona-e'latena
ya'nikto'nan ye·'lana
ho' ha'lawo·tinan a·'łea'up̄a
ḵ̄ä'pin a·'ho'i
o'neał e'ʻkuna·'wap̄a
a·'wan o'neał eʻkwikuna
e'la yä'lu
k̄äłhoku t̄e'wus a'ḵä
hon o'neał a·'ḵ̄änapḵä
yam t̄e'kohanan tca'we
a'wan ḵ̄ä'cima t̄e'li'tokwi
ḵ̄ä'pin a·'ho'i
o'neał kwa'toḵ̄äna
i·'tinan i·'łaḵ̄iḵ̄äp̄a
t̄e'k̄ohanana
hon i·'yona-e'latena.
yam ha'lawo·tinan·e
ło·''o
u'tenank·e
yam t̄e'wusu ya'nuła'kona

---

25 The eastern road. The Beast Gods dwell at Cipapolima, in the east. All curing rituals are oriented toward the east, as all katcina are oriented toward the southwest.

26 The house of the patient.

27 The prayer meal contains bits of ground shell or turquoise and a few threads pulled from the garment offered to the medicine man in payment for his services in curing.

Four times drawing them toward me,
Here in the hollow of the life-giving left hand
Of my fathers,
Life-giving priests,
I laid the prayer meal,
The shells,
The riches.

Then taking the prayer meal,[28]
The shells,
The riches,
Yonder to the east,
For the second time
With prayers
I made my road go forth.
Where my father's life-giving road comes in
Standing facing them,
I offered them prayer meal.
Thus anxiously waiting,
We have passed our days.[29]
Then when all their days were past,[30]
After our moon mother,
At her sacred place,
Still small, appeared,
And now yonder in the east
Standing fully grown makes her days,[31]
Now our spring children,
Whoever truly desires in his heart to grow old,
Taking prayer meal,
Taking shell,
Taking corn pollen,
Yonder with prayers

a·'witela'ma
a·'wana' u'łana
hon a·'tatc i'lap̂ona
o'naya·'nak̭ä a·'ciwan·i
li·'wan a·'wan we'cik̭a o'na ya·'nak̭ä a'stecokta'a
ha'lawo·tinan·e
ło·''o
u'tenan·e
i'tiułak̭̂äp̂a
ha'lawo·tinan·e
ło·''o
u'tenan i·'łeana
le'hokᵘ t̂e'luwankwin ta''na
kwilik̭̂änana
t̂e'wusa'k̭a
ho' o'neał kwai''ik̭äkä
yam a·tatcu
a·'wan o'naya·nak̭ä o'neał i'nakwi
ya'nikto·na ye·'lana
ha'lawo·tinan a·'łea'up̂a
a'nt̂sume'na
hon t̂e'wanan a·'teak̭ä
łokwa le·'wi t̂e'wak̭ä te'a'ana

hon ya'onak̭ä tsit i'lap̂ a·'te'ona
yam t̂e'łaci·'nakwi
kɔ·'wi t̂sa'na ye'tsak̭̂äna
li·wan t̂e'luwankwin ta''na
i'tiułana ho''i ya·'k̭̂änak̭ä t̂e'-wanan a'cap̂a
ho''na·wan k̭̂ä'nakwe·nan tca'we
hoł tcuw hi'yawołucna
ła'cina tse''ma'kona
ha'lawo·tinan i·'łeana
ło·'' i·'łeana
o'nean i·'łeana
le'hokᵘ t̂e'wus a'k̭ä

[28] The patient expectorates into the package of meal. Thus his sickness is removed, and the father "takes it out to the east."

[29] The four days during which the society holds its ceremonies of curing in the home of the patient. Only the officers and possessors of esoteric knowledge are present. The sacred paraphernalia of the society is set up, songs are sung, the Beast Gods are invoked, and finally the agency of sickness is withdrawn from the patient. The ceremonies are held for four consecutive nights, and last from midnight until dawn.

[30] The days of waiting until the novice was ready to assume his obligations.

[31] The time is now approaching the full moon. The ceremonies of initiation will begin with the making of prayer sticks by all members of the society on the day following the visit of the father to the home of the novice.

One by one shall make their roads go forth.[32]
Yonder where they have stood since the first beginning
Our fathers,
The forest,
The brush,
Those who have been given domain
Yonder on all the mossy mountains,
There we passed them on their roads.
At the feet of some lucky one,
Offering prayer meal,
Shells,
Corn pollen,
Even among their sharp fingers
We looked about.
Breaking off the straight green shoots of some lucky one,
We drew them toward us.
Even those standing there quietly,
Holding their long life,
Their old age,
Their waters,
Their seeds,
The divine ones made their roads come hither.
Near by into the house of our fathers,
Our mothers,
The clan of the sun,[33]
Into their house the divine ones brought their road
And there sat down quietly.
This many days,
Anxiously waiting
With us, their children, they passed their days.
And now that their appointed time had come,

o'neał kwai·'ilek̯äna·wa
hoł tci'mik̯ana'k̯äꝑa
hon a·'tatc i'laꝑona
ŧa'wił-ꝑɔ·'ŧi
ła'kwił-ꝑɔ·'ŧi
la'łhok^{u} a'wico yä'la'kona
u'loʻna ya'niktcia'kona
a·'wona-e'latena
hoł tcuw ha'lowi'li'kona
an sa'kwia
ha'lawo·tinan·e
ło·'o
o'nean a·'łeakna
a'si k̯ä'tsowakwinte
i'yun'ulapnak̯ä.
hoł tcuw ha'lowi'li·'kona
a·'k̯äwułkwiʻnakna
a·'wanaʻ-u'łak̯äꝑa
yam łu'wała'ꝁi'konate
yam o'naya·nak̯ä
yam ła'ciak̯ä
yam k̯ä'cima
yam ŧo'waconan łe'aꝑa
k̯ä'pin a·'ho'i o'neał i'k̯äna
la'lik hon a·'tatc i'laꝑona
hon a·'tsit i'laꝑona
yä'tok̯' a'nota
a·'wan he'coŧakwi
k̯ä'pin a·'ho'i
o'neał kwa'toꝁäꝑa
i'ŧinan ła'ꝁikna
le'si ŧe'wanan·e
a'ntsumeʻna
ho''na tca'wilaꝑa ŧe'wanan a·'teak̯ä te'kwi
k̯e·s le'n hai'tokwin te''tciꝑa

[32] The frequent changes of tense in the following passages are confusing, but have been retained in the translation because they are so characteristic a feature of the poetic style. It reflects the very slight importance attached to clarity and coherence.

Willow sticks may be gathered at any time, and kept by a man in the house in which he lives until ready for use. He must have them in readiness for the prayer-stick making, which starts shortly after sunrise the following day.

[33] An attempt on the part of the speaker to conceal his identity. He was neither a member of the Sun clan nor living in a Sun clan house.

Next day,
After our fathers,
Our ancestors,
Those who here had belonged to societies,
The divine ones,
After they first had taken hold of their plume wands,
We of the daylight,
Meeting one another,
With our warm human hands,
Embraced them.
For our fathers,
Our children,
Those who here belonged to societies,
For their ceremony
We shall give our plume wands human form.
With the massed cloud robe of our grandfather,
Male turkey,
With eagle's mist garment,
With the striped cloud wings
And massed cloud tails
Of all the birds of summer,
With these four times wrapping our plume wands,
We shall give them human form.
With the one who is our mother,
Cotton woman,
Even a roughly spun cotton thread,
A soiled cotton thread,
With this four times encircling them and tying it around,
With hanging rain feather,
We shall give our plume wands human form.
Saying, let it be now,
Taking our child's prayer meal,

Wherever we think, let it be here,
Our earth mother
We shall pass on her road.
Offering our plume wands,
We shall make their days.[34]
When there remains a little space,

t̄e'wan yä'ton·e
hon a·'tatc i'lap̄ona
ho''na·wan a·'łaci'na·we
li·'łno ti'k̯än i'lapkona

k̄ä'pin a·'ho'i
k̯e·'la yam te'lik̯inan ya't̄ena
t̄su'mek̄änapk̯ä te'a'ana
t̄e'k̄ohanana
hon i·'yona-e'latena
yam a'sin k̄ä'łnak̯ä
a·'wiyat̄en t̄su'mek̄änapk̯ä
yam a·'tatcu
yam tca'we
li·łn ti'k̯än i'lapkona

a·'wan hai'to
hon te'lik̯inan a·'ho' a·ya·k̄äna·wa

yam nan i'li te''ona

tɔn ɔts an a'wełuyan p̄a''in·e
k̄ä'k̄äl an ci'pololon u'tcun·e
la'łhok[u] ɔ'lo'ik̄aiak̯ä wɔ·'we
a·'wan ła'pihanan la'taw·e
a·'wan a'wełuyan· k̄äten a'k̯ä
a'k̯ä a·'witela'ma
te'lik̯inan a·'p̄a'un a·'ho' a·'ya·k̄äna
yam tsit i'li te''ona
pi'tsem o'k̯ä
kɔ·'t̄i pi''lenapte
pi''le ci'k̯änapte
a'k̯' a·'witela'ma
pa'nulapnan i·'kwian te''tcina
k̄ä'cima la'cowa
te'likinan ho''i ya·'k̄äna·wap̄a

hoł k̯ä·'k̄i k̯e·si' le''anak̄äp̄a
yam t̄e'apk̄unan ha'lawo·tinan·e
i·'łeana
hoł li·ła le''hatina
yam a'witelin tsi'ta
ho' o'na-e'latena
hon te'lik̯inan a·'łeana
hon a·'wan t̄e'wanan a'cna·wap̄a
hon yä'tok̯ä tatc i'lap̄ a·'te'ona

[34] The four-day retreat, which begins when the prayer sticks are planted shortly before sunset on the day following this speech. The novice has prayer sticks made for him by his ceremonial father. In the afternoon he is summoned to the ceremonial house of the society to receive them. He then goes with his father and officers of the society to plant in a shrine at Badger place, about 2 miles southeast of Zuñi. From the time of the planting until the conclusion of the ceremonies he must do no work, especially lift no heavy weights. He eats and sleeps very little and is untouchable, like one who has had contact with the dead. At the same time other members of the society plant in their fields or at Red Earth and after their supper return with their bedding to the society house for a four nights' retreat. The days are spent in preparation for the great ceremony of the last night.

Ere our sun father goes in to sit down at his sacred place
Then our father [35]
Will spread out his fathers' mist blanket,
Their perfect cloud house he will prepare,
Their rainbow bow he will lay down,
Their lightning arrow he will lay down,
And there will sit down quietly.
Far off from all directions
Our fathers will make their roads come forth.
Making their roads come hither
They will sit down quietly.
Sitting behind them
This many days,
Anxiously waiting
We shall pass our days.
When we reach their appointed time,[36]
Yonder from all directions
The ones who are our fathers,
Life-giving priests,
Life-giving p̃ekwins,
Life-giving bow priests,
All the Beast Priests,
The divine ones,
With no exceptions,
All will make their roads come hither.
Near-by, into the rain-filled rooms
Of their daylight fathers,
Their daylight children,
They will bring their roads.
At the place where they sit down quietly,
Our child will pass his fathers on their road.
Into a being like themselves [37]
They will transform him.

yam te'łaci·nakwi
i·'muna kwa'tok̭ätun te'kwi
kɔ·w a'nt̃e'we'tcikwi
hon tatc i'lap̃ a·'teona
yam a·'tatcu
a·'wan ci'pololon p̃e'wuna
a·'wan a'wełuyan k̭̃ä'kwen ya·'na ye'lete'una
a·'wan a'mitolan pi''łan a''una
a·'wan wi'lolonan co'l a''una
t̃i'nan ła'k̭̃up̃a
la'łhok[u] le'si te'kwi
hon a·'tatc i'lap̃ona
o'neał kwai''ik̭̃äna
o'neał i'k̭̃äna
i·'t̃inan i·'łak̭̃ik̭̃äp̃a
a·'wan ma'si'a
i'miałana
le'si t̃e'wanan·e
a'nt̃sume'na
hon t̃e'wanan a·'tek̭̃äna
hoł a·'wan hai'tokwin te''tcip̃a
la'łhok[u] le'si te'kwi
hon a·'tatc i'lap̃ona
o'naya·'nak̭ä a·'ciwan·i
o'naya·nak̭ä p̃e'kwi·we
o'naya·nak̭' a·'pi'ła·ci'wan·i
le· we·m a·'ciwan·i
k̭̃ä'pin a·'ho'i
kwa tcuw i'metcam·e
o'neał i'k̭̃äna
la'lik yam t̃e'k̃ohanan a·'tatcu
yam t̃e'k̃ohanan tca'we.
a·'wan k̭̃ä'cima t̃e'li'tonankwi
o'neała kwa'tok̭̃äna
i·'t̃inan i·'łak̭̃ik̭ä te'kwi
ho''na·wan t̃e'apk̃unan·e
yam a·'tatcu
a·'wona-e'latep̃a
yam ko'nhoł ho''i te''ona
ho''i ya·'k̭̃äna·wap̃a

[35] The p̃ekwin of the society, who sets up the altar and makes the meal painting. This is done before the novice is summoned to plant his prayer sticks.

[36] The fourth night of the retreat, when the ceremony of initiation takes place.

[37] The painting of the face and the body of the novice. There is power inherent in body paint.

Then sitting among his fathers,
Even at their valuable place,
Throughout a blessed night.
With us, their children,
They will come to day.
Next day, when yet a little space remains
Ere our sun father
Comes out standing to his sacred place,
Then with that through which our roads are fulfilled,
With clear water,
We shall add to the breath of our child.[38]
For since our breath is valuable,
Our child
Into his body
Will inhale our breath.
At the very place where he sees our spring
He will sit down as one of us.
That his road may be fulfilled,
Seeking that,
With our thoughts bent to that,
We shall always live.
Anxiously awaiting the time ordained for this,
We shall pass our days.
For even while I call myself poor,
Yonder on all sides,
Asking for life from those whom my thoughts embrace,
I shall add to your breath.
From the priest of the north,
From the priest of the west,
From the priest of the south,
From the priest of the east,
From the priest of the above,
From the priest of the below,
Asking their long life,
Their old age,
All their good fortune whereof they are possessed,

Asking for their breath,
And into my warm body,
Drawing their breath,
I shall add to your breath.

yam a·'tatcu
a·wan t̑e''ya t̑ewapte
i'me a'kcuna
t̑e'łinan k̑ɔ'kci
hon tca'wilap̑ a·'want̑e'wana
t̑e'wap yä'ton·e
hon yä'tok̭ä tatc i'lap̑ a·'te'ona
yam t̑e'łacinakwi
ye·'lana kwai''ik̭atun te'kwi
kɔ·w a'nt̑e'we'tcikwi
yam a'k̭ i·yona-ya·'k̭äna·wona

k̭ä'cima k̭ɔkc a'k̭ä
yam t̑e'apk̑unan·e
ho''nan p̑i''nan te'liuna·wap̑a
ho''na·wan p̑i''nan t̑e''yap̑a
ho''na·wan t̑e'apk̑unan·e
yam ce'łnakwi
p̑i''na ya'nhakuna kwa'tok̭äna·wa
hoł yam k̭änakwe·nan tu'nak̭ä te''a
im a'kcite
o'naya''ak̭a a'ntapana

tse'mak-t̑e'łakwi
hon a·'tek̭än·a
t̑e'wuna' lek̑on hai'to
a'nt̑sume'na
hon t̑e'wanan a·'tek̭än·a
ta''tcic te'wuko'liya le''kwanante
la'łhok[u] le'si te'kwi
yam tse''mak-t̑e'łakwi'kona
ho' t̑e'k̑ohanan yai'ncemana
t̑o''na·wan ho' p̑i''nan te'liana·wa
picl a·'ciwan·i
k̭älici a·'ciwan·i
a'laho a·'ciwan·i
t̑e'mak̑o a·'ciwan·i
i'yam a·'ciwan·i
ma'nilam a·'ciwan·i
a·'wan o'naya·nak̭ä
a·'wan ła'ciak̭ä
a·'wan kwa'hoł te'mła te'n·i ha'lowilin·e
i'lap̑ a·'te'ona
p̑i''na yai'ncemana
yam t̑e'huł k̭ä'łnakwi
p̑i''na yanhakuna kwa'tok̭'äna
t̑o''na·wan hon p̑i''nan te'liana·wa

[38] At dawn the head of the novice is washed by two sisters of his ceremonial father. During the washing of the head his society name is called in a song. Thus his rebirth is symbolized.

To this end, May you be blessed with life.	t̑e'wuna' t̑o' t̑e'k̭̑ohanan a'nik- tcia'tu.
Now we go.[39]	son a·'wa· ne·

The Society Father Blesses the Novice at the Close of His Initiation

On the following morning the members of the society make prayer sticks at their society house. They plant late in the afternoon and go into retreat in their ceremonial room. The novice has prayer sticks made by his ceremonial father, with whom he goes to plant at Badger Place. He observes a strict retreat in his own house. Each night he is brought to the society room to practice dancing and to be purified for his initiation.

Each member of the society makes prayer sticks for the novice to plant the last day. His father prepares his mi'le, the feathered ear of corn which will be his personal fetish, his medicine bag, and the eagle feathers that form part of his regalia. He makes or purchases the hand-woven blue breechcloth which forms his ceremonial costume. At the boy's house preparations for the feast are under way.

On the fourth night he is summoned by his father. At the society house he is clothed and his face and body are painted with sacred paint. Then he is brought into the ceremonial room to meet his fathers, the Beast Gods. He dances all night with two women of the clan of his ceremonial father. At dawn the two women wash his head at the altar, while the choir calls his new name. At the conclusion of this the ceremonial father hands the boy the medicine bag, eagle feathers, four ears of corn which have been lying on the altar, the mi'le, and the bundle of prayer sticks. They clasp hands over these sacred objects while the father repeats a long prayer, reviewing the events which have led up to this moment. At the conclusion all inhale the blessing of the newly consecrated mi'le.

The boy takes his sacred possession to his house and returns to the society room, where his relatives serve a sumptuous feast. About noon he goes with his ceremonial father and the head of the society to a shrine on Badger Place where he plants the bundle of prayer sticks. Then for four days he must abstain from animal food in addition to the usual requirements of sexual continence and gentleness. On the fourth morning his father takes him out toward the east and removes from his hair the downy feather which he has worn as a pledge of his abstinence. He takes the boy to his house, where his head is washed by his wife. On this day there are elaborate exchanges of

[39] The man leaves at once. The women of the boy's family immediately start preparations for his initiation, including the preparation of food for the two great feasts they must provide, and the grinding of meal to be given to his ceremonial father.

gifts of food between the women of the boy's family and those of the father's.

The following prayer, dictated by a member of the Great Fire Society, is said by the ceremonial father at the presentation of the mi'le, at the moment when he receives the novice into full membership in the society.

Now this many are the days
Since something made our child sick.
When his spirit failed
And his breath failed,
That by which we live,
That of which is made the flesh of these, my children,
The flesh of the white corn,
Prayer meal,
You prepared.
And taking shells,
The flesh of our mother, white shell woman,
Who, though abiding far off, in the west,
In all the village branches,[40]
Saying, "Let it be here,"
Has washed the cuticle from her body,
Taking even a single borrowed shell,
The shell,
The rich clothing.
You sent forth with prayers.[41]
Among all your fathers,
Life-giving priests,
Life-giving p̄ekwins,
Life-giving bow priests,
Society priests,
Society p̄ekwins,
Society bow priests
You looked about.
Now since nothing was clear to you,
The divine ones
Chose me from all.
Then my daylight children revealed themselves to you
And you also chose me from among them all
And let me know of it.
When my fathers had come out one by one
From wherever they abide,
Taking my prayer meal,
Yonder toward the east
I made my road go forth.[42]
Standing facing my fathers
I offered them prayer meal.
The divine ones took my prayer meal.
Then they leading,
I following at their backs,
With prayers we made our roads come hither.
Here into the rain-filled rooms
Of their daylight children
The divine ones entered.[43]
They sat down quietly.
Here we of the daylight met one another
I sat down quietly.
Taking up our prayer meal,
Our shells,
Our rich clothing,
Upon which we had breathed our prayers,
In the hollow of the life giving left hand
Of my fathers, life giving priests,
I placed the prayer meal,
The shells,
The rich clothing,
Then when my fathers took hold of their prayer meal,
Their shells,
Their rich clothing,
We of the daylight
With the prayer meal,
With the shells,
With the rich clothing,
We held one another fast.
Desiring our fathers' long life,
Desiring their old age,
Desiring their medicine,
Sending forth our prayers for these,
With prayer meal,

[40] The pueblos to the east, whence shells and turquoise are secured by trade. Wherever White Shell Woman bathes she leaves the rubbings from her body, the white olivella shells, which are ground down for wampum.

[41] Literally, "to set up before the door," used of any person or object appointed to intercede with outside forces.

[42] With the package of meal received from the patient's family, the shaman goes to the east to pray for divine help.

[43] The first visit to the patient.

With shells,
With rich clothing
We held one another fast.
Taking my child's prayer meal,
His shells,
His rich clothing,
Yonder toward the east,
With prayers I made my road go forth.[44]
Where the life-giving road of my fathers comes in,
I passed them on their road.
With my child's prayer meal,
With his shells,
With his rich clothing
For my child
I asked for life.
Then I returned to my own house.
As the sacred words of the divine ones circulated,[45]
We in the daylight,
Letting one another know,
Anxiously waiting we came to evening.
Following after those whom our thoughts embrace,[46]
The ones who were to have their days,
Male willow,
Female willow,
Breaking off straight young shoots,
Of whichever ones were lucky,
And drawing them toward us,
With our warm human hands
We held them fast.
With the massed cloud robe of our grandfather,
Male turkey,
With eagle's mist garment,
With the striped cloud wings
And massed cloud tails
Of all the birds of summer,
Four times with these wrapping the plume wands
We gave them human form;
With our mother,
Cotton woman,
Even a roughly spun cotton thread,
Four times encircling them and tying it around,
With a rain-bringing hair feather,
We gave them human form;
With the flesh of our two mothers,
Black paint woman,
Clay woman,
Clothing their plume wands with their flesh,
We gave them human form;
With the mucous of our fathers,[47]
Life-giving priests,
We gave them human form.
Saying, "Let it be now,"
And taking our plume wands,
The divine ones leading,
We following at their backs,
Hither with prayers
We brought our roads.
Into the rain-filled rooms
Of our daylight children [48]
The divine ones entered;
With their hands
They removed the source of sickness from our child,
The one who had been suffering from some evil sickness.
Then our child
With his spittle
Finished their plume wands.
Taking the plume wand,
After having removed the sickness from our child,
The one who had been suffering with some evil sickness,
Taking the plume wand,
We made our road go forth.
Saying, "Let it be here,"
I met those who are our fathers,
Life-giving priests,
Life-giving p̄ekwins,
Life-ġiving bow priests;
And furthermore our ancestors,
Those who here belonged to societies,
Those who were society chiefs,
Those who were society p̄ekwins,

[44] He goes out to the east a second time, "to take out the sickness."

[45] He notifies important members of the society that the society has been summoned to cure, while at the same time the supernaturals assemble.

[46] Heads of the society go after willow sticks of which to make prayer sticks. In the text of the following passage all pronouns are omitted, implying a third person subject. They have been restored in the translation in the interest of intelligibility. Such changes of person are characteristic.

[47] Medicine roots which are used on prayer sticks for special occasions. The use of these medicines, the way of making these prayer sticks, and the prayers which give them power are some of the most carefully guarded secrets in Zuñi ritual.

[48] The second visit to the patient. The physician rubs his body with the medicated prayer stick. The patient expectorates on it. The physician takes it out immediately.

Those who were society bow priests,
Those who with thoughts embracing,
Held in their keeping our world;
And furthermore our ancestors,
Those who had knowledge of how to care for us,
And the Beast Priests.
Where they were all fittingly gathered together,
None being absent,
There I passed them on their roads.
I gave them the plume wands.
My fathers took firm hold of my plume wands.
Yonder at the place of their first beginning,
At Cipapolima,
While Iyatiku Poceyanki [49]
By means of my plume wands sent word about,
Anxiously waiting
They came to evening.
When our sun father
Had gone in standing to his sacred place,
And our night fathers,
Our night mothers,
Coming out rising to their sacred place,
Passed us on our roads,
Saying, "Let it be now,"
Our father,
Our mother,
The perfectly robed ones [50]
Both of them we made arise.
They leading,
Near by into the rain-filled rooms of our daylight fathers,
Our roads entered.[51]
Sitting down quietly,
Again for the second time
Taking our child's prayer meal,
And giving it to our fathers,
Here in the hollow of their life-giving left hand,
The prayer meal,
The shell giving to them,
We held one another fast.
Saying, "Let it be now,"
Our father,
Our mother,
The perfectly robed,
We made arise.
With these leading,
Far off to the east,
With prayers we made our road go forth.[52]
Where our fathers' life-giving road comes in,
We passed them on their roads.
Standing face to face
Our child's prayer meal,
His shells,
We gave to our fathers.
And adding my own words
In accordance with whatever had already been said to make the prayer meal a being potent in prayer,
I asked for life for my child.
There we met our fathers,
Life-giving priests;
And furthermore, our ancestors,
Those who here belonged to societies,
The ones who had attained the far off place of waters;
And furthermore our relatives,
Those who used to know how to care for us;
Where none were missing
But where all abide holding their long life,
Holding their old age,
We passed them on their roads;
All the Beast Priests
Holding their weapons [53]
We met;
With these all leading,
We following at their backs,
Hither with prayers we came.[54]
Into their daylight children's water-filled rooms,
Their seed-filled rooms,
The divine ones entered.
After they had sat down quietly
We, the daylight people,

49 Described as a single individual with two names. "Some one who knows about medicine." Iyatiku is the "mother corn" of the Keres. Po'ciyanki is the culture hero of all the eastern Pueblos.

50 The mi'le "and something else." What, could not be learned.

51 The first night visit to the patient.

52 He goes out with corn meal for the second time to pray for divine help.

53 Sa'wanikä, any weapon including the claws of animals, and, abstractly, power.

54 He returns to the house of the patient.

Met one another.
Sitting down quietly,
Our fathers, life-giving priests,
Built[55] with their hand their massed cloud house,
Spread out their mist blanket,
Sent forth their life-giving road,
Prepared their perfect spring.
Sitting down quietly,
These, the divine ones,
Looked over their child.
Then also these same ones
Let their hands go first,
Their breath go first
While our hands followed.
For among all the corn priests' ladder descending children,
Among all the little boys and little girls,
And those whose roads go ahead,[56]
Was one, who even though a valuable person,
Because he became angry over something,
Used his power to harm our child.
The power of this foolish one,
Our fathers, the divine ones,
The Beast Priests,
Brought forth standing
Into the daylight of our sun father.[57]
Then with his fathers' water of life,
With their flesh,[58]
Our child nourished himself.
When the day had advanced a little,
When the night had advanced a little,
Our child's sickness grew less,
His breath became better.
That his road may be fulfilled
Reaching to where the road of his sun father comes out,
That he may stand firmly upon his earth mother,
Hoping for this we shall live.
When he said, let it be now,[59]
And after our moon mother,
Yonder in the west still small,
Had first appeared,
And when a little space yet remained
Until, standing against the eastern sky,
She should come to maturity.
At that time our spring children,[60]
Whoever of them had thought to grow old,
Taking prayer meal,
Taking shells,
Taking corn pollen,
Made their roads go forth.
Wherever they met their fathers of the bush,
At the feet of the lucky one
Prayer meal, shell,
Corn pollen,
They offered.
Breaking off the straight young shoots
Which they drew toward them,
With their warm human hands,
They held them fast.
With the massed cloud robe of our grandfather,
Male turkey,
Eagle's mist garment,
And the striped cloud wings
And massed cloud tails
Of all the birds of summer,
With these four times wrapping their plume wands,
They gave their plume wands human form.
With the one who is our mother,
Cotton woman,
Even a roughly spun cotton thread,
Four times encircling the plume wand
And tying it around,
And with a rain-bringing hair feather,
They gave their plume wands human form.
With the flesh of our two mothers,
Black paint woman,
Clay woman,
Clothing their plume wands with flesh,
They gave their plume wands human form.
Saying, "Let it be now,"
And taking our plume wands,

---

[55] The altar is set up in the patient's room.

[56] The aged.

[57] The cause of sickness is drawn from the body of the patient. (See p. 531.)

[58] The patient drinks from the medicine bowl on the altar an infusion of medicine roots in water. The ceremony described above is repeated on four consecutive nights.

[59] When the patient decided to fulfill his pledge of membership.

[60] The members of the society start their preparations for the initiation ceremonies. The final ceremonies take place at the full moon.

And taking our child's prayer meal,[61]
Yonder with prayer
One by one we made our roads go forth.
Meeting our earth mother,
And meeting our ancestors,
Our children,
Those who here belonged to societies,
And furthermore our fathers,
The Beast bow priests,
We offered them plume wands.
When there remained yet a little space.
Ere our sun father,
Went in to sit down at his sacred place,
From far off on all sides
Our fathers,
Life giving priests,
The divine ones,
With not one missing,
Making their roads come forth,
They made their roads come hither.
Into the rain-filled rooms of their daylight mothers,
They made their roads enter.[62]
Perpetuating their rite
According to the first beginning,
They fashioned their cloud house,
They spread out their mist blanket,
They sent forth their life-giving road,
They fashioned their spring,
They spanned their rainbow bow,
They set their lightning arrow,
They sat down quietly,
And at their feet we sat down.
This many days
Anxiously we have waited.[63]
Now, indeed, when the last of all their days was past,
Our child having made his road come in,[64]
Even where the precious road of his fathers enters,
Into a being like themselves
Our fathers transformed [65] their child.
Then a blessed night they spent
With us who are their children.
Next day,
While yet a little space remained
Ere our sun father
Should come out standing to his sacred place,
With our clear water,
With that by which we have being,
With this we took hold of our child.[66]
After the divine ones first added their breath,
Then also praying in the same words,
We added to the breath of our child.
Our child taking his fathers' breath,
Into his body will draw their breath.
And since our breath is valuable,
Where he sees our spring,
Even there he will sit down among us;
Then seeking always the ways of prolonging life,
With thoughts bent on this, we shall live.
Then also, that on following this we may bend our thoughts,
For this in plain words I sent forth my prayers.
He give us this child
That for a long time
In bonds of affection
We may live together,
These clear words were spoken,[67]
And to your fathers,
Wherever they stay,
You sent your clear words forth.
Indeed, even while I call myself poor,
Far off on all sides,
I have as my fathers life-giving priests.
Asking for their life-giving breath,
Their breath of old age,
Their breath of waters,
Their breath of seeds,
Their breath of riches
Their breath of fecundity,
Their breath of strong spirit,
Their breath of power,
Their breath of all good fortune whereof they are possessed,
Asking for their breath,

[61] As soon as the altar is set up in the society room the father or uncle of the novice is summoned. He again gives the boy's ceremonial father a packet of prayer meal, thanking him for having cured his child. This meal is later distributed among all present.

[62] The retreat of the society begins. Their room becomes taboo to outsiders because of the presence of the divine ones.

[63] Three nights.

[64] On the fourth night.

[65] The novice is clothed and painted.

[66] His head is washed.

[67] By the man who first summoned the society for the curing rites

Into our warm bodies taking their breath,
We shall add to your breath.
Then also far off on all sides
I have fathers:
Priest of the north,[68]
Priest of the west,
Priest of the south,
Priest of the east,
Priest of above,
Priest of below;
Our sun father,
Our moon mother,
The sky,
The Milky Way,
The Great Bear,
The Pleiades,
The seed stars,[69]
And all the little sparkling stars,
Priests,
Asking for their life-giving breath,
Their breath of old age,
Their breath of waters,
Their breath of seeds,
Their breath of fecundity,
Their breath of riches,
Their breath of strong spirit,
Their breath of power,
Their breath of all good fortune whereof they are possessed,
Asking for their breath,
Into our warm bodies taking their breath,
We shall add to your breath.
Do not despise the breath of your fathers,
But draw it into your body.
That our roads may reach to where the life-giving road of our sun father comes out,
That, clasping one another tight,
Holding one another fast,
We may finish our roads together;
That this may be, I add to your breath now.
To this end:
May my father bless you with life;
May your road reach to Dawn Lake,
May your road be fulfilled.

ma' les'i t̂e'wanan·e
now this much time

ho''na·wan t̂e'upk̂unan·e
our child

i'me' kwa'tikoł we'ak̭äk̭ä
perhaps some kind sickness because of

tse''mak i·'natina
spirit failing

yan'hak̂un i·'natina
breath failing

t̂on yam a·'teonak̭ä
ton your means of being

hom lu'knio tca'we
my these children

yam a'k̭·ä a·'ci'na ya·'na t̂owa k̂ohan an ci''nan·e
their with it flesh completed corn white its flesh

ha'lawo·tinan·e
prayer meal

ye'lete'unapk̭ä
(you) prepared

li'wan k̭ä'liciankwin ta''na
hither in the west direction

---

[68] The title "priest" seems to be applied to anyone endowed with the means of securing or bestowing blessings, regardless of whether they are human or immortal. The reference here is to supernaturals.

[69] Un unidentified constellation.

hon tsit i′lap̑a
we mother having

k̑o′hak̑w o′k̭ä
white shell woman

ho′łomacko′na i′młak̑inte
far off even though she stays permanently

le′ łu′walan ya·′tci hoł li·′ła le′′hatina
all village branches wherever here thus thinking

ło′ i′cuk̭äna′kona
shell which was rubbed off from her

to′pacoł yam ło·′ i′lop̑i′kona
just one your shell the one which was borrowed

ło·′o
shell

u′tenan·e
clothing

t̑e′wus ya′nułana
prayer appointed

le· yam a·′tatcu
all your fathers

o′na·ya·′nak̭ä a·′ciwan·i
life-giving priests

o′na·ya·′nak̭ä p̑e′kwi·we
life-giving speakers

o′na·ya·′nak̭ä a·′pi′ła·ci′wan·i
life-giving bow priests

le· ti′k̭ä a·′ciwan·i
all society priests

ti′k̭ä p̑e′kwi·we
society speakers

ti′k̭ä a·′pi′ła·ci′wan·i
society bow priests

t̑on a·′wunu′lapnapk̭ä.
you looked about among them

k̭es kwa′hoł yu′′he·tonan te′amap̑a
now something clear not being

k̭ä′pin a·′ho′i
raw persons

hom le′n a′nawana·′wap̑a
me thus having guessed

t̑e′k̑oha′nan hom tca′we
daylight my children

t̑om ya′nłi′to‘na
to you revealing

hom le′n a′nawana·′wap̑a
me thus having guessed

hom yu·′′ya·k̭äna·′wap̑a
me having let know

6066°—32——52

la'łhokᵘ hom a·'tatcu
yonder my fathers

hoł yam t̂i'nan-ła'k̂i'kona
wherever where they stay quietly

o'neała· kwai'ile-k̭äna·'wap̂a
roads having made come out severally

yam ha'lawo'tinan i·'łeana
my prayer meal taking

lehokᵘ t̂e'luankwin ta'ʻna
yonder to the east direction

ho' o'neał a'k̭äk̭ä.
I road made go

yam a·'tatcu
my fathers

ya'niktoʻna ye·'lana
face to face standing

ho ha'lawo·tinan a·'łea'up̂a
I prayer meal having given to them

k̭ä'pin a·'ho'i
raw persons

ho'man ha'lawo·tinan i·'łeana
my prayer meal taking

o'neał eʻk̂una·wap̂a
road going ahead

a·'wa ma'sikwin e'layälu
their back (at) following

k̂a'łhok t̂e'wus'ak̭ä hon o'neał a·k̭änapk̭ä.
hither prayer with we road made go

li'ł yam t̂e'k̂ohanan tca'we.
here their daylight children

a·'wan k̭äcima t̂e'li'tonankwi
their water room in

k̭ä'pin a·ho'i
raw persons

o'neała kwa'tok̭äna
roads making come in

i't̂inan-ła'k̭ik̭äp̂a
having sat down quietly

hon t̂e'k̂ohanana
we daylight in

i'yona-e'latena
one another meeting

ho i'miłak̂up̂a
I having sat down quietly

yam ha'lawo·tinan·e
our prayer meal

ło·''o
shell

u'tenan·e
clothing

yam t̂ewusu ya′nuła’kona
our prayers the ones that were appointed

a·′wana’u′łana
drawing toward (us)

hon a·′tatc i′lap̂ona
we fathers the ones [we] have

o′naya·nak̯ä a·′ciwan·i
life-giving priests

li′wan a·′wan we′cik̯ä o′naya·′nak̯ä a′stecokta’a
here their left life-giving palm

ha′lawo·tinan·e
prayer meal

ło·′’o
shell

u′tenan·e
clothing

i′tiułak̯ä tea’ana
placed against when it was

hon a·′tatc i′lap̂ona
we fathers the ones [we] have

yam ha′lawo·tinan·e
their prayer meal

ło·′’o
shell

u′tenan·e
clothing

ya′t̂ena-t̂su′mek̯änapk̯ä te′a’ana
they held fast when it was

t̂e′k̂ohanana
in the daylight

hon ha′lawo·tinan ak̯·ä
we prayer meal with

ło·′ ak̯·ä
shell with

u′tenan ak̯·ä
clothing with

hon i′wiyat̂ent̂su′mek̯äk̯ä
we one another held fast.

yam a·′tatcu
our fathers

a·′wan o′naya·′nak̯ä a′ntecemana
their long life desiring

a·′wan łaciak̯ä a′ntecemana
their old age desiring

a·′wan a′kwa·n a′ntecemana
their medicine desiring

t̂ewusu p̂enan kwai’ik̯äna
prayer words sending out

ha′lawo·tinan ak̯·ä
prayer meal with

ło·'' ak̭·ä
shell with

u'tenan ak̭·ä
clothing with

hon i'wiyat̂en-t̂su'mek̭äk̭ä.
we one another held fast.

yam t̂eapk̂unan an ha'lawo·tinan i·'łeana
our child his prayer meal taking

ło·' i·'łeana
shell taking

u'tenan i·'łeana
clothing taking

le'hok t̂e'luankwin ta'na
yonder to the east direction

t̂e'wusak·ä ho' o'neałan kwai''ik̭äk̭ä
prayer with I road made go out.

yam a·'tatcu
our fathers

a·'wan o'naya·'nak̭ä o'neałan i'na'a
their life-giving road coming in

ho' a·'wona-e'latena
we on their roads passed.

yam t̂e'apk̂unan an ha'lawo·tinan ak̭·ä
our child his prayer meal with

an ło·'' ak̭·ä
his shell with

an u'tenan ak·ä
his clothing with

yam t̂e'apk̂unan·e
our child

ho' an t̂e'k̂ohanan ce'mana
I for him life asking

yam he'cot̂akwi
my house to

ho' o'neał i'k̭äk̭ä.
I road made come.

k̭äpin a·'ho'i
raw persons.

a·'wan t̂e'wusu p̂e'nan i'tulohap̂a
their prayer word having gone around

t̂e'k̂ohanana i'yu'ya·k̭äna
in the daylight letting one another know

a'nt̂sume'na hon su'nhak̭änapk̭ä.
anxiously we came to evening.

tem t̂a a·'tapana
then again following them

tse''mak-t̂e'łakwi
where our thoughts touch

yam t̂ewanan i'lit̂un'ona
their days the ones who are to have

pi'lotsi te'ona
willow male being

p̣i'lok̯a te''ona
willow female being

hoł tcuw ha'lowi'li'kona
whoever the lucky one

a'k̯̑ewułkwi'nakna
shoots pulling

a·'wana-u'łak̯äna
drawing them toward him

yam a'sin k̯̑äłnak·ä
his hand warm with

a·'wiyat̑en-t̑su'mek̯̑äk̯a.
he held them fast

yam nani'li te''ona
his grandfather the one who is

to'n'ots an a'wełuyan p̑a'in·e
turkey male his cloud robe

k̯̑ä'k̯̑äl an ci'pololon u'tcun·e
eagle his mist garment

lałhok o'lo'ik̯aiak̯ä wo'we
yonder summer birds

a·'wan ła'pihanan la'tan·e
their striped cloud wing

a·'wan a'wełuyan k̯ä'ten ak·ä
their cumulus cloud tail with

a'witela'ma
four times

te'lik̯inan a·'p̑a'una
prayer stick wrapping them

a·'ho a·'ya·k̯̑äna
persons finishing them

yam tsit'ili te''ona
our mother the one who is

p̑i'tsem ok̯ä
cotton woman

k̑o't̑i p̑i''lenapte
rough cotton cord even

a'k·ä a'witela'ma pa'nulap i'kwian-te''tcina
with it four times going around belt reaching

k̯̑ä'cima la'cowa
rain hair feather

ho''i ya·'k̯̑äna·'wap̑a
person finishing it

yam tsi't' i'lite''ona
our mother the one who is

ha'kwin o'k̯ä
black paint woman

he'teł o'k̯ä
clay woman

a·′tcian ci′nanak·ä
their flesh with

a′k̭·ä te′lik̭inan i·′ci′nana
with it prayer stick giving it flesh

ho′′i ya·′k̭äk̭ä
person he finished it.

yam a·′tatcu
our fathers

o′na·ya·′nak̭ä a·′ciwan·i
life-giving priests

a·′wan pi′k̭än a′k̭ä ho′′i ya·′k̭äp̄a
their mucous with person having finished it

hoł k̭ä·′k̭i k̭e·′si le′anak̭äp̄a
whenever now having said

te′lik̭inan i·′łeana
prayer stick taking

k̭ä′pin a·′ho′i
raw persons

o′neał e′ʻk̄una·wap̄a
road going ahead

a·′wa ma′sikwi e′layälu
their back at following

k̄ä′łhokᵘ t̄e′wusak̭·ä
hither prayers with

hon o′neał a·′k̭änapk̭ä.
we road made go.

yam t̄e′k̄ohanan tca′we
their daylight children

a·′wan k̭ä′cima t̄e′li′tonankwin
their water inner room (to)

k̭ä′pin a·′ho′i
raw persons

o′neała kwa′tok̭äna
roads making come in

yam a′s·in ak̭·ä
their hand with

yam t̄e′apk̄unan·e
their child

kwa′hoł we′ak̭ä sa′mu a′k̭ä ho′′i te′a′kona
some sickness evil with person the one who had been

ła′panaʻna·wap̄a
having drawn out

ho′′na·wan t̄eapk̄unan·e
our child

yam pi′k̭än ak̭ä
his mucous with

te′lik̭inan ya·′k̭äp̄a
prayer stick having finished

te′lik̭inan i·′łeana
prayer stick taking

yam t̂e'apk̂unan·e
our child

kwa'hoł we'ak̭ä sa'mua·k̭·ä ho'i te'a'kona
something sickness evil with it person the one who had been

ła'pana'na
drawing out

te'lik̭inan i·'łeana
prayer stick taking

hon o'neała kwai'ik̭'änapk̭ä.
we road made go out.

hoł li·'ła le''hatina
wherever here thinking

hon a·'tatc i'lap̂ona
we fathers the ones [we] have

o'naya·'nak̭a a·'ciwan·i
life-giving priests

o'·naya·'nak̭ä p̂e'kwi·we
life-giving speakers

o'naya·'nak̭ä a·'p̂i'ła·ci'wan·i
life-giving bow priests

le·'stiklea ho''na·wan a·'łacina·we
furthermore our ancestors

li·'ła ti'k̭än i'lap̂kona
here societies the ones who belonged to

ti'k̭än a·'mosi'k̭ä
society they were chiefs

ti'k̭än p̂e'kwi· tea'k̭a
society speakers they were

ti'k̭än pi'ła·ci'wan·ik̭äk̭a
society bow priests they were

i'tsemak t̂e'łakwi u'lo'ni'lap̂ a·'te'ona
their thoughts touching the world holding the ones who are

le'stiklea ho''na·wan a·'łacina·we
furthermore our ancestors

ho' a'nilik̭' a·wanikwa'kona
people holding the ones who knew how

we·'ma' a·'ciwan·i
beast priests

kwa tcuw i'metcame ha'p̂ona k̂ɔ'kcikwi
not anyone left behind gathered together well where

ho a·'wona-e'latena
I on their roads passing them

ho te'li·k̭inan a·'łeap̂a
I prayer stick giving to them

hom a·'tatcu
my fathers

ho'man te'lik̭inan ya't̂ena-t̂su'mek̭äna
my prayer stick holding fast

lehoł yam tcimik̭äk̭atekwi
there their the place of the first beginning

ci′papo′limakwi
at Cipapolima

i′yätiku po′ceyäŋk̂i

---

ho′man te′lik̂inanak·ä
my prayer stick with

ya′cu’ i′tulo‘k̂äna
talk sending around

a′nt̂sume‘na su′nhak̂änapk̂ä
anxiously they came to evening.

hon yä′tok̂ä tatc i′lap̂ a·′te’ona
we sun father having the ones who are

yam t̂e′łacinakwi ye·′lana kwa′tok̂äp̂a
his ancient place standing having gone in

hon t̂e′ĥiak̂’ a·′tatc i′lap̂ona
we night fathers the ones (we) have

hon t̂e′ĥiak̂’ a·′tsit i′lap̂ona
we night mothers the ones (we) have

yam t̂e′łacinakwi i′łuwakna kwai’ina
their ancient place arising coming out

ho’n a·′wona-e′latena·wap̂a
us on our roads having passed

hoł k̂ä·′k̂i k̂e·si le′anak̂äp̂a
whenever now saying this

yam tatc i′li te′’ona
our father having the one

yam tsit i′lite′ona
our mother the one who is

p̂a′’i ya·′na
robed completely

a·′tciana e′lemak̂äna
both making arise

a·tci o′neał e′‘kwik̂äna
their road going ahead

la′lik yam t̂e′k̂ohanan a·′tatcu
near by our daylight fathers

a·′wan k̂ä′cima t̂e′li’tokwi
their water room to

hon o′neał kwa′tok̂äna
we road making go in

i′t̂inan-ła′k̂ikna
sitting down quietly

tem ta yam t̂e′apk̂unan an ha′lawo·tinan·e
and also our child his prayer meal

kwi′lik̂änana
the second time

li′wanem yam a·′tatcu
hither our fathers

a·′wan we′cik̂’ o′naya·nak̂’ a′stecokta
their left life-giving hollow of the hand

ha'lawo·'tinan·e
prayer meal

ło·' ak̲' iyanhai'tena·   i'wiyaten-t̂su'mek̲äna
shell   with presenting to one another   holding one another fast

hoł k̲ä·'k̲i k̲e·'si le''anik̲äp̂a
whenever   now   saying

yam tatc i'li   te''ona
our   father having the one who is

yam tsit i'li   te''ona
our   mother having   the one who is

p̂a''i ya·'na
robed   completely

a·'tciana   e'lemak̲äna
both   making arise

a·'tciana   o'neał   e''kwik̲ana
their   road   going ahead

lehok   t̂e'luankwin   ta'na
yonder   to the east   direction

t̂e'wus a'k̲·ä hon o'neała kwai''ik̲änapk̲ä.
prayers   with   we   roads   made go out.

hoł yam a·'tatcu
where   our   fathers

a·'wan o'naya·'nak̲ä o'neałan i'nakwi
their   life-giving   road   where it comes

a·'wona-e'latena
on their roads passing them

ya'nikto·na   ye·'lana
face to face   standing

yam t̂e'apk̲unan an ha'lawo·tinan·e
our   child   his   prayer meal

ło·''o
shell

yam a·'tatcu hon a·'łeana
our   fathers   we   giving to them

tem t̂a hołnoko'lea ha'lawo·tinan t̂ewus' a'nuł ho''i ya·'k̲ä
and   also   whatever   prayer meal   prayer   appointed person   made

te'a'kona
one it was

p̂e'na yałtona
word   laying on top.

yam t̂e'apk̲unan·e
our   child

hon an t̂e'kohanan ce'mana
we   for him   life   asking

ho''na·wan a·'tatcu
our   fathers

o'naya·'k̲a a·'ciwan·i
life-giving   priests

le'stiklea ho''na·wan a·'łacina·we
furthermore   our   ancestors

li·'łno ti'k̭än i'lapkona
here society the ones who had

lehoku k̭ä'cima t̃e''wok̭änap̃käna
yonder water place the ones who won

le'stiklea ho''na·wan i'yanik̭ina·we
furthermore our relatives

ho' a'nilik̭' a·'wanikwa'kona
us looking after the ones who knew how

kwatcu'wa le·w i'metcame
no one so many missing

yam o'naya·'nak̭ä łe'ap̃a
their long life carrying

yam ła'ciak̭a łe'ap̃a
their old age carrying

ho'n a·'wona-e'latena·wap̃a
us on (our) roads having passed

le·w we·'ma a·'pi'ła·ci'wan·i
all beast bow priests

yam sa'wanik̭ä łe'ap̃a
their weapons carrying

ho'n a·'wona-e'latena·wap̃a
us on (our) roads having passed

lu'kniak̭on o'neała e''k̃una·wap̃a
these roads making go first

a·'wa ma'sikwi e'layä'lu
their back at following

k̭ä'łhoku t̃e'wus ak·ä
hither prayers with

hon o'neał a·'k̭änapk̭ä
we road made go.

yam t̃e'k̭ohanan tca'we
their daylight children

a·'wan k̭ä'cima t̃e'li'tonankwi
their water inner room (in)

a·'wan t̃o'waconan t̃e'li'tonankwi
their seed inner room (in)

k̭ä·'pin a·'ho'i
raw persons

o'neała kwa'tok̭äna
roads making come in

i't̃inan-i'ła'k̭ik̭ä te'a'ana
they sat] down quietly when it was

t̃e'k̃ohanan a'k̭' a·'ho'i
daylight with persons

hon i'yona-e'latena
we one another meeting

i·'t̃inan i'łak̃ikna
sitting down quietly

hon a·'tatc i'lap̃ona
we fathers the ones [we] have

o′naya·′nak̭ä a·′ciwan·i
life-giving priests

yam a′s·in a′k·ä
their hand with

yam a′wełuyan k̭ä′kwe ya·′k̭äna
their cloud house having completed

ci′pololon p̂e′wuna
mist blanket spread out

o′naya·′nak̭ä o′neałan a·′k̭äna
life-giving road sending out

k̭ä′nakwe·nan ya·′na ye′lete′una
spring complete having prepared

i′t̂inan ła′k̭ikna
sitting down quietly

lu′kniak̂o k̭ä′pin a·′ho′i
these raw persons

yam t̂e-apk̂unan·e
their child

u′nulapna·′wap̂a
having looked all over

tem t̂a lu′kniak̂onte
and also these here

a·′wan a′s·in e′ʿkwik̂una
their hand going ahead

a·′wan ya′nhak̂una e′ʿkwik̂una
their breath going ahead

hon a·′was-yä′luk̭a.
our hands followed.

le·w t̂o′wa ci′wan an łe′tsilon p̂a′ni·nan tcawe
all corn priest his ladder descending children

ko·w a′ktsik̭ ła′na
somewhat boy large

ko·w k̭ä′tsik̭ ła′na
somewhat girl large

a·′won-e′ʿkwinte te′ʿya ho′′i te′ante
even those whose roads go ahead valuable person even though he is

kwa′tikoł a′k̭·ä i′k̭en i′samut̂ina
something because of heart becoming angry

yam sa′wanik̭äk̭ä
his weapons with

ho′′na·wan t̂e′apk̂unan·e
our child

a′nat̂suma′kona
the one who injured (him)

k̭ä′pin a·′ho′i
saw persons

yu·′′ya·nam an sa′wanik̭ä
foolish one his weapons

hon a·'tatc i'lap̑ona
we fathers the ones [we] have

we·'ma a·'p̑i'ła·ci'wan·i
beast bow priests

yam yä'tok̯ä ta'tcu an t̑e'k̑ohanakwi
their sun father his daylight (in)

lu'wana kwai'ik̯ana·wap̑a
standing having made come out

ho''na·wan t̑e'apkunan·e
our child

y·am a·'tatcu
his fathers

a·'wan k̯ä''kwin·e
their living water

a·'wan ci''nan·e
their flesh

i'k̯ä'k̑up̑a
drinking in

ko·'wi yä'ton a·'nap̑a
little day having gone

ko·'wi t̑e'łinan a·'nap̑a
little night having gone

ho''na·wan t̑e'apk̑unan·e
our child

an we'ak̯ä k̯ä'suana
his sickness decreasing

an ya'nkak̑unan i'k̑okcuk̯äna
his breath becoming better

yam yä'tok̯ä ta'tcu an o'neałan kwa''inakwi o'na ya·'na'a
his sun father his road where it comes out [his] road completed

yam a'wit̑elin tsi'tana
his earth mother (on)

e'layäłto ło·''otip̑a
standing up strong

a'ntsume'na hon t̑ewanan a·'tek̯än·a
eagerly we time shall live

hoł k̯ä·'k̯i k̯e·'si le''anak̯äp̑a
whenever now having said

hon ya'onak̯ä tsit i'lap̑ a·'teona
we moon mother having the ones

li'wan k̯ä'liciankwin ta''na
hither to the west direction

ko·'wit̑sa'na ye'tsak̯äna
very small making herself visible

t̑e'luankwin ta''na i'tiułana
(in) the east direction standing against

ho''i ya·'k̯ät̑unte'kwi ko·w a'nte'we'tcikwi
person about to become complete little space still remained for her

ho’’na·wan k̃ä’nakwe·nan tca’we
our spring children

hołtcu’wa ła’cina tse’’makona
whoever growing old the ones who thought

he’lawo·tinan i·’łeana
prayer meal taking

ło·’ i·’łeana
shell taking

o’nean i·’łeana
corn pollen taking

o’neała kwai’’ik̃äna
roads making go out

hoł yam a·’tatcu
where their fathers

ła’kwił p̃ot̃i
brush full of

a·’wona-e’latena
on their roads passing (them)

hołtcuw’ ha’lowi’li’kona
whoever the one that was lucky

an sa’kwia
his feet

ha’lawo·tinan ło·’’o
prayer meal shell

o’nean·e
corn pollen

a·’łeakna
giving to them

a·’k̃ewułkwi‘nakna
the young shoots pulling

a·wana-uła’kona
the ones he drew toward him

yam a’s·in k̃äłn ak̃·ä
his hand warm with

a·’wiyat̃en-t̃su’mek̃äna
holding one another fast

yam nan i’li te’’ona
his grand father the one who is

ton ots an a’wełuyan p̃a’in·e
turkey male his cumulus cloud robe

k̃ä’k̃äl an ci’pololon u’tcun·e
eagle his mist garment

la’łhoku o’lo’ik̃aiak̃ä wo’we
yonder summer birds

a·’wan ła’pihanan la’tane
their striped cloud wing

a·’wan a’wełuyan k̃ä’ten·e
their cumulus cloud tail

a’k̃’ a·’witela’ma
with them four times

te′lik̑inan a·′p̄a’una
prayer stick clothing (them)

a·′ho’ a·′ya·k̑äna
persons completing them

yam tsit i′li te′ona
their mother having the one who is

p̄i′tsem ok̑ä
cotton woman

k̄o′ti p̄i′′lenapte
even a rough cotton cord

a′witela’ma pa′nulapna ikwian-te′′tci·na
four times going around tied around reaching

k̑ä′cima la′cowa
water hair feather

te′lik̑inaw’ ho′′i ya·′k̑äna·wap̄a
prayer sticks having made them into persons

yam tsit i′li te′ona
their mothers having the one who is

ha′kwin o′k̑’ä
black paint woman

he′teł o′k̑ä
clay woman

a·′tcian ci′′nan te′lik̑inan i′ci’nana ho′′i-ya·′k̑äp̄a
their flesh prayer stick getting flesh into persons having made them

hoł k̑ä·′k̄i k̑e·′si le’anak̑äp̄a
whenever now having said

te′lik̑inan i·′łeana
prayer sticks taking

yam t̄eapk̄unan an ha′lawo·tinan i·′łeana
our child his prayer meal taking

le′hok^u t̄e′wus a′k·ä
yonder prayer with

hon o′neała kwai′ilek̑äna·wap̄a
we roads having made go out severally

yam a′witelin tsit o′na-elatena
our earth mother on her road passing

yam a·′łacina·′we
our ancestors

yam tca′we
our children

li·′łno tik̑′än i′lap̄kona
here societies the ones who belonged to

le′stiklea yam a·′tatcu
furthermore our fathers

we·′ma a·′p̄i’ła·ci′wan·i
beast bow priests

hon a·′wona-e′latena
we on their roads meeting them

hon te'lik̭inan a·'łeana·wap̑a
we prayer stick to them having given

hon yä tok̭ä tatc i'lap̑'a·'te’ona
we sun father having the ones who are

yam t̑e'łaci'nakwi i·'muna kwa'tok̭ät̑untekwi
his ancient place sitting down about to go in when it was

ko·w a'nteʻwe'tcikwi
little space yet remained for him

la'łhok^{u} le'si te'kwi
under so many directions

ho’'na·wan a·'tatcu
our fathers

o'naya·'nak̭ä a·'ciwan·i
life-giving priests

k̭̑ä'pin a·'ho’i
raw persons

kwa le'nhoł tcuw i'metcame
not of all no one left behind

o'neała kwai’'ik̭äna
roads making come out

oneał i·'k̭̑äna
road making come

yam t̑e'k̑ohanan a·'tsita
their daylight mothers

a·'wan k̭̑äcima t̑e'li’tonankwi o'neała kwa'tok̭̑äna
their rain inner room (in) road making come in

yam ko’ tcimik̭ä’kowa te'liaʻna
their something according to the first beginning imitating

a'wełuyan k̭ä'kwe ya·'k̭̑äna
cumulus cloud house making

ci'pololon p̑e'wuna
mist blanket spread out

o'naya·'nak̭ä o'neałan a·k̭̑äna
life-giving road sending out

k̭̑ä'nakwai’inan ya·'k̭̑äna
spring making

yam a'mitolan pi’łan a’'una
their rainbow bow putting down

yam wilolonan co’l a’'una
their lightning arrow putting down

i't̑inan-iła'k̭̑ik̭̑äp̑a
having sat down quietly

a·'wan sa'kwia i·'mi ałana
their feet at sitting down on it

le·'si t̑e'wanan·e
this much time

a'nt̑sumeʻna hon t̑e'wanan a·'tek̭̑äna
eagerly we time living

k̭es le'nhoł a·'wan te'mła t̑ewak̭a te'a’ana
now all their everything time past when it is

ho’na·wan t̂e′apk̂unan·e
our child

yam a·′tatcu a·′wan o′neałan kwa′tona te′ʻyapte
his fathers their road coming in even being valuable

o′neała kwa′tok̯äp̂a
roads making come in

hon a·′tatc i′lap̂ona
we fathers the ones [we] have

yam ko′nhoł ho’i te′’ona
their some kind person being

yam t̂e′apk̂unan·e
their child

ho’i- ya·′k̯̂äna·′wap̂a
having made him into a person

t̂e′łinan k̂o′kci
night good

ho’na tcawilap̂ a·′want̂ewana
us children with coming to day

t̂e′wap̂ yä′ton·e
the next day

hon yä′tok̯ä tatc i′lap̂ a·′te’ona
we sun father having the ones

yam t̂e′łacinakwi
his ancient place

ye·′lana kwai′’ik̯at̂ekwi
standing came out when it was

ko·w’ a′nteʻwetcikwi
little space was left for him

yam k̯ä′cima k̂o′kcak̯·ä
our water clear with

yam ak̯·’ o′nawi′lap̂ a·′teona
our with it living the ones who are

hon a′k̯·a yam t̂e′apk̂una ya′tena-t̂sumek̯äna·wap̂a
we with it our children having held fast

k̯ä′pin a·′ho’i k̯e·′la yam p̂inan te′lianapk̯ä t̂e′a’ana
saw persons first their breath added when it was

tem t̂a lukniak̂onte
and also these here

t̂e′wus a·′p̂ek̯äna
prayers speaking

yam t̂e′apk̂unan hon an p̂i′nan te′liana·′wap̂a
our child we his breath having added (to)

yam a·′tatcu
his fathers

a·′wan p̂i′’nan a′naʻna
their breath taking to him

yam ce′łnakwinte p̂i′’nan a′le’ton·a
his inside his body breath inhaling

ho′’na·wan p̂i′’nan te′ʻyap̂a
our breath being valuable

hołyam k̯ä'nakwe·nan t̂u'nak̯a te'a'ante
wherever spring he saw even where it is

i'mi-a'kcikna
sitting down among [us]

o'na-ya·'ak̯ä a'nt̂apana
prolonging life following

hon te'tse'ma' te'łakwik̂än·a
we shall be bending our thoughts (to it)

tem t̂a hon a·'tapana tse''mak-t̂e'łakwit̂u'n'ona'kä
and also we following [this] in order that it may be that toward which our thoughts bend

yu·''he·to t̂e'wusu p̂e'nan kwai''i·k̯äk̯ä
plain prayer words came forth

ho'n t̂e'apk̂unan i'yanhaitek̯a
to us child he gave

ta'canakwi ya'cuwa k̂ɔ'kci
for a long time talking together kindly

yam a·'teat̂un'onak̯ä
in order that it may be thus

yu·''he·to t̂e'wusu p̂e'nan kwai''ina
plain prayer words coming forth

yam a·'tatcu a·'tekwi
your fathers where they are

t̂om t̂e'wusu p̂e'nan kwai''ik̯änapk̯ä.
for you prayer words sent forth.

ta'tcic te'wuko'lia le'k̂wanante
while poor even though saying

la'łhok[u] le'si t̂e'kwi ho' a·'tatc i'li
yonder all directions I fathers have

o'na ya·'nak̯ä a·'ciwan·i
life-giving priests

a·'wan o'na ya·'nak̯ä p̂i''nan·e
this life-giving breath

a·'wan ła'ciak̯ä p̂i''nan·e
their old age breath

a·'wan k̯ä'cima p̂i''nan·e
their waters breath

a·'wan t̂o'waconan p̂i''nan·e
their seeds breath

a·'wan u'tenan p̂i''nan·e
their wealth breath

a·'wan t̂e'apk̂unan p̂i''nan·e
their children breath

a·'wan tse''makwin t̂su'me p̂i''nan·e
their spirit strong breath

a·'wan sa'wanik̯ä p̂i''nan·e
their power breath

a·'wan kwahoł te'mła te'n·i ha'lowilin p̂i''nan i'lap̂ a·'teona
their something everything at all good luck breath whatever they have

p̄i''na· yai'ncemana
breaths asking from them

yam t̄e'hul k̯äłnakwi
my body cavity warm in

p̄i''nan a'na'kwa'tok̯äna
breath drawing in

t̄o'man łon p̄i''nan te'liana·wa.
for you we breath will add (to).

tem t̄a la'łhok[u] le'si te'kwi ho a·'tatc i'li
and also yonder in all directions I fathers have

pi'cle a·'ciwan·i
north priests

k̯ä'lici a·'ciwan·i
west priests

a'laho a·'ciwan·i
south priests

te'mak̄oha a·'ciwan·i
east priests

i'yam a·'ciwan·i
above priests

ma'nilam a·'ciwan·i
below priests

yä'tok̯ä tatc i'lap̄a
sun father having

ya'onak̯a tsit i'lap̄a
moon mother having

a''p̄oyan·e
sky

yu'piyałan·e
Milky Way

kwi'lilek̯akwi
the seven [Ursa Major]

i'pilak̯a
the close together [the Pleiades]

k̄u'pa·kwe
the seeds

la'łhok[u] le· t̄su'hap̄a mo'yatcuwe
yonder are sparkling stars

a·'ciwan·i
priests

a·'wan o'na-ya·'nak̯ä p̄i''nan·e
their life-giving breath

a·'wan ła'ciak̯ä p̄i''nan·e
their old age breath

a·'wan k̯ä'cima p̄i''nan·e
their waters breath

a·'wan t̄o'waconan p̄i''nan·e
their seeds breath

a·'wan t̄e'apk̄unan p̄i''nan·e
their children breath

a·'wan u'tenan p̂i''nan·e
their clothing breath

a·'wan tse''makwin t̂su'me p̂i''nan·e
their spirit strong breath

a·'wan sa'wanik̭ä p̂i''nan·e
their power breath

a·'wan kwa'hoł te'mła te'n·i ha'lowilin p̂i''nan i'lap̂ a·'te'ona
their something everything at all good luck breath that they have

p̂i''nan yai'necemana
breath asking from them

yam t̂e'huł k̭äłnakwi p̂i''nan a'na'kwa'tok̭äna
our body cavity warm breath drawing in

to'man łon p̂i''nan te'liana·wa.
for you we breath will add (to).

eł yam a·'tatcu a·'wan p̂i''nan ya'tcita'nam·e
do not your fathers their breath (do not) despise

yam ce'łnakwi
your inside of body

p̂i''nan a'na·'kwatok̭äna
breath drawing in

hoł yam yä'tok̭ä ta'tcu
where your sun father

an o'naya·'nak̭ä o'neałan kwai''inakwi o'neał u'ła
his life-giving road where it comes out road touching

i'p̂iya-t̂su'mep̂a
hand in hand fast

i'yakna ło·''op̂a
holding one another tight

yam i'yona ya·'k̭äna a·'teat̂un'onak̭·ä
your roads finishing that (you) may be the ones

t̂oman łon p̂i''nan te'liana·wa k̭e·'si.
for you we breath add to now.

t̂e'wuna' hom tatcu
finally my father

tom t̂e'k̂ohanan a'niktcia't'u
you life may he grant

hoł t̂e'luaiyan k̭aiakwi o'neał te''tcina
somewhere dawn lake road reaching

t̂o o'na ya·'t'u
you road may [be] finished

Prayer of a Society Chief During His Winter Retreat

At the winter solstice all the societies observe retreats. After the images of the war god have gone into the kiva on the night before the first great prayer stick planting they hold late meetings at which special prayers are said for rain. There are special and very secret songs that are sung on this night only. They do not go into retreat formally until the next night. Three nights are spent mainly in preparation for the great ceremony of the last night at which the sick are cured. On this night the beast gods are present in all the society houses, and take possession of those who have the secret knowledge of how to invoke them.

The following prayers purport to be those spoken by the heads of the Cuma·kwe and Ant Societies, respectively, at some time during this four-day retreat. The man who dictated it was not a member of either society and did not state the precise use of the prayers. Nor were my other informants familiar with them. Such prayers might be used on any one of a great number of occasions.

My life-giving fathers,
At the place called since the first beginning Tcipia,
You dwell.
Where the deer stands,
At Dry place you dwell.
My fathers,
Life-giving priests, there you dwell.
This day,
Here at Itiwana,
Our daylight fathers,
Our mothers,
Our children,
In their inner rooms
For their fathers,
Life-giving priests,
Perpetuating the rite handed down since the first beginning,
Have spread out your cloud blanket,
Your life-giving road they have made.
Your spring they have made.
Perpetuating the rite handed down since the first beginning
You have sat down quietly before it;
At your back,
At your feet,
We shall sit down beside you.
Desiring your waters,
Your seeds,
Your riches,
Your long life,
Your old age,
Desiring these, I set you down quietly.
As you sit here quietly
As I wish, according to my words,
You will take us to be your children.

o'naya·naḳä hom a·'tatcu
ḳä·'k̄ä tci'mik̄aḳä tci'pia

t̄on a·'teaiye
nat̄sik e'lawa
t̄e'k̄usnawa t̄on a·'teaiye.
hom a·'tatcu
o'naya·naḳä a·'ciwan·i t̄on a'teaiye.
lu'ḳä yä'ton·e
li·'ła i'tiwan·a
t̄e'k̄ohanan yam a·'tatcu
yam a·'tsita
yam tca'we
a·wan t̄e'li'to'a
hom a·'tatcu
o'naya·naḳä a·'ciwani·i
lu'ḳä yä'ton·e
yam ko''nhoł tci'mik̄äḳä te'lia'na
yam a'wełuyan p̄e'wuna
yam o'naya·naḳä o'neałan ya·''na'a

yam k̄ä'nakwe·nan ya·'na'a
yam ko''noł tci'mik̄a'kowa te'lia'na

t̄on i't̄inan ła'k̄iḳä.
t̄o''na·wan ma'si'a
t̄o''na·wan sa'kwi'a
i'miya'wełana
t̄o''na·wan k̄ä'cima
t̄o''na·wan t̄o'waconan·e
u'tenan·e
o'naya·naḳä
ła'ciaḳä a'ntecemana
t̄o''na ho' t̄inan-ła'k̄u

t̄on i·'t̄inan ła'kikna
ko'nhoł ho' a'ntecema p̄e'yenak̄owa
ho''na t̄on tca'wila·wa

So that all my children
May be saved.
All will be happy.
Safely they will bring forth their young.
So that all my children may finish their roads,
So that they may grow old,
So that you may bless us with life,
So that none of my spring children
May be left standing outside.
So that you may protect us (I have done this).
May our roads be fulfilled;
May we grow old;
May our roads reach to dawn lake;
May we grow old;
May you bless us with life.

a'k̯a hom tca'we te'mła a·'te'ya-k̯̂äna
te'mła i·'k̯̂etsana
e'letokna t̂e'apkuna·wa
a'k̯ä hom tca'we te'mła a·'wona-ya·''an·a
a·'łacian·a
ho''na t̂e'k̂ohanan t̂on ya'niktcia-na·wa.
a'k̯ä hom k̯̂ä'nakwe·nan tca'we
kwa tcu'hoł e'la ła'tsina te'amek̯̂äna
a'k̯ä ho''na a·'te'yak̯̂äna
hon a·'wona-ya·t'u
hon a·'łacit'u
te'luwaian k̯̂ai'kwi o'neała te''tcina
hon a·'łacit'u
ho''na ton t̂e'k̂ohanan ya'niktci-an·a.

Prayer of the Chief of the Ant Society

At the place of the first beginning,
Ci'papolima,
Life-giving priests, abide.
My fathers,
Beast priests,
Mountain lion,
Bear,
Badger,
Wolf,
My father above,
Knife wing,
Shrew,
My fathers,
Over all this great world you go about.
Rattlesnake yellow,
Blue,
Red,
White,
Many colored,
Black.
Here at the place of your first beginning,
Ci'papolima,
In your inner room, you live.
Your massed cloud blanket is spread out.

k̯ä'k̯̂ä tcimik̯̂ak̯ä
ci'papo'lima
o'na ya·'nak̯ä a·'ciwan·i a·'teaiye.
hom a·'tatcu
we·'ma· a·'ciwan·i
ho'ktitaca
ai'nce
to'naci
yu'nawik̂o.
i'yamakwi tatc-i'li te''ona
a'tciala'tap̂a
k̯̂ä'lutsi
hom a·'tatcu
le· u'lo'nan ła'na t̂on a·'waiuy'a.
tci'tola łu'ptsina
l̂i''ana
a'hona
k̂o'hana
i'to'pan'ona
k̂wi'n·a
te'mła l̂i'ła k̯ä·'k̯̂ä tci'mik̯̂äk̯ä
ci'papolima
t̂e'li'ta t̂on a·'teaiye.
t̂o''na·wan̯ a'wełuyan p̂e'wi'a

Your life-giving road goes forth.

None of you are missing,
But all stay quietly.
Perpetuating your rite according to the first beginning,
You live.
My fathers,
Life-giving priest,
With none missing, you live.

Yonder my sacred word will reach.
To you I speak my sacred words.
My fathers,
Life-giving priest,
Perpetuating your rite according to the first beginning,
You live.
Here at Itiwana we live.
Here in the daylight we live.
My fathers,
Life-giving priest,
Where none are missing,
You live.
Listen to my sacred words.
There you live.
To you I speak.
Mindful of my words,
My country,
Itiwana,
Cover with your clouds,
Cover with your rains,
All of your children preserve.

Reaching to Dawn Lake,
May our roads be fulfilled.
May we grow old
May our peoples' roads all be fulfilled.
May they be preserved.

t̑o′'na·wan o′na ya·nak̭ä o′neałan a·′naiye
eł kwa tcu′hoł i′metcam·e.
te′mła t̑i′nan ła′k̭̑iye
yam ko′nhoł tci′mik̭̑ä'kowa te′liaʻna
t̑on a·′teaiye.
hom a·′tatcu
o′naya·nak̭ä a·′ciwan·i
eł kwa tcu′hoł i′metcam·e
t̑on a·teaiye.
la′k̑on t̑e′wu′su p̑ena· te′'tcina
t̑o′'na ho' t̑e′wusu a·′wamp̑e′ye'a.
hom a·′tatcu
o′naya·nak̭ä a·′ciwan·i
yam ko′'nhoł tci′k̭̑ä'kowa te′liaʻna

t̑on a·′teaiye.
li·ła i′tiwan·a hon a·′teaiye
t̑e′k̑ohanan hon a·′teaiye
hom a·′tatcu
o′na ya·nak̭ä a·′ciwan·i
eł kwa tcu′hoł i′metcam·e
t̑on a·′teaiye.
ho′man t̑e′wusu p̑e′na· yu'hatia·wa
t̑on a·′teaiye.
t̑o′'na ho' a·wamp̑e′ye'a
ho′man p̑e′na t̑on i·′hatiana·
hom u′loʻnakwi
i′tiwan·akwi
t̑on lo·′nana·wa
t̑on łi′tona·wa
t̑e′apk̑una·we
te′mła a·′teʻyak̑äna
t̑e′luwanan·e k̭̑ai′akwi te′'tcina
hon a·′wona-ya·tʻu
hon a·′łacitʻu
ho′'na·wan a·′ho′i
te′mła a·′wona-ya·tʻu
a·′teʻyatʻu.

Prayers for Collecting Medicine (Cactus Society)

The expedition for gathering medicine roots camps the first night about sixteen miles east of Zuñi. Before eating, the customary offerings of food are set aside. After singing four songs, the head of the expedition prays:

Now this night,
Our night fathers.
Our mothers,

ma' lu′k̭ä t̑e′łinan·e
hon t̑e′łia'k̭ a·′tatc i′lap̑ona
hon a·′tsit i′lap̑ona

Rising a little, have come standing to their sacred place.
The song sequence of our fathers

You have heard.
You who are our fathers,
Beast bow priests,
Your hand leading,
Our hands following,
Desiring your medicine,
Hither we take our roads.
Do not think to withhold it from us because of something,
For verily,
Desiring my fathers' flesh,

That by which my children may fulfill their thoughts,
To-morrow, throughout a good day,
A beautiful day,
With us your children
You will come to evening.
And when that day shall have passed,
Anxiously waiting,
We shall pass our days.

yam t̃e'łacinakwi
kɔ·w i·'łuwak̯na k̯̃e'atop̃a
yam a·'tatcu
a·'wan i'piclenan te'na· pi''lan·e
t̃o' yu''hatiak̯̃änapk̯ä.
t̃o''na hon a·'tatc i'lap̃ona
we·'ma· a·'p̃i'łaci'wan·i
to''na·wan a'sin e''kwi'kona
ho''na·wan a'si yä'luk̯̃än·a.
t̃o''na·wan a'kwan a'ntecemana
li·'łno hon a·'wonaiye.
eł kwa kwa'hoł a'kä i·'yat̃suma te'·amek̯̃äna
k̯es e'leanici
yam a·'tatcu
a·'wan ci''nan a'ntecemana
hom tca'we tse''makwi ya·'k̯̃änapkona'kä
t̃e'wan yä'ton·e
yä'ton k̃ɔ'kci
yä'ton tso''ya
ho'n tcawi'lap̃a
t̃on su'nhak̯̃äna·wa
isk̯än t̃e'wanan a·'tunte'kwi

a'nt̃sume'na
hon t̃e'wanan a·'tek̯̃än·a.

He takes the offering, burns it at a little distance from camp, and sitting down, waits for some omen.

Now this night
Our night fathers,
Our mothers,
Rising a little have come standing to their sacred place.
Bringing food
Hither with prayers
We made our road come forth.
Wherever, thinking "Let it be here,"
Our earth mother,
We passed on her road.
Sitting down on the bare ground,
(We came to you,)
Our ancestors,
The ones who here used to belong to societies,
The ones who used to understand medicine,
You who now have attained the far off place of waters;

ma'lu'k̯ä t̃e'łinan·e
hon t̃e'łiak̯̃ a·'tatc i'lap̃ona
hon a·'tsit i'lap̃ona
yam t̃e'łacinakwi
kɔ·w i·'łuwak̯na k̯̃e'atop̃a
i'·tonak̯' ho' i·'łeana
k̯̃ä'łhok^{u} t̃e'wus a·k̯ä
hon o'neała kwai''ik̯̃änapk̯ä.
hoł li·'ła le''hatina

yam a'witelin tsi'ta
hon o'na-e'latena
an i't̃at̃on i·'tinakna

yam a·'łacina·we
li''łno ti'k̯än i'lapkona

a'kwa· yai'yu'ya·n a·'tea'kona

le'hok^{u} k̯̃ä'cima te''wok̯̃änapkona

Having passed you on your roads,
We shall add to your hearts.
Adding to your hearts
Your long life,
Your old age,
Your waters,
Your seeds,
Your medicine
You will grant to us,
How the days will be
You will make known to us.
Knowing that, we shall live.

t̂o'n hon a·'wona-e'latena
t̂o'n hon a·'wik̭ena te'liana·wa
i'k̭en i·'telia·na
yam o'na-ya·nak̭ä
yam ła'ciak̭ä
yam k̭̂ä'cima
yam t̂o'waconan·e
yam a'kwan·e
ho''na t̂on ya'nhaitena·wa.
ko''nhoł t̂e'wanan te'atun'ona
ho''na t̂on ai'yu'ya·k̭̂äna·wap̂a
u's ai'yu'ya·na
hon t̂e'wanan a·'tek̭̂än·a

After praying, he waits for an omen. Next day they look for the plants. A young man going for the first time gives his ceremonial father a package of prayer meal, saying:

Now this day,

Our sun father
Having come out standing to his sacred place,
And having yet a little ways to go,
To go in to sit down at his other sacred place,
Bringing prayer meal which I have prepared,
Here near by,
At the very edge of the wilderness,
I have passed you on your road.
Desiring our fathers' medicine

We hold one another fast.
Desiring the medicine of our ancestors,
The ones who here belonged to societies,
The ones who used to understand medicine,
The beast priests.
Desiring their medicines,
With prayer meal,
With shells,
With rich clothing,
We hold one another fast.
My father,
You will cleanse your thoughts,
You will cleanse your heart,
So that somehow we may be the children of the divine ones.

ma 'lu'k̭ä yä'ton·e
hon yä'tok̭ä tatc i'lap̂ a·'te'ona
yam t̂e'łacinakwi
ye·'lana kwai''ik̭̂äna

t̂opak̭ä yam t̂e'łacinakwi
i·muna kwatok̭ätun te·kwi
kɔ·w a'nt̂e'wetcikwi
yam ha'lawotinan ye'lete'u'kowa i·'łeana
ło'kwa le·'wi te'a'a
t̂e'lupałtantapte
t̂om o'na-e'latena
yam a·'tatcu
a·'wan a'kwan a'ntecemana
hon i·'wiyat̂en-t̂su'mek̭̂äk̭ä.
ho''na·wan a·'łacina·we

li·'łno ti'k̭än i'lapkona

a'kwa· yai'yu'ya·na a·'tea'kona

we·ma· a·'pi'ła·ci'wan·i
a·'wan a'kwan a'ntecemana
ha'lawo·tinan a'k̭ä
ło·' a'k̭ä
u'tenan a'k̭ä
hon i·'wiyat̂en-t̂sumek̭̂äk̭ä
hom ta'tcu
t̂o' tse''mak i·'k̂ɔkcuna
t̂o' i'k̭e·n i·'k̂ɔkcuna
ko''lea k̭̂ä'pin a·'ho'i
ho' tca'wila·wa.

Perhaps, if we are fortunate,
Because of our thoughts
Our spring children may multiply.[70]

Among all the little boys
And all the little girls,
And those whose roads go ahead,
Our spring children have multiplied.
In order that this toward which our thoughts bend may be accomplished,
Desiring our fathers' medicine,
We have made our roads come hither.
My father,
For you I have finished all these words.
Even while I call myself poor,
Yonder on all sides
From those whom my thoughts embrace,
I shall ask for light;
I shall add to your breath.
Asking for the breath of the priest of the north,
The priest of the west,
The priest of the south,
The priest of the east,
The priest of above,
The priest of below.
Asking for their life-giving breath,
Their breath of old age,
Their breath of waters,
Their breath of seeds,
Their breath of fecundity,
Their breath of riches,
Their breath of strong spirit,

Their breath of power,
Their breath of all good fortune whereof they are possessed—
Asking for this,
Into my warm body
I shall draw their breath.
In order that our roads may reach
To where the road of our sun father comes out,
In order that we may finish our roads,
For this I add to your breath.
To this end, my father,

ho'nkwat hon ha'lowilap̑a
ho' tse''makwin a'k̭ä
ho''na· k̭̑ä'nakwe·na t̑e'apk̑una· ci'wunak̭̑äna.
kɔ·w a·'waktsik a·'łana
kɔ·w a·'k̭ätsik a·'łana
a·'won-a·'weʻkwinte
ho''na·wan k̭̑änakwe·na t̑e'apk̑unan ci'wunapk̭ä
i'sk̑ɔn tse''mak t̑e'łakwi yam a·'teatun'on a'k̭ä
yam a·'tatcu
a·'wan a'kwan a'ntecemana
k̭̑äłhok[u] hon o'neał a·'k̭̑äk̭ä

hom ta'tcu
le·'wi t̑o'man ho' p̑e'nan ya·'k̭̑äk̭ä.

ta'tcic ho' te'wuko'liya le'kwanante
la'łhok[u] le'si te'kwi yam tse''makt̑e'łakwi'kona
ho' t̑e'k̑ohanan yai'ncemana
t̑o'man ho' p̑i''nan te'liana·wa.
picl a·'ciwan·i

k̭̑ä'lici a·'ciwan·i
a'laʻ a·'ciwan·i
t̑e'mak̑o a·'ciwan·i.
i'yam a·'ciwan·i
ma'nilam a·'ciwan·i
a·'wan o'na-ya·'nak̭ä p̑i''nan·e
a·'wan ła'ciak̭ä p̑i''nan·e
a·'wan k̭̑ä'cima p̑i''nan·e
a·'wan t̑o'waconan p̑i''nan·e
a·'wan t̑e'apk̑unan p̑i''nan·e
a·'wan u'tenan p̑i''nan·e
a·'wan tse''makwin t̑su'me p̑i''nan·e
a·'wan sa'wanik̭ä p̑i''nan·e
a·'wan kwa'hoł te'mła p̑i''nan i'lap̑ a·'te'ona
yai'ncemana
yam t̑ehuł k̭̑ä'łnakwi
p̑i''nan a'naʻkwatok̭̑äna
yam yä'tok̭ä ta'tcu·
an o'neał an kwai''inakwin o'neał te''tcina
yam i·'yona-ya·'k̭̑änaptun'ona

t̑o'man ło p̑i''nan te'lian·a
t̑e'wuna' hom ta'tcu

[70] By means of medicine knowledge he will secure new members for the society.

May you be blessed with light.

t̃om t̃e'k̃ohanan a'niktciatu.

To this the father replies:

Now indeed
Our fathers' medicines

To one another we give.
Our fathers' life-giving breath,
Their breath of old age,
(We give to one another.)
When, among all the corn priests' ladder descending children,
Some evil causes sickness,
When the spirit fails,
Then, desiring their fathers' long life,
Desiring their old age,
Desiring their medicine,
Among all their fathers,
Society priests,
Society p̃ekwins,
Society bow priests,
They will look about.
Even though you do not know of it,
If the divine ones choose you,

When they summon you
You shall not think to refuse.
With prayer meal,
With shell,
With rich clothing,
They will bind you fast.
Then seeking these wherever they are,
Even though the night be dangerous,
Following your fathers,

Even to all the places where you did not think to enter,
Seeking these,
Living for their thoughts,
Thus shall you live.[71]

ma' la'k̭iman·te
yam a·'tatcu
a·'wan a'kwan·e
hon i'yan hai·'tek̭ä
hon a·'tatc i'lap̃ona
a·'wan o'naya·nak̭ä p̃i''nan·e
a·'wan ła'ciak̭ä p̃i''nan·e
le· t̃o'wa ci'wan an łe'tsilon p̃a'ni·nan tca'we
kwa'tik we'ak̃ä k̭ä
tse''mak i·'natina
yam a·'tatcu
a·'wan o'naya·nak̭ä a'ntecemana
a·'wan ła'ciak̭ä a'ntecemana
a·'wan a'kwan a'ntecemana
le· yam a·'tatcu
ti'k̭ä a·ciwan·i
ti'k̭ä p̃e'kwi·we
ti'k̭ä a·'pi'ła·ciwan·i
a·'wan u'lapnak̃än·a.
tekwant te'atip̃a
k̃ä'pin a·'ho'i
hoł t̃om a'nawana
t̃o·m a'ntecematina'k̃äp̃a
kwa t̃o' e'łamana tse''ma'cukwa
ha'lawo·tinan a'k̭ä
ło·' ak̭ä
u'tenan a'k̭ä
t̃om ya't̃ena-t̃su'mek̃änak̃äp̃a
lu'kni a·'t̃apana

hoł t̃e'łiak̭ä a't̃anapte

yam a·'tatcu
a·'wan e'la yä'lu
hoł yam kwa kwa'totun te'amek̭ä te''a'konatapte
lu'kni a·'t̃apana
lu'kni a·'wan tse''makwin a'k̭ä
t̃o' ho''i te'k̃än·a

[71] Dictated by a member of the Cactus Society. The remaining prayers were withheld.

Prayer for Stalking Deer

When a hunter sees deer tracks he crouches down in the trail and offers prayer meal to the deer, with the request that he may reveal himself. The following text is taken from a folk tale in which success in hunting is the test imposed on suitors. Several suitors fail because they neglect to offer prayer meal to the prey.

This day	lu'k̯ä yä'ton·e
He who holds our roads,	ho'n a·'wona·wi'lona
Our sun father,	ho''na·wan yä'tok̯ä ta'tcu
Has come out standing to his sacred place.	yam t̑e'łacinakwi ye·'lana kwai''ik̯̑äk̯ä.
Now that he has passed us on our roads,	ho'n a·'wona-e'latek̯atea'a
Here we pass you on your road.	li'ł t̑o''na ho' a·'wona-e'latek̯ä.
Divine one,	k̯̑ä'pin ho''i
The flesh of the white corn,	t̑o'wa k̑o'han an ci''nan·e
Prayer meal,	ha'la wo·tinan·e
Shell,	ło·''o
Corn pollen,	o'nea·we
Here I offer to you.	li·łt̑o''na ho' a·'łea'up̑a
With your wisdom	yam a'nikwanan a'kä
Taking the prayer meal,	ha'lawo'tinan·e
The shell,	ło·''o
The corn pollen,	o'nean i'łeana
This day,	lu'k̯ä ya'ton·e
My fathers,	hom a·'tatcu
My mothers,	hom a·'tsita
In some little hollow,	hoł ko·'wi t̑e'coka t̑sa'na
In some low brush,	ła·-t̑sana
You will reveal yourselves to me.	hom t̑o' ai'yetsak̯ak̯̑äna·'wap̑a
Then with your flesh,	t̑o''na·wan ci''nan a'k̯ä
With your living waters,	t̑o''na·wan k̯̑ä''kwin a'k̯ä
May I sate myself. In order that this may be	yam yu·''yackwi te'atun'onak̯ä
Here I offer your prayer meal.	li·ł t̑o''na ho' ha'lawo·tinan a·'łea'u.